30106024542291

AF748658

EUROPEAN CONSUMER LAW

Ius Communitatis Series, Volume 5

EUROPEAN CONSUMER LAW

Norbert Reich
Hans-W. Micklitz
Peter Rott
Klaus Tonner

2nd edition

intersentia
Cambridge – Antwerp – Portland

Intersentia Publishing Ltd.
Trinity House | Cambridge Business Park | Cowley Road
Cambridge | CB4 0WZ | United Kingdom
Tel.: +44 1223 393 753 | Email: mail@intersentia.co.uk

Distribution for the UK:
NBN International
Airport Business Centre, 10 Thornbury Road
Plymouth, PL6 7 PP
United Kingdom
Tel.: +44 1752 202 301 | Fax: +44 1752 202 331
Email: orders@nbninternational.com

Distribution for the USA and Canada:
International Specialized Book Services
920 NE 58th Ave. Suite 300
Portland, OR 97213
USA
Tel.: +1 800 944 6190 (toll free)
Email: info@isbs.com

Distribution for Austria:
Neuer Wissenschaftlicher Verlag
Argentinierstraße 42/6
1040 Wien
Austria
Tel.: +43 1 535 61 03 24
Email: office@nwv.at

Distribution for other countries:
Intersentia Publishing nv
Groenstraat 31
2640 Mortsel
Belgium
Tel.: +32 3 680 15 50
Email: mail@intersentia.be

European Consumer Law. 2nd edition
Norbert Reich, Hans-W. Micklitz, Peter Rott and Klaus Tonner

© 2014 Intersentia
Cambridge – Antwerp – Portland
www.intersentia.com | www.intersentia.co.uk

Artwork on front and back cover: Titian, The Girl with a Platter of Fruit, 1555-1558, © bpk / Gemäldegalerie, Staatliche Museen zu Berlin / photo: Jörg P. Anders

ISBN 978-1-78068-086-6
D/2014/7849/6
NUR 828

British Library Cataloguing in Publication Data. A catalogue record for this book is available from the British Library.

No part of this book may be reproduced in any form, by print, photoprint, microfilm or any other means, without written permission from the publisher.

SERIES PREFACE

The role of European law is becoming more and more central in comparative law, in the law of the other Member States and as an outstanding model for legal policy. Insiders have known for a long time that in almost all core areas of law, the important spurs to reform have been coming from Europe and that European law increasingly dominates the cornerstones of our legal systems. Therefore, a discussion of European law involves addressing the main problems and guiding principles but, in practical terms, it also increasingly entails raising questions that are threatening to revolutionise national legal traditions and render entire libraries obsolete.

Since 2002, the year marking the introduction of the Euro, a new law of obligations has been in place in Germany, with the old codifications in France and Austria following to a lesser extent. The next years were characterised by unrestricted cross-border mobility of court decisions; re-writing of core areas of company law such as accounting, cross-border mobility, but as well the promulgation of supranational types of company, with some of the largest German enterprises becoming 'European Companies' (SE); and also cross-border crediting of contributions to social security systems becoming a reality. The law on competition and subsidies has been primarily European for a long time and its mighty implementing mechanisms – overriding Heads of State – fill title pages. The same applies to intellectual property law, foreign exchange law, banking and insurance law and environmental law. These have become genuinely European subjects. Then, in the last years, the cross-border arrest warrant fundamentally changed European Criminal Law; anti-discrimination law is all encompassing; there is now a proposal for a European Optional Contract Law (Code); the Lisbon Treaty – though formally not a constitution – installed a new institutional setting strengthening democratic legitimacy and powers of the European Union; and the financial and state debt crises, not even ten years after the introduction of the Euro, triggered measures which considerably strengthened and broadened financial stability schemes at the EU level, from banking law to capital market law and collaboration with respect to systemic risk. The near future will show whether Europe is to have an institutionalised economic collaboration for its political economy ('true economic government') in some way, reflecting the now global importance of the Euro and the responsibility attached to it!

European law – in all legal areas – has long since assumed dimensions that make it absolutely necessary to refer to more than a single book. This series, now beginning its second edition, is structured so as to provide the relevant European complement to a traditional legal area. It offers the internal market package organised in this way, with those areas being chosen for users that have a significant internal market dimension. In comparison with a multi-volume looseleaf work, it has advantages not only in terms of price, but also in that it puts a greater emphasis on classification and limits the material to the essential, which is important in an overflowing area such as European law, of which only very few people manage to preserve an overview.

The dynamic nature of European law is impressive, as its development hurtles along, gathering momentum. There is a need for direction. A serious application of law can no longer focus solely on national transposition. The original, the European guideline, which *de facto* almost always has to be directly applied (even in national legal processes), must be considered. Such direction can best be provided by presenting the contents of European law in context and in the necessary detail – in the present case, up to twelve individual volumes. Some of the volumes have already had considerable success in one national market and are now presented to a pan-European public.

The volumes cover the most important topics in the 'Europeanisation' of law. For practitioners – solicitors and barristers, corporate lawyers, judges or lawyers in state authorities or ministries – who do not wish to turn a blind eye to European law, these volumes provide a reliable treatment of the important problems, with sufficiently detailed references. They provide practitioners with all they need on the EU level, and moreover give comparative law and legal policy insight. As a series, they give an overview of those areas most affected by European law. Likewise, they provide advanced students with material for excellent examination results. Students must study European law seriously as part of their main subject if they really wish to specialise in this in the future and do more than pass their examination with an average result. Works with comparative law and interdisciplinary aspects also prepare students for a possible period of study abroad, help them to analyse law in terms of function and also support studies in related subjects. Thus, IUS COMMUNITATIS makes European substantive law accessible in the form of the classic systematic textbook and specialist work.

All volumes on the applicable law of the Union begin by presenting the necessary tools: in each case, the EC/EU law and the instruments whereby this law enters into the national legal systems are introduced. In all volumes, a thorough description of the EC/EU law rules forms the core of the discussion. However, economic or other interdisciplinary references of significance to the legislation in question are also explained, i.e. what the rules are intended to achieve and, where there are lacunae, the various models that exist and are discussed throughout Europe. European law is, indeed, a law in the making. Each legal area is presented in a logical order, as an organic whole; this implies that the approximated or harmonised law forms only the skeleton or hard nucleus and is supplemented by comparative law explanations where harmonisation is not advanced. In this way, the relationship to national law becomes clearer and the ability of readers to deal with European law will improve, as they are given a coherent picture rather than the fragmentary one often complained of. These are to be textbooks, discussion books and, above all, practical books – sufficiently condensed to contain all the necessary details and yet clear in their outlines. This was the objective we strive for and the challenge. The authors and the editor (Stefan.Grundmann@rewi.hu-berlin.de) thank those who have criticised and inspired us and who may do so in the future.

The entire IUS COMMUNITATIS series owes much to the Thyssen Foundation, which considered the European aspect and in particular the connection with comparative law so important that it generously supported a good number of the volumes. As the editor, I should like to express my deepest thanks.

Berlin, Spring 2014 Stefan Grundmann

AUTHORS' PREFACE

European or, more exactly EU, consumer law has developed over time. It found its official recognition in Articles 3t and 153 of the EC Treaty, now Articles 12 and 169 of the Treaty on the Functioning of the European Union (TFEU). Consumer law now constitutes a separate subject matter which the authors *Hans-W. Micklitz* and *Norbert Reich* tried to analyse in 1,250 pages in the fourth German edition of *Europäisches Verbraucherrecht* of 2003. Clearly there was no chance to translate and update this bulk of material for the English-speaking reader. There was also a need to strengthen research on EU consumer law by including our colleagues *Peter Rott* from the University of Copenhagen and *Klaus Tonner* from Rostock University in the team of authors.

For the English edition, the authors, in cooperation with the publisher, decided to prepare a comprehensive version which we call *European Consumer Law*, comprising the central areas of EU consumer law which are of relevance beyond the jurisdiction of the EU itself. This implies two things:

- selection of relevant subject matter; and
- updating the subject matter according to new developments in EU law, which has been done in the second edition after the first was published in 2009.

The result is a completely re-conceptualised and rewritten work which is at the same time "more" and "less" than a mere translation of the original German version:

- It is "more" in its comprehensive, updated analysis of EU consumer law as of mid-2013;
- It is "less" in that we limit ourselves to 450 instead of 1,250 pages, implying a reduction only in size rather than intellectual spirit!

In selecting the materials, the authors decided on what is called a "horizontal approach" in EU jargon. This means that we have chosen such legal materials and instruments as are related to the position of the consumer – as an individual and as a member of a rather "diffuse group" – in the EU context in a broad and general manner without reference to the sometimes very specific legal regulation of business activities or consumer transactions. This method can be explained by briefly referring to the main content of the nine chapters.

Chapter 1 (Norbert Reich in cooperation with Hans Micklitz) gives an overall description of EU consumer protection, its development in politics and law, its basic concepts, a theory of consumer rights, the instruments of consumer law, in particular EU Directives, and finally the concept of the "consumer" as "passive economic citizen" who is the central protective subject of law itself. It has been updated with more recent concepts like the "vulnerable consumer" and "weaker consumer". The last section contains a conceptual and reformist outlook on the "future orientation of EU consumer law".

Chapter 2 (Hans-W. Micklitz) is concerned with advertising and commercial practices law. Alongside specific regulation of TV advertising, medicines and foodstuff advertising, discussion of which has been deliberately excluded due to their highly specific character, emphasis has been put on a thorough analysis of Directive 2005/29/EC on unfair commercial practices (UCPD), which has introduced a comprehensive fairness approach to B2C marketing practices. In the second edition the discussion has been updated with references to ECJ case law. This is supplemented by an analysis of Directive 97/55/EC (now Directive 2006/114/EC) on comparative advertising.

Chapter 3 (Hans-W. Micklitz) takes up a similar "horizontal" approach with regard to pre-formulated contract terms which were adopted in 1993 via the Unfair Contract Terms Directive 93/13/EEC and which have received much attention in the ECJ's judicial practice, to be reported and analysed in some detail here. The second edition demonstrates the increased impact of the case law of the ECJ on both procedural and substantive matters of unfair terms regulation in the EU.

Chapter 4 (Hans-W. Micklitz in collaboration with Norbert Reich) is concerned with the "horizontal" consumer sales Directive 1999/44/EC which has introduced certain basic and therefore mandatory consumer rights with regard to the most important transactions in which consumers usually engage. Recent case law of the ECJ has focused on clarifying and improving the remedies offered to the consumer. Other types of consumer contracts like package holidays, timeshare, services of general interest, etc. which are also regulated in EU law had to be omitted due to their rather specific character. However, a last section draws the attention of the reader to the debate on developing special rules concerning digital content contracts with consumers which have entered EU law via the back door of the draft Regulation on a Common European Sales Law (CESL).

Chapter 5 (Peter Rott) is devoted to the analysis of the Directive 2008/48/EC on credit agreements for consumers (CCD) that aims at "total harmonisation" and thereby sets a precedent for future EU instruments in the field of consumer contract law. The chapter also refers to other instruments that regulate financial services, such as the proposed Mortgage Credit Directive and payment services.

Chapter 6 (Hans-W. Micklitz) takes up product liability, regulated by the rather "old" Directive 85/374/EEC which had been amended once by Directive 1999/34/EC after the BSE scandal. Some case law of the ECJ has emerged which, to the surprise of many observers, postulated that the Directive, even though it only takes a very limited and reduced approach to product liability, has introduced "complete" and not just "minimum" harmonisation within its scope of application, but more recent judgments have tried to limit this approach. This obviously creates tensions with existing Member State product liability laws which may be more advantageous to the consumer who is injured by a defective product. In contrast, the important area of "service liability" has not yet found an appropriate legal instrument in the EU. Therefore the authors decided to include an Annex (6.39–6.52) with a proposal for a regulation/directive based on an extensive comparative study done by *Magnus/Micklitz* on "Liability for the Safety of Services" in 2006 for the EC Commission, relating to consumer services like health, leisure, tourism and general interest.

Chapter 7 (Norbert Reich) is concerned with cross-border consumer transactions, cross-border breach of consumer law and litigation in cases which are provoked by the fact that harmonisation of law in the area of consumer law (and other areas like EU commercial or financial services law) does not lead to uniform standards but must be governed by the traditional mechanisms of private international law. This area which had been a *domaine reservé* of Member States has experienced a complete paradigm change resulting from two important new regulations: Regulation (EC) No 593/2008 (Rome I) with regard to contractual obligations and Regulation (EC) No 864/2007 (Rome II) with regard to non-contractual obligations, including tort, product liability and unfair competition, which are not specifically directed at consumer law but have a direct impact on its realisation. With regard to cross-border litigation, Regulation (EC) No 44/2001 (to be superseded by Regulation (EU) 1215/2012 which does not change consumer jurisdiction) has established special rules on jurisdiction for disputes arising out of consumer contracts, and ECJ case law is emerging concerning the effect of internet contracts on jurisdiction and conflict of law. The chapter also refers to Regulation (EC) No 1896/2006 on a European order for payment procedure and Regulation (EC) No 861/2007 on a European small claims procedure.

Chapter 8 (Norbert Reich) takes up different mechanisms of individual and collective consumer protection via remedies and procedures which are promoted, encouraged or even prescribed by the EU. However, effective and equivalent consumer protection as a fundamental requirement of EU law and as a fundamental right of consumers, must, via adequate alternative dispute resolution mechanisms and court procedures, be guaranteed by Member States themselves. Directive 2013/83 on consumer ADR and Regulation (EU) 594/2013 on consumer ODR try to establish common standards for out-of-court consumer redress, including binding consumer arbitration.

Chapter 9 (Klaus Tonner) takes as a starting point the recent Consumer Rights Directive 2011/83 (CRD) which has fully harmonised information and withdrawal rights of distance and off-premises contracts. Its main impact will be felt in e-commerce which therefore has been placed at the centre of attention of the chapter. However, the CRD, with its broad if not comprehensive approach, has an impact on other areas, e.g. sales law, and must be made consistent with other Directives, in particular the E-commerce Directive 2000/31 and the Service Directive 2006/123/EC.

It should be pointed out to the interested reader that EU consumer law, like any other EU law, has three specific characteristics which are quite unique and make understanding it sometimes rather difficult:

- As far as consumer law is based on EU Directives, these must be implemented by Member States before they create rights in favour of consumers and obligations on businesses. Failure to do so adequately may allow consumers to seek compensation from Member States that have breached Union law. Member State courts must – "as far as possible" – interpret and apply their national law in accordance with EU law.
- Member States usually have different options available to them for implementation, depending upon the extent of harmonisation provided by the Directive. The "old approach" (with the exception of product liability) was concerned with "minimal harmonisation"; the new approach, as taken up by the UCPD, CCD and the CRD, focuses on "complete" harmonisation which in the end became a "targeted harmonisation". Attempts of the Commission, however, to impose "full harmonisation" on the central Directive 93/13 on unfair terms in consumer contracts (Chapter 3) and Directive 99/44 on sales of consumer goods (Chapter 4) fortunately have failed.
- The final arbiter in interpreting EU consumer law is the European Court of Justice (ECJ). Therefore much reference is made to the steadily growing case law of the ECJ without which EU consumer law could not be understood. However, while the case law of national courts plays a central role in understanding, interpreting and implementing EU law, it was not possible to adequately study all details of it.

Hopefully the book will contribute to the understanding of EU consumer law!

Each author is responsible for his own chapter, but they all have tried to coordinate their views and opinions as far as possible. Norbert Reich served as general editor of the second edition.

Spring 2014

Hans-W. Micklitz, Florence
Norbert Reich, Hamburg
Peter Rott, Copenhagen
Klaus Tonner, Rostock

TABLE OF CONTENTS

CHAPTER 2. UNFAIR COMMERCIAL PRACTICES AND MISLEADING ADVERTISING

CHAPTER 5. CONSUMER CREDIT

Peter Rott . . . 197

CHAPTER 7.
CROSS-BORDER CONSUMER PROTECTION

LIST OF ABBREVIATIONS

AcP	Archiv für die civilistische Praxis
ADR	alternative dispute resolution
AmJCompL	American Journal of Comparative Law
BB	Betriebs-Berater
BGB	Bürgerliches Gesetzbzuch (German Civil Code)
BGH(Z)	Bundesgerichtshof (German Federal Court), Zivilsachen (civil law reports)
BKR	Zeitschrift für Bank- und Kapitalmarktrecht
BR Drucks.	Bundesrats-Drucksache (Second Chamber of German Parliament, printed matter)
BT Drucks.	Bundestags-Drucksache (First Chamber of German Parliament, printed matter)
BVerfG(E)	Bundesverfassungsgericht (Federal Constitutional Court, reports of cases)
CESL	Common European Sales Law
CFR	Common Frame of Reference
CISG	Convention on the International Sale of Goods
CMLR	Common Market Law Reports
CMLRev	Common Market Law Review
COM	(EU) Commission document
CRD	Consumer Rights Directive (2011/83/EU)
DCFR	Draft Common Frame of Reference
DJT	Deutscher Juristentag (German Law Associations Meeting)
EBLRev	European Business Law Review
ECHR	European Convention of Human Rights
ECJ	Court of Justice of the EU
ECR	European Court Reports
ed(s)	editor(s)
EFTA	European Free Trade Area
ELJ	European Law Journal
ELRev	European Law Review
EP	European Parliament
ERA	Europäische Rechtsakademie (European Legal Academy)
ERCL	European Review of Contract Law
ERPrL	European Review of Private Law

EuR	Europarecht
EWS	Europäisches Wirtschaftsrecht
EUI	European University Institute, Florence
EuLF	The European Legal Forum
EUVR	Zeitschrift für Europäisches Unternehmens und Wirtschaftsrecht (Journal of European Consumer and Market Law)
EuZA	Europäische Zeitschrift für Arbeitsrecht
EuZW	Europäische Zeitschrift für Wirtschaftsrecht
EWS	Europäisches Wirtschafts- und Steuerrecht
GPR	Gemeinschaftsprivatrecht
ICLQ	International Law Quarterly
IFTTA Law Rev	IFTTA (International Forum of Tour and Travel Advocats) Law Review, supplement to the journal Reiserecht aktuell
IP	intellectual property
JCP	Journal of Consumer Policy
Juridica Int.	Juridica International (Tartu, Estonia)
JZ	Juristenzeitung
KritJ	Kritische Justiz
LQR	Law Quarterly Review
MLR	Modern Law Review
MPI	Max-Planck-Institut
NJW	Neue Juristische Wochenschrift
nyr	not yet reported (in ECR)
NZG	Neue Zeitschrift für Gesellschaftsrecht
OFT	Office of Fair Trading
OJ L/C	Official Journal of the EU, series legislation or communication
OxfJLSt	Oxford Journal of Legal Studies
PECL	Principles of European Contract Law
PICL	Principles of International Contract Law
RabelsZ	Rabels Zeitschrift für ausländisches und internationales Privatrecht
RIW	Recht der Internationalen Wirtschaft
RMC	Revue du marché commun
RTDEur	Revue Trimestrielle du droit européen
SI	Statutory Instrument (UK)
TEU	Treaty on European Union
TFEU	Treaty on the Functioning of the EU
UKHL	UK House of Lords cases
UKSC	UK Supreme Court cases
VersR	Versicherungsrecht
VuR	Verbraucher und Recht

WiscIntLJ	Wisconsin International Law Journal
WM	Wertpapier-Mitteilungen
YEL	(Oxford) Yearbook of European Law
ZBB	Zeitschrift für Bankrecht und Bankwirtschaft
ZEuP	Zeitschrift für Europäisches Privatrecht
ZIP	Zeitschrift für Wirtschaftsrecht
ZVerglRWiss	Zeitschrift für vergleichende Rechtswissenchaft
ZVersWiss	Zeitschrift für die gesamte Versicherungswissenschaft

TABLE OF EU LEGISLATION*

REGULATIONS

* The bold numbers are the main references.

DIRECTIVES

Council Directive 76/768/EEC of 27 July 1976 on the approximation of the laws of Member States relating to cosmetic products, OJ L 262, 27.09.1976, 169, amended by Directive 93/35/EEC of 14 June 1993 on the approximation of the laws of Member States relating to cosmetic products, OJ L 151, 23.06.1993, 32: *2.3*

Council Directive 83/189/EEC of 28 March 1983 laying down a procedure for the provision of information in the field of technical standards and regulations, OJ L 109, 26.04.1983, 8: *1.33*

Council Directive 84/450/EEC of 10 September 1984 relating to the approximation of the laws, regulations and administrative provisions of the Member States concerning misleading advertising OJ L 250, 19.09.1984, 17: *2.1, 2.3, 2.29, 2.51, 8.29*

Council Directive 85/374/EEC of 25 July 1985 on the approximation of the laws, regulations and administrative provisions of the Member States concerning liability for defective products [1985] L 210, 1885, 9: *1.32, 6.3–6.36, 7.1, 7.27*

Council Directive 85/577/EEC of 20 December 1985 to protect the consumer in respect of contracts negotiated away from business premises OJ L 372, 31.12.1985, 31: *1.27, 1.31, 5.21, 7.22, 9.1*

Council Directive 87/102/EEC of 22 December 1986 on the approximation of the laws, regulations and administrative provisions of the Member States concerning consumer credit, OJ L 42, 12.02.1987, 48: *2.14, 5.2, 5.14, 5.19, 5.23, 5.34, 7.22*

Council Directive 89/552/EEC of 3 October 1989 on the coordination of certain provisions laid down by law, regulation or administrative action in Member States concerning the pursuit of television broadcasting activities, OJ L 298, 17.10.1989, 23: *2.14, 7.28*

Council Directive 90/314/EEC of 13 June 1990 on package travel, package holidays and package tours, OJ L 158, 23.06.1990, 59: *1.9, 1.27, 1.31, 2.14, 6.37, 7.22, 8.10, 9.4*

Council Directive 92/59/EEC of 29 June 1992 on general product safety, OJ L 228, 11.08.1992, 24: *6.2*

Council Directive 93/13/EEC of 5 April 1993 on unfair terms in consumer contracts, OJ L 95, 21.04.1993, 29: *1.13, 1.31,* ***3.5–3.29****, 4.1, 7.22–7.23, 8.30, 8.35, 9.1*

Council Directive 93/22/EEC of 10 May 1993 on investment services, OJ L 141, 11.06.1993, 27: *5.1*

Council Directive 94/19/EC of 30 May 1994 on deposit guarantee schemes, OJ L 135, 31.05.1994, 5: *1.9*

Directive 94/47/EC of the EP and the Council of 26 October 1994 on the protection of purchasers in respect of certain aspects of contracts relating to the purchase of the right to use immovable properties on a timeshare basis, OJ L 280, 29.10.1994, 19: *1.27, 2.14, 5.25, 7.17–23*

Directive 95/46/EC of the EP and of the Council of 24 October 1995 on the protection of individuals with regard to the processing of personal data and on the free movement of such data, OJ L 281, 23.11.1995, 31: *1.14*

Directive 97/5/EC of the EP and the Council of 27 January 1997 on cross-border credit transfers, OJ L 43, 14.02.1997, 25: *5.1*

Directive 97/7/EC of the EP and of the Council of 20 May 1997 on the protection of consumers in respect of distance contracts, OJ L 144, 04.06.1997, 19: *1.9, 1.27, 2.14, 2.34, 5.25, 7.1, 7.23, 9.2*

Directive 97/36/EC of the EP and of the Council of 30 June 1997 amending Council Directive 89/552/EEC on the coordination of certain provisions laid down by law, regulation or administrative action in Member States concerning the pursuit of television broadcasting activities, OJ L 202, 30.07.1997, 60: *7.28*

Directive 97/55/EC of the EP and the Council of 6 October 1997 on comparative advertising, OJ L 290, 23.10.1997, 18: *2.2, 2.36–2.39, 2.52, 8.29*

Council Directive 98/6/EC of 16 February 1998 on consumer protection in the indication of the prices of products offered to consumers, OJ L 80, 18.03.1998, 27: *1.23, 1.27*

Directive 98/27/EC of the EP and the Council of 19 May 1998 on injunctions for the protection of consumers' interests, OJ L 166, 11.06.1998, 51: *1.16, 2.14, 8.33–8.38, 9.17*

Directive 98/37/EC of the EP and the Council of 22 June 1998 on the approximation of the laws of the Member States relating to machinery, OJ L 207, 22.06.1998, 1: *8.7*

Directive 98/43/EC of the EP and of the Council of 6 July 1998 on the approximation of the laws, regulations and administrative provisions of the Member States relating to the advertising and sponsorship of tobacco products OJ L 213, 30.07.1998, 9 (annulled by ECJ case C-376/98): *1.11, 1.22*

Directive 1999/34/EC of the EP and of the Council of 10 May 1999 amending Council Directive 85/374/EEC on the approximation of the laws, regulations and administrative provisions of the Member States concerning liability for defective products, OJ L 141, 04.06.1999, 20: *6.3*

Directive 1999/44/EC of the EP and of the Council of 25 May 1999 on certain aspects of the sale of consumer goods and associated guarantees, OJ L 171, 07.07.1999, 12: *1.31, 2.14, 4.1–4.36, 7.1, 7.22–7.23, 8.35, 9.1*

Directive 2000/31/EC of the EP and of the Council of 8 June 2000 on certain legal aspects of information society services, in particular electronic commerce, in the Internal Market, OJ L 178, 17.07.2000, 12: *1.27, 2.14, 7.24, 8.21, 9.18*

Council Directive 2000/43/EC of 29 June 2000 implementing the principle of equal treatment between persons irrespective of racial or ethnic origin, OJ L 180, 19.07.2000, 22: *1.27*

Directive 2001/29/EC of the EP and the Council of 22 May 2001 on the harmonisation of certain aspects of copyright and related rights in the information society, OJ L 167, 22.06.2001, 10: *1.42*

Directive 2001/34/EC of the EP and of the Council of 28 May 2001 on the admission of securities to official stock exchange listing and on information to be published on those securities, OJ L 184, 06.07.2001, 1: *2.14*

Directive 2001/95/EC of the EP and of the Council of 3 December 2001 on general product safety, OJ L 11, 16.01.2002, 4: *6.2*

Directive 2002/22/EC of the EP and the Council of 7 March 2002 on universal service and user's rights relating to electronic communication networks and services, OJ L 108, 24.04.2002, 51: *1.40, 8.3*

Directive 2002/58/EC of the EP and of the Council of 12 July 2002 concerning the processing of personal data and the protection of privacy in the electronic communications sector, OJ L 201, 31.07.2002, 37: *2.14, 9.11*

TABLE OF ECJ/CJEU CASES

Date	Case number	Parties	Reference ECR	Paragraph number
04.12.1974	41/74	*Yvonne van Duyn v Home Office*	1974, 1337	1.29
30.07.1976	21/76	*Handelskwekerij G. J. Bier v Mines de potasse d'Alsace SA*	1976, 1735	6.36, 7.42
06.10.1976	14/76	*De Bloos v Boyer*	1976, 1497	7.32
16.12.1976	33/76	*REWE v Landwirtschaftskammer Saarland*	1976, 1989	8.3
16.12.1976	45/76	*Comet v Produktschap voor Siergewassen*	1976, 2043	8.3
25.10.1977	26/76	*Metro v Commission (Metro/Saba I)*	1977, 1875	1.25
09.03.1978	106/77	*Amministrazione delle Finanze dello Stato v Simmenthal SpA*	1978, 67	8.3
21.06.1978	150/77	*Bertrand v Paul Ott KG*	1978, 1431	7.32, 7.34
20.02.1979	120/78	*Rewe Zentral AG v Bundesmonopolverwaltung für Branntwein (Cassis de Dijon)*	1979, 649	1.4, 8.39
22.02.1979	133/78	*Gourdain v Nadler*	1979, 733	7.32
21.05.1980	125/79	*Denilauer v S.N.C. Couchet Frères*	1980, 1553	7.32, 8.41
23.03.1982	102/81	*Nordsee v Reederei Mond*	1982, 1095	8.24
14.07.1983	201/82	*Gerling Kreditversicherung et al. v Amministrazione del Tesoro dello Stato*	1983, 2503	7.32
10.04.1984	14/83	*Colson et al. v Land Nordrhein-Westfahlen*	1984, 1891	1.34
13.02.1985	293/83	*Françoise Gravier v City of Liège*	1985, 593	1.15
07.03.1985	48/84	*Spitzley v Sommer Exploitation SA*	1985, 787	7.32
15.05.1986	222/84	*Johnston v Chief constable of the Royal Ulster Constabulary*	1986, 1651	8.2
12.03.1987	178/84	*Commission v Germany (Beer case)*	1987, 1227	2.30, 8.39
22.10.1987	314/85	*Foto Frost v Hauptzollamt Lübeck*	1987, 4199	8.5
25.02.1988	331/85 376/85 378/85	*Bianco & Girare v Directeur Général des Douanes*	1988, 1099	8.3
27.09.1988	189/87	*Kalfelis v Bankhaus Schroeder et al.*	1988, 5565	7.42
02.02.1989	186/87	*Cowan v Trésor public*	1989, 195	1.13

Date	Case number	Parties	Reference ECR	Paragraph number
07.04.1989	326/86 66/88	*Francesconi*	1989, 2087	8.15
16.05.1989	382/87	*Buet & Educational Business Services v Ministère Public*	1989, 1235	1.23, 1.36, 2.18
16.11.1989	360/88	*Commission v Belgium*	1989, 3803	1.20
13.12.1989	204/88	*Ministère public v Jean-Jacques Paris*	1989, 4361	2.33
13.12.1989	322/88	*Grimaldi v Fonds de Maladies Professionnelles*	1989, 4407	3.24, 8.23a
11.01.1990	220/88	*Dumez-France v Helaba*	1990, I-49	7.42
07.03.1990	362/88	*GB-Inno-BM v Conféderation du commerce luxemb.*	1990, I-667	1.11, 2.3, 2.33
19.06.1990	213/89	*The Queen v Secretary of State for Transport, ex parte Factortame*	1990, I-2433	8.3, 8.5
13.11.1990	C-106/89	*Marleasing v Comercial Internacional de Alimentacion*	1990, I-4135	1.28, 1.34
12.12.1990	C-241/89	*SARPP v Chambre syndicale des raffineurs et al.*	1990, I-4695	2.30
13.12.1990	C-238/89	*Pall v Dahlhausen*	1990, I-4827	2.3, 2.30
15.01.1991	C-372/89	*Gold-Ei v Überwachungsstelle für Milcherzeugnisse*	1991, I-43	2.33
21.02.1991	C-143/88 C-92/89	*Süderdithmarschen v Hauptzollamt Itzhoe;* *Zuckerfabrik Soest v Hauptzollamt Paderborn*	1991, I-415	8.3, 8.5
14.03.1991	C-361/89	*Di Pinto*	1991, I-1189	1.23, 1.37, 1.39, 2.18, 5.11
18.06.1991	C-369/89	*Piageme v Peters (Piageme I)*	1991, I-2971	1.13
04.10.1991	C-159/90	*Society for the protection of Unborn Children v Grogan*	1991, I-4685	1.11
19.11.1991	C-6/90 C-9/90	*Andrea Francovich et al. v Italian Republic*	1991, I-5357	1.35, 4.34, 8.3, 8.5
16.01.1992	C-373/90	*Criminal proceedings against X (Nissan)*	1992, I-131	1.34, 2.3, 2.31
17.06.1992	C-26/91	*Handte v Traitements Medano-chimiques*	1992, I-3967	6.1, 7.42
13.01.1993	C-293/91	*Commission v France*	1993, I-1	6.32
19.01.1993	C-89/91	*Shearson Lehmann Hutton v TVB Treuhandgesellschaft*	1993, I-139	1.37, 7.36
21.04.1993	C-172/91	*Sonntag v Waidmann*	1993, I-1963	8.41
18.05.1993	C-126/91	*Schutzverband gegen Unwesen in der Wirtschaft v Yves Rocher*	1993, I-2361	2.3, 2.31

Date	Case number	Parties	Reference ECR	Paragraph number
02.08.1993	C-271/91	*Marshall v Southampton Health authority et al.*	1993, I-4367	1.33
24.11.1993	C-267/91 C-268/91	*Keck and Mithouard*	1993, I-6097	2.31
02.02.1994	C-315/92	*Verband sozialer Wettbewerb v Clinique Laboratories*	1994, I-317	2.3
24.03.1994	C-275/92	*HM Customs & Excise v Schindler*	1994, I-1039	2.13
13.04.1994	C-128/92	*H. J. Banks v British Coal Corporation*	1994, I-1209	8.12
14.07.1994	C-91/92	*Paola Faccini Dori v Recreb Srl.*	1994, I-3325	1.33, 1.34
09.08.1994	C-359/92	*Germany v Council*	1994, I-3681	1.21, 6.11
06.04.1995	C-241 + 242/91P	*RTE + ITP v Commission (Magill)*	1995, I-743	1.42
10.05.1995	C-384/93	*Alpine Investments v Minister van Financiën*	1995, I-1141	1.4
15.06.1995	C-85/94	*Piageme v Peters (Piageme II)*	1995, I-2957	1.13
06.07.1995	C-470/93	*Verein gegen Unwesen im Handel v Mars*	1995, I-1923	2.3, 2.27
09.11.1995	C-465/93 C-466/93	*Atlanta et al. v Bundesamt für Ernährung*	1995, I-3761	1.19, 8.5
14.12.1995	C-312/93	*Peterbroeck, Van Campenhout & Cie SCS v Belgian State*	1995, I-4599	8.3
14.12.1995	C-430/93 C-431/93	*Van Schijndel and van Veen v Stichting Pensioenfonds Fysio-therapeuten*	1995, I-4705	8.3
15.12.1995	C-415/93	*Union royale belge des sociétés de football association et al. v Jean-Marc Bosman*	1995, I-4921	1.16, 8.12
05.03.1996	C-46/93 C-48/93	*Brasserie du Pêcheur v Germany; The Queen v Secretary of State for Transport / Factortame et al.*	1996, I-1029	1.35, 8.7, 8.10
07.03.1996	C-192/94	*El Corte Ingles v Rivero*	1996, I-1281	1.33, 8.27
30.04.1996	C-194/94	*CIA v Signalson*	1996, I-2201	1.33
23.05.1996	C-5/94	*The Queen v Ministry of Agriculture ex parte: Hedley Lomas*	1996, I-2553	8.7
11.07.1996	C-427/93	*Bristol-Myers Squibb v Paranova*	1996, I-3457	2.3
12.07.1996	C-180/96	*United Kingdom v Commission*	1996, I-3903	1.17
08.10.1996	C-178/94	*Dillenkofer et al. v Federal Republic*	1996, I-4845	1.9, 1.35, 8.7
12.11.1996	C-84/94	*United Kingdom v Council*	1996, I-5755	1.8, 1.23
12.12.1996	C-3/95	*Reisebüro Broede v Sandker*	1996, I-6511	1.4

Date	Case number	Parties	Reference ECR	Paragraph number
20.02.1997	C-106/95	*Mainschiffahrts-Genossenschaft v Gravières Rhénanes*	1997, I-911	7.5
20.03.1997	C-24/95	*Land Rheinland-Pfalz v Alcan Deutschland*	1997, I-1591	8.3
13.05.1997	C-233/94	*Germany v EP + Council*	1997, I-2304	1.5
29.05.1997	C-300/95	*Commission v United Kingdom*	1997, I-2649	6.29
03.07.1997	C-269/95	*Benincasa v Dentalkit*	1997, I-3767	1.37, 7.36
09.07.1997	C-34/95 C-35/95 C-36/95	*Konsumentenombudsmannen v De Agostini Forlag and TV Shop Sverge*	1997, I-3843	7.28
10.07.1997	C-261/95	*Palmisani v Istituto nazionale della previdenza sociale*	1997, I-4025	8.3
04.11.1997	C-337/95	*Parfums Christian Dior v Evora*	1997, I-06013	2.38
17.03.1998	C-45/96	*Bayr. Hyp.- und Wechselbank v Dietzinger*	1998 I-1199	9.4
16.07.1998	C-210/96	*Gut Springenheide et al. v Oberkreisdirektor Steinfurt, Lebensmittelüberwachung*	1998, I-4657	1.17, 2.27, 2.31
16.07.1998	C-355/96	*Silhouette*	1998, I-4799	1.42
26.11.1998	C-7/97	*Oscar Bronner v Mediaprint*	1998, I-7791	1.42
24.11.1998	C-274/96	*Bickel and Franz*	1998, I-7637	1.13
28.01.1999	C-303/97	*Verbraucherschutzverein v Sektkellerei Kessler*	1999, I-513	1.11, 2.3, 2.27
23.02.1999	C-63/97	*BMW v Deeni*	1999, I-905	2.39
16.03.1999	C-159/97	*Trasporti Castelletti Spedizioni Internazionali v Hugo Trumpy*	1999, I-1597	7.5
22.04.1999	C-423/97	*Travel Vac SL v Manuel José Antelm Sanchis*	1999, I-2195	9.4, 9.13
27.04.1999	C-99/96	*Mietz v Intership Yachting Sneek BV*	1999, I-2277	7.35
01.06.1999	C-126/97	*ECO-Swiss v Benetton*	1999, I-3055	7.46
03.06.1999	C-33/97	*Colim NV v Bigg's Continent Noord NV*	1999, I-3175	1.13
15.06.1999	C-140/97	*Rechberger et al. v Austria*	1999, I-3499	1.9, 1.33, 8.10
13.11.1999	C-369/97 C-376/97	*Arblade + Leloup*	1999, I-8453	7.12
13.01.2000	C-220/98	*Estée Lauder v Lancaster Group (Lifting)*	2000, I-117	1.11, 2.3, 2.23, 2.27
23.03.2000	C-208/98	*Berliner Kindl Brauerei AG v Andreas Siepert*	2000, I-1741	5.2
04.04.2000	C-465/98	*Verein gegen Unwesen in Handel und Gewerbe Köln v Adolf Darbo AG*	2000, I-2297	2.27

Date	Case number	Parties	Reference ECR	Paragraph number
06.06.2000	C-281/98	*R. Angonese v Cassa di Risparmio de Bolzano*	2000, I-4139	8.12
27.06.2000	C-240–244/98	*Océano Grupo Editorial v Quintero et al.*	2000, I-4941	1.9, 1.33, 3.21
26.09.2000	C-443/98	*Unilever*	2000, I-7435	1.33
05.10.2000	C-376/98	*Germany v EP and Council (re tobacco advertising)*	2000, I-8419	1.11, 1.22, 2.18
09.11.2000	C-381/98	*Ingmar Ltd. v Eaton Leonard Technologies*	2000, I-9305	7.12
10.05.2001	C-144/99	*Commission v Netherlands*	2001, I-3541	3.12, 3.16, 3.21
10.05.2001	C-203/99	*Veedfald v Århus Amtskommune*	2001, I-3569	6.21, 6.23, 6.34
20.09.2001	C-453/99	*Courage v Crehan*	2001, I-6297	8.13
09.10.2001	C-377/98	*Netherlands v EP and Council*	2001, I-7079	1.22
25.10.2001	C-112/99	*Toshiba v Katun*	2001, I-7945	2.37
22.11.2001	C-541/99 C-542/99	*Cape Snc v Idealservice; Idealservice v OMAI*	2001, I-9049	1.37, 1.39, 3.14
13.12.2001	C-481/99	*Heininger v Bayerische Hypothekenbank*	2001, I-9945	1.9, 1.36, 5.21, 9.4, 9.13
19.02.2002	C-309/99	*Wouters et al. v Algemeine Rad van de Nederlandse Orde*	2002, I-1577	1.12, 8.12
05.03.2002	C-386/00	*Axa Royale Belge v Geores Ochoa et al.*	2002, I-2209	3.18
12.03.2002	C-168/00	*Leitner v TUI Deutschland*	2002, I-2631	1.41
25.04.2002	C-154/00	*Commission v Greece*	2002, I-3879	6.30
25.04.2002	C-183/00	*Gonzalez Sánchez v Medicina Asturia*	2002, I-3901	6.30
25.04.2002	C-52/00	*Commission v France*	2002, I-3827	1.30, 5.11, 6.30
07.05.2002	C-478/99	*Commission v Sweden*	2002, I-4147	2.42, 3.24
11.06.2002	C-96/00	*Rudolf Gabriel*	2002, I-6367	7.37
17.09.2002	C-334/00	*Officine Meccaniche Tacconi v Wagner Sinto Maschinenfabrik*	2002, I-7357	7.30, 7.42
01.10.2002	C-167/00	*Verein für Konsumenteninformation v Henkel*	2002, I-8111	7.34, 8.26, 8.40
21.11.2002	C-473/00	*Cofidis S.A. v Jean Louis Fredout*	2002, I-10875	3.10, 3.22
10.12.2002	C-491/01	*The Queen v Secretary of Health ex parte BAT*	2002, I-11453	1.6
08.04.2003	C-244/00	*Van Doren + Q. v Lifestyle sports + sportswear et al.*	2003, I-3051	2.51
08.04.2003	C-44/01	*Pippig v Hartlauer Handelsgesellschaft et al.*	2003, I-3095	2.37, 2.51
12.06.2003	C-112/00	*Eugen Schmidberger v Austria*	2003, I-5659	1.16

Date	Case number	Parties	Reference ECR	Paragraph number
30.09.2003	C-224/01	*G. Köbler v Austria*	2003, I-10239	8.7
06.11.2003	C-243/01	*Gambelli et al.*	2003, I-13031	2.13
07.01.2004	C-100/02	*Gerolsteiner v Putsch*	2004, I-691	2.29
04.03.2004	C-264/02	*Cofinoga Mérignac v Sachithanathan*	2004, I-2157	3.18, 5.2
25.03.2004	C-71/02	*Herbert Karner Industrie-Auktionen v Troostwijk GmbH*	2004, I-3025	1.11, 1.31
01.04.2004	C-237/02	*Freiburger Kommunalbauten v Hofstetter*	2004, I-3403	3.21
29.04.2004	C-418/01	*IMS Health v NDC Health*	2004, I-5939	1.42
10.06.2004	C-168/02	*Rudolf Kronhofer v Marianne Maier*	2004, I-6009	7.42
13.07.2004	C-429/04	*Bacardi France v TF1*	2004, I-6613	7.28
09.09.2004	C-70/03	*Commission v Spain*	2004, I-7999	3.20
14.09.2004	C-19/03	*VZ HH v O2*	2004 I-8183	1.19
05.10.2004	C-397/01	*Bernhard Pfeiffer et al. v Deutsches Rotes Kreuz*	2004, I-8835	1.32
05.10.2004	C-442/02	*Caixa-Bank v Ministère de L'Economie*	2004, I-8961	1.4
12.10.2004	C-222/02	*Peter Paul et al. v Germany*	2004, I-9425	1.33, 8.7
20.01.2005	C-27/02	*Engler v Janus Versand*	2005, I-481	7.8, 7.37
20.01.2005	C-464/01	*Johann Gruber v BayWa AG*	2005, I-439	1.36, 1.37, 3.14, 7.8, 7.15, 7.36
27.01.2005	C-125/04	*Denuit, Betty Cordenier v Transorient Mosaïque Voyages et Culture*	2005, I-923	8.24
01.03.2005	C-281/02	*Andrew Owusu v N.B. Jackson et al.*	2005, I-1383	7.32
10.03.2005	C-336/03	*Easy Car v OFT*	2005, I-1947	1.9, 9.14
27.04.2005	C-159/02	*Gregory Paul Turner v Felix Fareed Ismail Grovit et al.*	2005, I-3565	7.32
07.07.2005	C-147/03	*Commission v Austria*	2005, I-05969	1.15
12.07.2005	C-154/04 C-155/04	*Alliance for Natural Health et al. v Secretary of State for Health*	2005, I-6451	1.6
13.10.2005	C-73/04	*B. + M. Klein v Rhodos Management*	2005, I-8667	7.33
25.10.2005	C-350/03	*Schulte v Deutsche Bausparkasse Badenia*	2005, I-9215	1.9, 1.36, 5.18
25.10.2005	C-229/04	*Crailsheimer Volksbank eG v Klaus Conrads et al.*	2005, I-9273	5.18
06.12.2005	C-453/03	*ABNA et al. v Secretary of State for Health et al.*	2005, I-10423	8.5
10.01.2006	C-302/04	*Ynos kft v János Varga*	2006, I-371	3.29

Date	Case number	Parties	Reference ECR	Paragraph number
10.01.2006	C-344/04	*The Queen and IATA, ELFAA v Dpt. of Transport*	2006, I-403	1.6, 1.28, 1.39, 7.21, 8.5
10.01.2006	C-402/03	*Skov Æg v Bilka Lavprisvarehus A/S; Bilka Lavprisvarehus v Mikkelsen et al.*	2006, I-199	1.32, 6.18,629
09.02.2006	C-127/04	*O'Byrne v Sanofi*	2006, I-1313	6.9, 6.24, 6.31
06.03.2006	C-338/04 et al.	*M. Placanica*	2006, I-1891	2.13
14.03.2006	C-177/04	*Commission v France*	2006, I-2461	1.32, 6.32
07.04.2006	C-212/04	*K. Adeneler/ELOG*	2006, I-6057	1.34
13.07.2006	C-295–298/04	*Vicenzo Manfredi et al. v Lloyd Adriatico Assicurazioni*	2006, I-6619	8.3
19.09.2006	C-356/04	*Lidl and Colruyt (Lidl I)*	2006, I-8501	2.38. 239
26.10.2006	C-168/05	*Elisa Maria Mostaza Claro v Centro Movil Milenium*	2006, I-10421	1.1, 1.9, 3.21, 3.27, 7.41, 7.44, 8.25
23.11.2006	C-238/05	*Asnef v Ausbank*	2006, I-11125	1.2, 1.25
13.03.2007	C-432/05	*Unibet v Justitiekanslern*	2007, I-2271	8.2, 8.9
17.04.2007	C-470/03	*A.G.M.COS.MET v. Suomen Valtio & T. Lehtinen*	2007, I-2749	8.7
19.04.2007	C-381/05	*Landtsheer*	2007 I-3114	2.38
26.04.2007	C-348/04	*Boehringer Ingelheim v Swingward*	2007, I-3391	1.42
28.06.2007	C-331/05P	*Internationaler Hilfsfonds v Commission*	2007, I-5475	8.27
04.10.2007	C-429/05	*Rampion v Franfinance*	2007, I-8017	3.29, 5.24
11.12.2007	C-438/05	*ITF & FSU v Viking*	2007, I-10779	1.12, 8.12
18.12.2007	C-351/05	*Laval v et al. v Svenska Bygnaddsarbetareförbundet*	2007, I-11767	1.12, 8.12
29.01.2008	C-275/06	*Promusicae v Telefonica*	2008, I-271	1.42
17.04.2008	C-404/06	*Quelle AG v Bundesverband der Verbraucherzentralen*	2008, I-2685	4.24
17.07.2008	C-94/07	*Raccanelli v MPG*	2008, I-5939	8.12
16.12.2008	C-205/07	*Gysbrechts*	2008, I-9947	1.31
23.04.2009	C-261 + 299/07	*VTB-VAB v Total Belgium NV*	2009, I-2949	2.11, 2.17, 2.44, 2.46
23.04.2009	C-509/07	*Luigi Scarpelli v NEOS Banca SpA*	2009, I-3311	5.24
14.05.2009	C-180/06	*Renate Ilsinger v Martin Dreschers*	2009, I-3961	7.37
04.06.2009	C-243/08	*Pannon v Erzsébet Sustikné Győrfi*	2009, I-4713	3.29
16.07.2009	C-189/08	*Zuid Chemie v Phillippos Mineralenfabriek*	2009, I-6917	7.42

Date	Case number	Parties	Reference ECR	Paragraph number
03.09.2009	C-489/07	*Pia Messner v Fa. St. Krüger*	2009, I-7315	9.14
06.10.2009	C-40/08	*Asturcom v Christina Rodrigues Nogueria*	2009, I-9579	3.29, 7.41, 8.25
19.11.2009	C-402 + 432/07	*Sturgeon et al.*	2009, I-10923	1.41
02.12.2009	C-358/08	*Aventis Pasteur*	2009, I-11395	6.31
17.12.2009	C-227/08	*Martin*	2009, I-11939	3.29
14.01.2010	C-304/08	*Plus Warengesellschaft*	2010, I-217	2.11, 2.44
11.03.2010	C-522/08	*Telekomunikacja Polska*	2010, I-2079	2.15
18.03.2010	C-317/08	*Alassini et al. v Telecom It.*	2010, I-2213	1.18, 8.3
03.06.2010	C-484/08	*Caja de Ahorros y Monte de Piedad de Madrid v Ausbanc*	2010, I-4785	3.12
08.06.2010	C-58/08	*Vodaphone et al. v Secretary of State*	2010, I-4999	1.10, 1.21
21.10.2010	C-467/08	*Padawan*	2010, I-10055	4.35d
09.11.2010	C-137/08	*VB Penzügyi Lizing v Schneider*	2010, I-10847	3.24a, 3.27, 3.29a
09.11.2010	C-540/08	*Mediaprint*	2010, I-10909	2.11, 2.44
16.11.2010	C-76/10	*Pohotovost' s. r. o. v Iveta Korčkovská*	2010, I-11557	3.29, 5.15, 5.34, 5.42
18.11.2010	C-159/09	*Lidl II*	2010, I-11761	2.28
07.12.2010	C-585/08 + 144/09	*Peter Pammer et al. v Reederei Karl Schlüter et al.*	2010, I-12527	7.17a
01.03.2011	C-236/09	*Ass. Belge Tests Achats*	2011, I-773	1.18
12.03.2011	C-122/10	*Konsumentombudsmannen v Ving Sverige AB*	2011, I-3903	2.34
16.06.2011	C-65 + 87/09	*Gebr. Weber et al. v J. Wittmer et al.*	2011, I-5257	4.24a
30.06.2011	C-288/11	*Wamo v JBC NV and Modemakers Fashion*	2011, I-5835	2.44
25.10.2011	C-509/09 + 161/10	*eDate Advertising et al.*	2011, I-10269	7.24
21.12.2011	C-495/10	*Centre Hospitalier universitaire de Besancon v Thomas Dutrueux et al.*	2011, I-nyr	6.22
15.03.2012	C-488/11	*Perenicova*	2012, I-nyr	3.6
26.04.2012	C-488/11	*Invitel*	2012, I-nyr	3.22b, 3.26, 3.27, 3.29
14.06.2012	C-618/10	*Banco espanol di credito v Camino*	2012, I-nyr	3.22a, 3.29, 5.42
05.07.2012	C-49/11	*Content Services*	2012, I-nyr	8.23c

Date	Case number	Parties	Reference ECR	Paragraph number
12.07.2012	C-602/10	*SC Volksbank România SA v Autoritatea Naţională pentru Protecţia Consumatorilor – Comisariatul Judeţean pentru Protecţia Consumatorilor Călăraşi*	2012, I-nyr	5.3, 5.11, 5.34
06.09.2012	C-190/11	*D. Mühlleitner v A. u. W. Yusufi*	2012, I-nyr	7.17a
23.10.2012	C-581 + 629/10	*Nelson et al. v Lufthansa*	2012, I-nyr	1.41
06.12.2012	C-169/11	*EU v Otis et al.*	2012, I-nyr	8.13
17.01.2013	C-206/11	*Köck*	2013, I-nyr	2.44
23.01.2013	C-283/11	*Sky Österreich v ORF*	2013, I-nyr	1.11
31.01.2013	C-12/11	*Mc Donagh v RyanAir*	2013, I-nyr	1.41
21.02.2013	C-472/11	*Banif Plus Bank Zrt v Csaba Czipai, Viktória Czipai*	2013, I-nyr	3.29, 5.42
14.03.2013	C-415/11	*Mohammed Aziz v Catalunyacaixa*	2013, I-nyr	1.9, 3.21a, 3.29a, 5.42, 8.5a
21.03.2013	C-92/11	*RWE Vertrieb v VZ NRW*	2013, I-nyr	3.11, 3.17, 3.18. 3.24a, 3.26
11.04.2013	C-361/11	*K. Berger v Freistaat Bayern*	2013, I-nyr	1.14
30.05.2013	C-488/11	*Asbeek*	2013, I-nyr	3.6, 3.14, 3.15, 3.22a
18.07.2013	C-265/12	*Citroen Belux*	2013, I-nyr	2.16
03.10.2013	C-32/12	*Soledad Duarte Hueros v Atoiciba et al.*	Opinion of AG Kokott	4.28a
17.10.2013	C-218/2	*L. Emrek v V. Sabranovic*	2013, I-nyr	7.17a
17.11.2013	C-391/12	*RLvS mbH*	2013, I-nyr	2.11
21.11.2013	C-482/12	*Peter Macinský, Eva Macinská v Getfin*	Opinion of AG Wahl	3.21
05.12.2013	C-508/12	*Walter Vapenik v Josef Thurner*	2013, I-nyr	7.36
05.12.2013	C-413/12	*Ass. de Consumidores Independientes (ACI) de Castilla y Leon v Anuntis Segundanamo Esp.*	2013, I-nyr	3.27, 8.26, 8.40
12.12.2013	C-470/12	*Pohotovost' v Mifoslav Vasuta*	Opinion of AG Wahl	3.27
19.12.2013	C-281/12	*Trento Svilupo and Centrale Adriatica*	Opinion of AG Kokott	2.26

CHAPTER 1
ECONOMIC LAW, CONSUMER INTERESTS, AND EU INTEGRATION

Norbert Reich and Hans-W. Micklitz

CONTENTS

This is an ex-library book and may have the usual library/used-book markings inside.This book has hardback covers. In good all round condition. No dust jacket.

ORDER NUMBER

PO NYAATP08

BOOK NUMBER

3993889

BAY NUMBER

820-1

AUTHOR	Reich, Norbert
TITLE	European Consumer Law

Bibliography:

Acquis group (ed.), *Principles of the Existing EC Contract Law (Acquis Principles)*, 2007; G. Alpa, *The Future of European Contract Law*, in: Twigg-Flesner et al. (eds.), *The Yearbook of Consumer Law 2008*, 19–34; A. Anderman, *EC Competition Law and Intellectual Property Rights*, 2000; F. Benyon (ed.), *Services and the EU Citizen*, 2013; T. Bourgoignie, *Eléments d'une théorie de droit de la consommation*, 1988; T. Bourgoignie/D. Trubek, *Consumer Law, Common Market and Federalism*, 1987; F. Cafaggi (ed.), *The Institutional framework of European Private Law*, 2006; J. Calais-Auloy/H. Temple, *Droit de la consommation*, 8th ed. 2010; D. Caruso, The Baby and the Bath Water – A Critique of European Contract Law, *AmJCompL* 2013, 475; P. Craig/G. de Burca, *Cases and Materials on EU Law*, 4th ed. 2004, 5th ed. 2011; A. Dashwood, *From Duyn to Mangold via Marshall: Reducing Direct Effect to Absurdity? Cambridge Yearbook of European Legal Studies*, Vol. 9, 2006–2007, 81; S. Douglas-Scott, *Constitutional Law of the EU*, 2002; J. Drexl, *Die wirtschaftliche Selbstbestimmung des Verbrauchers*, 1998; U. Everling/W.-H. Roth (eds.), *Mindestharmonisierung im Europäischen Binnenmarkt*, 1997; H. Faber, Elemente verschiedener Verbraucherbegriffe, *ZEuP* 1998, 854; W. van Gerven, Of rights, remedies and procedures, *CMLRev* 2000, 501; S. Grundmann, Information, party autonomy and economic agents in European contract law, *CMLRev* 2002, 269; S. Grundmann, *Europäisches Schuldvertragsrecht*, 1999; S. Grundmann/W. Kerber/S. Weatherill (eds.), *Party Autonomy and the Role of Information in the Internal Market*, 2001; S. Grundmann/F. Ochmann, German Contract Law Five Years after the Fundamental Contract Law Reform, *ERCL* 2007, 446; G. Hadfield/R. Howse/M. Trebilcock, Information-Based Principles for Rethinking Consumer Protection Policy, *JCP* 1998, 131; J. Handler, *Social Movements and the Legal System – A Theory of Law Reform and Social Change*, 1978; B. Heiderhoff, *Grundstrukturen des nationalen und europäischen Verbrauchervertragsrechts*, 2004; B. Heiderhoff/M. Kenny, The Commission's 2007 Green Paper on the Consumer Acquis: deliberate deliberation?, *ELRev* 2007, 740; N. Helberger et al., Digital Content Contracts for Consumers, *JCP* 2013, 37; N. Helberger et al., *Digital Consumers and the Law*, 2013; T. Hervey, Community and National Competence in Health after Tobacco Advertising, *CMLRev* 2001, 1421; M.W. Hesselink, Consumer Protection, Citizenship, or Justice?, *ERPrL* 2007, 323–348; E. Hondius, The Notion of Consumer: EU vs. Member States, *Sydney Law Review* 2006, 89–98; E. Hondius, The protection of the weak party in a harmonised European contract law, *JCP* 2004, 245; G. Howells/H.-W. Micklitz/T. Wilhelmsson, *European Fair Trading Law*, 2006; G. Howells/T. Wilhelmsson, EC Consumer Law – Has it Come of Age?, *ELRev* 2003, 370; G. Howells/T. Wilhelmsson, *EC Consumer Law*, 1997; G. Howells/S. Weatherill, *Consumer Protection Law*, 2005; N. Huls (ed.), *Over indebtedness of consumers in the EC Member States*, 1996; J. Karsten, Passengers, Consumers, and Travellers, *JCP* 2007, 117–136; J. Karsten/A.R. Sinai, The Action Plan on European Contract Law: Perspectives for the Future of European Contract and Consumer Law, *JCP* 2003, 159; V. Kendall, *EC Consumer Law*, 1995; M. Kenny, *The Transformation of Public and Private EC Competition Law*, 2002; L. Krämer, *EEC-Consumer Law*, 1986; L. Krämer, The European Union, Consumption, and Consumer Law, in: *Liber amicorum Bernd Stauder*, 2006, 177–194; L. Krämer/H.-W. Micklitz/K. Tonner (eds.), *Law and Diffuse Interests in the European Legal Order – Recht und diffuse Interessen in der Europäischen Rechtsordnung, Festschrift für N. Reich*, 1997; M. Kuneva, The European Contract Law and Review of the Consumer

Acquis, *ZEuP* 2007, 955–960; L. Loacker, Verbrauchervertrage mit gemischter Zwecksetzung, *JZ* 2013, 234; B. Lurger, *Grundfragen der Vereinheitlichung des Vertragsrechts in der EU*, 2002; A. Maack, *Die Durchsetzung des AGB-rechtlichen Transparenzgebots in internationalen Verbraucherverträgen*, 2001; U. Magnus/ H.-W. Micklitz, *Liability for the Safety of Services*, 2006; H.-W. Micklitz, The Concept of Competitive Contract Law, *PennState IntLRev* 2005, 549; H.-W. Micklitz, *The Politics of Judicial Co-operation in the EU*, 2005; H.-W. Micklitz, The Principles of European Contract Law and the Protection of the Weaker Party, *JCP* 2004, 339; H.-W. Micklitz, *Internationales Produktsicherheitsrecht*, 1995, H.-W. Micklitz, *The Relationship Between National and European Consumer Policy – Challenges and Perspectives*, in: Twiggg-Flesner et al. (eds.), *The Yearbook of Consumer Law 2008*, 35–66; H.-W. Micklitz, Commentary before §§13 BGB, in: *Münchner Kommentar zum BGB*, 6th ed. 2012; H.-W. Micklitz (ed.), *Social Justice in EU Private Law*, 2011; H.-W. Micklitz, *Brauchen Unternehmen und Verbraucher eine neue Architektur des Verbraucherrechts*, Gutachten 69. Dt.- Juristentag 2012; H.-W. Micklitz, Do Consumers and Businesses Need a New Architecture of Consumer Law, *YEL 2013*, 266; H.-W. Micklitz/N. Reich (eds.), *Public Interest Litigation before European Courts*, 1996; H.-W. Micklitz/N. Reich, Europäisches Verbraucherrecht – Quo vadis? (Überlegungen zum Grünbuch der Kommission zur Überprüfung des gemeinschaftlichen Besitzstandes im Verbraucherschutz v. 8.2.2007), *VuR* 2007, 121; H.-W. Micklitz/N. Reich/S. Weatherill, EU Treaty Revision and Consumer Protection, *JCP* 2004, 367; H.-W. Micklitz/N. Reich, Cronica de una muerte anunciada – The Commission Proposal on a Directive of Consumer Rights, *CMLRev* 2009, 471; R. Okedij, Access to Copyrighted Digitalised Information Works, in: Maskus/Reichmann (eds.), *International Public Goods and Transfer of Technology*, 2005, 142; P. Oliver/M. Jarvis, *Free Movement of Goods in the EC*, 4th ed. 2003, 5th ed. 2010; E. Paasavirta/I. Rissanen (eds.), *Principles of Justice and the Law of the EU*, 1995; M. Poiares Maduro, *We the Court. The European Court of Justice and the European Economic Institution*, 1998; H. Pelkmans, *The Institutional Economics of European Integration*, in: Cappelletti et al. (eds.), Integration through Law, I/1, 1986; S. Prechal, *Directives in EC Law*, 2nd ed. 2005; M. Radeideh, *Fair Trading in EC Law – Information and Consumer Choice in the Internal Market*, 2005; S. Rachagan (ed.), *Consumer Protection in the WTO Era*, 1999; I. Ramsay (ed.), *Consumer Law in the Global Economy*, 1997; N. Reich, *General Principles of EU Civil Law*, 2013; N. Reich, EU Strategies in Finding the Optional Consumer Law Instrument, *ERCL* 2012, 1–29; N. Reich, The Social, Political and Cultural Dimension of EU Private Law, in: R. Schulze, *European Private Law – Current Status and Perspectives* 2011, 57; N. Reich, Crisis or Future of European Consumer Law, in: Twiggg-Flesner et al. (eds.), *The Yearbook of Consumer Law 2009*, 2008, 3; N. Reich, Protection of Consumers' Economic Interests by EC contract law – some follow-up remarks, *Sydney Law Review* 2006, 37; N. Reich, The Constitutional Relevance of Citizenship and Free Movement in an Enlarged Union, *ELJ* 2005, 675; N. Reich, A European Contract Law or an EU Contract Law Regulation for Consumers?, *JCP* 2005, 383; N. Reich, The "Courage" doctrine: Encouraging or discouraging compensation for antitrust injuries?, *CMLRev* 2005, 35; N. Reich, The Consumer as Citizen, the Citizen as Consumer, in: *Liber amicorum Jean Calais-Auloy*, 2004, 943; N. Reich/H.-W. Micklitz, *Europäisches Verbraucherrecht*, 4th ed. 2003; H. Rösler, *Europäisches Konsumentenvertragsrecht*, 2004; H. Rösler, Auslegungsgrundsätze des Europäischen Verbaucherprivatrechts in

Theorie und Praxis, *RabelsZ* 2007, 495; M. Ross, Promoting Soldiarity: From Public Services, to a European Model of Competition, *CMLRev* 2007, 1057–1080; P. Rott, Minimum harmonisation for the completion of the internal market?, *CMLRev* 2003, 1107; P. Rott, Consumers and Services of General Interest: Is EC Consumer Law the Future?, *JCP* 2007, 49; U. Rörig, *Die Direktwirkung von Richtlinien in Privatrechtsverhältnissen*, 2001; B. Schäfer/C. Ott, *Economic Analysis of Civil Law*, 2008; H. Schulte-Nölke/C. Twigg-Flesner/M. Ebers (eds.), *EC Consumer Law Compendium*, 2008; H. Schulte-Nölke/R. Schulze (eds.), *Europäische Rechtsangleichung und nationale Privatrechte*, 1999; R. Schulze (ed.), *Common Frame of Reference and Existing EC Contract Law*, 2008; D. Staudenmeyer, The Place of Consumer Contract Law Within the Process on European Contract Law, *JCP* 2004, 269; E. Steindorff, *EG-Vertrag und Privatrecht*, 1996; J. Stuyck, EC Competition law After Modernisation: More than Ever in the Interest of Consumers, *JCP* 2005, 1; J. Stuyck, European Consumer Law after the Treaty of Amsterdam: Consumer Policy in or beyond the Internal Market?, *CMLRev* 2000, 357; J. Stuyck, Patterns of justice in the European Constitutional Charter: minimum harmonisation in the field of consumer law, in: Krämer et al., *Law and diffuse interests*, 1997, 279; M. Tamm/K. Tonner, *Verbraucherrecht – ein Handbuch*, 2012; E. Terryn et al. (Al.), *Landmark Cases of EU Consumer Law – In Honour of Jules Styck*, 2013; K. Tonner/K. Fangerow, Directive 2011/83 on consumer rights: a new approach to European consumer law?, *EuVR* 2012, 67; T. Tridimas, *General Principles of Community Law*, 2nd ed. 2006; C. Twigg-Flesner, No sense of purpose or direction? The modernisation of European Consumer Law, *ERCL* 2007, 198; C. Twigg-Flesner, *The Europeanisation of Contract Law*, 2008; C. Twigg-Flesner, Time to Do the Job Properly – The Case for a New Approach to EU Consumer Legislation, *JCP* 2010, 355; H. Ulrich, Intellectual Property, Access to Information, and Antirust, in: Dreyfus/Zimmermann/First (eds), *Expanding the Boundaries of IP*, 2001, 367; H. Unberath/A. Johnston, The Double-Headed Approach of the ECJ concerning Consumer Protection, *CMLRev* 2007, 1237; T. Vissol (ed.), *The Euro: Consequences of the Consumer and the Citizen*, 1999; S. Weatherill, The CRD: How and why a quest for 'coherence' has (largely) failed, *CMLRev* 2012, 1279; S. Weatherill, *EU Consumer Law and Policy*, 2005, 2nd ed. 2013; S. Weatherill, *Justifying Limits to Party Autonomy in the Internal Market – EC-Legislation in the Field of Consumer Protection*, in: Grundmann/Kerber/Weatherill (eds.), *Party Autonomy*, 2001, 173; S. Weatherill, *Consumer Policy*, in: Craig/de Burca (eds.), *The evolution of EU Law*, 1999, 693; J.H.H. Weiler/N.J.S. Lockhart, Taking rights seriously. Seriously: The European Court and its fundamental rights jurisprudence, *CMLRev* 1995, 51; T. Wilhelmsson, The Abuse of the 'Confident Consumer' as Justification for EC Consumer Law, *JCP* 2004, 317; T. Wilhelmsson, Private Law in the EU: Harmonised or Fragmented Europeanisation?, *ERPL* 2002, 77; T. Wilhelmsson, Full Harmonisation of Consumer Contract Law?, *ZEuP* 2008, 225; T. Wilhelmsson, *Is There a European Consumer Law – and Should There Be One? Centro di studi e ricerche di diritto comparato e straniero, No. 41*, Rome 2000; T. Wilhelmsson, *Social Contract Law and European Integration*, 1994; T. Wilhelmsson (ed.), *Perspectives of Critical Contract Law*, 1993; T. Wilhelmsson/E. Punio/A. Pohjolainen (eds.), *Private Law and the Many Cultures of Europe*, 2007; C. Willett, Can Disallowance of Unfair Contract Terms Be Regarded as a Redistribution of Power in Favour of Consumers?, *JCP* 1994, 471.

I. ECONOMIC LAW AND CONSUMER INTERESTS IN THE COMPLEX RELATIONS OF COMMUNITY/UNION, MEMBER STATES AND UNDERTAKINGS

1.1 The present book addresses and systematises the central areas of European economic law from the perspective of the consumer as a typically *homo oeconomicus passivus*, i.e. as a "passive market participant". In essence, consumer law purports to guarantee and protect the autonomy of the individual, who appears in the market without any profit-making intentions, primarily against undertakings which engage actively in the market and also against Member States and the Community, now Union.[1] It proceeds by providing the following:

(1) guarantees of consumers' freedom of choice and decision, in particular by preventing fraudulent misrepresentation and by providing material information about products, services and markets;
(2) protection of legitimate expectations against suppliers of products and services;
(3) protection of special legal interests such as health and safety of products and services;
(4) judicial protection and access to justice including collective legal protection and alternative dispute resolution mechanisms.

The protection of legal interests is tied into a network of relations which also concern the consumer's freedom of decision and his legitimate expectations. Within the Single European Market, namely the Internal Market, the Community itself, the Member States and undertakings play an active role. These relations frame markets for consumer goods and services within the EU as a whole. In different areas and to differing degrees, they also grant subjective rights to the European citizen or resident, to some extent also collective rights of consumer organisations and business organisations against undertakings, associations of undertakings, Member States and the EU itself.

The legal relations between the Union, Member States and undertakings were determined by a set of legal rights and duties. The consumer rights as an individual or as a collective supplement the principle of private autonomy which is generally recognised by EU law.[2] Undertakings, Member States and the Union are addressees of those rights which purport to grant freedom of decision,

[1] For an overview of the abundant literature emphasising different aspects of consumer protection in the EU see: Reich, *Liber amicorum Calais-Auloy*, 943; Howells/Wilhelmsson, *EC Consumer Law*; Micklitz, *PennState IntLRev* 2005, 549; Stuyck, *CMLRev* 2000, 367; Drexl, 44; Radeideh; Weatherill, *EU Consumer Law and Policy*.

[2] Reich, *General Principles of EU Civil Law*, Chapter 1 on "framed autonomy".

guarantee legitimate expectations, protect health and safety interests and make access to justice possible.

The Lisbon Reform Treaty of 13 December 2007,[3] which entered into force on 1 December 2009, has not changed the basic regulatory structure of the Internal Market. Article 3(3) TEU repeats that "the Union shall establish an internal market". Article 4(2) TEU lists the internal market and consumer protection as areas of "shared competence" between the Union and the Member States. The "Community" was renamed the "Union"; both terms will be used with an identical meaning in this paper. The EC Treaty was renamed and rearranged as the "Treaty on the Functioning of the EU" (TFEU), headed by the more general "Treaty on European Union" (TEU). The Charter of Fundamental Rights of 2000 in its 2007 version was incorporated into Union law as having same legal value (Article 6(1) TEU).

The relationship between Member States and undertakings centres around implementation of protective provisions under Union law which also serve the consumer's interests. Despite the significance of health and safety interests of consumers, however, the main objective of those provisions is primarily the free access of undertakings to the Internal Market in the sense of Article 26(2) TFEU.

From this point of view, European economic law becomes the law of the Internal Market,[4] which *indirectly protects consumer interests*. The interests promoted and protected thereby could be described as "diffuse"[5] as they are not restricted to specific interest groups or a clearly definable set of people; they potentially apply to any citizen or resident whatever their nationality. A policy which employs economic law for the protection of such interests purports to enhance "quality of life".[6] According to the preamble of the EC Treaty the "contracting parties" affirm, *inter alia*, "as the essential objective of their efforts the constant improvements of the living and working conditions of their peoples". Article 3(3) TEU insists somewhat more "socially and ecologically minded" on the "sustainable development of Europe based on balanced economic growth ... It shall combat social exclusion and discrimination, and shall promote social justice and protection". Neither has had any clear impact on the existing regime of EU consumer law, perhaps with the exception of consumer over-indebtedness, where the European Commission has adopted resolutions

---

3 OJ C 306 of 17 December 2006.

4 Cf. Stuyck, *supra* note 1, 389; critique Howells/Wilhelmsson, *ELRev* 2003, 370.

5 This is not to say that "diffuse interests" need to be restricted to consumer protection; Handler's assessment, *Social Movements and the Legal System – A Theory of Law Reform and Social Change*, includes "environmental policy", "civil rights" and "social welfare". Cf. also the first German edition of this book: Reich, *Förderung und Schutz diffuser Interessen durch die EG*, 1987.

6 See ECJ, 26 October 2006, C-168/05, *Elisa Maria Mostaza Claro v Centro Movil Milenium* [2006] ECR I-10421 at para 37.

aimed at overcoming a possible exclusion of over-indebted consumers from the market.[7]

Quality of life is a very broad term. Here it will be defined as the right to information, freedom of choice and decision with regard to marketing activities and contracting by undertakings active on the Internal Market, protection of legitimate expectations, legal protection, and access to justice as well as to ADR mechanisms in favour of the European *homo oeconomicus passivus*. The following paragraphs provide a brief overview of the different stages of the development of EU consumer law as part of European economic law. The significance has shifted from an initial indirect recognition of consumer interests as a regulatory element of Community – now Union – law to an increase in its autonomy by creating certain consumer rights which lately, however, have been put under pressure because of the efficiency and competence critique insisting on the concept of "internal market" as the basis for consumer protection. Accordingly, the question of the relationship between Union and national consumer law, including in particular the legal effects of directives, becomes of primary importance. There is a problematic general shift from minimum to complete harmonisation measures implying a slow but steady "competence creep" towards the EU[8] accompanied by reduced power for Member States in consumer legislation. We will briefly examine the different "consumer concepts" within EU law and finally give a critical assessment of future perspectives of an ever more efficiency-driven EU consumer law, where new types of "governance" like self-regulation are given a more prominent position.

II. THE INITIAL "PRODUCTIVIST CONCEPT" OF THE EEC TREATY AND THE PROBLEM OF THE PROMOTION OF CONSUMER INTERESTS

1.2 Initially the Treaty on the European Economic Community (EEC) was aligned "productively", i.e. focusing on the supplier.[9] In its institutions and legal structure it primarily concentrated on the producer of economic value, for whom it purported to make available more extensive areas for production and distribution. To that extent the understanding of integration as governed by the Treaty was aimed towards the achievement of a "Common Market", to become later the "Internal Market". Integration within the then EEC was purported to be primarily market related and to implement the fundamental freedoms in favour

---

7 G. Comparato, EU's steps towards a financially inclusive European private law, EUI-ERPL Working Paper, 2014 forthcoming.

8 Weatherill, *ERCL* 2006, 136 at 139.

9 Weatherill, *supra* note 1, 1–33, describing the evolution of Community consumer policy.

of the active market participant. EEC "fundamental rights" were formulated as market access rights.

This realisation does not stand in contradiction to the fact that the "Internal Market" is only the means to an increase in quality of life in terms of consumer welfare, as stated in the preamble and in Article 2 of the EEC Treaty. Article 3 of the EEC Treaty stated clearly that this objective was primarily to be achieved by implementing production-related measures. In other words, the promotion of quality of life was dependent on the promotion of a European policy focusing on production and distribution. The "raising of the standard of living and quality of life" according to Article 2 of the EEC Treaty had been subordinated to an integration mechanism related to production without constituting an independent and specific policy element.

To that extent the original conception of integration of the European Economic Community was in accordance with the classical notion of free trade: consumer welfare and quality of life were to appear quasi-automatically as the results of market freedoms,[10] provided certain conditions were present (openness of the market under a system of competition and non-discrimination).

According to the original concept of the Treaty, the "four freedoms" – free movement of goods, persons (as self-employed persons by establishment or as workers), services and capital – concerned conditions for production and distribution. The concept was addressed to the "active market participant". Producers, traders, importers, service providers and workers were to be released from national – and therefore artificial – boundaries and to be allowed to engage in a larger marketing area, i.e. the internal market. To that extent they indirectly promoted various consumer welfare interests in terms of an increased individual freedom of choice.

At first glance, the remaining Community policies appeared to be less production-orientated. However, they are mainly addressed to active economic subjects, in particular to undertakings. This is particularly so in relation to competition policy, which the Treaty regards as a system to protect competition within the Single European Market against distortion (Article 3(g) EC formerly Article 3(f) EEC Treaty, now Article 3(3) TEU), i.e. the policy is imposed on undertakings as freedom of competition but also grants them freedom of market access. This is so because it is addressed towards producers, service providers, traders, importers and other economic subjects who want to avoid distortion of competition by interfering with their economic activities. To that extent competition policy supplements the other freedoms as governed in the Treaty.[11] Neither a Member State nor private barriers shall obstruct or limit the freedom to conduct business in an internal market. Compared to this, in the scope of

---

10 Cf. Pelkmans, The Institutional Economics of European Integration, in: Cappelletti et al. (eds.), *Integration through Law*, I/1, 318.

11 For a conceptual account, see Reich, *supra* note 2, para 1.14.

assessing competition-restricting measures, the role of the consumer or customer is reduced to allowing them a "fair share of the resulting benefit" as evidenced by the non-coincidental formulation of Article 81(3) EC. According to the ECJ in its *Asnef* case,[12] the "beneficial nature of the effect on all consumers in the relevant markets … must be taken into consideration, not the effect on each member of that category of consumers", in the case at hand concerning the effect of a register of debtors on access to credit.

1.3 These findings merely illuminate the European Economic Community's – renamed European Community (EC) after the Maastricht Treaty of 1992 – difficulties in establishing and enforcing an autonomous policy promoting the protection of consumer interests. The development of consumer policy as an independent policy and area of law took place concurrently with intensified integration, even if this autonomy remains constantly precarious.[13] Five stages may be determined: the European Commission developed a catalogue of "consumer rights" in two consumer-political programmes dated 1975 and 1981.[14] The Commission based the catalogue on international discussions and applied it to the EC.[15] It demanded the realisation of five fundamental rights in favour of the consumer, and to that extent is supported by the Council of Ministers, then the highest European legislative organ; these were:

(1) the right to protection of health and safety;
(2) the right to protection of economic interests;
(3) the right of redress;
(4) the right of information and education; and
(5) the right to representation (right to be heard).

On the one hand these rights are derived from the economically weaker position of the consumer and from the overwhelming bargaining strength of the supplier on the other hand. A precise catalogue containing measures shall assist in realising these rights.

1.4 Initially, court rulings of the European Court of Justice (ECJ) did not directly deal with cases of consumer interests. These cases were concerned with the justification of measures taken by Member States, the effect of which was the restriction of the free movement of goods and services contrary to Article 34 and

12 ECJ, 23 November 2006, C-238/05, *Asnef-Aquifax v Ausbank* [2006] ECR I-11125 at para 70.
13 For the development cf. the overview provided in Stuyck, *supra* note 1, 377.
14 OJ C 92, 25 April 1975 and OJ C 133, 3 June 1981.
15 Evidence in Bourgoignie/Trubek, *Consumer Law, Common Markets and Federalism*, 89–110; Krämer, *EEC Consumer Law*, 15–53; Reich, *SydLRev* 1992, 21; Reich, *SydLRev* 2006, 37.

Article 56 TFEU. Compared to the strict exceptions contained in these Articles, since its decision in *Cassis de Dijon*[16] the ECJ has developed the broader *principle of consumer protection as an independent reason of justification* against national restrictions to free movement provided they are proportionate and non-discriminatory under Community law. This case law, originally developed for the free movement of goods, has since been made applicable *ceteris paribus* to the free movement of services and establishment.[17] Consumer protection has thus gained autonomous importance within the system of legal protection under Community law and legitimises both measures taken by Member States and the Community.[18] In relation to consumer interests, which have not been sufficiently articulated at Community level, the ECJ functions as a guardian ensuring true consumer protection or, in other words, the ECJ functions as a critic of disguised provisions which actually safeguard special interests in a protectionist way. This was and still is done by a rigid control of Member State measures under the *proportionality* principle.[19]

1.5 In the 1980s the EEC was increasingly concerned with the issue of opening the markets and there emerged the concept of a "Single European Market" or "Internal Market"[20] which had been applied beforehand in judicial decisions. Specific protective policies were only of relevance for the Community to the extent that they increased the freedom of choice of individual consumers; the approach is a liberal one related to free trade rather than a social state protective approach.

Initially, the Single European Act of 1987[21] pursued this concept in Article 14 EC (formerly Article 8a EEC), establishing firmly the objective of achieving the Single European Market by 31 December 1992 in terms of free movement of goods, persons, services and capital. It therefore set up a particular competence granting the Community a majority vote in the Council of Ministers combined with a qualified right to veto of Parliament by means of the so-called cooperation proceedings. The newly drafted Article 100a EEC (Article 95 EC = 114 TFEU) granted the Council of Ministers in cooperation with the European Parliament comprehensive powers to enact "measures" establishing and enhancing the

16 ECJ, 20 February 1979, 120/78, *REWE v Bundesmonopolverwaltung* [1979] ECR 649.

17 ECJ, 10 May 1995, C-384/93, *Alpine Investments BV v Minister van Financien* [1995] ECR I-1141 at paras 43–46; ECJ, 12 December 1996, C-3/95, *Reisebüro Broede v Sandker* [1996] ECR I-6511 at para 38; ECJ, 5 October 5004, C-442/02, *Caixa-Bank v Ministère de l'Economie* [2004] ECR I-8961.

18 Unberath/Johnston, *CMLRev* 2007, 1237, however, criticise the "double headed approach" of the ECJ by taking a stricter view on the legitimacy of Member States than of Community measures.

19 Weatherill, *supra* note 1, 42–48, explaining the *Cassis* principle.

20 The Commission's White Paper 1985, COM (1985) 310 final.

21 OJ L 169, 29 June 1987.

functioning of the internal market. These measures were subject to two limitations:

(1) The Commission shall proceed from a "high level of protection" with regard to its proposals *inter alia* in the area of consumer protection. However, this principle will not be legally binding on the other organs, in particular the European Parliament and the Council of Ministers.
(2) Single Member States may derogate as per Article 100a(4) EEC = 114(4) TFEU subject to requirements which do not concern the protection of the economic interests of the consumer – as opposed to those contained in consumer-political programmes of the EC – but which are limited to the protection of the consumer's health and safety.[22]

Consumer policy in the triple sense of freedom of choice, legitimate expectations and protection of legal interests plays an increased role in the extraordinarily dynamic realisation of the internal market. The following overview shows that with an increasing extension of the areas of policy and authoritative powers of the Community, consumer interests will gradually be further included in the law of the internal market. The internal market was to become a "social face".[23]

1.6 The fourth stage subsequent to the signing of the Maastricht Treaty on 7 February 1992, coming into force on 1 November 1993, established the express acknowledgment of consumer protection as an independent principle under Community law as per Article 129a EEC = Article 169 TFEU, read together with Article 3(s) EEC.[24] It was clarified that consumer policy was based on a double foundation: as an internal market policy on the one hand and as specific action to support consumer policy measures taken by Member States on the other.

As the Community's power with regard to consumer protection is not exclusive, it is bound by the principles of subsidiarity and proportionality, as set out in Article 3(b) Maastricht Treaty (Article 5 EC = 5 TEU):

> "In areas which do not fall within its exclusive competence, the Community shall take action, in accordance with the principle of subsidiarity, only if and in so far as the objectives of the proposed action cannot be sufficiently achieved by the Member States and can therefore, by reason of the scale or effects of the proposed action, be better achieved by the Community. Any action by the Community shall not go beyond what is necessary to achieve the objectives of this Treaty."

---

22 Details in de Ruyt; Stuyck, *supra* note 1, 378.
23 Micklitz, *The Politics of Judicial Co-operation in the EU*, 7–10.
24 Details in Stuyck, *supra* note 1, 379 ff.

Subsidiarity remains predominantly a political term, which the institutions of the Community have to take into consideration when exercising their powers. The extent to which it is justiciable is limited, that is in terms of the scope of the general system of legal protection of the Community and more widely of the Union.[25] According to the ECJ it suffices if a directive's (indirect) reference to the principle of subsidiarity results from the recitals.[26] The legislative margin of appreciation of the Community organs can generally not be attacked by the courts of the Community. However this does not apply to the criteria for the exercise of the powers, the choice of the appropriate decision-making procedure and the obligations to indicate reasons and to publish as per Articles 253/254 EC = 296/297 TFEU. The ECJ reviews the application of the correct procedure but not the merits of the act.[27] The decision on what is necessary according to the principle of subsidiarity is not subject to the scrutiny of the ECJ.[28] With regard to proportionality, the Court, in its *IATA* judgment of 10 January 2006, concerning the legality of the Overbooking and Cancellation Regulation (EC) 261/2004[29] referred to the "immediate objective pursued by the Community legislature … to strengthen protection for passengers who suffer cancellation of, or long delays to, flights by redressing, in an immediate and standardised manner, certain damage caused to passengers placed in such circumstances" (para 82).

1.7 A further stage of the development of an independent consumer policy is determined by the Treaty of Amsterdam 2 October 1997, which came into force on 1 May 1999. The former Article 129a was amended by Article 153 EC = 169 TFEU, autonomous consumer rights were established and the Community's powers extended. A separate "Subsidiarity Protocol" was intended to limit the insecurities connected with the exercise of the term "subsidiarity". In particular the Community was required to apply flexible instruments in areas not exclusively subject to its powers – such as consumer policy – and to give preference to directives over regulations, "other things being equal" according to para 6.

---

25 Reich, *supra* note 2, 44–45; Weatherill, in: Grundmann/Kerber/Weatherill (eds.), *Party Autonomy*, 173, 192; Weatherill, *supra* note 1, 23.

26 ECJ, 13 May 1997, C-233/94, *Germany v European Parliament and the Council* [1997] ECR I-2304 at para 26 on the Directive on deposit-guarantee schemes.

27 Stuyck, *supra* note 1, 397.

28 ECJ, 10 December 2002, C-491/01, *The Queen v Secretary of Health ex parte BAT* [2002] ECR I-11453 at para 182; ECJ, 12 July 2005, C-154 + 155/04, *Alliance for Natural Health et al. v Secretary of State for Health* [2005] ECR I-6451 at paras 105–107.

29 ECJ, 10 January 2006, C-344/04, *The Queen and IATA, ELFAA v Dpt. of Transport* [2006] ECR I-403, OJ L 46, 17 February 2004, 1.

The new, extended legal framework of consumer policy will be illustrated by a textual comparison of Article 129a Maastricht Treaty and Article 153 EC, now Article 169 TFEU:

Article 129a(1)	**Article 153(1–3)**
The Community contributes to the attainment of a high level of consumer protection by …	In order to promote the interests of consumers and to ensure a high level of consumer protection, the Community shall contribute to protecting the health, safety and economic interests of consumers as well as to promoting their right to information, education and to organise themselves in order to safeguard their interests.
	Consumer protection requirements shall be taken into account in defining and implementing other Community policies and activities.
	The Community shall contribute to the attainment of the objectives referred to in paragraph 1 through:
(a) measures adopted pursuant to Article 100a in the context of the completion of the internal market;	(a) measures adopted pursuant to Article 95 in the context of the completion of the internal market;
(b) specific action which supports and supplements the policy pursued by the Member States to protect the health, safety and economic interests of consumers and to provide adequate information to consumers.	(b) measures which support, supplement and monitor the policy pursued by the Member States.

The Nice Treaty from 26 January 2001 – which came into force on 1 February 2003 – maintained the importance of consumer protection with the appropriate legal framework *tel quel*.

The consolidated version of the Lisbon Reform Treaty renumbered Article 153 EC to Article 169 TFEU without change, but moves the horizontal provision of para 2 to a new Article 12 TFEU. In Article 4(2)(f) TFEU consumer protection is expressly included in the field of "shared competences" between the Union and Member States. This seems to indicate a more prominent role for consumer protection in the policy objectives and the competence structure of the Union. Article 38 of the Charter contains the principle of consumer protection whereby "Union policies shall ensure a high level of consumer protection" without elevating it to the status of a subjective right in the sense of Article 52(2) Charter.

1.8 It remains within the margin of appreciation of the Community/Union legislator to decide on the measures for the achievement of a particular regulatory objective.[30] The Commission, Parliament and – less actively so – the Council submit action programmes on a regular basis.[31] On 2 October 2001, the Commission brought up for discussion a "Green Paper on EU Consumer Protection"[32] which mainly deals with the introduction of a general clause in market behaviour law and the coordination of implementation of consumer legislation.

The statement of the Commission from April 2002 on the "Consumer political strategy 2002–2006"[33] announced a rethinking of the traditional "minimum protection approach". It writes:

> "We must go further to enable consumers and business to realise the benefits of the internal market. Central to this is the establishment of common protection rules and practices across Europe. This means moving away from the present situation of different sets of rules in the Member States towards a more consistent environment for consumer protection across Europe".

It cites three medium-term objectives: an evenly high level of consumer protection throughout the entire EC, effective enforcement of legal provisions for the protection of the consumer, and an appropriate level of participation of consumer associations in shaping EC policy.

A Communication of 6 April 2005[34] on "Healthier, safer, more confident consumers: a Health and Consumer Protection strategy" proposed several measures by the Community to be taken between 2007 and 2013. It is mostly concerned with health aspects, but has also proposals concerning general consumer policy which signal a substantial withdrawal of an activist approach based on positive consumer protection measures. It wants to support a truly internal market for consumers:

> "Consumer confidence as a basic requirement of markets is better understood; but it has not been reflected in all policy areas … Market integration results in economic benefits for consumers (greater choice of goods and services; competition on merit; lower prices; higher standards of living). Internal market policies must ensure that these benefits are realised, including on the quality of goods and services. The Internal market cannot function properly without consumer confidence. Adequate consumer protection is necessary for growth and competitiveness."

---

30 Explicitly by the ECJ, 12 November 1996, C-84/94 *UK v Council* [1996] ECR I-5755 (Directive 93/104/EEC concerning certain aspects of the organisation of working time).

31 For example, Council Resolution of 28 June 1999 on Community consumer policy 1999 to 2001, OJ C 206, 21 July 1999.

32 COM (2001) 532 final.

33 COM (2002) 208, 12.

34 COM (2005) 115 final, 10.

The Commission Green Paper of 8 February 2007 "on the Review of the Consumer Acquis"[35] insists that a "consumer's confidence in the internal market must be stimulated by ensuring a high level of protection across the EU. Consumers should be able to rely on the equivalent rights and have resort to the equivalent remedies if something goes wrong."

1.8a In more general terms, the Commission has taken up its full harmonisation approach in its most recent EU Consumer Policy Strategy 2007–2013[36] where it links consumer confidence to an "equally effective protection" respectively "equally high level of protection" which will also allow businesses, in particular SMUs to "sell anywhere on the basis of a single, simple set of rules". Consumer confidence is indeed important for an internal market, but it should not serve as a pretext for simply relying on market forces to achieve such confidence and avoiding active support measures or limiting them to full harmonisation.[37]

On 22 May 2012[38] the Commission published a paper on "A European Consumer Agenda – Boosting confidence and growth". It defined four goals, namely:

- improving consumer safety;
- enhancing knowledge;
- improving implementation; and
- aligning rights and key policies to economic and social change.

The Lisbon Treaty did not change the architecture of EU consumer law. The competences remained the same. The highly controversial shift of the "social market economy" in Article 3(3) TEU and its impact on competition law does not, or at least not yet, affect consumer law. Much more important are the less visible changes which go back to the Lisbon Council Conclusion 2000 introducing the language of the "making the EU the most competitive economy of the world". This rhetoric has been confirmed in the Europe 2020 agenda.[39] The European Commission as a policy maker and driving force behind consumer legislation is using the "economic efficiency rhetoric" not only to shift the focus from minimum to maximum harmonisation but also to introduce a new thinking into consumer law, which brings European consumer law closer to the

---

35 COM (2006) 744 final, 4; critical remarks by MICKLITZ/REICH, *VuR* 2007, 121; TWIGG-FLESNER, *ERCL* 2007, 198; HEIDERHOFF/KENNY, *ELRev* 2007, 740; TWIGG-FLESNER, *Europeanisation of Contract Law*, 172–180.

36 COM (2007) 99 final, 4.6 of 13 March 2007.

37 WILHELMSSON, *JCP* 2004, 317.

38 COM (2012) 225 final.

39 A European Strategy for smart, sustainable and inclusive growth, http://ec.europa.eu/commission_2010-2014/president/news/documents/pdf/20100303_1_en.pdf (accessed 31 January 2014).

American understanding.[40] However, the ECJ seems to be sticking to the idea that consumers are the weaker parties and that they need to be protected, even *ex officio* via the judiciary.[41]

III. CONSUMER RIGHTS UNDER PRIMARY EU LAW

1. CONSUMER POLICY AS AN INDEPENDENT COMMUNITY/UNION POLICY

a) Consumer protection in the internal market: a contradiction in itself?

1.9 The Maastricht Treaty very strongly stressed the "auxiliary character" of consumer policy which was related to the legislation of the internal market on the one hand and to the policy of the Member States on the other. Contrary to environmental policy which was of great relevance in the Treaty of Maastricht (as previously seen in the Single European Act) consumer policy took the role of the "little sister" which had to be subordinate to the other policies.[42] Thus, it is not surprising that the principle of subsidiarity was used to attack the independence of Community consumer policy albeit without success.

During the proceedings on the validity of Directive 94/19/EC of 30 May 1994 on deposit-guarantee schemes,[43] the ECJ[44] gave its point of view on the relevance of consumer policy in the scope of the harmonisation of the internal market. The Directive is based on Article 57 EEC (now Article 50 TFEU) and on Article 100a EEC (now Article 114 TFEU). However the ECJ took the opportunity to make some general remarks on the relationship: harmonisation of legislation – consumer protection:

> "In that regard it suffices to point out that, although consumer protection is one of the objectives of the Community, it is clearly not the sole objective. As has already been stated, the Directive aims to promote the right of establishment and the freedom to provide services in the banking sector. Admittedly, there must be a high level of consumer protection concomitantly with those freedoms; however, no provision of the Treaty obliges the Community legislature to adopt the highest level of protection which can be found in a particular Member State. The reduction in the level of protection which may thereby result in certain cases through the application of the

40 The American Law Institute has established a working group which shall elaborate a 'restatement of consumer law.' For an overview see Caruso, Black Lists and Private Autonomy in EU Contracts Law, in: Leczykiewicz/Weatherill (eds.), *The Involvement of EU Law in Private Law Relationships*, 291; Caruso, *AmJCompL* 2013, 475.

41 Micklitz/Reich, *CMLRev* 2014 forthcoming.

42 Cf. Stuyck, *supra* note 1, 367.

43 OJ L 135, 31 May 1994, 5 as amended by Directive 2009/14/EC, OJ L 68, 13 March 2009, 3.

44 ECJ, 13 May 1997, *Germany v Council* [1997] ECR I-2405 at para 48.

> second subparagraph of Article 4(1) of the Directive does not call into question the general result which the Directive seeks to achieve, namely a considerable improvement in the protection of depositors within the Community."

In the context of Germany's state liability for violating the time period allowed for implementing the safeguarding of solvency per Article 7 of Directive 90/314/EEC[45] of 13 June 1990 on package travel, package holiday and package tours, the ECJ had the opportunity to consider the significance of consumer protection within the Community. In the *Dillenkofer* decision[46] of 8 October 1996 it stated:

> "The purpose of Article 7 is accordingly to protect consumers, who thus have the right to be reimbursed or repatriated in the event of the insolvency of the organizer from whom they purchased the package travel. Any other interpretation would be illogical, since the purpose of the security which organizers must offer under Article 7 of the Directive is to enable consumers to obtain a refund of money paid over or to be repatriated. That result is, moreover, confirmed by the penultimate recital in the preamble to the Directive, according to which both the consumer and the package travel industry would benefit if organizers were placed under an obligation to provide sufficient evidence of security in the event of insolvency. In that connection, the German and United Kingdom Governments' argument that the Directive, which is based on Article 100a of the Treaty, is aimed essentially at ensuring freedom to provide services and, more generally, freedom of competition cannot be valid. First, the recitals in the preamble to the Directive repeatedly refer to the purpose of protecting consumers. Secondly, the fact that the Directive is intended to assure other objectives cannot preclude its provisions from also having the aim of protecting consumers. Indeed, according to Article 100a(3) of the Treaty, the Commission, in its proposals submitted pursuant to that article, concerning inter alia consumer protection, must take as a base a high level of protection."

The ECJ uses this and numerous other decisions that have been reached on the interpretation of directives in order to illustrate that it considers consumer policy to be particularly important within the legal system of the Community. In order to justify specific mandatory provisions protecting consumers as contained in contract law, the ECJ refers *inter alia* to the consumer's "weaker position of bargaining powers and less information".[47] According to its consumer-friendly case law, the ECJ in its *Heininger* judgment[48] has insisted that derogations from a

45 OJ L 158, 23 June 1990, 59.

46 ECJ, 8 October 1996, C-178/94 et al. [1996] ECR I-4845 at paras 36–39; confirmed in ECJ, 15 June 1999, C-140/97, *Rechberger* [1999] ECR I-3499 at para 51.

47 ECJ, 27 June 2000, C-240–244/98, *Oceano Grupo* [2000] ECR I-4941 at para 23; Directive 93/13/EEC, more recently ECJ, 14 March 2013, C-415/11, *M. Aziz v Catalunyacaixa* [2013] ECR I-nyr.

48 ECJ, 13 December 2001, C-481/99, *Heininger v Bayrische Hypothekenbank* [2001] ECR I-9945; Rösler, *RabelsZ* 2007, 495; critique Riesenhuber, *JZ* 2005, 829; follow-up by ECJ, 25 October 2005, C-350/03, *Schulte v Deutsche Bausparkasse Badenia* [2005] ECR I-9215 at para 101;

consumer protection directive "must be interpreted strictly" (para 31). It has also thrown out the argument that considerations of consumer protection must be sacrificed on the altar of legal certainty:

> "Finally, as regards the argument that it is essential, for reasons of legal certainty, to restrict the period within which the right of cancellation may be exercised, such reasons cannot prevail since they imply a limitation of the rights expressly conferred on consumers by the doorstep selling directive in order to protect them against the risks arising from the fact that the credit institutions have chosen to enter into agreements away from their business premises. If those institutions choose such methods in order to market their services, they can easily safeguard both the interests of consumers and their own requirements as to legal certainty by complying with their duty to supply consumers with information." (para 47)

This judicial safeguarding of consumer protection contributed to consumer policy emerging from its formerly neglected position and to being independently positioned in the Treaty of Amsterdam. This was confirmed in the *Claro* judgment[49] concerning consumer protection against unilaterally imposed arbitration clauses. Even though the ECJ did not pass judgment on the compatibility of such clauses with EC law, it insisted that once this court is convinced of the unfairness of the clause, overriding concerns of consumer protection according to Article 3(1)(t) EC as implemented by Directive 93/13, "as measure which is essential to the accomplishment of the tasks entrusted to the Community and, in particular, to raising the standard of living and the quality of life in its territory… [require the court] to assess of its own motion whether a contractual term is unfair, compensating in this way for the imbalance which exists between the consumer and the seller or supplier" (para 37).

More recent decisions seem to apply a stricter review of the exercise of legislative powers of the Community with regard to consumer protection in a broad sense. This is particularly so in connection with the protection of health against tobacco advertising. This has revived discussion on the justification of an autonomous consumer policy under Community law.[50] Weatherill responded to critics that measures taken by the Community under consumer law are justified "to promote consumer confidence in the viability of the market as a legitimate

---

somewhat differently ECJ, 10 March 2005, C-336/03, *easyCar v OFT* [2005] ECR I-1947 at para 28 against the opinion of AG Stix-Hackl aiming at balancing the interests of consumers and car rental companies in the interpretation of the term "transport services" thus excluding a cancellation of the consumer under Directive 97/7/EC (1.27).

49 ECJ, 26 October 2006, C-168/05, *Elisa Maria Mostaza Claro v Centro Movil Milenium* [2006] ECR I-10421.

50 Cf. the critical remarks of Hadfield/Howse/Trebilcock, 131; Hesselink, 323 at 329: "consumer protection becomes market protection"; Schäfer/Ott, *Economic Analysis of Civil Law*, 9; for a different view on "paternalism", see Kerber/Vanbergh in: Grundmann/Kerber/Weatherill, *Party Autonomy*, 7; critique also from an environmental point of view by Krämer, *FS Stauder*, 177.

objective of law making under Article 95".[51] The authors of this chapter have drawn attention to the tendencies under Community law to grant EU citizens in terms of Article 20 TFEU subjective rights, mostly with regard to non-discrimination under Article 18 TFEU. This is consistent with the vesting of independent rights in the consumer as a "passive market participant".[52] The extent of those rights might be disputed as far as the political sense or the economic expenses of such measures are concerned. However this does not alter their legal admissibility provided that the provisions regulating competence are adhered to.

b) Consumer policy and subsidiarity

1.10 The wording of Article 169(1) TFEU illustrates unmistakably that consumer protection forms an autonomous policy area within the Community. The Community is neither the holder of a monopoly, nor does it possess exclusive jurisdiction as it merely "makes a contribution" as exemplified in Article 3(t) EC. The objective of the contribution is to promote the consumer's interests, generally in order to guarantee a high (even though it is not the highest) level of consumer protection. It concerns the relationship of responsibilities which are to be taken by the Community and the Member States in the area of consumer protection. It is for that reason that the principle of subsidiarity needs to be understood as a rule of responsibility and "comparative efficiency" rather than a rule of exclusion.[53]

According to the wording of Article 5(2) TEU, the principle of subsidiarity is generally applicable to the area of consumer policy because the Community lacks exclusive jurisdiction. However, the provisions on joint action in the area of consumer protection are specified to such an extent by the precise wording of Article 169 TFEU and further supplemented by the principle of a minimum level of protection Article 169(4) TFEU that the principle of subsidiarity does not imply any additional restraints of power. At most, the principle of subsidiarity may be of significance during the drafting and implementation stage with regard to preference given to directives over regulations, renunciation of exaggerated attention to detail and occasionally drawing on voluntary codes of conduct, as set out in the Subsidiarity Protocol attached to the Treaty of Amsterdam. It was modified by Protocol (No 2) on the "Application of the Principles of Subsidiarity and Proportionality" attached to the Lisbon Treaty, trying to involve national parliaments in the monitoring process – so far with little success. However, this

---

51 Weatherill, *supra* note 25, 194; somewhat more cautious in Weatherill, *supra* note 1 (1st ed.), 77–78.

52 Reich, *supra* note 1, 943; Micklitz, in: Micklitz (ed.), *The Many Concepts of Social Justice in EU Private Law*, 2011, 34: "The European Model as Access Justice".

53 Micklitz, The EU as a Federal Order of Competences and the Private Law, in: Azoulai (ed.), *The Question of Competence in the European Union*, 2014 forthcoming.

is an issue concerning the legislative margin of appreciation and is thus only limited subject to judicial review, as the ECJ has said in many judgments.[54]

2. THE CONSUMER RIGHT TO INFORMATION

a) *The information paradigm of EU consumer law*

1.11 The consumer policy programmes of 1975 and 1981 mention the right to information as one of the five consumer rights.[55] Prior to the ECJ *GB Inno* decision[56] this right had merely been included in a non-binding Community document. However, in this decision the ECJ upgraded the importance of the right to information to the extent that it became the measure for limitations by Member States of the free flow of information. Therefore the decision could be understood as recognition, under Community free movement law, of the consumer right to information at least with regard to measures by Member States restricting the free movement of goods. A further embodiment of the right of unrestricted flow of information – also in trade – arises indirectly from Article 10(1) ECHR (European Convention on Human Rights) which, in connection with Article 6(3) TEU also binds the organs of the Community; it may only be restricted by reasonable and proportionate measures in the public interest.[57] According to the ECJ's case law, the free movement of services includes the right of the (potential) recipient and consumer to make use of services within the entire Community area without being limited by discriminatory or disproportionate measures by Member States. Services cannot be provided without information, notwithstanding whether or not information is concerned a service for consideration.[58]

---

54 ECJ, 8 June 2010, C-58/08, *Vodafone et al. v Secretary of State* [2010] ECR I-4999 at para 77.

55 Overview cf. Reich, *supra* note 2, 294; limitations: Howells/Wilhelmsson, *European Consumer Law*, 9.

56 ECJ, 7 March 1990, C-362/88 [1990] ECR I-667.

57 Cf. comprehensively the opinion of AG Fennelly of 15 June 2000 in the case C-376/98, *Germany v EP and Council*, nullity of Directive 98/43/EC relating to the advertising and sponsorship of tobacco products [2000] ECR I-8149 at para 153. The ECJ does not mention this issue in its decision of 5 October 2000. See also ECJ, 25 March 2004, C-71/02, *Herbert Karner Industrie-Auktionen v Troostwijk GmbH* [2004] ECR I-3025 at paras 50–52. See also Reich, *supra* note 2, 2.6–2.7. A different approach has been suggested by the opinion of AG Trstenjak of 17 July 2008 in C-205/07, *Gysbrechts* concerning the minimum protection clause in the Distance Selling Directive 97/7/EC which would be set aside by primary law on free movement of goods. In its judgment of 16 December 2008, the Court followed suit: [2008] ECR I-9947 concerning the Belgian prohibition of prepayment clauses before the lapse of the withdrawal period under the Distance Selling Directive 97/7 which was said to be conforming to the proportionality principle of EU law, while the prohibition to take the credit card number as security was said to be disproportionate.

58 In the decision concerning the prohibition of abortion under Irish law of 4 October 1991, C-159/90, *Grogan* [1991] ECR I-4685.

Secondary law contains extensive provisions on information of different depth in numerous, or, more precisely, in an endless number of provisions on advertising law, contract law, labelling law and data protection law. Thus it is possible to refer to an *information paradigm* of EU consumer protection.[59] The consumer-political model applied by the ECJ, most prominently in the field of unfair commercial practices, is the "average consumer who is reasonably well informed and reasonably observant and circumspect".[60]

Access to information is a citizen's right under Article 11 of the EU Charter and indirectly also a consumer right, as the ECJ confirmed in its *Sky* judgment[61] where it wrote:

> "In the light, first, of the importance of safeguarding the fundamental freedom to receive information and the freedom and pluralism of the media guaranteed by Article 11 of the Charter and, second, of the protection of the freedom to conduct a business as guaranteed by Article 16 of the Charter, the European Union legislature was entitled to adopt rules such as those laid down in Article 15 of Directive 2010/13, which limit the freedom to conduct a business, and to give priority, in the necessary balancing of the rights and interests at issue, to public access to information over contractual freedom." (para 66)

b) *The right to information as a subjective right*

1.12 The consumer right to information is to be "promoted" by the Community/Union; by virtue of this it must not be disturbed or limited. The obligation to promote an independent individual legal claim of the consumer corresponds with other provisions under Community law which purport to secure and enhance the consumer's legal position in the market. The best-known provisions include the prohibition of discrimination on the ground of nationality and sex in the relevant sphere of application of the Treaty. According to the established practice of the ECJ they are directly horizontally applicable. The principles of this practice[62] can be transferred *ceteris paribus* to the consumer right to information. In addition Article 21 TFEU might be hinted at; this grants the right of free movement as an individual right under Community law and independent of secondary subsequent provisions.[63]

---

59 Reich, *Bürgerrechte in der EU*, 280; Howells/Micklitz/Wilhelmsson, *European Fair Trading Law*, 123–146; Unberath/Johnston, *CMLRev* 2007, 1237 at 1250: "preference for the provision of compulsory information over more severe marketing restrictions".

60 ECJ, 16 July 1998, C-210/96, *Gut Springenheide* [1998] ECR I-4657 at para 31; ECJ, 28 January 1999, C-303/97, *Kessler* [1999] ECR I-513 at para 36; ECJ, 13 January 2000, C-220/98, *Lifting* [2000] ECR I-117; cf. Stuyck, *supra* note 1, 389; Reich, *supra* note 2, 297; Weatherill, *supra* note 1, 57–59, doubts Howells/Wilhelmsson, *supra* note 1, 315.

61 ECJ, 23 January 2013, C-283/11, *Sky Österreich v ORF* [2013] ECR I-nyr; comment Reich, in: Terryn et al., *Landmark Cases of EU Consumer Law – In Honour of Jules Stuyck*, 35.

62 Reich, *supra* note 59, 158, 212.

63 Cf. Reich, *ELJ* 2005, 675.

Article 153 EC contained in the Treaty of Amsterdam, after Lisbon Article 169 TFEU, represents another important codification of *subjective rights.* The provisions which are directly applied by the Community in favour of citizens, in particular in the areas of free movement, labour and consumption, provide guarantees with a character similar to fundamental rights. These rights are protected *vis-à-vis* the Community, Member States and other individuals against unjustified limitations. This protective function of guarantees under Community law against limitations organised under private law has been stressed by the ECJ in its *Bosman* decision.[64] The consequences of those limitations also apply to *(collective) restrictions of the flow of information* against consumers, for example by standard business conditions which are not materially justified.[65]

c) *Comprehensibility and language of the information*

1.13 The consumer right to information will only be satisfied if the information is made available in a comprehensible language – in the case of illiterate, blind or deaf people by use of the appropriate media, i.e. symbols. This concerns a problem which Community law has to deal with in different contexts. As for the diversity of languages in the Community and the numerous minorities and groups, a satisfying solution has not yet been found. However, some remarks are purported to point at the diverse character of the problems without providing a solution.

Primary law is mainly concerned with the question of to what extent national linguistic provisions, such as in French or Italian law, and more recently extensive language legislation of new Member countries (e.g. Poland and Latvia)[66] violate the fundamental freedoms. Obviously this depends on the strictness of the national regulation and the extent to which it affects the free movement of goods and services. The ECJ pursued a rather liberal approach by not completely overruling mandatory linguistic provisions, for example on presentation, labelling or advertising. However, it insists on an opening clause if consumer information can be achieved by different, less limiting means.[67] On

---

64 ECJ, 15 December 1995, C-415/93 [1995] ECR I-5432.

65 The horizontal effect of the personal freedoms with regard to collective restrictions was recognised by ECJ, 19 February 2002, C-309/99, *Wouters* [2002] ECR I-1577 at para 120 and later extended to collective action by labour unions against the fundamental freedoms, ECJ, 11 December 2007, C-438/05, *ITF & FSU v Viking* [2007] ECR I-10779; ECJ, 18 December 2007, C-351/05, *Laval v Bygnadds* [2007] ECR I-11767, see Reich, *German Law Journal*, 2008, 125.

66 Micklitz, *ZEuP* 2003, 635; Reich, *PennState JIntL* 2005, 587.

67 See the somewhat protracted *Piageme* controversies, ECJ, 18 June 1991, C-369/89, *Piageme I* [1991] ECR I-2971 at para 13; ECJ, 15 June 1995, C-85/94, *Piageme II* [1995] ECR I-2955 at paras 15 and 29 concerning the imposition of a mandatory language requirement of the area in which the product is marketed beyond the "easily understood language" which may be another language, maybe even English as *lingua franca* of the EU.

balance, the different legal interests need to be balanced, i.e. free movement on the one hand and effective consumer information on the other. This has been pointed out by the ECJ in its *Colim* decision:[68]

> "Save where it can be transmitted effectively by the use of pictograms or signs other than words, information which traders are obliged to communicate to the purchasers or, as the case may be, to the end user is of no practical use unless it is given in a language which can be understood by the persons for whom it is intended." (para 29)

The legal situation arising from secondary law is extremely confusing and unclear.[69] Directive 93/13/EEC on unfair terms in consumer contracts and subsequent directives which were relevant for the Treaty require certain information to be given in a manner "comprehensible" to the consumer. Therefore the conclusion could be drawn that information needs to be provided in a comprehensible language independent of the law applicable to the particular contract.[70] Reference to international private law is of no assistance, unless considering establishing a special connection to the language issue.[71] Directive 99/44/EC allows for or requires Member States to implement linguistic regulations for particular types of contracts such as guarantees when purchasing consumer goods.

It appears that a solution could only be reached if the requirement of comprehensibility could be specified in a way that considers both the consumer right to information as a subjective right and the market freedom of the supplier.[72] However, Member States' interest in implementing a linguistic and cultural policy is not considered a legitimate objective in consumer matters. The internal market is purported to pierce through and abolish national borders and thus is an inappropriate instrument to enforce interests which are mainly of a cultural and educational character.

A new development towards language legislation can be seen in the case law concerning citizenship.[73] The Court followed this approach in the *Bickel and Franz* judgment of 4 November 1998.[74] Both persons, Mr Bickel being a lorry driver of Austrian nationality and Mr Franz a German tourist, violated Italian law while in the province of Bolzano, where German is spoken. By special regulation based on an Italian–Austrian agreement concluded well before their

68 ECJ, 3 June 1999, C-33/97 [1999] ECR I-3175.

69 Details Rott, *ZVerglRWiss* 1999, 382; Maack, *Die Durchsetzung des AGB-rechtlichen Transparenzgebots*, 62: relevance of the language accepted by the consumer; Twigg-Flesner, *supra* note 35, 70.

70 Reich, *supra* note 59, 326.

71 Possible special connection cf. Rott, *supra* note 69, 392–399.

72 Rott, *supra* note 69, 407.

73 Reich, *supra* note 63, 679 ff.

74 ECJ, 24 November 1998, C-274/96, *Criminal proceedings against H.O. Bickel und U. Franz* [1998] ECR I-7637.

membership of the EU, the German language is to have the same status as Italian in the Alto Adige region. This means that German-speaking Italian citizens are entitled to a court hearing in German. Could this also be extended to the defence of Mr Bickel and Mr Franz before a local court in the province of Bolzano? Both AG Jacobs and the Court were willing to extend the prohibition against discrimination in Article 18 TFEU to all nationals coming under the free movement rules. AG Jacobs referred to *Cowan*[75] and extended it to the right of a Union citizen accused in criminal proceedings – a reasoning transferable to consumer matters concerning legal protection in general. Both the Advocate General and the Court agreed that refusing to allow German-speaking citizens from Austria or Germany to use their mother tongue in the province of Bolzano, where this was allowed for German-speaking Italians, amounted to discrimination based on nationality. The Court said:

> "In that regard, the exercise of the right to move and reside freely in another Member State is enhanced if the citizens of the Union are able to use a given language to communicate with the administrative and judicial authorities of a state on the same footing as its nationals." (para 16)

d) *Limitations of the right to information: right to data protection*

1.14 It goes without saying that the right to information is subject to certain restrictions. The provisions under Community law which expressly or impliedly justify the limitation of freedoms also apply to the consumer right to information. This is particularly so for public policy, public security or public health reasons governed by Article 36 TFEU for the free movement of goods as well as for Articles 52/62 TFEU on the free provision of services. If an unlimited consumer right to information resulted in the frustration of Community or national precautionary measures in the area of health, security or environment, or even in the violation of fundamental constitutional values such as the right to privacy or copyright, then that right must yield to higher-ranking interests. These restrictions need to comply with the general principle of proportionality under Community law.

Data protection, which has been recognised under primary law in Article 286 EC, can legally restrict the consumer's right to information. However, such a restriction of the consumer right to information only arises in cases under secondary law under Directive 95/46/EC on the protection of personal data of 24 October 1995.[76] Data protection under Article 286 EC did not establish a general principle; it merely referred to existing secondary law which applies to data processing throughout the Community. Therefore Article 286 EC only

---

[75] ECJ, 2 February 1989, 186/87, *Cowan v Trésor public* [1989] ECR 195.

[76] OJ L 281, 23 November 1995, 31.

protects natural persons and data related to them; for example, information on the business activities of an undertaking is excluded. Article 16(1) TFEU now provides that "[e]veryone has the right to the protection of personal data concerning them". Furthermore, information which is of assistance to the consumer, such as information on the quality, reliability or health risk of particular products or undertakings, will typically be admissible under secondary law as a legitimate exercise of public authority.[77] A further imminent restriction of the right to information results from the specific character as a *consumer* information. It thus needs to relate to consumer interests as listed in Article 169(1) TFEU, i.e. economic consumer interests as well as the protection of health and safety. Political and social information is not included.

3. CONSUMER RIGHT TO EDUCATION, ASSOCIATION, PROTECTION OF LEGITIMATE EXPECTATIONS AND EFFECTIVE JUDICIAL PROTECTION

a) The right to education

1.15 The right to education in Article 169 TFEU is closely connected to the right to information and extends it. Other than that it refers to the Member States, in this area the Community/Union does not possess any particular powers. Article 165 TFEU on education, vocational training and youth and Article 167 TFEU on "culture" expressly exclude harmonisation measures, which could result in a "right" in a subjective sense. Discrimination on the grounds of nationality as per Article 18 TFEU constitutes the only prohibition as already established in the *Gravier* decision,[78] a reasoning which has been confirmed in the judgment against Austria concerning discriminatory restrictions of access to its higher education system.[79] Thus consumer education to promote "domestic" products or services would not only constitute a violation of the fundamental freedoms but also of the granting of a right to education free from discrimination unless such education would be justified by other legal interests; for example it must be possible to indicate to children – and adults – that from an ecological point of view it does not seem sensible to buy Irish butter – given congestion on European roads – if the same product could be obtained from a domestic producer.

---

[77] ECJ, 11 April 2013, C-361/11, *K. Berger v Freistaat Bayern* concerning public warnings of foodstuff unfit for human consumption under Article 14 of the Foodstuff Regulation (EC) No. 178/2002 (OJ L 31, 1 February 2001, 1), even if there is no danger to the health of consumers.

[78] ECJ, 13 February 1985, 293/83 [1985] ECR 593.

[79] ECJ, 7 July 2005, C-147/03, *Commission v Austria* [2005] ECR I-5969.

b) *The right to form associations*

1.16 The consumers' right to organise themselves corresponds with the constitutional law of the Member States and is acknowledged under Community law, Article 11 ECHR and Article 12(1) of the Charter of Fundamental Rights of the European Union.[80] With this provision the EU legislator clarifies that consumer associations fall within the sphere of application of the Treaty and therefore must not be treated differently because of their "nationality". These associations can act across the borders in any form in the Community, enlist members, practise in court, etc.

An independent "right of legal representation" as demanded in the consumer-political programmes of the EC cannot be derived therefrom. The action programme of the Commission from April 2002[81] at least announced that it would give consumer associations an appropriate role in shaping EU policy. Community law, however, does not impose itself on internal regulations of consumer associations. The way these associations safeguard their members' rights is determined by their constitutions and by the applicable domestic law. Community law can specify and extend the legal position by provisions under secondary law; cf. Directive 98/27/EC of 19 May 1998 (now Directive 2009/22/EC)[82] on applications for an injunction in the interest of the consumer. A right for consumer associations to take legal action against unfair marketing practices can only be derived from secondary, not primary, Community law. However, Regulation 2006/2004/EC on consumer protection co-operation[83] has shifted the focus from private to public enforcement, as each and every Member State had to designate a competent authority for the enforcement of cross-border consumer issues (details 8.42).

c) *Protection of legitimate expectations*

1.17 Article 169 TFEU does not contain further rights in favour of the consumer. A right to health, safety and safeguarding of economic interests cannot be directly derived from Article 169 TFEU in a way granting a subjective claim the violation of which would give rise to Member State or Community liability per Article 340 TFEU.[84] Only secondary Community law may establish subjective rights, in particular through product liability law (details Chapter 6).

---

80 Cf. ECJ, 15 December 1995, C-415/93, *Bosman* [1995] ECR I-5432 at para 79 under reference to Article 11 ECHR; similar, ECJ, 12 June 2003, C-112/00, *Eugen Schmidberger v Republik Österreich* [2003] ECR I-5659 at para 79 for details.

81 COM (2002) 208, 28.

82 OJ L 166, 11 June 1998, 51 (Directive 98/27/EC).

83 OJ L 364, 9 December 2004, 1.

84 Further considerations in: Micklitz, *Internationales Produktsicherheitsrecht*, 169.

Article 168 TFEU on health services does not contain a subjective legal claim to a high standard of health protection either. Harmonisation measures are expressly excluded. Consumer health protection may take priority over economic and social difficulties of a country (cf. the United Kingdom and mad cow disease) with regard to ordering provisional measures based on the precautionary principle.[85]

Primary and secondary law taken together will provide a consumer's right to legitimate expectations.[86] This right is mirrored in product liability law on the one hand and in consumer contract law on the other. The general clause is to be specified according to the particular area. On balance it results in weighing the undertaking's interests in market access (subject to as few restrictions as possible) on the one hand and the consumer interest in assertion of lawful claims on the other. A similar process of weighing interests may also arise within provisions under consumer law: between the right to freedom of choice and information on the one hand and the protection of specific interests, such as particular advertising practices, on the other.

d) *Judicial protection and access to justice*

1.18 A consumer right to judicial protection and access to justice has been required in the appropriate consumer programmes but is not expressly included in Article 169 TFEU. This right is rather derived from the system of legal protection under Community law. In principle the system peaks in effective legal protection and is derived from Articles 6 and 13 ECHR which have to be respected by Union law under Article 6(3) TFEU. Article 47 of the Charter of Fundamental Rights of the European Union contains an express recognition that "[e]veryone whose rights and freedoms guaranteed by the law of the Union are violated has the right to an effective remedy before a tribunal". Member States must "provide remedies sufficient to ensure effective legal protection in the fields covered by Union law": Article 19(1)(2) TEU. In recent cases – many more are to be expected in the near future – the ECJ has referred to Article 47 to guarantee the consumer access to effective legal protection, which however may include the obligation to first make use of an out-of-court ADR (alternative dispute resolution) or ODR (online dispute resolution)

---

85 ECJ, 12 July 1996, C-180/96R, *United Kingdom v Commission* [1996] ECR I-3903 at paras 63 and 93.

86 Wilhelmsson, in: Paasivirta/Rissanen (eds.), *Principles of Justice and the Law of the EU*, 325 ff.; Micklitz, in: Krämer et al. (ed.), *Recht und diffuse Interessen*, 1997, 245; Micklitz, *Yearbook of European Law*, 2000, 167, 188–196; Howells/Wilhelmsson, *supra* note 1, 320; Stuyck, *supra* note 1, 392; doubts cf. Roth, in: Schulte-Nölke/Schulze (eds.), *Europäische Rechtsangleichung und nationale Privatrechte*, 45.

procedure with certain conditions like fairness, cost-efficiency, possibility to go to court, etc.[87]

These rights, however, do not only exist in favour of the consumer but in favour of the Union citizen and legal resident in general, such as restrictions on his freedom to move, or prohibitions of discrimination on the ground of sex in access to and supply of goods and services according to Council Directive 2004/113/EC of 13 December 2004.[88]

Specific rules on legal protection and access to justice are either ancillary provisions to consumer protection directives or are based on the new competence of the EC under Article 65 EC in the field of judicial cooperation in civil matters "having cross border implications". Denmark does not participate in this mechanism. The UK and Ireland may opt in to the measures taken under these provisions, which they have typically done so far. Article 81 TFEU now allows for measures "ensuring an effective access to justice". It mentions in particular the "development of alternative methods of dispute settlement".[89]

e) *The so-called sectoral clause*

1.19 Article 12 TFEU contains a sectoral clause known from the area of environmental law:

> "Consumer protection requirements shall be taken into account in defining and implementing other Union policies and activities."

The clause applies to Union organs conducting policies in the scope of their competence, for example transport policy, competition policy, regional and environmental policy. It applies to any Union institution not only to the Commission but in particular to Parliament and the Council in their function as legislators in the appropriate proceedings. The clause is not subjectively safeguarded, i.e. its exercise cannot be controlled by affected individuals or associations unless subject to regulations or directives under secondary law. It does not establish an additional power with regard to Member States.[90]

Experiences with a similar type of sectoral clause in Article 11 TFEU in the area of environmental law[91] produce scepticism as far as the integration of consumer policy into other Community policies is concerned. It played a role in

---

87 ECJ, 18 March 2010, C-317/08 et al., *Alassini et al.* [2010] ECR I-2213; for a discussion of the effectiveness principle see Reich, *supra* note 2 at Chapter 4.

88 OJ L 373, 21 December 2004, 37; for its importance see ECJ, 1 March 2011, C-236/09, *Ass. Belge Test-Achats* [2011] ECR I-773; Reich, 3.15–3.21.

89 For proposals in this vein see Micklitz/Reich/Weatherill, *JCP* 2004, 384; see in more detail Chapter 8.

90 Weatherill, *supra* note 1, 66.

91 Details in Krämer, *EC Environmental Law*, 2004, 351.

measures for the introduction of the euro, which touched on consumer interests regarding transparency, continuance of contracts and the avoidance of passing on of costs.[92]

Its legal significance is limited to a duty to give reasons in terms of Article 296(2) TFEU, according to which regulations, directives and decisions adopted jointly by the European Parliament and the Council, and such acts adopted by the Council or the Commission, shall state the reasons on which they are based. This duty to give reasons, which is independent of formal requirements and textual balancing, is subject to judicial review by the ECJ in proceedings on the avoidance of directives or decisions in the scope of its jurisdiction.[93] This power, however, does not extend to a substantive review of Community policies as to their "consumer political conformity".

IV. "MEASURES" OF CONSUMER POLICY: A QUESTION OF COMPETENCE

1. HARMONISATION MEASURES ACCORDING TO THE "OLD LAW"

1.20 The question of competence was of less importance in the early days of Community consumer policy as the latter was based on the general competence to approximate as per Article 100 EEC, 94 EC, 115 TFEU. It purported harmonisation of the legal and administrative provisions of the Member States contained therein by means of directives as far as they "directly" affected the establishment and functioning of the internal market. Unanimity among Member States was required; the European Parliament had only an advisory role. Enacting directives – including in the area of consumer protection – led to time-consuming negotiations but guaranteed stability of the compromises reached and was not questioned by an action before the ECJ to have the compromise declared void. With regard to harmonisation measures, such as in the area of advertising, the ECJ, in turn, was satisfied that it had certain effects on competitive conditions in the internal market that justified the need for harmonisation.[94]

92 Cf. the detailed documentation in the special volume published by Vissol, *The Euro: Consequences for the Consumer and the Citizen*, including articles by Servet, Théret, Pepermans, Müller-Peters, Burgoyne, Colicelli, Plaza and Reich. The importance of continuity of contracts after introduction of the euro has been stressed by the ECJ, 14 September 2004, C-19/03, *VZ HH v O2* [2004] ECR I-8183.

93 Stuyck, *supra* note 1, 386; compare limitations ECJ, 9 November 1995, C-466/93, *Atlanta* [1995] ECR I-3791.

94 ECJ, 16 November 1989, C-360/88, *Commission v Belgium* [1989] ECR I-3803: failure to implement Directive 84/450/ECC relating to the approximation of laws, regulations and administrative provisions of the Member States concerning misleading advertising.

2. COMPETENCE IN THE INTERNAL MARKET AND ITS RESTRICTIONS

1.21 The question of competence became imperative with the introduction of majority decisions contained in the Single European Act with regard to measures concerning the achievement of the Single European Market as per Article 100a EEC, 95 EC, 114 TFEU.[95] The margin of competence was broadly drafted embracing any measure having as their object the establishment and functioning of the internal market. This did not only include provisions on the promotion of the free movement but also provisions purporting to harmonise the differing competition conditions which had been established by the particular consumer protection legislation of Member States.

According to Article 114(3) TFEU the Commission is obliged to apply a high level of protection when making proposals *inter alia* on consumer protection. The ECJ established an independent consumer lawmaking power thereof in the area of product safety:[96]

> "The free movement of goods can be secured only if product safety requirements do not differ significantly from one Member State to another."

Community measures are not restricted to the enactment of directives as in Article 115 TFEU; the Community may also enact regulations[97] and decisions. According to the "Subsidiarity Protocol", directives shall be preferred to regulations, "other things being equal".

The ECJ reviews the measures for their proportionality, i.e. suitability, necessity and proportionality in the narrow sense, but grants the Community institutions a wide margin of appreciation. This is particularly so in the area of consumer protection. On this point the ECJ has not frequently engaged in judicial review, so the margin of competence has thus been of less relevance.[98]

1.22 According to present law the majority of measures of Union consumer policy will be enacted on the basis of the competence of the internal market of Article 114 TFEU/169(2)(a) EC. These competences are not unlimited despite the wide interpretation given in earlier Court decisions, as can be seen in the judgement of 5 October 2000 on advertising and sponsorship of tobacco products.[99] In particular it concerned the complaint of the Federal Republic of Germany against Directive 98/43/EC of 6 July 1998 relating to the approximation

---

95 As pointed out by Weatherill, *supra* note 25, 191.

96 ECJ, 9 August 1994, C-359/92, *Germany v Council* [1994] ECR I-3681 at paras 34 and 37.

97 In this sense the *Vodafone* judgment, *supra* note 51.

98 Reich, *EuZW* 1991, 203, 208; Unberath/Johnston, 1237 at 1282.

99 ECJ, 5 October 2000, C-376/98, *Germany v EP and Council* [2000] ECR I-8149; cf. Hervey, *ELRev* 2001, 101; Weatherill, *supra* note 1, 73–79.

of laws, regulations and administrative provisions of Member States relating to the advertising and sponsorship of tobacco products,[100] which almost entirely prohibited advertising and sponsoring of tobacco products. Article 168 TFEU had been ruled out as a legal basis as the Community's competence to protect health did not embrace the enactment of harmonisation measures. After all, only the general clause regarding internal market policies in connection with the free movement of services remained. The ECJ insisted that Article 114 TFEU may not simply be invoked because of differences in Member State legislation; otherwise the powers of the Community would be without limitations, contrary to Article 4(1) TFEU. The ECJ then criticised that the Directive did not abolish existing obstacles to the free movement of goods and services. Furthermore, it found that there was no evidence proving that the different existing advertising rules in the Member States resulted in an "appreciable"[101] distortion of competition. However, in certain areas the ECJ allowed Community bans on advertising, such as in the area of print advertising and the sponsoring of sporting events. Nonetheless, the ECJ was incapable of distinguishing admissible and inadmissible provisions of the Directive, since this concerned a legislative issue. Thus Directive 98/43/EC was declared void in its entirety.

The significance of the tobacco decision for consumer policy in the Community on the basis of internal market competence is controversial. *Roth*[102] alleges that the Directives on (consumer) contract law will be of short duration, considering the latest court decisions of the ECJ, as they do not provably contribute to the free movement or elimination of distortion of competition; they "merely" concern legal protection. The coordination of the different legal systems in the Community should be realised by international private law if necessary with consideration of consumer protection as per Article 5 of the Rome Convention on the Law Applicable to Contractual Obligations (now the Rome I Regulation), not by harmonisation of laws. Other authors, such as *Grundmann* and *Kerber*,[103] primarily refer the Community competence to information-type regulations; otherwise the principle of *pacta sunt servanda* applies, instead of imposing mandatory standards on consumers that restrict their free choice.

This point of view is not supported by the practice of the ECJ; rather, it is to be objected to.[104] In a somewhat different, yet related, context, the ECJ stated in

---

100 OJ L 213, 30 July 1998, 9.

101 This criteria was not repeated in the later *BAT* judgment of 13 December 2002, C-491/01, ECR I-11453 at para 60.

102 Roth, in: Ernst/Zimmermann (ed.), *Zivilrechtswissenschaft und Schuldrechtsreform*, 2001, 225, 231–235; Roth, *JZ* 2001, 475, 477.

103 Grundmann/Kerber, in: Grundmann/Kerber/Weatherill (eds.), *Party Autonomy*, 264, 281–283 considering financial services; Grundmann, *CMLRev* 2002, 269.

104 Reich, *RabelsZ* 2002, 531.

its decision on the validity of Directive 98/44/EC on the legal protection of biotechnological inventions that:[105]

> "The purpose of harmonisation is to reduce the obstacles, whatever their origin, to the operation of the internal market which differences between the situations in the Member States represent."

In the area of consumer protection the obstacles result from the different levels of protection which undermine the trust of the consumer in the functioning of the markets, increase misallocations based on false or incomplete information and limit the consumer's passive market freedoms. This is not to say that in an individual case the legal instrument which is to be examined satisfies the test of proportionality; such an examination requires Community competence in the first place.

The Commission has taken the tobacco judgment as a justification of its recent policy to propose *full instead of minimum harmonisation measures.*[106] In para 104, the Court criticised Directive 98/43/EC as not providing for a so-called "internal market clause", e.g. a provision allowing tobacco advertising complying with the Directive to freely circulate in the internal market. This seems to contradict the practice of consumer protection directives to provide for minimum harmonisation. But this argument is mistaken. Consumer protection measures as described here – information, advertising, contract standards, liability rules and judicial protection – do not directly influence free movement as such, but only regulate the consequences of marketing products and services in the internal market. They may create additional transaction costs and risks for undertakings if the standards differ, but even with full harmonisation there will never be uniformity of legal standards in the internal market due to prior existing differences in law and regulation.[107]

3. "MEASURES" INSTEAD OF "SPECIFIC ACTIONS"

1.23 Article 169(2)(b) TFEU provides for "measures" and abolishes the misleading and imprecise term "specific actions". Despite the interpretative difficulties mentioned above, it has been argued with regard to Community law that besides promotional and financial support measures, legislative instruments

---

[105] ECJ, 9 October 2001, C-377/98, *NL v EP and Council* [2001] ECR I-7079.

[106] COM (2002) 208 final; critique MICKLITZ/REICH/WEATHERILL, *JCP* 2004, 367 at 385; WILHELMSSON, *JCP* 2004, 317; see also see remarks by WEATHERILL, *supra* note 1, at 84–89 taking a differentiated view point.

[107] This has been shown in HOWELLS/MICKLITZ/WILHELMSSON, *supra* note 59, 70–82 with regard to the "complete harmonisation clause" of the Unfair Commercial Practices Directive 2005/29/EC.

may be enacted which enable a Community consumer policy to be independent of the internal market. This affirms the approach taken in Directive 98/6/EC of 16 February 1998 on consumer protection in the indication of the prices of products offered to consumers,[108] which however has not been repeated with regard to other legislative acts. The only restriction of this competence is that the measure has to "support, supplement and monitor" the policy pursued by Member States. This requirement will be easily fulfilled today since all Member States – partly through EC activities – have their own body of consumer law which may be complemented by additional Community measures. The legislative procedure for harmonisation measures under Article 114 TFEU and genuine consumer protection measures under Article 169(2)(b) TFEU is the same. In both cases, the Community legislator has a prerogative to assess on what legal basis to conduct a measure and what measures are appropriate, e.g. a regulation, a directive or a "soft law" instrument (recommendation, code of conduct, etc.).[109] On the other hand, the measures under Article 169(2)(b) will always set "minimum" standards according to Article 169(4) TFEU. This would to some extent render superfluous the debate between "minimum" and "full" harmonisation.[110]

A minimum standard of harmonisation refers to the power of Member States to extend the scope of application as regards the subject matter and the person affected "upwards", i.e. they are entitled to raise but not to lower the level of protection.[111] They are, however, subject to general Community law, for example the general principles of free movement of goods and services and avoid discrimination.[112]

4. "MONITORING" MEASURES

1.24 Measures taken by the Community do not only serve to promote and supplement but also to "monitor" the policy of the Member States. What is the relationship of this particular competence and the general reviewing powers of the Commission under Article 17 TFEU? It is possible that the Community specifies its reviewing powers in appropriate secondary legal instruments and separates these powers from the regular infringement proceedings before the

108 OJ L 80, 18 March 1998, 27.

109 Cf. ECJ, 12 November 1996, C-84/94, *United Kingdom v Council* [1996] ECR I-5755, considering Directive 93/104/EEC concerning certain aspects of the organisation of working time.

110 Reich, *JCP* 2005, 383.

111 ECJ, 16 May 1989, 382/87, *Buet* [1989] ECR I-1235; ECJ, 14 March 1991, C-361/89, *di Pinto* [1991] ECR I-1189.

112 Cf. Stuyck, in: Krämer et al. (eds.), *Law and Diffuse Interests*; ECJ, 25 March 2004, C-71/02, *Herbert Karner v Troostwijk GmbH* [2004] ECR I-3025 at para 34.

ECJ as per Article 258 TFEU.[113] In particular, monitoring is used to examine whether the Member States actually secure the consumer protection of their citizens, a power which had been granted to the individual States. Financial incentives, development programmes, selective support of consumer projects, etc., may be made dependent on whether Member States meet their obligations arising from consumer policy directives.

These competences have been of less significance so far. This may be so as the Commission, as the "guardian" of the Treaties, prefers the (well-established) procedure under Article 258 TFEU in cases of breaches of the Treaty obligations under Article 4(3) TFEU, and as it can apply for interim measures (Article 278 TFEU). The obligation on the Member States to report on the implementation of measures as contained in more recent directives is certainly of significance insofar as it represents enhanced monitoring. There is a certain tendency in DG Sanco to use new modes of soft enforcement which might be regarded as a form of monitoring.[114] However, no reference is made to Treaty articles on which such measures could be based.

5. CLASSIFICATION OF THE DIFFERENT POLICIES

1.25 Three approaches to the possibility of action for EU organs to support and protect consumer interests in the internal market have emerged from the discussion on integration as led in the EU.

- The opening of the market as *"negative" integration*, i.e. abolishing (national) restrictions on free movement of goods and services which do not pursue the achievement of a legitimate policy objective such as consumer protection within the limits of the non-discrimination and proportionality principles; the effects on consumer protection are only indirect and sometimes may even threaten overly protective Member State policies.[115]
- "Integration by promoting competition" and thereby increasing free choice of the consumer in the sense of Article 101(3) TFEU. Consumer interests only have an indirect importance in assessing potential effects of restrictions on competition as far as they seem to increase consumer welfare by "ensuring continued supply and the provision of a wider range of goods".[116] It will not

113 Stuyck, *supra* note 1, 388.
114 http://ec.europa.eu/consumers/index_en.htm; see the activities reported under the heading of "Consumer Research".
115 For an assessment, see Unberath/Johnston, 1237 with detailed references.
116 For a short overview, see Stuyck, *JCP* 2005, 1; the leading case has been ECJ, 25 October 1977, 26/76, *Metro v Commission* (usually referred to as *Metro-Saba I*) [1978] ECR 1875 at para 47; ECJ, 23 November 2006, C-238/05, *Asnef v Ausbank* [2006] ECR I-11125 at para 70.

be discussed in this context how far competition law can have an indirect effect on consumer welfare.[117]

- The regulation of information and marketing practices, establishment of legitimate expectations, protection of legal interests and the facilitation of access to justice through important *"positive" integration measures* will be the focus of the next sections.

6. OVERVIEW OF "POSITIVE" INTEGRATION MEASURES OF EC CONSUMER LAW AND POLICY

1.26 *Positive integration measures* based on secondary law, notably directives, tend to *directly* protect and improve the legal and economic position of consumers,[118] namely misleading advertising, unfair commercial practices and comparative advertising (Directive 2005/29/EC, see Chapter 2), "horizontal consumer contract law" in particular the elimination of unfair terms in consumer contracts (Directive 93/13/EC, see Chapter 3), and the guarantee of certain quality standards in the most common consumer contract, i.e. consumer sales (Directive 99/44/EC, see Chapter 4), consumer credit (Directive 2008/48/EC, Chapter 5) and other financial services, liability for defective products and services (Directive 85/374/EEC, Chapter 6), protection in cases of cross-border contracting, marketing and injury through rules of private international law (Rome I and Rome II Regulations, 593/2008 and 864/2007, see Chapter 7), legal protection of (individual and collective) consumer interests (Directive 2009/22/EC on injunctions, Regulation 2006/2004 on Consumer Enforcement Co-operation, recently the Consumer ADR Directive 2013/11 and ODR Regulation 524/2013, see Chapter 8), and last but not least the Consumer Rights Directive 2011/83 concerning consumer information both in general and with special regard to "off-premises" and distance contracts (Chapter 9).

1.27 The following other EC directives specifically concerned with consumer protection deserve attention; some of them have been under Commission review and led to new instruments:[119]

117 For a skeptical view see Cseres, Towards a European model of economic justice: the role of competition law, in: Micklitz (ed.), *The Many Concepts of Social Justice in European Private Law*, 2011, 405.

118 A detailed study of the relevant consumer directives and their implementation in Member State law has been done by Schulte-Nölke et al., *Consumer Law Compendium*, 2008; for a recent overview, see Twigg-Flesner, *supra* note 35, 54–61.

119 Green Paper on the review Consumer Acquis COM (2006) 744 final of 8 February 2007; critical remarks by Micklitz/Reich, *VuR* 2007, 121; Twigg-Flesner, *ERCL* 2007, 198; Heiderhoff/Kenny, 740; Twigg-Flesner, *supra* note 35, 172–180.

- Directive 85/577/EEC of 20 December 1985 to protect the consumer in respect of contracts negotiated away from business premises (now replaced via the Directive 2011/83/EU of 25 October 2011 on Consumer Rights);[120]
- Directive 90/314/EEC of 13 June 1990 on package travel, packaged holidays and package tours (under review);[121]
- Directive 94/47/EC of 26 October 1994 on the protection of purchasers in respect of certain aspects of contracts relating to the purchase of the right to use immovable properties on a timeshare basis (now replaced by Directive 2008/122/EC of 14 January 2009);[122]
- Directive 97/7/EC of 20 May 1997 on the protection of consumers in respect of distance contracts (now replaced by Directive 2011/83/EU of 25 October 2011 on Consumer Rights);[123]
- Directive 98/6/EC of 6 February 1996 on price indications (under review);[124]
- Directive 2002/65/EC of 23 September 2002 concerning distance marketing of consumer financial services.[125]

Several other directives have specific provisions concerning consumer transactions, e.g.:

- Directive 2000/31/EC of 8 June 2000 on electronic commerce in the internal market (Chapter 9);[126]
- Directive 2000/43/EC of 29 June 2000[127] and Directive 2004/113/EC of 13 December 2004[128] concerning discrimination on grounds of race, ethnic origin and sex in the supply of goods and services available to the public;
- Directive 2006/123/EC of 12 December 2006 on services in the internal market (Chapter 9);[129]
- Directive 2007/64/EC of 13 November 2007 on payment services in the internal market.[130]

---

120 OJ L 372 of 31 December 1985, 85, OJ L 304, 22 November 2011, 64.

121 OJ L 158, 23 June 1990, 90; a new proposal has been published as of 9 July 2013, COM (2013) 512 final.

122 OJ L 280, 29 October 1994, 94; OJ L 33, 3 February 2009, 10.

123 OJ L 144, 4 June 1997, 19; OJ L 304, 22 November 2011, 64.

124 OJ L 80, 18 March 1996, 27.

125 OJ L 271, 9 October 2002, 16.

126 OJ L 13, 17 July 2000, 12.

127 OJ L 180, 19 July 2000, 22.

128 OJ L 373, 21 December 2004, 37.

129 OJ L 376, 27 December 2006, 36.

130 OJ L 319, 5 December 2007, 1.

LEEDS UNIVERSITY LIBRARY

In special fields like passenger protection,[131] directly applicable regulations have been adopted, based on Article 91/100(2) TFEU or its predecessors, which relate to transport. Examples of the use of regulations for the consumer interest are:

- Regulation (EC) 261/2004 of 11 February 2004 on compensation and assistance to passengers in the event of denied boarding and of cancellation and long delays of flights;[132]
- Regulation (EC) 1371/2007 of 23 October 2007 on rail passengers' rights and obligations;[133]
- Regulation (EC) 1177/2010 of 24 November 2010 on passengers travelling by sea and inland waterways;[134]
- Regulation (EC) 181/2011 of 16 February 2011 on passengers in bus and coach transport.[135]

V. THE POSITION OF THE CONSUMER UNDER THE LAW OF EU DIRECTIVES

1. PREVALENCE OF DIRECTIVES IN EU CONSUMER POLICY

1.28 Positive integration refers to *direct support* of consumer interests through an independent consumer policy of the EU. It does not negatively treat measures by the Member States restricting the opening of the market and thereby indirectly consumer choice, nor does it leave the marketing objectives under competition conditions to the undertakings in the scope of competition policy. Instead it attempts to provide independent information and to pursue autonomous protective objectives. It therefore normally makes use of directives as per Article 288 TFEU. In the meantime, alternative instruments have been discussed, such as the so-called "co-regulations",[136] which, however, did not gain importance in consumer law.

Directives are binding on Member States (including all State organs and courts)[137] – but only as to the result to be achieved, leaving some choice as to

---

131 See Karsten, in: Benyon (ed.), *Services and the EU Citizen*, 34, insisting that passenger rights are a new field of a broadly understood consumer protection.

132 OJ L 46, 17 February 2004, 1; confirmed by ECJ, 10 January 2006, C-344/04, *The Queen and IATA, ELFAA v Dpt. of Transport* [2006] ECR I-403. A new proposal has been published by the Commission, COM (2013) 130 of 13 March 2013.

133 OJ L 315, 3 December 2007, 14.

134 OJ L 344, 17 December 2010, 1.

135 OJ L 55, 28 February 2011, 1.

136 Cf. the considerations in Green Paper on EU Consumer Protection, COM (2001) 531, 5 October 2001, 6, 14.

137 ECJ, 13 November 1990, C-106/89, *Marleasing* [1990] ECR I-4135.

form and method open to them. Their appearance is twofold, taking an integration-political point of view: they purport to open the markets on the one hand and thereby to achieve the internal market as per Article 26 TFEU. On the other hand, they pursue certain protective objectives as set out in Article 114(3) and Article 169 TFEU, provided the EU limitations on competence are respected. The opening of the market and positive integration are interlinked. This is enhanced by the Community legislator; in order to establish his competences he may even refer to the harmonisation of competition conditions if in fact the creation of certain Community minimum standards in consumer protection are of importance, for example in the area of misleading advertising and other types of unfair commercial practices. It is also conceivable that in the future the EU legislator will rely more on Article 169(2)(b) and thereby adopt independent consumer protection measures which support actions of Member States, including regulations and directives with minimum protection standards under Article 169(4) TFEU.

2. LEGAL EFFECTS OF DIRECTIVES

1.29 The legal effects of directives are determined according to Article 288(3) TFEU. The wording seems – in deliberate distinction from regulations – not to include a so-called "direct effect" or "direct applicability" of directives by the national courts without having been transformed by the national legislator beforehand. In its *Van Duyn* decision[138] the ECJ already objected to this formalistic *argmentum e contrario* and drew attention to the protective effects of directives which the courts were required to enforce (theory of *effet utile* under EU law). It stated the following:

> "If, however, by virtue of the provisions of Article 189 (now Article 288 TFEU) regulations are directly applicable and, consequently, may by their very nature have direct effects, it does not follow from this that other categories of acts mentioned in that article can never have similar effects. It would be incompatible with the binding effect attributed to a directive by Article 189 to exclude, in principle, the possibility that the obligation which it imposes may be invoked by those concerned. In particular, where the community authorities have, by directive, imposed on member states the obligation to pursue a particular course of conduct, the useful effect of such an act would be weakened if individuals were prevented from relying on it before their national courts and if the latter were prevented from taking it into consideration as an element of community law. Article 177, which empowers national courts to refer to the court questions concerning the validity and interpretation of all acts of the community institutions, without distinction, implies furthermore that these acts may be invoked by individuals in the national courts. It is necessary to examine, in

[138] ECJ, 4 December 1974, 41/74 [1974] ECR 1337.

every case, whether the nature, general scheme and wording of the provision in question are capable of having direct effects on the relations between member states and individuals". (para 12)

1.30 The *direct effect of directives*[139] is the subject of an intensive and controversial discussion which will be documented only briefly here. As a general requirement, the following conditions must be met. The appropriate test is threefold:

(1) the time allowed for implementing the Directive has elapsed;
(2) the Directive contains sufficiently precise and mandatory obligations of the Member States which depends on the individual provisions;
(3) these obligations must be unconditional, i.e. not require further implementing measures.

For the purposes of this article it may be summarised in four stages.

a) "Minimum" vs. "total" and "targeted" harmonisation

Prior to raising the issue of direct effect, the extent and intensity of harmonisation of the Directive is to be determined and compared with the existing law of the Member State. Only to the extent to which EU law pursues a *harmonisation effect* may it be referred to as having direct effect. This effect results from the Directive itself or from the general provisions on competence under EU law.

aa) Minimum harmonisation as the traditional starting point

1.31 In the field of *economic consumer protection*, *minimum directives* have traditionally been enacted on a regular basis, setting certain *minimum standards* for all EU Member States. Therefore, at the beginning of its consumer policy, the E(E)C used the instrument of "minimum harmonisation", e.g. in the early Directives 85/577/EEC on doorstep sales and 90/314/EEC on package holidays. Later instruments like Directives 93/13/EEC on unfair terms and 99/44/EC on consumer sales continued this principle, which allows for different approaches provided that the basic threshold of protection is maintained. Member States remain free to create different levels of protection, in particular maintaining higher levels of protection for their citizens or increasing them in later legislation. The distortions of competition resulting therefrom need to be accepted as far as they result from minimum harmonisation. They are, however,

---

139 Comprehensive discussion PRECHAL, *Directives in EC Law*, 2006, 255–261; REICH, *supra* note 2, 19–22.

subject to restrictions under Community law, such as the principle of proportionality.[140] Contrary to Grundmann[141] the legal effect of the "higher" standards is not limited to cross-border transactions of goods and services, but also applies to domestic marketing.

On the other hand – which some proponents of the "internal market philosophy' see as a disadvantage – harmonisation will therefore only be partial and sometimes create new "disharmonies". Therefore, in its review of the existing "consumer *acquis*", the Commission seems to favour "full harmonisation".

bb) Total harmonisation "targeted" at specific areas as the "new" approach

1.32 More recent directives, such as Directive 2005/29/EC concerning unfair commercial practices, Directive 2008/48/EC on consumer credit, Directive 2008/122/EC on time sharing, and – albeit to a limited extent – Directive 2011/83/EU on consumer rights (replacing Directive 85/577/EC on door-to-door selling and Directive 97/7/EC on distance selling) purport the enforcement of the principle of *complete or full harmonisation.* In its original proposal on a Consumer Rights Directive of 8 October 2008,[142] the Commission wanted to adopt the full harmonisation approach to all areas covered, including unfair terms and consumer sales. This proposal, due to criticism from academia[143] and political bodies, could not succeed. Full harmonisation was limited to so-called off-premises and distance contracts, while a more targeted approach was taken in other areas, including the concept of consumer itself (for details see Chapter 9). In the harmonised field – the "target area of harmonisation" – the Member States would then lack the power to establish a "higher standard of protection" in favour of the consumer. The relevant directives will usually define as precisely as possible the harmonised field and frequently allow different options to Member States, about which they must inform the Commission.

The consequences of such an approach – which are problematic from a consumer-political point of view – can be illustrated by the example of product liability law. The relevant Directive – 85/374/EEC of 25 July 1985 – merely allows the Member States the continuance of "any rights which an injured person may have according to the rules of the law of contractual or non-contractual liability or a special liability system existing at the moment when this Directive is notified", per Article 13. Member States are prohibited from maintaining or introducing strict liability systems, a proviso strictly applied by the ECJ

---

140 Cf. the different arguments voiced in Everling/Roth; ECJ, 25 March 2004, C-71/02, *Herbert Karner v Trosstwijk GmbH* [2004] ECR I-3025 at para 34; for a different approach see opinion of AG Trstenjak of 17 July 2008 in C-205/07 *Gysbrechts*, *supra* note 57.

141 *Europäisches Schuldvertragsrecht*, 1999, 81–88.

142 COM (2008) 614.

143 See Micklitz/Reich, *CMLRev* 2009, 471 with further references.

prohibiting any extension of liability to suppliers or the introduction of a product monitoring duty for producers. On the other hand, the traditional tort system remains untouched, which creates problems of delimitation between "strict" and "fault-based" liability.[144]

b) *"Horizontal (negative) direct effect"?*

1.33 In the traditional doctrine of EC law, a directive can only have "vertical direct effect", that is it creates rights for citizens against the state. A Member State that does not comply with its obligations under a directive cannot use its non-compliant law to impose obligations on individuals or restrict rights which a person should have had if the Directive had been correctly implemented. The concept of "state" is a broad one, including the scenario that the state acts in the form of a subject under private law, or if it directs the activity of a private person.[145]

On the other hand, this doctrine excludes the so-called "horizontal direct effect" which has been stressed by the ECJ in its *Dori* decision of 14 July 1994.[146] The ECJ refers to the doctrine of legal sources of Community law which grants regulations, but not directives, the ability to establish direct obligations against private persons. Article 169 TFEU does not alter the legal situation under EU law in terms of the relations between consumers and undertakings since the provision in itself is too ambiguous to impose legal obligations.[147]

Borderline cases have been before the ECJ where directives can be applied as at least allowing a "negative horizontal direct effect". The leading ECJ case is *Unilever.*[148] It concerned the effect on a remedy for breach of contract because the product (virgin olive oil) did not conform to the recently amended Italian standards which, however, had not been notified to the Commission, in violation of the relevant Directive, 83/189/EEC. The Court wrote, referring to its earlier *CIA* judgment,[149] concerning the consequences of a failure to notify the Commission of a technical regulation or standard under Directive 83/189/EEC on relations between private parties:

> "Thus, it follows from the case-law of the Court that the inapplicability of a technical regulation which has not been notified ... can be invoked in proceedings between

---

144 ECJ, 20 April 2002, C-52/00, *Commission v France* [2002] ECR I-3827 at paras 22–23; ECJ, 10 January 2006, C-402/03, *Skov v Bilka Lavprisvarehus and Bilka Lavprisvarehus v Jette Mikkelsen et al.* [2006] ECR I-199; as a follow-up 14 March 2006, C-177/04, *Commission v France* [2006] ECR I-2461 and critique Reich, *VuR* 2006, 241.

145 Dashwood, 81; see ECJ, 2 August 1993, C-271/91, *Marshall v. Southampton Health Auth.* [1993] ECR-I 4367.

146 ECJ, 14 July 1994, C-91/92 [1994] ECR I-3325; differing opinion of the AGs Lenz, Jacobs and van Gerven.

147 ECJ, 7 March 1996, C-192–94, *El Corte Inglés* [1996] ECR I-1281.

148 ECJ, 26 September 2000, C-443/98 [2000] ECR I-7535.

149 ECJ, 30 April 1996, C-194/94, *CIA Security v Signalson and Securitel* [1996] ECR I-2201.

> individuals ... Whilst it is true ... that a directive cannot of itself impose obligations on an individual and cannot therefore be relied on as such against an individual... that case-law does not apply where non-compliance with Article 8 or Article 9 of Directive 83/189, which constitutes a substantial procedural defect, renders a technical regulation adopted in breach of either of those articles inapplicable. In such circumstances, and unlike the case of non-transposition of directives ..., Directive 83/189 does not in any way define the substantive scope of the legal rule on the basis of which the national court must decide the case before it. It creates neither rights nor obligations for individuals." (paras 49–51)

The distinction of the Court between non-implementation of a directive which cannot as such impose obligations, and non-notification in breach of a directive which may be directly held against private parties in an action for breach of contract, is not convincing. In both cases, non-compliance of a Member State with obligations contained in a directive – whether substantive or procedural ones – has effects on private relations, at least in a "negative way", that is, a remedy which one party would normally have had under national law if the directive had been applied or implemented correctly, is excluded. The directive does not create obligations as such, but it modifies them.

This differentiation was further developed by AG Saggio in his opinion of 16 December 1999 in the *Oceano* case.[150] With regard to the legal effects of the Unfair Contract Terms Directive 93/13/EC on a jurisdiction clause to the detriment of the consumer, he distinguished between the effects of "substitution" and "elimination":

> "It should further be noted that a solution of this kind, which distinguishes between the 'substitution effect and the 'exclusionary effect of a directive which has not been transposed within the prescribed period, already appears in embryo in the Court's case-law concerning the consequences of a declaration of failure to fulfil an obligation under the Treaty". (para 38)

While indeed a directive cannot "substitute" national law to create obligations as such, it may very well eliminate provisions of national law which restrict rights arising out of a directive, thereby merely "extending" or modifying already existing but not "enacting" or "imposing" obligations on the other party. This approach can be based on the precedence of EU law over Member State law.[151]

---

150 ECJ, 27 June 2000, C-240–244/98, *Océano Group Ed. v Rocio Murciano Quintero et al.* [2000] ECR I-4941.

151 See Reich, *supra* note 2, para 3.6, concerning the effects of the Age Discrimination Directive 2000/78/EC in employment law, based on constitutional principles and Article 21 of the Charter; there are still no parallel developments with regard to consumer law directives.

c) "Directive conforming" (consistent) interpretation

1.34 The prohibition of horizontal direct effect needs to be supplemented, as the ECJ has consistently held that national law needs to be interpreted "in the light of the wording and the purpose of the Directive".[152] This applies to both the law implementing the directive and earlier law.[153] This entails an obligation on the national judge under Article 4(3) TFEU to find the necessary provisions in his legal protection system to bridge legal protection gaps which have arisen as a result of non-implementation or implementation which is inconsistent with EU law. This requirement merely applies "*so far as it is possible*", i.e. an interpretation *contra legem* is not required. The question of the extent to which national law can be interpreted in a way which is compatible with EU law is decided at national rather than Union level. If national law can be read in conformity with Union law, then the national judge has to apply an interpretation in accordance with EU law because of the principle of priority of the latter. This is particularly so for an interpretation which has been offered by the ECJ even though it used to follow another point of view in earlier decisions. In the *DRK* case[154] the Court insisted that:

> "if the application of interpretative methods recognised by national law enables, in certain circumstances, a provision of domestic law to be construed in such a way as to avoid conflict with another rule of domestic law or the scope of that provision to be restricted to that end by applying it only in so far as it is compatible with the rule concerned, the national court is bound to use those methods in order to achieve the result sought by the directive. In such circumstances, the national court, ... must, when applying the provisions of national law specifically intended to implement the directive, interpret those provisions so far as possible in such a way that they are applied in conformity with the objectives of the directive." (paras 117–118)

The principle of interpretation that conforms to EU law is therefore to be understood by way of an obligation on the national judge to use the full range of interpretative methods – including those of a teleological restriction (as in this case) – to make sure that national law conforms to EU directives with direct effect – even if this amounts to imposing a burden on a private party. Therefore, the original distinction between denying the horizontal effect of directives and imposing an EU law-conforming interpretation of national law loses much of its importance, at least in relations governed by civil and commercial law.

---

152 ECJ, 10 April 1984, C-14/83, *Colson* [1984] ECR 1984, 1891.

153 ECJ, 13 November 1990, C-106/89, *Marleasing* [1990] ECR I-4135; ECJ, 16 January 1992, C-373/90, *Nissan* [1992] ECR I-131; ECJ, 14 July 1994, C-91/92, *Dori* [1994] ECR I-3325 at 27.

154 ECJ, 5 October 2004, C-397/01 et al., *Bernhard Pfeiffer et al. v Deutsches Rotes Kreuz* [2004] ECR I-8835; similarly the later judgment of the ECJ, 7 April 2006, C-212/04, *K. Adeneler v ELOG* [2006] ECR I-6057.

d) *State liability as a remedy of last resort*

1.35 If the theory of direct effect cannot be invoked by the consumer against the undertaking, even though the Directive wanted to give subjective rights to the consumer, then state liability as a remedy of last resort may arise against the Member State for having failed to implement a Directive properly or not at all. In its *Francovich* decision, the ECJ established that an individual citizen who has suffered damage through a Member State's failure to properly implement a directive has a right to compensation against the State.[155] This right to compensation requires that it should be possible to identify the persons protected and the content of those rights under EU law on the basis of the provisions of the Directive, whereas the debtor cannot be determined; the rule in question which has been breached must intend to confer rights upon individuals. Furthermore, the violation of EU law, for example the Directive which had not been implemented properly or not at all, must be "*sufficiently qualified*". This will be the case if the Member State "manifestly and gravely" violated its obligation to implement a directive. Finally, there must be a "direct causal link" between the breach of the State's obligation and the harm suffered.[156] Fault of the organs or agents of a Member State is not required. State liability is of particular significance where the Directive prescribes protection of the consumer against the bankruptcy of a trader, for example ensuring the minimum claims of depositors and investors against credit institutions or investment firms by establishing specific schemes (but not mere violation of state supervisory duties),[157] or in contracts for package tours with regard to security for money paid over.[158]

VI. CONSUMER CONCEPTS IN COMMUNITY LAW

1. THE "INFORMED CONSUMER" STANDARD

1.36 Community and now Union law proceed from the premise of an "informed consumer". Consumer protection as social protection of disfavoured or minority groups, is generally a matter of the Member States in the scope of minimum harmonisation.[159] Under the new law of "total or targeted

155 ECJ, 19 November 1991, C-6 + 9/90, *Francovich* [1991] ECR I-5357; confirmed by ECJ, 14 July 1994, C-91/92, *Dori* [1994] ECR I-3325 as a substitute for the missing horizontal direct effect.

156 ECJ, 5 March 1996, C-46 + 48/93, *Brasserie du Pêcheur* [1996] ECR I-1029.

157 ECJ, 12 December 2004, C-222/02, *Peter Paul* [2004] ECR I-9425.

158 ECJ, 8 October 1996, C-178/94 et al., *Dillenkofer* [1996] ECR I-4845; ECJ, 15 June 1999, C-140/97, *Rechberger* [1999] ECR I-3499.

159 Especially ECJ, 16 May 1989, C-382/87, *Buet* [1989] ECR I-1235; thereto Stuyck, in: Krämer et al., *Law and Diffuse Interests*, 287; Howells/Wilhelmsson, *supra* note 1, 315–320;

harmonisation", this depends on its scope. In the area of consumer credit under Directive 2008/48/EC, questions of social protection of the consumer-debtor against usury, default and insolvency are left to Member State law. EU consumer protection policy and law usually belong to economic, not social, law.

The Community/Union legislator – and to an even larger extent the Commission – rely on the effects of the internal market and competition in order to support consumer welfare. A guarantee of the right to free choice constitutes the core issue of a European economic constitution for liberal authors,[160] as it establishes the individual rights of the citizens to participate in cross-border transactions in accordance with Community law. Consumer protection extends these liberties as "freedom of choice and decision" to "passive citizens".[161] According to this point of view it may also distort integration where freedom of contract is excessively limited.[162]

The measures of the Community in the scope of consumer protection demonstrate an element focusing on information – if not exclusively – which is expressly repeated in Article 169 TFEU.[163] They are thus in accordance with a market economy. Socio-political, distributive demands are less important.[164] In this field, the Member States – taking into account in particular the principle of subsidiarity – are required to take action. For this reason, Wilhelmsson[165] objects to an excessive unification of European contract law where "social values" would not be adequately considered.

2. THE "VULNERABLE" CONSUMER STANDARD

1.36a Vulnerable consumers are those who cannot, or can no longer, cope with the requirements of the modern consumer society. These consumers run the risk of being isolated from social and economic life, be it by over-indebtedness, illness or a lack of possibilities to communicate. This also includes the growing problem of "social deprivation". This group of consumers was once the focus of the national consumer policies of the 1960s and 1970s. It was exactly this political movement that concentrated on the right to protect the weak. Consumer policy and consumer law policy will always try to integrate this group of vulnerable consumers. In the Lisbon Strategy, the EU explicitly mentioned for

---

Weatherill/Micklitz, in: Grundmann/Kerber/Weatherill, *Party Autonomy*, 173, 185–187, 197, 200; Hondius, *JCP* 2004, 245.

160 Critical discussion thereof in Kenny, 86–93; Lurger, 396–400.

161 Reich, *ZEuP* 1994, 387.

162 Kirchner, in: Grundmann/Kerber/Weatherill, *Party Autonomy*, 165.

163 Grundmann/Kerber/Weatherill (eds.), *Party Autonomy*.

164 Cf. Wilhelmsson, *Social Contract Law and European Integration*; differing opinion Willet, 471.

165 *ERPL* 2002, 77, 84; similar view Reich, *supra* note 110, 383.

the first time the existence of different types of consumers. It speaks of humans "living below the poverty line and in social exclusion".[166]

Improved information and market transparency are of little help to vulnerable consumers when it comes to leading a self-determined life. It is rather the targeted promotion of infrastructure and intelligent, realistic schemes for providing advice that enable consumers to participate independently in economic and social life. If one declares inclusion and social participation to be the objective then one also has to take care of "vulnerable" consumers.[167] Amazingly enough, the vulnerable consumer has entered the European consumer policy agenda. Recital 34 of the Consumer Rights Directive 2011/83/EU (CRD, see Chapter 9) insists that:

> "In providing that information, the trader should take into account the specific needs of consumers who are vulnerable because of their mental, physical or psychological infirmity, age or credulity in a way which the trader could reasonably be expected to foresee. However, taking into account such specific needs should not lead to different levels of consumer protection."

However, the Recital did not make it into the specific information requirements of the CRD.

The legalisation of this new type of consumer is closely linked to the liberalisation of the energy and telecommunications markets, which was so strongly promoted by the European Commission after the adoption of the Single European Act led to the creation of new structures. The guarantee of supply for everybody was added to the concept of universal services. This obligation not only refers to vulnerable consumers, but includes them in its protective realm. For the first time the concept appears in Directive 2002/22/EC on universal services and users' rights relating to electronic communications networks and services (Universal Service Directive).

Article 1(1) of the Universal Service Directive aims at ensuring the availability throughout the Community of good quality publicly available services through effective competition and choice and, further, aims to deal with circumstances "in which the needs of end-users are not satisfactorily met by the market". According to the seventh recital, the Directive's focus is to ensure the "same conditions [of] access, in particular for the elderly, the disabled and for people with special social needs". Directive 2009/140/EC has not changed the terms defined in Article 2 of Directive 2002/21/EC. For the first time disabled

[166] COM (2010) 2020 3 March 2010, www.europarl.europa.eu/summits/lis1_en.htm (accessed 31.07.2012).

[167] www.bmelv.de/SharedDocs/Downloads/EN/Ministry/Trusting-Vulnerable-Responsible-Consumer.pdf.

persons are granted special rights in Articles 7/23a of the amended Universal Service Directive 2009/136/EC of 25 November 2009.[168]

In the Internal Market in Electricity Directive 2003/54/EC and the Internal Market in Natural Gas Directive 2003/55/EC, the so-called second generation of the liberalisation of the energy markets, the European Commission coined the notion of the "vulnerable customer".[169] In view of the increasing problems of social exclusion as a consequence of the liberalisation of the Single European Market the EU has even tightened its approach in the Directive 2009/72/EC of 13 July 2009.[170] However, the EU leaves it to the Member States to substantiate the term "vulnerable consumer" as per Article 3(7) Directive 2009/72/EC.

The conceptual differentiation in Directive 2005/29/EC on Unfair Commercial Practices can also be considered to belong to the border areas of traditional contract law understanding. Interestingly the Directive does not speak of the "vulnerable consumer", but of "consumers whose characteristics make them particularly vulnerable" to unfair commercial practices. This term is taken to include consumers with characteristics such as "age, physical or mental infirmity or credulity that render them susceptible".[171] The law does not define the "normal addressee of advertisement", who in the Directive is spoken of as an "average consumer".

The practical impact of the vulnerable consumer standard is still hard to evaluate. However, it is clear that European consumer law has again changed its outlook. Today it is fair to assume that the vulnerable consumer concept stands side by side with the informed consumer concept.

3. THE "WEAKER" CONSUMER IN THE CASE LAW OF THE ECJ

1.36b As far as application and interpretation of European consumer law directives is concerned, the practice of the ECJ regarding contract law particularly emphasises the *protection of the consumer as weaker party* in contract law.[172] In the *Schulte* case,[173] the ECJ required Member States "to ensure that their legislation protects consumers who have been unable to avoid exposure to such risks [incurred because of not knowing of their right of cancellation under the Doorstep Directive 85/577], by adopting suitable measures to allow them to avoid bearing the consequences of the materialisation of those risks".

168 OJ L 337, 18 December 2009, 11; for an evaluation see Nijenhuis, in: Benyon, *supra* note 134, 56.

169 Compare Article 3(5) Directive 2003/54/EC and Article 3(3) 2003/55/EC: "vulnerable consumer respectively vulnerable customer".

170 OJ L 211, 14 August 2009, 55.

171 Compare Directive 2005/29/EC Article 5(3): "particularly vulnerable".

172 ECJ, 13 December 2001, C-481/99, *Heininger* [2001] ECR I-9945 at para 38.

173 ECJ, 25 October 2005, C-350/03, *Schulte v Deutsche Bausparkasse Badenia* [2005] ECR I-9215 at para 101.

Lurger[174] rightly describes this approach as the *"principle of solidarity and fairness"*.

The ECJ has quite often been criticised, in particular from the perspective of consumer law activists, for not being ready to really engage with the consumer problems in the litigation and for being all too often prepared to merge consumer protection interests with internal market requirements. One outstanding example is the rise and fall of the so-called *Heininger* saga, where even a whole series of references to the ECJ did not lead to real improvement of the legal position of consumers.[175] More recently, however, the ECJ has appeared to take a more active stand in protecting consumer interests. The new battlefield is Directive 93/13/EC where an amazing number of references, in particular from the new Member States, but also from Member States suffering from the euro crisis, is met with the readiness of the ECJ to take consumer protection "much more seriously".[176] In order to understand its protective ambit, at least in the words of the ECJ in interpreting the Unfair Terms Directive, a quotation from the *Penzügij Lizing* case[177] will be helpful; this quote has been repeated time and again where the concept of the "consumer as the weaker party" has been used to justify a specific type of interpretation:

> "according to settled case-law, the system of protection introduced by the Directive is based on the idea that the consumer is in a weak position vis-à-vis the seller or supplier, as regards both his bargaining power and his level of knowledge. This leads to the consumer agreeing to terms drawn up in advance by the seller or supplier without being able to influence the content of those terms … The Court of Justice has also held that, on account of that weaker position, Article 6(1) of the Directive provides that unfair terms are not binding on the consumer. As is apparent from case-law, that is a mandatory provision which aims to replace the formal balance which the contract establishes between the rights and obligations of the parties with an effective balance which re-establishes equality between them … In order to guarantee the protection intended by the Directive, the Court has also stated that the imbalance which exists between the consumer and the seller or supplier may be corrected only by positive action unconnected with the actual parties to the contract."

This case law is seemingly only concerned with Directive 93/13/EC. However, it can be seen as a general approach to the objectives of EU consumer law by the ECJ, framing party autonomy in B2C transactions in favour of the consumer as

---

[174] See *supra* note 144, 380; see also Reich, *supra* note 2, Chapter 2 insisting on a "Principle of Protection of the Weaker Party" in EU civil law.

[175] Micklitz, The Relationship between National and European Consumer Policy – Challenges and Perspectives, *Yearbook of Consumer Law 2008*, 2007, 35–66.

[176] Micklitz/Reich, *CMLRev* 2014, forthcoming; the leading case is *Aziz*, C-415/11, *supra* note 47 and 3.

[177] ECJ, 9 November 2010, C-137/08, *VB Penzügji Lizing v Schneider* [2010] ECR I-10847 at para 46.

the typically weaker party in relation to the business or professional partner who is seen to be regularly in a stronger bargaining position.

It is hard to predict where the development will lead, but quite obviously the ECJ sets the protective standards itself. Seen this way, the ECJ turns into a some sort of social manager which counterbalances the much harsher and market-orientated philosophy in particular of the European Commission, if not the European legislator.

4. "CONSUMER" AS A LEGAL CONCEPT: A NARROW OR A WIDE DEFINITION?

1.37 As with the Member States, EU law only at first glance recognises a uniform concept of "consumer" which would form the basis of all legal instruments.[178] Depending on the method of integration and the concrete objective of a Community/Union measure, different "consumer" concepts are employed – which are usually restricted to so-called B2C (business-to-consumer) transactions, but in some cases, however, cover any customer or end user, whether private or professional. The following overview provides a first point of reference:

(1) In the field of protection of economic interests, in particular in contract law, the notion of the term "consumer" is most unambiguous. Consumer is any natural person who upon the conclusion of a contract is acting for purposes which are outside his trade, business or profession. The term "consumer" is *functional-occupation related*, like the term "undertakings" in the field of competition law. Activities which relate to a business, a profession or work are excluded even if the acting party as such is not experienced in legal matters.[179] According to the narrow interpretation of the ECJ, legal entities are not included.[180]
(2) Depending on the protective purpose of the measure, this definition may be extended by national law in the scope of minimum harmonisation to other persons worthy of protection.[181] EC law however will generally not by itself protect so-called "small traders" but leaves this to Member States as part of minimum harmonisation.
(3) In the field of financial services, and in particular in payment, insurance and investment law, which are not covered in this book, the term "consumer" is

---

178 On this, Stuyck, *supra* note 1, 392; Faber, 854; Micklitz, Commentary before §§13 BGB, in: *Münchner Kommentar zum BGB*, para 88; Drexl, 433.

179 ECJ, 14 March 1991, C-361/89, *di Pinto* [1991] ECR I-1189; ECJ, 3 July 1997, C-269/95, *Benincasa* [1997] ECR I-3767 (in the context of the Brussels Convention, see 7.31).

180 ECJ, 22 November 2001, C-541 + 542/99, *Idealservice* [2001] ECR I-9049.

181 See the detailed references in Schulte-Nölke/Ebers, 672–687.

interpreted widely as also extending to clients, policyholders and investors. The specific purpose of the business is therefore irrelevant. As can be seen from Recitals (13) and (17), the Directive 2011/83/EU on consumer rights has confirmed the discretion left to Member States, even in fully harmonised fields of consumer law. It should be noted, however, that institutional clients, policyholders and investors are usually excluded.

(4) In the field of product liability the protection of any person who might come into contact with a defective or hazardous product is of paramount importance. It is irrelevant, however, what function they are carrying out in doing so. Consumer protection equals the protection of any natural person, irrespective of the job that they are performing. This applies exclusively to damage caused by death or personal injuries. Protection of property is functionally limited.

1.38 With this said, it should now be possible to establish a core notion of "consumer" under Community law as a "passive market participant",[182] the hallmarks of which are as follows:

- consumers are generally only natural persons;
- the activities of consumers are to be functionally distinguished from those of undertakings, self-employed persons and employees as described by the fundamental freedoms of Community/Union law;
- the applicability of consumer provisions to "mixed purposes" will depend on the predominance of one or the other purpose; there is, according to the case law of the ECJ with regard to the Brussels Convention, no presumption that the consumer as private person acts for private purposes;[183]
- the role of the consumer is not restricted to personal activities but may also serve the consumption of others provided this is done outside his trade, profession or business; and
- in the field of the non-economic protection of legal interests, in particular product liability, the term "consumer" is independent of any activity and may be employed in relation to any natural person.

In conclusion, the term "consumer" in Article 169 TFEU and "citizen of the Union" in Article 20 TFEU are substantially concurrent: each describes a subject with a certain legal status as determined by EU law which goes beyond the scope of the classical fundamental EU freedoms. Freedom of movement – with regard to the Community citizen – and rights based on information and protection of legitimate interests – with regard to the consumer – constitute the central

---

182 Reich, *supra* note 5, 389.

183 See ECJ, 20 January 2005, C-464/01, *Johann Gruber v BayWa AG* [2005] ECR I-439. Recital (17) of the Consumer Rights Directive 2011/83/EU provides for an extension to so called "double-purpose" contracts, see however the criticism by Loacker, *JZ* 2013, 234.

reference points for the granting of subjective rights which can be further developed by a network of derivative secondary law. Both the EU consumer and the citizen benefit from the EU principle of effective legal protection and access to justice, but this must be ensured mainly by the Member States themselves and not by the EU. Article 47 of the Charter of Fundamental Rights enhances the European impact on effect legal protection and access to justice for both.[184]

VII. FUTURE ORIENTATIONS OF EU CONSUMER POLICY AND LAW: A CRITICAL OVERVIEW

1. FROM CONSUMER LAW TO USER PROTECTION?

a) *The role of the "passive market citizen"*

1.39 In EU consumer law, a narrow definition of the consumer has mostly been used. With some slight variations, a consumer is a natural person who in the type of transaction covered by a directive is acting outside their business or profession. In the case law of the ECJ, this definition has been interpreted as not covering non-profit legal persons, commercial persons acting outside their normal business, and assignees of consumer contracts.[185] Mixed contracts depend on what element is most prominent – there is a presumption that the contract has been concluded for business or professional purposes which must be refuted by the consumer.[186] This case law creates a number of arbitrary delimitations and excludes persons who are also in need of protection. It should not be forgotten that this narrow definition was first developed in matters of jurisdiction where, according to the Court, not only questions of consumer protection, but also of legal and procedural certainty concerning the place where a case is to be heard must be taken into account. Since the Brussels Convention[187] Regulation (EC) 44/2001[188] takes as a starting point the rule "*actor sequitur forum rei*", meaning that the domicile of the defendant is usually relevant in determining jurisdiction within the EU (details 7.34). Any rule departing from this principle, like in the area of consumer cases, is an exception and must be

---

184 Reich, *supra* note 2, Chapter 4 on the "Principle of Effectiveness".

185 ECJ, 22 November 2001, C-541 + 542/99, *Idealservice* [2001] ECR I-9049; ECJ, 14 March 1991, C-361/89, *di Pinto* [1991] ECR I-1189; ECJ, 19 January 1993, C-89/91, *Shearson Lehmann Hutton v TVB Treuhandgesellschaft* [1993] ECR I-139.

186 ECJ, 20 January 2005, C-464/01, *Johann Gruber v Bay Wa AG* [2005] ECR I-439; the same direction Heiderhoff/Kenny, 740 at 745.

187 [1998] OJ C 27/1 (consolidated version).

188 Council Regulation (EC) No 44/2001 of 22 December 2000 on jurisdiction and the recognition and enforcement of judgments in civil and commercial matters OJ L 12, 16 January 2001, 1.

interpreted narrowly in the interests of legal certainty.[189] This argument, however, is not true for consumer transactions where only the position of the "non-professional market participant" outside the courtroom is at stake, like in all transactions which are pre-determined by the marketing strategies of a business (including use of pre-formulated terms) where the receiving party (the consumer or user) is usually in a "take it or leave it" situation.

It should also not be forgotten that such a narrow interpretation of the consumer concept as advocated by the ECJ is not in itself written into Article 169 TFEU which leaves it to the discretion of the EU legislator or Member States to define the concept of consumer. The Court, in cases involving marketing practices and consumer contracts, had no problems with allowing Member State law, since it is closer to real consumer problems than EC law, to extend the consumer concept to other persons acting without professional expertise.[190] Member State law has done so extensively[191] by allowing different rules on the personal application of a consumer protective measure, thereby of course creating distortions of competition in the internal market which are not "popular" with EC institutions. This explains attempts at a "full harmonisation" of the consumer concept.

This book suggests that one should not be too concerned with the purpose of the transaction but rather with the *position of the person in the marketplace*. The consumer in this sense is the "passive market citizen", the *homo oeconomicus passivus*, who enters into transactions to satisfy his/her needs without producing the product or service him/herself. Some areas of EU law seem to recognise this broadening of the concept of consumer by being concerned with user protection in general. The most obvious example is Directive 2006/123/EC on services in the internal market.[192] Articles 19–22 contain detailed rules protecting the "recipient of services" against discrimination, and providing assistance and detailed information on services covered by the Directive;[193] these rules are not limited to the traditional consumer. Similar principles are emerging in the area of tourist and passenger protection.

Similar rules can be found in directives on financial services like payment,[194] insurance or investment. It is usually the non-professional user of services who

---

189 ECJ, 3 July 1997, C-269/95, *Benincasa* [1997] ECR I-3767 at paras 14–17.

190 ECJ, 14 March 1991, C-361/89, *di Pinto* [1991] ECR I-1189.

191 For France see CALAIS-AULOY/TEMPLE, *Droit de la consommation*, paras 12–15 ("*extensions possibles de la notion du consommateur*"); for the UK, HOWELLS/WEATHERILL, 593, also including persons setting up a business; for Germany, GRUNDMANN/OCHMANN, *ERCL* 2007, 452–456 who insist that recent German case law has narrowed the concept of consumer, thus following the case law of the ECJ; for an overall discussion see HONDIUS, *SydLRev* 2006, 89; EBERS, in: SCHULTE-NÖLKE (ed.), *Consumer Law Compendium*, 670, insisting that Member States must be allowed to extend the concept of consumer beyond the Directives at 687.

192 *Supra* note 129.

193 ACKERMANN, Das Informationsmodell im Recht der Dienstleistungen, *ZEuP* 2009, 230–267.

194 See Directive 2007/64/EC, *supra* note 130 concerning "payment service users" with some special rules concerning "consumers". In the meantime, the Commission has published on 8 May 2013 a "Proposal for a Directive on the comparability of fees related to payment

falls within the sphere of application, whatever the sphere of use of this service, e.g. for his/her profession, work or household, which may not be known to the trader or important for qualifying the transaction as "consumer" or "non-consumer". What is more important is the professional expertise of the provider vs. the non-professional activity of the user to determine the scope of application of a protective measure. This widens the concept of consumer law, but makes sure at the same time that rules on information, mandatory standards and legal protection cannot depend on the rather imprecise intention on the possible use of a certain product or service.

b) *Access to services of general interest and to payment services*

1.40 Services of general interest like communication, energy and transport have only recently come within the scope of Community law, together with a trend for deregulation and privatisation of these services. While in the "old days" these services were highly regulated by public law, the new regime, which is more concerned with competition and choice, had to develop standards of its own, in particular by also transposing, somewhat hesitantly, the idea of *solidarity* to a more economic and competitive understanding of public services, thus including questions of consumer – or rather user – access and quality.[195]

The most important elements of this strategy[196] have been, on the one hand, the internal market approach, and on the other, the so-called "universal service obligation" on providers.[197] The impact therefore is on free choice in access to services and in non-discriminatory treatment without distinguishing between consumers in the traditional sense and other users. Under the Universal Services Directive 2002/22/EC of 7 March 2002 (now Directive 2009/140/EC)[198] and the revised Electricity Directive 2009/72/EC, "household customers" should not be prevented from switching to another provider through direct or indirect impediments.[199]

1.40a The "universal" or public service obligations concern access to services which should be open to anybody, the details of which are to be regulated by Member States. The contract cannot easily be terminated; freedom of contract is suspended by mandatory rules in favour of non-professional users. The

---

accounts, payment account switching, and access to payment account with basic features", COM (2013) 266.

195 Ross, *CMLRev* 2007, 1057 at 1070 insisting on the applicability of the general norm of Article 16 EC.

196 Consumer Policy Strategy, COM (2002) para 3.1.5; also EU Consumer Policy Strategy 2007–2013 COM (2007) 99 at 8.

197 Rott, *JCP* 2007, 53.

198 OJ L 108, 24 April 2002, 51.

199 Rott, *JCP* 2007, 56; Micklitz, Do Consumers and Business need a New Architecture for Consumer Law? A Thought Provoking Impulse, *Yearbook of European Law*, 2013, 266 (294).

provisions on user protection, however, are rather weak at an EU level: Member States must only ensure that there are "adequate safeguards to protect vulnerable consumers, including appropriate measures to help them to avoid disconnection" under Article 3(3) of Directive 2009/72/EC. Annex A gives consumers "a right to a contract" with some basic information. They must be given notice "of any increase of charges" and have the right to withdraw from contracts if they do not accept the new conditions, but there is no right to be informed about the calculation of the increase of charges nor is there any right to challenge it. The Unfair Terms Directive 93/13/EEC is a weak substitute in this field, even though it may be applied in principle, in particular the transparency principle of Article 4 (details 3.17). The EU legislator seems to have confidence in competition; however, competition is particularly distorted in the area of energy supply.[200]

It should also be mentioned that Directive 2007/64/EC[201] on payment services contains in Article 20 provisions on "access to payment systems", which come close to a "universal service obligation" to be determined by Member States among the different providers as can be seen in the recent Commission proposal of 8 May 2013 (1.39).

c) *Passengers, tourists and travellers*

1.41 Another area where EC law has extended the traditional borders of consumer law is concerned with passenger rights in transportation, in particular air transport. The role of the passenger does not depend on whether he/she undertakes a trip "outside" or "within" his/her business or profession; delays, cancellations and accidents concern him/her regardless of the purpose of the trip. Therefore, Regulation (EC) 261/2004[202] provides for detailed remedies for the passenger in the event of overbooking, delays and cancellations. This Regulation has not been based on the EC's internal market or consumer competence, but on its competence in the area of transportation (Article 91/100 TFEU). This power of regulation has been upheld by the ECJ.[203] A number of important ECJ judgments have extended the scope of application of Regulation 261/2004 in favour of the "stranded" air passenger, in particular extending the right of compensation in cases of long delays and not only of cancellations,[204] and in favour of assistance to be given a passenger due to the closure of air space during the eruption of the

200 Rott, *JCP* 2007, 57.
201 *Supra* note 130.
202 *Supra* note 132.
203 ECJ, 10 January 2006, C-344/04, *IATA and ELFAA v Department for Transport* [2006] ECR I-403.
204 ECJ, 19 November 2009, C-402/07 + C-432/07, *Sturgeon and Others* [2009] ECR I-1092, confirmed by ECJ, 23 October 2012, C-581 + 629/10, *Nelson et al. v Lufthansa et al* [2012] ECR I-nyr.

Icelandic volcano Eyafjallajokull.[205] In the area of railway passenger rights, Regulation (EC) 1371/2007[206] has been adopted. As Karsten[207] writes:

> "The body of EC consumer law, as widely understood, is expanding into new areas. However, an enlargement of consumer law, narrowly understood, and a change of the narrow notion of 'consumer' have not accompanied this growth. Rather, in passenger law, traditional EC consumer law has developed as an independent branch. Passenger law is thereby generally adding to the edifice of consumer law; though without touching its core domain of 'shopping law'".

A certain precedent for this extension had been set already by Directive 90/314/EEC on package holidays. The definition of consumer, according to Article 2(1) has been extended to:

> "the person who takes or agrees to take the package ('the principal contractor'), or any person on whose behalf the principal contractor agrees to purchase the package ('the other beneficiaries') or any person to whom the principal contractor or any of the other beneficiaries transfers the package ('the transferee')".

The rules in the Directive concerning liability and compensation are mandatory and – with minor exceptions – cannot be waived by contract clauses (Article 5(4)). They have even been extended to cover non-material damage.[208] These provisions are usually regarded as "extensions" of the consumer concept which, being exceptions to the general rule, must be interpreted narrowly.[209] But the argument could be turned upside down: the above-mentioned provisions on the position of users of services demonstrate that a narrow definition of the consumer which is limited to the intended specific (professional or private) use of a service will not be sufficient to clarify the protective ambit of a regulation. Therefore the *general position of the non-professional user* should be taken as a starting point for defining the personal sphere of application of a consumer protective rule which may be narrowed down in certain circumstances.

With regard to contracts of carriage, Article 5 of the Rome I Regulation 593/2008 of 17 June 2008 on the law applicable to contractual obligations (7.18) contains special rules that aim to protect passengers, whatever the purpose of their trip, against choice-of-law clauses that have no connection to transportation.

---

205 ECJ, 31 January 2013, C-12/11, *McDonagh v Ryan Air* [2013] ECR I-nyr.

206 *Supra* note 133.

207 Karsten, *JCP* 2007 at 135; Karsten, *supra* note 131, 37, speaks of a "consumerisation of transport law", including also passengers for professional purposes which would not come under the narrow consumer definition of the *acquis*.

208 ECJ, 12 March 2002, C-168/00, *S. Leitner v TUI* [2002] ECJ I-2631.

209 For the relevance of his argument, see Reich, *supra* note 2, para 2.12.

d) *IP users?*

1.42 Intellectual property matters have so far hardly been discussed from the perspective of consumer protection, even though the consumer – or rather the non-professional user – will usually have to pay the "price" for the use, copy or purchase of a product or service protected by an IP right, or otherwise be excluded from its use. This price may be directly calculated as a licence fee, possibly imposed by a rights-management institution or may be part of the overall purchase itself. Consumers or potential users may simply be denied access at the discretion of the rights holder, which is particularly relevant for "information goods" in the so-called "information society"; EU law does not include a "fair use" principle.[210] Protection is exclusively attributed to the rights holder, not to the user, as can be clearly seen from Directive 2004/48/EC,[211] which does not even mention user rights.

It was only the Court of Justice which, in its controversial *Magill* case[212] gave user rights an adequate footing under the competition rules. The Court had to evaluate the practice of (market dominating) Irish radio and TV stations invoking their copyright to refuse to release their programmes to independent consumer magazines. The Court followed the Commission and the CFI against the opinion of AG Gulmann in holding that this practice amounted to an abuse of Irish radio and TV stations' dominant position on the regional market for programme magazines:

> "The appellants' refusal to provide basic information by relying on national copyright provisions thus prevented the appearance of a new product, a comprehensive weekly guide to TV programmes which the appellants did not offer and for which there was potential consumer demand". (para 54)

The judgment aroused and still arouses protests among the IP community, which does not seem to recognise user rights and prefers unlimited protection of

---

210 The leading US Supreme Court case concerning fair use is *Campell v Acuff-Rose Music, Inc.* (1980) 510 U.S. 580, explaining the "four factor test". For its (reduced) relevance in US and TRIPS law, Okedij, Access to Copyrighted Digitalised Information Works, in: Maskus/Reichmann (eds.), 2005, 142, pleading for an "international fair use doctrine" at 182, and insisting on an access rule for copyrighted digital works at 187.

211 Directive 2004/48/EC of the EP and the Council of 29 April on the enforcement of intellectual property rights OJ L 157, 30 April 2004, 45; corrigendum L 195, 2 June 2004, 16.

212 ECJ, 6 April 1995, C-241 + 242/91P, *Radio Telefis Eireann (RTE) and Independent TV Publications Ltd (ITP) v Commission* [1995] ECR I-743.

IP rights.[213] The Court in later cases had to clarify its case law by insisting it did not want to attack the very substance of IP rights.[214]

Similar controversies were provoked by the rules on exhaustion for intellectual property rights as developed by the case law of the ECJ. They have an indirect effect on consumer protection because they preclude the rights holder from invoking his IP right to control or limit the distribution of a protected product within the internal market, or to cash-in twice for its licensing once the product has been placed on the market with his consent.[215] With regard to copyright, in *Laserdisken* the ECJ[216] insisted that the exhaustion of the right of distribution guaranteed under Directive 2001/29/EC of 22 May 2001 on copyright in the information society[217] is limited to the internal market; only the placement on the internal market (including the EEA), not on the world market, is a valid reason for exhaustion. This territorial limitation of exhaustion obviously limits the access of consumers to copyrighted products already put on non-EU/EEA markets.[218]

Also directly important for consumer protection, e.g. right to information and education under Article 169(1) TFEU, are those cases where questions of "fair use" in the area of copyright are in conflict with the protection of the rights holder. This includes cases of non-commercial use, e.g. the reproduction of copyrighted material already in circulation for personal purposes, the citation, caricature or parody of a work in later personal creations and the use of copyrighted material for educational purposes. Usually questions of "fair use" are not regarded as part of consumer law, but have been defined by Member States as exceptions to their general rules on copyright. In our opinion, this view is too narrow because the position of the consumer as the non-active market citizen is greatly influenced by the corresponding rights of the IP holder. In many cases his right to receive information, which was recognised by the Court in its *Laserdisken* judgment,[219] will be greatly influenced by the extent of

---

213 Anderman, *EC Competition Law and Intellectual Property Rights*, 178; Schmidt, *ECLR* 2002, 210 at 215: lack of clarification of exceptional circumstances; for differentiated view insisting on the limits of antitrust, see Ulrich, Intellectual Property, Access to Information, and Antirust, in: Dreyfus/Zimmermann/First (eds.), *Expanding the Boundaries of IP*, 2001, 367 at 381–398.

214 ECJ, 26 November 1998, C-7/97, *Oscar Bronner GmbH & Co KG v Mediaprint* [1998] ECR I-7791; later ECJ, 29 April 2004, C-418/01, *IMS Health v NDC Health* [2004] ECR I-5939 at para 38 where the Court develops three conditions for abuse: the refusal prevents the emergence of a new product for which there is potential consumer demand; this refusal is unjustified: it excludes competition on a secondary market.

215 Reich, *Understanding EU Law*, 2005, 170–173; for an example, see ECJ, 26 April 2007, C-348/04, *Boehringer Ingelheim et al. v Swingward et al.* [2007] ECR I-3391.

216 ECJ, 12 September 2006, C-479/04, *Laserdisken* [2006] ECR I-8089.

217 OJ L 167, 22 June 2001, 10.

218 This argument was used by the EFTA Court in its *Maglite* opinion of 3 December 1997, cited by AG Jacobs in his opinion of 29 January 1998 in ECJ, 16 July 1998, C-355/96, *Silhouette* [1998] ECR I-4799 at 4813.

219 *Supra* note 216 at para 64.

copyright protection and by the possibility of invoking a "fair use" exception for non-commercial, that is, personal purposes.

Directive 2001/29/EC has to some extent "communitarised" these exceptions with the intention of creating an internal market, a concept justified by the Court in its *Laserdisken* judgment. But Directive 2001/29/EC also left the question of "fair use" (a concept not mentioned in the Directive) to the Member States – quite to the opposite of the idea of creating a "single market" for copyright in the information society. Article 5(3) contains numerous exceptions to the reproduction and public communication right enshrined in copyright which must be invoked by the Member States, e.g. for the sole purpose of illustration for teaching for scientific research duly quoting the source, quotations for review and criticism in accordance with "fair practice" (Article 5(3)(d)), use for the purpose of caricature, parody or pastiche (k), use in connection with the demonstration or repair of equipment (l), and use for educational and similar purposes. Under the so-called "three step-test", these exceptions must however not conflict with "normal exploitation" of the work and "not unreasonably prejudice the legitimate interests of the rightholder" (Article 5(5)). It is quite obvious that the EC legislator does not have faith in the Member States, which may possibly extend user rights to the detriment of rights holders.[220] Article 6(3) allows for "technological measures" to prevent a circumvention of protected copyright, including *access control*. Article 6(4) exceptionally requires Member States to "take appropriate measures to ensure that rightholders make available to the beneficiary the above mentioned exceptions", but it is not clear how this can be implemented. At the moment this seems to be a dead letter provision making free access practically impossible as provided in the "fair use" provisions.

From a broadly understood consumer law approach, the non-harmonisation of these exceptions is regrettable. It means that the non-professional user is subject to different national regimes which may not even be very effective in allowing access in areas expressly covered by the Directive, while the rights holder enjoys a broad protection with at least comparable standards. EU law does not even try to adequately balance these interests. There is an urgent need to realign copyright protection with user's and consumer rights.[221] The only option to avoid "over-protection" of rights holders and "under-protection" of consumers and users against their right to free access to information is to limit the threshold of copyright itself.[222] Article 2 talks of "works" of authors, but does not define their originality or individuality as the basis of protection. This must still be

220 Criticism of this "three step" test by Okediji, *supra* note 210, 170, pleading for a "proportional approach to access" at 184.

221 For details see now the excellent paper by Helberger et al, *JCP* 2013, 37.

222 Reich/Micklitz, *Verbraucherrecht*, 279 making the criticism that the right of the user concerning access to information has been regulated in a rather restrictive manner.

done by applicable Member State law which uses different thresholds in this respect but which should not be "levelled up" to the detriment of users.

Important litigation involving a balancing between the protection of rights holders under Directive 2004/48/EC on the one hand and the protection of users concerning their personal data relating to the use of the internet by means of connections provided by a telephone company, arose in *Promusicae*.[223] The question put before the ECJ concerned the obligation of Member States to allow rights holders or their management societies access in civil infringement proceedings to user data stored by internet providers. The Court did not give a straightforward answer, but required Member States and their courts in answering such a request to balance the two opposing fundamental rights, namely of rights holders to an effective protection of their intellectual property, and "a further fundamental right, namely the right that guarantees protection of personal data and hence of private life." Indirectly the Court has recognised user rights at least insofar as their personal data are concerned. However this protection is not absolute and has to be balanced against the protection of rights holders. The Court did not say how this conflict is to be settled, but left this to Member States. It did not voice opposition to a provision in applicable Member State law which allowed access to personal data only in criminal, not in civil, proceedings.

2. CONSUMER LAW AND CONTRACT LAW IN THE EU

1.43 Within the process initiated by the European Commission of preparing a so-called "Common Frame of Reference" for European contract law,[224] a group of researchers has been established to review and consolidate the "consumer *acquis*" and to make proposals for a legislative initiative on a Community level. The so-called Acquis Group[225] published a comprehensive draft on the *acquis* principles, relating mostly to consumer law, at the beginning of 2007.[226] The principles take up some of the criticism voiced against the existing EC consumer law directives, to eliminate certain contradictions and to extend their sphere of

223 ECJ, 29 January 2008, C-275/06, *Productores de Musica de Espana (Promusicae) v Telefonica de Espana* [2008] ECR I-271 at para 63.

224 Communication from the Commission to the Council and the EP on European Contract Law, COM (2001) 398 final of 11 July 2001; Action Plan, COM (2003) 68 final of 12 February 2003; The Way Forward, COM (2004) 651 final of 11 November 2004; First Annual Progress Report, COM (2005) 456 final of 23 September 2005; a critical overview has been given by Reich, *WiscInt LJ* 2007, 425.

225 See their website: http//:acquis.jura.uni-bielefeld.de.

226 For a detailed comment, see Acquis Group (ed.), *Principles of the Existing EC Contract Law (Acquis Principles)*, 2007. Some reservation has been voiced by Jansen/Zimmermann, *JZ* 2007, 1131 because of their going beyond the *acquis* by developing some general principles of contract law. See also Wilhelmsson/Twigg-Flesner, *ERCL* 2006, 441; Twigg-Flesner, *supra* note 35, 140–164.

application by trying to create a "general part of European consumer contract law" – a strategy certainly to be welcomed even though a political agreement and a legal structure still have to be debated and found.

Some remarkable innovations of the principles should be mentioned insofar as they are relevant in this context for the future of European consumer law:

- According to Article 1:201, "consumer" means any natural person who is *mainly* acting for purposes which are outside the person's business activity; this would extend the existing narrow definition mainly into the area of "mixed contracts".
- Article 2:201 contains a general pre-contractual informational duty on businesses towards consumers, which is specified in detail in later provisions; there is a special rule in Article 2:203 concerning information that should be provided to disadvantaged consumers.
- Article 2:206 contains a duty to provide and express information in clear and intelligible language; this seems to refer also to the language issue.
- Chapter 6 consolidates the law of "non-negotiated terms", without however transforming the indicative list of Directive 93/13/EEC (*infra* 3.23) into a "black or grey list".

1.43a The *acquis* principles were included in the draft Common Frame of Reference (DCFR) elaborated by a number of EU civil law scholars under the leadership of Professor van Bar in a reform process of EU civil law initiated by several papers of the EU Commission. In 2007/8 a first interim draft CFR[227] was presented to the Commission, which was followed in 2008/9 by a final version,[228] supplemented by six copious volumes of notes and explanations.[229] An intense academic debate followed.[230] It is not necessary to go into this discussion in more detail. However, three points should be noted because they are of relevance for the following discussion on a future EU consumer law:

---

227 Bar/Clive/Schulte-Nölke (eds.), *Principles, Definitions and Model Rules on European Private Law – Draft CFR Interim Outline Edition*, 2008.

228 Bar/Clive/Schulte-Nölke (eds.), *Principles, Definitions and Model Rules on European Private Law – Draft CFR Outline Edition*, 2009.

229 Bar/Clive/Schulte-Nölke (eds.), *Principles, Definitions and Model Rules on European Private Law – Draft CFR Full Edition*, 2009.

230 For example see Micklitz/Cafaggi (eds.), *European Private Law after the CFR*, 2010; Eidenmüller et al., The CFR for European Private Law – Policy Choices and Codification Problems, *OxfJLS* 2009, 659–708; Jansen/Zimmermann, A European Civil Code in all but name, *CLJ* 2010, 98; Hesselink, The CFR as a source of European Private Law, *Tulane LRev* 2009, 919–971; Cherednychenko, Fundamental Rights, Policy Issues and the DCFR, *ERCL* 2010, 39; Vogenauer, CFR and UNIDROIT-Principles of International Commercial Contract: Coexistence, Competition, or Overkill of Soft Law, *ERCL* 2010, 143; Larouche/Chirico (eds.), *Economic Analysis of the DCFR*, 2011; Wagner (ed.), *The CFR – A View from Law and Economics*, 2009; not to mention the many French, German, and Italian contributions.

- The principles and provisions of the DCFR go far beyond mere contract law; they contain rules on the law of obligations in general (e.g. on non-contractual obligations like tort, unjust enrichment), on a number of specific contracts beyond sales law, particularly in the area of services, and on transfer of property and security interests in movables. Some scholars criticised the authors for "over-fulfilling" the mandate given by the Commission.
- The DCFR aims to integrate and in some cases improve mandatory consumer law provisions, particularly to integrate those from the *acquis* into the general rules of EU civil law. Therefore, Article I.-1:105(1) of the DCFR provides that: "A 'consumer' means any natural person who is acting *primarily* for purposes which are not related to his or her trade, business or profession". This definition is broader than the traditional one used in the *acquis* to allow the inclusion of so-called "double purpose contracts" which usually would not come within the scope of the consumer protective provisions of EU law according to the *Gruber* case law of the ECJ mentioned above.[231]
- The legal character of the DCFR remains unclear. In its early communications, the Commission regarded it as a "toolbox" for future legislation – a somewhat dismissive term for the enormous scholarly work which went into it. But the Commission certainly did not want to endorse the work formally because of a "competence gap" in the EU Treaties regarding general contract and even more private law legislation in the EU. This had not been changed by the Lisbon Treaty on European Union, rather to the contrary: Article 5 TEU insisted on a narrow reading of EU competences based on the principle of "conferral" and limited by the provisions on subsidiarity and proportionality mentioned above.

1.43b With Commissioner Reding taking office as DG Justice in 2009, the development of a European civil law has gained pace. She appointed a group of experts which transformed the draft *Academic* Common Frame of Reference into a *Political* Common Frame of Reference, which served the European Commission as a starting point to present its draft on a Common European Sales Law (CESL) in November 2011.[232] The publication of the CESL or, as it is also called, the Optional Instrument (OI) triggered a Europe-wide discussion at an academic and political level, with an endless number of publications. At the time of writing the legal status of the CESL/OI is still unclear; its EU constitutional status is in doubt.[233] Given the highly controversial nature of the

---

231 *Supra* note 183.

232 COM (2011) 635 final. The literature discussing fundamental problems and detailed provisions of CESL has become unmanageable.

233 Reich, *supra* note 2, paras 6.14–6.19.

ongoing discussions in the European Parliament and in the Council,[234] it seems premature to engage in a more detailed analysis of the respective articles of the CESL/OI. For the purposes of this introduction it suffices to recall the major possible innovations or changes:

- The CESL/OI would introduce a new layer for EU sales and related service contracts, for B2SMU (small and medium undertakings) and B2C transactions, mainly with regard to cross border sales via the internet,
- The CESL/OI would leave it to the supplier in the consumer sales contract to choose the CESL as the common legal order, provided the consumer has been given the necessary information and has given his consent. This requirement is rather formal as the consumer would not be able to induce the supplier to conclude the contract based on CESL because of its high level of consumer protection. The concept of "optional" is somewhat misleading because it is limited to the part of the supplier, not the consumer.
- The CESL/OI would confirm the narrow interpretation of the term "consumer" as provided for by the ECJ in *Gruber*. The rather innovative information duty does not seem to have survived the current legislative process.

3. REVIEW OF EUROPEAN CONSUMER CONTRACT LAW: TOWARDS FULL HARMONISATION OF THE *ACQUIS* OR A EUROPEAN CONSUMER PROTECTION REGULATION?

a) *Commission attempts at reviewing the "consumer acquis"*

1.44 In its activities directed towards a Common Frame of Reference, the Commission published a "Green Paper on the Review of the Consumer *Acquis*" in 2007.[235] The Commission presented options for further work – on the one hand, a vertical approach, and on the other, a mixed approach consisting of a horizontal instrument combined with, where necessary, vertical action to regulate "the main consumer contractual rights and remedies", for example with regard to consumer sales.[236] The more ambitious intention to structure, systemise, if not to merge, the major consumer contract law directives into one have failed. The so-called Consumer Rights Directive 2011/83/EU (Chapter 9) unites doorstep and distant selling under one umbrella. The practical outcome is

234 As to the state of affairs (1 February 2014): www.europarl.europa.eu/oeil/popups/ficheprocedure.do?lang=en&reference=2011/0284(COD).

235 COM (2006) 744 final of 8 February 2007; see for an official explanation Kuneva, *ZEuP* 2007, 955.

236 COM (2005) 456, 9–10.

therefore nearer to the first option, namely a vertical approach limited to particular consumer problems.

With regard to the extent of harmonisation, the Commission presented three options[237]:

(1) full harmonisation similar to the recently enacted directives;
(2) minimum harmonisation with a mutual recognition clause; or
(3) minimum harmonisation combined with the country-of-origin approach.

The traditional minimal harmonisation approach was no longer even discussed, even though it is part of Article 169(2)(b) TFEU. Options 2 and 3 contradict the recent Rome I Regulation (EC) 593/2008 (7.17), which has expressly provided for a minimum protection clause of the law of the consumer's country of residence, thereby expressly excluding the mutual recognition or country-of-origin principle for contract law. Therefore the approach taken by the Commission in the area of consumer contract law has met overwhelmingly with criticism.[238] The Consumer Rights Directive discussed above (1.26) opted for a compromise between targeted and minimum harmonisation.

b) Option for an EU Consumer Protection Regulation as an alternative?

1.45 As an alternative to the ongoing Commission work, it seems as if Article 169 TFEU would and should become the main vehicle for consumer protection in the EC and for reviewing the existing somewhat incoherent and inconsistent *acquis*. This however was and is not the case. The main reason is the ambivalent, double-faced nature of Article 169 itself in para 2, either referring in (a) to measures concerning the internal market itself, or in (b) to "supporting and supplementing measures" linked to consumer policies pursued by the Member States. Since the Commission is the main player in proposing legislative measures, it has the freedom to choose its legislative basis for measures, depending on its priorities, and these were clearly with the aim of establishing the "internal market" and making it work by eliminating existing limits to free movement and distortions of competition, and not in pursuit of an independent, autonomous consumer policy. In effect, only one directive – Directive 98/6/EC[239] on unit pricing – is based on Article 169(2)(b) TFEU respectively its predecessor. But this precedent did not have any successor; it is now under reconsideration, which may easily change its legislative basis.

The legal limits of Article 169(2)(b) TFEU have never been tested, but there seems to be an overwhelming agreement that the room left to EU legislation is

[237] COM (2006) 744, 10.
[238] Micklitz/Reich, *VuR* 2007, 121; Wilhelmsson, *ZEuP* 2008, 225.
[239] *Supra* note 124.

rather small and will in particular limit "innovative legislation", that is, legislation to create new rights and obligations of consumers and business in areas not yet covered by Member States.[240] Reich has argued that Article 169(2)(b) could at least be used to codify and amend at least the existing EC consumer contract law:[241] since all Member States now have – either on their own or by implementing EU directives – their own national consumer law, the general principles of an overall EU approach to consumer protection based on information and fairness before entering into and within transactions, and specific rules on "cooling-off" periods in direct and distance marketing, on unfair terms, and on legitimate quality expectations as rather well-developed areas of EU consumer contract law, could easily be elaborated and "codified".

A somewhat similar proposal was promoted by Twigg-Flesner,[242] suggesting the creation of a cross-border-only consumer law regulation. It could be based on the traditional internal market competence of Article 114 TFEU. It would create uniform standards for cross-border marketing which would not depend on applicable national consumer law according to Article 6 of the Rome I Regulation 598/2008.

At the time of writing none of these proposals seem to have a chance of being realised. The EU institutions are awaiting the outcome of the legislative process of the CESL (*supra* 1.43b), keeping in mind that the mandate of the European Parliament will end in May 2014 and will not be able to terminate its deliberations.

240 Weatherill, *supra* note 1, 74; for more extensive reading, see Stuyck, *supra* note 1, 387: it is sufficient that a policy (not a law) of Member States already exists.

241 Reich, *JCP* 2005, 400 with detailed proposals; similar Rösler, *RabelsZ* 2007, 502.

242 Twigg-Flesner, *JCP* 2010, 355.

CHAPTER 2
UNFAIR COMMERCIAL PRACTICES AND MISLEADING ADVERTISING

Hans-W. Micklitz

CONTENTS

Bibliography:

A. Bakardjieva, *Fair Trading in Flux? National Legacies, Institutional Choice and the Progress of Europeanisation*, PhD thesis, 2003; E. Balate (ed.), *Unfair Advertising and Comparative Advertising*, 1987; A. Beater, *Unlauterer Wettbewerb*, 2002; A. Beater, *Verbraucherschutz und Schutzzweckdenken im Wettbewerbsrecht*, 2000; A.-D. Bruun Nielsen, *Analysis of the possibility of introducing a general clause on good market behaviour into Community law – Report for the Nordic Council of Ministers*, February 2000; J. Calais-Auloy/H Temple, *Droit de la consommation*, 8th ed., 2010; J.M. Clark, *Competition as a Dynamic Process*, 1961; H. Collins (ed.), *The Forthcoming EC Directive on Unfair Commercial Practices, Contract, Consumer and Competition Implications*, 2004; H. Collins, EC Regulation of Unfair Commercial Practices, in: Collins (ed.), *The Forthcoming EC Directive*, 2004, 1; L.W. Craig/W.W. Park/J. Paulsson, *International Chamber of Commerce Arbitration*, 3rd ed. 2000; N. Gomez, The Unfair Commercial Practices Directive: A Law and Economics Perspective, *ECRL* 2006, 1; F. Henning-Bodewig, *Unfair Competition Law European Union and Member States*, 2006; G. Howells, The Rise of European Consumer Law – wither National Consumer Law?, *Sydney L Rev* 2006, 63; G. Howells, Co-regulation's role in the Development of European Fair Trading Laws, in: Collins (ed.), *The Forthcoming EC Directive on Unfair Commercial Practices, Contract, Consumer and Competition Implications*, 2004, 119; G. Howells/H.-W. Micklitz/T. Wilhelmsson, *European Fair Trading Law – The Unfair Commercial Practices Directive*, 2006; B. Keirsbilck, *The New European law on unfair commercial practices and competition law*, 2010; B. Keirsbilck, *The Implementation of the Unfair Commercial Practices Directive in the United Kingdom, Germany and the Netherlands*, De wet handelspraktijken anno 2008, 219–298; L. Krämer, *EEC Consumer Law*, 1986; T. Lettl, *Der lauterkeitsrechtliche Schutz vor irreführender Werbung in Europa*, 2004; H.-W. Micklitz/J. Kessler (eds.), *Marketing Practices Regulation and Consumer Protection in the EC Member States and the US*, Vol. 10, 2002; H.-W. Micklitz/B. Monazzahian/C. Rössler, *Door to Door Selling – Pyramid Selling – Multilevel-Marketing, A Study Commissioned by the European Commission*, Vols. I and II, November 1999, http://europa.eu.int/comm/dgs/health_consumer/library/surveys/sur10_01.html; H.-W. Micklitz/S. Weatherill, *European Economic Law*, 1997; H.-W. Micklitz/N. Reich/S. Weatherill, EU Treaty Revision and Consumer Protection, *JCP* 2004, 367; E. Millan/R. Elliott, Offensive Advertising, Public Policy, and the Law: The Rulings on the Zagorka Case, *JCP* 2004, 475; M. Radeideh, *Fair Trading in EC Law – Information and Consumer Choice in the*

Internal Market, 2004; N. Reich, *Understanding EU Law*, 2nd ed. 2005; N. Reich, The November Revolution of the European Court of Justice, *CMLRev* 1994, 459; J. Stuyck, Comment to Case C-71/02, *Herbert Karner Industrie-Auktionen GmbH v. Troostwijk GmbH*, *CMLRev* 2004, 1686; J. Stuyck/E. Terryn/T. v. Dyck, Confidence Through Fairness? The New Directive on Unfair Business-To-Consumer Commercial Practices in the Internal Market, *CMLRev* 2006, 107; C. Twigg-Flesner/D. Parry/G. Howells/ A. Nordhausen, *An Analysis of the Application and Scope of the Unfair Commercial Practices Directive, A Report for the Department o f Trade and Industry*, 18 May 2005, www.dti.gov.uk/; E. Ulmer, *Das Recht des unlauteren Wettbewerbs in den Mitgliedstaaten der Europäischen Wirtschaftsgemeinschaft*, 1965; S. Weatherill, Who is the "average consumer", in: Weatherill (ed.), *The Regulation of Unfair Commercial Practices under the EC Directive 2005/29/EC: New Rules and New Techniques*, 2007; S. Weatherill, *EU Consumer Law and Policy*, 2005, 2nd ed. 2013; T. Wilhelmsson, *The Informed Consumer v the Vulnerable Consumer in European Trade Practices Law – a Comment*, Yearbook of Consumer Law 2006.

I. INTRODUCTION

1. SUMMARY OF THE LEGISLATIVE HISTORY OF DIRECTIVE 84/450/EEC

2.1 The principle of fairness in competition had already been contained in the Preamble of the EC Treaty which came into force on 1 January 1958.[1] The Treaty in itself does not govern any individual provisions on the law on unfair competition; however as per Article 3(g) EC the establishment of a system ensuring that competition in the internal market is not distorted is one of the aims of the Community. Pursuing this approach, the European Commission asked the Munich University Institute for International Intellectual Property Law to deliver an opinion comparing the law of unfair competition within the former six EEC Member States. Professor Eugen Ulmer was in charge of the project; in 1965 the first volume on comparative law was published. Ulmer could proceed from a "legally intact world" therein. Despite differing national provisions, all states were parties to the Paris Convention for the Protection of Industrial Property and there was a "common legal understanding". Furthermore the "prudent businessman" was understood to be the protective object and was to be protected against unfair competition by his business rivals. Ulmer suggested the conclusion of a treaty (under international law) between the six EEC members which was to govern a legally compelling general clause supplemented by specific individual elements. A treaty would be given priority over a directive as the latter would only be binding on the EEC Member States with regard to the objective as

1 See for an account of the European approach on advertising regulation, Weatherill, *EU Consumer Law and Policy*, 216.

per Article 189(3) EEC (now Article 288 TFEU), and as the main focus of competition law – the solution of a problem – is closely related to the choice of instruments. The general clause was to be in accordance with the general clause contained in Article 10*bis*(2) Paris Convention for the Protection of Industrial Property. Accordingly "honest practices" (*anständige Gepflogenheiten*, *usages honnêtes*) would be the central element. The European Commission then developed a working document taking into consideration these suggestions.[2] Simultaneously, trade and industrial associations were surveyed.[3] Concluding from the comments made by trade and industry and jurisprudence, the Commission[4] declared that it was time to deal with the harmonisation of the law on unfair competition in its entirety. The preparatory work of the Commission did not contain a consumer policy element.

The consumer protection movement at the beginning of the 1970s and the accession of then new Member States to the EC (Denmark, the UK and Ireland) led to a change in approach. The traditional understanding of unfair marketing practices law as a means to regulate the relationship between competitors became less relevant, and consumer protection against misleading – and initially unfair – advertising was focused on instead.

By realising the economic fundamental rights of the consumer in the first Consumer Policy Programme in 1975 (see 1.3), the Commission produced a first draft proposal for a directive which was amended in 1979 subsequent to the delivery of the opinions of the Economic and Social Committee and of the European Parliament.[5] The discussions in the Council lasted for more than five years. They illustrate the difficulties which arise in developing a common denominator for differing legal and consumer policy concepts. In particular, the United Kingdom resisted the introduction of the "fairness" concept, being unfamiliar with the term "unfair competition" or "unfair advertising", which included a general prohibition of comparative (non-misleading) advertising; it had delegated the control of advertising to an independent self-regulatory authority (ASA, Advertising Standards Authority) which is mainly financed by business.[6]

Diverging opinions arose in the Council with regard to the extent of the legal progress to be made by the Directive. Thus some of the Commission's proposals for reform as contained in the consumer policy discussion triggered protest, such as the general freedom of (genuine) comparative advertising (Article 4 of the draft of 1979), the prohibition of partially fraudulent misrepresentation (Article 3(1)) or the prohibition of omitting material information (Article 3(2)), the general right to action for consumer associations (Article 5), the introduction of the shifting of the burden of proof (Article 6) and the right of consumer

2 Document No. XIV/5593/68-D, 11 April 1968.
3 Document No. 2.715/XIV/70-D.
4 Document No. XIV/156/72-D, 28 February 1972.
5 OJ C 194, 1 August 1979, 3.
6 Cf. Krämer, *EEC Consumer Law*, 205.

associations to bring an action against measures of self-monitoring authorities (Article 7). These suggestions had been criticised by other observers as being not much more than a measure of traditional information policy trying to increase market transparency in favour of consumers. These proposals, however, were watered down prior to the final decision-making in the Council of Ministers which required unanimity as per Article 100 EEC.

Directive 84/450/EEC relating to the approximation of the laws, regulations and administrative provisions of Member States concerning misleading advertising[7] which had been adopted in 1984 concluded the first stage of the approximation work. It was envisaged as a minimum directive, i.e. exceeding provisions in favour of the interests stated in Article 1, namely consumers, persons carrying on a trade or business or practising a craft or profession, and the interests of the public in general remain unaffected (Article 7). Furthermore it merely established minimum standards for misleading, but not unfair, advertising. For this reason the freedom of non-deceptive comparative advertising as contained in the draft to the Directive had been removed; however the issue is now dealt with in a separate directive (see 2.2). Directive 84/450 has now become Directive 2006/114/EC.[8]

2. THE DEVELOPMENT OF DIRECTIVE 97/55/EC CONCERNING MISLEADING ADVERTISING SO AS TO INCLUDE COMPARATIVE ADVERTISING

2.2 Directive 84/450/EEC concerning misleading advertising excluded comparative advertising from its scope of application and thus reaffirmed the diverse legal regimes within Member States.[9] The development of the internal market and the tendencies of liberalising commercial practices of the ECJ and French Cour de cassation,[10] not so the German Bundesgerichtshof, as well as the increasing regulatory – or more precisely deregulatory –intervention of the EC institutions, required a review of the general prohibition of comparative advertising as enforced in some Member States, such as Germany, Belgium and Italy.

Subsequent to intensive preparatory work, the Commission produced a proposal for a directive on comparative advertising in 1991.[11] It did not contain a complete liberalisation of (non-misleading) comparative advertising; however if comparative advertising was based on a comparison of substantial, material

7 Directive 84/450/EEC of 10 September 1984 relating to the approximation of the laws, regulations and administrative provisions of Member States concerning misleading advertising, OJ L 250, 19 September 1884, 17.

8 OJ L 376, 27 December 2006, 21.

9 Evidence in Balate.

10 Conseil Constitutionnel, 15 January 1992, No. 91–303 DC.

11 OJ C 180, 11 July 1991, 1.

and verifiable aspects, and those chosen in a fair way of competing goods or services, if there was no confusion among consumers, if it did not discredit competitors and if it was not "mainly aimed at" taking undue advantage of the reputation of another brand, then it was to be allowed. However, these imprecise and far-reaching criteria risked encouraging Member States which had pursued a strict approach to comparative advertising to continue their practice, thus making liberalisation ineffective. This interpretation would have been contrary to the *effet utile* of a future directive.

On the other hand, legal doctrine criticised the admissibility of weak forms of comparative advertising where the addressee is clear from the circumstances but not clearly stated. This kind of comparative advertising without clear comparison would "simply" be contrary to the principles of non-price competition. This criticism appeared to be overstated as the draft prohibited advertising which was "mainly aimed at taking undue advantage of the reputation of other brands" (see current case law, 2.38).

The proposal also regulated comparative tests carried out by third parties which were to be allowed for marketing use only if the institute conducting the test approved of it. Approval could be related to payment. However this would have been contrary to the character of a product test, as objective consumer information independent of a competitor. In the interest of consumers a complete prohibition on commercial purposes of comparative tests carried out by third parties would have been appropriate; such use converted the initial informative element of neutral product tests into a marketing instrument and thus created new risks of confusion. This draft proposal has been criticised as it would have established an exemption to the right of information about test results which would have gone beyond the system. The draft aimed at complete, as opposed to minimum, harmonisation in order to prohibit Member States from applying stricter standards in the interest of purported consumer protection.

The discussion about the "principle of subsidiarity" (1.6), however, resulted in revising the proposal by simplifying it. On 21 April 1994[12] the Commission presented the amended version. The basic principle of the Directive emerging from the general advertising directive was not to be changed. However, the Commission purported to promote voluntary self-monitoring "taking into consideration the principle of subsidiarity and proportionality". Comparative advertising was not to be permitted generally but under "certain very stringent conditions". That is the reason why the criteria for comparative advertising were drafted stricter to the extent that they "shall be allowed only provided that it objectively compares the material, relevant, always verifiable, fairly chosen and representative features".

---

12 COM (1994) 151 final = OJ C 136, 19 May 1994, 4.

It must not refer to the personality or personal situation of a competitor. Provisions on comparative tests carried out by third parties have been deleted. The draft passed the legislative procedure and was finally adopted on 6 October 1997.[13] However the Commission could only partly carry out its initial intention to promote extrajudicial settlements in Member States. Unlike Directive 84/450/EEC on misleading advertising, Directive 97/55/EC on comparative advertising claims complete harmonisation. The Directive does not really explain the reason why comparative advertising requires complete harmonisation in contrast to the regulation on misleading advertising. Recital (18) merely refers to the fact that Directive 84/450/EEC should not apply to comparative advertising "given that the objective of amending the said Directive is to establish conditions under which comparative advertising is permitted".

3. RELATIONSHIP WITH PRIMARY COMMUNITY LAW

2.3 Primary Community law on free movement of goods and services (1.29–1.38) is the standard by which the legality of secondary Community law is measured. Relating to the Directive on misleading advertising, a collision between the remaining national regulatory competences under the concept of minimum harmonisation as enshrined in Article 7 of Directive 84/450/EEC and Article 28 EC comes into view. There are opinions that where there is a specific Community regulation, national provisions are to be measured according to that Community standard rather than to Articles 28 or 30 EC. Otherwise the ECJ would replace the national standard as granted by the Community legislator per Article 7 of Directive 84/450/EEC with its own criterion for deception. This line of reasoning, however, denies that the prohibition of Article 28 EC does not merely apply to national measures but also to measures taken by Community organs.[14] To that extent the Directive is to be interpreted according to superior Community law.

This consequence becomes even more important as the ECJ justifies its autonomous interpretation of misleading advertising from different sources: from the applicability of Article 28 EC (ex-Article 30 EEC) to non-misleading comparative price analysis according to *GB-Inno*[15] and *Yves Rocher*,[16] to a non-misleading labelling in *Mars*[17] (1.32), to the absence of a trademark in *Pall v Dahlhausen*,[18] from the interpretation of Article 2 of Directive 84/450/EEC in

---

13 OJ L 290, 23 October 1997, 18.

14 ECJ, 11 July 1996, C-427/93, *Bristol-Myers Squibb v Paranova* [1996] ECR I-3457 at para 36.

15 ECJ, 7 March 1990, C-362/88, *GB-Inno* [1990] ECR I-667.

16 ECJ, 18 May 1993, C-126/91, *Yves Rocher* [1993] ECR I-236.

17 ECJ, 6 July 1995, C-470/93, *Mars* [1995] ECR I-1923.

18 ECJ, 13 December 1990, C-238/89, *Pahl v Dahlhausen* [1990] ECR I-4844.

the case of misleading advertising for car imports in *Nissan*,[19] from the interpretation of Directive 76/768/ECC on the approximation of the laws of Member States relating to cosmetic products in the light of Articles 30/36 EC for the labelling of cosmetic products in *Clinique*[20] and *Lifting*,[21] as well as from the interpretation of Article 13(2)(b) Council Regulation (EEC) No. 2333/92 in *Sektkellerei Kessler*.[22] The diversity of legal sources raises the question of the inner consistency of the term "misleading advertising" which is not restricted to the scope of application of Directive 84/450/EEC but refers to Community law as such. This is the only way of appropriately approaching this term.

4. THE WAY AHEAD: DIRECTIVE 2005/29/EC ON UNFAIR COMMERCIAL PRACTICES (UCPD)

2.4 Calculated from the date of the adoption of the misleading directive, it took nearly 20 years until the European Commission, with the adoption of Directive 2005/29/EC concerning unfair commercial practices, eventually reached its primary objective of establishing a comprehensive legal regime governing unfair commercial practices – comprehensive insofar as the Directive is not limited to misleading advertising, but also covers unfair advertising. Nevertheless, an unregulated area remains insofar as Directive 2005/29/EC only applies in the B2C context for which it contains an exclusive set of regulations and replaces the old Directive 84/450/EC that from now on will only apply in the B2B context. In the UCPD the underlying concept is based on a combination of full harmonisation and the single market principle, i.e. the country of origin principle (2.19).

The story begins in 2001 with the Green Paper on EU Consumer Protection.[23] The Follow Up Communication published in 2002[24] was already much more concrete on the different regulatory options. The first Proposal of 18 June 2003[25] put forward the general prohibition of "unfair commercial practices" in the form of – henceforth based on the secondary Community Law – a comprehensive blanket clause, i.e. the prohibition of unfair commercial practices (Article 5) on top of the substantive provisions. The blanket clause found its specification in the prohibition of misleading advertising, now subdivided into the prohibitions of "misleading actions" (Article 6) and "misleading omissions" (Article 7). Completely new was the prohibition of

19 ECJ, 16 January 1992, C-373/90, *Procureur de la République (Nissan)* [1992] ECR I-131.
20 ECJ, 2 February 1994, C-315/92, *Clinique* [1994] ECR I-317.
21 ECJ, 13 January 2000, C-220/98, *Estée Lauder v Lancaster Group [Lifting]* [2000] ECR I-117.
22 ECJ, 28 January 1999, C-303/97, *Sektkellerei Kessler* [1999] ECR I-117.
23 COM (2001) 531 final.
24 COM (2002) 289 final.
25 COM (2003) 356 final.

so-called "aggressive commercial practices" (Article 8), in particular of the "use of harassment, coercion and undue influence" (Article 9). Annex I of the Directive contained a list of commercial practices that pursuant to Article 5(4) "*shall in all circumstances be regarded as unfair*". Moreover, the Commission sought to combat unfair commercial practices by – voluntary – codes of conduct for businessmen on a national and Community level (Article 10). Article 11 contained the obligation of Member States to ensure that, in the interest of consumers, adequate and effective means exist to combat unfair commercial practices and to guarantee the compliance with the provisions of the Directive (cf. for the legal protection 7.32). The main features of the structure of the first proposal were not modified during the entire process of legislation.

On 9 November 2004, about a year after the presentation of the first proposal, Member States already agreed in the Council on a Common Position. Remarkably, the project itself was not much debated, either in the European Parliament or in Member States. The political debate focused on three issues: (1) Member States were critical of the combination of full harmonisation and the single market clause (see more comprehensively, 2.17); the Commission, along with the United Kingdom, the Netherlands, Luxembourg and Estonia, regarded this as necessary. (2) Germany and Austria did not give up their opposition to the limitation of the scope of application to B2C relations. In addition, within the Scandinavian practice there was the understanding that "slavish imitation", plagiarism or denigration, i.e. classic B2B matters, could very well mislead consumers. (3) Denmark and Sweden were, and still are, critical of the principle of full harmonisation, because they fear a decrease of consumer protection in certain areas.

On 11 May 2005, the Directive was quietly passed by the Council. Nevertheless, the fast adoption could not fully conceal the ongoing discord relating to questions of principle. In particular, the United Kingdom, Luxembourg and Lithuania criticised the lack of the country of origin principle; Denmark and Sweden voted against the Directive, because it is oriented towards full harmonisation; Spain, Portugal and Italy criticised the lack of a definition of the reference to a consumer concept. The Directive had to be implemented by 12 June 2007; the implemented provisions were applicable from 12 December 2007.[26] Within the B2C context it replaces Directive 84/450/EEC which has now become Directive 2006/114/EC.[27] The legal situation with regard to comparative advertising is somewhat confusing. Directive 2006/114/EC integrates the Directive 97/55/EC on comparative advertising but only with regard to B2B relationships. In B2C relationships, Directive 2005/29/EC applies, which contains a set of minimum rules on comparative advertising.

---

26 This will be difficult and further divergences are the obvious result: KEIRSBILCK.

27 OJ L 376, 27 December 2006, 21.

II. THE PURPOSE OF DIRECTIVE 2005/29/EC

2.5 The UCPD aims to develop the fairness of commercial practices in the internal market. The protection of particular interests is limited to those of consumers.[28] The fourth recital in the preamble to the Directive describes consumers at first as the potential victims of uncertainty as to which national rules apply in the Community to unfair commercial practices. Pursuant to the fifth recital, these uncertainties shall be eliminated on a high level of consumer protection. The interaction of legal uncertainty that impairs the internal market and its elimination on a high level of consumer protection reappears in the eleventh and twelfth recitals. Only by this high standard could the fragmentation of the internal market as a result of different concepts of fairness be overcome and trade barriers eliminated. Competitors are only indirectly protected in the sixth recital. Their interests are not subject to the Unfair Commercial Practices Directive.

1. PROTECTION OF CONSUMERS' ECONOMIC INTERESTS

2.6 The sixth recital specifies the objective of consumer protection to the extent that the law governing unfair commercial practices focuses only on the consumers' economic interests. Thereby, however, the Directive is inconsistent because No. 17 of the Annex prohibits as unfair false claims that a product is able to cure illness, dysfunction or malformations. Does this not refer to health protection? No. 12 prohibits the making of a materially inaccurate claim concerning the nature and extent of the risk to the personal security of the consumer or his family if the consumer does not purchase the product. This relates in fact to overall security matters in terms of public policy, not to product safety, but it has a substantial relation to health.

2. MAIN PURPOSE OF THE UCPD: FREEDOM OF DECISION-MAKING, MARKET TRANSPARENCY AND INFORMATION

2.7 The UCPD itself furnishes the elements for substantiating its protective purpose, namely freedom of decision-making, market transparency and consumer information. These three elements suggest that only those advertising efforts that transport information fall under the scope of the Unfair Commercial Practices Directive. Such a perception is however already incorrect for the reason

[28] See on the regulatory technique GOMEZ, 1.

that the parameters need not be fulfilled cumulatively. The freedom of decision-making can in theory also be affected by advertising efforts that transport not information but emotions. The assessment of advertising efforts that make a socio-political reference is more difficult. Given Community law's tendency to extend the concepts of common or internal market to regulatory areas that are discussed in the Member States under different policy categories, the control area that is provided by the protection of consumers' economic interests appears extremely broad. As far as the reference exceeds the market context, one has to bear in mind that the European law governing unfair commercial practices does not provide standards for the measuring of taste and decency. This complex matter stays in the hands of the Member States (2.23).

Consumer information is the central parameter of consumer protection, not only for shaping the law of unfair commercial practices. Without information the consumer is unable to make rational decisions. At the same time, providing information requires that the consumer has the capacity to process the information intelligently and in a timely manner. Here one can clearly recognise the normative reference based on information that underlies the consumer concept. The decisive question is how much information and education a consumer can expect from the advertiser. However, *de lege lata* there is no general obligation for the advertiser to inform the consumer accurately and comprehensively by means of advertising.[29] The UCPD largely comes close to such a principle in particular by codifying the so-called misguidance as an omission (cf. 2.35).

3. INTERNAL MARKET REFERENCE AND GENERAL INTEREST

2.8 The relationship between the internal market as a concept of law and the general interest is precarious. Defining the general interest at least sector-specifically has again and again challenged the Commission. The UCPD avoids any reference to the general interest. In fact, in some Member States the general interest served as a gateway for taking non-competition objectives into account. At the European level, things are different as difficulties arise in defining a European general interest. By referring to the internal market and to the consumer as a market-citizen who is reduced to his economic interests, the UCPD pushes Community law into areas of national unfair commercial practices law that until today constituted a domain of national regulations of general interest. The borderline of the internal marked concept is reached where the UCPD leaves to Member States a residual competence to answer the questions of taste and decency (cf. 2.23). Admittedly this can only be a small

29 For a different reading see however Radeideh.

area, as the internal market reference releases a broad area of social life that up to now was excluded from the application of the national regulations under the aspect of protecting the general public.

4. THE RELATIONSHIP OF THE PROTECTIVE PURPOSES TO EACH OTHER

2.9 The recitals in the preamble of the Directive do not give much information about the relationship of the protective purposes to each other. In particular, the argument exists that consumer interests are to be given prevalence. This is based on the pivotal position of the information paradigm in the concept of workable competition within the internal market and therefore also on the law of fair trading.[30] The counter-argument is obvious: the workings of competition shall not be subject to an exogenic result-control of the competition processes. At the same time the protection of institutions and individuals are not to be played off against each other. For the institutional element of ensuring a workable competition and the individual guarantee of market-related freedoms are mutually dependent on each other. The decision about a possible prevalence gains practical importance in connection with the proportionality test that is required under Community law.

III. THE SCOPE OF DIRECTIVE 2005/29/EC

1. PERSONAL SCOPE OF APPLICATION

2.10 To the disappointment of Germany and Austria, the Unfair Commercial Practices Directive does not cover B2B relations. Apparently none of the other 23 Member States has argued in support of this position. Typical of most statements was the assumption of equality of consumers' and competitors' interests. The logical result is a spill-over of unfair competition concepts from the B2B relations towards the B2C area. Central to the discussion have been the issues of "slavish imitation" and of denigration; this is where Community law – even from the consumers' viewpoint – produces protection gaps that can only be closed under an extensive interpretation of the UCPD.

The legal definition of the consumer in Article 2(a) ties in with the manifold and not always totally coherent descriptions in different consumer protection directives (cf. 1.48). The consumer is defined in a negative way. Under the secondary law, only a natural person is considered a consumer "who … is acting for purposes which are outside his trade, business, craft or profession". In 2011

30 Beater, *Unlauterer Wettbewerb*, §13, paras 34 *et seq.*

the European Commission started the consultation with the overall objective to adopt appropriate legislation to unfair B2B practices.[31]

The term trader is defined as "a natural or legal person who, in commercial practices covered by this Directive, is acting for purposes relating to his trade, business, craft or profession and anyone acting in the name of or on behalf of a trader". The term "trader" appears in different consumer protection directives as a complementary term to consumer. The European trader is defined by his function. He is the bearer of the market communication in terms of workable competition. The European law of unfair commercial practices does not distinguish between small traders and big business. All traders have to deal with the dynamics of the internal market. Thus the European law on unfair commercial practices cannot set up protection for medium-sized businesses. Even those acting in the name of or on behalf of a trader are defined as traders. They are to be considered as indirect addressees of the Directive, irrespective of the kind of legal relation towards the trader on whose behalf they are acting.

2. FACTUAL SCOPE OF APPLICATION

2.11 Article 2(d) contains a legal definition of the term commercial practices. Accordingly, "business to consumer commercial practices … means any act, omission, course of conduct or representation, commercial communication including advertising and marketing, by a trader, directly connected with the promotion, sale or supply of a product to consumers". The definition is complemented by Article 3(1), which extends the scope of application to commercial practices before, during and after a commercial transaction relating to a product. The general ban on unfair commercial practices applies outside contractual relations as well as after conclusion of a contract and even during its execution. The ECJ has confirmed the broad scope of application.[32] This is particularly true with regard to sales promotion measures, which were initially subject to an envisaged separate EU measure. In a whole series of judgments the ECJ has submitted sales promotion measures to the Directive 2005/29/EC.[33] However, Directive 2005/29/EC may not be relied on against newspaper publishers, with the result that, in those circumstances, that directive must be interpreted as not precluding the application of a national provision under which those publishers are required to identify specifically, in this case through the use

31 COM (2012) 702 final.

32 ECJ, 4 January 2010, C-304/08, *Plus Warengesellschaft* [2010] ECR I-217 at para 36; ECJ, 9 November 2010, C-540/08 *Mediaprint* [2010] ECR I-10909 at para 17; ECJ, 17 January 2013, C-206/11, *Köck* [2013] ECR I-nyr at para 26.

33 ECJ, 24 April 2009, C-261–299/07 *VTB-VAB* [2009] ECR I-2949; ECJ, 4 January 2010, C-304/08, *Plus Warengesellschaft* [2010] ECR I-217; ECJ, 9 November 2010, C-540/08 *Mediaprint* [2010] ECR I-10909.

of the term "advertisement" (*Anzeige*), any publication in their periodicals for which they receive remuneration, unless it is already evident from the arrangement and layout of the publication that it is an advertisement.[34]

The subsequent part of the definition of commercial practices in the second clause of Article 2(d) encounters difficulties. According to the wording, commercial practices have to be "directly" connected with the promotion, sale or supply of a product to consumers. The terms have to be seen in a chronological order. Promotion can be considered as being the pre-contractual, sale as being the contractual and supply as being the post-contractual phase. By this the mistaken term "sale" can be corrected, which suggests a contract in terms of the law of obligations, meaning passage of title in return for payment. In doing so, such practices can also be covered by the scope of application, which do not have a direct link to the contractual transaction.

The usage of imprecise terms continues in wording according to which only such practices are covered that are connected with the promotion, sale or supply of a product to consumers. Article 2(c) provides a legal definition in this respect. Accordingly, product means "any goods or service including immovable property, rights and obligations". Immovable property probably means real estate. The Directive does not define the meaning of "rights". However, licensing of copyright, trademarks, designs, patents and similar intellectual property may be considered to be covered. Hence, it creates no difficulties in subsuming such situations under the scope of application, where a commercial practice stands in relation to the sale of a computer to a consumer while at the same time a simple licence for the utilisation of software is granted. The respective rules on unfair competition within the European trademark and copyright law take precedence over those rules of the UCPD (2.13).

3. LIMITATION OF THE SCOPE OF APPLICATION

2.12 Article 3(2) to (7) formulates different category groups, which are related to the Directive, but which shall not fall under its scope of application. In this respect, the Directive differs between national and European rules, which remain "without prejudice", which are "more specific", which are not to be applied and which are "more restrictive or prescriptive".

a) National and Community law regulations that are not pre-empted by the Directive

2.13 According to Article 3(2), especially the law of contracts, and in particular the rules on the validity, formation or effect of a contract, are to be considered.

---

34 ECJ, 17 October 2013, C-391/12, *RLvS Verlagsgesellschaft mbH* [2013] ECR I-nyr.

According to the ninth recital of the Directive, this also covers rules on intellectual property rights. Article 3(7) makes it clear that there is no contradiction of the rules determining the jurisdiction of the courts under Council Regulation (EC) No. 44/2001 (see 7.34). Article 3(8) excludes establishment and authorisation requirements, codes of conduct and other specific rules for regulated professions from the scope of application in order to uphold the high integrity standards that Member States may, in conformity with Community law, impose on members of such professionals (cf. Article 2(l)). According to its ninth recital, the Directive shall not conflict with rules that are in conformity with Community law. This formulation refers obviously to the decisions of the ECJ in *Schindler, Gambelli* and *Placanica* cases,[35] where the ECJ on the one hand granted Member States the right to organise gambling activities themselves, but on the other hand tied this right to a series of conditions, the most important being that they must really protect the public against the dangers of gambling and betting, but not simply to raise revenue by excluding foreign providers.

b) Priority of special EC provisions

2.14 Directive 2005/29/EC forms a *lex generalis* in relation to those provisions of Community law which regulate special aspects of unfair commercial practices (Article 3(4)). Thus the Directive only applies if there are no guidelines under Community law that refer specifically to certain questionable unfair practices. According to the tenth recital of the Directive, this applies to Directive 97/7/EC on the protection of consumers in respect of distance contracts (now Directive 2011/83 on Consumer Rights),[36] to Directive 98/27/EC (now 2009/22/EC) on injunctions for the protection of consumers' interests (8.33)[37] and to Directive 2002/65/EC on the distance marketing of consumer financial services.[38] This list is not to be understood as complete, for Directive 89/522/EEC on Television (now Directive 2010/13/EU on Audiovisual Media Services),[39] the future Nutrition and Health Claims Regulation and the different directives on contract

[35] ECJ, 24 March 1994, C-275/92, *Schindler* [1994] ECR I-1039; ECJ, 6 November 2003, C-243/01, *Piergiorgio Gambelli* [2003] ECR I-13031; ECJ, 6 March 2006, C-338 et al., *Placanica* [2006] ECR I-1891.

[36] Directive 97/7/EC of the European Parliament and of the Council of 20 May 1997 on the protection of consumers in respect of distance contracts, OJ L 144, 4 June 1997, 19; Directive 2011/83/EU of the European Parliament and the Council of 25 October 2011 on Consumer Rights OJ L 304, 22 November 2011 64, repealing Directive 97/7/EC.

[37] Directive 98/27/EC on injunctions for the protection of consumers' interests of 19 May 1998, OJ L 166, 11 June 1998, 51; now Directive 2009/22/EC of 23 April 2009 OJ L 110, 1 May 2009, 30.

[38] Directive 2002/65/EC of the European Parliament and of the Council of 23 September 2002 concerning the distance marketing of consumer financial services and amending Council Directive 90/619/EEC and Directives 97/7/EC and 98/27/EC, OJ L 271, 9 October 2002, 16.

[39] Council Directive 89/552/EEC of 3 October 1989 on the coordination of certain provisions laid down by Law, Regulation or Administrative Action in Member States concerning the

law, as far as they contain regulations on commercial practices like for example Directive 87/102/EEC on consumer credit (now Directive 2008/48/EC),[40] Directive 90/314/EEC on package travel,[41] Directive 94/47/EC on timeshares (now Directive 2008/122/EC),[42] Directive 99/44/EC on the sale of consumer goods[43] and Directive 2000/31/EC on e-commerce,[44] also belong to this category. Moreover, the relevant provisions of Directive 2002/58/EC concerning the processing of personal data[45] and the protection of privacy in the electronic communications sector, and of Directive 2001/34/EC on the admission of securities to official stock exchange listings[46] should be mentioned. The same applies to the relevant provisions of the regulations and directives of the secondary European trademark and copyright law concerning unfair commercial practices. In *Telekomunikacja Polska*[47] the ECJ held that provided the Directive 2009/25/EC applies, there is no room for deviating national rules on unfair commercial practices even if these can be based on derogations in secondary Community law.

c) The escape clause (minimum/maximum harmonisation)

2.15 It was fiercely disputed whether the Directive should aim at maximum harmonisation. In the end the majority of Member States have not resisted maximum harmonisation, with the exception of Denmark and Sweden. The

---

pursuit of television broadcasting activities OJ L 298, 17 October 1989, 23–30; now Directive 2010/13/EC of 10 March 2010, OJ L 95, 15 April 2010, 1.

40 Council Directive 87/102/EEC of 22 December 1986 for the approximation of laws, regulations and administrative provisions of the Member States concerning consumer credit, OJ L 42, 12 February 1987, 48 as amended; now Directive 2008/48/EC of 23 April 2008, OJ L 133, 22 May 2008, 66, repealing Directive 87/102/EC.

41 Council Directive of 13 June 1990 on package travel, package holidays and package tours, OJ L 158, 23 June 1990, 59, currently under revision; new Commission proposal COM (2013) 513 of 9 July 2013.

42 Directive 94/47/EC of the European Parliament and the Council of 26 October 1994 on the protection of purchasers in respect of certain aspects of contracts relating to the purchase of the right to use immovable properties on a timeshare basis, OJ L 280, 2 October 1994, 83, now Directive 2008/122/EC of 14 January 2009, OJ L 33, 3 February 2009, 10.

43 Directive 1999/44/EC of the European Parliament and the Council of 25 May 1999 on certain aspects of the sale of consumer goods and associated guarantees, OJ L 171, 7 July 1999, 12.

44 Directive 2000/31/EC of the European Parliament and of the Council of 8 June 2000 on certain legal aspects of information society services, in particular electronic commerce, in the Internal Market, OJ L 178, 17 July 2000, 16.

45 Directive 2002/58/EC of the European Parliament and of the Council of 12 July 2002 concerning the processing of personal data and the protection of privacy in the electronic communications sector, OJ L 201, 31 July 2002, 37.

46 Directive 2001/34/EC of the European Parliament and of the Council of 28 May 2001 on the admission of securities to official stock exchange listing and on information to be published on those securities, OJ L 184, 6 July 2001, 1.

47 ECJ, 11 March 2010, C-522/08, *Telekomunikacja Polska* [2010] ECR I-2079 at para 31 with regard to Article 17 Directive 2002/22/EC on Universal Services; see Namysłowska, *GRUR Int.* 2010, 1033.

search for a political compromise led to a transition period of – formerly – six years, in which national provisions can still be applied, as long as they (a) cover the scope of application of the Directive; (b) are more restrictive or prescriptive than the Directive; (c) were enacted for the implementation of the Directive; and (d) contain minimum harmonisation clauses. In order to claim continuance for such national provisions, those provisions must be "essential" to ensure that consumers are adequately protected against unfair commercial practices and they must be "proportionate" to the attainment of this objective.

As far as Member States make use of that exception provision, they shall notify the Commission according to Article 3(6) without delay of any national provisions applied on the basis of paragraph 5. According to the clear wording, the rule does not refer to the notification of new national provisions, but to the notification of the application of already existing provisions. Member States would have to notify the Commission if a court or a regulatory authority makes use of a national provision. Within the EC, this would probably apply to hundreds of decisions. The Commission tries to establish a basis for putting an end to the national "solos" after six years. This can only succeed if the Commission sets up a database comparable to that of the CLAB (3.31).

Theoretically, the derogation can be prolonged. However, this requires that the Commission comes – under the review pursuant to Article 18 – to the conclusion that such a prolongation is necessary. The Commission holds the decision-making competence and it would take much effort by Member States to regain it in the Council. So far no such prolongation is in sight.

d) *Special provisions for financial services, precious metals and health-related rules*

2.16 Article 3(9) of the UCPD sets up a special rule for commercial practices in relation to financial services as defined in Directive 2002/65/EC and for immovable property. Here, Member States retain the power to impose requirements that are more restrictive or prescriptive. In *Citroen Belux*[48] the ECJ confirmed the exclusion of financial services from the scope of application.

According to Article 3(10) it does not apply to the application of such laws, regulations and administrative provisions of Member States relating to the certification and indication of the quality of articles of precious metal. The Directive does not give an explanation for this exception, even though deception of consumers by incomplete or false information is likely to occur especially in this area. It constitutes an astonishing rule in the face of cross-border jewellery purchases.

Article 3(3) leaves Community and national rules relating to health and safety aspects of products unaffected. This evolves last but not least from the

[48] ECJ, 18 July 2013, Case C-265/12, *Citroën Belux* [2013] ECR I-nyr.

circumstance that the UCPD aims solely at the protection of economic interests of the consumers.

IV. MINIMUM/MAXIMUM HARMONISATION AND INTERNAL MARKET CLAUSE IN THE UCPD

2.17 The UCPD provides for full or maximum harmonisation and it establishes in Article 4 the internal market clause, which means that it combines maximum harmonisation and the country of origin principle. The shift from minimum to maximum harmonisation is of utmost importance for European consumer law (see already 1.22).[49] It constitutes in itself a paradigm shift which deserves careful analysis as it requires a re-balance of the regulatory competences between the European Community and Member States. The first two references go to the heart of the concept of maximum harmonisation.[50]

Tying together maximum harmonisation and the country of origin principle considerably affects the level of enforcement of consumer protection legislation in the EU. The country with the lowest enforcement level could then become the "leader" in giving shape to the interpretation of the rules of the UCPD.

1. THE BACKGROUND TO THE DEBATE

2.18 There is a broader background to the maximum/minimum debate. There had been a long established policy of the European Commission to strive for minimum harmonisation in the field of consumer law (1.42). This is particularly the case with regard to consumer contract law. Minimum harmonisation seemed to be the political consensus between Member States and the European Commission. It allowed the setting up of a common platform within the European Community equally valid for all Member States, but it enabled Member States to maintain or introduce stricter standards. In *Buet*[51] the ECJ had recognised the competence of Member States to set tighter standards on doorstep selling under Directive 85/577/EEC (now Directive 2011/83/EU) within the limits of the proportionality principle. However, times are changing. There were early announcements indicating the policy shift. Yet the Commission took the decisive step in its consumer policy programme of 2002–2006. Here it clearly established full harmonisation as the new objective of its politics on commercial

---

49 For a critique see Howells, *Sydney L Rev* 2006, 79–86.

50 ECJ, 23 April 2009, Joined Cases C-261, C-299/07, *VTB-VAB v Total Belgium* [2009] ECR I-02949; see in more detail 2.44.

51 ECJ, 16 May 1989, 382/87, *Buet* [1989] ECR I-1235; also ECJ, 14 March 1991, C-361/89, *di Pinto* [1991] ECR I-1189.

practices and on consumer contract law (1.32).[52] Obviously, the Commission intended to stop Member States protecting their "consumer-gardens". The decisive breakthrough, however, came with the UCPD in B2C relations.[53]

For quite a long time little attention was devoted to a principle already enshrined in the Single European Act, namely the concept of mutual recognition of Member States' fair trading rules. However, two important exceptions were made, namely in Directive 89/552/EEC on television without frontiers (now Directive 2010/13/EU) and Directive 2000/31/EC on e-commerce.[54] Here the Community introduced the country of origin principle in the Television Without Frontiers Directive as well as in the E-Commerce Directive. Both of the Directives concern so-called "multi-state acts of advertising", i.e. the single advertising act emanating from one country has an effect on the markets of several other EU and third countries simultaneously, as is generally the case in cross-border media (also in all kinds of commercial communications) and in Europe-wide marketing concepts. If the principle of country of determination were to apply, advertisers would be obliged to know the advertising and "fairness" law rules in every country where their marketing has any perceptible effects. The larger the number of legal systems referred to, the less practicable it becomes to assess the lawfulness of advertising for each place of business separately. The use of the principle of the country of determination raises particular difficulties in cases where the accessibility of the advertisement may no longer be controlled (e.g. advertising on the internet, where advertisers cannot prevent users from a specific country from accessing their websites).[55] On the other hand, one has to consider the risk for consumers of a so-called "race to the bottom".

Whilst both directives strengthened the legitimacy of the country of origin principle in regulating marketing practices, the principle alone was not agreed as an appropriate means to substitute the harmonisation policy. In its constant endeavour to foster the completion of the internal market, the European Commission received support from the ECJ in its famous *Tobacco Advertising* judgment.[56] It is in this context that the idea arose within the legal department of the European Commission to combine maximum harmonisation and the country of origin principle. The legal service of the European Commission understands from *Tobacco Advertising* that there can be no harmonisation in the sense of Article 95 EC without guaranteeing the free movement of products and services in the entire internal market (1.22).

[52] Consumer Policy Strategy (2002–2006), OJ C 137, 8 June 2002, 2.

[53] OJ L 149, 11 June 2005, 22.

[54] See Reich, *Understanding EU Law*, 128–134.

[55] For the conflict-of-law provisions of Rome II see 7.28.

[56] ECR, 5 October 2000, C-376/98, *Germany v European Parliament and Council* [2000] ECR I-8419.

2. MAXIMUM HARMONISATION AND INTERNAL MARKET CLAUSE

2.19 Article 4(1) taken with Article 4(2) of the Proposal from June 2003 aimed at a rather radical realisation of the country of origin principle. Article 4 states: "(1) Traders shall only comply with the national provisions, falling within the field approximated by this Directive, of the Member State in which they are established. The Member State in which the trader is established shall ensure such compliance. (2) Member States shall neither restrict the freedom to provide services nor restrict the free movement of goods for reasons falling within the field approximated by this Directive." In Recitals (20) and (47) of the Proposal, the Commission justified its intention according to which other Member States must not impose additional requirements on the trader who complies with the provisions of the country of origin. This only would allow legal certainty which traders need when entering into cross-border transactions with consumers. It is further stated that Member States need to ensure that traders established in their territories comply with their national provisions regardless of whether the consumers targeted or reached by their commercial practices reside in their territory or in other EU member countries. With the help of the internal market clause, possible differences between Member States should be abolished.

The consequences of such a provision supported the worst expectations of the critics of the country of origin principle or, on the other hand, the hopes of its supporters. The following scenario might describe the conflict potential: a competent court of one of the 25 Member States decides on the compliance of a commercial practice with the general clause in Article 5(2). No competent court of another Member State could challenge that decision, by the decision. If the latter wanted to rule on an identical commercial practice, then, in order to review the decision of the former, it would only be possible to address the ECJ which would then need to review whether Community law was interpreted correctly.

There is no doubt that the internal market clause was at the centre of the discussions during the legislative process. The majority of Member States – explicit supporters of the proposal of the Commission remained the United Kingdom, Luxembourg and Latvia – have, during the negotiations, enforced the cancellation of Article 4(1). Only the wording of Article 4(2) was kept and its place was slightly changed. There is substantial controversy in legal doctrine over whether the internal market clause had been given up or whether it is still alive albeit in a reduced form. It remains to be seen whether the above-mentioned scenario could become reality. The last word will be for the ECJ. The first reference procedure will not deal with Article 4(2) but with the maximum harmonisation approach, in particular with regard to sales promotion measures (see under 2.44).[57]

---

57 ECJ, 23 April 2009, Joined Cases C-261/07, C-299/07, *VAB v Total Belgium* [2009] ECR I-02949.

V. THE CONCEPT OF FAIR TRADING IN THE UCPD

1. THE THREE-LEVEL STRUCTURE OF THE GENERAL CLAUSE

2.20 The comprehensive general clause of Article 5 prohibiting "unfair commercial practices" defines the general legal framework. As regards the substantive provisions of the European fair trading system, the Commission has decided – in conformity with the principal concept of the (continental) European Member States[58] – in favour of a general clause of "unfair commercial practices". It was purported to include the different general clauses and principles of Member States in a harmonised European framework simplifying the normative orientation of the market users, be it traders or consumers.[59] Pursuant to Article 5(2), a commercial practice shall be unfair if it is contrary to the requirements of professional diligence (a), and if it materially distorts or is likely to materially distort the economic behaviour with regard to the product of the average consumer whom it reaches or to whom it is addressed, or of the average member of the group when a commercial practice is directed towards a particular group of consumers (b). The requirements set out in Article 5(2) must be satisfied cumulatively to justify unfairness.

On the second level, the Directive deals with those advertising practices which are particularly unfair. According to Article 5(3) commercial practices are unfair which are misleading in terms of Article 6 (misleading actions) and Article 7 (misleading omissions) or aggressive in terms of Article 8 (aggressive commercial practices) and Article 9 (harassment, coercion and undue influence).

The third level is represented by Annex I to the Directive according to which 28 individually listed misleading and aggressive trading practices are unfair *per se*. This illustrates the judgment that there are commercial practices which do not need to be individually assessed. Listing such discriminating market practices is a model which is new to some Member States.

2. CONCEPTUAL BASIS OF THE TERM "FAIRNESS"

2.21 The challenge of the Directive is to put the term "fairness" into a concrete form within a European context. A positive description of the term "fairness" within a European context automatically leads to conflicts with national standards. The reason is that Member States have been using and are still using unfair commercial practices law to deal with advertising measures that heavily

58 Cf. Micklitz/Kessler; Henning-Bodewig.

59 Recital (30).

affect moral values, such as discrimination against women.[60] This was made possible through an understanding of unfair marketing practices law that might equally deal with non-market-related values. The Directive does not delimit the concept of fairness from non-market-related moral values, from taste and decency and from national cultures. Therefore it must refer to economic theory which underpins and could guide European fair trading law, in order to distinguish fairness from morality. At least Recital (7) which refers to taste and decency provides a possible solution for how to manage a possible interplay of European and national taste or decency.

a) *European fairness as an autonomous concept*

2.22 At an early stage the question was raised as to whether it could be concluded from the character of the UCPD as a framework directive that the term "fairness" could be given shape through the respective national concepts.[61] If this were true, then the Community legislator would have given up the idea that it could be the purpose and objective of the Directive to create a Community law standard. Therefore the opposite is the case. Without exception, all the statements of the Commission show that it considers regulating unfair trading law uniformly as the only way to abandon the remaining barriers of intra-Community trade. Any other interpretation would be contrary to the objective of the Directive. It would leave room for Member States to interpret the general clause in the light of their traditions and cultures – a result which the Commission clearly wanted to avoid.

Closely connected to the possible framework character of the Directive is the second question of whether it is of significance for the development of European unfair trading law what wording is used to describe the term "fairness". There is a certain preparedness in legal doctrine to argue in this direction. This reading cannot be followed. European fair trading law requires a common wording of the concept of "fairness" in order to strike down the risk which results from the infiltration of non-market related moral values by way of reference to *bonos mores* and the like as in traditional unfair competition law in Germany (under the old law), Austria and Belgium.

b) *European fairness, national morals, taste, decency and cultural values*

2.23 The UCPD refers in a confusing way to fairness, morals, taste and decency as well as national cultures, without giving any hint of what might be understood by these broad and ideology-laden concepts. However, the development of an autonomous terminology requires that it is possible for the 28 Member States to

60 Millan/Elliott, 475.

61 See Barkadjieva.

agree on a yardstick for how to define the term "fairness" in a positive way. A possible and necessary demarcation between fairness on the one hand and non-market related morals on the other, is not easy to draw.[62] There is a universal freedom of communication which is invoked as a constitutional and human right by those benefiting from it, whereas critics rely on the diverging national morals in the respective legal systems. The universal freedom of communication influences the term "fairness" as a non-moral element of integrity. Fairness then means universal economic clarity, unambiguousness and transparency in the sense of workable competition.[63] The degrees of freedom which can be or must be granted to Member States which fall below (or above?) a European doctrine of fairness are nothing else but culture-specific variations of occidental codified customs, i.e. tradition in each aspect.

Such an understanding helps to draw a demarcation line between the European concept of fair trading based on market freedoms and competition, and national non-market related values which remain outside the Directive. The problem remains, however, that Member States may use the open-ended wording of European unfair commercial practices law to establish their own rules and to narrow down the freedom of market communication which is at the heart of the UCPD. That is why the term "fairness" as applied in the UCPD cannot be given a non-market-related moral implication. It must rather be applied as a means to realise competition in the internal market. The Directive strives for freedom in market communication and "demoralises" unfair commercial practices law.[64] That is why, for example, sex discrimination in advertising is not a matter of concern for the European approach on unfair commercial practices. Such a reading is confirmed in the second sentence of Recital (7) stating that the Directive does not relate to taste and decency, which vary widely among Member States. All parties involved in the making of the UCPD were aware of the fact that it was not intended to interfere with national customs and habits – in other words, with national morals.

The relationship between fairness and culture appears Recital (18), which refers to the formula the ECJ found in *Lifting*:[65] "In order to apply that test [the average consumer test] to the present case, several considerations must be borne in mind. In particular, it must be determined whether social, cultural or linguistic factors may justify the term 'lifting', used in connection with a firming cream, meaning something different to the German consumer as opposed to consumers in other Member States, or whether the instructions for the use of the product are in themselves sufficient to make it quite clear that its effects are short-lived, thus neutralising any conclusion to the contrary that might be

62 See WILHELMSSON, in: HOWELLS/MICKLITZ/WILHELMSSON (eds.), Chapter 3(d).
63 See *supra* note 30 at para 2.9.
64 See for a somewhat more sceptical reading, WILHELMSSON, *supra* note 62, Chapter 3(d) (i)-(iii).
65 ECJ, 13 January 2000, C-220/98, *Lifting* [2000] ECR I-117 at para 29.

derived from the word lifting." The very broad exemption could be read so as to strengthen Member States' leeway in giving their own reading of whether a certain commercial practice affects national values, such as morals and even culture. At the end of the day, the ECJ will have to decide whether Member States are referring to morals, taste, decency and culture as a pretext to protect national industries or whether they are legitimately defending national non-market-related values.

c) Elements of the general clause

2.24 The general clause in Article 5 consists of three parts. Article 5(2)(a) refers to the requirements of professional diligence (see 2.25), and Article 5(2)(b) to the economic behaviour of the consumer, which is further defined in Article 2(h) and (e) (see 2.7). Article 5(3) constitutes a special need for protection of vulnerable consumers (see 2.27).

3. REQUIREMENTS OF PROFESSIONAL DILIGENCE

2.25 Article 2(h) defines professional diligence as a "standard of special skill and care which a trader may reasonably be expected to exercise towards consumers, commensurate with honest market practice and/or the general principle of good faith in the trader's field of activity". The first draft proposal referred to customary market practice, being understood as good business conduct, due diligence or the like.[66] The reference has been heavily criticised as it was said to risk setting in stone the *status quo* of what is customary in a particular area. The final version clarifies that commercial practices combine facts and norms, e.g. existing codes of practice, and the need to test them against the yardstick of fairness.

However, this is not the only difficulty. The reference to "professional diligence" has been heavily attacked as it supports a concept according to which the UCPD establishes a traditional reading of protecting individuals and competitors in terms of Article 10*bis*(2) of the Paris Convention (see 2.1). The counter-argument, however, that the criterion of professional diligence is incompatible with the objective of consumer protection, carries more weight. Consumers do not establish honest market practice and they are not involved in developing codes of practice. The European Commission originally had in mind the intention of complementing the binding rules laid down in the Directive on unfair commercial practices with codes of conduct. The reference to professional diligence makes sense only if there are European codes of conduct and if they have been developed with due consideration of professional and consumer

66 Article 2598 of the Italian *codice civile* refers to "*correttezza professionale*".

interests. The contrary is true (see 2.47). The gap that still remains can be bridged to a certain extent by way of applying the advertising rules of the International Chamber of Commerce in Paris.[67]

The term "professional diligence" is of no relevance for the prohibition of misleading actions, of misleading omissions and of aggressive commercial practices. These practices are regarded as *per se* violations. This consequence was clearly stated in Recital (57) of the first draft proposal. A similar wording is not contained in the final version of the Directive. The contrary cannot be concluded by virtue of Article 7(4)(d) either, according to which the trader is required, in the event of an invitation to purchase, to provide information about the arrangements for payment, delivery, performance and the complaints-handling policy, if they depart from the requirements of professional diligence. This negative exception is unlikely to be suitable as an *argumentum e contrario* for making professional diligence a decisive criterion when examining misleading advertising.

4. MATERIAL DISTORTION OF THE ECONOMIC BEHAVIOUR OF THE CONSUMER

2.26 Article 5(2) refers to the material distortion of the economic behaviour of the consumer which is defined in Article 2(e) as using a commercial practice to appreciably impair the consumer's ability to make an informed decision, thereby causing the consumer to take a transactional decision that he would not have taken otherwise. The significance of the threefold terminology, namely relating to economic behaviour, informed decision, and transactional decision, should not be overestimated. On a scale, economic behaviour seems to be the widest and transactional decision the narrowest of the three, with informed decision ranking in the middle. All three terms have in common the intention of ensuring the consumer's autonomy during pre-contractual negotiations.[68] One could now argue the difference between behaviour and decision. However, it is not the consumer's behaviour which is of concern but rather, in pursuance of the objective of the Directive, his behaviour in the market. The consumer can only influence his behaviour if he does not merely "behave", i.e. remains in the pre-contractual study of the advertising practices which surround him but if he is willing to take decisions; therefore he requires information. Only an informed decision furthers workable competition. Therefore it seems sensible to understand the three terms as a whole.[69]

67 Craig/Park/Paulsson.

68 The definition is problematic with regard to the evaluation of after-sales practices which do not distort the pre-contractual process of taking a decision, Twigg-Flesner/Parry/Howells/Nordhausen, 2.39, p. 14.

69 See now AG Kokott 19 December 2013, C-281/12, *Trento Svilupo and Centrale Adriatica* [2013] ECR I-nyr.

Distortion of economic behaviour has an objective side, as it concerns the autonomy of the consumer, and a subjective side – a possible intent or fault on the consumer's side. Article 2(e) defines "to materially distort the economic behaviour of consumers" as using a commercial practice *to* appreciably impair the consumer's ability to make an informed decision. The word "to" suggests such a subjective intentional requirement of commercial practice. However, it is also possible to conclude quite the contrary from a systematic reading of the definitions and the formally limited significance of the definition of the term "transactional decision" for the interpretation of Article 5(2). The Directive on unfair commercial practices is meant to "demoralise" unfair trading law (see 2.23). There must be no intention or any other subjective element in Community law when determining whether there is a violation.

The restriction of the prohibition of unfair advertising to "material" distortion purports to free the cross-border transaction from the necessity that any, even very minor, distortions will be judged as being unfair. The same is true with regard to misleading actions and omissions under Articles 6(1) and 7(1) as well as aggressive commercial practices under Articles 8 and 9. Only significant distortions are likely to cause the consumer to take a decision that he would not have taken otherwise. Therefore the commercial practice must be apt to distort the consumer's ability to take an informed decision.[70] In principle, the Directive proceeds from the assumption that a sufficiently informed consumer cannot be distorted in taking his decision. In *Pall v Dahlhausen* the ECJ explained that statements about the origin of the trademark which are misleading are not apt to trigger a misconception which would be relevant to the consumer in taking his transactional decision. Despite the fact that the case *in concreto* concerned the evaluation of the existence of a risk of confusion under trademark law, a general legal principle can be derived from the case: not every omitted or even false piece of information is "material" in terms of the relevance threshold. The materiality threshold is inseparably connected with the model of the informed consumer (see 2.27).

According to Article 5(2) 2nd dash of the Proposal, unfair commercial practices not only need to be material but also actually distorting. An unfair commercial practice shall be regarded unfair "if it materially distorts or is likely to materially distort the economic behaviour with regard to the product of the average consumer whom it reaches or to whom it is addressed". There is an almost identical reference to the "factual context" in Article 6(2) (misleading actions) and Article 7(1) (misleading omissions). The UCPD proceeds from an interaction between normative requirements on the consumer and his actual behaviour. The legislator has put the significance of the intervention threshold into perspective. It is therefore irrelevant whether the commercial practices distort the consumer materially; they need to be prone to distort him.

70 Recital (54).

Community law requires the national enforcement authorities to take a prognostic decision on the possibility of a material distortion.

5. THE "AVERAGE CONSUMER" AND PARTICULARLY VULNERABLE GROUPS

2.27 Unfairness is generally measured against the model of the "average consumer" as developed by the ECJ, i.e. the "average consumer, who is reasonably well-informed and reasonably observant and circumspect" in terms of the established case law of the ECJ. The average consumer is the measure of all things.[71] Recital (18) refers explicitly to the ECJ's construction of an average consumer; however, an explicit reference in the text has been skipped due to pressure from some Member States in the law-making process. Whether the elimination affects the yardstick of control, is a matter of controversy in legal doctrine.[72]

However, to the extent that commercial practices are addressed to a special group of consumers then the yardstick is the understanding of the average member of the respective group. Article 5(3) refers to consumers which because of their mental or physical infirmity, age or credulity are particularly vulnerable to commercial practices or the underlying product. The measure has a normative component as it purports to evaluate the advertising measure. Recitals (18) and (19) provide an insight into the objectives of this provision. The Community is obviously thinking of children and seniors, who should not be protected to a greater extent *per se* but only if commercial practices or products are particularly appealing to the groups affected. Such an understanding is supported by Article 16 of the Consolidated Broadcasting Directive 89/552/EEC, which states that television advertising must not cause minors physical or psychological damage.

The decision as to whether an advertisement is aimed at particularly vulnerable consumer groups is difficult to make. The evaluation of spill-over effects is remarkably problematic. Advertisements which are addressed to adults can also reach children. Depending on the interpretation, the yardstick of control varies. According to Article 5(3) it is necessary to distinguish whether the trader could reasonably be expected to foresee that the commercial practices can materially distort the economic behaviour not of all consumers taken as a whole, but only of a clearly identifiable group of consumers who are particularly

---

71 See ECJ, 6 July 1995, C-470/93, *Mars* [1995] ECR I-1923; ECJ, 16 July 1998, C-210/96, *Gut Springenheide* [1998] ECR I-4657; ECJ, 28 January 1999, C-303/97, *Sektkellerei Kessler* [1999] ECR I-117; ECJ, 13 January 2000, C-220/98, *Lifting* [2000] ECR I-117; ECJ, 4 April 2000, C-465/98, *Darbo* [2000] ECR I-2297.

72 See Wilhelmsson, 211; Weatherill, in: Weatherill (ed.), *EU Consumer Law and Policy*, 2nd ed. 2013, 243.

vulnerable. The indication in Article 5(3) and the Recitals that the practices cause or are likely to cause distortion with regard to this group suggests that there is a subjective element in the design and choice of the advertising measure and that it pursues a particular objective.

6. RELATIONSHIP BETWEEN THE COMPREHENSIVE GENERAL CLAUSE AND THE SPECIAL GENERAL CLAUSES

2.28 Whether a commercial practice violates the general clause, i.e. must be regarded as unfair, has to be decided on a case-by-case basis. The situation is different with regard to misleading and aggressive practices. Article 5(3) declares that "misleading" or "aggressive" marketing strategies in terms of Articles 6 to 9 are always regarded as unfair.[73] This is also true by virtue of Article 5(5) for commercial practices listed in Annex I which are not "particularly" unfair but which "shall in all circumstances be regarded as unfair" (see 2.45). It is therefore irrelevant whether these practices contradict the "requirements of professional diligence" or whether they are likely to "materially distort" the economic behaviour with regard to the product. In particular, those countries which are experienced in dealing with a general clause objected to the idea that it could be possible without considering the concrete circumstances to label commercial practices to be misleading or aggressive *per se*. The tone of criticism becomes harsher when the legal qualification of the list of incriminating practices as laid down in the Annex is discussed. However, it should not be forgotten that the 28 incriminated advertising practices will help to clear unfair practices from the European-wide internal market. Too much leeway to Member States might put the overall objective into jeopardy.

There is substantial controversy on the interrelationship between the comprehensive general clause in Article 5 and the special general clauses in Articles 6 to 9. The overall idea behind the Directive is to establish a common framework on how unfair commercial practices should be dealt with. Therefore the special prohibitions contained in Articles 6 and 7 or 8 and 9 together with the corresponding lists should be read so as to limit the residual function of the general clause. Cases of misleading or aggressive advertising which are not regulated cannot become the subject matter of a review of fairness through the backdoor by using the general clause. The general clause only applies in extreme and obvious cases to close regulatory gaps. The general clause serves as a safety net. Therefore a Member State which imposes a prohibition on the basis of Article 5(2) which goes beyond Articles 6 to 9 and Annex I is under substantial pressure to justify the prohibition under the provisions of EC law. However,

[73] Recital (56) of the Proposal.

whilst the purpose of the Directive seems clear, legal doctrine all over Europe is divided over the role and function of the general clause.[74]

VI. THE CONCEPT OF MISLEADING ADVERTISING IN DIRECTIVE 2005/29/EC

2.29 With the adoption of the UCPD, different measures for judging misleading advertisements were established, depending on whether the addressee of the advertisement is a consumer or an entrepreneur. It remains within the authority of every Member State to impose these measures on B2B relations. Theoretically this is possible, but it requires a precise examination of the measures formulated in Articles 6 to 9. The European Community has decided in favour of a division that reflects a different protection purpose and different personal and factual scope of applications, but not different concepts of deception.

Primarily important for the term "misleading" used in B2C relations is the distinction between *action* and *omission*. Whether there is misleading advertising by action or by omission, either Article 6 or 7 is to be applied. Even though both articles overlap to a great extent, the requirements are not totally equal. Thus the question arises as to whether in fact actions can be distinguished from omissions to the same degree as the Directive. In fact the boundaries are rather blurred. Practices that are not demonstrably false, but which are capable of misleading the consumer, may result from the quantity provided or withheld. In this way, the distribution of half-truths surely is an action; the repressed part of such information is at the same time an omission. In such cases it seems to be a matter of taste as to whether to categorise such practices as acts or omissions.

1. THE CONCEPT OF MISLEADING COMMERCIAL PRACTICES

2.30 Article 6 (misleading actions) and Article 7 (misleading omissions) are based on the same concept. Article 6 says: "A commercial practice shall be regarded as misleading if it contains false information and is therefore untruthful or in any way, including overall presentations deceives or is likely to deceive the average consumer, even if the information is factually correct". Article 7 holds a "commercial practice as misleading if, in its factual context, taking into account of all its features and circumstances and the limitations of the communication medium, it omits material information that the average

---

[74] See Stuyck/Terryn/van Dyck, 106.

consumer needs, according to the context, to take and informed transactional decision". Both Articles 6 and 7 then list a set of criteria to define the elements which have to be taken into account whether there is a misleading action or misleading omission. The concept of misleading commercial practices ties both notions – actions and omissions – together.

The crucial question is whether there is an autonomous notion of the term "misleading" under Community law which functions as a standard for courts and administrative authorities of Member States in order to attack misleading advertising in the internal market on the one hand and to combat disguised segregation practices on the other hand which arise through exaggerated strictness of the prohibition of misleading advertising (see 2.23). The ECJ indicated in a number of judgments all dealing with the notion of misleading advertising, though in varying contexts, that it purports an autonomous development of the term considering both elements of advertising law equally, i.e. the protection of the interests of consumers, competitors and the general public on the one hand, and the opening of markets in furtherance of the internal market on the other. The *proportionality* principle will be taken into account for the prohibition of misleading advertising. The ECJ held that consumer habits may change and that the internal market is a factor which may trigger such a change. This is the reason why the Federal Republic of Germany could not rely on the argument that consumers would consider "beer" to be in accordance with the purity requirement, otherwise they would be misled.[75] The decision merely referred to labelling provisions. However as labelling is to be understood as a "statement" in terms of the Directive, these principles also apply to misleading advertising.[76] These principles have been confirmed and further developed in later decisions. The *Pall v Dahlhausen* case[77] concerned the risk of being misled by unauthorised utilisation of the ® mark in Germany which had been legally acquired abroad. The prohibition of that kind of advertising was considered a "measure having equivalent effect" not being justified by mandatory requirements of consumer protection and the fairness of commercial transactions. The invocation of Directive 84/450/EEC justifies the prohibition.

Therefore the decisive elements are stated which characterise the further discussion on the term misleading: mere aptness to mislead on the one hand, or actual misleading on the other; the model of the careless, uninformed consumer, or a consumer who is reasonably well informed, observant and circumspect; prohibition of misleading advertising; or requirement of information. Not least because of a variety of preliminary proceedings initiated by Member States'

---

75 ECJ, 12 March 1987, C-178/84, *Commission v Germany (purity requirement for beer)* [1987] ECR I-1227 at para 32.

76 Cf. Directive 79/112/EEC; ECJ, 12 December 1990, C-241/89, *SARPP* [1990] ECR I-4695 at para 32.

77 ECJ, 13 December 1990, C-238/89, *Pall v Dahlhausen* [1990] ECR I-4827.

courts, the ECJ has clarified basic disputes to an extent that it seems that the initiative has been transferred to the Community legislator.

2. MISLEADING COMMERCIAL PRACTICES: ABSTRACT OR CONCRETE?

2.31 In some Member States the notion of the term "misleading" is empirical in its origin as opposed to the European one which is normative. Accordingly these national courts proceed from a *subjective/concrete* risk of being misled:[78] *subjective* as it ascertains consumer expectations by conducting a public opinion poll if necessary and as it regards deception possible even in the case of objectively true advertising statements; *concrete* as merely the provable risk of deceived consumer expectations will give rise to strike down the practice. If a consumer feels subjectively misled, then he is indeed misled. The ECJ, on the other hand, determines misleading advertising according to *objective/concrete* criteria – *Yves Rocher*,[79] *Mars*[80] and *Lifting*:[81] *objective* as according to its function, meaning that the ECJ does not decide the merits of a case but provides guidance on the interpretation of Community law; *concrete* as the ECJ requires that the consumer has been provably misled, i.e. *in concreto*. However, it took a series of court decisions to overcome the most basic uncertainties in the application of the misleading doctrine.

The *Nissan* decision[82] represents the high-water mark of a controversial discussion about the notion of the term misleading, i.e. about the question of whether Community law will allow an abstract risk to suffice or if it requires actual proof of being misled. The case concerned a French car dealer engaging in parallel imports of Nissan cars from Belgium to France. In its advertisements the car dealer failed to disclose *inter alia* that the trimmings of the imported cars were inferior to those of the models intended for the French market. A French court submitted the question to the ECJ of whether the defendant's non-disclosure of the minimum trimmings amounted to misleading advertising with regard to the car price. The ECJ stated that misleading advertising with regard to the price was only given if it could be proven that a significant part of the consumers to whom the advertisement was addressed to make the purchase decision not knowing that the lower car price was accompanied by the inferior trimmings of the cars sold by the parallel importer. The absence of an indication of the lack of warranty and inferior trimmings does not render advertising which is addressed to consumers familiar with the particularities (and risks!) arising

---

78 ECJ, 18 May 1993, C-126/91, *Yves Rocher* [1993] ECR I-2361.
79 Ibid.
80 ECJ, 6 July 1995, C-470/93, *Mars* [1995] ECR I-1923.
81 ECJ, 13 January 2000, C-220/98, *Lifting* [2000] ECR I-117.
82 ECJ, 16 January 1992, C-373/90, *Nissan* [1992] ECR I-131.

from parallel imports. It seems questionable whether the ECJ accepted even the abstract risk of being misled. In legal literature the reach and effect of the decision has been subject to a highly controversial debate. It took a number of further judgments before the point could be clarified.

Irrespective of the *Keck* doctrine,[83] the case law of the ECJ[84] pursued its search for an autonomous concept of misleading advertising; however it failed to settle the discussion about the interplay between objective/subjective and abstract/concrete danger. German courts had prohibited the utilisation of the term "*Clinique*" which was employed throughout the Community in connection with cosmetic products as it allegedly misled consumers about medical characteristics. Estée Lauder therefore had to employ the term "*Linique*". Thus the marketing of a product group throughout the Community became impossible. This not only violated Article 28 EC and Directive 76/768/EEC on the approximation of the laws of Member States relating to cosmetic products but also the term misleading as contained in Directive 84/450/EEC which was interpreted in terms of market segregation rather than consumer protection. The German prohibition of the term "*Clinique*" could not be upheld.[85] The ECJ obviously proceeded from the fact that the German consumer could not be misled by the term "*Clinique*".

This reading is consistent with the *Mars* decision of 6 July 1995[86] which involved the question of whether an advertisement with the text "+10%" was misleading, if for the purpose of a short-term advertising campaign for an ice cream bar the contents had been increased. The submitting court found a misleading effect in the new wrapper which was held to be apt to raise the expectation in the consumer that the product would be sold for the same price as before – which would amount to prohibited price fixing – or that the design of the indication "+10%" would give the impression that the volume or weight of the product had been enlarged or increased significantly. The ECJ stated that an interdiction possibly imposed on the trader not to increase prices would be advantageous to the consumer and thus provide him with protection against misleading advertising. The design of the indication was not misleading, as reasonably circumspect consumers can be deemed to know that there is not necessarily a link between the size of publicity markings relating to an increase in a product's quantity and the size of that increase.

In *Gut-Springenheide*[87] the ECJ had to decide whether Article 10(2) of Council Regulation 1907/90 required a concrete risk of being misled or whether

---

[83] ECJ, 24 November 1993, C-267 + 8/91, *Keck and Mithouard* [1993] ECR I-6097; for an overview of the follow up cases, see opinion of AG Bot of 8 July 2008 in C-110/05 *Commission v Italy*.

[84] ECJ, 2 February 1994, C-315/92, *Verband sozialer Wettbewerb v Clinique* [1994] ECR I-317.

[85] On the significance of this, Reich, *CMLRev* 1994, 487.

[86] ECJ, C-470/93, *Mars* [1995] ECR I-1923.

[87] ECJ, 16 July 1998, C-210/96, *Gut Springenheide* [1998] ECR I-4657.

an abstract risk sufficed. The ECJ emphasised[88] that the mere potential of being misleading was of relevance. If the facts necessary to making a decision on a possible misleading effect are missing then the ECJ leaves it to the discretion of the national courts to decide whether the disputed description, brand or advertising statement have actually misled the consumers concerned. Thus the ECJ refrains only in individual cases from a normative stipulation of the potential to be misled and leaves it to the national courts to decide whether to take expert opinions or consumer inquiries into consideration. The formulation "it could be misleading only in so far as it would have deterred a significant number of consumers" must be understood this way. Under Community law, advertising is not only misleading if it actually misleads consumers but also if the ECJ normatively establishes the general propensity of an advertising measure to produce misleading effects, however leaving it to the national courts to produce concrete evidence. The national courts can require the services of an expert opinion or a consumer survey in order to assess whether an advertising statement is misleading. This task sharing between the ECJ and the national courts has been forcefully confirmed in *Sektkellerei Kessler*[89] and *Lifting*.[90] Therefore a mere abstract danger to the consumers does not suffice to qualify a commercial practice as misleading *vis-à-vis* consumers or being likely to mislead consumers. There must be a concrete danger for consumers to take a transactional decision he would not have taken otherwise. Whether or not this is the case remains to be decided by the national courts. The UCPD, though quite sceptical of empirical evidence,[91] mirrors the current state of the ECJ's case law.

If a minority of consumers has been misled, then the effect of the prohibition needs to be balanced against the principles of free movement of goods and services and often it needs to be restricted. Contrary to some Member States' law, the subjective risk of deception is not primarily decisive but the objective falsity of the advertising statement needs to be determined according to the general principles of Community law. The criterion for the risk of being misled is the average consumer who is reasonably well informed, observant and circumspect rather than the uninformed and careless consumer. Only the misleading of a significant number of consumers incurs the prohibitive effect whereby the consumers' previous knowledge is decisive.

---

88 As early as in Recital (15) to *Nissan* the ECJ left it to the national courts to decide, in the circumstances of the particular case and bearing in mind the consumers at whom the advertising is directed, whether the latter could be misleading insofar as it "would have deterred a significant number of consumers from making a purchase".

89 ECJ, 28 January 1999, C-303/97, *Sektkellerei Kessler* [1999] ECR I-513.

90 ECJ, 13 January 2000, C-220/98, *Lifting* [2000] ECR I-117.

91 See Recital (18).

3. INFORMATION REQUIREMENTS AND MISLEADING OMISSIONS (ARTICLE 7)

2.32 Member States disagree on the need to oblige suppliers to provide the consumer with adequate information via advertising measures. The ECJ had a number of occasions on which to give its own view on the interrelationship of the prohibition of misleading advertising and the need to disclose information (see 2.35); however, it did not take a clear position. The Directive on unfair commercial practices pushes the development into the direction of a general information duty. The regulatory means is the verdict on misleading omissions in Article 7 UCPD.

a) *Developments of case law*

2.33 Prior to the adoption of the UCPD the ECJ had not had the opportunity to deliver an opinion on the question whether and if necessary under which circumstances the autonomous term of "misleading" under Community law establishes a "requirement to inform". Nonetheless three elements can be extracted from the established practice of the ECJ which refer to the coherence between information and clarification:

(1) the informed consumer is required to obtain missing information – *Nissan* and *Lifting*;[92]
(2) true information must not be withheld from the consumer – *GB-Inno*;[93]
(3) the reasonable consumer is required to identify objectively false information – *Mars*.

Could it be concluded that the ECJ condenses the prohibition of misleading into a requirement to inform? A principle of the *true advertising* cannot be derived from *GB-Inno*.[94] The ECJ has rejected such an idea in *Jean Jacques*[95] and *Goldei*.[96] However, a normatively determined reasonable consumer can only fulfil his role as a vehicle in realising the internal market if the information is available to him which he needs to do so, i.e. if he has the right to information. This obligation to inform merely constitutes the reverse of the normative consumer image. Article 169 TFEU allows further development of ECJ case law. Article 169 TFEU grants the consumer a subjective right to information, the contents of which is further defined in secondary provisions under Community law (1.12). The newly adopted UCPD fits very well into such a perspective.

92 ECJ, 13 January 2000, C-220/98, *Lifting* [2000] ECR I-117.
93 ECJ, 7 March 1990, 362/88, *GB-Inno* [1990] ECR I-667.
94 Ibid.
95 ECJ, 13 December 1989, 204/88, *Jean Jacques* [1989] ECR I-4361.
96 ECJ, 15 January 1991, 372/89, *Goldei* [1991] ECR I-43.

b) *Misleading omissions (Article 7)*

2.34 Article 7 distinguishes between four forms of omissions: (1) omitting material information in paragraph 1; (2) hiding or providing material information in an unclear, incomprehensible, ambiguous or untimely manner in paragraph 2; (3) hiding information about limitations of space or time in paragraph 3; and (4) hiding material information in the case of an *invitation to purchase*. Contrary to misleading actions, the list of sanctioned practices does barely contain references on misleading omissions. Explicit prohibitions that amount to omissions are completely missing. Nos. 5, 6 and 28 in the Annex mention the term "invitation", but the examples at best provide assistance in determining what the Community legislator regards as an invitation to purchase.

This presumably clear structure turns out to be inconsistent. In paragraph 1, the question already arises as to how the information that is described as material differs from the equally named term in Article 6(1)(b). The Directive does not provide any guidance in this relation. Article 7(2) mingles the terms "action" and "omission". Without doubt, the hiding of information is an omission. Within Community law, this term has not played any role in the area of unfair practices so far.[97] Providing information, on the other hand, is targeted to an action. The contradiction may always be solved by combining Article 7(2) with Article 7(1). This seemed to be the intention of the legislator, too, since he talks of "also". Paragraph 3 generalises the legislative approach – well known from the Directive 97/7/EC on distant selling – that aims at the harmonisation of pre-contractual information. For the first time, the Commission reveals what already became apparent since the adoption of the Distance-Sale and the E-Commerce Directive: the complete and systematic harmonisation of the pre-contractual phase. The term "invitation" must be interpreted autonomously.

However, the ultimate question remains whether Article 7 establishes a general duty of disclosure, at least concerning such information that the consumer needs for his informed decision, i.e. Article 2(e). The answer can only be given by consideration of the concept of the European consumer. The informational obligations constitute compensation for the liberal concept of an understanding, alert and averagely informed consumer. The view on the conception of Article 7 underlines – in spite of all its structural deficits – the importance of an information paradigm, which develops more and more an information right (see 1.11). While Article 7 abstains from establishing clear informational obligations in the case of jump-advertising initiated by the trader, the informational obligations imposed on the trader increase within the narrower phase of contractual conclusion. Even though Article 7(1) and (2) –

[97] See opinion of AG Saggio, *Commission/Austria (money laundering)* [2000] ECR I-783 at para 4, and CFI, *SA Cimenterieres CBR et al.* [2000] ECR, II-491.

pursuant to their wording – generally apply to commercial practices, where the trader "omits material information" and that thus constitutes "misleading omissions", they point towards an information obligation. The special rule of Article 7(4)(1), which is designed as a *lex specialis,* specifies the essential requirements in the case of an "invitation to purchase". According to the wording, a misleading omission in the pre-contractual phase is only possible where the requirements of an *invitatio ad offerendum* are fulfilled. This would lead to a paradoxical result since such a – literal – interpretation of the clause would exclude major parts of the suppliers' advertisement from the scope of application of Article 7. Furthermore, such interpretation would thwart the aim of Article 7(1). Moreover, Article 7(4) imposes "*in the case of an invitation to purchase*" a special rule that demands the disclosure of the following information, unless it arises directly from the circumstances. Compared to the phrase of the first draft "*in the case of an invitation to submit an offer*", the adopted one is rather wide and adjusts the various facts of Article 7. *Ving Sverige*[98] provided the ECJ with the opportunity to clarify the meaning of an invitation to purchase. The preliminary reference of the Swedish Ombud aimed at examining the admissibility of the entry-level prices which often work to entice the consumer but which are then not available on the market. The ECJ here rejected the right of the consumer to be provided with clear-cut information; however, it left a margin of discretion to the national courts.

c) Misleading through violations of informational obligations established in specific laws

2.35 Article 7(5) continues a legislative approach that could already be deduced from and established under existing Community law. With the help of the unfair commercial practices law, violations of pre-contractual and also of post-contractual informational obligations shall be sanctioned. Thus Community law combines contract law with the law of unfair commercial practices. Article 7(5) deals with violations of those informational duties combined in Annex II as marketing instruments, i.e. as instruments of commercial communication. Hence the borderlines between advertisement and contract law become further blurred both in the phase of contractual initiation and in contractual performance. The catalogue of given informational obligations is not limited to the pre-contractual phase, as for example is shown by those duties which are to be observed according to Directive 97/7/EC on distance selling.

According to Article 7(5), only the violation of such duties that are based on Community law count as misleading. If Member States have already established information requirements based on minimal rules that go further than Community law requirements, a violation of these rules does not count as

98 ECJ, 12 May 2011, C-122/10, *Konsumentombudsmannen v Ving Sverige AB* [2011] ECR I-3903.

misleading omissions under EC law.[99] Though Member States may enact advanced informational duties within the scope of application of the respective Directive, legal protection is supposed to be warranted through contractual means.[100] Via Recital (15) of the Directive, the Community legislator tries to limit Member States' competences in formulating adequate sanctions. That way, Article 7(5) creates conflicts on two sides. On one hand, the foreclosure of national informational duties creates indirect pressure to harmonise those duties, too; on the other hand, the relation between contract law and the law of unfair commercial practices becomes more precarious, since Community law has to be adjusted with the harmonised national law, but also with the non-harmonised national law.

Annex II lists 13 directives in chronological order. The scope of the provisions is extremely wide. The Commission has decided in favour of a chronological order according to the date of publication. First, the consumer-relevant directives that contain informational duties are listed. Systematically examined, the Annex extends to methods of contract conclusion – distance sales, distance sales in financial services and e-commerce, but not door-to-door sales – to special types of contracts – package holidays, timeshares, consumer credit, insurance, life insurance and indemnity insurance – and to capital market information, undertakings for collective investment in transferable securities and securities. The reference to the Directive on indication of prices and the broad reference to the Community code relating to medical products for human use constitute an exceptional position. While the Directive on indication of prices can be regarded as a method of contracting, the reference to pharmaceuticals poses directly the question of why other product-related informational rules (e.g. for food and cosmetics) are not listed.

VII. COMPARATIVE ADVERTISING IN DIRECTIVE 2006/114/EC

2.36 Directive 97/55/EC modified Directive 84/450/EEC, Directive 2006/114/EC integrated Directive 97/55/EC but only with regard to B2B relations. Article 6(2)(a) Directive 2005/29/EC prohibits comparative advertising in B2C relations. In consumer practice, however, the rules on comparative advertising in B2B relations are of much greater importance. That is why they are presented here. Indirectly they also affect the very rudimentary rules of Article 6(2)(a) Directive 2005/29/EC. Case law from the ECJ is only available with regard to the old Directive 97/55/EC which covered both B2B and B2C relations. The cases refer to the numbering in the Directive 97/55/EC; in the text that follows I use

99 This is the meaning of Recital (15).

100 Wilhelmsson, in: Howells/Micklitz/Wilhelmsson, European Directive, Chapter 5(c)(v).

the new numbering under Directive 2006/114/EC. In essence, what was Article 3(a) Directive 97/55/EC has become Article 4 Directive 2006/114/EC. The numbering of (a)–(g) has also changed, but not the content.

1. THE CONCEPT OF COMPARATIVE ADVERTISING

2.37 The objective is defined in Article 1 as the protection of consumers, persons carrying on a trade or business or practising a craft or profession and the interests of the public in general against misleading advertising and the unfair consequences thereof and to lay down the conditions under which comparative advertising is permitted. Article 2(c) contains a definition of comparative advertising: "Any advertising which explicitly or by implication identifies a competitor or goods or services offered by a competitor." In both *Toshiba*[101] and *Pippig*[102] the ECJ clearly rejected efforts to narrow the term "comparative advertising" in order to limit the Directive's scope of application. In *Toshiba* the producer of branded goods could only indirectly be identified; in *Pippig* there was no indication of the producer's name. Hence, in both cases additional efforts were necessary to identify the producers of the comparative products. A wide definition will make it possible to cover all sorts of comparative advertising with the effect that comparative advertising is already existent if there is a declaration that – even if only indirectly – refers to a competitor or the goods or services which he offers. This shows that the ECJ analyses advertising, its identifiability and comparison using a comprehensive view.

The actual core of the Directive is Article 4 Directive 2006/114/EC, which states the requirements which must be met for comparative advertising to be admissible. Article 4(1)(a)–(h) conclusively enumerates the various possibilities under which undertakings can legally engage in comparative advertising. Each letter has its own origin. All in all it represents an attempt to reduce the different legal traditions to a common denominator. The facts at stake can be structured according to their purposes; the principle of proportionality serves as a catalyst. Whenever comparative advertising is suited to support rational consumer conduct, and if it does not interfere with the good reputation of the affected competitor more than necessary to achieve this purpose, then the consumer interest will decide the issue in favour of the admissibility of comparative advertising.

Comparative advertising which is unsuited to function as a basis for rational consumer decisions is misleading advertising as defined Article 4(1)(a), the comparison of goods intended for different purposes as regulated in (b) and (d), as well as advertising which does not objectively compare one or more material,

101 ECJ, 25 October 2001, C-112/99, *Toshiba v Katun* [2001] ECR I-7945.

102 ECJ, 8 April 2003, C-44/01, *Pippig* [2003] ECR I-3095, 3144.

relevant, verifiable and representative features as regulated by (c). Comparisons which exceed the mark of what is necessary are those which discredit or denigrate the trademarks, trade names, other distinguishing marks, goods, services, activities, or circumstances of a competitor as regulated in (h) or which do take unfair advantage of the reputation of a competitor – (e) and (f).

However, as the EC legislator decided to introduce a separate provision into Directive 2005/29/EC, Article 6(2)(a), which prohibits comparative advertising that creates confusion with any products, trademarks or trade names, there was a need to narrow down Article 3(a)(h) to protect traders from this sort of confusion.

The dichotomy of strengthening the rational consumer conduct on the one hand, versus the prohibition on discrediting and damaging the reputation of a competitor on the other suggests that both purposes are equally significant. However, it also indicates the difficulties which arise from the concrete assignment. Even if comparative advertising purports to support rational consumer conduct, the comparison in itself constitutes denigration and damage of reputation. Between both poles there exists a strained relationship. Consumers want not only a communication of facts in the comparison but also an assessment of the comparison as made by the advertiser. The more drastic the assessment, the more "informative" the advertisement. In turn the competitor will do everything in his power to restrict the comparative advertising to the communication of the mere facts. From his point of view a comparison of figures and facts may be acceptable as long as the consumer is required to draw his own conclusions. Such comparative advertising could easily adopt the character of labelling requirements which are purported to inform the consumer but which do not actually contain practical information as the labelling requirements do not assess the mere facts.

Therefore, the central question is when the competitor is visible and what types of comparisons are or are not covered by the Directive. This is a vital decision. Either it falls within the scope of application of the Directive with all the consequences, i.e. in particular with the consequence of a transfer of legitimacy requirements on indirect comparisons with the result of increased informational rights for the consumers, or the issue remains outside the Directive. In principle, an indirect reference to the competitor is sufficient. The borderline is reached where the potential addressee cannot be determined, i.e. if any reference is missing. Then advertising without any comparison has to be assessed as such. In *Toshiba* the ECJ held an indirect comparison to a competitor or his goods or services to be sufficient. According to the words of the ECJ it is unimportant whether the comparison lies in a direct comparison between the competitors or between the offered goods and services of the competitors.[103] In *Pippig* the ECJ affirmed this approach. Any comparative advertisement will

103 ECJ, 25 October 2001, C-112/99, *Toshiba v Katun* [2001] ECR I-7945, at 31.

highlight the advantages of the goods or services offered by the competitor compared to those of other competitors. In order to achieve this, the statements need to emphasise the differences between the compared goods or services by pointing out their main features. A comparison with the competitor follows automatically from such a description. Accordingly, within the scope of application of Directive 2006/114/EC, no distinction may be made between the different parts of the comparison, i.e. between the specifications of the offer of the competitor, the specifications of the offer of the competitor and the relation between those two offers.

2. STRENGTHENING OF THE RATIONAL DECISION-MAKING PROCESS

2.38 Misleading comparative advertising is hardly suited to support the consumer in making his market decision, as stated in Article 4(a). There was strong resistance in some Member States against the legalisation of comparative advertising. However, after the adoption of Directive 97/55/EC those Member States had to give way to the new approach, due to its purpose to completely harmonise the term of comparative advertising. This has been made abundantly clear by the ECJ in *Pippig*. In reference to the historical development, the ECJ refers to the purpose of Directive 97/55/EC (now Directive 2006/114/EC) to reach a complete harmonisation of the conditions under which comparative advertising can be assumed. Such a harmonisation naturally requires that it is to be determined in which cases comparative advertising is admissible within the Community. This leads to the result and the main assumption that "stronger national regulations for the protection against misleading advertising are not to be applied to comparative advertising with respect to form and content of the comparison".[104]

Article 4(a) is to be taken with (g), respectively with Article 6(2)(a) of Directive 2005/29/EC, according to which there must be no creation of confusion in the market place between the advertiser and a competitor or between the advertiser's trademarks, trade names, other distinguishing marks, goods or services and those of a competitor. According to the rationale of the Directive, the differentiation between misleading and confusion is of less significance except for the fact that Article 4(h) prohibits comparative advertising causing actual confusion. Despite timely criticism, the legislator abstained from clarifying by an appropriate formulation that advertising measures which were designed to merely confuse were also included. The systematic reading of the provisions contained in Directives 2006/114/EC and 2005/29/EC proceeds from the inclusion of advertising measures which merely incur a risk of confusion.

[104] AG Tizzano in C-44/01, *Pippig* [2003] ECR I-3095, 3117, at 44.

A major controversy has arisen regarding the question of to what extent it should be qualified as misleading if a supplier of a generic product or of a less well-known trademark refers to an established and well-known trademark or to another sign of distinction. Two fields of problems are to be identified: on the one hand, the question of whether the trademark may be mentioned at all, and, on the other hand, of whether it has to be mentioned. The supplier of a generic product or of a less-known trademark tends to avoid mentioning the products and the producers they refer to. In *Toshiba*, the defendant Katun had confined itself to naming the identification numbers of the products of Toshiba; in *Pippig*, the defendant Harflauer refrained from mentioning the name of the producer (Zeiss).[105] Toshiba argued that the reference to the identification numbers was misleading; *Pippig* protested against the notion that comparative advertising has to mention the name of the producer. Both situations have in common the fact that the producers of brand articles insisted on the explicit mentioning of their trademarks, in order to claim at the same time that mentioning the trademark was illegal as it took unfair advantage of the trademark. The ECJ finally accepted that the use of a trademark of such a product to which the comparison refers is legal as far as is necessary in order to inform the market about the nature of the goods or the object of the services offered.[106] At the same time, it yielded to the arguments of the producers of brand articles insofar as it agreed that an omission of such indication is to be considered as misleading if the trademark is capable of significantly influencing the decision of a buyer to make a purchase. This is supposed to always be the case if the comparison regards competing products, whose respective trademarks show significant differences concerning their outlook.[107] In *Lidl I*[108] and *Lidl II*[109] the ECJ has concretised the requirements. The threshold for misleading advertising is passed if the selection of the products that are compared yields the impression of representativity. With this, the ECJ has indirectly established a duty to mention the trademark, which can hardly be avoided, even if the final decision is up to the national courts in view of the concrete circumstances of the single case.

Article 4(b) requires that it compares goods or services meeting the same needs or intended for the same purpose. The question of whether the comparison

---

105 For different types of advertising, see ECJ, 8 April 2003, C-44/01, *Pippig* [2003] ECR I-3095 at para 13.

106 ECJ, 8 April 2003, C-44/01, *Pippig* [2003] ECR I-3095 at para 50, with reference to ECJ, 25 October 2001, C-112/99, *Toshiba v Katun* [2001] ECR I-7945. However, in *Toshiba* the ECJ did not make such a clear statement as the ECJ now maintains in *Pippig*; see opinion of AG Tizzano, C-44/01 [2003] ECR I-3095, 3110, at 28; on the question of whether the parallel importer may advertise his product at all, see ECJ, 4 November 1997, C-357/95, *Christian Dior* [1997] ECR I-6013.

107 ECJ, 8 April 2003, C-44/01, *Pippig* [2003] ECR I-3095, 3148 at para 53, as confirmed in *Lidl II*: ECJ, 18 November 2010, C-159/09 [2010] ECR I-11761 at para 50.

108 ECJ, 19 September 2006, C-356/04, *Lidl I* [2006] ECR I-8501 at paras 83–84.

109 ECJ, 18 November 2010, C-159/09, *Lidl II* [2010] ECR I-11761 at para 50.

is admissible or not depends on the functional interchangeability of the products. To that extent there is a parallel with the establishment of the relevant market in the competition rules.[110] However this practice has risks as the ECJ tends to narrow the relevant market which might be admissible and sensible in antitrust law but might result in unnecessary restrictions in the law on fair trading. The ongoing liberalisation by the Community legislator of the law governing gifts and discounts allows the advertiser to compare prices with or without considering gifts. A comparison might contain relevant information for the consumer even if the products are not interchangeable. Difficulties arise from Article 4(d) which restricts Article 4(b) to the extent that the comparison needs to refer to products with the same designation if products with designation of origin are to be compared. The provision originates from Article L. 121–10 Code de la consommation[111] and thus it might be explained as to why certain product groups need to be protected against comparative advertising. According to Article 4(d) the comparison of a Bordeaux wine with an Australian Cabernet Sauvignon would be inadmissible. By applying this provision, consumer protection in terms of a logical decision-making process falls by the wayside. The German legislator refrained from implementing this provision.

Lidl I and *Lidl II* define the benchmark for admissible comparisons. The ECJ accepted that the competitor compares two selections of foodstuff provided the products are individually identifiable. This is a rather consumer-friendly decision as it allows for comparing a collection of products without mentioning each product individually.

According to Article 4(c) advertising is admissible if it objectively compares one or more material, relevant, verifiable and representative feature of goods or services. This provision enumerates a number of characteristics which need to be met. "Material" and "relevant" should be understood as a pleonasm as a differentiation seems not to make much sense. It is the purpose of the provision merely to admit those comparisons which do not restrict themselves to trivialities, i.e. which concern the price or the quality. Such features will be "representative" simultaneously so as to insert three terms in order to express one and the same. Contrary to that, the feature "verifiable" has to be interpreted separately. In this connection the question arises when the statement will be verifiable, who will be in a position to verify it and according to which standard the verification is to be conducted. In this respect Article 4(c) results in the consequence that comparative image advertising is prohibited under Community law. The same has to apply to advertising measures which appeal to the subjective perception and the subjective sensation of the consumer. It might rightly be disputed whether image or emotional advertising are supportive of a rational decision-making process; probably it is not. However with the

110 Reich, *supra* note 54.

111 Cf. Calais-Auloy/Temple, 141.

prohibition of image or emotional advertising a main feature of advertising no longer applies, i.e. the pleasure and desire for advertising, in particular comparative advertising. *Landtsheer*[112] opens the door for the admissibility of comparative advertising without comparison.

The consumer is the addressee of advertising in Article 4(c). He needs to conduct the examination and the standard is the informed average consumer (see 2.27). He might only examine comparative advertising if the advertising statement itself communicates the relevant information which is required to draw a comparison. AG Tizzano, as confirmed by the ECJ, has argued in *Lidl*[113] "that the condition concerning the verifiability of the advertiser's statements can be held to have been observed not only, of course, when all the elements of the comparison are included directly in the advertisement but also when the advertisement indicates where and how an average consumer can find those elements easily or in any case clearly makes it possible for the consumer to ascertain what they are from the context and the circumstances of the case". This goes very much along with the information-based philosophy behind the UCPD. The consumer needs to responsibly fulfil the role and function in the internal market as conferred upon him, i.e. he must be in a position to easily obtain the necessary information. In *Lidl I* and *Lidl II*[114] the ECJ has confirmed such an understanding.

3. THE REQUIRED EXTENT OF THE COMPARISON

2.39 An advertising measure in terms of Article 4(a), (b), (d) or (c), is generally admissible. The restrictions which arise from the Directive apply only if the required extent has not been exceeded.

Article 4(d) of Directive 97/55/EC prohibits comparative advertising which discredits or denigrates the trademarks, trade names, other distinguishing marks, goods, services, activities or circumstances of a competitor. Any comparison, however harmless, discredits the goods, services or activities of a competitor. This is, after all the purpose of the comparison. This functional approach has not been followed by Article 4(d). The emphasis is rather put on the manner how, by which means, and with which words the comparison is explained. The objective truth of a statement may be insulting in the context. Irrespective of the situation, the core issue regards the horizon according to which it is determined whether the comparison "discredits" and/or "denigrates" the products of the competitors. The competitor's threshold will be significantly

112 ECJ, 19 April 2007, C-381/05, *Landtsheer* [2007] ECR I-3114 at para 41.

113 Opinion of 29 March 2006, ECJ, 19 September 2006, C-356/04, *Lidl v Colruyt* [2006] ECR I-8501.

114 *Supra* notes 108 and 109.

lower than the consumer's. This might even apply to the average informed competitor standard in comparison to the average consumer who is reasonably well-informed, observant and circumspect. The rational decision-making process of the consumer is not necessarily influenced by emotionally burdened statements; on the contrary, the goodwill of the competitor is heavily strained. In its interpretation the ECJ should allow itself to be influenced by the consideration that advertising measures represent a means to inform which is safeguarded in the constitutions of Member States[115] and in the ECHR.[116] A wider interpretation seems appropriate to sacrifice hastily the protective purpose at the altar of misconceived consumer interests. In *Pippig*[117] the ECJ at least partly put an end to its prior manoeuvre. According to the ECJ, a denigration does not already follow from the fact that the advertiser has decided on a selected range of goods for comparison with his – lower priced – products. The decision of the advertiser is autonomous. This statement is rather striking in the view of the circumstances of the case, where a test buyer had decided on eyeglasses with exceptionally expensive lenses, which are rarely demanded in combination with the particular frame. According to the opinion of the ECJ, it contradicts the aims of the Directive if it can be demanded that the advertiser restrict himself to mentioning only average prices. The ECJ further refused to find it denigrating or discrediting if additional to the mentioning of the competitor's name, its logo and a picture of the shop façade was used. The following limitation – inasmuch as the advertisement acknowledges the legitimacy of the approach of Community law – can only refer to the kind of display of the logo or the facade of the building.[118] The ECJ has thereby given priority to consumer protection. *Lidl I* and *Lidl II*[119] confirm the existing case law but allow for a clarification. The selection of the products chosen for comparison may not produce misleading assumptions on the general price level.

Article 4(e) prohibits comparative advertising which takes unfair advantage of the reputation of a trademark, trade name or other distinguishing marks of a competitor or of the designation of origin of competing products. Irrespective of the fact that Article 4(e) refers to the fairness of advertising measures, it presents the opportunity, at least theoretically, to counteract a liberalisation of comparative advertising. There are good reasons to doubt whether taking advantage of the reputation of a competitor should have been regulated at all. The Community legislator, however, has decided in favour of a prohibition of taking advantage of the reputation and thus generated the question whether Article 4(e) is intended for the protection of trademarks rather than on the liberalisation of comparative advertising – in particular the comparison of well-

115 Thus the decision of the BVerfGE, WRP 2001, 129 – *Benetton-Werbung*.
116 Cf. Micklitz/Weatherill, 231, 279.
117 ECJ, 8 April 2003, C-44/01, *Pippig* [2003] ECR I-3095.
118 Ibid, 3156, at paras 80–83.
119 *Supra* notes 108 and 109.

known brands and generic products, or luxurious products and low-price products (see on no-name products 2.38). Article 4(e), in particular taken together with (f), creates legal uncertainty with regard to the limitations of the comparability of brand-name products in general. Consumer protection can only be served by applying an interpretation which allows the comparison of prices in the sensitive field of protection of trademarks in order to enable rational consumer decision-making. To the extent that the designation of the name serves to enable the comparison for the consumer, in particular to clarify the different products in the comparison and its suppliers, the possible taking advantage of the reputation of a competitor must be accepted. From this starting point it must be decided whether the specific use of the distinctive sign of the branded product is necessary in order to make the comparison transparent for the consumer.

Given the open standards it is hardly surprising that Article 4(e) has been subject to court decisions by the ECJ. In *Toshiba*[120] the ECJ had to decide the question of whether the manufacturer of spare parts was allowed to use the same order numbers as the original offeror or – more generally speaking – the admissibility of a comparison of a generic product and a brand-name product. The ECJ held that stating the article number of the manufacturer of the device alongside the article number of the competitor allows for the assertion that both products are similar in technical features and thus constitutes a comparison in terms of Article 4(c). The question of whether it represents an unfair taking advantage of the reputation of a competitor in terms of Article 4(e) will depend on the overall representation of the advertisement. If it allows for confusion with the product of the original manufacturer or if it suggests an association with the original spare parts, then it might constitute a case of taking unfair advantage of the reputation of a competitor. If the comparison becomes impossible without referring to the article numbers of the original manufacturer, then the comparison should be admissible. The decision has brought no clarification with regard to the limitations. Thus it is not surprising that the national courts asked for an answer to the question of, if so, under which circumstances the comparison of a branded product with generic goods is unfair.

Pippig deals with a situation where the trademark of a well-known producer was compared to one of a less-known producer. The case did not fall within the category of taking unfair advantage of the reputation of a trademark according to Article 4(e), but in the category of denigration and discrediting according to Article 4(h). Nevertheless, the principles established for Article 4(e) can be transferred; the ECJ should be following the dictum of *Toshiba*, that is to say that the traditional law of unfair commercial practices including comparative advertisement has no function in trademark law. That would have made it necessary to draw a parallel with Article 6(1)(c) of the trademark Directive

120 ECJ, 25 October 2001, C-112/99, *Toshiba v Katun* [2001] ECR I-7945.

89/104/EEC (now Directive 2008/95/EC), in order to maintain a coherence between both fields of law. In *Gerolsteiner*[121] the ECJ defined the term "honest practice" in that direction, namely in that it equals the duty not to act in contradiction of the legitimate interests of the owner of the trademark. Thus the Directive on comparative advertising concretises the term "honest practice" of Article 6(1)(c) of Directive 89/104/EWG (Directive 2008/95/EC) in the market. The ECJ has in *Gerolsteiner* given priority to the law of unfair commercial practices over the law of trademarks.[122]

VIII. AGGRESSIVE COMMERCIAL PRACTICES IN DIRECTIVE 2005/29/EC

2.40 Besides the comprehensive general clause on the ban of unfair commercial practices and the specific general clause on the ban of misleading actions or omissions, the ban of aggressive commercial practices is now established, which is likewise conceived as a specific general clause.

1. AGGRESSIVENESS AS A NEW PROHIBITION CLAUSE

In Articles 8 and 9, the Directive creates a new prohibition clause, which so far has not been known in the legal systems of Member States.[123] Article 8 significantly expands the scope of application of Directive 2005/29/EC. However, that innovation did not come as a surprise, since the Commission had announced it in the Green Paper.[124] The Commission was able to rely on the approval of Member States, since "aggressive practices" are not acceptable. Behind this diffuse consensus lies a rethinking of the conceptual patterns of the law of unfair commercial practices. The liberalisation of the law of unfair commercial practices has released a significant potential for aggressiveness. Paradigmatic for this trend are the possibilities opened up to advertisers since the abolition of the law on discounts and on promotional gifts. Promotional actions in particular demonstrate a paradigm change. Similar tendencies appear with the use of devices of modern communication, such as e-mail or mobile phones for the purpose of advertisement. The only question is where the borderline is to be drawn between the advertisement which is "allowed" within the legal system, and where it is not to be tolerated. In a way, every kind of

121 ECJ, 7 January 2004, C-100/02, *Gerolsteiner* [2004] ECR I-691.
122 Ibid, at para 20. Such a reading can be supported by reference to ECJ, 23 February 1999, C-63/97, *BMW v Deenik* [1999] ECR I-905, 941, at para 39.
123 Howells, in: Howells/Micklitz/Weatherill, Chapter 6.
124 COM (2001) 531 final, Recital No. 41, 42, COM (2002) 289 final, Follow-up Communication No. 25 with Annex No. 2, 2.3.

advertisement is to a certain degree aggressive. "A little bit" aggressive is socially tolerated and desirable for the advertisers. It is helpful to distinguish between the content of the advertisement and the way it calls the consumer's attention.[125]

2. AGGRESSION AND CULTURE

2.41 "Aggression" as a social phenomenon contains a strongly marked, culture-specific component, which manifests itself in significant perception differences concerning the aggression and the intrusion potential of advertisements. Thus it is the logical consequence that the liberalised law on sales discounts and on gifts comes before the new prohibition. Greece judges, for example, giving away a CD with a newspaper to be a particularly aggressive form of advertisement. At the same time, such a practice seems very common in the United Kingdom. In addition, in Germany there was no criticism voiced when an established newspaper gave away the first volume of an encyclopaedia to its subscribers. Similar problems exist in the evaluation of so-called cold calling, i.e. telephone calls for the purpose of advertisement without prior notice (see 1.36 with reference to *Alpine Investments*). Its legal treatment is the subject of much discussion in Europe. The Austrian and German ban on telephone advertisements is said to be a refuge of consumer protection. Member States with a liberal tradition are hardly able to comprehend the German-Austrian position. Cultural differences appear in the treatment of direct marketing, i.e. especially with door-to-door sales. The Scandinavian nations have strong reservations against door-to-door sales. Germany bans commercial selling in public places. The Commission seems to be aware of the diverse value judgments concerning commercial practices within the different Member States and acknowledges that for example the direct commercial approach in public can be unwanted for cultural reasons.[126]

Besides those culture-specific differences in the perception, which to a certain degree can be objectified, subjective perception differences also play a significant role. With a keen mind, the consumer can fend off a misleading infringement of his freedom of choice. Fending off aggression takes more than just a keen mind. Fending off telephone advertisement, direct action or a sales approach in public requires a cessation of communication. It can be questioned whether the concept of the average circumspect and informed consumer is sufficient or if it needs a completion as a normative category. When the Community legislator strikes a new path in Articles 8 and 9 UCPD, this is to be understood as a reaction to the changes in the advertising industry itself. It might be off the mark to hastily characterise the new rule on aggressive

125 Howells, in: Howells/Micklitz/Wilhelmsson, Chapter 8(d)(iv).
126 Recital (7) Directive 2005/29/EC.

advertisement as "old wine in new skin". Such a treatment does not cope with this new phenomenon and the defiance for the legal system connected to it. Community law requires an autonomous definition of the term "aggressive commercial practice" and a critical examination of the German legal position.[127]

3. FUNCTION AND SYSTEM OF ARTICLES 8 AND 9

2.42 In spite of the embodiment of the legal ban, the Commission has to deal with the phenomenon that there still are significant differences in the national legal systems. This appears on the one hand with the still unfinished discussion on legal rules concerning promotional actions, which has many parallels to the rule on aggressive advertisements.[128] On the other hand, the Commission had to deal with precarious forms of direct and distance communication (door-to-door sales, street advertisements, cold calling), but it could only establish minimal harmonisation. In the face of these circumstances, the new rule can only be the first step, which will continue to keep courts busy in the future.

Article 8 is to be understood as the basic rule which defines aggressive practices.[129] Article 9 gives corresponding criteria, in order to establish whether a harassment, a constraint or an unlawful influence is present. Those are applicable for all three groups. In this respect, Articles 8 and 9 complement one another.

According to Article 8, a commercial practice shall be regarded as aggressive if, in its factual context, taking account of all its features and circumstances, by harassment or coercion, including the use of physical force, or undue influence, it significantly impairs or is likely to significantly impair the average consumer's freedom of choice or conduct with regard to the product and thereby causes him or is likely to cause him to take a transactional decision that he would not have taken otherwise. Thus an aggressive practice is said to exist if three requirements are met: (1) there must be harassment, coercion or undue influence; (2) the consumer's freedom of choice or conduct must be significantly impaired; and (3) it must cause him to take a transactional decision that he would not have otherwise taken.

According to Article 9, five factors are to be considered to conclude that a harassment, coercion or undue influence is present: (a) the timing, location, nature or persistence of the use; (b) the use of threatening or abusive language or

---

127 See Howells, in: Howells/Micklitz/Wilhelmsson, Chapter 8(a)(iii), who speaks of an "underdeveloped concept".

128 Initially the European Commission intended to regulate sales promotion measures as well. The proposed draft, however, raised considerable objections from the Member States. In September 2005 the European Commission announced the intention to withdraw the draft, see COM (2005) 462 final (27 September 2005).

129 Twigg-Flesner/Parry/Howells/Nordhausen, 3.24 *et seq.*, 45 *et seq.*

behaviour; (c) the exploitation by the trader of any specific misfortune or circumstance of such gravity as to impair the consumer's judgment, of which the trader is aware, to influence the consumer's decision with regard to the producer; (d) any onerous or disproportionate non-contractual barriers imposed by the trader where a consumer wishes to exercise rights under the contract, including rights to terminate a contract or to switch to another product or another trader; and (e) any threat to take any action that cannot legally be taken. Nos. 24 to 31 in the Annex, which list the *per se* prohibited practices, specify the aggressive practices, which under any circumstances, i.e. without consideration of the single case are to be considered unfair. This aim is also once more emphasised by Recital (17) of the Directive.

Article 2(j) offers a legal definition for the term "undue influence".[130] Accordingly, undue influence means "exploiting a position of power in relation to the consumer so as to apply pressure, even without using or threatening to use physical force, in a way which significantly limits the consumer's ability to make an informed decision". Parallel definitions for the terms harassment and coercion are missing. The reasons for this omission remain strangely unexplained. They only repeat the wording of Articles 8 and 9, without adding any sort of explanation as to what is to be understood by harassment or coercion.

IX. ANNEX I OF DIRECTIVE 2005/29/EC: STRUCTURE AND CONCEPT

2.43 The commercial practices listed in Annex I constitute something like a black list of incriminated practices. By use of this list the European legislator attempts to adjust the market. The black list is meant to be a helpful guide, especially in countries with no prior experience with the general clause of Article 5. Directive 93/13/EEC on unfair terms in consumer contracts served as a blueprint (see 3.23). Since 2011 the European Commission has published judgments from Member State courts which are publicly accessible.[131]

1. THE CONCEPT OF THE LIST AND NATIONAL LAW

2.44 The list establishes binding standards that Member States have to implement into national law. The UCPD differs from Directive 93/13/EEC. On the basis of its indicative character the ECJ decided that there was no obligation for implementation of the list.[132] Apart from the fact that the consequences for

130 Article 2(j) talks of "undue influence", while Article 2(e) refers to an "appreciable … impair[ment]", the latter only being important for Articles 8 and 9.

131 https://webgate.ec.europa.eu/ucp/.

132 ECJ, 7 May 2002, C-478/99, *Commission v Sweden* [2002] ECR I-4147.

the development of the law on unfair business terms are problematic, the legal position of the UCPD appears different. The practices listed in Annex I set binding standards that Member States may not deviate from.

The first two references from Belgian courts[133] concerned the question of whether the list pre-empts the possibility for Member States to define more stringent standards. At issue were Belgian prohibitions on joint offers which reach beyond the standards set in the list. Initially the European Commission intended to adopt a separate regulation on sales promotion. As this project has been abandoned, the ECJ has to decide whether maximum harmonisation means that joint offers may only be restricted in the limits of the list or whether Member States may refer to the general clause to set tighter standards.[134] A third reference comes from the German Supreme Court[135] pointing in the same direction. The court asks whether Article 5(2) of the Directive pre-empts Member States from prohibition sweepstakes *in abstracto* without providing evidence that the consumer has been unduly influenced *in concreto*. Again, the reach of the maximum harmonisation doctrine is at stake here. From the beginning the ECJ took a firm stand against abstract *per se* prohibitions against national sales promotion measures. Much to the surprise of the Member States, the ECJ held the Directive to be applicable and declared this type of sales prohibition measures as not being in compliance with the Directive.[136]

2. "CONSIDERED UNFAIR" – "CONSIDERED MISLEADING" – SCOPE FOR INTERPRETATION

2.45 "Considered unfair" leads to the perception that the misleading practices listed do not require further construction under the misleading criteria of the Directive. Thus the relevant threshold or the reference to the "average consumer" model would not apply. The list describes in conjunction with Article 5(5) abstract criteria for risk. There is no room for taking further criteria outside the interpretation of each number into account.

The logic of such argumentation cannot be completely denied. Practices that are not directly covered by one of the prohibition clauses would then automatically be legalised. This seems possible in situations where the practice touches the matter

133 ECJ, 23 April 2009, Joined cases C-261, C-299/07, *VTB-VAB v Total Belgium* [2009] ECR I-02949.

134 See on this issue already, Stuyck/Terryn/van Dyck, 107, at 149 *et seq*.

135 Bundesgerichtshof, Beschluss vom 5.6.2008, *Europäische Zeitschrift für Wirtschaftsrecht* 2008, 542.

136 ECJ, 23 April 2009, Joined Cases C-261, C-299/07, *VTB-VAB v Total Belgium* [2009] ECR I-02949 at para 50; ECJ, 4 January 2010, C-304/08, *Plus Warengesellschaft* [2010] ECR I-217 at para 37; ECJ, 9 November 2010, C-540/08 *Mediaprint* [2010] ECR I-10909 at para 18; ECJ, 30 June 2011, C-288/10, *Wamo* [2011] ECR I-5835 at para 31; ECJ, 17 January 2013, C-206/11, *Köck* [2013] ECR I-nyr.

described but does not fulfil all of its requirements. The list has so far had a negative publicity effect. It shall document which practices are under no circumstances tolerated within the Community. Remaining gaps can in narrow confines be closed via usage of the general clause (for role and function of the general clause see 2.20).

The regulatory technique causes difficulties. Annex I names commercial practices which are in all circumstances considered unfair, but then distinguishes only between misleading and aggressive practices. Examples of unfair practices that are neither misleading nor aggressive are not given. Practical problems arise insofar as it is not clear whether the incriminated practices only apply in cases where the consumer is misled or irrespective of a deception. A good example is the prohibition of progressive customer promotion ("pyramid selling") in No. 14 of the Annex that does not cover all the relevant situations if one focuses only on deception.[137] From the perspective of the Directive's conception, only a holistic view can be appropriate. That means that the elements of the prohibition of misleading consumers and the prohibition of aggressive promotion, which are suitable for an interpretation, can be used for the construction of the various incriminated practices. On the other hand it is not possible to use the general clause as laid down in Article 5, because it has only a reserve function. This general clause remains applicable in narrow confines, but it can be seen that a commercial practice has to be sanctioned mainly under the concept of unfairness pursuant to Article 5; it thus remains no more than a supplement to the list of prohibited practices.

3. EXCLUSIVE OR NON-EXCLUSIVE

2.46 From the very beginning of the legislative process, the Commission took the position that it had to be an exclusive list. Recital (17) refers to a full list of all such practices. The wording and the lack of the word "especially" suggest that the list shall in fact be exclusive. But such a reading is not persuasive from any point of view. It would deprive the UCPD of any meaning; for the Directive shall – even if only in a limited way – guarantee an adjustment to the development of the forms of advertising. From a historical perspective such a reading is not convincing, because, for example, the European Parliament wanted to have several additional clauses included in the list. Pursuant to the spirit and the purpose of the Directive, it must be possible to amend the list; the question concerns the way this should be done. An amendment would be possible in the form of a final decision by the ECJ if the Court regards itself as competent to decide the case in full.[138] The passage, which was finally included, goes on to clarify that the list can only be lengthened (or shortened) by amending the UCPD.

---

137 See Micklitz/Monazzahian/Rössler.

138 Wilhelmsson, in: Howells/Micklitz/Wilhelmsson, Chapter 5(d)(i).

X. CODES OF PRACTICE IN DIRECTIVE 2005/29/EC

2.47 Over and over again the Commission has tried to grant codes of practice within the system of the European unfair practices law a clearly guaranteed legal status. Theoretically, this would have been possible by a Co-Regulation.[139] As regards content, it concerns the attempt to combine elements of binding law with the setting of voluntary standards. The European Commission little by little had to reduce its demands during the legislative process. Eventually, the Commission failed in its efforts for a stronger legal and conceptual integration of the codes in connection with the UCPD.[140]

1. FUNCTION OF THE CODES OF PRACTICE

2.48 According to Article 10, the UCPD shall not exclude the control of unfair commercial practices by code owners and recourse to such bodies by the persons or organisations referred to in Article 11 if proceedings before such bodies are in addition to the court or administrative proceedings referred to in Article 11. The provision itself is hardly comprehensible. One can only understand its content against the background of the debate in the Green Paper[141] and the follow up Communications[142] about the significance of codes of practice and the version of Article 10 in the first proposal of June 2003. There, the codes were specified even more precisely. National codes and codes on a Community level were explicitly mentioned. This passage was deleted without substitution. Actually, according to the Commission's view, the Community wide codes were meant to quicken the formation of a European unfair commercial practices law.

2. SUBSTANTIVE REQUIREMENTS AND LEGAL CONSEQUENCES OF A BREACH

2.49 Article 2(f) provides a legal definition for codes. Accordingly, a "code of conduct" means an agreement or set of rules not imposed by law, regulation or administrative provisions of a Member State, which defines the behaviour of traders who undertake to be bound by the code in relation to one or more particular commercial practices or business sectors. The negative part of the

---

139 Le Livre blanc sur la gouvernance européenne COM (2001) 428 final, in particular Suivi du Livre blanc sur la gouvernance européenne – Pour un usage mieux adapté des instruments, COM (2002) 278 final, 5 June 2002, recours encadré à un mécanisme de corégulation, see Howells, in: Collins (ed.), *The Forthcoming EC Directive*, 119.

140 Howells, in: Howells/Micklitz/Wilhelmsson, Chapter 7(d).

141 COM (2001) 531 final.

142 COM (2002) 289 final.

definition is self-evident, because otherwise it would constitute mandatory law, i.e. statutes or regulations. The specification is remarkable in that a code in terms of the Directive presupposes that the traders undertake to be bound by it. The definition does not state what this means in particular. One should, however, be able to have regard to Article 6(2)(b)(i). A mere goodwill declaration is not sufficient, but rather there must be a clear-cut obligation, compliance with which is reviewable.[143] Even with clarification of the jungle of terms used in accordance with voluntary self-binding mechanisms, one should not overlook the fact that basically an adjustment of terms within the Community context is necessary. It is mostly in older directives governing the law on unfair commercial practices that the concept of "code" appears without the existence of such clarification.

Neither Article 10 nor the Recitals make a statement about the scope of application or define the codes' substantive requirements. Thus Article 10 applies to codes of practice that refer to unfair business practices at large (B2B and B2C). One can hardly imagine that the codes address only consumers. The necessary revision must be made pursuant to Article 6(2). Substantive requirements follow indirectly from the definition of "code owners" – Article 2(g) – according to which codes must also include monitoring measures for their compliance. An open question is whether codes of practice may go further than the practices mentioned in the UCPD, i.e. whether they may voluntarily prohibit practices that are legal under Community law. Given the importance that the consumer has for the realisation of the law of market communication, caution must be exercised. Over-ambitious prohibitions may easily pursue other objectives than protection of the consumer.

The procedure for setting up the codes is regulated in neither Article 10 nor Article 2(f). In light of the UCPD's explicit purpose and its limitation to B2C it would have been self-evident for the Commission to give higher significance to the possible participation of consumer organisations. The rest of the debate in the Green Paper is to be found in Recital (20). Accordingly – as cited at the end in the third sentence of the rationale – "consumers' organisations could be informed and involved in the drafting of codes of conduct".[144] This, indeed, is an extremely vaguely formulated objective that carefully avoids naming the addressee of this objective.

Indirectly this is achieved pursuant to Article 10. There, the code owners are mentioned. According to Article 2(g) this includes any entity, including a trader or group of traders, which is responsible for the formulation and revision of a code of conduct and/or for monitoring compliance with the code by those who have undertaken to be bound by it. Under the circumstances this can only apply to national and European trade associations. Member States' role remains largely

143 Howells, in: Howells/Micklitz/Wilhelmsson, Chapter 7(h).

144 Recital (20).

unclear. Article 10 explicitly mentions that Member States may "encourage" the setting up of codes of practice.

Article 6(2) functions as a link to the legal definition of codes of conduct. Accordingly, the non-compliance with a code by which a trader declared to be bound and to which he has referred in his commercial practices, is to be regarded as misleading. The *per se* assumption of unfairness stays in the draft that became law, but unlike in the original proposal the formula can no longer be reversed. As long as the codes substantiate the professional "due diligence" standard and thereby can decide what is right and wrong, and fair and unfair, traders can consider themselves secure as long as they comply with the self-made rules. The codes' modified meaning, in particular in connection with the professional due diligence in terms of Article 5(2), has the effect that a trader who undertakes to be bound by the code and who complies with the standards stipulated therein does not automatically act lawfully.[145] Article 6(2)(b) does not constitute a safe harbour for traders.

XI. BURDEN OF PROOF IN DIRECTIVES 97/55/EC (NOW 2006/114/EC) AND 2005/29/EC

2.50 The burden of proof as provided in the UCPD and in Directive 97/55/EC (2006/114/EC) concerning comparative advertising are not adjusted to each other. This arises from the different purposes and protection goals of unfair/misleading advertising on one hand and comparative advertising on the other.

1. THE REGULATION IN DIRECTIVE 2005/29/EC

2.51 Basically, the burden of proof of the unfairness of a commercial practice still rests with the plaintiff. This legal consequence was explicitly emphasised in the first proposal's Recital (69). Otherwise the facilitative regulation in Article 12 of the adopted version of the Directive, which literally implements Article 6 of Directive 84/450/EEC (now Article 7 Directive 2006/114/EC), remains in place.

In fact, the discretionary scope is much narrower than the formulation of Article 12 suggests. The weights have been shifted, not only because in *Pippig*[146] the ECJ for the first time explained the importance of Article 6 of Directive 84/450/EEC (now Article 7 of Directive 2006/114/EC), but also because Recital (21) of the UCPD lays the decision about the allocation of the burden of proof in the hands of Member States and simultaneously emphasises the need to "enable courts and administrative authorities to require traders to produce evidence as

145 See Collins, in: Collins (ed.), *The Forthcoming EC Directive*, 1, 30.

146 ECJ, 8 April 2003, C-44/01, *Pippig* [2003] ECR I-3095.

to the accuracy of factual claims they have made". This wording is much more precise than Recital (16) of Directive 84/450/EEC. There it reads: "The advertiser should be able to prove, by appropriate means, the material accuracy of the factual claims he makes in his advertising, and may in appropriate cases be required to do so by the court or administrative authority". Apart from the revised perspective – in the UCPD the emphasis lies on the institutions that are authorised to intervene – also the limitation on "appropriate cases" was omitted. The Recitals strengthen an interpretation under which Member States' discretionary scope for the allocation of the burden of proof is gradually confined.

2. THE REGULATION IN DIRECTIVE 97/55/EC (NOW 2006/114/EC)

2.52 Directive 97/55/EC brought about a significant change to the burden of proof rule in Article 6 of Directive 84/450/EEC (now Article 7 Directive 2006/114/EC). Accordingly, Member States delegate authority to the courts, which can request the advertiser, in cases of comparative advertising, to provide corresponding evidence on short notice. The Directive must be subdivided. In the case of misleading advertising there are good reasons and recent trends in case law that argue for a placing of the burden of proof on the advertiser, at least insofar as the advertising has a verifiable factual core. In the case of comparative advertising things are quite clear. If there is a conflict, the advertiser has to prove that the comparative information he submitted can be verified. Article 6 as it is formulated in Directive 97/55/EC (now Article 7 Directive 2006/114/EC) has shifted the burden of proof to the advertiser's disadvantage, which is just and equitable. Thus the person who makes a statement must also be able to provide evidence of its trueness.

The significance of the burden of proof rule became obvious in *van Doren v Lifestyle*.[147] Even though the decision does not deal with comparative advertising it does nevertheless apply insofar as the ECJ addressed the problem of parallel imports. The national court brought the question before the ECJ whether Articles 28 and 30 EC (now 30 and 34 TFEU) are to be construed in such a way that they allow the application of national regulations according to which a person who invokes an exhaustion of trademark law pursuant to Article 7 of Directive 89/104/EEC has to demonstrate and, if necessary, to prove that the goods he distributes were already put on the market within the European Economic Area beforehand by the owner of the trademark or with his consent. Advocate General Stix-Hackl regards, with good reason, a burden of proof rule that as a result prohibits parallel imports as being incompatible with Community

[147] ECJ, 8 April 2003, C-244/00, *van Doren* [2003] ECR I-3051.

law.[148] The ECJ assented to this conclusion. It concluded that a burden of proof rule that generally obliges a third person who is sued by the trademark owner to bring evidence for the exhaustion of the trademark right, because it constitutes a legal exception, is incompatible with Article 5 and Article 7 of the First Trademark Directive 89/104/EEC (now 2008/95/EC); Articles 28 and 30 EC (now Articles 30 and 34 TFEU) could however make a modification necessary. The onus is, the ECJ continues, on the trademark owner to provide evidence that the goods were originally put on the market by him or with his consent outside the European Economic Area, if the third person were able to prove that there would be an actual risk of market segregation if he were obliged to provide such proof. If the trademark owner manages to provide such evidence, the onus is on the third person to prove that the trademark owner has consented to the good's further distribution within the European Economic Area.

148 Ibid.

CHAPTER 3

UNFAIR TERMS IN CONSUMER CONTRACTS

Hans-W. Micklitz

CONTENTS

Bibliography:

H.E. Brandner/P. Ulmer, The Community Directive on Unfair Terms in Consumer Contracts: Some Critical Remarks on the Proposal Submitted by the EEC Commission, *CMLRev* 1991, 647; S. Bright, Winning the battle against unfair contract terms, *Legal Studies* 2000, 331; D. Brock, *Der Schutz der Verbraucher vor mißbräuchlichen Klauseln im französischen Privatrecht*, 1998, 107–118; F. Brunetta d'Usseaux, Formal and substantive aspects of the transparency principle in European private law, *Consumer Law Journal* 1997, 231; J. Calais-Auloy/H. Temple, *Droit de la consommation*, 8th ed. 2010; 157; H. Collins, Good Faith in European Contract Law, *Oxford Journal of Legal Studies* 1994, 229; R. Damm, Europäisches Verbrauchervertragsrecht und AGB-Recht, *JZ* 1994, 161; C. Erwine/J. Hunter, Completion of the Internal Market and Consumer Protection, *JCP* 1994, 207; J. Ghestin/I. Marchessaux-van Melle, *La Semaine Juridique* 1995, Ed. E No. 481, 319; St. Grundmann, *Europäisches Schuldvertragsrecht*, 1999; D. Hoffmann, *AGB-Kontrolle im öffentlichen Sektor*, in: Lehofer/Meyer (eds.), *Geschäftsbedingungen in Österreich und der Europäischen Union, Verbraucherrecht und Verbraucherpolitik, Jahrbuch des österreichischen Konsumentenrechts*, Vol. 17, 1998, 65; E. Hondius, *Unfair Terms in Consumer Contracts*, 1987; G. Howells/S. Weatherill, *Consumer Protection Law*, 3rd ed. 2005; H.-W. Micklitz, A Common Approach to the Enforcement of Unfair Commercial Practices and Unfair Contract Terms, in: van Boom/Akseli/Garde (eds.), *Experiencing Unfair Commercial Practices – On the impact of the 2005 UCP Directive on marketing, sales practice, enforcement strategies and national legal system*, forthcoming 2014; H.-W. Micklitz/M. Radeideh, The European database on unfair terms in consumer contracts, *JCP* 2005, 325; H.-W. Micklitz/N. Reich, Von der Klausel- zur Missbrauchskontrolle, *EWuZW* 2013, 457; H.-W. Micklitz/N. Reich, The Court and the Rosebud (The Sleeping Beauty), *CMLRev* 2014 forthcoming; H.-W. Micklitz/N. Reich, Luxemburg ante portas – jetzt auch im deutschen "runderneuerten" AGB-Recht?, in: Wurmnest et al. (ed.), *Festschrift für Ulrich Magnus*, 2014, 631; C. Pavillon, ECJ 26 October 2006, Case C-168/05 *Mostaza Claro v. Centor Movil Milenium SL* – The Unfair Contract Terms Directive: The ECJ's Third Intervention into Domestic Law, *ERPL* 2007, 736; T. Pfeiffer, in: Grabitz/Hilf II/Wolf, *Das Recht der Europäischen Union, Kommentar, A 5, Klauseln in Verbraucherverträgen*, 1999; N. Reich, More Clarity after 'Claro'?, *ERCL* 2007, 41; N. Reich, *General Principles of EU Civil Law*, 2013; N. Reich et al., *Understanding EU Law*, 2nd ed. 2005; N. Reich, L'information du consommateur, in: Serra/Calais-Auloy, *Concurrence et Consommation*, 1994, 23; N. Reich/H.-W. Micklitz, *Europäisches Verbraucherrecht*, 4th ed., 2003; P. Rott, Informationspflichten in Fernabsatzverträgen als Paradigma für die Sprachenproblematik im Vertragsrecht, *ZVerglRWiss* 98 (1999), 382; P. Rott/B. Butters, Öffentliche Versorgungsbedingungen und Vertragsgerechtigkeit im Lichte des Gemeinschaftsrechts, *VuR* 1999, 107; M. Schilling, Inequality of Bargaining Power versus Market for Lemons: Legal Paradigm Change and the Court of Justice Jurisprudence on Directive 93/13 on unfair terms, *ELR* 2008, 336; J. Schmidt-Salzer, EG-Richtlinie über mißbräuchliche Klauseln, Inhaltskontrolle von AVB und Deregulierung der Versicherungsaufsicht, *VersR* 1995, 1261; J. Stuyck, Joined Cases C-240/98 to C-244/98, *Océano Grupo Editorial SA vs. Rocio Murciano Quintero* and *Salvat Editore SA vs. José M. Sànchez Alcón Prades et al.*, *CMLRev* 2001, 719; M. Tenreiro, *Les clauses abusives dans les contrats avec les consommateurs*, 1993; E. Terryn et al. (eds.), *Landmark Cases of EU Consumer Law – In Honour of Jules Stuyck*, 2013; S. Whittaker, Unfair Contract Terms, Public Services and the Construction of a European Conception of Contract, *LQR* 2000, 95; T. Wilhelmsson, Public Interest Litigation on Unfair Terms, in: Micklitz/Reich (eds.), *Public Interest Litigation before European Courts*, Vol. 2, 1996, 385; T. Wilhelmsson, *Critical Studies in Private Law*, 1992; T. Wilhelmsson, *Social contract law and European integration*, 1994; T. Wilhelmsson, Control of Unfair Contract Terms and Social Value: EC and Nordic Approaches, *JCP* 1993, 435; T. Wilhelmsson, The Proposal of an Unfair Terms Directive – a Nordic Perspective, *ECLJ* 1992, 77; C. Willett, *Fairness in Consumer Contracts, The Case of Unfair Terms*, 2007.

I. THE STARTING POINT

3.1 The legislatures of the Member States of the European Community had dealt intensively with the regulation of unfair contractual terms between 1970 and 1990. Justification for a consumer policy intervention can be found in the asymmetry of economic powers, which was only possible because of the principle of contractual freedom: contracts are pre-formulated by one contractual party, in particular by undertakings or their associations, and are unilaterally imposed on the other party, in particular on consumers, without negotiation. During that process the undertaking primarily considers its own rationalisation interest and its interest of shifting the risk. The "costs of the transaction" thereby saved will benefit the undertaking and not necessarily the consumer or the public in general.

The other contracting parties – in particular economically weaker and legally ignorant consumers – lack bargaining power and economic incentives to enforce their own and more advantageous conditions. There is no collectivisation of consumer interests in the form of special representation that participates in contractual negotiations, unlike in the field of employment law.[1] This is the reason why pre-formulated contractual terms constitute a unilateral use of economic power where utilised against private ultimate consumers. These terms do not share the guarantee of contractual fairness which according to the liberal doctrine characterises freely negotiated contracts based on self-determination.

For the EC, the issue of approximating Member State laws on contractual terms, irrespective of their form, must be achieved against the background of the respective substantive contract law. A term which might be offensive in one legal system might be acceptable under another provided that corresponding legal remedies provide adequate protection for the consumer. Exemption terms in standard business conditions might violate the "*ordre public*" *per se*. The prohibition of those terms could be of completely different significance depending on the legal system, as the provisions of contract law against which the exemption clause is to be measured might be different themselves.

The consumer policy programmes of the EC provided a common base of action for the suppression of unfair contractual terms, in which, however, the Commission did not produced concrete proposals until 1990. Previously, in 1984, it published a Green Paper in which it suggested two possibilities for action to be considered.[2] First, the enactment of a directive on unfair terms which would contain a definition of terms alongside a so-called black list of terms – according to the example of the German Law governing Standard Business Conditions (AGBG-Gesetz of 1974) – and which should be prohibited throughout the Community (e.g. the complete exemption of contractual obligations). The second option concerned negotiations between trade associations and consumer associations which are conducted under the supervision of a governmental authority. Reference was made to the UK Office of Fair Trading which negotiates the so-called Codes of Practice with supplier associations and the Nordic *ombud*-model which applies standards of conduct of the consumer-ombudsman. These kinds of negotiations could apply at Community level tailored to specific trades, such as cars, electronic devices and package tours.

---

1 Cf. the attempt by Calais-Auloy, 115.

2 COM (1984) 55, 9 February 1984.

1. THE PROPOSALS OF THE COMMISSION

3.2 A comparative law analysis conducted by the Dutch legal expert Professor Hondius[3] provided the Commission with a basis to legitimate Community-wide action. However, the internal negotiations in the Commission were characterised by conflicts on the legal basis, its competences, the extent and intensity of the Community initiative which had not been overcome until the presentation of the first proposal of a directive on 14 September 1990.[4] Overall this proposal had been critically assessed by the Economic and Social Committee[5] as well as by the European Parliament[6] and this resulted in amendments. The scientific, legal and policy discussion indicated the conceptual and textual problems with the proposal.[7] This discussion influenced the further negotiations within the Commission.

3.3 On 5 March 1992 the Commission presented a new proposal.[8] This was based on Article 100a EEC (now Article 114 TFEU) and thus had to specify reasons that the distortion of competition as provoked by the differing legal provisions compellingly justified Community measures of a high level of protection. The proposal suggests a nexus between the opening of the internal market for consumer goods and services, and the protection of the consumer against unfair terms. The extended freedom of choice of the consumer as a Union citizen (or resident) is to be accompanied by an increased protective standard relating to unfair terms. This is shown in three ways:

(1) initially, general criteria are defined according to which contractual terms may be unfair; however, contrary to the initial proposal there is a differentiation between "individually negotiated" and "not individually negotiated" (i.e. standard) terms;
(2) at Community level a "black list" is to be established which prohibits a minimum number of unfair terms *per se*; and
(3) the Member States are responsible for effective protection of the consumer rights which are to be established this way.

Article 3 of the proposal defined a non-individually negotiated contractual term as unfair:[9]

3 Hondius.
4 OJ C 243, 28 September 1990, 2.
5 Opinion of 24 April 1991, OJ C 159, 17 June 1991, 34.
6 Opinion of 20 November 1991, OJ C 326, 16 December 1991, 108.
7 European Consumer Law Group, JCP 1991, 107; Brandner/Ulmer, *CMLRev* 1991, 647; Wilhelmsson, *ECLJ* 1992, 77.
8 COM (1992) 66 OJ C 73, 24 March 1992, 7.
9 Considerations in Wilhelmsson, *ECLJ* 1992, 85 ff.

> "if, of itself or in combination with another term or terms of the same contract, or of another contract upon which it is dependent, contrary to the requirements of good faith:
> - it causes to the detriment of the consumer a significant imbalance in the parties' rights and obligations arising under the contract, or
> - It causes the performance of the contract to be significantly different from what the consumer could legitimately expect."

Additionally, it is required that terms be in plain, intelligible language; the requirement of transparency shall be included in Community law. Community law should only regulate contracts entered into between commercial suppliers and consumers; so-called small (scale) traders and self-employed persons, etc. are not subject to the scope of protection of the Directive. On the other hand, the activities of publicly owned business should be included (Article 2(c)); however it is unclear to which extent public services were covered (13.15).

Strikingly contrary to German and French law, but in a similar way to English law, Article 4 of the proposal contained criteria for the unfairness of terms in individual contracts. Two requirements need to be met cumulatively:

- it causes the performance of the contract to be unduly detrimental to the consumer, and
- it has been imposed upon the consumer as a result of the economic power of the seller or supplier and/or the consumer with economic and/or intellectual weakness.

If this provision had been incorporated into Community law it would have constituted the acknowledgment of an element under Community law of *Sittenwidrigkeit* according to German law, *abus de faiblesse* according to French law, or "unconscionability" according to the common law standard. These contain open concepts which need to be specified by case law and whose significance depends on the legal system.

In the amended proposal, the concretising of the general clauses was dealt with in an appendix. According to the appendix, two terms which are also considered unfair in individual contracts are distinguished – in this case the preponderance of one contractual party over the other is presumed under Community law – as are those terms which are only considered unfair in standard business conditions.

The proposal contained a number of requirements for Member States in order to prevent the use of unfair terms in contracts. This included in particular the right granted to the purchaser in Article 6 to receive goods which are in compliance with the contract and to find appropriate remedies in the event of defects. If guarantees are provided (there is no requirement to do so), certain minimum requirements need to be met, i.e. they must be granted either for a minimum of twelve months or for the ordinary duration, provided it is less than twelve months. Member States are required to prohibit the use of unfair terms in order to secure effective legal protection; this should also include a sort of legal action taken by consumer associations within the Community.

2. THE DELIBERATIONS IN THE COUNCIL OF MINISTERS

3.4 The deliberations on the proposal in the Council led to discussions among Member States on the scope of application of the Directive and the extent of review. The common position of the Council of 22 September 1992[10] contained a compromise and entailed a significant reduction of the scope of application and the level of protection. According to Recital (12) it is justified by the principle of "partial harmonisation". In detail the following points need to be emphasised:

(1) The Directive shall only be applicable to pre-formulated terms, not to individually negotiated contracts.
(2) The element of unfairness is to be determined as a combination of the above alternatively stated elements and thus simultaneously narrowed down (Article 3(1)).

Recital (13) refers to the necessity of an "overall evaluation of the different interests involved". This is constituted by the principle of good faith which may be satisfied by the seller or supplier:

> "where he deals fairly and equitably with the other party whose legitimate interests he has to take into account".

(3) Review is not applicable to terms which "reflect mandatory statutory or regulatory provisions and the provisions or principles of international conventions" (Article 1(2)). Thus the standard business conditions of public utility undertakings and public transport enterprises are not within the scope of application of the Directive, provided they are based on governmental or international legal instruments – even if they exclude rights from consumers in an inappropriate manner.
(4) Review is not applicable to the price/quality ratio and to the main subject matter of the contract provided that "the term is in plain intelligible language".
(5) Statutory warranty provisions are no longer included; they are to be considered in particular directives. In fact, their failed regulation has been the starting point for the creation of Directive 99/44/EC on the sale of

10 Council document 8406 January 1992, *JCP* 1992, 469.

consumer goods, which is the focus of the attention of Member States (see 4.1).

(6) The appendix functions as per Article 3(3) only as an indication of a non-exhaustive list of terms "which may be regarded as unfair". This legitimises their prohibition by Member States without expressly prohibiting them (grey indication list instead of black list).

(7) According to Article 8 the Directive is drafted as a minimum directive to the extent that it is compatible with Community law – in particular Article 28 EC (now Article 34 TFEU on the free movement of goods).

Overall, the common position is characterised by a significant reduction in scope of protection, protective purpose and enforcement of protection which makes it more difficult to achieve the actual purpose of the Directive, i.e. to provide consumers and sellers or suppliers with minimum standards for the drafting of B2C contracts within the internal market. The Commission rightly expressed its regrets about this reduction but did not succeed in putting its proposals through the Council – similar to the European Parliament.

3. THE PROTECTIVE PURPOSE OF DIRECTIVE 93/13/EEC OF 5 APRIL 1993

3.5 Council Directive 93/13/EEC relating to the approximation of the laws and administrative provisions of Member States concerning unfair terms in consumer contracts,[11] which was adopted on 5 April 1993, purports to aim at partial harmonisation of consumer contract law in Member States. It pursues the protection of the consumer as a contractual party that is normally the weaker party.[12] This protective ambit is thus narrower than the purpose of the varying legislation of Member States, in particular where the protective purpose is meant to cover any pre-formulated contractual term notwithstanding the qualification of the contracting parties. However, as regards the intensity of review, it differentiates between the persons affected (sellers or suppliers on the one hand and consumers on the other). Because of the principle of minimum harmonisation, Member States may include persons in their legislation which are outside the notion of the term "consumer". In terms of the interpretation of the Directive, the consumer policy protective purpose must not be forgotten, which – like other consumer protection directives – requires an autonomous interpretation.[13]

The protective purpose is also expressed in the recitals, in particular in (6) and (8) to (10):

---

11 OJ L 95, 21 April 1993, 29.

12 For a critical review of the consumer related purpose, Schilling, 336.

13 Reich, *General Principles of EU Civil Law*, at para 2.12.

> "Whereas, in order to facilitate the establishment of the internal market and to safeguard the citizen in his role as consumer when acquiring goods and services under contracts which are governed by the laws of Member States other than his own, it is essential to remove unfair terms from those contracts."

> "Whereas the two Community programmes for a consumer protection and information policy underlined the importance of safeguarding consumers in the matter of unfair terms of contract; whereas this protection ought to be provided by laws and regulations which are either harmonized at Community level or adopted directly at that level. Whereas in accordance with the principle laid down under the heading 'Protection of the economic interests of the consumers', as stated in those programmes: 'acquirers of goods and services should be protected against the abuse of power by the seller or supplier, in particular against one-sided standard contracts and the unfair exclusion of essential rights in contracts'. Whereas more effective protection of the consumer can be achieved by adopting uniform rules of law in the matter of unfair terms."

Through such minimum protection the Community legislator hopes to promote and enhance of cross-border transactions (Recital (5)):

> "Whereas, generally speaking, consumers do not know the rules of law which, in Member States other than their own, govern contracts for the sale of goods or services; whereas this lack of awareness may deter them from direct transactions for the purchase of goods or services in another Member State."

From such legislation the Council moreover expects to combat distortions of competition in order to thereby justify its competence under Article 100a EEC (now Article 114 TFEU).

II. THE SCOPE OF APPLICATION OF DIRECTIVE 93/13/EEC

1. OBJECTIVE SCOPE OF APPLICATION

3.6 The Directive determines its objective and subjective scope of application autonomously and in distinction from the relevant provisions of Member States. It covers all types of sale and service contracts, unless specifically exempted (3.10–3.13). In *Asbeek*,[14] the Court confirmed that it also "applies to residential tenancy agreements".

[14] ECJ, 30 May 2013, C-488/11 [2013] ECR I-nyr.

In *Pereničova*,[15] the ECJ was given the opportunity to engage in a discussion on the relationship between unfair terms and unfair commercial practices. The *Pereničova* case dealt with the control of unfair commercial practices required in Directive 2005/29/EC (2.4) and its impact on the validity of an incorrect statement on the annual percentage rate (58.76% instead of the indicated 48.63%) in the context of an *individual* litigation relating to a B2C credit agreement under Slovakian law So what is at stake is the degree to which unfair commercial practices might have an impact on the validity of *individual* and maybe even *standardised* contractual relations. The ECJ[16] focuses exclusively on Article 4(1) of Directive 93/13/EEC, according to which it is possible to include a commercial practice deemed to be unfair in the assessment of the unfairness of the contract terms as "one element among others" (ECJ, *Pereničova*, Recital (43)). The AG emphasises[17] that "Article 4(1) of Directive 93/13/EEC can be regarded as something of a gateway for assessments under the legislation on fair trading practices." What both the AG and the ECJ are advocating is a more consistent approach to unfair commercial practices and unfair terms, which raises complicated questions on the relationship between the two directives.[18]

a) Standard contracts

3.7 First of all, so-called standard contracts are subject to the Directive, i.e. standard business conditions which have been pre-formulated for a number of cases and which are used by the supplier against the consumer. French law refers to "*contrats d'adhésion*" where contractual terms are normally not negotiated. Contracts are marketing instruments of undertakings which standardise performances and conditions and typically only consider the marketing interest of the party wishing to rely upon them. The Directive recognises the particular relevance and, to a certain extent, the risk of standard contracts at two points, namely in Article 3(2) by introducing a shifting of the burden of proof:

> "Where any seller or supplier claims that a standard term has been individually negotiated, the burden of proof in this respect shall be incumbent on him."

According to Article 7(2), Member States are required to introduce special procedures with regard to standard contract terms so that contractual terms "drawn up for general use" could be removed from the contracts.

---

15 ECJ, 15 March 2012, C-453/10 [2012] ECR I-nyr.

16 Ibid, at 43.

17 Ibid, at 124.

18 For a deeper reading Micklitz, in: Boom/Akseli/Garde.

b) *Pre-formulated terms*

3.8 The Directive also applies to terms which have not been individually negotiated, Article 3(1) without falling within the definition of "standard contracts". According to this definition:

> "A term shall always be regarded as not individually negotiated where it has been drafted in advance and the consumer has therefore not been able to influence the substance of the term, particularly in the context of a pre-formulated standard contract. The fact that certain aspects of a term or one specific term have been individually negotiated shall not exclude the application of this Article to the rest of a contract if an overall assessment of the contract indicates that it is nevertheless a pre-formulated standard contract."

The legal definition and the legislative history of the Directive show that the Community legislator intended to introduce into Community law a special category falling between genuine individual contracts, namely agreements, and standard business conditions. This category consists of so-called "pre-formulated (individual) terms". These can be formulated in advance by sellers or suppliers and third parties, such as handbooks or computer programmes, by advisory professions such as notaries or lawyers, or by associations and the like. The mode of pre-formulation is irrelevant.

The drafters of the Directive seem to proceed from the fact that an additional element is required that is supplementary to the pre-formulation in order to make the Directive applicable, namely that the consumer was unable to influence the pre-formulation. The connection of this element with the scope of application is unclear, as it will be difficult to prove such a nexus. Thus it appears correct to consider pre-formulation as a presumption that under normal circumstances the consumer had no opportunity to have an impact on a contract's contents. This would accurately reflect the typical negotiation situation between the consumer and the sellers or suppliers, in which contractual conditions and terms are not negotiated specifically but rather use is made of pre-formulated contracts for reasons of rationalisation in order to save on transaction costs. According to Community and now Union law, this is so irrespective of whether this is applied only in individual cases or in the majority of them.

c) *Individual terms*

3.9 The contents of genuine individual terms are not subject to review. It is difficult to understand, however, when such individual terms in consumer contracts exist. They are in any event not subject to review provided they concern the price/quality ratio and the main subject matter of the contract. Thus there is no need to interpret the term "pre-formulation" strictly. Contracts between private persons which are based on individual negotiations are not included in any event, so that the need for a strict interpretation of the scope of application does not arise therefrom either. Therefore it is correct to proceed from the fact that with regard to the relation between the consumer and the seller/supplier any term is subject to review. In the event that a single term had been individually negotiated, the remaining terms will be subject to review as per Article 3(2).

2. EXCEPTIONS TO THE SCOPE OF APPLICATION

a) Mandatory statutory or regulatory provisions and the provisions or principles of international conventions

3.10 The Directive expressly excludes two kinds of terms from review of contents even if they are pre-formulated (Article 1(2)):

> "Contractual terms which reflect mandatory statutory or regulatory provisions and the provisions or principles of international conventions to which the Member States or the Community are party, particularly in the transport area, shall not be subject to the provisions of this Directive."

These legally binding provisions arise from mandatory regulatory provisions of Member States provided that they are applicable to the contract under the rules of private international law. Contrary to the usual priority of Community law over the law of Member States, the Community legislator expressly recognises the prerogative of the contractual law of the Member States which needs to be in accordance with primary Community/Union law. Therefore, discriminatory contractual provisions of the Member States cannot exclude review irrespective of Article 1(2) of Directive 93/13/EEC.

The question remains as to what might be understood by "mandatory statutory or regulatory provisions". Recital (13) seems to contain a clarification according to which the term "mandatory statutory or regulatory provisions" should also include rules which apply between the contractual parties by virtue of law unless otherwise agreed upon. The Recital does not constitute an official definition; it can be employed with regard to the interpretation of the Directive but is not binding on the ECJ. In applying this argument, standard terms contained in contracts on the delivery of energy which are concluded by way of issuing an ordinance might be considered a "mandatory statutory or regulatory provision". However, this is not the only possible interpretation. Recitals (14) and (16) conflict with such an understanding and might be read so as to include mandatory provisions which are imposed on the consumer by an ordinance.

In *Cofidis*[19] the ECJ had the opportunity to comment on the meaning of the term "mandatory statutory or regulatory provisions" in Article 1(2). The main concern of the case was the question of whether the ECJ had jurisdiction to measure the provisions governed in Article 311–37 of the French Code de la consommation against the regulations of Directive 93/13/EEC according to which claims arising from a consumer credit contract need to be brought to court within two years of the occurrence of the event prompting the dispute. Advocate General Tizzano[20] believed that the Directive was not applicable because the terms disputed in *Cofidis* were not covered by the scope of application of the Directive. They were subject to Article 4(2) which excludes a review of the main subject matter of the credit contract and furthermore must be regarded as mandatory in the sense of Article 1(2). The ECJ circumvented the issue and confirmed the admissibility of the claim, indicating that the disputed terms not only followed mandatory statutory or regulatory provisions but that their wording was ambiguous and therefore fell within the scope of application of Directive 93/13/EEC.[21] That is why *Cofidis* might be read so as to include the control of mandatory provisions. However, it should be reiterated that the ECJ did not really tackle the issue of the meaning of Article 1(2).

RWE[22] offered the ECJ for the first time the opportunity to explicitly discuss the scope and reach of Article 1(2) with regard to "mandatory statutory or regulatory provisions".

Referring to the opinion of AG Trstenjak and without much ado, the ECJ responded to the referring question of the German Federal Court (Bundesgerichtshof, BGH)[23] that "it may legitimately be supposed that the national legislature struck a balance between all the rights and obligations of the parties to certain contracts", provided the particular contract at stake is meant to be covered by the respective statutory rule.[24] If, however, the legislator has exempted a particular contract from the scope of application and the supplier intends to extend the scope of the statutory price regulation to a type of contract which comes under the scope of the Directive, the exemption of the control does not apply. The ECJ recognises the risk that the supplier might try to circumvent the purpose of the Directive.[25]

Finally, terms which were based on international conventions are excluded from review. Naturally it is implied that these conventions are in accordance

---

19 ECJ, 21 November 2002, C-473/00, *Cofidis S.A. v Jean Louis Fredout* [2002] ECR I-10875.

20 Opinion 18 April 2002, C-473/00, *Cofidis S.A. v Jean Louis Fredout* [2002] ECR I-10875 at paras 40 and 42.

21 Ibid, at para 22.

22 ECJ, 21 March 2013, Case C-92/11, *RWE Vertrieb AG v Verbraucherzentrale Nordrhein-Westfalen e.V.* [2013] ECR I-nyr.

23 Ibid, at para 23.

24 Ibid, at para 28.

25 Ibid, at para 30.

with Community law. Except for a few exceptions,[26] this provision has not been of practical relevance so far.

b) Review of price and main subject matter

3.11 A further exception from review as regards the contents is stated in Article 4(2):

> "Assessment of the unfair nature of the terms shall relate neither to the definition of the main subject matter of the contract nor to the adequacy of the price and remuneration, on the one hand, as against the services or goods supplies in exchange, on the other, in so far as these terms are in plain intelligible language."

The restriction, which was not included until it was discussed in the Council, purports to exclude the so-called main subject matter of the contract from the review process with the express reservation that (pre-formulated) terms are in plain intelligible language. In *Cofidis*[27] Advocate General Tizzano considered finance terms which merely stipulate the interest rate, the contractual penalty and the amount to be within the scope of application of Article 4(2) of the Directive. This assessment, which lacks further reasoning, might be justified by the interest rate and the amount. It is hardly applicable to contractual penalties, however. The ECJ avoided taking a clear position,[28] meaning that Article 4(2) has not yet been concretised by case law.

In *Ausbanc*[29] the ECJ confirmed that the minimum standard of harmonisation allows the Member States to submit core terms to control if they so decide. The Caja de Ahorros had unsuccessfully argued that Article 4(2) would set mandatory standards from which no deviation to the benefit of the consumer might be possible.

c) Employment, succession and company law

3.12 The Directive does not contain any further express exceptions from its scope of application, for example for contracts in the field of employment, succession, company and insurance law. However Recitals (10) and (19) contain misleading formulations which could be considered as exceptions:

---

26 Pfeiffer, in: Grabitz/Hilf II/Wolf, A 5, Article 1, paras 28–37.

27 AG Tizzano, opinion 18 April 2002, C-473/00, *Cofidis S.A. v Jean Louis Fredout* [2002] ECR I-10875 at para 41.

28 Ibid, at paras 21–22, 26.

29 ECJ, 3 June 2010, Case C-484/08, *Caja de Ahorros y Monte de Piedad de Madrid v Asociación de Usuarios de Servicios Bancarios (Ausbanc)* [2010] ECR I-04785 at paras 28, 29.

> "Whereas as a result *inter alia* contracts relating to employment, contracts relating to succession rights, contracts relating to rights under family law and contracts relating to the incorporation and organization of companies or partnership agreements must be excluded from this Directive."

These formulations are merely indirectly confirmed in the Directive and thus can only function as an explanation but not as an official exclusion of the stated contracts from the scope of application. It is relevant whether contracts relating to employment, to the incorporation and organisation of companies or to rights under family law are entered into between "sellers or suppliers" and "consumers" which will normally not be the case. In employment and company law there are arrangements, however, where certain terms do not put a private contractual party in the position of an employee or a person having a holding in the company, but rather in the position of a consumer. This is so, for example, with regard to terms on the purchase of goods or services in the context of an employment relationship, or possibly a private investment in a mutual fund.

d) Insurance law

3.13 The "exception for insurance contracts" has been misleadingly formulated and appears in different versions in the different official languages of the EC.[30] It reads:

> "In insurance contracts, the terms which clearly define or circumscribe the insured risk and the insurer's liability shall not be subject to such assessment since these restrictions are taken into account in calculating the premium paid by the consumer."

This is the reason why the importance of this recital should not be overestimated. Again, the only concern regards the question to which extent the "price/quality ratio" can be reviewed by the means of controlling pre-formulated terms. This needs to be done according to the criteria of Article 4(2) of Directive 93/13/EEC, i.e. the first stage is to assess the transparency of, for example, the exclusion of risks. Then it must be ascertained what constitutes the "consideration" and remuneration in insurance law. On the one hand, differentiated distinction should be drawn between primary risk descriptions and exclusion of benefits, obligations and the like on the other. It goes without saying that the particularities will depend on the insurance law of Member States. This issue has not been the subject of case law of the ECJ. However, in *Commission v Netherlands*[31] Advocate General Tizzano drew attention to the significance of completely excluding insurance contracts from the scope of application of the

---

30 GRUNDMANN, 268, para 28.

31 Opinion, 23 January 2001, C-144/99, *Commission v Netherlands* [2001] ECR I-3541.

Directive for consumer protection, but without making any conclusion. The ECJ did not consider the issue in its decision.[32]

3. SUBJECTIVE APPLICATION CRITERIA

a) *The concept of "consumer"*

3.14 Article 2 of Directive 93/13/EEC stipulates that the provisions contained therein merely apply to contractual terms in contracts concluded between sellers or suppliers and consumers. The term consumer is similarly defined as in other European directives.

> "Consumer means any natural person who, in contracts covered by this Directive, is acting for purposes which are outside his trade, business or profession."

Private tenants come under the notion of the consumer.[33] In mixed contracts, in particular with regard to self-employed persons, the known problems of demarcation arise, which the ECJ resolves by applying a strict interpretation focusing on the protective purpose. In *Idealservice*[34] the ECJ refused to define as a consumer a businessman who had acquired a vending machine for beverages for his colleagues. "Consumer" in terms of Article 2(b) means only natural persons. The reasoning presented by the French and Spanish governments, that the concept of consumer allowed for a broader interpretation, was rejected by the ECJ.[35]

With regard to mixed contracts, case law concerning the interpretation of the consumer provisions of Article 13 the Brussels Convention of 1968 (7.36) on jurisdiction in civil matters may be relevant. In *Gruber*,[36] the Court applied Article 13 only in cases where the professional activity to which the contract relates is merely marginal and ancillary. Should the consumer deceive the other party as to the true nature of the contract – for example by pretending that the contract is part of a professional activity when the professional activity is only of minor importance – he has waived his protection and the good-faith contract partner is not subject to the special jurisdiction of Articles 13 and 14.

The law of Member States is not prevented from extending the scope of application to activities which are not relevant to consumers; either where the contract has a dual purpose (Recital (17) of the Consumer Rights Directive 2011/83/EU, 1.38) or where certain people appear worthy of protection irrespective

---

32 ECJ, 10 May 2001, C-144/99, *Commission v Netherlands* [2001] ECR I-3541.

33 ECJ, 30 May 2013 C-488/11, *Asbeek* [2013] ECR I-nyr.

34 ECJ, 22 November 2001, C-541 + 542/99, *Cape Sne v Idealservice* [2001] ECR I-9049.

35 Ibid, paras 14–15.

36 ECJ, 20 January 2005, C-464/01, *Johann Gruber v Bay Wa AG* [2005] ECR I-439.

of their consumer character, for example small traders, franchisees, farmers and the like (Recital (13) of the CRD).

b) Seller or supplier, in particular public undertakings and landlords

3.15 The concept of "seller" or "supplier" whose pre-formulated terms are subject to review reads:

> "Seller or supplier means any natural or legal person who, in contracts covered by this Directive, is acting for purposes relating to his trade, business or profession, whether publicly owned or privately owned."

On the one hand, terms which have been formulated in advance by private persons are excluded. On the other hand, the Directive clarifies that the pre-formulated terms of any trade, business or profession are subject to the Directive irrespective of their legal form. Generally exceptions will not be made. However, the seller or supplier is required to formulate the contracts in advance; performances which are rendered under public or social security law are excluded from the scope of application of the Directive.

The question of whether standard business conditions of public utility undertakings in the form of an ordinance or a similar administrative act fall within the scope of application of the Directive is disputed. General opinion is that such ordinances need to be seen as mandatory statutory or regulatory provisions in the meaning of Article 1(2) and thus are not subject to the scope of application of the Directive.[37] However there are counter-arguments which make the term of mandatory statutory or regulatory provisions appear in a different light, at least in connection with Article 2(c).[38] Recitals (14) and (16) seem to start from a wider scope of application in terms of the subject matter. Recital (13), however, supports rather a strict interpretation of Article 1(2).

The main focus of interest in the controversy is the term "mandatory statutory or regulatory provisions". It appears feasible to refer to the legally dogmatic approach which the ECJ had developed to the restriction of the scope of application of Article 28 EC (now Article 34 TFEU).[39] Accordingly only those provisions of Member States which are based on "mandatory requirements" within the meaning of the *Cassis de Dijon* doctrine will be exempted from Community/Union law. Standard business conditions, even if they are adopted in the form of mandatory law, could then be examined in order to find out whether the terms in question fully consider the interests of the general public. Directive 93/13/EEC might contribute to giving shape to the notion of "interests

---

37 Pfeiffer, in: Grabitz/Hilf II/Wolf, note 26 and Article 2, paras 23–24.

38 Cf. in particular Rott/Butters; Whittaker, 95.

39 For the first time Hoffmann, in: Lehofer/Mayer, 68.

of the general public".[40] However, the whole debate has lost impetus as public utilities are under pressure to be privatised. Private companies, however, would come under the scope of application in any event.

In *Asbeek*[41] the ECJ held that landlords acting for professional purposes come under the scope of the Directive. There was nothing in the Directive which could justify an exemption of this type of service providers.

III. THE CONCEPT OF UNFAIRNESS

1. UNFAIRNESS IN THE FORMAL SENSE: THE SO-CALLED REQUIREMENT OF TRANSPARENCY

a) *The significance of the requirement of transparency*

3.16 The concept of unfairness as employed and concretised in Articles 3–5 of Directive 93/13/EEC consists of a formal and substantive element. The requirement of transparency is comprehensively formulated in Article 5:

> "In the case of contracts where all or certain terms offered to the consumer are in writing, these terms must always be drafted in plain, intelligible language. Where there is doubt about the meaning of a term, the interpretation most favourable to the consumer shall prevail. This rule on interpretation shall not apply in the context of the procedures laid down in Article 7(2)."

The general significance of the principle of transparency has been clarified by the case law of the ECJ.[42] It is of such paramount importance for the implementation of the Directive into national law that Member States are required to include this principle in their legislation. A mere reference to the established practice of the courts will not suffice. Therefore the ECJ has settled a long and controversial discussion which had been of significance and which went beyond Directive 93/13/EEC. The opinion of the Advocate General in *Commission v the Netherlands* is even more explicit, stating that the seller or supplier should be required *from the start* to ensure that clauses are drafted in plain, intelligible language. Furthermore, he should be responsible for ascertaining that prior to the conclusion of the contract the consumer is in a position to obtain the information necessary to make a decision with full knowledge of the subject matter. The ECJ thus fully relies on the reasoning of the Advocate General.[43]

---

40 Thus the objections of Rott/Butters, 115 can be counteracted with the fact that the referral to general welfare is not of assistance in the concretising of the reviewing standard.

41 ECJ, 30 May 2013, C-488/11 [2013] ECR I-nyr.

42 ECJ, 10 May 2001, C-144/99, *Commission v Netherlands* [2001] ECR I-3541.

43 Ibid, para 20.

At the same time the ECJ clarified that the requirement of transparency applied to terms which usually had not been subject to review under Article 4(2).[44] In *RWE*[45] the ECJ confirmed this reasoning. Price clauses which come under the scope of application can be submitted to a severe transparency test. Therefore the price/quality ratio and the main subject of the contract which is determined by an opaque term will be subject to the reviewing process.

b) *Plain intelligible language*

3.17 Directive 93/13/EEC makes concrete the principle of transparency. It is to be characterised as a sub-category of good faith through the principle of legitimate expectations.[46] This proceeds from two standards – *plainness* and *intelligibility* – which need to be assessed separately.[47]

Plainness refers to the legal effect of a term, including its consequences. The consumer needs to know what to expect, for example with regard to an exemption clause. Ambiguous formulations must not put the seller or supplier in a position to improve his legal position at the consumer's expense. Intelligibility refers to the legibility; it purports to eliminate from the contract the so-called "small print" which the consumer cannot readily understand. The user is required to design the standard business conditions plainly, both from an editing and optical point of view. However, the requirement of intelligibility also contains a qualitative element. According to its purpose the requirement of intelligibility entails a requirement for information. Terms must not mislead the consumer about the scope of his rights and obligations.[48]

Whether the linguistic intelligibility is also of concern cannot be unequivocally answered with the help of the text of the Directive. In theory the language issue could be dealt with by referring to the principles of private international law.[49] However "intelligibility" includes the linguistic element in order to attain the protective ambit of the Directive. If the seller or supplier is aware of circumstances under which a term is linguistically not intelligible for the consumer or if he could have known about that fact using reasonable care, then the former is required to make a translation or to otherwise ensure its intelligibility. The user of a term is responsible for ensuring that the consumer obtains the contract in an intelligible language, preferably in his mother tongue.[50]

---

44 Ibid, para 19, referring to the opinion of AG Tizzano, 23 January 2001, para 27.

45 ECJ, 21 March 2013, C-92/11, *RWE Vertrieb AG v Verbraucherzentrale Nordrhein-Westfalen e.V.* [2013] ECR I-nyr.

46 Wilhelmsson, in: Micklitz/Reich (eds.), 385.

47 Pfeiffer, in: Grabitz/Hilf II/Wolf, A 5, Article 5, paras 8–9.

48 The argument of Pfeiffer, in: Grabitz/Hilf II/Wolf, para 10 is convincing.

49 On the issue of international private law, see Rott, 382.

50 Hesitantly, Pfeiffer, in: Grabitz/Hilf II/Wolf, *supra* note 47, para 20.

c) *Contractual transparency and transparency of markets*

3.18 *Contractual* transparency has been primarily referred to in previous discussions on the role and function of the principle of transparency. The question as to what could be required from the user of standard business conditions in order to increase the plainness and intelligibility of his provisions constitutes the focus of consideration. The consumer who is to assess his legal position with the help of the information provided to him is set as the standard.[51] At the heart of contractual transparency is "bilateral". The *institutional* dimension of the principle of transparency, the transparency of markets, is lessened. The consumer is to be put in a position where he can assess his legal position with the help of the information provided in order to make a decision on the conclusion of the contract or to assess the risk of a possible withdrawal form the contract; both fall under the consumer's own responsibility. From this perspective the opinion of the Advocate General in *Commission v the Netherlands* gains importance, namely that transparency needs to be established *prior* to the conclusion of the contract.[52]

At present, transparency of markets as an objective of contract law has not been acknowledged, although the European principle of transparency is rooted in competition law.[53] The establishment of transparency in order to maintain competition within the Community arises from the differing directives in the field of consumer law which formulate the requirements to inform specifically about products or standards. The origins of competition law are embedded in the widely known consequence that the price and the main subject matter are subject to review insofar as both have to be transparent. Indications of prices and performances need to be made in a manner allowing for actual information of the consumer. This is the only way to guarantee competition between potential suppliers.

A first step in this direction has been made by the ECJ in the *Axa Royale* decision.[54] It concerned the question of how to interpret Article 31(3) of Directive 92/96/EEC on direct life insurance according to which Member States are allowed to demand additional information from the insurance company only if "it is necessary for a proper understanding by the policyholder of the essential elements of the commitment". A general and vague indication as to the termination of the contract as contained in Belgian law does not suffice; the different remedies:

---

51 Ibid, para 6.

52 ECJ, 10 May 2001, C-144/99, *Commission v Netherlands* [2001] ECR I-3541 at para 20, in which the ECJ refers to para 31 of the opinion.

53 Reich, in: Serra/Calais-Auloy, 23. On the development of the principle of transparency as a legal principle independent of directives, see Wilhelmsson, *Social contract law and European integration*, 123, 131.

54 ECJ, 5 March 2002, C-386/00, *Axa Royale Belge SA v Georges Ochoa und Stratégie Finance SPRL* [2002] ECR I-2209.

> "enable him [the consumer] to select the contract best suited to his requirements so that he can profit fully from the greater choice of contracts and the increased competition in the single assurance market". (para 28)

This reasoning is based on the consideration that the principle of transparency has a competitive function: the consumer needs to be in a position to decide whether or not to enter into a more advantageous contract. This decision has opened up new perspectives with regard to the scope of application of Directive 93/13/EEC. Transparency no longer solely depends on the plainness and intelligibility of the standard business conditions, i.e. on contractual transparency. It will also depend on the question of whether the information contained has been processed in a way that enables the consumer to compare the legal situation, i.e. that there exists transparency of competition. In *Cofinoga*,[55] the European Court of Justice explicitly recognised the twofold function of the transparency principle.

In *RWE*[56] the ECJ considerably strengthened the role and function of the transparency principle. The point at stake was how concrete the information of price increase clauses in gas supply contracts might be and whether and to what extent a certain lack of transparency can be compensated for by a right to cancel the contract after notification of the price increase.

The ECJ went a long way in providing guidance to the national court.[57] The contract must set out "in transparent fashion the reasons for and the method of the variation of the charges for the service to be provided" so that the consumer can foresee the forthcoming charges. It is only on provision of such precise information that the consumer will be able to terminate the contract. The ECJ understands the transparency principle as a duty to disclose relevant information which enables the consumer – at least in theory – to compare different contracts in order to be able to calculate the potential risk of a price increase. It has to be recalled that the policy of the European Union aims at establishing competitive structures on the energy market and to allow the consumer to easily switch contracts and look for the best conditions offered. This objective would be compromised if the consumer gets caught in opaque price increase clauses.

2. SUBSTANTIVE CRITERIA

The major idea the current author wishes to put forward is that the Directive spells out a common concept of control for all sorts of unfair contract terms be

---

[55] ECJ, 4 March 2004, C-264/02, *Cofinoga Mérignac SA v Sylvain Sachithanathan* [2004] ECR I-2157.

[56] ECJ, 21 March 2013, C-92/11, *RWE Vertrieb AG v Verbraucherzentrale Nordrhein-Westfalen e.V.* [2013] ECR I-nyr, paras 49–59; detailed comments by MICKLITZ/REICH, *EuZW* 2013, 459.

[57] ECJ, 21 March 2013, C-92/11, *RWE Vertrieb AG v Verbraucherzentrale Nordrhein-Westfalen e.V.* [2013] ECR I-nyr, paras 49–51.

they standardised or not. Such a reading of the Directive entails the need to develop a common concept of control which overcomes the restrictions enshrined in the distinction between individual and collective litigation. The idea of a joint concept heavily affects national justification patterns as will be shown.

a) *Abuse control of unfair terms rather than control of standardised terms*

3.19 The understanding of Directive 93/13/EEC differs between Member States, both in the way in which the Directive has been implemented and in the legal doctrine. The two camps may be described as follows: on the one hand there are those who defend the idea that Directive 93/13/EEC deals with the control of standardised terms only. Member States are then free to decide whether they want to extend the control to individually negotiated terms. On the other hand there are those who defend a broader view and start from the premise that the harmonisation envisaged by the Directive reaches beyond the control of standardised terms. This is not the place to fully develop this argument.[58] However, it is necessary to demonstrate the main strands which justify a broader reading of the Directive, i.e. a shift not only in the scope of the Directive but in the regulatory policy which should guide its enforcement.

The starting point for discussion is Recital (9) which reads as follows: "acquirers of goods and services should be protected against the abuse of power by the seller or supplier, in particular against one-sided standard contracts and the unfair exclusion of essential rights in contracts." The wording suggests two things: that (i) the control is related to unfair terms, and that (ii) it is bound to the abuse of power. Taken literally it challenges any approach which binds the control of contract terms to its collective character. Instead the Directive introduces the idea of "abuse of power" which is not at all easy to apply in an EU legal environment.

Second, Directive 93/13/EEC proceeds from a role-related protection model.[59] The connection of the control power to the abuse of bargaining powers represents an obvious expression thereof. The control power given the competent entities is not restricted to standard contract terms but equally covers individually negotiated terms. Therefore an approximation of the standards applicable to both proceedings is given; the differentiation between individually negotiated terms and pre-formulated standard business conditions becomes less relevant.

Third, the category of pre-formulated individual contracts overrides the distinction between individually negotiated terms and standardised contract conditions. This has to be understood as a compromise between the supporters

58 See Micklitz, in: Reich/Micklitz, §§ 13.16–13.23.

59 Recital (9).

of an all-embracing system of terms control and the opponents defending a distinction between individual and standardised terms. One German author[60] refers to pre-formulated individual contracts as an "academic cabinet of oddness". However, the notion hides an important shift in regulatory policy. The traditional separation between individual terms and standardised terms is fading.

Fourth, there are a number of discrepancies enshrined in the terminology of the Directive which support a *common* concept of review of individual and standardised terms. Article 7(1) requires the Member States to provide adequate and effective means to "prevent the continued use of unfair terms in contracts concluded with consumers by sellers or suppliers". Here the wording literally concerns unfair terms only, whereas Article 3(2) speaks of a pre-formulated standard contract (and not standard contract terms). The broader wording refers to the original approach of the Commission as laid down in the proposal which aimed at the control of unfair terms as such.[61] According to Article 7(2) courts or administrative bodies shall decide "whether contractual terms drawn up for general use are unfair." Theoretically this could only refer to terms which are employed in "a number" of cases. Recital (23), however, is not of further assistance in defining what is meant by "general use".

All in all, one might therefore argue that the concept of control enshrined in the Directive reaches beyond the distinction of standardised terms and individual terms, and allows for the establishment of a genuine European concept which ties the control of unfair terms to the abuse of power. It is here that a strong link to the rationality doctrine might be created. European consumer law is very much bound to the completion of the internal market. Abuse of power in private law relations and abuse of power in competition law are interrelated. As the rationality doctrine underpins the internal market programme, so it makes its mark on the ideology behind Directive 93/13/EEC on unfair terms in consumer contracts. The ECJ seems ready to move in precisely this direction.[62]

b) *Yardstick of control*

3.20 The argument goes that there is a common standard of control against which individual terms *and* standardised terms may be measured independently of the type of litigation, be it individual or collective. Individual litigation means that unfair terms have become the subject of dispute in court proceedings between two private parties – the consumer and the supplier. Collective litigation

---

60 Schmidt-Salzer, 1261.

61 Proposal for a Council Directive on unfair terms in consumer contracts, COM (1990) 322 final – SYN 285, Official report of the Bundesrat (BR-Drucks.) 611/90.

62 Micklitz/Reich, in: Wurmnest et al. (ed.).

concerns unfair terms which are challenged in court by either consumer or business organisations[63] or public authorities.

Individual litigation: Articles 3(1) and Article 4(1) contain standards for the assessment of the unfairness of a term. According to the prevailing understanding in legal doctrine, Article 4 merely refers to the review of actions taken by an individual.[64] The European Court of Justice regards the *contra proferentem* rule as a substantial part of the protection of the consumer interest.[65] It has, however, not yet had the opportunity to decide on the reach of Article 4(1) and its impact on collective litigation. Another point of discussion is to what extent the time at which the contract has been concluded might be taken into consideration. Wilhelmsson[66] points out that the Scandinavian countries also consider imbalances occurring during the performance of the contract. This, however, is not the view of EU law as unequivocally stated in Article 4.

The question of whether or not a common standard of control might be applied to both types of litigation is linked to whether the standard of unfairness is a concrete-individual or an abstract-general one.[67] This highly controversial issue is connected to the debate over whether the circumstances of the case at issue have to be taken into consideration only in individual litigation or whether they may equally determine collective litigation. Legal doctrine, at least in a country such as Germany, tends to link individual litigation to a concrete-individual test and collective litigation to an abstract-general test. Similar developments are reported in France.[68] It has already been made clear that such a formalistic distinction has led to a deadlock in the control of unfair terms.

The deficiencies in the control of unfair contract terms have been recognised. A German author, Damm,[69] pleads for a "*sozialbereichspezifische Generalisierung der Benachtei-ligungsfrage*" (social sector specific generalisation of the detriments).[70] The idea behind this is to find a compromise between the concrete-individual and the abstract-general test. Damm starts from the control of standardised terms. These should not be legally analysed without taking the context in which they are applied into consideration. However, "taking into consideration" does not mean taking account of all the detailed individual

63 There is no current policy in the EC directives which contain rules on collective enforcement. Article 7 of Directive 93/13/EEC addresses consumer organisations only.

64 Pfeiffer, in: Grabitz/Hilf II/Wolf, A 5, Article 4, No. 3.

65 ECJ, 9 September 2004, C-70/03, *Commission v Spain* [2004] ECR I-7999.

66 Wilhelmsson, *JCP* 1993, 435, 440; Wilhelmsson, *Critical Studies in Private Law*, 148.

67 References of the discussion in Pfeiffer, in: Grabitz/Hilf II/Wolf, *supra* note 64, Nos. 1–4.

68 See with regard to France, Brock, 107–118. However, English legal doctrine puts much more emphasis on the substance of the test and on the notion of "fairness", see Collins, 239, 245; Howells/Weatherill, 363; for a deeper analysis of the new concept in the light of the common law tradition, Willett, 161.

69 Damm, 172.

70 Cautious approach by Pfeiffer, in: Grabitz/Hilf II/Wolf, *supra* note 64, No. 5, who analyses the coherence between concrete-individual and general-abstract rules.

circumstances but rather generalising the individual circumstances in a way which allows the drawing of a realistic (concrete) but general picture of the socio-economic environment. This line of argument, which has been triggered by Article 4 of the Directive, allows control of unfair terms to be made parallel regardless of whether they are used in individual or collective litigation.

Collective litigation: according to the current author's point of view, Article 4 applies to collective actions as well. This results from abuse control under which concrete individual circumstances can and should also be taken into consideration in collective litigation. Directive 93/13/EEC requires an *area/ sector-related* or *type of contract-related* differentiation of the control standards. However, collective actions cannot be individualised to the degree that the legal position of an individual consumer could be taken into account. It is only possible to generalise the individual-concrete approach in terms of branch- or sector-related control. Such an approximation of control standards would enhance the efficiency of collective and individual actions.

c) *The scope of review by the ECJ*

3.21 The reviewing competence of the ECJ in relation to Directive 93/13/EEC is the subject of controversial debate. The problem is that a general clause needs to be concretised in order to become practical. The ECJ's only involvement in this concretising issue is that it might be required to provide answers for how to interpret Community and now Union law within the scope of the preliminary ruling procedure of Article 234 EC, now Article 267 TFEU. However, its powers do not include the interpretation of the law of Member States (implementing the directives). Theoretically, this maxim is easy to rationalise, but is of less importance in practical borderline cases.

With regard to interpreting the general clause of Article 3 itself, the ECJ has taken a somewhat conflicting and ambiguous point of view. The first litigation came before the Court in *Océano.*[71] Several Spanish clients were sued by a book-club company at its place of business but not their residence, because a jurisdiction clause was inserted into the standard contract form. The Spanish judge was not sure whether he could raise the issue of his territorial incompetence *ex officio* because he regarded the jurisdiction clause to be unfair under Article 3(2) of Directive 93/13/EEC and No. 1(q) of the so-called indicative list of the Annex. The Court gave a somewhat unclear answer:

> "A jurisdiction clause must be regarded as unfair within the meaning of Article 3 of the Directive (93/13/EEC) *in so far as* it causes, contrary to the requirement of good faith, a significant imbalance in the parties' rights and obligations existing under the contract to the detriment of the consumer."

---

71 ECJ, 27 June 2000, Joined Cases C-240–244/98, *Océano Grupo editorial v Rocio Murciano Quintero et al.* [2000] ECR I-4491; comment Stuyck, 719.

The Court insisted on the protective ambit of Directive 93/13/EEC. This means that the judge should be able to raise *ex officio* the potential unfairness of the jurisdiction clause, and that he should apply and interpret his national law in conformity with Community law (this is settled case law now, see 3.29). However, the Court did not completely condemn the jurisdiction clause, but left it to the national judge, depending on the circumstances of the case. There is, however, a strong likelihood that such unilateral clauses are unfair because they contradict the principle of effective judicial protection (7.1–7.11).[72]

In the case of *Freiburger Kommunalbauten*,[73] the municipal construction company had sold Mr and Mrs Hofstetter a parking space to be built by the company. Under the relevant clause, the full price was due on delivery of a security by Freiburger Kommunalbauten, irrespective of any progress made in the construction. The German Federal Court was inclined to the view that the clause was not unfair, but was not free from doubt and therefore referred it to the ECJ. To the surprise of observers, both AG Geelhoed and the Court declined to review the clause but left this to the national courts. This means that the ECJ cannot decide on the unfairness of a particular clause without knowing the national law that forms the background of the decision and the circumstances of the individual case. The reference procedure of Article 234 EC is limited to interpreting Community law, but not deciding questions between both national and EU law. The Court implicitly opted for a theory of judicial restraint in contract law matters.

One could have argued that there is an important difference between *Océano* and *Freiburger Kommunalbauten*. In the former, the Court was able to refer to the indicative list as a yardstick, whereas there was no yardstick available in *Freiburger Kommunalbauten*. However, in *Claro*[74] the ECJ confirmed *Freiburger Kommunalbauten*. At stake was the admissibility of arbitration clauses. The law in the Member States differs widely.[75] The ECJ could have referred to No. 1(q) but left the final decision, just as in *Freiburger Kommunalbauten*, to the Member States' courts.

3.21a In the last five years the ECJ has been offered the opportunity to develop its case law much further and it has found two ways to overcome the obvious contradiction between *Océano* and *Freiburger Kommunalbauten*. The first and now relatively established means is to upgrade the role and function of the indicative list (see under 3.24). The second, and much more difficult, method started in *Mohamed Aziz*,[76] where for the first time ever Advocate General

[72] Reich, *General Principles of EU Civil Law*, para 4.15.

[73] ECJ, 1 April 2004, C-237/02, *Freiburger Kommunalbauten GmbH Baugesellschaft & Co KG/ Ludger und Ulrike Hofstetter* [2004] ECR I-3403.

[74] ECJ, 26 October 2006, C-168/05 *Elisa Maria Mostanza Claro v Centrol Movil Milenium* [2006] ECR I-10421.

[75] See for an overview Reich, *ERCL* 2007, 41.

[76] ECJ, 14 March 2013, C-415/11 [2013] ECR I-nyr.

Kokott and the ECJ were asked to analyse the guiding importance of the general fairness test – in the language of Directive 93/13/EEC, good faith and significant imbalance.

According to the present author, *Freiburger Kommunalbauten* would already have given the ECJ the opportunity to engage in an analysis of the deeper meaning of the so-called general clause, but the ECJ decided not to do so – maybe in light of the uproar against *Océano*. The then UK House of Lords – now the Supreme Court – refused twice, in *First National*[77] and in the *Bank Charge*[78] case, to refer precisely this question to the ECJ. In *Mohamed Aziz* the referring Juzgado de lo Mercantil No. 3 de Barcelona did not explicitly mention the general clause, Article 3 of the Directive. All the Juzgado did was to ask, "how is the concept of disproportion to be understood with regard to"[79] the three concrete contract terms enumerated there. The starting point in the eyes of the referring court is therefore not the meaning of broad principles such as "good faith" and "insignificant imbalance" whose application in the national context is linked to strong conceptual and even ideological conflicts. In a clever move, the potential "disproportion" guides the opinion of Advocate General Kokott on which the ECJ relies in key parts of the judgment.

The AG begins her analysis with a clarification of the function of the fairness test as enshrined in Articles 3 and 4 of Directive 93/13/EEC. Both the AG and the ECJ say nothing about the ongoing academic debate on what good faith means and whether and to what extent good faith and significant imbalance have a similar or even the same meaning. However, they both take "significant imbalance" as their starting point – without mentioning good faith directly. The key argument deserves to be quoted in full:[80]

> "(68) As stated by the Advocate General in point 71 of her Opinion, in order to ascertain whether a term causes a 'significant imbalance' in the parties' rights and obligations arising under the contract, to the detriment of the consumer, *it must in particular be considered what rules of national law would apply in the absence of an agreement by the parties in that regard* [emphasis added]. Such a comparative analysis will enable the national court to evaluate whether and, as the case may be, to what extent, the contract places the consumer in a legal situation less favourable than that provided for by the national law in force. To that end, an assessment should also be carried out of the legal situation of that consumer having regard to the means at his disposal, under national legislation, to prevent continued use of unfair terms.

77 Judgment of the House of Lords of 25 October 2001, *The Director General of Fair Trading v First National Bank plc* [2001] UKHL 52.

78 Judgment, 25 November 2009, *Office of Fair Trading (Respondents) v Abbey National plc & Others (Appellants)* [2009] UKSC 6, on appeal from [2009] EWCA Civ 116.

79 ECJ, 14 March 2013, C-415/11 *Mohammed Aziz* [2013] ECR I-nyr at para 31.

80 Ibid, at para 68.

> (69) With regard to the question of the circumstances in which such an imbalance arises 'contrary to the requirement of good faith', having regard to the sixteenth recital in the preamble to the directive and as stated in essence by the Advocate General in point 74 of her Opinion, the national court must assess for those purposes whether the seller or supplier, dealing fairly and equitably with the consumer, *could reasonably assume* [emphasis added] that the consumer would have agreed to such a term in individual contract negotiations."

In the application of the fairness test, the national legal order seems to form the major reference point for the ECJ. At first glance, this makes sense; however, the difficulty might arise that the national order provides for standards that might be regarded as "unfair" perhaps not in the reference order but in the legal order of another Member State. Implicitly, the ECJ seems to be prepared to take the national default rules enshrined in a codified legal system as a yardstick to measure whether a deviating standard term can be justified. This sounds very much like the typical line of reasoning of lawyers who are trained in civil legal thinking and it sets aside the differences between Member States which have a codified private legal order and those which have not.[81]

The ECJ has embarked on a difficult journey and we may wonder where this journey will lead us to. However, one thing is for sure: *Freiburger Kommunalbauten* belongs to the past. The ECJ is ready to give shape to the criteria – even beyond the indicative list – of what good faith and significant imbalance might mean in a genuinely autonomous EU understanding.

3. THE CONSEQUENCES OF UNFAIR TERMS

3.22 Article 5(2) provides that where there is doubt about the meaning of a term, the interpretation most favourable to the consumer shall prevail. The so-called *contra proferentem* rules as applied in most Member States are thus present throughout the Community.[82] However, the opinion of Advocate General Tizzano in *Commission v the Netherlands*[83] that Article 5(3) of Directive 93/13/EEC has to be implemented by the Member States is not unproblematic. According to Article 5(3) the *contra proferentem* rule is not applicable to actions against consumer associations. The Advocate General focuses on the wording of the Directive rather than refer to the legal understanding which prevails in some Member States that the differentiation between individual litigation, where the rule applies, and collective litigation where it does not, is no longer appropriate.

81 Weatherill, *ERCL* 2010, 74 makes that point in discussing the role and function of general principles of private law.

82 ECJ, 10 May 2001, C-144/99, *Commission v Netherlands* [2001] ECR I-3541, para 19, referring to AG Tizzano.

83 Ibid, at para 20, referring to AG Tizzano, para 30.

A legal comparison would have allowed dealing more substantially with the practical relevance of the interpretation rules, rather than being formally focused on the Directive, producing results prejudicial those to whom protection had been promised. The idea of a common concept of control which applies equally to both types of litigation seems to be the sole solution.

The legal consequences of formally or substantively unfair terms arise from Article 6(1):

> "Member States shall lay down that unfair terms used in a contract concluded with a consumer by a seller or supplier shall, as provided for under their national law, not be binding on the consumer and that the contract shall continue to bind the parties upon those terms if it is capable of continuing in existence without the unfair terms."

Article 6 lays the definition of the legal in the hands of Member States, the powers of which are not unlimited, however. The so-called principle of partial nullity is rooted in Community law. Thus the contract shall continue to be binding without the (formally or substantively) unfair terms, provided the term can be separated from the context.

3.22a In *Banco Español*[84] the ECJ decided against the power of the national courts to "save" a standard term in contract by changing its content so as to bring it into line with the requirements of the Directive. The decision under Article 6 one is an either/or decision. *Either* the clause is non-binding because it is unfair *or* it is binding because it is fair. The Court used strong language to make its point:[85] "as the Advocate General observed in points 86 to 88 of her Opinion, that, if it were open to the national court to revise the content of unfair terms included in such contracts, such a power would be liable to compromise attainment of the long-term objective of Article 7 of Directive 93/13". The supplier of standard terms could then rely on courts to adjust the terms. The deterrent effect of the potential non-binding effect of a term would get lost. In *Asbeek*[86] the ECJ confirmed its position. The reasoning of the ECJ allows for the conclusion that any attempt by national courts to rescue the incriminated term is not allowed under EU law. This would mean in particular that German courts can no longer use the so-called *ergänzende Vertragsauslegung* (supplementary interpretation of the contract) as a doctrinal instrument to protect suppliers against the potential negative effects of a non-binding term, which could lead to restitution claims.[87]

---

84 ECJ, 14 June 2012, C-618/10, *Banco Español* [2012] ECR I-nyr.
85 Ibid, at paras 65–73, in particular para 69.
86 ECJ, 30 May 2013, C-488/11 [2013] ECR I-nyr.
87 See Micklitz/Reich, in: Wurmnest et al. (ed.), 633.

3.22b The *Invitel*[88] case deals with a *collective* action of the Hungarian National Consumer Protection Office against a telecommunications services provider, which used a unilateral price amendment clause without a valid reason and without explicitly describing the method by which prices could vary. The consequences of a potential prohibition of the collective action on *individual* contracts with the defendant business company are of particular interest. Most contract lawyers might consider the problem as being commonly known. What is at stake? Judgments are binding *inter partes* only. If the parties are the consumer agency and a company, the final judgment of the competent court might bind only these two parties. But what about the potential effect of the collective action, more precisely of an action for an injunction, on individual contracts which contain precisely the term which has been declared void in the collective action?

Article 6(1) Directive 93/13/EEC plays a decisive role. According to its wording, this rule is *not* restricted to *individual* procedures but, due to Article 7(2), is deeply linked to actions for injunctions. The AG argues:[89] "These terms are therefore intended for use in a large number of consumer contracts. They can therefore be combated effectively only if the decision of the national court finding a particular term to be unfair is accorded fairly wide applicability." And the ECJ decided[90] that these terms "are not binding on either the consumers who are parties to the actions for an injunction or on those who have concluded with that seller or supplier a contract to which the same GBC apply".

The AG focuses on the *effet utile* of the directive which requires an extension of *res judicata* (*Rechtskrafterstreckung*). Whereas the AG explicitly excludes third parties not involved in the proceedings, since their right to be heard has not been respected, the ECJ does not comment on this question despite referring directly to the AG[91] (Recital (39)), although it does limit the effects "on those who have concluded with that seller or supplier a contract".

The submission of the Hungarian court does not require a distinction to be drawn between the two forms of extension of *res judicata*, as the relevant Hungarian law does not include third parties. The addressee of the extension of *res judicata* is the same user of the term, not the term itself declared illegal, even if the incriminated contract is applied literally identical by another businessman.

However, the ECJ's formulation in Recital (40) leaves more leeway (open wording) and would make it theoretically possible to extend the *effet utile* to the term, regardless of the original user, for example if a Member State wants to use some sort of system of *ex parte* court order by which each and every trader has to abstain from using the banned terms, with the penalty being fines or other

88 ECJ, 26 April 2012, C-472/10, *Invitel* [2012] ECR I-nyr.
89 Ibid, at para 51.
90 Ibid, at para 38.
91 Ibid, at para 39.

sanctions, that seems to be up to that Member State. It is hardly comprehensible why a user who applies the same incriminated term should be allowed to refer to a "legitimate interest".

3.22c Are Member States now *obliged* to give *erga omnes* effect to actions for injunctions declaring a contract term to be unfair or are they only *entitled* to do so since the Directive lays down minimum requirements only? Let us recall what AG Trstenjak says:[92] "They [these unfair terms] can therefore be combated effectively only if the decision of the national court finding a particular term to be unfair is accorded fairly wide applicability". The ECJ confirmed this argument.[93]

The opinion of the AG and the ECJ judgment read together suggest that the Member States are under an obligation to extend *res judicata* beyond the contracting parties. Both seem to start from the premise that adequate and effective protection under Article 7 cannot be limited to the parties to the litigation but must include all those who have concluded a consumer contract with the same supplier. Some uncertainty results from the operative provisions of the judgment. Both the AG and the ECJ formulate it as follows: "Article 6(1) of Directive 93/13, read in conjunction with Article 7(1) and (2) thereof, must be interpreted as meaning that:- it does not preclude the declaration of invalidity of an unfair term included in the standard terms of consumer contracts in an action for an injunction." This formula does not have any equivalent in the judgment, where the minimum character of the Directive and the potential link to the extension of *res judicata* are not discussed. One might therefore wonder whether further clarification is needed in order to decide the mandatory character of the extension to third parties. Even if the Member States are obliged to introduce an extension of *res judicata*, they have substantial leeway in how to shape the extension. This goes together with the principle of procedural autonomy as stressed by the AG.[94]

IV. THE SO-CALLED INDICATIVE LIST

3.23 The problem of any general clause-style provision is that it requires extensive concretising by case law in order to create legal certainty and commitment for individual conflicts arising between sellers or suppliers and consumers. More important is the so-called "indicative list" which, according to Article 3(3), is merely "an indicative and non-exhaustive list of the terms which may be regarded as unfair". In *Commission v Kingdom of Sweden*, brought

92 Ibid, at paras 51 and 58.
93 Ibid, at paras 37, 38, 39.
94 Ibid, at para 38.

against the latter for failure to fulfil its obligations, the ECJ not only determined the legal nature of the indicative list but also decided on the obligation of the Member States to adopt the appendix in their statutory provisions.[95] In conclusion, the ECJ confirmed both the indicative nature of the list and also denied that there existed an obligation to effect formal implementation.[96]

1. THE LEGAL NATURE OF THE INDICATIVE LIST

3.24 From the start, the discussions focused on the possible legal effect of the appendix – the reason being that the ECJ had granted in *Grimaldi*[97] certain legal effect to recommendations in terms of Article 249(4) EC which were designed to be non-mandatory. As the indicative list has more weight than a recommendation because it concretises the general clause, it certainly has an indirect binding effect. In legal literature it has been argued that the list contains a concretising and presumptive effect with regard to unfairness.[98] *Wilhelmsson*[99] stressed that the notion of an "indicative list" does not exclude legal effect from the beginning, for example on courts. If legal effect is to be excluded from the list, then reasonable grounds need to be produced. The list can be used in interpreting national law which has been implemented to carry out Community law.

This reading was confirmed by the ECJ in *Océano* where it is referred to No. 1(q) in order to justify the adverse effect for the consumer of the jurisdiction clause. In *Commission v Kingdom of Sweden* the ECJ mentions again the list's "indicative and exemplary character".[100] Contrary to Advocate General Geelhoed, however, the ECJ refrains from referring to a presumptive effect.[101] For the ECJ it is decisive that a term contained in the list is not necessarily considered unfair and *vice versa*, that is, a term not contained in the list can still be considered unfair.[102]

The list refers to the symmetry of rights and obligations of the contractual parties as laid down in the contractual terms. Such an understanding concretises the formula under Article 3(1). The presumptive effect of the indicative list can be rebutted if Article 4(1) applies. The seller or supplier bears the burden of proof that the particular circumstances laid down in Article 4(1) are present. The Member States have a margin of appreciation with regard to the interpretation of

95 ECJ, 7 May 2002, C-478/99, *Commission v Kingdom of Sweden* [2002] ECR I-4147.
96 Ibid, at para 20.
97 ECJ, 13 December 1989, C-322/88 [1989] ECR 4407.
98 Pfeiffer, in: Grabitz/Hilf II/Wolf, A 5, paras 78 *et seq.*
99 Wilhelmsson, *Social Contract Law*, 67 ff.
100 ECJ, 7 May 2002, C-478/99, *Commission v Kingdom of Sweden* [2002] ECR I-4147 at para 22.
101 Opinion 31 January 2002, *Commission v Kingdom of Sweden* [2002] ECR I-4147 at para 28.
102 ECJ, 7 May 2002, C-478/99, *Commission v Kingdom of Sweden* [2002] ECR I-4147 at para 20.

the indicative list.[103] At the same time the ECJ extended its own margin of appreciation without explicitly expressing it.

3.24a In the meantime the ECJ has revised its earlier case law. While still not granting the indicative list a presumptive effect, the ECJ has upgraded the importance of the indicative list considerably to overcome the clash between no control (*Freiburger Kommunalbauten*) and full control (*Océano*). In *Pénzügyi*[104] the ECJ set a new tone, continued this line of reasoning in *Invitel*,[105] and came close to a result of orientated guidance in *RWE*[106] and *Mohamed Aziz*.[107] What the ECJ in effect is doing is assessing the incriminated term against the respective points of the indicative list, thereby providing its own interpretation of the respective rules. This move is being disguised as "guidance", but in practice there is quite often not much room left for the national court which remains formally responsible for applying the understanding of the ECJ to the concrete circumstances of the case.

2. IS THERE AN OBLIGATION TO IMPLEMENT FOR THE MEMBER STATES?

3.25 The question of whether the Member States are required to implement the indicative list as an indicative or exemplary list is to be considered separate from the legal effect. Tenreiro,[108] who attended the legislative procedure of the Directive, indicated at an early stage that the Member States were required to at least print the indicative list in the process of implementing the Directive, even if it was not declared to be mandatory. In this way the contractual parties or the courts dealing with the legal dispute should be put in a position to concretise the general clause which is mandatory under Community law with the help of the indicative list. Accordingly, the official report from the Commission on the implementation of Directive 93/13/EEC proceeds from an express implementation of the appendix.[109] However the Commission could not carry its legal view in the legal proceedings of the *Commission v Kingdom of Sweden*. In accordance with the opinion of the Advocate General, the ECJ rejected the argument of the Commission. The complete effectiveness of the Directive could be guaranteed without the list in the appendix becoming part of the provisions implementing the Directive.

---

[103] This aspect has been particularly emphasised by Stuyck, 728–729.

[104] ECJ, 9 November 2010, C-137/08 [2010] ECR I-10847.

[105] ECJ, 26 April 2012, C-472/10 [2012] ECR I-nyr.

[106] ECJ, 21 March 2013, C-92/11 [2013] ECR I-nyr.

[107] Opinion of AG Kokott at para 84, ECJ at paras 74 and 75, C-415/11.

[108] Tenreiro, 1.

[109] COM (2000) 248 final, 18.

As regrettable as this rejection decision may be from the Commission's point of view, the obligation imposed on Member States to guarantee that the consumer is informed about the function and contents of the appendix still represents the main statement of the decision.[110] Precise requirements cannot be extracted from the decision. The chosen means of implementation needs to ensure that the general public can acquire knowledge of the list. Sweden referred to the list as stated in the *travaux préparatoires* as well as to the comprehensive information campaign of Swedish consumer associations and the availability of the material on the internet.

3. THE CONTENT OF THE INDICATIVE LIST

3.26 The terms stated in Appendix 1 are of differing character. They mainly concern the one-sidedness of the drafting of the contract of the seller or supplier *vis-à-vis* the consumer, for example excluding or limiting legal liability in the event of personal injury (lit. a), excluding or limiting the legal rights in the event of total or partial non-performance, or inadequate performance including warranty rights (lit. b), lapsed terms (lit. d), lump sum damages (lit. e), termination terms (lit. f, g), extending rights (lit. h), reservation of right of modification (lit. j, k), terms on increasing the price (lit. l), shortening of the time period for asserting a legal claim (lit. q) and the like. With regard to financial services, Annex 2 establishes a certain facilitation in favour of the providers of financial services for clauses on termination and on the reservation of the right to modification; here information provided in due time will suffice to exclude unfairness of the term. Furthermore, it is admissible that the seller or supplier reserves the right:

> "to terminate unilaterally a contract of indeterminate duration without notice where there is a valid reason, provided that the supplier is required to inform the other contracting party or parties thereof immediately."

This far-reaching exception appears particularly problematic as it imposes termination on the consumer if the seller or supplier no longer wishes to fulfil the contract in the form concluded. The central principle of contract law as applied in all Member States, namely *pacta sunt servanda*, is considerably narrowed down as a consequence.

The indicative list is gaining importance as an overall benchmark in consumer contracts (3.24a). Now the ECJ has started to give shape to the content

[110] ECJ, 7 May 2002, C-478/99, *Commission v Kingdom of Sweden* [2002] ECR I-4147 at para 22 referring to the opinion of AG Geelhoed, para 48.

of the list. *Océano*[111] provided the opportunity to determine the importance of Annex 1(q). It concerned the assessment of a national jurisdiction clause which required the consumer to sue the seller or supplier at his residence. By referring to Annex 1(q) the ECJ declared such jurisdiction clauses unfair in terms of Article 3. In *Pénzügyi* the ECJ confirmed its reasoning with regard to Annex 1(q).[112] More importantly since the ECJ has upgraded the indicative list, more and more references can be found in the judgments to the various incriminated terms. In *Invitel* the ECJ referred to Annex 1(j) and Annex 2(b) and (d),[113] in *RWE* Annex 1(j) and Annex 2(b) and (c)[114] and in *Mohamed Aziz* Annex 1(e) and (q).[115] The pending but not yet decided cases will provide the ECJ with further opportunities to interpret the indicative list. Over time the ECJ will generate a European understanding of the list as a whole. This development was hard to foresee a couple of years ago.

V. LAW ENFORCEMENT

1. ADEQUATE AND EFFECTIVE MEANS OF LAW ENFORCEMENT: ASSOCIATIONS AND AUTHORITIES WITH STANDING TO SUE

3.27 Article 7 obliges Member States to introduce adequate and effective means of law enforcement. In essence it obliges Member States to introduce actions for an injunction. The primary addressees of the right to action are consumer organisations. In addition, Member States may grant identical powers to public authorities (see in more detail 8.42).

Invitel[116] gave the ECJ the opportunity to clarify the means of collective redress available under the Directive. The referring court had also sought an answer on means of collective redress aiming in one form or another for a refund of costs and expenses charged via contract terms which turn out to be unfair and void. Whilst the ECJ clearly confirmed that Member States are entitled to introduce collective actions beyond actions for injunction, it is much less clear whether and to what extent the ECJ is paving the way for a genuine European means of collective redress. *Invitel* can at best be understood as a first step in that direction, but further references would be needed to test the potential of the Directive.[117]

111 ECJ, 27 June 2000, Joined Cases C-240–244/98, *Océano Grupo editorial v Rocio Murciano Quintero et al.* [2000] ECR I-4491 at para 24.
112 ECJ, 9 November 2010, C-137/08 [2010] ECR I-10847.
113 ECJ, 26 April 2012, C-472/10 [2012] ECR I-nyr.
114 ECJ, 21 March 2013, C-92/11 [2013] ECR I-nyr.
115 AG Kokott at para 84, ECJ at paras 74 and 75, C-415/11.
116 ECJ, 26 April 2012, C-472/10, *Invitel* [2012] ECR I-nyr.
117 Micklitz/Reich, in: Wurmnest et al. (ed.), 631.

3.27a *Asociación de Consumidores Independientes de Castilla y León*[118] raised the question of whether EU law precludes the Spanish procedural rules under which an action for an injunction initiated by a consumer protection association must be brought before the courts where the defendant is established. The respective situation is purely internal and did not arise in a cross-border context. The ECJ held that EU law does not lay down rules attributing territorial jurisdiction for actions for an injunction and did not find a breach of the principles of equivalence and effectiveness. Unlike individual proceedings where the consumer is the weaker party, in the case of collective actions initiated by consumer protection associations, there is no need for protection. The CJEU thereby deprived consumer protection associations of the possibility to initiate actions for an injunction at the place of their main office.

The preliminary references of the Slovak court in *Pohotovost'*[119] will give the ECJ the opportunity to further clarify the role of consumer protection associations under the Directive. In particular, the ECJ will have to address the question of whether the Member States have to grant consumer protection associations the right to intervene in individual enforcement proceedings in order to assist consumers in pursuing their claims. According to Advocate General Wahl this issue is not addressed by Directive 93/13/EEC and Articles 38 and 47 of the Charter do not support a different interpretation of the Directive. The Advocate General adopts a strict division of roles between the national courts and consumer protection associations under the Directive: compensating the imbalance between an individual consumer and a seller or supplier is restricted to the national court, which has to assess of its own motion whether a contractual term is unfair and has to ensure that the consumer is not bound by an unfair term. Consumer protection associations, on the other hand, must initiate proceedings against unfair terms in their own right, preventing the continued use of unfair terms independent from individual proceedings. However, in line with the principle of minimum harmonisation, the Member States are not precluded from granting consumer protection associations leave to intervene into legal proceedings.

2. LIMITATION PERIOD

3.28 The Directive is silent as to whether Member States are authorised to restrict the period in which consumers or legitimate associations need to assert the ineffectiveness of the term. Referring to Article 6, Advocate General Tizzano

118 ECJ, 5 December 2013, C-413/12, *Asociación de Consumidores Independientes de Castilla y León v Anuntis Segundamano España SL* [2013] ECR I-nyr.

119 Opinion 12 December 2013, C-470/12, *Pohotovost' s.r.o. v Miroslav Vašuta* [2013] ECR I-nyr.

stated in *Cofidis*[120] that a limitation period of two years is not compatible with Community law as effective legal protection could only be guaranteed if the unfairness of a term could be asserted without being subject to time restrictions. The Advocate General considered the obligation of the courts to review the unfairness *ex officio*, as formulated by the ECJ in *Océano*,[121]to support his point of view. The principle of legal certainty requires validity in the consumer interest too,[122] and in this respect it did not justify the introduction of a limitation period. The ECJ concurred with AG Tizzano by insisting that a restriction of the courts' power not to review terms *ex officio* or by way of defence of a consumer was likely to interfere with the effectiveness of the purported protection of Articles 6 and 7 of the Directive.[123]

3. REVIEW *EX OFFICIO*

3.29 The Directive does not establish whether the consumer needs to refer to the unfairness of the term or whether courts are required or allowed to review unfairness *ex officio*. This legal question was focused upon in *Océano*. The ECJ[124] confirmed the possibility to review *ex officio* referring to the weaker position of the consumer who possessed less information. If the consumer was required to assert the unfairness of a term, then the legal knowledge of the consumer would be decisive.

Although the ECJ does not articulate an obligation for the judge to perform a review, the question still arises as to whether circumstances could be conceived in which he would be required to act *ex officio* and whether his margin of appreciation would become nearly zero. The reasoning behind *Océano* about the rights granted to the consumer which are generally granted under Community law could be of significance, for example the right to revoke a contract. Thus in *Océano* the ECJ established a rule which required concretisation. This did not result from a reference of a local Hungarian court[125] – the first from a new Member State – which wanted to know the effects of an unfair clause: must there be an express declaration of the consumer, or does it cease to bind the consumer *ipso iure*? Here the ECJ denied the applicability of Directive 93/13/EEC to legal questions which emerged prior to the accession. However, in *Claro*[126] the ECJ

120 Opinion 18 April 2002, C-473/00, *Cofidis S.A. v Jean Louis Fredout* [2002] ECR I-10875 at paras 55–63.

121 ECJ, 27 June 2000, Joined Cases C-240–244/98, *Océano Grupo editorial v Rocio Murciano Quintero et al.* [2000] ECR I-4491 at paras 21–24.

122 Ibid, at para 62.

123 Ibid, at para 35.

124 Ibid, at paras 25–27.

125 ECJ, 10 January 2006, C-302/04, *Ynos kft v János Varga* [2006] ECR I-371.

126 ECJ, 26 October 2006, C-168/05, *Elisa Maria Mostanza Claro v Centrol Movil Milenium* [2006] ECR I-10421; on which Reich, *ERCL* 2007, 41, and Pavillon, 735.

underlined the obligation of Member States' courts to control unfair terms in consumer contracts *ex officio*.

In a whole series of follow-up references – *Pannon*,[127] *Asturcom*,[128] *Pénzügyi*,[129] *Pohotovost'*,[130] *Invitel*,[131] *Banco Espanol*[132] and *Banif*[133] – the ECJ confirmed and developed more and more sophisticated criteria for the new procedural remedy. So far, the ECJ has imposed an obligation on the national judge in a judicial order for payment procedure in *Banco Espanol*,[134] and in *inter partes* proceedings where the consumer objected against an order of payment in *Pénzügyi*.[135] In *Invitel* the ECJ extended the *ex officio* doctrine to the action for injunction, thereby interlinking individual and collective redress. What remains to be decided is the degree to which the *ex officio* doctrine can be extended beyond the scope of the Unfair Contract Terms Directive to all EU rules which provide for a mandatory level of protection, not only in consumer law but also in labour law, anti-discrimination law, environmental law – in short, wherever the EU sets binding standards. *Martin*[136] confirmed the applicability to doorstep selling, *Rampion*[137] to consumer credit, and *Duarte Hueros*[138] to consumer sales. This means that at least in the area of consumer law it seems fair to speak of a comprehensive and all-encompassing procedural remedy.

4. LEGAL PROTECTION IN ENFORCEMENT PROCEEDINGS

3.29a In *Aziz*, the ECJ ruled on the compatibility of the Spanish mortgage enforcement proceedings with Directive 93/13/EEC. According to the Spanish Civil Procedure Code, the debtor may not object to the unfairness of a term of the loan agreement in the mortgage enforcement proceedings. An objection to an unfair term is only possible in separate declaratory proceedings which, however, do not lead to a suspension of the enforcement proceedings. Differently from *Pénzügyi*[139] and *Banco Español*,[140] the case did not deal with the duties of

[127] ECJ, 4 June 2009, C-243/08 [2009] ECR I-4713.
[128] ECJ, 6 October 2009, C-40/08 [2009] ECR I-9579.
[129] ECJ, 9 November 2010, C-137/08 [2010] ECR I-10847.
[130] ECJ, 16 November 2010, C-76/10 [2010] ECR I-1155.
[131] ECJ, 26 April 2012, C-472/10 [2012] ECR I-nyr.
[132] ECJ, 14 June 2012, C-618/10 [2012] ECR I-nyr.
[133] ECJ, 21 February 2013, C-472/11 [2013] ECR I-nyr.
[134] ECJ, 14 June 2012, C-618/10 [2012] ECR I-nyr at paras 42 and 43.
[135] ECJ, 9 November 2010, C-137/08 [2010] ECR I-10847 at para 56.
[136] ECJ, 17 December 2009, C-227/08 [2009] ECR I-11939.
[137] ECJ, 4 October 2007, C-429/05 [2007] ECR I-8017.
[138] ECJ, 3 October 2013, C-32/12, *Soledad Duarte Hueros v Autociba SA and Automóviles Citroën España SA* [2013] ECR I-nyr.
[139] ECJ, 9 November 2010, C-137/08 [2010] ECR I-10847.
[140] ECJ, 14 June 2012, C-618/10 [2012] ECR I-nyr.

national courts to carry out an assessment of the unfairness of contract terms of their own motion. The ECJ established a new remedy, which connects the enforcement proceedings with the declaratory proceedings. The principle of effectiveness requires that the court hearing the declaratory proceedings has the possibility of staying the enforcement proceedings (provisionally) in order to stop enforcement until it has been assessed whether a term is unfair. If considered to be admissible, the preliminary reference in *Macinský and Macinská*[141] will give the ECJ the opportunity to consolidate its ruling in *Aziz*. The Slovak rules at stake enable a creditor to enforce a secured claim based on an unfair term in a consumer contract through the sale of immovable property by means of an out-of-court procedure. The question is whether it is compatible with Directive 93/13/EEC for a Member State to require consumers to make the first move to suspend or halt the enforcement of a contract which allegedly contains an unfair term. Advocate General Wahl did not consider it excessive to require consumers to initiate legal proceedings against the trader to suspend or halt the out-of-court enforcement procedure in the form of a public auction.

VI. REFORM OF THE UNFAIR TERMS DIRECTIVE 93/13/EEC

3.30 According to Article 9, the Commission is obliged to submit a report on the implementation of the Directive to the Council. In preparation of the report the Commission organised a conference in Brussels on 1–7 July 1999, the topic being "The 'Unfair Terms' Directive – Five Years on – Evaluation and future perspectives".[142] The results served as a basis for its report on the implementation of Directive 93/13/EEC one year later.[143] The purpose of the report is twofold. On the one hand it fulfils the Commission's obligation to report on the implementation of the Directive; on the other the Commission links the legal situation *de lege lata* with a discussion of subjects that need to be approached *de lege ferenda*. For this purpose the Commission established nine subject categories, with the structure of each being identical. To begin with, the legal situation in the Member States is analysed, then questions on the need for reform are formulated.

The nine subject categories concern the following main areas: (1) current limitations on the Directive's scope – individually negotiated terms, the exclusion concerning mandatory provisions, exclusion as regards the price and the subject matter of the contract; (2) the notion of "unfair term" and the list in

141 Opinion of 21 November 2013, Case 482/12, *Peter Macinský, Eva Macinská v Getfin s.r.o., Financreal s.r.o.*

142 Published under this title by the European Commission in 2000.

143 COM (2000) 248 final, 27 April 2000.

the Annex; (3) the principle of transparency and the right to information; (4) sanctions; (5) the national systems for striking out unfair terms; (6) towards a "positive" system for eliminating unfair terms; (7) towards a European system for the elimination of unfair terms; (8) the more problematic sectors – utilities and financial services; and (9) the future of the database the European Commission has set up to collect data on national court decisions within the scope of application of the Directive.[144]

3.31 The very same issues are now subject to the ongoing revision of the *acquis communautaire*[145] (see 1.41). Originally the European Commission intended to integrate Directive 93/13/EEC into a coherent EU consumer law approach that brings together at least four directives: 93/13/EEC on unfair terms, 99/44/EC on consumer sales, 85/577/ECC on doorstep and 97/7/EC on distance selling. These efforts have failed, not least due to strong resistance from Member States and from consumer lawyers. What has remained is the insertion of the notification duty under Article 8(a) of the amended Directive 93/13/EEC. Member States have to inform the European Commission if they extend the scope of application to core terms and whether they introduce a black or grey list of incriminated terms. It remains to be seen whether the CESL, if it is adopted, will lead to amendment of the Unfair Terms Directive (see 1.43b and 4.1b) The finally adopted Directive 2011/83/EU on consumer rights is bound to develop a common regulatory scheme on doorstep and distance selling (see under Chapter 9).

Today it seems as if the ECJ has taken the lead in using Directive 93/13/EEC as a horizontal tool to give shape to the level of consumer protection in the EU, filling step by the step the gaps and uncertainties left in the 20-year-old legislation. In the last five years (2008–2013) the ECJ has had to decide 12 preliminary references, and many more are pending. Through their preparedness to make active use of the preliminary reference procedure, the national courts have awakened the sleeping beauty that is the Unfair Terms Directive.[146] A closer look at the substance of the cases might provide a partial explanation. Most of the cases deal with financial matters in a broad sense. The sector-specific directives on consumer credit, for example (see 5.42), suffer from the fact that they do not tackle the really sensitive issues like consumer-debtor default, acceleration clauses, penalty payments and the like. In times of economic crisis, the broad scope of application of the Directive on unfair terms turns out to serve as a means of last resort.

144 See MICKLITZ/RADEIDEH, 325.

145 See COM (2006) 744 final.

146 MICKLITZ/REICH, *CMLRev* 2014 forthcoming.

CHAPTER 4
SALE OF CONSUMER GOODS

Hans-W. Micklitz and Norbert REICH

CONTENTS

Bibliography:

S. Augenhofer, Bedeutung von Werbeaussagen – sowohl des Verkäufers als auch des Herstellers – für die Begründung von Gewährleistungsrechten, *JBl* 2001, 82; H. Beale/G. Howells, EC Harmonisation of Consumer Sales Law – A Missed Opportunity?, *JCL* 1997, 21; R. Bradgate/C. Twigg-Flessner (eds.), *Blackstone's Guide to Consumer Sales and Associated Guarantees*, 2003; A.-D. Bruun Nielsen, Directive 1999/44/EC of the European Parliament and the Council on certain aspects of the sale of consumer goods and associated guarantees and its influence on Danish law, *ERPL* 2001, 189, 190; O. Calliano, A Critical First Glance at the CESL Project by the Digital Consumer Law Approach, in: Moccia, *The Making of European Private Law: Why, How, What, Who*, 2013, 217; U.P. Gruber, Montagefehler und fehlerhafte Montageanleitung, *VuR* 2002, 120; S. Grundmann, From Traditional to Modern Sales Law, in: Terryn et al., *Landmark Cases of EU Consumer Law – in Honour of Jules Stuyck*, 2013, 725; S. Grundmann, Germany and the Schuldrechtsmodernisierung 2002, *ERCL* 2005, 149; S. Grundmann, Generalreferat: Internationalisierung und Reform des deutschen Kaufrechts, in: Grundmann/Medicus/Rolland (eds.), *Europäisches Gewährleistungsrecht: Reform und Internationalisierung des deutschen Schuldrechts, Hallesche Schriften zum Recht*, Vol. 13,

2000, 281; S. Grundmann, *Europäisches Schuldvertragsrecht*, 1999; S. Grundmann/C.M. Bianca (eds.), *EU-Sales Directive – Commentary*, 2002; N. Helberger et al., Digital Content Contracts for Consumers, *JCP* 2013, 37; N. Helberger et al., *Digital Consumers and the Law*, 2013; E. Hondius, De consumentenkoop in Europees perspectief/naar een richtlijn consumentenkoop en consumentengaranties, *Tijdschrift voor Consumentenrecht* 1996, 245; R.H.C. Jongeneel, The sale of goods in the Netherlands Civil Code: A contribution to the discussion about the Green Paper on guarantees for consumer goods and after-sales services, *Consumer Law Journal* 1995; G. Lastowka, *Virtual Justice*, 2010; H.-W. Micklitz, *Social Justice in European Private Law, Yearbook of European Law 1999/2000*, 167–204; H.-W. Micklitz/N. Reich, Cronica de una muerta anunicada, *CMLRev* 2009, 471; H.-W. Micklitz/N. Reich, The Commission Proposal for a Regulation on CESL – Too Broad or not Broad Enough?, *EUI/Law Working Papers 2012/04*, www.ssrn-id2013183[1].pdf; N. Reich, *General Principles of EU Civil Law*, 2013; N. Reich, Transformation of Contract Law in the New Member Countries, *PennState JIntLaw* 2005, 587; H. Rösler, Sale of Consumer Goods, in: *The Max Planck Encyclopedia of European Private Law*, 2012, 1500; P. Rott, A New Social Contract Law for Public Services? – Consequences from Regulation of Services of General Economic Interest in the EC, *ERCL* 2005, 323–345; P. Rott, Minimum Harmonisation for the Completion of the Internal Market? The Example of Consumer Sales Law, *CMLRev* 2003, 1107; P. Rott/C. Twigg-Flessner, *No Closer to Harmonisation? The Implementation of Directive 99/44/EC into English and German Law Three Years On, Yearbook of Consumer Law*, 2007, 121; A.K. Schnyder/R.M. Straub, Das EG-Grünbuch über Verbrauchsgütergarantien und Kundendienst – Erster Schritt zu einem einheitlichen EG-Kaufrecht, *ZEuP* 1996, 8; R. Schulze (ed.), *Common European Sales Law – A Commentary*, 2013; D. Staudenmayer, *EG-Richtlinie 1999/44/EG zur Vereinheitlichung des Kaufgewährleistungsrechts*, in: Grundmann/Medicus/Rolland (eds.), *Europäisches Gewährleistungsrecht: Reform und Internationalisierung des deutschen Schuldrechts*, Hallesche Schriften zum Recht, Vol. 13, 2000, 27; M. Tenreiro, La proposition de directive sur la vente et les garanties des biens de consommation, *Revue Européenne de Droit de la Consommation* 1996, 187; E. Terryn et al. (eds.), *Landmark Cases of EU Consumer Law – in Honour of Jules Stuyck*, 2013; C. Twigg-Flesner, The EC-Directive on Certain Aspects of the Sale of Consumer Goods and Associated Guarantees, *Consumer Law Journal* 1999, 7, 177; C. Twigg-Flesner/R. Bradgate, The EC-Directive on Certain Aspects of the Sale of Consumer Goods and Associated Guarantees – all Talk and No Do?, *Web JCLI* 2000(2), 1; L. Vékás/M. Paschke (eds.), *Europäisches Recht im ungarischen Privat- und Wirtschaftsrecht*, 2004; S. Watterson, Consumer Sales Directive 1999/44/EC – The impact on English Consumer Law, *European Review of Private Law* 2001(9), 197; H.P. Westermann, Vorschlag für eine Einpassung der Kaufgewährleistungs-Richtlinie ins deutsche Recht, in: Grundmann/Medicus/Rolland (eds.), *Europäisches Gewährleistungsrecht: Reform und Internationalisierung des deutschen Schuldrechts*, Hallesche Schriften zum Recht, Vol. 13, 2000, 251; A. Zaccaria, Umsetzungsüberlegungen zur Kaufgewährleistungs-Richtlinie in Italien, in: Grundmann/Medicus/Rolland (eds.), *Europäisches Gewährleistungsrecht: Reform und Internationalisierung des deutschen Schuldrechts*, Hallesche Schriften zum Recht, Vol. 13, 2000, 181; B. Zahn, Verträge über digitale Inhalte, *ZEuP* 2014, 77.

I. INTRODUCTION

4.1 The Directive on the sale of consumer goods and associated guarantees originates from the lengthy preparation of the passing of Directive 93/13/EEC on unfair terms in consumer contracts (3.4). The difficulty is that this Directive eliminates terms in consumer contracts without providing provisions which apply to those terms which have been declared invalid. This was the starting point for the Commission to approximate the laws of Member States concerning warranties via the back door.[1] The Council has objected to the Commission's suggestion but at the same time has given a mandate to research the legal situation in the Member States and to draft its own proposal for a directive on consumer sales and guarantees. The research was carried out by the Centre de Droit de la Consommation of the Université Catholique de Louvain-la-Neuve on behalf of the Commission.[2] Based on the findings, the Commission, today Directorate-General SANCO, represented by D. Hoffmann and M. Tenreiro, delivered the so-called Green Paper on guarantees for consumer goods and after-sales services of 15 November 1993.[3] In 1994, the Commission financed a conference, organised by Sheffield University, to analyse the potential effects of the proposals as contained in the Green Paper on the legal systems of Member States. The results have since been published.[4] In October 1994, during the consumer forum in Brussels, the then Commissioner announced the drafting of a directive and commissioned a work force consisting of well-known scholars from various Member States to prepare a first draft. This draft purported to implement the guidelines of the Green Paper into legal provisions; it was circulated amongst scholars but has never been published. Within the Commission the draft had only limited support. The main criticism concerned the inclusion of the producer as a possible defendant for liability claims. For a long time it appeared as if the Commission could not reach a compromise on one draft. Surprisingly, however, in 1996 a slimmed-down proposal for a directive on the sale of goods and associated guarantees was presented to the public.

The preparatory work of the Commission has not been closely scrutinised, with the exception of the thorough analysis of the Green Paper by Schnyder and Straub.[5] The draft proposal of the Directive started a general discussion, the focus of which was the possible effects on private national law; only M. Tenreiro[6] considered the European dimension of the draft. Legal doctrine appears to be

---

1 OJ C 73, 24 March 1992, 7.

2 Etude sur un régime juridique pour les garanties et services après vente? Rapport Final, Avril 1993, Convention B-5-1040/92/007568, unreported.

3 COM (1993) 509 final.

4 Cf. the reports and the analyses of the Green Paper which are printed in Consumer Law Journal, Vol. 3 Nos. 3 and 4, 1995.

5 Schnyder/Straub, 8.

6 Cf. Tenreiro, 187–225; also Hondius, 245.

more sensitive to the issue since the passing of Directive 93/13/EEC. The European Community, in the form of the Commission, fulfils:

> "the concern, as expressed by the European Parliament, to *unconditionally* [emphasis added] work towards an approximation of the private laws of Member States on Community level".[7]

The Green Paper aimed at a dramatic modernisation of contract law both in the areas of *statutory* and *commercial* guarantees, whereas the first public draft proposal aimed simply at a humble amendment of national provisions in the area of the sale of consumer goods. The draft proposal for the Directive did not include differentiate between *statutory* and *commercial* guarantees to prevent, as stated in the recitals:

> "difficulties in connection with certain legal traditions in which the institution '*statutory guarantee*' is unknown. It is for that reason that the term '*guarantee*' is exclusively used to refer to commercial guarantees".[8]

The draft proposal therefore did not amount to more than an adaptation of the UN Convention for the International Sale of Goods of 1980 (CISG) to the "consumer level" without providing innovative solutions. Justice is not done to the mass character of consumer contracts by a concept which is limited to dogmatising privity of contract and excludes the liability of the producer – despite the fact that the Commission has made a politically clever move by following the CISG.

The draft proposal was not altered during the legislative process, except for some minor amendments. Directive 1999/44/EC on the sale of consumer goods and associated guarantees was adopted on 20 May 1999.[9] Member States were required to implement it into their national law by 1 January 2002. The majority of Member States have acted in the meantime, including the new member countries.[10] In Germany the Directive has legitimised the modernisation of the law of obligations.[11] Currently, there appears to be no other directive which has attracted so much attention. The Directive on the "sale of consumer goods and associated guarantees" strongly intervenes in national civil law.[12] It has enhanced the debate in the European Union over the feasibility of a single

---

7 Cf. COM (1995) 520 final, OJ C 307, 16 October 1996, 8, referring to the two Decisions of the European Parliament from 26 May 1989, OJ C 158, 26 June 1989, 400 and from 6 May 1994, OJ C 205, 25 July 1994, 518.

8 Cf. COM (1995) 520 final.

9 OJ L 171, 7 July 1999, 12.

10 Reich, 587.

11 Grundmann, *ERCL* 2005, 149.

12 Rott/Twigg-Flessner, 121.

European contract law, which has resulted in the Commission proposal of a Regulation on a Common European Sales Law (1.43b).

4.1a With its proposal on a Consumer Rights Directive (CRD) of 8 October 2008[13] (9.2) the Commission wanted to substantially modify Directive 99/44/EC by reducing established consumer rights and by basing EU legislation on the full harmonisation principle (1.32). The final version of the CRD, namely Directive 201/83/EU has taken a more targeted approach, with a few changes to Directive 99/44/EC concerning delivery and risk taking, and which will be discussed in Chapter 9 (9.16). The scope and central concepts of Directive 99/44/EC have not been touched, including the minimum harmonisation approach which leaves Member States a wide discretion, in particular concerning remedies beyond the minimum threshold of Article 3 of the Directive itself (4.23–4.28).

4.1b The proposed Regulation on a Common European Sales Law (CESL, 1.43b), also as a parallel regime to B2C sales law, would be available to parties to cross-border contracting if they were to decide to opt in. It would to some extent set aside Member State sales law based on the implementation of Directive 99/44/EC applicable under the conflict of law provisions of Regulation (EC) 593/2008, in particular Article 6 (7.17–7.17b). This is however not the place to discuss the rather detailed proposals of the Commission, although their impact on digital content contracts will be considered below (4.35a-4.35e).

II. SCOPE OF APPLICATION

1. SCOPE OF APPLICATION CONCERNING THE SUBJECT MATTER

4.2 As regards the subject matter, the Directive applies to sales contracts for consumer goods, which are defined in Article 1(2)(b) as "any tangible movable item", as well as contracts for the supply of consumer goods to be manufactured or produced (Article 1(4)).

a) Consumer goods

4.3 The Directive applies to new and second-hand goods.[14] On the one hand this results from the lack of an express limitation in relation to new goods and on the other hand from the existence of exceptions for second-hand goods (Articles 1(3) and 7(1)(2); cf. also Recitals (8) and (16)) which shall account for the special interests in the sale of second-hand goods.

---

13 Critique Micklitz/Reich, *CMLRev* 2009, 471 at 501.

14 Luna Serrano, in: Grundmann/Bianca, Article 1, para 28.

Consumer goods are only tangible objects. Intangible goods and rights (licences, patents and copyrights) are excluded from the scope of application of the Directive.[15] This raises problems concerning the law of digital content contracts (for details see 4.35a–e). Water and gas are only covered by the Directive to the extent that they are "put up for sale in a limited volume or set quantity", cf. Article 1(2)(b)(2), e.g. a bottle of mineral water or a canister of propane gas for camping purposes.[16] Utility contracts for water and energy (electricity and gas) are excluded from the scope of application of the Directive.[17] This is all the more important as the European Union has liberalised the energy markets in the EU via the so-called third generation Electricity and Gas Directives containing contract law provisions in the Annex under the heading of "Consumer Protection Measures".[18]

The wording "movable" objects results in the exclusion of contracts for the sale of real estate.[19] Sales by way of execution or otherwise by authority of law (Article 1(2)(b)(1) 1st dash) are also excluded

b) Guarantee

4.4 The scope of application of the Directive also includes "guarantees", in earlier versions called "commercial" guarantees, which are defined in Article 1(2)(e) as:

> "any undertaking by a seller or producer to the consumer, given without extra charge, to reimburse the price paid or to replace, repair or handle consumer goods in any way if they do not meet the specifications set out in the guarantee statement or in the relevant advertising".

It is of paramount importance for common law jurisdictions to exclude so-called "extended *warranties*" which need to be paid for by the consumer. The text of the Directive is unequivocal and legal questions arising from the purchase of guarantees are not dealt with by the Directive.[20]

c) Second-hand goods sold at public auction

4.5 Article 1(3) allows Member States to provide that second-hand goods "sold at public auction where consumers have the opportunity of attending the sale in

---

15 Luna Serrano, in: Grundmann/Bianca, Article 1, para 30.

16 Staudenmayer, in: Grundmann/Medicus/Rolland, 27, 33.

17 Luna Serrano, in: Grundmann/Bianca, Article 1, para 34.

18 Directives 2009/72/EC and 2009/73/EC of the EP and the Council of 13 July 2009 concerning common rules for the internal market of electricity and gas and repealing Directives 2003/54/EC and 2003/55/EC, [2009] OJ L 211/55 (Electricity), L 211/94 (Gas).

19 Luna Serrano, in: Grundmann/Bianca, Article 1, para 30.

20 Beale/Howells, 20, 37; Luna Serrano, in: Grundmann/Bianca, Article 1, para 20, 23 *et seq.*; Malinvaud, in: Grundmann/Bianca, Article 6, para 13; Twigg-Flesner, 177, 185 ff.

person" are not covered by the term "consumer goods".[21] This mainly has an effect on the trade of art and antiques. Auctions over the internet cannot be excluded under Article 1(3).

d) *Contracts for the supply of consumer goods to be manufactured or produced*

4.6 The types of contract to which the Directive applies have been extended and clarified. The Directive not only applies to consumer goods already in existence but also to consumer goods which are to be manufactured or produced (Article 1(4)) that is, contracts for work and materials and contracts for work and services fall within the scope of application of the Directive.[22] However, Article 2(3) clarifies that the seller is not liable for the defective performance of those contracts where it results from materials delivered by the consumer.

2. SCOPE OF APPLICATION CONCERNING THE PERSON AFFECTED

a) *The consumer*

4.7 Article 1(2)(a) defines "consumer" as:

> "any natural person who, in the contracts covered by this Directive, is acting for purposes which are not related to his trade, business or profession".

This means that the Directive neither applies to contracts between sellers and tradesmen insofar as the purpose of the contract indirectly refers to a professional activity (mutual commercial transaction – B2B)[23] nor does it apply to contracts between consumers (mutual consumer transaction – C2C), nor to contracts between private sellers and commercial buyers (reversed consumer purchase – C2B) as these transactions fall foul of the requirement that the transactions have to be related to the seller's trade, business or profession. The question of how to deal with a mixed purchase purpose or a mixed use of consumer goods has been made the responsibility of the national courts; Recital (17) of the CRD seems to allow an extensive interpretation (1.37).[24] Similar problems of definition of (mixed) consumer contracts exist in unfair terms legislation (see 3.14). The European Court of Justice has taken a rather restrictive attitude in the interpretation of the Brussels Convention (see 7.36) which in our opinion is not applicable to contractual relations B2C.

---

21 In detail: Luna Serrano, in: Grundmann/Bianca, Article 1, para 37 *et seq.*

22 Luna Serrano, in: Grundmann/Bianca, Article 1, para 16; Westermann, in: Grundmann/Medicus/Rolland, 259.

23 Luna Serrano, in: Grundmann/Bianca, Article 1 para 60 *et seq.*

24 Grundmann, *Europäisches Schuldvertragsrecht*, 2.12, para 15.

b) *The seller*

4.8 "Seller" is defined in Article 1(2)(c) as:

> "any natural or legal person who, under a contract, sells consumer goods in the course of his trade, business or profession".

In essence the term "seller", as defined in paragraph 2(c), corresponds to the terms "seller" or "supplier" as used in Directive 93/13/EEC. The term describes the contractual counterparty of the consumer and its definition is the opposite of the term "consumer".

c) *The producer*

4.9 The circle of addressees is completed by defining "producer" following Article 3(1) and (2) of Directive 85/374/EEC concerning product liability (6.13). According to Article 1(2)(d), "producer" in terms of the Directive means the manufacturer of consumer goods, the importer of consumer goods into the territory of the Community/Union or any person purporting to be a producer by placing his name, trademark or other distinctive sign on the consumer goods.

For the actual producer, the question arises as to whether only the manufacturer of the final product is to be considered a possible producer or whether the term "producer" extends to the manufacturer(s) of basic materials or intermediary products. According to a German author,[25] any producer of movable goods within the chain of delivery can be considered a producer in terms of Article 1(2)(d) if he causes non-conformity of the final product with the contract pursuant to Article 4. He supports his argument by reasoning that the term "producer" in Article 1(2)(d) refers to the "producer of consumer goods" and consumer goods are defined in paragraph 2(b) as any movable tangible object (subject to further specifications). In support of further identifying the term "importer", which is not expressly defined in the Directive, Article 3(2) of the Product Liability Directive can be cited.

III. CONFORMITY OF THE CONSUMER GOODS WITH THE CONTRACT

4.10 The regulation of conformity with the contract is entirely tailored to the industrial mass production of the goods. According to Article 2(1) of Directive 1999/44/EC, the seller must deliver goods to the consumer which are in conformity with the contract of sale. What is meant by this is illustrated by the conditions set out in Article 2(2) on the conformity of the consumer goods with

---

25 AnwKomm-BGB-*Pfeiffer*, Kauf-RL Article 1, para. 38.

the contract[26] which apply cumulatively.[27] If these conditions are met, there is a rebuttable[28] presumption that the goods are in conformity with the contract. In cases where the conditions are not met, the goods will only be in conformity with the contract if the circumstances support such an assumption. Moreover, the presumption of Article 2(2) has the effect that the elements listed (with the exception of point (b)) need to be considered under national law in cases of liability for non-conformity with the contract – regardless of whether they are considered contractually agreed under national law or not. Except for Article 2(2)(b), the remaining conditions are objective and therefore need no agreement. The term "defect", which forms the basis for liability, follows Article 35 CISG and is amended by including advertising (Article 2(2)). The legal inclusion of incorrect installation as a case of lack of conformity is new and less well-known (Article 2(5)) and has been amended during the conciliation proceedings by the so-called "IKEA clause" (Article 2(5) s. 2).

1. DESCRIPTION, SAMPLE OR MODEL: ARTICLE 2(2)(A)

4.11 Article 2(2)(a) proceeds from a description, sample or model given[29] by the seller. The conformity of consumer goods with the contract is presumed if the goods correspond with the description given by the seller and possesses the qualities of the samples or models provided.

2. FIT FOR ANY PARTICULAR PURPOSE FOR WHICH THE CONSUMER REQUIRES THEM: ARTICLE 2(2)(B)

4.12 Article 2(2)(b) requires that the consumer goods are fit for a agreed particular purpose, i.e. a purpose which is different from a purpose for which goods of the same type are normally used,[30] point (c). However, under normal circumstances the normal use will be required in addition to point (b).[31] If the consumer has specific expectations regarding the use of the goods, then he must communicate those to the seller and the latter must agree to them. Unilateral expectations are insufficient.[32] Not only express but also implied agreements will suffice if the latter complies with national law.[33]

---

26 Grundmann, in: Grundmann/Bianca, Article 2, para 18.

27 Recital 8, the problem of the conformity with the contract, cf. Grundmann, in: Grundmann/Bianca, Article 2 para 9; Stijns/van Gerven, in: Grundmann/Bianca, Article 7, para 24 *et seq.*

28 Bradgate/Twigg-Flesner (eds.), 41 ff; Twigg-Flesner/Bradgate, 1, 9.

29 Similar view also Bradgate/Twigg-Flesner (eds.), 56; Twigg-Flesner/Bradgate, 1, 12.

30 Bradgate/Twigg-Flesner (eds.), 58; Watterson, 197, 205.

31 Grundmann, in: Grundmann/Bianca, Article 2, para 24.

32 Grundmann, in: Grundmann/Bianca, Article 2, para 25.

33 Bradgate/Twigg-Flesner (eds.), 58; zur Bedeutung von Article 2 Abs. 2 lit b); Twigg-Flesner/Bradgate, 1, 13.

3. FIT FOR NORMAL USE: ARTICLE 2(2)(C)

4.13 Article 2(2)(c) refers to the purposes for which goods of the same type are normally used. It relates to the intention of those regularly acting in the particular market.[34] Article 2(2)(c) is almost identical to Article 35(a) CISG. If the consumer goods are regularly used in more than one way, then they must be equally suited for all these purposes.[35]

4. NORMAL QUALITY AND PUBLIC STATEMENTS: ARTICLE 2(2)(D)

4.14 According to Article 2(2)(d), conformity of the consumer goods with the contract is presumed if it is shown in quality and performance:

> "which are normal in goods of the same type and which the consumer can reasonably expect, given the nature of the goods and taking into account any public statements on the specific characteristics of the goods made about them by the seller, the producer or his representative, particularly in advertising or on labelling".

Normal quality refers to the average quality customary in a particular market unless the circumstances require a different quality. In comparison to Article 2(2)(c), point (d) 1st alternative constitutes a residual category which is intended to apply to any relevant quality which could be reasonably expected.[36] The inclusion of advertising statements to determine conformity with the contract constitutes a truly innovative element. However, it is only possible to consider those advertising statements or statements regarding particular product features made on the label which can be objectively measured or substantiated. There is no lack of conformity where there is mere sales talk without factual background ("flowery advertisements")[37] which is merely intended to create trust or other feelings in the observer of the advertisement.[38] What the consumer can "reasonably expect" is to be determined against the notion of a reasonable regular consumer who can judge the situation and is able to criticise.[39]

The views on the importance of Article 2(2)(d) differ. On the one hand the provision is objected to partly because it abolishes the distinction between the

---

34 GRUNDMANN, in: GRUNDMANN/BIANCA, Article 2, para 26.

35 TWIGG-FLESNER/BRADGATE, 14.

36 GRUNDMANN, in: GRUNDMANN/BIANCA, Article 2 para 26.

37 TWIGG-FLESNER/BRADGATE, 1, 16: "mere puffs".

38 AUGENHOFER, *JBl* 2001, 82, 85; GRUNDMANN, in: GRUNDMANN/BIANCA, Article 2 para 37.

39 AUGENHOFER, *JBl* 2001, 82, 84 ff.

declaration of intention and advertising, and on the other the provision partly denies any innovative character regarding the national legal situation.[40]

Irrespective of any criticism, the wording of the provision still contains elements of the concept of legitimate expectations.[41]

Under Article 2(4) the seller is not bound by public statements of the producer or its representative if he shows that:

> "he was not, and could not reasonably have been, aware of the statement in question [1st dash], by the time of conclusion of the contract the statement had been corrected [2nd dash], or that the decision to buy the consumer goods could not have been influenced by the statement [3rd dash]."

The conditions apply alternatively, i.e. if one of the conditions is met, this will suffice.

In particular, the burden of proof that the consumer was not influenced by an advertisement could be difficult to discharge, given that an advertisement in its nature purports to convince the consumer to buy the product. Article 2(2)(d) and Article 2(4) therefore constitute a rebuttable presumption that advertising impacts on the consumer.[42]

Note that the presumption of the lack of conformity cannot be rebutted by the seller by simply proving that the purchase decision *was* not influenced by the public statement; the seller is required to prove that the consumer *could not have been influenced*.[43]

5. INCORRECT INSTALLATION OR INCORRECT INSTALLATION INSTRUCTIONS

4.15 According to Article 2(5) s. 2 the seller is liable for a defect caused by incorrect installation if the installation forms part of the contract of sale of the goods and the goods were installed by the seller or were under his responsibility. The term 'installation' is not defined in the Directive. Article 2(5) s. 2 constitutes liability of the seller if the product, intended to be installed by the consumer, is installed by him and the incorrect installation results from a shortcoming in the installation instructions (so-called IKEA clause). Under the Directive, the seller is liable for installation instructions which ordinarily are not provided by himself but by the producer, irrespective of any fault.

---

40 With regard to Germany, Westermann, in: Grundmann/Medicus/Rolland, 259. For Austria cf. Augenhofer, *JBl* 2001, 82, 88. In Denmark and the Netherlands a comparable provision already existed, cf. Jongeneel, 143, 145 ff; Bruun Nielsen, 189, 190.

41 Cf. Micklitz, 167.

42 Twigg-Flesner/Bradgate, 1, 15.

43 Bradgate/Twigg-Flesner (eds.), 62; Twigg-Flesner/Bradgate, 1, 16.

IV. TIME AND PRESUMPTION OF LACK OF CONFORMITY

4.16 The time set for determining the conformity of the consumer goods with the contract is the "time at which the goods were delivered" (Article 3(1)), now defined by Article 18 of the CRD (9.16).

Concerning the time of the lack of conformity with the contract, the presumption of Article 5(3) applies in favour of the consumer according to which, unless proved otherwise, any lack of conformity which becomes apparent within six months of delivery of the goods shall be presumed to have existed at the time of delivery. The duration of the period of six months is determined by way of the burden of proof and the setting-off in connection with restitution. The latter argument is less plausible as the calculation within six months is as difficult as within 24 months. The six-month period is a cut-off period which is not linked to the appearance of the defect. In fact, the timely limited shifting of the burden of proof provides for the consumer an incentive to assert a claim, or, more likely, to enquire whether there is a claim to benefit from the privilege. The boundaries between the factual necessity to examine consumer goods and to notify a defect have become blurred. The presumption does not apply without restrictions. It is inapplicable in circumstances where the presumption is incompatible with the "nature of the goods" or "the nature of the lack of conformity". Because of the restriction on the "nature of the goods" the application of the shifted burden of proof to second-hand goods is subject to restrictions as it is impossible to apply those features of new goods; however, a certain use is required.

V. STATUTORY EXCLUSION OF LIABILITY FOR LACK OF CONFORMITY

4.17 The seller is liable to the consumer for any lack of conformity, irrespective of whether he is at fault or not (Article 3(1)). The seller's liability for lack of conformity of the consumer goods with the contract shall be restricted if, at the time the contract was concluded, the consumer was aware, or could not reasonably have been unaware of, the lack of conformity, or if the lack of conformity has its origin in materials supplied by the consumer (Article 2(3)). The requirement to "not reasonably be unaware of" needs to be treated sensitively.[44] Opinions on whether this requirement as it stands covers obvious lack of conformity or gross negligence[45] or if any negligence suffices, differ

44 Twigg-Flesner, 177, 182.

45 Grundmann, in: Grundmann/Bianca, Article 2 para 52.

significantly.[46] Considerations regarding unawareness take account of equitable principles which are linked to the degree of the consumer's attention. This becomes even more evident as the defect must become "obvious" to the consumer. Therefore the consumer does not bear the burden of conducting an investigation.[47] "Becoming obvious" would only extend to obvious defects which compared to gross negligence would constitute an even more severe measure.

VI. THE OBLIGATIONS OF THE SELLER: ARTICLE 2; AND THE RIGHT OF REDRESS: ARTICLE 4

1. SELLER'S OBLIGATIONS

4.18 Article 2 defines the obligations of the seller under the concept of "conformity". Unlike in traditional contract law concepts the seller is also liable to the extent stated under Article 2(2)(d) for advertisements by the producer. This extension of liability is put into perspective by Article 2(4), according to which the seller can avoid liability for the conduct of the producer which results in the lack of conformity with the contract under the conditions listed in that paragraph. Whether or not the provision will remain without relative consequences depends on the threshold which is to be applied. Pursuant to Article 2(2)(d), the seller is responsible for rebutting the presumption of the lack of conformity with the contract. Direct liability of the producer or other links in the distribution chain for lack of conformity is not provided for by the Directive. One should also note Recital (23), according to which it may be necessary to provide for the producer's direct liability for defects for which he is responsible.

Pursuant to Article 2(4) it is required of the seller that "he was not, and could not reasonably have been, aware of the statement in question". Irrespective of the qualification of the measure of negligence, this provision forces the seller to remain up-to-date with advertising statements made by the producer. To this extent Article 2(4)(a) constitutes an obligation to obtain information, the violation of which is sanctioned by way of liability for lack of conformity.[48] Pursuant to Article 2(4)(b) the seller can object to liability under certain circumstances where he can show that by the time of conclusion of the contract the statement had been corrected. Complicated legal questions arise under Article 2(4)(c). The decision of the consumer to buy will have been impacted upon "in any form" by the advertising statement as this is what such a statement aims for and how it justifies the expenses. Whether or not the decision to buy has been

46 The discussion in Italy, cf. ZACCARIA, 189.

47 GRUNDMANN, in: GRUNDMANN/BIANCA, Article 2 para 52.

48 GRUNDMANN, in: GRUNDMANN/BIANCA, Article 2 para 41.

made by way of a statement under Article 2(2)(d) remains circumstantial. This is what the consumer will ordinarily allege in his favour and what the seller will ordinarily reject. To this extent the significance of the rebuttal pursuant to Article 2(4)(c) is hard to assess.

2. THE RIGHT TO REDRESS IN ARTICLE 4

4.19 Article 4 contains a provision which applies where the seller is liable to the consumer for the lack of conformity caused by a third party. Pursuant to Article 4(1) the final seller shall be entitled to pursue remedies against the producer, a previous seller in the same chain of contracts or any other intermediary for an act or omission resulting in the lack of conformity. The person or persons liable against whom the final seller may pursue remedies, together with the relevant actions and conditions of exercise shall be determined by national law. Beyond the relationship between the final seller and the consumer, the Directive also regulates the relationship between businessmen (B2B). It is the purpose of Article 4 to prevent the final seller's liability for damage which was actually caused by the misconduct of a third party.

The extent of the obligation to implement Article 4 is subject to discussion. Member States are required, however, to provide the final seller with a right of redress against persons in the distribution chain, whereas it is at Member States' discretion to provide the details of the right of redress (Article 4 s. 2). It is insufficient, however, if national law merely provides a right of redress.[49] As regards the *effet utile*, the final seller is to be furnished with an effective right to redress.

a) Requirements on the right to redress

4.20 In order for the final seller to assert a claim to redress, there must be a liability claim by a consumer for lack of conformity caused by the conduct of a third party, but not the delivery of non-conforming goods from a previous seller to the final seller. Therefore, the provision also applies where the goods delivered were in conformity with the contract, but where the previous seller or producer has otherwise caused liability of the final seller against the consumer.

b) Persons subject to the right to redress

4.21 Article 4(1) lists the potential persons subject to the right to redress: the producer, a previous seller in the same chain of contracts, or any other intermediary. The term "producer" is defined in Article 2(2)(b). The meaning of

---

49 Zaccaria, 193.

the term "previous seller" in the chain of distribution depends on the contractual relations within the chain. Persons other than previous sellers in the chain that come into contact with the goods may also be liable, such as persons responsible for the transport, carriers and persons acting as sales agents or brokers, as well as importers that are not part of the chain.

The Directive does not require the provision of direct action against the producer. Article 12 obliges the Commission, however, to pursue the question of the extent to which liability of the producer is to be included at a later point in time.

c) Subject to the disposition of the parties?

4.22 The opinions on whether Article 4 allows for a disposition of the parties to exclude liability of the final seller vary considerably. As Article 4 constitutes a "may provision", and pursuant to Recital (9) the principle of freedom of contract shall remain unaffected, it could be concluded that one could regard the provision to be subject to the disposition of the parties.[50] However, Member States are required to introduce a right to redress. The question remains, however, as to what good is a statutory right to make redress in favour of the final seller if it may be contractually waived, e.g. by way of an exclusion clause? Recital (9) seems to require *express* renouncement for an exclusion to take effect. This wording appears to hinge upon an individual agreement rather than exclusion in the standard terms and conditions.[51]

VII. REMEDIES OF THE CONSUMER: ARTICLE 3

4.23 Upon the insistence of the Federal Republic of Germany in the common position of the Council, the initially planned fourfold right of the consumer to choose was abandoned in favour of a hierarchy of remedies. Pursuant to Article 3(3) the consumer can only assert his rights progressively. In the case of a lack of conformity, the consumer can first require the seller to repair the goods or to replace them. If such a claim is not appropriate, or where the repair or replacement are not completed within a reasonable time or cause the consumer significant inconvenience, then the consumer has a right to reduction of the price or rescission of the contract.[52]

---

50 Bridge, in: Grundmann/Bianca, Article 4, para 33; Staudenmayer, 42 ff.

51 Bradgate/Twigg-Flesner (eds.), 228.

52 Also Bradgate/Twigg-Flesner (eds.), 88; Twigg-Flesner/Bradgate, 1, 16; Westermann, in: Grundmann/Medicus/Rolland, 266.

1. REPAIR AND REPLACEMENT: THE *WEBER/PUTZ* DOCTRINE

4.24 Pursuant to Article 3(2) 1st alternative, in the case of a lack of conformity, the consumer is entitled to have the goods brought into conformity free of charge by repair[53] or replacement. Precisely this question was the subject of the first reference by the German Supreme Court to the ECJ. German law entitled the seller, where goods not in conformity are replaced, to payment of compensation for the benefits derived by the purchaser from the use of those goods until their replacement with new goods – a provision repealed by later legislation. This happened after ECJ confirmed in *Quelle*[54] that the Community legislature intended to make the "free of charge" aspect of the seller's obligation to bring goods into conformity an essential element of the protection afforded to consumers by the Directive. Otherwise the consumer might be deterred from making use of his/her rights.

4.24a The *Weber* and *Putz* cases[55] decided by the ECJ on 16 June 2011 against the critical opinion of AG Mazak of 18 May 2010 are a good, and at the same time controversial, example of the impact of EU law on traditional ideas on remedies in sales law beyond the wording of Directive 99/44/EC. They concern reimbursement of additional costs by the consumer for replacing a defective product and installing an improved one, for example by tearing off and replacing defective tiles used for floor panelling, or by disconnecting and reconnecting a dishwasher that did not function. AG Mazak rejects this claim under EU law, but the ECJ upheld it as a causal consequence of the seller's obligation to deliver a product that conforms to its specifications. The reasoning of the Court is surprisingly short and based on the rather vague provisions in the Directive that repair and replacement should be done within "a reasonable time", "free of charge" and "without significant inconvenience to the consumer", even if the contract did not include installation services. This creates a *strict liability regime* for the seller, not only for the act of replacing the defective product itself, but also for the resulting follow-up costs even after the transfer of the risk. In order to avoid the seller being over-charged, the Court referred to the possibility of bringing a recourse action against the previous seller or producer according to

[53] Legal definition in Article 1(2)(f) as "bringing consumer goods into conformity with the contract of sale".

[54] ECJ, 17 April 2008, C-404/06 *Quelle AG v Bundesverband der Verbraucherzentralen* [2008] ECR I-2685; the German Federal Court (Bundesgerichtshof – BGH) followed suit in its judgment NJW 2009, 427.

[55] Joined Cases C-65/09 + C-87/09, *Gebr. Weber et al. v J. Wittmer et al.* [2011] ECR I-5257, comments with different approaches by Johnson/Unberath, *CMLRev* 2012, 793; Grundmann, in: Terryn et al. (ed.), 725; Reich, *General Principles of EU Civil Law*, paras 4.18–4.19.

Article 4 of Directive 99/44/EC (para 48, *supra* 4.19). The Court was also asked whether Article 3(3) of Directive 99/44/EC was to be read as an "absolute" or as a "relative" defence for the seller in relation to the impossibility of repairing or replacing the defective product. The "dominant opinion" (*herrschende Meinung*) of German law at the time, under the implementing provision of §439 BGB, understood it as an "absolute proportionality test": if one of the remedies was impossible and the other disproportionate in terms of cost, this had the consequence of a total loss of first-stage remedies under sales law; the consumer could only terminate the contract or receive a price reduction; damages could only be recovered under existing (German) law requiring that the seller be at fault, a possibility that would usually be excluded because the seller did not produce the good himself and did not know (nor should have known) of the defect. The Court however opted for a "relative proportionality defence" as corroborated by Recital (11): even if one remedy (repair) would be impossible and the other (replacement) result in disproportionate costs for the seller, the consumer would not completely lose his first-stage remedies; the disproportionate cost of replacement (including costs for disconnecting and reconnecting) would only allow the seller to reduce them "to an amount proportionate to the value the goods would have if there were no lack of conformity and the significance of the lack of conformity" (para 74). The reference point is not therefore the (possibly much higher) cost of removal of the defective product or/and the installation of a conforming product, but its lower net value. This seems to be a fair balancing of the different interests of the parties.

The judgment is an important step in improving consumer's remedies, while at the same time trying to balance the interests of both parties in case of excessive costs of removing respectively reinstalling the defective good. The German Federal Court (BGH), in its judgment of 21 December 2011,[56] followed suit under the principle of consistent interpretation (1.34) by extending the scope of replacement from merely meaning disconnection to also including reconnection, a possibility thus far rejected in its earlier case law. The BGH also followed suit concerning the "relative proportionality test" under Article 3(3) of Directive 99/44/EC, and interpreted §439 BGB restrictively using the method of "teleological reduction" of German law which it had already applied in its follow-up judgment to *Quelle*. It discussed in detail the different proposals in legal writing on how to implement the proportionality criteria; it found a reimbursement of €600 to be adequate for the value of non-defective tiles (€1,200).

---

[56] BGH, VIII ZR 70/08 NJW 2012, 1073; the BGH however did not extend this principle to B2B transactions, VIII ZR 226/11 of 17.10.2012, EuZW 2013, 157.

a) *The right of the consumer to choose*

4.25 Initially the consumer has the discretion to choose between repair and replacement[57] as expressly shown by the wording of Article 3(3) ("or") and the history of origin of this particular provision. The Commission proposal of the CRD (*supra* 4.1a) wanted to change this in favour of the seller and to the detriment of the consumer, which was severely criticised by the present authors[58] and was not taken up in the final text of the CRD.

b) *Exclusion of the obligation to remedy by the seller*

4.26 The right of the consumer to choose is limited by the reservation of the possibility and the reasonableness of the remedy. A situation of non-conformity only needs to be remedied where repair or replacement is neither impossible nor unreasonable.[59] The question of whether an action is possible is to be assessed for each alternative individually whereas reasonableness is to be assessed by comparing the two alternatives.

The seller can only be required to remedy the situation if this is objectively possible. According to Recital (16), replacement will ordinarily[60] be excluded for second-hand goods so that the consumer is limited in his right to repair. The same applies to the purchase of specified goods.

Whether and when a remedy is considered 'unreasonable' is further defined in Article 3(3)(2) and Recital (11). Reasonableness is to be assessed according to objective criteria; a remedy shall be deemed disproportionate if it imposes costs on the seller which, in comparison with the alternative remedy, are unreasonable (unreasonably high replacement costs for simple repairs and *vice versa*), cf. Recital (11), with the qualifications given in the *Weber/Putz* judgment (4.24a). In assessing the reasonableness test, the criteria set out in Article 3(3)(2) need to be considered, such as the value of the goods if there was no lack of conformity (1st dash), the significance of the lack of conformity (2nd dash) and whether the alternative remedy can be achieved without significant inconvenience to the consumer (3rd dash). From the seller's point of view, repair will be most appropriate for high-quality and long-life goods, and replacement will be the best alternative for cheap, low-quality, mass-produced products for reasons of cost.[61] From a consumer's point of view, any lack of conformity is inconvenient.

---

57 Bradgate/Twigg-Flesner (eds.), 88; Staudenmayer, 38.

58 Micklitz/Reich, *CMLRev* 2009, 471 at 503.

59 Cf. Bradgate/Twigg-Flesner (eds.), 88; Twigg-Flesner/Bradgate, 1, 17.

60 An example where as an exception this is inapplicable, Twigg-Flesner/Bradgate, 1, 17 ff. Bradgate/Twigg-Flesner (eds.), 91.

61 This principle will lead to a fair solution in most cases but not in all. It might be possible that a defect might be easily repairable whereas the repair of severe defects in high-quality goods might be unreasonably expensive, Twigg-Flesner/Bradgate, 1, 18.

In the case of goods of daily use this inconvenience may be significant.[62] The Directive lists undefined terms "impossible", "unreasonable", "disproportionate" and "significant inconvenience", all of which await further definition under Union law.

c) *Execution of the remedy*

4.27 If, after having taken into account the reasonableness test, the consumer is referred to repair or replacement, then any repair or replacement shall be completed within "a reasonable time" and without "any significant inconvenience" to the consumer (Article 3(3)). Both criteria have their own relevance and their requirements need to be examined individually. Otherwise the distinction in Article 2(5) would be senseless, according to which the consumer is entitled to either have the price reduced or the contract rescinded if either the seller has not completed the remedy within a reasonable time (2nd dash) or if the seller has not completed the remedy without significant inconvenience to the consumer (3rd dash).

The Directive does not set out the start date for this period; it merely needs to be reasonable. It appears that the consumer will start the period by asserting his claim. Whether the period is reasonable is determined according to the type of goods, the consumer's intended purpose for the goods (a car, for example, is more important than a toaster) as well as according to the type of defect. The more difficult it is to remedy the defect, the more time the seller will be allowed to remedy the situation.

The consumer is already caused significant inconvenience where the repair fails, i.e. if the goods cannot be repaired on the first attempt. Such a reading is supported by the fact that the consumer is not required to grant a grace period. Significant inconvenience also extends to the limitation of the use of other goods of the consumer (e.g. damage of other legal interests) or a non-pecuniary personal effort as, for example, the "running about".

The seller is required to complete the repair or the replacement free of charge (Article 3(2)). He bears all necessary costs, in particular the cost of postage, labour and materials, cf. Article 3(4). Depending on the particular facts, further costs which the consumer incurs in realising his rights are also included, such as travel expenses, mailing costs and so forth.

The question of whether the consumer should pay compensation for the use he has had of the goods since they were delivered to him, if the non-conforming goods are replaced, has been decided in the negative by the above-mentioned *Quelle* judgment (4.24).

In the event of incorrect installation instructions in accordance with the terms of Article 2(5) s. 2, the question arises as to what the consumer can require

62 Cf. Twigg-Flesner, 177, 184; Bradgate/Twigg-Flesner (eds.), 95.

by way of replacement. As long as the product has not been installed, the consumer can require a correct installation instruction or a correction or explanation of the instruction. Where, however, because of incorrect installation instructions there has been an inappropriate installation, then the question arises as to whether the consumer can require the seller to install the product. Pursuant to Article 3(3) the consumer can require the consumer goods to be repaired or replaced free of charge. However, the goods installed, not the installation instruction, is to be considered as consumer goods. The claim to have the goods repaired therefore relates to the installed goods in their entirety.[63]

2. REDUCTION OF THE PRICE AND RESCISSION (TERMINATION) OF THE CONTRACT

4.28 The "second level" remedy of the consumer is the right to an appropriate reduction of the price or rescission (termination) of the contract. The consumer's right to claim compensation is not governed by the Directive but by Member State law. The transition from the first to the second level of remedy was the subject of political discussions, the result of which is a detailed regulation which leaves little discretion to Member States.[64] Only if the consumer is entitled to neither repair nor replacement (1st dash), or if the seller has not completed the remedy within a reasonable time (2nd dash), or if the seller has not completed the remedy without significant inconvenience to the consumer (3rd dash) may the consumer require an appropriate reduction of the price or have the contract rescinded without having to satisfy further requirements; in particular there is no need to grant a grace period to the seller (Article 3(5)). The consumer can assert his second-level rights immediately if, for example, he cannot claim repair or replacement because such a claim is impossible pursuant to paragraph 3. If the seller fails to complete the repair or replacement, or if it is without effect, or where further waiting is pointless or unreasonable for the consumer, the consumer has a direct right to have the price reduced or the contract rescinded. According to the wording of the Directive, significant inconvenience may even result in a reduction of the price or rescission of the contract where the seller actually successfully repairs or replaces the goods. If, however, from the outset it is obvious that repair or replacement can only be completed by causing significant inconvenience, the consumer must be directly entitled to have the price reduced or have the contract rescinded. The consumer is not entitled to

63 Gruber, *VuR* 2002, 120, 123.

64 Cf. Staudenmayer, 37, who refers to the relationship between the compromising and the limitation of the margin of appreciation of the Member States regarding the implementation; Rott, *CMLRev* 2003, 1107.

have the contract rescinded if the lack of conformity is minor (Article 3(6)), but may only claim a price reduction.

The conditions set out in Article 3(5) apply alternatively and the consumer is entitled to his second-level rights if one of the conditions set out in Article 3(5) is not met. The legal details of the right to rescission, as well as the modalities of the execution of the right, i.e. in particular questions regarding the compensation for the use where the contract is rescinded,[65] are at the discretion of Member States. This might result in an unequal treatment of distance contracts and normal sales contracts.

As regards the reduction of the price, the Directive merely requires that it must be appropriate, an indication that its extent is not provided by the Directive.

4.28a The relation between the rights to rescission and to reduction of the price in case of minor defects according to Article 3(6) has been before the Court in the *Duarte* case.[66] The question was posed by a Spanish court which, under its procedural provisions, could not allow a consumer who has originally claimed termination of the contract however being rejected because of a mere minor defect, to switch remedies. Since the consumer had not expressly asked for a reduction of the price, she was barred from doing so in later proceedings. AG Kokott and the Court found the Spanish rule to violate the "effectiveness principle" under EU law (8.3) which should allow the consumer to at least ask for a price reduction if termination was impossible.

VIII. THE DOUBLE PERIOD AND THE PERIOD FOR ASSERTING A CLAIM: ARTICLE 5

4.29 Again, the initial approach as contained in the Commission proposal has been significantly altered as insisted on by some Member States like Germany. Unlike the Roman legal system, German law does not distinguish between the period in which the defect must occur (cut-off period) and the period in which to assert a claim (limitation period). Under the initial approach the two periods diverge. The now relevant Article 5(1) s. 1 establishes a two-year cut-off period. The lack of conformity which already existed at the time of the delivery of the goods needs to become apparent within two years of the delivery of the goods. A lack of conformity which existed at the time of the delivery (Article 3(1)) becomes "apparent" if it was obvious from the beginning, or a latent defect becomes apparent within a two-year period.[67] The consumer is not required,

65 This consequence is made clear in Recital (15).

66 ECJ, 3 October 2013, C-32/12, *Soledad Duarte Hueros v Atoiciba et al.* [2013] ECR I-nyr.

67 Hondius, in: Grundmann/Bianca, Article 5, para 7.

however, to notify the seller.[68] Instead, pursuant to the second sentence, Member States are given the discretion to grant a limitation period which shall not expire within a period of two years from the time of delivery, instead of a cut-off period or in addition thereto.

Member States may provide that, in the case of second-hand goods, the time periods may be shortened to one year (Article 7(1)(2)). Article 5(1) complements the lengths and starting points of both periods. In practice a limitation period which is identical in length to a cut-off period effectively results in a shortening of the cut-off period, since the consumer is required to take the necessary steps under national law – ordinarily this will be the starting of court or similar proceedings – to assert his claim before the expiry of the limitation period.[69] The Directive does not contain any provision on how to suspend or interrupt the running of the two periods of Article 5(1). Recital (18) clarifies that Member States may provide for suspension or interruption of the period in accordance with their national law.

The option granted to Member States in Article 5(2), which allows them to provide that the rights of the consumer depend on the notification of the lack of conformity within two months, does not fit the concept. Initially the Commission intended to make notification binding in exchange for the fourfold right of the consumer to freely choose his or her remedy. The consumer was to be placed in a strong legal position but at the same time required to notify possible defects to the non-conforming seller.[70] According to the view of the Commission, by inserting different levels of remedies, the justification for an introduction of a duty to notify became obsolete. Article 5(2)(1) and (2) as well as Recitals (19) and (20) illustrate the discrepancy of the compromise formula in the final text of the Directive.[71] It remains unclear whether the duty to notify requires the consumer to examine the consumer goods. The response should not solely be looked for in Article 5(2) but also in the system of the Directive which links the justification and realisation of the different remedies with the requirement that the consumer is not reasonably unaware of the lack of conformity. Article 5(2) refers to a period of two months from the date on which the consumer detected such a lack of conformity. This entails a reference to Article 2 which in turn relates to Article 2(3). This means that the consumer is not required to conduct a thorough examination of the goods and to search for latent defects. The consumer is not subject to a duty to investigate; rather he is merely subject to a qualified duty to notify.

---

68 Westermann, in: Grundmann/Medicus/Rolland, 272.

69 Staudenmayer, 40; Westermann, in: Grundmann/Medicus/Rolland, 273.

70 This interrelation is particularly referred to by Staudenmayer, 41.

71 Staudenmayer, 42; Westermann, in: Grundmann/Medicus/Rolland, 274. In Article 5(2)(3) it is announced that not later than 7 January 2003, the Commission shall prepare a report on the use made by Member States.

IX. "COMMERCIAL" GUARANTEES: ARTICLE 6

4.30 The Directive requires Member States to introduce a guarantee which accompanies the contract. A definition is given in Article 1(2)(e). Considering that the first proposal of the Commission did not measure up to the regulatory attempts as contained in the Green Paper, the regulation of the commercial guarantee has been further limited in the final version of the Directive. It is no longer required for the guarantee to put the beneficiary in a better position than he would otherwise have been in under national law.[72]

Pursuant to Article 6 the offerer is unilaterally bound by his guarantee statement, and more importantly by an associated guarantee.[73] An offerer who advertises an extensive and long-lasting guarantee will be liable in respect of that advertised guarantee even if the guarantee form provides for significantly less liability.

Article 6(2) to (4) contain formal requirements for contractual guarantees. Pursuant to Article 6(2) 1st dash the guarantee shall state that the consumer has legal rights under applicable national legislation governing the sale of consumer goods and make clear that those rights are not affected by the guarantee.[74] The principle of transparency is intended to prevent consumers being misled by a guarantee given by the seller or the producer (cf. Recital (21)). The guarantee shall also set out the essential particulars necessary for making claims under the guarantee, notably the duration and territorial scope of the guarantee, as well as the name and address of the guarantor (Article 6(2) 2nd dash). These details must be given in plain, intelligible language.[75] At the request of the consumer, the guarantee shall be made available in writing or feature in another durable medium available and accessible to him (Article 6(3)).[76] The language clause of Article 6(4) gives Member States the discretion that the guarantee is to be given in one or more official languages of the Community for goods brought into circulation in their territory.[77]

If the guarantee fails to meet the requirements set out in paragraphs 2 to 4, it will remain valid as per Article 6(5), and the consumer can still rely on the guarantee and require that it be honoured.[78] However, in such a case the Directive fails to provide a sanction against the offerer. This flaw has been repeatedly criticised from early on.[79] An appropriate provision has not been inserted however, not even in the form used in the numerous consumer law

72 In detail: Malinvaud, in: Grundmann/Bianca, Article 6, para 31 *et seq.*
73 Ibid, Article 6, para 15.
74 Ibid, Article 6, para 24 *et seq.*; Staudenmayer, 43.
75 In greater depth: Malinvaud, in: Grundmann/Bianca, Article 6, para 28 *et seq.*
76 See also Ibid, Article 6, para 18 *et seq.*
77 Ibid, Article 6, para 20 *et seq.*
78 Ibid, Article 6, para 41.
79 Beale/Howells, 19, 21, 39 "a curiosity".

directives, i.e. that it is the obligation of Member States to ensure that consumer rights are appropriately and effectively enforced. The Directive has only been inserted in the Appendix to Directive 2009/22/EC (on cross-border injunctions for the protection of consumers' interests),[80] according to which cross-border violations of the principle of transparency may be pursued by way of legal action taken by an association or through the competent administrative authority. This represents a protective gap which needs to be bridged by Member States on their territory.

X. BINDING NATURE, MINIMUM PROTECTION, PIL, DUTY TO REPORT AND INFORM: ARTICLES 7, 8, 8A, 9, 11 AND 12

4.31 In essence, the provisions at the end of the Directive represent the general standard of the legislative technique regarding consumer law directives. Conflict of law provisions will be discussed in Chapter 7 (7.21).

1. BINDING NATURE, ARTICLE 7(1)

4.32 Pursuant to Article 7(1) the rights granted under the Directive in case of non-conformity of the delivered consumer good are binding and cannot be excluded or limited. The binding character is inherent in consumer law directives as it is purported to establish a level of protection that is not at the parties' disposition. The freedom to contract for national and international sales contracts is therefore significantly limited.[81] Contractual clauses or agreements made with the consumer prior to his notification of the lack of conformity by which the rights granted under the Directive are indirectly or directly restricted[82] will not be binding on the consumer.[83] This applies to sales contracts for new and second-hand goods irrespective of whether liability is affected through individual agreement or standard terms and conditions.[84] Article 7(1) allows the parties to make different agreements after the lack of conformity has been brought to the attention of the seller, as the consumer will have been informed about the lack of conformity.[85] Article 7(1) does not govern

---

80 OJ L 110, 1 May 2009, 30.

81 Stijns/van Gerven, in: Grundmann/Bianca, Article 7, para 13.

82 In detail: Stijns/van Gerven, in: Grundmann/Bianca, Article 6, para 23 *et seq.*; Bradgate/Twigg-Flesner (eds.), 139 ff.

83 In detail as regards the legal consequence of the missing binding of the consumer: Stijns/van Gerven, in: Grundmann/Bianca, Article 6, para 52 *et seq.*

84 Bradgate/Twigg-Flesner (eds.), 139.

85 Stijns/van Gerven, in: Grundmann/Bianca, Article 6, para 16 *et seq.*; Staudenmayer, 44.

the right of redress of the final seller. Article 7(1)(2) contains an exception which applies to second-hand goods only. Member States may provide that the contractual parties may agree on contractual terms or agreements which have a shorter time period for the liability of the seller, provided that the agreed period is not less than one year.[86]

2. THE MINIMUM PROTECTION CLAUSE

4.33 Article 8(1) clarifies that the rights resulting from this Directive are to be exercised without prejudice to other rights which the consumer may invoke under the national rules governing contractual or non-contractual liability.[87] The same applies to other questions regarding the law on the sales of goods, irrespective of whether they are regulated by national or Union law.[88]

Pursuant to Article 8(2), Member States may adopt or maintain in force more stringent provisions, compatible with the Treaty in the field covered by this Directive,[89] to ensure a higher level of consumer protection. The Directive approximates the main issues of the laws on the sale of goods, thereby establishing a minimum standard which might be raised but not lowered.[90]

The principle of minimum harmonisation as formulated in Article 8(2) needs to be further clarified with a view to implementation. It also becomes more important to think about how it can be assessed if and when national law is more beneficial to the consumer. The EU legislator, as well as relevant commentaries, consider it possible to distinguish a better solution from a minimum solution. This entails a further principle issue: the question of when a provision in a Directive effects an entire harmonisation contrary to the standard formula. This question arises in particular with regard to the core provisions of the Directive, Article 2 on the conformity of goods with the contract and Article 3 on remedies.[91]

86 See also Stijns/van Gerven, in: Grundmann/Bianca, Article 6, para 42 *et seq.*

87 In detail: Grundmann, in: Grundmann/Bianca, Article 2, para 1 *et seq.*

88 Ibid, Article 2, para 3; cf. Rott, 1107, 1128.

89 Cf. Rott, 1107, 1109 ff who analyses whether, if there is free movement of goods, Article 28 EC the competence rule of Article 95 EC or the Directive itself limits the adoption or maintenance of more stringent provisions.

90 Grundmann, in: Grundmann/Bianca, Article 6, para 10 *et seq.*

91 Rott, 1107, 1109.

3. THE DUTY TO REPORT AND INFORM

4.34 With Article 9 the Directive wanders on a new path. It obliges Member States[92] to take appropriate measures to inform the consumer of the national law transposing the Directive and to encourage, where appropriate, professional organisations to inform consumers of their rights. Obviously the duty to inform does not extend to a duty to inform the consumer about the Directive as such, irrespective of the fact that directives may take effect prior to implementation. The duty arose with the expiry of the implementation period on 1 January 2002 (Article 11).[93] By virtue of Article 9 the consumer is granted a subjective right to information by the State which had been unknown before, the violation of which can be sanctioned according to the *Francovich* doctrine.[94] The consumer can assert a claim for not having been appropriately informed about the timely implementation or for having been informed about the implementation, but national law does not acknowledge rights granted under the Directive.[95] Article 9 is a suitable area for the further development of the system of subjective rights. It remains to be seen, however, how potential damage to the consumer can be assessed.

4. REVISION OF THE CONSUMER SALES DIRECTIVE: A NEW ARTICLE 8A

4.35 Directive 99/44/EC belongs to the set of directives which were under revision under the draft CRD of 8 October 2008 which became the CRD 2011/83/EU (4.1a, 9.2).[96] The earlier debate focused on those issues which had been left undecided in the legislative process. The key point was whether and under what conditions the manufacturer might be held liable for defective products.[97] However, the European Commission has not yet come up with a proposal.

The CRD – as well as regulating consumer information (Articles 5–8), delivery (Article 18) and passing of risk (Article 20 – see 9.16) – has introduced an Article 8a into Directive 99/44/EC concerning the reporting obligations of Member States if they make use of the option of imposing more stringent information provisions than those provided in Article 5(1) to (3) for regular sales contracts and in Article 7(1) for off-premises sales contracts.

---

92 Sirena, in: Grundmann/Bianca, Article 9, para 6.

93 Ibid, Article 9, para 9.

94 Cf. ECJ, 19 November 1991, C-6/90 + C-9/90, *Francovich* [1991] ECR I-5357.

95 Sirena, in: Grundmann/Bianca, Article 9, para 15 *et seq.*

96 COM (2006) 744 final.

97 For a proposal in this direction see Micklitz/Reich, *supra* note 13, 508.

XI. OUTLOOK: DIGITAL CONTENT CONTRACTS

4.35a Provisions on digital content were first contained in the CRD 2011/83/EU: Recital (19) explains the new EU policy with regard to digital content. Article 2(11) defines "'digital content' as data which are produced and supplied in digital form". Article 5(1)(g) and (h) includes information requirements for contracts other than off-premises or distance ones, while Article 6(r) and (s) includes similar ones for off-premises and distance contracts (9.9). Articles 14(4)(b) and 16(m) contain special rules concerning withdrawal from digital content contracts.

These consumer information provisions for digital content were taken over and extended, in particular with regard to conformity and remedies in case of non-conformity, by the CESL (4.1b). Even though this chapter does not go into details of the sales law proposals of CESL, the extension of its legal regime to B2C digital content contracts is an interesting development.[98] This is notwithstanding the controversies surrounding the entire CESL project based on an "opt-in" application to cross-border transactions (1.43b). The EU legislator may want to use the proposal on digital content B2C contracts for a special directive containing mandatory provisions (4.35e).

4.35b Concerning definitions of digital content, Article 2(j) CESL is much more specific than the CRD:

> "[D]igital content means data which are produced and supplied in digital form, whether or not according to the buyer's specifications, including video, audio, picture or written digital content, digital games, software and digital content which makes it possible to personalise existing hardware of software; it excludes
> i) financial services, including online banking services:
> ii) legal or financial advice provided in electronic form
> iii) electronic healthcare services
> iv) electronic communication services and networks, and associated facilities and service;
> v) gambling;
> vi) the creation of new digital content and the amendment of existing digital content by consumers or any other interaction with the creation of other users."

Article 5(b) CESL seems to indicate that the EU legislator treats the supply of digital content like software, music, video, electronic games – with or without consideration, whether supplied online or on a tangible medium like a CD or DVD – as a sort of "quasi-sales contract". This seems to be a departure from the classical approach of licensing of intellectual property rights, which was regarded

98 In this sense Reich, *supra* note 55, 6.23.

as a contract of its own in most Member States.[99] It can be justified by the "commodification" (*Verdinglichung*) of digital content through modern technologies, in particular through downloading on the internet or streaming of videos, which makes digital content a candidate for a standardised transaction similar to the traditional sales concept. There are some exceptions to this new approach, in particular financial services and gambling.

4.35c Article 100 CESL extends the concept of conformity expressly to "digital content". Article 102 contains rules on third-party claims, some of which are specific to digital content in B2C transactions, namely (with exceptions for digital content supplied without a price in Article 107):

"– the digital content ... must be cleared of any right or not obviously unfounded claim of a third party ... under the law of the contract or, in case of absence of such agreement, under the law of the buyer's residence, provided ... the seller knew or could be expected to have known of at the time of the conclusion of the contract;
– liability of the seller is excluded only in cases of positive knowledge of the consumer;
– the provisions of this article may not be derogated from in B2C transactions."

It is not quite clear why the seller's conformity obligation, which is normally a strict one, in this case surprisingly depends on fault in contracts regarding digital content. In difference to normal sales contracts of movables, where the buyer acquires full rights of use and sale of the good, digital content contracts usually contain *use restrictions* on the consumer-buyer in general contract terms, for instance regarding copying and content modification. They are usually justified by the so-called Copyright in the Information Society Directive 2001/29/EC[100] because the contract on digital content also contains licensing elements protecting the right holder. They have to be evaluated using a "fairness" test.[101] Abuses seem to be frequent, but this needs to be studied separately, combining intellectual property with contract law concepts.[102]

Article 105(4) contains a specific mandatory clause on an obligation to update digital content, whereby the trader "must ensure that the digital content remains

---

99 See the study of Rott, "Extension of the Proposed Consumer Rights Directive to Cover the Online Purchase of Digital Products", study for BEUC, 2009; Grüber, *Digitale Güter und Verbraucherschutz*, 2010; Helberger et al., *Digital Consumers and the Law*, 21. See also the detailed "Amsterdam Study" on Future Rules for Digital Content Contracts, 2011, done for the Commission. See now Zahn, *ZEuP* 2014, 77 (90) for different types of digital contracts.

100 [2011] OJ L 167/10.

101 For a discussion of the problems under contract terms legislation in Germany, see Grüber, *supra* note 99, 116. The US law situation which allows a near to complete control by copyright owners over users, in particular with regard to so called "virtual worlds" (games etc.), has been critically discussed in the excellent study by Lastowka, 93, 179 ff.

102 For details see now Helberger et al., *JCP* 2013, 44.

in conformity with the contract throughout the duration of the contract". This right to an update depends of course on its (express or implied) terms and therefore may simply be avoided by omitting such a clause in the contract, even though the consumer may have expectations of its inclusion.[103]

4.35d The CESL does not seem to contain any specific remedies for non-performance of B2C contracts relating to the use of digital content even though the "digital buyer" enjoys a "right to require performance" under Article 110. Some remedies may relate to physical goods only, like repair. The right of termination in the event of non-insignificant non-performance is expressly also extended to "the supply of digital content" in Article 114(2) CESL.

If there has been a breach of information duties on digital content (Article 20(1)(g) and (h)), Article 29(1) CESL provides for liability of the trader "for any loss caused to the other party by such failure". This provision cannot be derogated from: Article 29(4). The concept of loss has been defined in Article 2(c) of the Proposal. On the other hand, once the professional seller has supplied the information as required, for example on lack of interoperability, the consumer will not have a remedy against the seller. The information requirement *de facto* functions as an exclusion clause under Article 99(3).[104]

4.35e Obviously, many other questions remain open, the most important being the relation between consumer and copyright law. The CESL does not contain any provisions concerning private copying of digital content; Member State legislation is divergent under Article 5(2)(b) of the Copyright in the Information Society Directive 2001/29/EC, where this is only optional and subject to "fair compensation".[105] Such limited protection of reasonable consumer expectations should be reconsidered.[106] Helberger et al. write:

> "Arguably, the reasonable consumer expectations standard counterweighs the copyrightholder-centered norms on private copying that prevail in the copyright-law analysis."[107]

In practice however, the real problem may lie with exclusion clauses which, according to Article 108 CESL, are forbidden in B2C contracts, but by an *argumentum e contrario* are allowed in B2B transactions. This makes the already difficult distinction between the types of transactions (4.7) even more crucial, but in the "virtual world" of the internet almost impossible to verify. It is therefore suggested that a presumption should be added that digital content

---

103 Helberger et al., *supra* note 99, 99 and 109.
104 Helberger et al., *supra* note 99, 48.
105 [2001] OJ L 167/10; ECJ, 21 October 2010, C-467/08, *Padawan* [2010] ECR I-10055.
106 Helberger et al., *supra* note 99, 97.
107 Helberger et al., *JCP* 2013, at 47.

contracts come under the B2C provisions, unless the commercial character of the transaction is obvious.

As a result, it is submitted that a separate EU directive (or EU regulation) should be included in the consumer *acquis* regulating digital consumer content contracts, based on Directive 2011/83, and including (improved) provisions taken from the CESL as mentioned above. It is not suggested that the Consumer Sales Directive 99/44/EC should be amended because of the hybrid character of digital content contracts.

CHAPTER 5
CONSUMER CREDIT

Peter Rott

CONTENTS

Bibliography:

J. Ady/E. Paetz, Die Umsetzung der Verbraucherkreditrichtlinie in deutsches Recht und besondere verbraucherpolitische Aspekte, *WM* 2009, 1061–1070; E. Balate/ P. Dejemeppe/F. de Patoul, *Le droit du credit à la consommation*, 1995; J. Benedict, Responsible Lending – Das europäische Vertragsrecht zwischen *caveat emptor* und *caveat creditor*!, *ZEuP* 2008, 394–410; U. Blaurock, Verbraucherkredit und Verbraucherleitbild in der Europäschen Union, *JZ* 1999, 801–809; E. Bonino, Finanzdienstleistungen – eine Priorität der Europäischen Verbraucherpolitik, *WM* 1996, 1617–1618; P. Bülow/M. Artz, Am Vorabend einer neuen Verbraucherkreditrichtlinie, *WM* 2005, 1153–1157; U. Burgard, Der Vorschlag der Kommission für eine Richtlinie über Zahlungsdienste im Binnenmarkt, *WM* 2006, 2065–2071; K.-H. Caspari, Anlegerschutz in Deutschland im Lichte der Brüsseler Richtlinien, *NZG* 2005, 98–103; Civic Consulting, Broad economic analysis of the impact of the proposed Directive on consumer credit, EP doc. PE 385.637; A. Danco, Die Novellierung der Verbraucherkreditrichtlinie, *WM* 2003, 853–861; F. Domke/A. Sperlich, Werbung für Verbraucherkredite mit Zinsangaben, *BB* 2010, 2069–2071; J.-U. Franck, Bessere Kreditkonditionen für Verbraucher durch mehr Regulierung?, *ZBB* 2003, 334–342; T. Gessner, Die Restschuldversicherung in der Äquivalenzprüfung des Darlehensvertrags, *VuR* 2008, 84–90; S. Grundmann, EC Financial Services and Contract Law – Developments 2002–2005, *ERCL* 2005, 482–494; S. Grundmann/J. Hollering, EC Financial Services and Contract Law – Developments 2005–2007, *ERCL* 2008, 45–64; B. Gsell/H. M. Schellhase, Vollharmonisiertes

Verbraucherkreditrecht – Ein Vorbild für die weitere europäische Angleichung des Verbrauchervertragsrechts?, *JZ* 2009, 20–29; C. HERRESTHAL, Die Verpflichtung zur Bewertung der Kreditwürdigkeit und zur angemessenen Erläuterung nach der neuen Verbraucherkreditrichtlinie 2008/48/EG, *WM* 2009, 1174–1180; S. HERRMANN, Der Verbraucherkreditvertrag, *VVF* 1996; J. HOFFMANN, Preiskontrolle oder Wettbewerb? – Zur Verordnung über grenzüberschreitende Zahlungen in Euro, *EuZW* 2002, 69–75; M. HOFFMANN, Der Diskussionsstand zur Reform der Verbraucherkreditrichtlinie, *BKR* 2004, 308–315; G. HOWELLS/T. WILHELMSSON, *EC Consumer Law*, 1997; W. KARTEN, Ökonomische Aspekte einer EU-Richtlinie zur Versicherungsvermittlung, *ZVersWiss* 2002, 43–60; K.-O. KNOPS, Restschuldversicherung im Verbraucherkredit, *VersR* 2006, 1455–1459; J. KÖNDGEN/O. STÖCKER, Die Eurohypothek – Akzessorietät als Gretchenfrage?, *ZBB* 2005, 112–120; P. LATHAM, Dispositions communautaires relatives au crédit à la consommation: la directive 87/102/CEE du 22 décembre 1986, *RMC* 1988, 219–224; R. METZ, Verbraucherrelevante europäische Rechtssetzung im Bereich Finanzdienstleistungen, *VuR* 2007, 361–363; G. NOBBE, Verantwortlichkeit der Bank bei der Vergabe von Krediten und der Heinnahme von Sicherheiten, *ZBB* 2008, 78–82; M. REHBERG, Transparenz beim Vertrieb von Finanzprodukten – Das Konzept der Kompensation mangelnder Produkt- durch Statustransparenz vor dem Hintergrund der aktuellen europäischen Rechtsentwicklung, *WM* 2005, 1011–1019; N. REICH, *Heininger* und das europäische Privatrecht, in: BUB et al. (eds.), *Zivilrecht im Sozialstaat, Festschrift für Peter Derleder*, 2005, 127–144; N. REICH/H.-W. MICKLITZ, *Europäisches Verbraucherrecht*, 4th ed. 2003; N. REICH/H.-W. MICKLITZ, Europäisches Verbraucherrecht – quo vadis? Überlegungen zum Grünbuch der Kommission zur Überprüfung des gemeinschaftlichen Besitzstandes im Verbraucherschutz vom 8.2.2007, *VuR* 2007, 121–130; U. REIFNER, Empfehlungen zum Vorschlag einer EU-Richtlinie zum Konsumentenkredit, *VuR* 2004, 11–15; U. REIFNER, Konsumentenkreditrichtlinie im Europaparlament – Zurück zu den Siebzigern?, *VuR* 2004, 85–90; K. RIESENHUBER, Information – Beratung – Fürsorge, Kritische Bemerkungen zum Vorschlag einer neuen Verbraucherkreditrichtlinie, *ZBB* 2003, 325–334; K. RIESENHUBER, *EU-Vertragsrecht*, 2013; C. RITZ, *Harmonisierungsprobleme bei der Umsetzung der EG-Richtlinie 87/102 über den Verbraucherkredit*, 1996; M. ROHE, Privatautonomie im Verbraucherkreditrecht wohin?, Zum Richtlinienvorschlag zur Harmonisierung der Rechts- und Verwaltungsvorschriften der Mitgliedstaaten über den Verbraucherkredit, *BKR* 2003, 267–273; P. ROTT, Mitverantwortung des Kreditgebers bei der Kreditaufnahme – Warum eigentlich nicht?, *BKR* 2003, 851–859; P. ROTT, Risikohaftung der Banken für Schrottimmobilien: Anmerkung zu EuGH, Rs. C-350/03 – Schulte und C-229/04 – Crailsheimer Volksbank, *GPR* 2006, 25–28; P. ROTT, Maximum Harmonisation and Mutual Recognition versus Consumer Protection: The Example of Linked Credit Agreements in EC Consumer Credit Law, *EuLF* 2006, I-61-I-68; P. ROTT, Europäisierung des Rechts der Finanzintermediäre, *EWS* 2008, 21–32; P. ROTT, Kreditvermittlung nach der Reform des Verbraucherkreditrechts, *VuR* 2008, 281–285; P. ROTT, Renationalisation of direct selling – The Impact of the new Consumer Rights Directive on financial services, *ERA-Forum* 2012(13), 35–44; P. ROTT/E. TERRYN/C. TWIGG-FLESNER, Kreditwürdigkeitsprüfung: Verbraucherschutzverhinderung durch Zuweisung zum Öffentlichen Recht?, *VuR* 2011, 163–169; B. STAUDER, La prévention du surendettement du consommateur, in: IMSAND (ed.), *La nouvelle loi fédérale sur le crédit à la consommation*, 2002, 105–144; A. TIFFE, Die

Zulässigkeit von Bearbeitungsgebühren bei Verbraucherdarlehen, *VuR* 2012, 127–133; R. Volante, Mortgage credit contracts and the Green Paper on Mortgage Credit – Controls on Transparency and Fairness, *ERCL* 2007, 150–178; K. Weyand, Informationspflichten bei der Werbung für Verbraucherkredite, *BKR* 2012, 197–199.

I. CONSUMER FINANCIAL SERVICES

5.1 Financial services have developed into a special category of consumer law that reflects best the current philosophy of the EU Commission in the field of consumer law. From a consumer perspective, the protection needs are particularly high in financial services. This has been recognised, for example, in Recital (9) of the Unfair Commercial Practices Directive 2005/29/EC. First of all, significant amounts of money may be at stake. Secondly, in particular in the fields of credit contracts and insurance contracts, the consumer may enter into long-term agreements over many years. Thirdly, financial services are particularly difficult to understand. They are intangible legal instruments that are only determined by the contract itself, and the terms of the contract are often not easy to grasp. Economic theory classifies many financial services as "credence goods", a category of goods in which the consumer is not only usually inexperienced but cannot evaluate straight after the conclusion of the contract either, in particular in cases where the effects of the contract only come to light much later, for example in insurance contracts.[1]

From an internal market perspective, which appears to be the currently prevailing perspective in EU consumer law, financial services are of great importance but are also ambiguous. Being intangible services, they are in principle ideal for being provided cross-border on the internal market since no transportation or similar costs arise. In reality, however, the markets for financial services used to be very much nationalised. One reason lies, again, in the complexity of the services, a factor that is aggravated when it comes to unknown financial services provided by foreign companies, and potentially in a foreign language.[2] Thus, consumer confidence in foreign providers of financial services tends to be lower than in national service providers. The other reason, that is commonly quoted, is that the diversity in the consumer protection laws of the Member States made it difficult for financial service providers to act safely in foreign markets and created enormous transaction costs. Therefore, cross-border competition used to take place in a different form: service providers established subsidiaries in other EU Member States, and this was supported by EU legislation that facilitated the establishment of subsidiaries through mutual recognition.

1 See, for example, Karten, 43.
2 See the proposal for the Insurance Mediation Directive, COM (2000) 511 final, at 9. See also Caspari, 99, on investment services.

Nevertheless, the EU made a first attempt to regulate in the field of consumer credit law in the aftermath of the first consumer protection programme of 1975[3] that ultimately led to the adoption of Directive 87/102/EEC. In the second half of the 1990s, the generation of EU legislation in the field of financial services sped up when the Commission made new efforts to create an internal market for financial services that included both the regulation of financial markets and the relationship between consumers and service providers. At the same time, EU financial services law became more and more separate from general consumer contract law.

In the economically important field of cross-border payment services, the EU first adopted Directive 97/5/EC on cross-border credit transfers.[4] After the introduction of the euro,[5] Regulation (EC) No. 2560/2001 on cross-border payments in euros[6] followed, since there was no longer any explanation for the high fees that many banks charged for cross-border payment in euros. A major coup in this area was Directive 2007/64/EC on payment services in the internal market,[7] which not only replaced Directive 97/5/EC but also created a whole institutional as well as a substantive law framework for cross-border payments, including detailed rules on the responsibilities of the payment service providers and their customers in the case of fraudulent use of payment cards.[8] Regulation (EC) No. 2560/2001 was in the meantime replaced by Regulation (EC) No. 924/2009,[9] which extended the rules on cross-border payments to cross-border direct debits.

Another important instrument in the field of financial services was Directive 2002/65/EC on the Distance Marketing of Financial Services[10] that harmonises, to a large extent, the diverse national rules on this particular distribution method. It covers, amongst other things, consumer credit as well as the whole field of banking and investment services, and also insurance contracts, and it is distinct from the general Distance Selling Directive 97/7/EC in that it generally follows the full harmonisation approach. The separation of general consumer law and financial services law in the area of direct marketing was completed with the Consumer Rights Directive 2011/83/EU that replaces the Doorstep Selling Directive 85/577/EEC and the Distance Selling Directive 97/7/EC and totally excludes financial services from its scope of application, the result being that there is no longer any special protection at the EU level in the event of the doorstep selling of financial services.[11]

---

3 The programmes for a consumer protection and information policy provided, *inter alia*, that a harmonisation of the general conditions governing consumer credit should be undertaken as a priority.

4 OJ L 43, 14 February 1997, 25.

5 Regulation (EC) No 1103/97 on certain provisions relating to the introduction of the euro, OJ L 162, 17 June 1997, 1.

6 OJ L 344, 28 December 2001, 13. See also J. Hoffmann, 69.

7 OJ L 319, 27 December 2007, 1.

8 On which see Burgard, 2065.

9 OJ L 266, 9 October 2009, 11.

10 OJ L 271, 9 October 2002, 16.

11 See Rott, *ERA-Forum* 2012(13), 35 ff.

Most recently, the EU Commission has started an initiative to regulate the retail banking market. In March 2013, the Commission tabled a proposal for a Directive on the transparency and comparability of payment account fees, payment account switching and access to a basic payment account.[12] The proposal combines a bundle of aims and objectives. Firstly, based on the finding that approximately 58 million European citizens do not have a payment account – which is, amongst other things, necessary to participate in the internal market – the Commission wants to introduce the right to a payment account with basic features at no or low fees. Secondly, the Commission wants to foster competition in the payment accounts market by increasing transparency of bank fees and by facilitating the process of switching to another service provider. Thirdly, the proposal aims at removing obstacles in the opening of a bank account abroad, obstacles that predominantly affect people working abroad.

In the field of investment on the capital market, the EU has adopted Directive 2004/39/EC on Markets in Financial Instruments (MiFiD Directive)[13] that replaced the earlier Directive 93/22/EEC on investment services in the securities field.[14] That area is also under review, and in October 2011 the EU Commission tabled proposals for a new Directive on markets in financial instruments that would replace the MiFiD Directive[15] and for a Regulation on markets in financial instruments.[16]

The focus on the internal market for financial services also extended to the field of consumer credit law. This field is in many ways paradigmatic for the development of EU consumer law and internal market law in the field of financial services and is therefore discussed in detail in this book. First, the achievements and the lacunae of the old Directive 87/102/EEC are outlined in brief (II). Then the reform process is discussed, with a focus on the highly controversial debates on the coverage of the Directive and of the envisaged degree of harmonisation (III), before the Consumer Credit Directive 2008/48/EC[17] is analysed in detail (IV). Finally, the most important features of the proposed Mortgage Credit Directive (V) and some credit-related unfair contract terms law cases (VI) are presented.

II. THE OLD DIRECTIVE 87/102/EEC

5.2 The old Consumer Credit Directive 87/102/EEC was negotiated and adopted before the European Single Act came into force. Thus, the Member States had to decide unanimously, and the negotiations were lengthy and

12 COM (2013) 266 final.
13 OJ L 145, 30 April 2004.
14 OJ L 141, 11 June 1993, 27.
15 COM (2011) 656 final.
16 COM (2011) 652 final.
17 OJ L 133, 22 May 2008, 66.

difficult.[18] As a result, the Directive provided for a fairly low level of consumer protection, which, however, did not do much harm since its Article 15 explicitly allowed Member States to maintain or introduce more stringent rules for the protection of consumers. Unlike other directives, the Consumer Credit Directive was only rarely subject to ECJ case law, which may again be related to its low level of consumer protection.

Like all EU consumer law instruments, the Directive had the twofold aim of reducing differences in the laws of the Member States that could lead to distortions of competition between creditors and also traders whose goods or services are financed by third parties (Recitals (1) to (4)) and of better protection of consumers (Recitals (9) and (10)). The provisions of the Directive predominantly followed the information paradigm, trying to ensure that the consumer is enabled to make informed decisions, which would also improve the functioning of the internal market. Moreover, it contained provisions that were meant to prevent contract terms that are disadvantageous to the consumer, and it required Member States to adopt certain regulatory measures in order to supervise the conduct of creditors and credit intermediaries.[19] In contrast, the Directive was not concerned with social elements such as protection from usury or protection from over-indebtedness.

The scope of application has sometimes been seen as the greatest achievement of the Directive. Credit agreements had been defined as agreements whereby a creditor grants or promises to grant to a consumer a credit in the form of a deferred payment, a loan or other similar financial accommodation. This definition was revolutionary in that it looked at the economic purpose rather than doctrinal categories such as sale, loan or leasing. In contrast, agreements for the provision on a continuing basis of a service or a utility are not deemed to be credit agreements even if the consumer has the right to pay for them by means of instalments. Rental contracts and leasing contracts under which title did not ultimately pass to the consumer were also excluded, and the same applies to consumer guarantee contracts, according to the judgment of the ECJ in *Berliner Kindl.*[20]

The most important instrument of the Directive was the regulation of advertisement and contractual information. To both, the annual percentage rate of charge (APR) was central,[21] which was defined as the total cost of the credit to the consumer expressed as an annual percentage of the amount of the credit granted. The problem was that initially the calculation of the APR was left to the Member States, which led to a lack of comparability of the APRs of different

---

18 See Latham, 219.

19 For an overview, see Reich, in: Reich/Micklitz, *Europäisches Verbraucherrecht*, 735.

20 ECJ, 23 March 2000, C-208/98, *Berliner Kindl Brauerei AG v Andreas Siepert* [2000] ECR I-1741.

21 See also ECJ, 4 March 2004, C-264/02, *Cofinoga Mérignac SA v Sylvain Sachithanathan*, [2004] ECR I-2157 at para 26.

Member States. With two amendments, by Directives 90/88/EEC[22] and 98/7/EC,[23] the calculation methods were harmonised. Still, the method then introduced was criticised for not including all the relevant costs of the credit and in particular the costs for credit insurance. Article 4(2) required some other information to be provided and under Article 4(3), further information *should* be given, where the Annex to the Directive provided for a long list of information that could be required by the Member States. As a result, the Member States introduced greatly diverging information obligations on creditors.

Besides information, the prominent means of consumer protection were the requirement of the contract to be concluded in writing, under Article 4(1), and the rules on linked credit agreements of Article 11 that were, however, fairly weak.[24] New to some legal orders was also the consumer's right to early repayment that was established in Article 8. Other provisions dealt with the assignment of the creditor's rights to a third person, ensuring that the consumer could still plead the defences that he had against the creditor (Article 9) and the protection of the consumer who makes payment by means of bills of exchange including promissory notes (Article 10). Finally, Article 12 required Member States to exercise official control over creditors and credit intermediaries.

The success or otherwise of Directive 87/102/EEC was first evaluated by the Commission in 1995.[25] To this end, the Commission analysed the implementation of the Directive in the Member States and found an enormously heterogeneous picture. Whilst some Member States had implemented the bare minimum of rules, others had created laws that resembled very little of the Directive. Whilst it had been obvious from the outset that the level of consumer protection established by the Directive was low, the Directive had also failed the goal of harmonising the laws of the Member States. At the same time, the Commission found that no EU-wide market for consumer credit had developed.

III. THE REFORM PROCESS AND THE HARMONISATION CONCEPT

5.3 In a way, the process for the reform of the Directive had already been initiated with the critical reports of the Commission concerning the limited success of Directive 87/102/EEC both in facilitating cross-border credit and in establishing a sufficient level of consumer protection in the field of consumer credit. The main conclusion that the Commission drew from this limited success

22 OJ L 61, 10 March 1990, 14.
23 OJ L 101, 1 April 1998, 17.
24 See *infra*, at 5.23.
25 See COM (1995) 117 final.

was that it was the diversity of national consumer credit laws that hampered the conclusion of cross-border credit contracts.[26]

In order to support the preparation of a proposal for a new Directive, the DG SANCO had commissioned a number of expert studies on particular issues, such as the calculation of the annual percentage rate of charge, on usury, on mortgage credit and on financial intermediaries.[27] In October 2002, the Commission then tabled its first proposal for a new Consumer Credit Directive.[28] This proposal was far more extensive than the old Directive, and since the Commission had identified the diversity of national consumer credit legislation as the main impediment for the creation of an internal market for consumer credit, the proposal aimed at total harmonisation of this field of law. This proposal was criticised from all sides. The representatives of the banking industry,[29] supported by a number of academics,[30] thought that the proposal was overly protective and created unacceptable burdens on the banking industry, in particular since it included rather far-reaching, although fairly undefined provisions that were meant to introduce a principle of "responsible lending".[31] Consumer representatives opposed the proposal in particular because of its total harmonisation approach since the proposed Directive would have disallowed more stringent consumer protection in its scope of application, thereby prohibiting certain national legislation that had already reached a higher level of consumer protection.[32] They were supported by representatives of some Member States.[33] The European Parliament, dominated by conservative and liberal members, supported the views of the banking industry. It rejected the proposal and reduced its content significantly.[34]

As a reaction, the Commission published an amended proposal[35] that was of an entirely different character. The provisions on responsible lending were eased, and the consumer protection provisions were thinned out. The Commission had also accepted that total harmonisation could not be achieved for political reasons, given the different national levels of consumer protection in credit law. It had therefore included certain options into the amended proposal. However, the Commission had also made an attempt to bring the concept of "mutual recognition" into the proposal. Under this concept, as enshrined in Article 21(2) of the amended proposal, Member States were supposed not to restrict the

26 See, in particular, COM (2002) 443 final, at 22.

27 See the references in COM (2002) 443 final, at 2, note 7.

28 COM (2002) 443 final.

29 See Danco, 853.

30 See Rohe, 267; Riesenhuber, 325.

31 On which see *infra*, at 5.16.

32 See also Grundmann, 488.

33 See, for example, the statement by the German Ministry of Justice of January 2003, available at www.bmj.bund.de/files/-/587/EURL_Stellungnahme.pdf.

34 European Parliament, 20 April 2004, Doc. P5_TC1-COD (2002)0222.

35 As a first step, the Commission explained the envisaged amendments in October 2004, COM (2004) 747 final, before it published a consolidated new text in October 2005, COM (2005) 483 final.

activities of creditors established in another Member State and operating within their territory in accordance with this Directive either through freedom of establishment or free provision of services. This principle of mutual recognition should not only apply to the admission, or supervision, of creditors as service providers but predominantly to consumer protection in private international law. Under the then applicable regime of the Rome Convention on the Law Applicable to Contractual Obligations[36] and its successor, the Rome I Regulation,[37] the choice of law by the parties to the contract may not deprive a consumer of the protection of the mandatory provisions of the law of the country of the consumer's habitual residence, and in the absence of a choice of law, a consumer contract is governed by the law of the country of the consumer's habitual residence. Thus, the so-called "passive" consumer who was in some way approached by the creditor in his home country may not lose the protection afforded to him by the mandatory consumer protection laws of his home country, and the consumer credit laws of the Member States are usually mandatory. The principle of mutual recognition would turn these rules on their head: where the rules established by the Member States differ, the less protective regime of the Member State in which the creditor is domiciled would apply.

Such a system would have created uncertainty amongst consumers. It was therefore heavily criticised in the literature.[38] An expert study commissioned by the European Parliament came to the conclusion that the principle of mutual recognition would have negative effects on the cross-border provision of financial services.[39] In the Common Position of September 2007, the principle of mutual recognition was therefore dropped. In contrast, the Common Position kept pursuing the goal of total harmonisation but with an increased number of options that are available. The legal uncertainty that is created by the use of options is compensated for by transparency requirements, although not across the board. According to Article 26, a Member State that makes use of regulatory choices referred to in a number of provisions shall inform the Commission thereof as well as of any subsequent changes. The Commission shall make the information public on a website or in another easily accessible way. Member States shall then take the appropriate measures to diffuse that information amongst national creditors and consumers. The options are also subject to special scrutiny in the Commission's review of the Directive, according to Article 27(2).

The harmonisation concept is now enshrined in Article 22(1): "Insofar as this Directive contains harmonised provisions, Member States may not maintain or introduce in their national law provisions diverging from those laid down in this Directive." Two questions remain: does the Directive contain a provision

36 Consolidated version in OJ 1998, C 27, 34.

37 On which see 7.16.

38 See Rott, *EuLF* 2006, I-61.

39 See Civic Consulting.

concerning a specific issue, and if so, is it "harmonised"? Clearly, there are certain issues that the Directive does not deal with at all, and these issues remain within the competence of the Member States, as Recital (9) confirms. The prime example is usury[40] where the policies of the Member States differ greatly.[41] Another example that is mentioned in Recital (9) is the possibility for Member States to maintain or introduce provisions on the cancellation of a contract for the sale of goods or supply of services if the consumer exercises his right of withdrawal from the credit agreement.[42] Other issues are the consequences of delayed performance by the consumer,[43] and rules on enforcement and insolvency.

In the case of *Volksbank România*, the question arose as to whether or not Member States were still allowed to prohibit certain bank charges. In fact, the Directive fully harmonised information obligations related to such charges, but does not mention their admissibility at all. Thus, the Court concluded that the Member States are not precluded by the Directive from regulating this issue.[44]

IV. THE NEW REGIME OF DIRECTIVE 2008/48/EC

5.4 The new Consumer Credit Directive 2008/48/EC was adopted in April 2008. It had to be implemented by 11 June 2010. The new directive does not apply to credit agreements existing on the date when the national implementing measures enter into force. The only exceptions are Articles 11, 12, 13 and 17, the second sentence of Article 18(1), and Article 18(2), which all apply to existing open-ended credit agreements from the date on which Directive 2008/48/EC is transposed into national law. Member States are however free to apply other provisions of the directive to contracts that have been concluded prior to the entry into force of the national implementation measures.

1. SCOPE OF APPLICATION

a) Personal scope of application

5.5 The personal scope of application of the Directive has not changed. It is only concerned with contracts between creditors and consumers, and Article 3(a) uses the narrow definition of consumer that is common in EU consumer law.

40 See COM (2002) 443 final, explanation of Article 30(1).

41 See COM (1995) 117 final, No 273.

42 See also *infra*, at 5.26.

43 The respective provisions of Articles 24 and 25 of the first proposal, COM (2002) 443 final, have been rejected by the European Parliament.

44 CJEU, 12 July 2012, Case C-602/10 *SC Volksbank România SA v Autoritatea Națională pentru Protecția Consumatorilor – Comisariatul Județean pentru Protecția Consumatorilor Călărași (CJPC)* [2012] ECR I-nyr.

b) *Credit agreements*

5.6 Like the old Directive, the new Consumer Credit Directive applies to credit agreements in their economic sense. Agreements for the provision on a continuing basis of services, such as insurance services (see Recital (12)), or for the supply of goods of the same kind, for example of beer or oil, where the consumer pays for the duration of their provision in instalments are explicitly excluded by Article 3(c). This exception does not, however, apply to the volumes of an encyclopaedia that are only parts of one set of goods.

c) *Exemptions*

5.7 Further exemptions are listed in Article 2(2) to (5). Article 2(2) provides for total exemptions where the Directive does not apply, whilst Article 2(3) and (4) contains partial exemptions, and optional exemptions are subject to Article 2(5) and (6). Whilst the Commission had tried, in its first proposal, to expand the scope of application drastically and to include even low-value credit contracts that, on aggregate, may also cause over-indebtedness, the list of exemptions in the final Directive is much longer than its predecessor.

aa) Total exemptions

5.8 As before, credit that is granted free of interest and without any other charges is excluded by Article 2(2)(f). In addition, this provision now exempts credit that has to be repaid within three months and where only insignificant charges are payable. Although not dealing explicitly with payment card credits, this provision covers debit card agreements and also many but not all credit card agreements. A similar type of exemption is Article 2(2)(j) on credit agreements which relate to the deferred payment, free of charge, of an existing debt.

As under the old Directive, Article 2(2)(b) exempts credit agreements the purpose of which is to acquire or retain property rights in land or in an existing or projected building. In contrast, credit agreements for the renovation or increase of value of an existing building, which had also been exempted under Article 2(1)(a) of Directive 87/102/EEC, are now within the scope of application.

Hiring agreements had always been excluded from the Consumer Credit Directive but the status of leasing agreements had not been entirely clear. Article 2(2)(d) now explicitly extends this exemption to leasing agreements where an obligation to purchase the object of the agreement is not laid down either by the agreement itself or by any separate agreement. The provision specifies that such an obligation shall be deemed to exist if it is so decided unilaterally by the creditor.

Article 2(2)(g) and (l) concern credit agreements that are concluded under conditions that are particularly favourable to consumers: credit that is granted by an employer to his employees as a secondary activity free of interest or at annual percentage rates that are lower than those prevailing in the market and which are not offered to the public generally, and credit agreements which relate to loans granted to a restricted public under a statutory provision with a general interest purpose, and at lower interest rates than those prevailing in the market or free of interest or on other terms which are more favourable to the consumer than those prevailing in the market and at interest rates not higher than those prevailing in the market.

The threshold of €200 has been maintained, whereas the much too low ceiling of €50,000 has been raised, after some bargaining between the Commission, the Council and the European Parliament, to €75,000 (after the Council had set it at €100,000 in its Common Position). Both figures relate to the "total amount of credit", which is defined, in Article 3(l), as the ceiling or the total sums made available under a credit agreement.

An entirely new exemption has been created for credit agreements which are secured either by a mortgage or by other comparable security commonly used in a Member State on immovable property or secured by a right related to immovable property. The Commission has argued that these types of credit agreements are so different from normal consumer credit contracts that they should be regulated in a separate legal instrument (see also Recital (14)), and indeed work is under way to deal with mortgage credit.[45] It should, however, be mentioned that the exemption of Article 2(2)(a) also covers consumer credit contracts over movables, for example, cars that are secured by a mortgage.

Furthermore, credit agreements upon the conclusion of which the consumer is requested to deposit an item as security in the creditor's safe-keeping and where the liability of the consumer is strictly limited to that pledged item are exempted, according to Article 2(2)(k), since the only thing the consumer can lose is the pledged item. Another new exemption is the one in Article 2(2)(i) on credit agreements which are the outcome of a settlement reached in court or before another statutory authority. And finally, Article 2(2)(h) gives the MiFiD Directive 2004/39/EC priority over the Consumer Credit Directive in cases where the investment firm or credit institution granting the credit is involved in a transaction of an instrument that comes under the MiFiD Directive.

bb) Partial exemptions

5.9 Article 2(3) provides for partial exemptions for overdraft facilities and where the credit has to be repaid on demand or within three months (but not within less than one month, see *supra* 5.7). Overdraft facilities are defined in Article 3(d) as explicit credit agreements whereby a creditor makes available to a consumer funds which exceed the current balance in the consumer's current

[45] See *infra*, at 5.38 *et seq.*

account. In particular, reduced information obligations are imposed on creditors, and no right of withdrawal is granted to the consumer.

Even less provisions apply, according to Article 2(4), in the case of the so-called overrunning, which Article 3(e) defines as a tacitly accepted overdraft whereby a creditor makes available to a consumer funds which exceed the current balance in the consumer's current account or the agreed overdraft facility. Apart from the specific provision of Article 18, only the provisions on the supervision of creditors and the chapter on implementing measures apply.

cc) Optional exemptions

5.10 Optional exemptions apply to the British mutual savings banks and to certain agreements that modify existing credit agreements. For the British mutual savings banks, Article 2(5) provides similar rules as Article 2(3) for overdraft facilities: reduced information obligations are imposed on creditors and no right of withdrawal is granted to the consumer. The same applies under Article 2(6) to credit agreements which provide for arrangements to be agreed by the creditor and the consumer in respect of deferred payment or repayment methods, where the consumer is already in default on the initial credit agreement but only where: (a) such arrangements would be likely to avert the possibility of legal proceedings concerning such default; and (b) the consumer would not thereby be subject to terms less favourable than those laid down in the initial credit agreement. Where the modifying credit agreement also falls under Article 2(3), this latter provision applies, which reduces the discretion for Member States.[46]

d) Barriers to more extensive national legislation?

5.11 An important issue for the Member States is whether or not the (narrow) scope of application of the Consumer Credit Directive prohibits wider national scopes of application.[47] In this respect, the recitals of the Directive offer some clarifications, although they are still incomplete.

The total exemptions of Article 2(2) are mentioned in Recital (10), according to which the Directive should be without prejudice to the application by Member States, in accordance with Community law, of the provisions of this Directive to areas not covered by its scope. Examples mentioned in Recital (10) are credit agreements involving amounts of less than €200 or more than €75,000. Thus, the Directive has no exclusive effect on the types of credit that have been exempted by Article 2(2). For example, Member States can extend the scope of application of the national implementation of the directive to credit contracts that are

---

46 See *infra*, at 5.11.

47 See generally Chapter 1, at 1.30.

excluded by Article 2(2).[48] Limitations merely stem from the four freedoms of the Treaty.

Relying on the judgment of the ECJ in *di Pinto*, this should also apply to the personal scope of application, for example, with a view to the protection of persons who wish to set up a business and need credit to do so,[49] although this is not explicitly mentioned in the recitals (unlike in the recitals to Directive 2002/65/EC on the Distance Marketing of Financial Services). In the case of *di Pinto*, the French Cour de cassation had referred the question to the ECJ of whether French law could protect a trader who was canvassed for the purpose of concluding an advertising contract concerning the sale of his business. The ECJ held that such a businessman was not to be considered a consumer even though this particular contract was not his usual business. Therefore, Directive 85/577/EEC did not protect him. Nevertheless, the ECJ held that the Directive did not prevent Member States from protecting traders from doorstep selling if they wished to do so. The reason was that the Directive did not apply at all to the instant case since the French scenario fell outside the scope of application of the Directive.[50]

The effect on national competence to legislate is different in areas where the Directive specifies the applicable provisions, as in Article 2(3) for overdraft facilities. Recital (11) clarifies that such partial exemptions offer no leeway for introducing those rules that have been explicitly ruled out. What remains possible is the maintenance or introduction of provisions that fall completely outside the scope of the Directive, such as usury laws. The same would seem to apply to the optional exemptions of Article 2(5) and (6). Here, ECJ case law on the Product Liability Directive 85/374/EEC springs to mind. This Directive is, according to the ECJ, also a total harmonisation instrument that contains some regulatory choices. According to the ECJ judgment in *Commission v. France*, these regulatory choices can only be implemented into national law as they are.[51] From a legal certainty perspective, this would have the advantage of only two possible solutions in the laws of the Member States, the choice of which the Member States have to communicate to the Commission under Article 26.

2. THE PROTECTIVE INSTRUMENTS

5.12 The protective instruments of the new Consumer Credit Directive have in parts been developed out of the old Directive. More instruments have been

---

48 CJEU, 12 July 2012, Case C-602/10 *SC Volksbank România SA v Autoritatea Națională pentru Protecția Consumatorilor – Comisariatul Județean pentru Protecția Consumatorilor Călărași (CJPC)* [2012] ECR I-nyr.

49 See also Bülow/Artz, 1153 f.

50 ECJ, 14 March 1991, C-361/89, *Criminal proceedings against Patrice di Pinto* [1991] ECR I-1189 at para 15.

51 ECJ, 25 April 2002, C-52/00, *Commission v France* [2002] ECR I-3827 at para 47.

added in order to reflect not only the changes on the consumer credit market but also more stringent national legislation since the Member States would not have agreed otherwise to the new Directive. The Directive also takes into account the rules on the distance marketing of financial services, as established by Directive 2002/65/EC (since it is the explicit aim of the EU to foster the cross-border conclusion of consumer credit contracts) and parallelises rules, in particular, in the field of pre-contractual information.

a) *Credit advertisement*

5.13 The legislator of Directive 87/102/EEC had already seen the dangers that are related to credit advertisement. Unaltered, the new Directive distinguishes advertisement with figures from advertisement without figures. Where no figures (interest rates, costs and so on) are given, only the provisions of the Unfair Commercial Practices Directive 2005/29/EC apply (see also Article 4(4)).[52]

If instead a credit advertisement indicates an interest rate or any figures relating to the cost of the credit to the consumer it shall include "standard information" that is detailed in Article 4(2). It has to include: (a) the borrowing rate, fixed or variable or both, together with particulars of any charges included in the total cost of the credit to the consumer; (b) the total amount of credit; (c) the annual percentage rate of charge; (d) if applicable, the duration of the credit agreement; (e) in the case of a credit in the form of deferred payment for specific goods or services, the cash price and the amount of any advance payment; and (f) if applicable, the total amount payable by the consumer and the amount of the instalments. An optional exemption applies in the case of an overdraft facility that comes under Article 2(3), where Member States may decide that the annual percentage rate of charge need not be provided.

The standard information has to be provided in a clear, concise and prominent way by means of a representative example. The proposal by the Council to require this information to be provided in a particular order, which would have facilitated the comparison of different offers,[53] was cancelled at the last minute by the European Parliament. Unlike, for example, under UK law,[54] a "representative" example does not require a fixed quota of credit agreements that are actually concluded under the "representative" conditions. Rather, Recital (19) confirms that it should correspond, for instance, to the average duration and total amount of credit granted for the type of credit agreement under consideration and, if applicable, to the goods purchased. The frequency of certain types of credit agreement in a specific market should also be taken into account. As regards the borrowing rate, the frequency of instalments and the

52 On which see *supra* 2.25.

53 See Franck, 341.

54 See Regulation 8 of the Consumer Credit (Advertisements) Regulations 2004, SI 2004/1484.

capitalisation of interest, creditors should use their conventional method of calculation for the consumer credit concerned. On that basis, the German Regional Court of Stuttgart held that advertisement for credit "from ... %" was prohibited.[55]

Where the conclusion of a contract regarding an ancillary service relating to the credit agreement, in particular insurance, is compulsory in order to obtain the credit or to obtain it on the terms and conditions marketed, and the cost of that service cannot be determined in advance, the obligation to enter into that contract shall also be stated in a clear, concise and prominent way, together with the annual percentage rate of charge, according to Article 4(3). This provision aims at making the costs of credit insurance transparent since credit insurance may amount to a significant part of the costs of a credit.[56] Consumer advocates have criticised the criterion "compulsory" because there is a danger that creditors will not make insurance formally compulsory but only require it "in the individual case".[57] It is then for the consumer, or for consumer associations, to prove that credit insurance is in fact required in virtually every "individual" case. At least, one could argue in favour of some alleviation of the burden of proof in circumstances where a creditor can be shown to have required credit insurance in a significant number of credit agreements.

The description of the standard information required appears to be exclusive. In contrast, according to Recital (18) Member States should remain free to regulate information requirements in their national law regarding advertising which does not contain information on the cost of the credit. This statement is however in contradiction with Directive 2005/29/EC that governs the field of advertising and that has established a harmonised EU-wide standard of fairness that would seem to prevent Member States from adopting divergent levels of protection.

b) Pre-contractual obligations

5.14 The new Consumer Credit Directive contains three types of pre-contractual obligations: (aa) pre-contractual information, (bb) pre-contractual advice and (cc) the duty of responsible lending.

aa) Pre-contractual information

5.15 As with all modern EU consumer law directives, and in particular following the structure of Directive 2002/65/EC on the Distance Marketing of

[55] LG Stuttgart, 22 September 2011, BKR 2012, 206; critique by Weyand, 197. On the German implementation of Article 4 see also Domke/Sperlich, 2069 ff.

[56] See Knops, 1455.

[57] See Knops, 1455; Gessner, 84, 86.

Financial Services, the new Consumer Credit Directive shifts information obligations to the time prior to the conclusion of the contract. According to Article 5(1), information must be provided in good time before the consumer is bound by any credit agreement or offer. Preferences expressed and information supplied by the consumer must be taken into account. Again, the purpose of these information requirements is the comparability of different offers, not only with a view to consumer protection but also for fostering competition between credit providers.

With up to 19 headings, the information obligation under Article 5(2) is extremely comprehensive, and many authors have doubted that the consumer would be able to understand and digest so much information.[58] In order to avoid information overload and to maintain, or allow, the comparability of different offers, the EU legislator therefore focuses on standardisation again. It has developed the Standard European Consumer Credit Information form set out in Annex II to the Directive that shall be used in supplying information, on paper or on another durable medium. If the creditor has supplied the Standard European Consumer Credit Information, he shall be deemed to have satisfied not only the requirements of Article 5(2) but also those of Article 3(1) and (2) of Directive 2002/65/EC (if the consumer credit contract is prepared and concluded exclusively by means of distance communication). Additional information which the creditor may provide to the consumer, in particular information that may be necessary under Article 3(3) and (4) of Directive 2002/65/EC, shall be given in a separate document which may be annexed to the Standard European Consumer Credit Information form, in order not to blur the comparability of the conditions of different credit offers.

The main points are the main characteristics of the creditor (Article 5(1) s. 4(b)) and the characteristics, the conditions and the costs of the credit, including the type of credit under Article 5(1) s. 4(a), the total amount of credit and the conditions governing the drawdown (s. 4(c)), the duration of the credit agreement (s. 4(d)), the borrowing rate, the conditions governing the application of the borrowing rate and, where available, any index or reference rate applicable to the initial borrowing rate, as well as the periods, conditions and procedures for changing the borrowing rate (s. 4(f)), the amount, number and frequency of payments to be made by the consumer and, where appropriate, the order in which payments will be allocated to different outstanding balances charged at different borrowing rates for the purposes of reimbursement (s. 4(h)), and, where applicable, the charges for maintaining one or several accounts recording both payment transactions and drawdowns, unless the opening of an account is optional (s. 4(i)).

The most important information on the costs of the credit, however, relates to the so-called annual percentage rate of charge (APR), which the creditor has to

---

58 See, for example, Riesenhuber, 328.

inform the consumer of under Article 5(1) s. 4(g) and has already been the most prominent piece of information to be provided under the old Directive 87/102/EEC. The APR is defined, in Article 3(i), as the total cost of the credit to the consumer, expressed as an annual percentage of the total amount of credit. The new Directive has made a fresh attempt to achieve better harmonisation of its calculations and has therefore specified, in Article 19, that the total cost of the credit to the consumer shall be determined. The notion of the total cost of the credit, as defined in Article 3(g), includes all the costs – including interest, commission, taxes and any other kinds of fees which the consumer is required to pay in connection with the credit agreement and which are known to the creditor – except for notaries' costs, that the creditor must, however, inform the consumer of under Article 5(1) s. 4(j). A new element of the APR is meant to prevent the disguise of credit costs as costs of maintaining an account. According to Article 19(2) para 2, the costs of maintaining an account recording both payment transactions and drawdowns, the costs of using a means of payment for both payment transactions and drawdowns, and other costs relating to payment transactions shall be included in the total cost of credit to the consumer unless the opening of the account is optional and the costs of the account have been clearly and separately shown in the credit agreement or in any other agreement concluded with the consumer.

Experience in the Member States showed, however, that for specific types of credit, namely for credit without fixed duration and for drawdowns, the assumptions were still not sufficiently concrete to eliminate discrepancies in their calculation. Therefore, the European Commission amended the Consumer Credit Directive with Commission Directive 2011/90/EU,[59] which added a number of new assumptions for the calculation of the APR.

The APR is of such importance that failure to calculate it correctly may trigger consequences in unfair contract terms law. In the case of *Pohotovost'*, the CJEU held that lack of information about the APR was suitable to render the determination of price unclear, depending on the circumstances of the case, and therefore not to be in plain and intelligible language in the terms of Article 4(2) of the Unfair Contract Terms Directive 93/13/EEC. Thus, if the national court came to the conclusion that the price of the credit was actually unclear, it could control the fairness of the price clause under unfair contract terms law, although the price of credit is normally, as a core term, exempted from the unfair contract terms law regime.[60]

What remains problematic is the issue of credit insurance and this is because they are only included in the total cost of credit, as defined in Article 3(g), if the insurance service is compulsory, which triggers the above-mentioned difficulty

---

59 OJ L 296, 15 November 2011, 35.

60 CJEU, order of 16 November 2010, C-76/10, *Pohotovost' s.r.o. v Iveta Korčkovská* [2010] ECR I-11557 at paras 56–63.

of proving the compulsory character of credit insurance. Thus, in many cases the APR will still not reflect the actual costs of credit, which will also hamper the comparability of the conditions of different offers. Also exempted are the charges payable by the consumer for non-compliance with any of his commitments laid down in the credit agreement and charges other than the purchase price which, for purchases of goods or services, he is obliged to pay whether the transaction is effected in cash or on credit. The creditor must however inform the consumer, under Article 5(1) s. 4(l), of the interest rate applicable in the case of late payments and the arrangements for its adjustment, and, where applicable, any charges payable for default. Moreover, the standard information must contain a warning regarding the consequences of missing payments, Article 5(1) s. 4(m). The creditor must also inform the consumer, under Article 5(1) s. 4(k), of the obligation, if any, to enter into an ancillary service contract relating to the credit agreement, in particular an insurance policy, with the well-known limitation that the conclusion of such a contract has to be compulsory in order to obtain the credit or to obtain it on the terms and conditions marketed.

A common standard in EU consumer law is the obligation to provide information on the absence or existence of a right of withdrawal, as established by Article 5(1) s. 4(o). Further legal information relates to the right of early repayment under Article 5(1) s. 4(p), the consumer's right to be supplied, on request and free of charge, with a copy of the draft credit agreement – provided the creditor is at the time of the request willing to proceed to the conclusion of the credit agreement with the consumer – under Article 5(1) s. 4(r), and the right to be informed immediately and free of charge, pursuant to Article 9(2), of the result of a database consultation carried out for the purposes of assessing his creditworthiness, under Article 5(1) s. 4(q). This latter right is meant to create transparency of the creditor's decision but fails to do so because the creditor only has to inform the consumer of the result but not of the grounds of the result.[61]

In principle, pre-contractual information must be supplied on paper or on a durable medium. However, since it is excessively difficult to supply up to 19 items of information via telephone, Article 3(3) of Directive 2002/65/EC on the Distance Marketing of Financial Services allows for some softening of the requirements for the conclusion of the contract via voice telephony by allowing reduced information to be provided before the contract is concluded, if the consumer explicitly consents to such reduced information. One indispensable item of information is the description of the main characteristics of the financial service in question. Article 5(2) of the Consumer Credit Directive now specifies, for the purposes of Article 3(3) of Directive 2002/65/EC, which characteristics of a consumer credit are the "main characteristics" and therefore states an exemption of Article 5(2).

---

61 See also the critique by Metz, 362.

Furthermore, Article 5(3) allows softening of the rules for all types of consumer credit contracts that are concluded at the consumer's request using a means of distance communication which does not enable the information to be provided in accordance with Article 5(1), which does not only cover voice telephony but also multimedia messaging services (MMS). In such a case, the creditor shall provide the consumer with the full pre-contractual information using the Standard European Consumer Credit Information form immediately after the conclusion of the credit agreement.

Independently from the means of communication used, the consumer has the right, according to Article 5(4), to be supplied free of charge with a copy of the draft credit agreement, unless the creditor is unwilling to proceed to the conclusion of the credit agreement with the consumer anyway.

In principle, it should be obvious that the list of information to be provided under Article 5(1) is exclusive, which is confirmed by Recital (32). In other words, the Member States cannot ask for more information to be provided. Whether or not this also applies to the information to be supplied under Article 5(2) in the case of voice telephony is less clear. The reason is that Article 5(2) specifies the information obligations under Article 3(3) of Directive 2002/65/EC, and this latter Directive allows Member States, according to its Article 4(2), to maintain or introduce more stringent provisions on prior information requirements, although "pending further harmonisation", which, for example, Germany has done. The correct solution to this might be that the main characteristics of a consumer credit, that have to be described under Article 3(3)(b) of Directive 2002/65/EC, are now fully harmonised by Article 5(2) of the new Consumer Credit Directive, whilst the Member States maintain their competence to require additional information to be supplied in distance contracts that are not related to the characteristics of the credit.

bb) Pre-contractual advice

5.16 A new pre-contractual obligation that has hitherto been unknown to many Member States is the duty to provide pre-contractual advice, under Article 5(6): Member States shall ensure that creditors and, where applicable, credit intermediaries provide adequate explanations to the consumer, in order to place the consumer in a position enabling him to assess whether the proposed credit agreement is adapted to his needs and to his financial situation. With this provision the EU legislator recognises that information alone may not be enough to secure a free and informed decision by the consumer.[62] The background is a consumer image that regards the consumer as not sufficiently informed but receptive to information. To this end, the creditor may have to explain the pre-contractual information to be provided in accordance with Article 5(1), the

[62] See also Recital (27).

essential characteristics of the products proposed and the specific effects that they may have on the consumer, including the consequences of default of payment by the consumer. The extent of this obligation is not entirely clear from the wording of Article 5(6). Whilst the English version of the Directive refers to "the proposed credit agreement", the German version speaks of the main characteristics "*der angebotenen Produkte*" (of the *products* offered). The latter term reflects the drafting history of Article 5(6), which was developed out of Article 6(3) of the first proposal by the Commission, which required the creditor to establish, among the credit agreements they usually offer or arrange, the most appropriate type and total amount of credit, taking into account the financial situation of the consumer, the advantages and disadvantages associated with the product proposed, and the purpose of the credit.[63] Moreover, Recital (27) states that the consumer may still need additional assistance in order to decide which credit agreement, within the range of products proposed, is the most appropriate for his needs and financial situation, and that therefore, Member States should ensure that creditors provide such assistance in relation to the credit products which they offer to the consumer. This means that the creditor would also have to give advice on alternative credit products that he usually offers.[64] In contrast, and this is also clear from the drafting history and from its origin in Article 6(3) of the first proposal from Belgian law, the creditor is not required to point out to the consumer more suitable credit products offered by his competitors.[65]

Under the total harmonisation approach of the Directive, Member States cannot go beyond the requirements of Article 5(6) but they are explicitly allowed to adapt the manner by which and the extent to which such assistance is given, as well as by whom it is given, to the particular circumstances of the situation in which the credit agreement is offered, the person to whom it is offered and the type of credit offered, which means that they may distinguish the "average consumer" from particularly vulnerable groups of consumers – an approach that has also been taken in the law of unfair commercial practices[66] and, to a certain extent, in the investment law of the MiFiD Directive 2004/39/EC.[67] Unlike the use of certain regulatory choices, such concretisation of the duty of pre-contractual advice does not need to be reported to the Commission under Article 26.

cc) Responsible lending

5.17 One of the most controversial initial proposals by the Commission was the proposal to introduce a duty of responsible lending. According to Article 9 of

63 For more details see Rott, *BKR* 2003, 856 ff.

64 Instead, one should not go so far as to require banks to calculate tax consequences and the like, see Grundmann, 488.

65 On Belgian law see Balate/Dejemeppe/de Patoul, n 199.

66 See Chapter 2, at 2.27.

67 On similarities and differences see Riesenhuber, 329.

the first proposal for a new Consumer Credit Directive, the creditor should have been assumed to have previously assessed, by any means at his disposal, whether the consumer can reasonably be expected to discharge their obligations under the credit agreement;[68] and as mentioned above, under Article 6(3) the creditor should have advised the consumer accordingly – a duty that forms part of a few legal orders, including Belgium and Switzerland[69] and that was also developed by French courts[70] but is unknown to most Member States.[71] With this proposal, the Commission aimed at avoiding the consumer's over-indebtedness by avoiding unreasonable credit contracts in the first place.

Not much is left of this proposal. Still, Article 8(1) requires that, before the conclusion of the credit agreement, the creditor must assess the consumer's creditworthiness. This shall occur on the basis of sufficient information, "where appropriate" obtained from the consumer and, "where necessary", on the basis of a consultation of the relevant database. Whilst Member States, in particular Belgium, whose legislation requires creditors to assess the creditworthiness of consumers on the basis of a consultation of the relevant database are allowed to retain this requirement, according to Article 8(1) s. 2, the total harmonisation character of the Directive prohibits Member States from introducing such an obligation in all cases (even where this is not "necessary" in the individual case). The duty to assess creditworthiness also applies in cases where the parties agree to a significant increase in the total amount of credit after the conclusion of the credit agreement.

Under Article 9, the Member States shall in the case of cross-border credit ensure access for creditors from other Member States to databases used in that Member State for assessing the creditworthiness of consumers. The conditions for access shall be non-discriminatory. Their particular usefulness, of course, depends on the type of database used. Databases that show all the credit obligations of a consumer[72] are certainly more useful than those databases that only show credit obligations that are defaulted. The Commission had planned to introduce centralised databases at the national level[73] but was stopped by the European Parliament.

Unlike Article 5(6) on the duty to advise, Article 8 does not call upon the Member States to concretise the requirements for the assessment of creditworthiness. Nevertheless, Recital (26) confirms that the Member States' authorities could give appropriate instructions and guidelines to creditors,

68 For details see Rott, *BKR* 2003, 851.

69 See Rott, *BKR* 2003, 851.

70 For an excellent overview, see Benedict, 394.

71 See, for example, the German leading case of BGH, 16 March 1989, WM 1989, 595. See also Nobbe, 80, for fundamental criticism of the concept of responsible lending.

72 See, for example, Swiss Consumer Credit Law, on which see Stauder, 105.

73 See Article 8 of the first proposal, COM (2002) 443 final. For critical comments see Danco, 854.

which again would not need to be communicated to the Commission, under Article 26, so that no full transparency would be achieved. In fact, such guidelines appear highly advisable to avoid legal uncertainty.[74]

The Directive does not state the legal consequences of the consumer's lack of creditworthiness. In the light of the image of the consumer who is able to digest information, one cannot lightly follow a prohibition of concluding a credit contract with such a non-creditworthy consumer.[75] The provision would, however, be utterly useless if there were no consequences attached to such a finding. Recital (26) gives weight to the importance of creditors not engaging in irresponsible lending or giving out credit without prior assessment of creditworthiness, and calls upon the Member States to carry out the necessary supervision to avoid such behaviour and to determine the necessary means to sanction creditors in the event of their doing so. Therefore, one may at least expect an obligation to give a warning to the consumer,[76] which is also mentioned in Recital (26).[77]

dd) Sanctions for the breach of pre-contractual obligations

5.18 As usual in EU consumer law, the Member States remain responsible for determining the legal consequences of the breach of pre-contractual obligations; see Article 23.

Controversies have arisen concerning the consequences of the breach of the duty to perform a creditworthiness assessment. In fact, the Member States have taken very different approaches in this respect. Whilst Belgium has maintained its previous contract law remedies and France has explicitly introduced the right of the court to order the partial or complete loss of the interest claim in such a situation,[78] the German legislator has explicitly treated the duty to assess the consumer's creditworthiness as a public law duty and implemented that duty in prudential supervision law.[79] This latter solution appears to be in breach of the Directive as it would deprive the consumer of an individual remedy, although at least one of the objectives of the creditworthiness assessment is the prevention of the consumer's over-indebtedness and the negative consequences for his or her private life.[80] Additional public law sanctions are of course possible and may be useful.

---

[74] For an account of the legal uncertainty that was created by the French case law on responsible lending, see Benedict, 403.

[75] See also Reifner, *VuR* 2004, 88; Grundmann/Hollering, 50.

[76] See also Hoffmann, 312.

[77] Against Herresthal, 1176, who argues that the concept of responsible lending has been entirely given up in the legislative process.

[78] Article L-311.47 Code de la consommation.

[79] §18 para. 2 Kreditwesengesetz. See also Ady/Paetz, 1064.

[80] See Rott/Terryn/Twigg-Flesner, 163 ff; against Nobbe, 80; Herresthal, 1176.

The penalties that are applicable to infringements of national implementing legislation must be effective, proportionate and dissuasive. Taking into consideration the judgments in the doorstep selling cases of *Schulte*[81] and *Crailsheimer Volksbank*,[82] one would expect, at the least, that creditors would be liable to compensate the damage that insufficient information, advice or warnings on the lack of creditworthiness result in.[83]

c) *Form and content of the contract*

aa) The content of the contract

5.19 The provision on the content of the contract was central to the old Directive but has lost much of its significance, in particular for the competition between creditors, due to the introduction of the above-mentioned pre-contractual information obligations. Nevertheless, the contract remains of importance for the precise determination of the mutual rights and obligations.

The content of the contract is specified in Article 10(2). The range of items to be included is far more extensive than it was under Article 4 of Directive 87/102/EEC. In parts, pre-contractual information has to be repeated. Other pieces of information must be concretised, in particular information on the right of withdrawal, on the right of early repayment, and on the right to terminate the contract agreement: see Article 10(2)(p), (r) and (s). According to Article 10(2)(q), the contract must also contain information concerning the rights resulting from Article 15 (on linked credit agreements) as well as the conditions for the exercise of those rights, and under Article 10(2)(t), the creditor shall inform the consumer as to whether or not there is an out-of-court complaint and redress mechanism for the consumer and, if so, the methods for having access to it. In fact, Article 24 requires Member States to ensure that adequate and effective out of court dispute resolution procedures for the settlement of consumer disputes concerning credit agreements are put in place, using existing bodies where appropriate.

A controversial issue was the introduction of a mandatory statement of account in the form of an amortisation table, which consumer representatives had long called for, in order to improve the transparency of credit agreements.[84] The Council had included such a requirement in Article 10, in its Common Position, but the European Parliament has weakened the provision in such a way

---

81 ECJ, 25 October 2005, C-350/03, *Elisabeth Schulte, Wolfgang Schulte v Deutsche Bausparkasse Badenia AG* [2005] ECR I-9215.

82 ECJ, 25 October 2005, C-229/04, *Crailsheimer Volksbank eG v Klaus Conrads, Frank Schulzke und Petra Schulzke-Lösche, Joachim Nitschke* [2005] ECR I-9273.

83 See also Reifner, *VuR* 2004, 14, against Nobbe, 80. On the potential consequences of insufficient information in the junk property cases see, for example, Reich, in Bub et al., 138 ff; Rott, *GPR* 2006 26.

84 See, for example, Reifner, *VuR* 2004, 14.

that an amortisation table must only be given on request of the consumer, a right of which the consumer must be informed under Article 10(2)(i). The amortisation table is free of charge and can be asked for at any time throughout the duration of the credit agreement; see Article 10(3).

bb) The form of the contract

5.20 Traditionally, the written form used to be an important means of consumer protection in credit law since it issues a certain warning to the consumer that he is about to do something of importance. This was also reflected in Article 4 of Directive 87/102/EEC. At the same time, the requirement of concluding a credit contract in writing is a barrier to the cross-border supply of credit, and in particular on concluding credit contracts on the internet. Therefore, some Member States had already abolished this requirement and allowed credit contracts to be concluded by electronic means if the parties so agreed.[85]

Despite intense resistance by some Member States, including Germany, against the abolishment of the written form requirement,[86] Article 10(1) s. 1 of the new Consumer Credit Directive now allows credit agreements to be drawn up on paper or on another durable medium, the latter being, according to Article 3(m), any instrument which enables the consumer to store information addressed personally to him in a way that is accessible for future reference for a period of time adequate for the purposes of the information and which allows the unchanged reproduction of the information stored, which includes, amongst other things, e-mails.

A somewhat cryptic provision is Article 10(1) para 2 s. 2, according to which Article 10 shall be without prejudice to any national rules regarding the validity of the conclusion of credit agreements which are in conformity with Community law. With a view to Recital (30), this provision refers to the conclusion of the contract by offer and acceptance and allows national rules that specify the binding effect of an offer, and its duration. In contrast, Member States are no longer allowed to require the written form of the credit contract, due to the total harmonisation approach of the Directive.[87] Compensation for that reduction in consumer protection shall be achieved through the above-mentioned extension of pre-contractual information and advice.

The abolishment of the written form requirement, however, does not extend to communication *after* the conclusion of the contract. For example, English law requires the written form for termination of the contract by the creditor. The

---

85 See, for example, the UK Consumer Credit Act 1974 (Electronic Communications) Order 2004, SI 2004/3236.

86 See only METZ, 362.

87 Against GRUNDMANN/HOLLERING, 49; GSELL/SCHELLHASE, 26.

reason is that the consumer may no longer have access to electronic communication once he has got into difficulties with repaying the credit.[88] Such legislation remains to be allowed in principle. The only problematic case is Article 13(1) para 2 and (2) on the creditor's right to terminate an open-ended credit agreement, which requires notice to be drawn up on paper or on another durable medium, which could be seen as a formal requirement of total harmonisation. Still, such notice needs to be communicated, and this is not possible in electronic form where the consumer no longer has access to electronic communication.

d) The right to terminate the contract

5.21 A new provision, Article 13, regulates the right of both creditor and consumer to terminate an open-ended credit agreement. According to Article 13(1) para 1, the consumer may effect standard termination of an open-ended credit agreement free of charge and at any time unless the parties have agreed on a period of notice, which may not exceed one month. In contrast, the creditor only has the right to terminate an open-ended credit agreement if the contract so provides. In that case, the period of notice may not be shorter than two months.

Where the consumer has not yet drawn down credit under an open-ended credit agreement, Article 13(2) allows the creditor to terminate the consumer's right to draw down, if so agreed in the contract and provided there are objectively justified reasons. Justified reasons may be, for example, suspicion of an unauthorised or fraudulent use of the credit or a significantly increased risk of the consumer being unable to fulfil his obligation to repay the credit.

Some Member States have introduced a certain minimum period that needs to elapse between the time that the creditor asks for reimbursement and the day on which the credit has to be reimbursed. Such consumer protection legislation may be maintained, according to Recital (9). What also remains untouched is national law in the area of contract law regulating the rights of the contracting parties to terminate the credit agreement on the basis of a breach of contract (see Recital (33)) but also the right to avoidance due to mistake, misrepresentation, fraud or duress.

e) The right of withdrawal

5.22 Unlike other EU consumer law directives, Directive 87/102/EEC did not provide a right of withdrawal, but the national laws of many Member States did.

---

88 See Department of Trade and Industry, the Consumer Credit Act 1974 (Electronic Agreements) Order 2004, Regulatory Impact Assessment, www.dti.gov.uk/files/file23061.pdf, No 2.2.

Thus it was clear from the outset that the right to withdrawal would be included in Directive 2008/48/EC.

The rules laid down in Article 14 largely follow the model of Article 6 of Directive 2002/65/EC, although the Consumer Credit Directive prevails over Directive 2002/65/EC, and also over the Doorstep Selling Directive 85/577/EEC,[89] according to its Article 14(4). Naturally, this only applies where the Consumer Credit Directive actually grants a right of withdrawal in the individual case.

According to Article 14(1), the period of withdrawal is 14 calendar days and the dispatch rule applies; see Article 14(3)(a) s. 2. This appears to have become the new standard in EU consumer law. The period begins to run, according to Article 14(1) para 2, on the day on which the contract is concluded, provided that the consumer has received the contractual terms and conditions and information in accordance with Article 10, otherwise on that later day. No rule is provided for the case that the contractual terms and conditions and information are not, or not properly, provided in accordance with Article 10, and that the period of withdrawal does therefore not commence. Therefore, the *Heininger* rule applies, according to which a period of withdrawal that has not commenced cannot end.[90]

The consequences of the withdrawal are set out in Article 14(3) and (4). The consumer has to pay to the creditor the capital and the interest accrued thereon from the date the credit was drawn down until the date the capital is repaid, without any undue delay and no later than 30 calendar days after the dispatch by him to the creditor of notification of the withdrawal. The interest shall be calculated on the basis of the agreed borrowing rate. The only other compensation to which the creditor may be entitled is compensation for any non-returnable charges paid by the creditor to any public administrative body. It may be remembered that the creditor has to inform the consumer of these consequences under Article 10(2)(q). One possible sanction for misinformation would be the loss of the claim for compensation, but the Member States are free to determine the appropriate sanction. Of course, the fact that Article 14(3)(b) requires the consumer to pay the agreed interest rate does not prohibit the Member States from holding usurious interest rates void.

Article 14(4) adds that the consumer who exercises his right of withdrawal shall not be bound either to an ancillary service relating to the credit agreement that is provided by the creditor or by a third party on the basis of an agreement between the third party and the creditor. This provision that has only been included towards the end of the negotiations relates to credit insurance contracts and ensures that the consumer is also released from this potentially very expensive ancillary contract.

89 Due to the replacement of Directive 85/577/EEC with the Consumer Rights Directive 2011/83/EU, which does not apply to financial services, the overlap no longer exists.

90 ECJ, 13 December 2001, C-481/99, *Georg Heininger and Helga Heininger v Bayerische Hypo- und Vereinsbank AG* [2001] ECR I-9945.

Two "French" exemptions are included in Article 14. First, under Article 14(7), true cooling-off periods, during which the performance of the contract may not begin, are not affected by Article 14(1) and continue to be allowed. The second one refers to French legislation on linked credit agreements: according to Article 14(2), where in the case of a linked credit agreement, national legislation already provides that funds cannot be made available to the consumer before the expiry of a specific period, Member States may exceptionally provide that the period referred to in paragraph 1 of this Article may be reduced to this specific period at the explicit request of the consumer. Under French law, this shorter period is three days.[91] Apart from these exemptions, the rules on the right of withdrawal are exclusive. More stringent rules, in particular a prohibition on charging the consumer interest, are not allowed any longer.

f) *The right to early repayment*

5.23 The right to early repayment already formed part of Directive 87/102/EEC. Nevertheless, the rules of the Member States specifying the consequences of early repayment, and in particular the creditor's claim for compensation, differed greatly,[92] and the new detailed rules established by Directive 2008/48/EC that were meant to harmonise totally the laws of the Member States in this field, were subject to fierce resistance from all sides. Political agreement could only be achieved through the inclusion of numerous regulatory choices.

The basic rule of Article 16(1) is that the consumer is entitled at any time to discharge fully or partially his obligations under a credit agreement, and that in such a case, he shall be entitled to a reduction in the total cost of the credit, such reduction consisting of the interest and the costs for the remaining duration of the contract. In return, the creditor is entitled, according to Article 16(2), to fair and objectively justified compensation for possible costs directly linked to early repayment of credit, but only if the early repayment falls within a period for which the borrowing rate is fixed. Article 16(2) para 2 fixes ceilings that depend upon the time between the early repayment and the agreed termination of the credit agreement. If this period exceeds one year, the compensation may not exceed 1% of the amount of credit repaid early; if the remaining period is less than one year, compensation may not exceed 0.5% of the amount of credit repaid early.[93] By no means may the creditor benefit from early repayment. Therefore, Article 16(5) disallows any compensation to exceed the amount of interest that the consumer would have paid during the period between the early repayment and the agreed date of termination of the credit agreement.

---

91 See also the report by Lechner, EP doc. A6-0504/2007, at 20.

92 See only COM (1995) 117, No 190 ff.

93 Initially, the Commission had proposed no compensation at all to be paid in that latter case where the remaining period is less than one year, see Article 16(2)(a) of the first proposal, COM (2002) 443 final.

Initially, the Commission had planned to require the creditor to prove that the reference interest rate applied by the European Central Bank to its most recent main refinancing operation carried out before the first calendar day of the half year in question is lower at the time of the early repayment than at the time of conclusion of the credit agreement. This was meant to prevent the creditor from obtaining compensation although no damage arises because the creditor can use the repayment to conclude a new credit contract at a higher interest rate. This rule was however deleted by the European Parliament. Instead, Article 16(2) now determines that the compensation should be "fair and objectively justified". Looking at Article 16 as a whole, it is clear that the "fair and objectively justified" compensation can be determined in a lump sum agreement. The Member States may provide that the consumer can, if the compensation claimed by the creditor exceeds the loss actually suffered, claim a corresponding reduction; see Article 16(4)(b). *Vice versa*, Member States have the regulatory option to allow the creditor to exceptionally claim higher compensation if he can prove that the loss he suffered from early repayment exceeds the amount determined under the lump sum agreement. In both cases, the "loss" shall consist of the difference between the initially agreed interest rate and the interest rate at which the creditor can lend out the amount repaid early in the market at the time of early repayment, and shall take into account the impact of early repayment on administrative costs.

Compulsory exemptions for the creditor's claim of compensation are laid down in Article 16(3); they include overdraft facilities and – unnecessarily when one looks at the requirements of Article 16(2) – the situation that the repayment falls within a period for which the borrowing rate is not fixed.

Finally, the Member States can – optionally – introduce thresholds of up to €10,000 within any period of 12 months. If the amount of the early repayment does not reach the threshold, the consumer shall not owe any compensation. Even with all these regulatory choices in place, the consumer's position in some Member States where strictly no compensation was owed in the event of early repayment deteriorated.[94]

g) Linked credit agreements

5.24 Linked credit agreements were also touched upon in Directive 87/102/EEC but Article 11 of that Directive provided little use for consumers.[95] In fact, the Commission stated in its first proposal for a new Consumer Credit Directive that a "number of Member States simply transposed Article 11 and created legislation that was ineffective", whereas other Member States have gone (far)

---

94 See, for example, old §489 para 1 of the German Civil Code.

95 For critical comments see Howells/Wilhelmsson, 208 ff.

beyond the requirements of that Directive.[96] Problematic issues were the very narrow description of the linked credit agreement[97] and the subsidiarity of the creditor's liability *vis-à-vis* the liability of the trader of the linked contract. The Commission therefore aimed at introducing the far-reaching model of joint and several liability – an attempt that had already failed in the negotiations for the old Directive[98] and that failed again after strong criticism from the banking industry.[99] The Commission then retreated towards the old system of Directive 87/102/EEC, which, under the total harmonisation approach of the new Directive, would have meant a mandatory ban on consumer protection in this field.[100] In its final version, Article 15 deals with two areas: with the effects of the withdrawal of a contract on the sale of goods or the provision of services on a linked credit agreement and with the consumer's claims against the creditor that arise from the linked contract on the sale of goods or the provision of services.

aa) The definition of the linked credit agreement

5.25 Directive 2008/48/EC provides, in Article 3(n), a new and much broader definition of the linked credit agreement. It is defined as an agreement where (i) the credit in question serves exclusively to finance an agreement for the supply of specific goods or the provision of a specific service, and (ii) those two agreements form, from an objective point of view, a commercial unit; a commercial unit shall be deemed to exist where the supplier or service provider himself finances the credit for the consumer or, if it is financed by a third party, where the creditor uses the services of the supplier or service provider in connection with the conclusion or preparation of the credit agreement, or where the specific goods or the provision of a specific service are explicitly specified in the credit agreement. Beyond this definition, Member States are free, according to Recital (10) to include agreements where the credit in question only serves partially to finance an agreement for the supply of specific goods or the provision of a specific service.[101] At the same time, the new definition seems to be narrower than Article 11(2) of the old Directive 87/102/EEC as interpreted by the ECJ in *Rampion and Godard*[102] since it talks of 'specific goods' and 'specific services'.

---

96 COM (2002) 443 final, at 22. See also Ritz; Herrmann; and Blaurock, 801; all on Germany, France and the UK.

97 Although the ECJ has applied that description in a very consumer-friendly manner, see ECJ, 4 October 2007, C-429/05, *Max Rampion, Marie-Jeanne Rampion, née Godard v Franfinance SA, K par K SAS* [2007] ECR I-8017; ECJ, 23 April 2009, C-509/07, *Luigi Scarpelli v NEOS Banca SpA* [2009] ECR I-3311.

98 See Latham, 224.

99 See, for example, Danco, 855 ff.

100 For a detailed analysis see Rott, *EuLF* 2006, I-61.

101 This has allowed Germany to maintain the definition provided by §358 para 3 of the Civil Code.

102 ECJ, 4 October 2007, C-429/05, *Max Rampion, Marie-Jeanne Rampion, née Godard v Franfinance SA, K par K SAS* [2007] ECR I-8017.

bb) The withdrawal from the linked contract

5.26 According to Article 15(1), the consumer who has exercised a right of withdrawal, based on Community law, concerning a contract for the supply of goods or services, shall no longer be bound by a linked credit agreement either. This type of connection had already been established by Directive 94/47/EC on timesharing (now replaced by Directive 2008/122/EC), Directive 97/7/EC on distance selling (now replaced by the Consumer Rights Directive 2011/83/EU) and Directive 2002/65/EC on the distance marketing of financial services.

The legal consequences are not entirely clear. Under Article 15(1), the consumer shall "not be bound" by the linked credit agreement. He may however wish to uphold the credit agreement. For example, he may have obtained very cheap credit that was meant to promote the sale of a certain product, for example, a 0% loan. The wording of Article 15(1) appears to suggest that the linked credit agreement is not necessarily void but that the creditor may remain bound to his agreement.

The exercise of a right of withdrawal that is not based on EU law but is of a purely national nature is not covered by Article 15(1). Thus, since this area is unregulated by the Consumer Credit Directive, it remains within the competence of the Member States.

cc) The effect of the withdrawal from the credit agreement on the linked contract

5.27 The effect of the withdrawal from the credit agreement on the linked contract is not regulated in Article 15. The respective proposal by the European Parliament[103] was expressly rejected by the Commission, in its amended proposal.[104] Thus, this issue remains within the competence of the Member States, as Recital (37) confirms.

dd) The consumer's claims against the creditor

5.28 Beyond the new definition of linked credit agreements, not much has changed in relation to the consumer's claims against the creditor in cases in which the goods or services covered by a linked credit agreement are not supplied, or are supplied only in part, or are not in conformity with the contract for the supply thereof. The subsidiarity requirement has been transferred into the new Directive and the consumer shall only have the right to pursue remedies against the creditor if the consumer has pursued his remedies against the supplier

103 See Article 16(2) of the position of the European Parliament of 20/4/2004, Doc. P5_TC1-COD (2002)0222.

104 COM (2004) 747 final, at 5.

but has failed to obtain the satisfaction to which he is entitled according to the law or the contract for the supply of goods or services. Member States have introduced diverging requirements on what the consumer has to do in order to obtain satisfaction from the supplier, ranging from litigation and failed attempts to execute a judgment to mere out-of-court attempts to pursue a remedy. According to Recital (38), the competence to specify the subsidiarity requirements remains with the Member States.

The other relevant issue is which remedies the consumer can pursue against the creditor, and again the Member States have introduced divergent remedies, ranging from joint and several liability under UK legislation to the mere right to reject further payment to the creditor, without the right to be reimbursed for payment that has already been made, which is the German solution.[105] Article 15(3) explicitly allows (in the UK) the rendering of the creditor jointly and severally liable in respect of any claim which the consumer may have against the supplier where the purchase of goods or services from the supplier has been financed by a credit agreement. Otherwise, the Member States shall determine to what extent and under what conditions those remedies shall be exercisable; see Article 15(2) s. 2. In conclusion, almost no harmonisation has been achieved in relation to this particular issue.

h) *Overdraft facilities and overrunning*

5.29 Overdraft facilities and overrunning enjoy special treatment in many respects. Overdraft facilities as described in Article 2(3) come under Article 6, as do the types of credit mentioned in Article 2(5) and (6), meaning that the creditor does not have to provide up to 19 items of information but only up to 12. Information on the repayment of the credit and so on is replaced by information on the conditions and procedure for terminating the credit agreement, under Article 6(1) para 2(g). Two items of information only apply in cases of overdraft facilities where an indication that the consumer may be requested to repay the amount of credit in full at any time and information about the charges applicable from the time such agreements are concluded and, if applicable, the conditions under which those charges may be changed must be provided, according to Article 6(1) para 2(h) and (k). Member States may decide, according to Article 6(3) that the APR need not be provided.

Special rules also apply to the content of the contract where Article 10(5) specifies the reduced number of details to be provided. In addition to this, Article 12 reflects the fact that the amount of credit changes with every drawdown performed by the consumer. Therefore, the consumer shall be kept regularly informed by means of a statement of account, on paper or on another durable medium, containing the following particulars: (a) the precise period to

[105] See BGH, 25 April 2006, *WM* 2006, 1066.

which the statement of account relates; (b) the amounts and dates of drawdowns; (c) the balance from the previous statement and the date thereof; (d) the new balance; (e) the dates and amounts of payments made by the consumer; (f) the borrowing rate applied; (g) any charges that have been applied; and (h) where applicable, the minimum amount to be paid. Article 12(2) protects the consumer from surprising changes of interest rates: the consumer shall be informed on paper or another durable medium of increases in the borrowing rate, or in any charges payable, before the change in question enters into force. The only exception is where the new interest rate is determined by a reference rate that has increased, the new reference rate is made publicly available by appropriate means and the information concerning the new reference rate is also kept available on the premises of the creditor.

If an agreement to open an account includes the possibility to overrun, Article 18 applies. According to Article 18(1), the creditor must provide, on paper or another durable medium on a regular basis, information as mentioned in Article 6(1) para 2(e), which includes the borrowing rate, the conditions governing the application of that rate, any index or reference rate applicable to the initial borrowing rate, the charges applicable from the time the credit agreement is concluded, and, where applicable, the conditions under which those charges may be changed. The same should apply if the possibility to overrun is given at a later date, in an amendment to the account contract. A possible sanction for failure to inform in accordance with Article 18(1) would be the loss of interest and charges.

Article 18(2) is meant to issue a warning to the consumer. In the event of a significant overrunning exceeding a period of one month, additional information obligations come into play. These relate to: (a) the overrunning itself; (b) the amount involved; (c) the borrowing rate; and (d) any penalties, charges or interest on arrears applicable. Article 18(2) reflects the fact that interest rates in the event of overrunning are usually much higher than interest rates in a "normal" credit contract. Some Member States even require the creditor to offer a normal credit product when the duration of the overrunning is significant. Such national legislation is not affected by the Directive, according to Article 18(3).

i) Credit intermediaries

5.30 Intermediaries in the field of financial services have attracted much attention in recent years.[106] Insurance intermediaries were given their own dedicated Directive 2002/92/EC on insurance mediation;[107] a reform of this Directive is envisaged in order to raise the minimum standards of consumer

106 On the development of EU law of financial intermediaries, see Rott, *EWS* 2008, 21.

107 OJ L, 15 January 2003, 3.

protection provided.[108] Intermediaries in the field of investment services have been imposed with new obligations under the MiFiD Directive 2004/39/EC. Credit intermediaries were already mentioned in the old Directive 87/102/EEC but only with a view to prudential supervision. They were then recognised to be a relevant issue for consumer law in the 1996 Green Paper "Financial Services: Meeting Consumers' Expectations".[109] In 2007, the Commission considered the proposal of a special Directive on credit intermediaries that would regulate their legal position in a comprehensive manner,[110] but no legislative initiative has followed. In the meantime, Directive 2008/48/EC has introduced some obligations on credit intermediaries, which are, unlike most other provisions, explicitly not meant to be exclusive; see Recital (17). They relate, predominantly, to pre-contractual information. In contrast, the regulation and control of intermediaries by public authorities that the Commission wished to include in the Directive[111] have been cancelled by the European Parliament.[112]

aa) The definition of the credit intermediary

5.31 A credit intermediary is defined, in Article 3(f), as a natural or legal person who is not acting as a creditor and who, in the course of his trade, business or profession, for a fee, which may take a pecuniary form or any other agreed form of financial consideration: (i) presents or offers credit agreements to consumers; (ii) assists consumers by undertaking preparatory work in respect of credit agreements other than as referred to in (i); or (iii) concludes credit agreements with consumers on behalf of the creditor. This definition is very broad. It covers the creditor's agents, in particular those employees that are involved in doorstep activities, but also independent brokers, regardless of whether they act only for one creditor, or a limited number of creditors, or whether they promise to search the whole credit market for the best available credit. Even traders that act as agents for creditors that finance, as third parties, their contracts on the supply of goods or services, are credit intermediaries in the terms of Article 3(f). The only exception is the legal profession.[113]

bb) Pre-contractual information and advice

5.32 First of all, the pre-contractual information obligations under Articles 5(1) and 6(1) and the duty of advice under Article 5(6) are not only imposed on

108 See the proposal for a new Directive on insurance mediation, COM (2012) 360 final.
109 COM (96) 209 final.
110 See the Commission's Green Paper on Retail Financial Services in the Single Market, COM (2007) 226 final, at 20.
111 See Article 28 of the first proposal, COM (2002) 443 final.
112 See M. Hoffmann, 314.
113 See also COM (2002) 443 final, explanations on Article 2.

creditors but also on credit intermediaries. Only the duty to assess the consumer's creditworthiness solely applies to creditors. The only credit intermediaries that are exempted from the mentioned obligations are those suppliers of goods or services that are acting as credit intermediaries in an ancillary capacity, according to Article 7. By this, the Directive means those traders whose activity as credit intermediaries is not the main purpose of their trade, business or profession, but who only hand over the credit application forms of the creditor. Obviously, in such a case the creditor himself remains responsible for pre-contractual information and advice.

Like the creditor,[114] the credit intermediary who infringes his pre-contractual obligations should be liable for the damage caused. The creditor and the credit intermediary would be jointly and severally liable in such a case since the creditor only fulfils his own pre-contractual information (through the credit intermediary) if the credit intermediary provides full and correct information and advice.[115]

As mentioned above, additional obligations may apply to the credit intermediary from national law on intermediaries. In particular, independent intermediaries would be expected to provide information not only about the credit products of one creditor but to give a comprehensive overview of the market. Failing this, they may enter liability which is not shared by the creditor who only has to consider his own products when giving advice to the consumer, under Article 5(6).[116]

cc) Status information and fees

5.33 Specific rules on credit intermediaries are laid down in Article 21, which aims at creating transparency. Under Article 21(a), the credit intermediary has to indicate in advertising and documentation intended for consumers, the extent of his powers, in particular whether he works exclusively with one or more creditors or as an independent broker. This aims at providing the consumer with an idea of the extent of the market overview provided by the credit intermediary, and therefore of the quality of his advice. In the field of financial intermediaries, status information is sometimes perceived to be more important than product information.[117]

The fee payable to the credit intermediary, if any, is regulated by Article 21(b) and (c). The consumer may only be charged a fee if the fee is disclosed to the consumer and agreed between the consumer and the credit intermediary on paper or another durable medium before the conclusion of the credit agreement.

---

114 See *supra*, at 5.4.
115 For details, see Rott, *EWS* 2008, 28.
116 For details, see Rott, *VuR* 2008, 281 ff.
117 See, for example, Rehberg, 1011.

The Member States can, however, also maintain or introduce the mandatory written form of the agreement.

The fee has to be communicated to the creditor by the credit intermediary, for the purpose of calculation of the APR. A previous version of Article 21, decided upon by the Council in its Common Position, under which the fee should only become payable if the credit intermediary does not receive a fee from the creditor and if the credit agreement was actually concluded, was not accepted by the European Parliament. Member States are however free to adopt such additional requirements.

j) *Enforcement*

5.34 Of course, the rules of the Directive are mandatory: Article 22(3). This includes a prohibition on circumventing the rules of the Directive, in particular by combining credit agreements that are within the scope of application with credit agreements that are outside. That prohibition also covers the rule of Article 14(2) of the old Directive 87/102/EEC, according to which the Directive could not be avoided by splitting credit agreements into small portions. The mandatory nature of the Directive extends to the impossibility of avoiding the rules of the Directive by choosing the law of a non-EU country.

The Directive does not specify remedies or sanctions but applies the usual formula, according to which sanctions should be "effective, proportionate and constitute a deterrent".

In addition to that, and following its case law in the area of unfair contract terms, the ECJ held in the case of *Rampion and Godard* that national courts had the right to apply the mandatory law of the Consumer Credit Directive of their own motion since consumers might not be aware of their rights under that Directive.[118] This was confirmed in *Pohotovost'*.[119]

Moreover, and in line with current policy on settlement of consumer disputes, Article 24 requires Member States to ensure adequate and effective complaints and redress procedures for the out-of-court settlement of consumer disputes concerning credit agreements. These procedures have now been fleshed out by the new Directive 2013/11/EU on consumer ADR and the new Regulation (EU) No. 524/2013 on consumer ODR (8.23a–e).

Member States are, however, free to determine whether such out-of-court dispute settlement procedures are mandatory prior to access to the court system.[120]

---

118 ECJ, 4 October 2007, C-429/05, *Max Rampion, Marie-Jeanne Rampion, née Godard v Franfinance SA, K par K SAS* [2007] ECR I-8017.

119 CJEU, 16 November 2010, C-76/10, *Pohotovost' s.r.o. v Iveta Korčkovská* [2010] ECR I-11557 at paras 56–63.

120 CJEU, 12 July 2012, C-602/10, *SC Volksbank România SA v Autoritatea Naţională pentru Protecţia Consumatorilor – Comisariatul Judeţean pentru Protecţia Consumatorilor Călăraşi (CJPC)* [2012] ECR I-nyr.

k) *Conclusions and perspectives*

5.35 It should be remembered that the aim, and indeed the justification, for the total harmonisation approach of the new Consumer Credit Directive is the establishment of an internal consumer credit market, in which cross-border consumer credit actually happens. That this can be achieved with the now enacted Directive has often been doubted.[121] Too great are the remaining legal differences in the national consumer credit laws, where the Directive does not provide harmonised provisions, for example, in national usury laws. The CJEU has added to this by accepting national prohibitions on certain bank charges in *Volksbank România*. The many regulatory choices that allow national legislators to maintain legal instruments that are particular to their legal order do not foster harmonisation either, but were of course the price for an agreement to be reached at all. Moreover, language barriers and local credit cultures remain present, and language barriers are of much greater significance to legal products, such as financial services, whose characteristics are determined by the terms of the contract, rather than to the market for goods. Thus, it would seem unlikely that an internal credit market will develop in the near future. What remains is an approximation of the consumer credit laws of the Member States, with significant improvements for many Member States that have until now operated at the low level of Directive 87/102/EEC, and with some restrictions on the most protective Member States.

V. MORTGAGE CREDIT

5.36 As mentioned above, mortgage credit was excluded from the Consumer Credit Directives, the argument being that it is so different from unsecured credit that it should not come under the same set of rules.

1. RECOMMENDATION 2001/193/EC

5.37 Instead, mortgage credit is the subject of the Commission Recommendation 2001/193/EC of March 2001 on pre-contractual information to be given to consumers by lenders offering home loans.[122] The Recommendation endorses a Voluntary Code of Conduct on Pre-Contractual Information for Home Loans that was agreed between European-wide credit sector associations and consumer organisations. The main aim of the Code of Conduct is to increase transparency and to assist in comparisons by consumers

[121] See, for example, Danco, 859; Rohe, 273; Franck, 339; Hoffmann, 310.
[122] OJ 2001, L 69/25.

between lenders. Standardisation applies both to the information to be supplied, and to the format in which it is supplied (in the form of a European Standardised Information Sheet or ESIS). A register of lenders complying with the Code was compiled by the European Commission.[123] The Recommendation (and the Code of Conduct) covers domestic as well as cross-border home loans but excludes credit agreements covered by the Consumer Credit Directive. The pre-contractual information to be supplied includes both general information and personalised information specific to the individual consumer. Overall, the Recommendation was not very successful. A study conducted by the Institute of Financial Services found insufficient compliance with the Recommendation.[124] The Commission has also concluded that implementation of the Code was inconsistent and sub-optimal.[125]

2. THE PROPOSED MORTGAGE CREDIT DIRECTIVE

5.38 During the negotiations for the new Consumer Credit Directive, the EU Commission had already launched a separate consultation process on mortgage credit, with the Green Paper on Mortgage Credit in the EU,[126] followed by the White Paper on the Integration of EU Mortgage Credit Markets.[127] Ultimately, the Commission published a proposal for a Directive on credit agreements related to residential property in April 2011.[128] By and large, the proposal follows the structure of the Consumer Credit Directive 2008/48/EC, but it is even more protective than the Consumer Credit Directive in that it includes warning requirements and strengthens the creditworthiness assessment. Moreover, it includes provisions related to authorisation and prudential supervision of mortgage lenders and of mortgage credit intermediaries.

a) Scope of application

5.39 The proposed Directive would fill the gap that was left by Directive 2008/48/EC. According to its Article 2(1), it would apply to: (a) credit agreements which are secured either by a mortgage or by another comparable security commonly used in a Member State on residential immovable property or secured by a right related to residential immovable property; (b) credit agreements the

123 ec.europa.eu/internal_market/finservices-retail/home-loans/code_en.htm#register.
124 IFF, Monitoring the uptake and the effectiveness of the Voluntary Code of Conduct on Pre-contractual Information for Home Loans, www.money-advice.net/media.php?id=611.
125 See the Proposal for a Directive on credit agreements related to residential property, COM (2011) 142 final, at 4.
126 COM (2005) 327 final. See also Köndgen/Stöcker, 112; Volante, 150.
127 COM (2007) 807 final.
128 COM (2011) 142 final.

purpose of which is to acquire or retain property rights in land or in an existing or projected residential building; and (c) credit agreements the purpose of which is the renovation of the residential immovable property a person owns or aims to acquire, which are not covered by Directive 2008/48/EC.

b) Substantive law

5.40 At the level of substantive law, the proposed directive would introduce requirements related to mortgage credit advertising that do not only go beyond the Unfair Commercial Practices Directive 2005/29/EC but that are also far more detailed than those established by Article 4 of the Consumer Credit Directive. Amongst others, Article 8 would require advertisement to include a warning, where applicable, concerning the risk of losing the immovable property in the event of non-observance of the commitments linked to the credit agreement when the credit is secured by a mortgage or another comparable security commonly used in a Member State on residential immovable property or secured by a right related to residential immovable property. As in general consumer credit law, under Article 9 the creditor would have to provide pre-contractual information in a standard form, the European Standardised Information Sheet (ESIS). The advice duty of the Consumer Credit Directive is also contained in Article 11 of the proposal, as is the duty to perform a creditworthiness assessment in Article 14. However, in the case of the proposed Mortgage Credit Directive, the creditor would have to refuse credit if the assessment of the consumer's creditworthiness results in a negative prospect for his ability to repay the credit over the lifetime of the credit agreement.

The proposal clearly separates advice from the selling of a credit. According to Article 17(1), service shall only be marketed as 'advice' if the remuneration of the individual providing the service is transparent to the consumer. Of the other consumer rights enshrined in the Consumer Credit Directive, the proposal only takes up the right to early repayment in Article 18. In contrast, no right of withdrawal would be granted.

The duties of credit intermediaries would also be more strictly regulated than in general consumer credit law. According to Article 10, the credit intermediary would have to provide, amongst other things, detailed information on his own person, his status or independence, and on potential fees. Moreover, they would have to comply with the duties to provide pre-contractual information and advice like creditors do.

c) Authorisation and prudential supervision

5.41 The proposal goes beyond the Consumer Credit Directive in also dealing with authorisation and prudential supervision of mortgage lenders and of mortgage credit intermediaries. To this end, Member States would have to designate a competent authority: Article 4. The rules appear to be inspired by the Insurance Mediation Directive 2002/92/EC and the MiFiD Directive 2004/39/EC, and it is not entirely clear to what extent they would affect the consumer-creditor relationship. Credit intermediaries would need to be authorised and registered: Article 19(f). Prerequisites are, according to Article 20, that they are of good repute and that they hold professional indemnity insurance. The staff of creditors and credit intermediaries would have to possess an appropriate level of knowledge and competence in relation to the offering or granting of credit agreements or the activity of credit intermediation: Article 6. Importantly, Member States shall also ensure that the manner in which creditors remunerate their staff and the relevant credit intermediaries and the manner in which credit intermediaries remunerate their staff do not impede compliance with the obligation to act in accordance with the best interests of the consumer; the relevant Article 5(2) seems to be leaning on Article 18 of the MiFiD Directive and to react to bonus systems that reward practices such as "churning". Authorisation requirements shall also be introduced for non-credit institutions that do not come under the prudential supervision system of the General Banking Directive 2006/48/EC.[129]

The proposal has met with considerable resistance from the banking industry, in particular related to the strict rules on creditworthiness assessment. Nevertheless, the European Parliament has approved the Commission proposal, although with numerous amendments;[130] thus, its adoption is expected in the near future.

VI. CREDIT-RELATED UNFAIR CONTRACT TERMS LAW

5.42 Unfair contract terms law has always played an important role in national consumer credit law. A number of cases have recently been referred to the Court of Justice. The relevant issues are manifold: they range from price variation clauses and bank charges to the preconditions and effects of the termination of the contract and the consequences of delayed payment. For example, German courts have held that a number of bank charges are against good faith because banks charge the consumer for "services" that they perform in their own interest, in particular when it comes to evaluating securities.[131] In *Banif Plus Bank*, the case turned on drastic consequences of the consumer's breach of his payment

129 OJ 2006, L 177/1; last amended by Directive 2011/89/EU, OJ 2011, L 326/113.

130 See European Parliament Doc. TA/2013/541/P7.

131 See BGH, 21 April 2009, *NJW* 2009, 2051; Tiffe, 127.

obligations.[132] In the case of *Banco Español de Credito*,[133] one of the issues at stake was an interest rate of 29% on delayed payment; which the national court considered excessive. In *Pohotovost'*,[134] the bank even charged 91.25% interest on delayed payment. In that latter case, the Court of Justice did not explicitly hold the sanction of 91.25% interest per annum to be unfair in terms of Article 3(1) of the Unfair Contract Terms Directive 93/13/EEC, given the fact that it is not competent to decide the case that is pending in the national court but only to give guidance on the correct application of the Directive (3.21). It is, however, quite obvious that this sanction is disproportionate in the terms of Article 3(3) taken with No. 1(e) of the Annex to Directive 93/13/EEC, in particular against the background of the applicable Slovakian law which only allowed a sanction of 9% per annum.

The same applies to mortgage credit where, in the case of *Aziz*,[135] besides important procedural issues, the consequences of delayed payment were at stake. Importantly, in that latter case, the Court of Justice has for the first time made explicit that unfairness must be judged, amongst other things, against the background of the national default rules that would apply in the absence of the contract term at issue, for example the default interest rate for late payment.

---

132 CJEU, 21 February 2013, C-472/11, *Banif Plus Bank Zrt v Csaba Czipai, Viktória Czipai* [2013] ECR I-nyr.

133 CJEU, 14 June 2012, C-618/10, *Banco Español de Crédito SA v Joaquín Calderón Camino* [2012] ECR I-nyr.

134 CJEU, 15 November 2010, C-76/10, *Pohotovost' s.r.o. v Iveta Korčkovská* [2010] ECR I-11557.

135 See, in particular, CJEU, 14 March 2013, C-415/11 *Mohamed Aziz v Caixa d'Estalvis de Catalunya, Tarragona i Manresa (Catalunyacaixa)* [2013] ECR I-nyr.

CHAPTER 6

LIABILITY FOR DEFECTIVE PRODUCTS AND SERVICES

Hans-W. Micklitz

CONTENTS

Bibliography:

M. Adams, *Ökonomische Analyse der Gefährdungs- und Verschuldungshaftung*, 1985; J.S. Borghetti, *La responsabilité du fait des produits*, 2004; J. Borghetti, The Scope of Application of the Directive on Product Liability and the Impact of the Directive on French Law, *ZEuP* 2011, 919;G. Brüggemeier, *Haftungsrecht*, 2006; G. Brüggemeier, Die Gefährdungshaftung der Produzenten nach der EG-Richtlinie, in: Ott/Schäfer, *Allokationseffizienz in der Rechtsordnung*, 1989; J. Calais-Auloy/H. Temple, *Droit de la consommation*, 8th ed. 2010; B. Dahl, *Consumer Litigation in Denmark*, 1981; P. Eklund, The Effect of the EEA Agreement on Consumer Protection Interests in Sweden, *JCP* 1994, 123; D. Fairgrieve (ed.), *Product Liability in Comparative Perspective*, 2005; J. Gesthin, Le nouveau Titre IV bis du Livre III du Code civil "De la responabilité du faits des produits défectueaux", *JCP* 1998 I, 148; J. Goldberg/B. Zipursky, The Easy Case for Products Liability Law, *Harv LRev* 2010, 1918; D. Harland, Reform of the Law of Product Liability in Australia, *JCP* 1992, 191; C. Hodges, *European Regulation of Consumer Product Safety*, 2005; E. Hondius, A Dutch DES Case: Pharmaceutical Producers Jointly and Severally Liable, *ConsLJ* 1994, 40; G. Howells, The Rise of European Consumer Law – Whither National Consumer Law?, *Sydney LRev* 2006, 64; G. Howells, *Comparative Product Liability*, 1993; G. Howells/S. Weatherill, *Consumer Protection Law*, 2005; J. Kellam, *The Contract-Tort Dichotomy as a Theoretical Framework for Product Liability Law*, 2000; J. Kellam/L. Nottage, Europeanisation of Product Liability in the Asia-Pacific Region, *JCP* 2008, 217; P.J. Kellam et al., Theories of Product Liability and Australian Consumer Law, *Competition and Consumer Law Journal* 2013, 1; L. Krämer, *EEC Consumer Law*, 1985; H.P. Lehofer, Minimum Implementation of Minimum Directives? Consumer Protection in Austria in the Context of European Integration, *JCP* 1994, 3; P. Lodrup, Product Liability in Norway, *JCP* 1991, 7; U. Magnus/H.-W. Micklitz, *Liability for the Safety of Services*, 2006; N. Reich, Competition between Legal Orders, *CMLRev* 1992, 861; N. Reich, Horizontal Liability in Secondary EC Law: Also a Critique of ECJ Case Law on Remedies for Compensation on Product Liability, Non-Discrimination, and IP law, in: *Liber amicorum Guido Alpa*, 2007, 846; N. Reich/H.-W. Micklitz, *Europäisches Verbraucherrecht*, 4th ed. 2003; N. Reich/H.-W. Micklitz, *Consumer Legislation in the EEC Countries – A comparative analysis*, 1981; M. Reimann, Product Liability in a Global Context: The Hollow Victory of the European Model, *ERPL* 2003, 123; W.-H. Roth, Freier Dienstleistungsverkehr und Verbraucherschutz, Verbraucher und Recht, *VuR* 2007, 16; H.-B. Schäfer/C. Ott, *Lehrbuch der ökonomischen Analyse des Zivilrechts*, 3rd ed. 2000; J. Stapleton, *Product Liability*, 1994; E. Steindorff, *EG-Vertrag und Privatrecht*, 1996; H.C. Taschner, Case-C-203/99, Henning Veedfald v. Arhus Amtskommune, judgment of the Court (Fifth Chamber) of 10 May 2001, *CMLRev* 2002, 385; M. Tulibacka, *Product Liability Law in Transition*, 2009; F. Graf v. Westphalen, *Produkthaftungshandbuch*, Vol. 2, 1999; S. Whittacker, Form and Substance in the Harmonisation of Product Liability in Europe, *ZEuP* 2007, 858; T. Wieckhorst, *Recht und Ökonomie des Produkthaftungsgesetzes*, 1994; T. Wilhelmsson, Products Liability in Finland, *JCP* 1991, 15.

I. THE WORK OF THE EC ON A DIRECTIVE ON PRODUCT LIABILITY

1. THE ECONOMIC AND LEGAL FUNDAMENTALS OF THE EUROPEAN APPROXIMATION WORK

6.1 Product liability law consists of legal rules granting compensation for harm which either a private consumer incurs from a shoddy product in his household or a bystander from the hazards of a defective product, or commercial customers incur from the use of a defective device or an employee from dangerous machinery. The legal systems of the Member States of the EC – now EU – provide for compensation rules in the respective legal systems (common law, codified law) which are rooted in either contract or tort.[1] The scope of application of contract law and in particular the law on the sale of goods is restricted – irrespective of national particularities – since it benefits the contractual parties; occasionally it benefits those with a close connection to the contract, such as relatives, tenants, etc. In French law as developed by courts, any member of a contractual chain *action directe*)[2] will be responsible to victims with the exception of those which have merely been near an accident. At the same time, contractual liability may be limited by exclusion clauses which will be subject to unfair terms legislation.

Because of the restriction of the protected circle of possible claimants as contractually specified, the law on product liability evolved from tort law based on a "strict" negligence theory. However, in the more recent legal theories and legal policy discussions of the Member States the differences between contract and tort law have become blurred.[3] The decisive legal development as promoted by case law is the *general duty of care* imposed on the producer and other persons involved in the chain of production and marketing *vis-à-vis* the ultimate consumer, user or victim irrespective of contractual relations. This amounts to a *safety obligation* of the producer and other persons putting a product onto the market *vis-à-vis* potentially injured persons. We will not go into detail of the somewhat complex and divergent development of this obligation in Member States, but focus exclusively on Community and now Union law.

---

1 Overview in REICH/MICKLITZ, *Consumer Legislation in the EEC Countries*, 106; HOWELLS, *Comparative Product Liability*; KELLY/ATTREE; FAIRGRIEVE (ed.).

2 ECJ, 17 June 1992, C-26/91, *Handte* [1992] ECR I-3967 with regard to the applicability of Article 5(3) of the Brussels Convention resp. Regulation 44/2001, see 6.34, 7.42; for an overview see CALAIS-AULOY/TEMPLE, 283–285.

3 See KELLAM.

2. CONSUMER INTERESTS IN PRODUCT LIABILITY LAW

6.2 Consumers have an interest in the functioning of the internal market in the EU, as already shown (1.5), i.e. the free movement of goods extends the possibility for the consumer to choose and thus exert competitive pressure on prices, quality, etc. The opening of the market which is linked to greater freedom of choice also results in an "extension of risks" to the detriment of potential victims of defective products. In an internal market the compensatory interests of the consumer arising from the damage incurred by defective products cannot be left to the free interplay of market forces. In addition, from a welfare point of view they require the establishment of minimum standards. In an internal market it is not clear why an Italian consumer should be satisfied by a lower protection standard regarding the same product defect than a French consumer. Positive integration in the internal market also requires *an increase* in protective standards in the field of compensation. Otherwise there will be the danger of a "negative competition of the legal systems" by a "race to the bottom" which cannot be balanced out by international procedural or private law.[4] The need for a regulation of product liability at EC/EU level is not only supported by the resolution of the compensatory issue, albeit at least by minimum, not necessarily uniform, standards, but also by the attempt to establish *safety standards* directly attached to the free movement of goods. The extended liberalisation by the EC/EU of the movement of goods is necessarily to be followed by duties to conduct, which spread the risks of defective and hazardous products appropriately. Thus the introduction of a Community/Union-wide harmonised product liability regime is the result of the extensive case law of the ECJ on the significance of Articles 28 and 30 EC (now Articles 34 and 36 TFEU) for the free movement of goods. By linking product liability to the objective existence of a defect and thus to the safety risk emerging from a product which freely circulates in the internal market, it simultaneously establishes the *marketing requirements* for products within the EC/EU. Therefore product liability is also an indirect safety regulation which appears in the guise of private law; the functioning of the internal market is thus directly effected.

From that the question arises the issue of whether safety standards are to be determined centrally by the EC/EU or locally by the courts of the Member States. The Community legislator had opted for a combination of *central and decentralised safety regulations* as expressed in Directive 92/59/EEC as amended by Directive 2001/95/EC on general product safety.[5] This Directive should be seen as a counterpart to the Product Liability Directive. It imposes a duty on

4 In particular Reich, *CMLRev* 1992, 861.

5 Council Directive 92/59/EEC of 29 June 1992 on general product safety, OJ L 228, 11 August 1992, 24; Directive 2001/95/EC of the European Parliament and of the Council of 3 December 2001 on general product safety, OJ L 11, 16 January 2002, 4. For an overview see Hodges.

manufacturers to put only safe products onto the market and it provides for the establishment of competent public authorities which have to monitor the market.[6]

3. THE DEVELOPMENT STAGES OF THE E(E)C: APPROXIMATION WORK

6.3 The work in the competent authorities of the E(E)C on the Directive on product liability started simultaneously with the "boom" in consumer policy caused by the preparatory works on the first consumer policy programme (1.3). Influenced by the general public concern about latent product risks, in particular pharmaceutical products, an extensive consumer political criticism about the flaws of the then existing product liability law occurred in many industrialised countries. Reform proposals aimed at an extension of liability of the producer for the safety and freedom from fault of the products. Concurrently with the EC initiative, work by the Council of Europe in Strasbourg on a Convention of the Member States on product liability took place.[7] Within the EC the task force consisting of members of the Commission and officials of the Member States presented a draft in 1974.[8] A second draft followed in 1975.[9] In 1976, the Commission published a first proposal for a directive.[10] In the scope of its restricted powers of cooperation with regard to European legislation, the European Parliament discussed the proposals in the following years and presented its opinion in 1979.[11]

At the same time at the E(E)C level, intensive "lobbying" conducted by industrial and consumer associations began. As a result of these publicly-led discussions and the debates in Parliament, the Commission presented a slightly modified proposal in 1979.[12]

The discussions in the Council of Ministers lasted for more than five years. The main points of debate had been:

- the concepts of defect (6.4) and producer (6.12);
- the possibility of the so-called state-of-the-art defence (6.28);
- the "opt-out" for agricultural and fishery products (6.20); and
- the relationship with existing or coming Member State law (6.30).

6 Micklitz, in: Reich/Micklitz, *Europäisches Verbraucherrecht*, §27.
7 Council, Proposal of a convention of 4 April 1975, DIR/JUR (75) 1.
8 EEC Doc. XI/334/74.
9 EEC Doc. XI/355/76.
10 OJ C 241, 14 October 1976, 9.
11 OJ C 127, 21 June 1979, 61.
12 OJ C 271, 26 October 1979, 3.

The finally adopted Directive 85/374/EEC[13] of 25 July 1985 on the approximation of the laws, regulations and administrative provisions of the Member States concerning liability for defective products is notable for its compromises on all of these questions, which will be discussed below.

However Directive 85/374/EEC did not bring the regulation of product liability in the E(E)C to a conclusion. It is based on a continuous evaluation which is *inter alia* illustrated by the obligation of the Commission to report as per Article 21 of the Directive. By means of this evaluation, the experience gained in practice has been included in its further development. By that an interrelation between national law and the Directive has been established.[14] The first report from the Commission[15] which had been based on a poll of approximately 400 individual persons, associations and undertakings illustrated that in the period up to 1994 the Directive had not significantly altered the situation. However, at that time, the first criticism of individual provisions and formulations appeared. In particular, the options and the different interpretation possibilities were objected to by lawyers and consumer associations. Irrespective of the criticism, the Commission did not feel the need to make alterations but expressly indicated that it would particularly observe the non-inclusion of agricultural primary production. This had no consequences until the occurrence of mad cow disease which damaged the faith of a large part of the European population in agriculture. The original option possible under Directive 85/374/EEC to exclude liability for primary agricultural and fishery products was abolished by Directive 99/34/EC.[16]

On 31 January 2001 the Commission produced its second report to the Council.[17] Unlike the first report, the second was based on a Green Paper which had been presented to the governments of the Member States, to undertakings and to industrial and consumer associations. They were asked to deliver an opinion on particular areas of product liability in order to assess the effects of the EC Directive and possible alterations. More than 100 opinions were received, which were then analysed in the Commission's report.

As a result it is shown that even ten years after the enactment of the Directive there has only been limited experience with implementation, a fact which is explained by the late implementation of the Directive by some of the Member States. Furthermore, many liability cases are settled out of court by insurance companies, about which no precise information is available. Moreover, the continuing applicability of national liability provisions based on contract or tort results in a relatively restricted application of the harmonised law. Even though the attitude towards significant aspects of liability under the EC Directive may vary, in particular between undertakings and consumer associations, the

13 OJ L 210, 7 August 1985, 29.
14 Also Wieckhorst.
15 COM (1995) 617 final.
16 OJ L 414, 4 June 1999, 20.
17 COM (2000) 893 final.

Commission still does not feel the need to make alterations; this is a result of the lack of practical experience with the Directive – an attitude which has not changed at the time of writing.

The following discussion analyses the different controversial points in the legislative work and the legal experiences gained so far. It will concentrate on the main, particularly controversial aspects of the Directive. Questions concerning compensation (the notion of damage, the extent of damage, the exclusion of damages and period of termination) shall be dealt with only in passing because they have been regulated incompletely in the Directive or left to Member State discretion, in particular regarding damages for pain and suffering as well as damages for loss of property (6.34). This is the reason why national tort and possibly contract law will still be applicable alongside the law as stated in the Directive (see 6.30).

II. THE SAFETY CONCEPT OF THE DIRECTIVE: WHAT IS A DEFECT?

1. THE NOTION OF DEFECT IN THE DIFFERENT PROPOSALS

6.4 The definition of defectiveness of products which should incur liability has been a central issue of the discussion. The increasing intensification of the discussion indicates a clarification which gave a more striking outline to the concept of no-fault liability for product risks. The draft of 1975 stated relatively imprecisely in Article 3:

> "A product is defective if it is not suited for the purpose as intended by the producer."

Two weaknesses of this definition are obvious. Firstly, it does not distinguish the safety of a product from its quality as employed in sales law. Secondly, the definition makes the notion of defect solely dependent on the determination of the producer, i.e. it does not include cases of misuse which is to be expected or misuse which is to be attributed to the producer; furthermore it does not establish what is to be understood by "intention" – only legal declarations or advertising addressed to the general public.

The proposal of a Directive of 1976 established a safety policy concept in Article 4 which had been maintained in later versions and which constitutes the core of Directive 85/374/EEC.

It reads:

> "A product is defective when it does not provide the safety which a person is entitled to expect, taking all circumstances into account."

In this definition a defect regarding quality or conformity as known in the law on the sale of goods (4.10) is clearly distinguished from a defect which leads to an unsafe product. It must be borne in mind that the safety concept which is rooted in the notion of defect refers equally to persons and things, even though personal integrity plays a more important role in the Member States than the mere protection of property. For this reason the Council of Europe excluded property damage from the draft convention. Another important extension is that the "safety concept" of a product is not only determined by the producer (for example by means of directions for use, warnings, etc.) but is also linked to consumer expectations. The term "person" is not determined; however, it obviously aims at the entire circle of potential users within the EC including their conduct, which can only be determined to a certain extent by the producer. Thus a product might be defective if it is not used as indicated by the producer, provided that the latter could link legitimate safety expectations to the product. The question remains whether liability will arise in cases of misuse (see 6.8).

This specific concept of "defect" has not been questioned in later modifications as such. Article 4 of the proposal from 1976 was somewhat specified in the amended proposal from 1979 to the extent that it refers to the "the use to which it could reasonably be expected that the product would be put" at the time of bringing the product into circulation. Article 6 of the final version of the Directive continues the original consumer-related definition with an indication as to the "presentation of the product", or "the use to which it could reasonably be expected that the product would be put", and "the time when the product was put into circulation"; these criteria are supposed to facilitate the burden of proof. Paragraph 2 of Article 6 is new, and according to it a product shall not be considered defective for the sole reason that a better product is subsequently put into circulation.

2. DEFECT AND EXPECTED SAFETY

a) *Construction, fabrication and instruction defects*

6.5 The Directive determines the contents and thus the protective purpose of product liability in the light of the notion of defect which is made dependent on the safety which a person is entitled to expect.

The expectations of the producer are one of the criteria, but not the decisive one, as clearly shown by Article 6(1)(a). If the presentation of the product as such is defective, i.e. insufficient instructions for its use and scope of application, warnings as regards the poisonous character of a pesticide or the side-effects of a pharmaceutical product, then there is a defect which will be generally specified as an "instruction defect" in the traditional discussion on conduct-related product liability. The Directive does not generally alter the law of the Member

States; it merely completes and supplements it. The Directive contains indications of objective fault liability.

The term "presentation" is to be interpreted widely; any description of the product is likely to influence the expectation of the consumer. Therefore, advertising statements or indications on the packaging are covered by the term "presentation". Statements made by a third party which the producer uses, such as advertising agencies or sellers, will be attributed to the producer.

Depending on the extent to which the producer indicates the risks of the product, safety expectations for it will be lower; however, a complete exemption from liability is prohibited. This is also the case if the product satisfies applicable safety regulations and has obtained certificates. The producer will still be required to warn about foreseeable risks.

Liability for defective or incomplete "presentation" may also arise if a particular compatibility with the environment or health is suggested (e.g. in product marketing) without this being the case. However the notion of harm as contained in the Directive is limited to bodily and certain property damage; environmental damage is not covered by the Directive (*infra* 6.30).

6.6 A defect is also present if the product is not in accordance with Community, national or usual industry standards. On the positive side, this means that the product must be in accordance with the "state of the art", otherwise the producer or the person named in the Directive will be liable. This is the case because the technical and scientific standards entrench the general safety expectations.

The defect may occur in the area of construction or manufacturing. Such defects include common design and/or fabrication defects such as the ignoring of safety standards (which are not mandatory but restate the scientific and technical knowledge at the time the product is put into circulation), offending hygiene regulations in connection with the production of food and pharmaceutical products, ignoring regulations for packaging of chemicals which require particular protection from children, etc.

A defect is also present if there are no appropriate safety regulations yet or if potential risk is unknown or undefined. However, the exemption of liability as per Article 7(e) of the Directive might apply if the state of scientific and technical knowledge at the time that the product was put into circulation was not sufficient as to enable the existence of the defect to be discovered. In this case a person, e.g. a consumer, can expect a product to be brought into circulation free of any unnecessary risks. No-fault liability purports to pass on the risk potential of development risks to the producer. This becomes truer the higher the production risks – for example with carcinogenic pesticides and chemicals or mutagenity of pharmaceutical products – or the more vulnerable the end consumer – for example children in relation to toys.

However the consumer cannot expect absolute safety. The boundaries are fluid and need to be determined by the courts on a case-by-case basis. This means that the standard is relative, open and "reflexive", which as illustrated by the Directive depends on the presentation, the foreseeable use, the intended circle of consumers and the like. In conclusion it can be said that the risk threshold is determined by courts which could lead to different standards in the internal market. Thus the protective purpose of the Directive takes priority over the integration intention of the Community/Union.

6.7 The adherence to generally recognised or legally required standards as an exemption for liability of the producer which would otherwise arise is to be considered according to the exclusion provision of Article 7(d). Accordingly the producer shall not be liable if he proves that "the defect is due to compliance of the product with mandatory regulations issued by the public authorities". Industry standards or standards of otherwise private standardising institutes (CEN, DIN) do not fall under the exemption. If these mere private standards have become part of a product regulation by the means of a so-called dynamic reference, for example in the scope of the new approach to technical standards and regulations in the EC, they will not become regulations "issued" by a public authority.

Administrative product controls (for example the licensing of pharmaceutical products or pesticides, type permits for cars) are legally not suitable to produce evidence in exoneration as per Article 7(d). In order to exempt the producer, he needs to base his product on a generally applicable mandatory regulation. This might be in the form of a regulation or a directive of the Community/Union but also regulatory acts issued by a Member State which of course must conform to EU law.[18]

Furthermore, a causal connection between the defect and the mandatory regulation issued by the public authorities is required. A German author concludes from this that the possibility to exempt is denied in cases where the producer could freely decide whether to use, for example, a positive list of preservatives specifically authorised for use in foodstuffs or a negative list of additives in cosmetics.[19] Such a restrictive interpretation requires concretisation according to the particular mandatory regulation issued by the public authorities which establishes a nexus of its regulative character. Positive or negative lists are merely of assistance in excluding additives which are potentially dangerous according to the state of the art. They do not contain a guarantee of safety as approved by the EC/EU or a national authority. The responsibility for defects always remains with the producer. Damages which occur as a result of their use

[18] The legal basis for this kind of action is Directive 2001/95/EC on product safety which introduced market surveillance systems and the obligations for Member States to give their national authorities the powers to take action against unsafe products.

[19] Krämer, 326.

are not to be attributed to the (positive or negative) list but to the autonomous decision of the producer.

The situation is different, however, if a mandatory regulation issued by the public authorities requires a particular presentation of the product. Such a case of causation between a mandatory regulation issued by the public authorities and a defect should instead be rare. If, for example, mandatory regulations issued by the public authorities require the installation of seatbelts in cars, and the latter are in accordance with the appropriate safety regulations, then the producer cannot be held liable by arguing that without seatbelts a particular injury would not have occurred. The producer will however be liable for the safety of the seatbelts irrespective of existing regulations.

b) Defects at the time of or subsequent to a product being put into circulation

6.8 The types of defects described are related to the time of putting the product into circulation. In the most recent discussion on product liability based on tort, situations were debated which go beyond these types and which concern risk potential which occurs subsequent to a product being put into circulation and must be met by duties to observe the product. Doing so (i.e. observing the product) is purported to compensate for non-liability in the case of development risk; this is because there is no violation of the producer's duty to make the product safe since the defect could not be foreseen. Such a duty might arise subsequently due to scientific publications on long-term side-effects or reports on undesirable side-effects, as has been recognised by the case law of Member States regarding tort liability.

An example of this may be cases where possible product risks may be presumed to exist at the time of the product being put into circulation but the where warnings signs are not clear enough to be recognised by the consumers or the consumer's agent (e.g. physicians).[20] Moreover, cases in which consumers divert a faultless product from its intended use, but where this should have been foreseen by the producer, have been the subject matter of case law in the Member States but have not yet reached the ECJ. Remote misuse will not give rise to liability according to the standard of tort law concerning improper conduct, for example the use of a solvent for the purpose of "sniffing". However there is a duty to prevent risks if the producer ignores these faulty developments, i.e. "the risk of misuse has already been correspondingly realized". Thus the producer is subject to a duty based on the general concepts of tort law to observe that the product is safe for persons. The intensity of this duty depends on the degree of risk and on the product; if life and health are endangered, the duty is more extensive and will apply earlier than in regard to property damage.

[20] See for a German discussion the decisions of the Federal Court (Bundesgerichtshof – BGH) BGHZ 59, 172; BGH, NJW 1992, 560 and BGH, NJW 1995, 1286.

The EC Directive, however, proceeds from the fact that the defect needs to be present at the time of putting the particular product into circulation (Article 7(b)). Subsequent risks which do not originate in the product itself but which are to be referred to as factors later do not subsequently render the product defective. This includes defects which result from improper handling by the injured party. It can be questioned, however, whether the subsequent risk originated in a defect in the product design. According to the systematic position of Article 7(b), such a situation is assumed; the producer is required to furnish complete counter-evidence.[21] If he successfully produces counter-evidence, then according to the Directive, product liability cannot be invoked. Thus the protection as provided by the Directive is incomplete; it is to be completed by the differing national law of the Member States which, however, has been condemned by the ECJ as going beyond the complete harmonisation concept in the Directive irrespective of Article 13 (*infra* 6.30).

6.9 A similar problem arises if at the time of putting the product into circulation the producer intended to distribute the product in a country with lower safety requirements rather than in the actual market country. Article 7(b) needs to be applicable even then if the product remains unaltered but its legal surroundings change. In the case of Article 7(b) the causation of the defect is not in the sphere of influence of the third-party producer. The producer will not be liable if according to his point of view, i.e. according to the requirement of the country of manufacture, there is no defect.

It is not clear, however, what is to be understood by the term "putting the product into circulation". The Directive does not give a definition of the term but it needs to be interpreted according to the protective purpose of the Directive. The question is whether this refers to a relative or an absolute moment. According to prevailing opinion the time proceeds from the set moment a product is put into circulation only once, i.e. when it knowingly leaves the sphere of influence of the producer (so-called "fabrication theory"), which has been confirmed by the ECJ.[22] According to this theory, the product which goes through cycles during its development, construction and marketing is put into circulation every time the product reaches the end of one of the above-mentioned cycles. Thus the time of putting the product into circulation can vary for the same product and is to be determined according to the type of defect. With regard to construction and instruction defects, a "flexible" term of putting a product into circulation applies: a product which had initially been constructed without defects, supplied with perfect instructions and which at the time of being put into circulation for the first time had been in accordance with the expected safety requirements can become defective upon the occurrence of

---

21 See for a controversial debate v. Westphalen, *Produkthaftungshandbuch*, 159.

22 ECJ, 9 February 2006, C-127/04, *O'Byrne v Sanofi* [2006] ECR I-1313.

subsequent risks and hazards if the product continues to be marketed in that state. A subsequent series of the product may not meet the legitimately expected safety requirements. As regards the burden of proof, the presumption of Article 7(b) is applied analogously, which goes beyond the scope of defect during the fabrication process. If it can be established that at the time the injury occurred the product was defective due to defective design, then there is the presumption that the product had been defective at the time of putting it into circulation. The producer thus needs to establish that the product originates from an (earlier) series which cannot be regarded as defective according to the then appropriate state of scientific and technical knowledge. *Vice versa* the producer must adapt his product to new requirements which emerge from a development in the state of scientific and technical knowledge either by furnishing additional warnings or even by a undertaking new construction. Safety standards are subject to alterations which may occur during the product life cycle. This may also mean that a producer may no longer market his initially faultless product if it is not in accordance with the "state of the art" without risking becoming liable.

Such an interpretation does not violate Article 6(2) of the Directive, according to which:

> "a product shall not be considered defective for the sole reason that a better product is subsequently put into circulation."

This provision merely concerns the comparison of the earlier product with a subsequent, improved and thus different product. However the provision is of no assistance in cases where the safety standard which can be legitimately expected from the same product alters over the course of time as knowledge of product risks also changes. The tightening of liability for construction defects by virtue of the Directive is no obstacle to innovation; instead it promotes and supports innovation in terms of risk research.

c) Products having no effect

6.10 The Directive is not unequivocal as regards cases where the defectiveness of a product rests in its insufficient effectiveness and thus leads to injuries to the health and property of the consumer. The distinction between "fit for purpose" (meaning conformity rooted in the law on the sale of goods, 4.10–4.15) and safety (as governed by product liability law) must not disguise the fact that both areas overlap if the "conformity" with the contract and with general standards constitutes the marketing purpose of the product. If a lack of conformity results in the harm of legally protected interests, e.g. life, health and property, then the product does not provide the safety a person could legitimately expect. Such wide interpretation is indicated by the presentation of the product as stated in

Article 6(1)(a) of Directive 85/374/EEC which promises implied effectiveness or freedom from harm arising from ineffectiveness. Ineffective products are therefore subject to product liability by virtue of the EC Directive – a view which, however, has not yet been supported by the case law of the ECJ.

d) *Territorial standard*

6.11 Finally the extent of the territorial standard as set by the Directive is to be analysed. In the Member States consumer expectations can vary; a risk which might just be acceptable in one country may already constitute a defect in another country. The Directive cannot directly bring about a compulsory approximation of the safety standards unless there are mandatory provisions applying throughout Europe. This is the case because national courts decide on the standard of safety which could legitimately be expected. Territorial differences are only acceptable within the strict boundaries of the case law on free movement of goods. Article 30 EC (now Article 34 TFEU) accepts different use patterns and safety customs for the "proportionality" test of differing national safety regulations which limit the free movement of goods which is also based on the mutual recognition of national safety requirements by the individual Member States (1.21). If the safety requirements set out by a Member State are met, then this will also apply to the other Member States. They can rely on the fact that the state in which the respective product had been produced guarantees that the product is sufficiently safe; the protective effect applies to the entire Community/Union. This means that the product merely has to meet the safety requirements of one Member State even if those are particularly low. However, the producer needs to bear in mind that a defect which had been detected in one Member State will "have an effect on" the entire internal market.[23] Directive 2001/95/EC on general product safety provides proceedings which apply Community/Union-wide to withdraw an unsafe product from the internal market. This wide interpretation of the term "defect" compensates to a certain extent for the renunciation of special product liability for "importers" within the single market by virtue of Article 3(2).

III. THE NOTION OF "PRODUCER"

1. IMPORTANCE OF THE CONCEPT FOR A SYSTEM OF "STRICT LIABILITY"

6.12 The notion of the producer provided significant legal-dogmatic and legal policy difficulties in the discussion. This results from the nature of no-fault

23 Cf. also ECJ, 9 August 1994, C-359/92, *Germany v Council* [1994] ECR I-3681.

product liability for safety defects which is neither linked to a contractual element nor to a wrong and thus is different from the responsibility regimes as provided by the Member States. The person responsible can therefore neither be determined by contractual bonds (possibly the contractual chain) nor by violation of functional duties of the producer to make the product safe for persons (as a producer, supplier, importer, dealer, seller, etc.). The attribution needs rather to be done according to the division of the production and distribution which as such provokes risks for the consumer. Such an allocation of risks needs to be economically efficient, i.e. to impose responsibility where damage can best be prevented and remedied incurring as little cost as possible.[24] At the same time it should not obstruct the free movement of goods within the EC/EU but, on the contrary, facilitate it and to provide the consumer with a solvent defendant[25] in the case of harm.

In the course of the discussions, the notion of the producer has been remarkably extended, which constituted a significant alteration of the law of the Member States. Article 2 of the first proposal referred to a producer as the person who has manufactured the defective product in its intended form and who has put it into circulation. This does not even indicate the problem of the division of production and distribution. According to the second proposal, the producer of any defective raw material or the manufacturer of a component part, as well as quasi-producers, are treated equivalently to the 'actual' producer. A quasi-producer is a person who presents himself as a producer by putting his name, trademark or other distinguishing feature on the product and thus identifies himself with the product and its defectiveness. Importers are also producers but only to the extent that they import goods into the EC/EU – not importers (exclusive distributors) within the EC/EU. By that a "parcelling out" of the liability of importers is to be avoided which would create additional trade barriers within the EC/EU.

The extension of the notion of the producer to the quasi-producer and the fictitious producer remained in the later versions until the final version of the Directive in 1986.

The Green Paper which had been published in 1999 put forward the question of whether sellers or suppliers in the distribution chain should also be subject to product liability insofar as their activities had an impact on the safety of the product. According to some of the opinions delivered, this question should be answered in the affirmative as this would achieve an approximation with the Directives 92/51/EEC, later 2001/95/EC, concerning product safety. The majority objected to such an extension as it was problematic to determine the extent of liability. Liability for damages could be restricted to typical activities such as

---

24 The economic analysis of third party liability law cf. extensively Schäfer/Ott, 110 ff, 309 ff; Brüggemeier, in: Ott/Schäfer; Adams.

25 However the Directive does not provide in particular for the case of insolvency as for example by establishing a compensation fund, possibly Article 13 of the Directive which constitutes a bar for the introduction of such systems in Member States.

storage or transport. However, unrestricted liability represented another possibility. If liability arose in the first case only, then this would be close to fault liability, which would be contrary to the spirit of the Directive. In its report the Commission thus came to the conclusion that an extension of liability to the supplier would not be justified. It referred in particular to the different purposes of the Directive concerning product liability and the Directive(s) concerning product safety, which justify the different treatment of supplier's liability. The Directive concerning product liability purports to provide compensation for harm occurring through defective products; thus, according to the point of view of the Commission, it does justice to the special position of the supplier in making him only secondarily liable.

2. THE CONCEPT OF "PRODUCER" IN DIRECTIVE 85/374/EEC

a) *Producer in a narrower and broader sense*

6.13 With regard to contractual or conduct-related product liability, determination of the term "producer" provides no difficulties. Product liability based on safety expectations which lead to a defect requires its own criteria for the attribution of liability. The *effet utile* of Community/Union law to provide the injured consumer with a solvent party against whom a claim may be asserted must not be abolished by an interpretation which implicitly relates to conduct-related liability based on a "duty of care".

The description of the term "producer" in Article 3(1) of Directive 85/374/EEC is conclusive, according to which any person who takes part in the production process is deemed to be a producer provided they are in control of putting the product into circulation.

Initially the determination of the final producer is less problematic. The producer is therefore whoever places the product on the internal market within the EU. Labelling obligations may allow identification of the producer, e.g. with regard to pre-packed groceries, cosmetics, pharmaceutical products. Problems exist if the product has been altered or repackaged. Then the differentiation between fault liability of the seller and no-fault liability of the producer becomes problematic. Other possible problem areas concern, e.g. final assembly and finishing work of the product or bottling.

The EC Directive refers to the producer of the final product. A product is considered to be final if it reaches the state in which it is to be distributed to the consumer without further modification, alteration or supplementation.

The targeted circle of purchasers is decisive for determining whether the activity is still to be related to the production or if it concerns mere distribution. In the latter case fault or contractual liability will apply. The characterisation of someone who merely contributes intellectually as a "producer" is furthermore questionable. According to the general view the terms "producer" and "product" are mutually dependent. This means that a person who merely contributes by means of intellectual activities cannot usually be considered a producer. But there may be exceptions to this principle.

6.14 Article 3(1) of the EC Directive refers to the producer in general and is not restricted to the production process as such. Thus the producer of (licensed) software is a producer and will be liable under Article 3(1) of the Directive if his product is defective. It is decisive that the person who produces an immaterial output presents himself as a producer.

With regard to franchising, not only the franchisee but also the franchisor may be liable for the sale of a defective product according to product liability law, as the franchisor allows the marketing of the product under its trademark without being the actual producer. The franchisor is responsible for quality controls. The franchisee is integrated into an extensive marketing and distribution set-up which is operated by the franchisor. It is therefore irrelevant that according to a particular franchise note, the sales contract of the consumer is entered into with the franchisee.

With regard to licensing, one must distinguish between agreements on technical innovations and transfer of technical knowledge. If the fact of the licensing appears on the outside, although there is no obligation in this regard, then the licensor will not be liable as a direct "producer", but may be regarded as a quasi-producer in the sense of Article 3(1) of the Directive which extends product liability to any person who, by putting his name, trademark or other distinguishing feature on the product, presents himself as its producer.

6.15 Problems will arise with regard to materials which are put into circulation by the seller or supplier's free will but which are not or are only partially intended for sale, for example samples on the one hand or waste and emissions on the other. The main criteria are always whether the product was put into circulation, which is the case with samples. On the other hand, even a wide interpretation of the EC Directive will not result in liability in case of harmful emissions as the polluter is not the "producer" of a product. Although he has added to the pollution of the environment he has not put a product into "circulation" (in terms of a market in an economic sense).

As regards waste it could be distinguished by whether or not it is suitable for "recycling", i.e. it can be at least indirectly integrated into circulation.[26] According to the Directive it would be obvious to distinguish according to whether or not contact of the waste with the consumer would be possible on the basis of the type of disposal. Insufficient disposal which at least renders contact

[26] Cf. Krämer, 322; v. Westphalen, *supra* note 21, 59.

– even if involuntary – with the consumer possible should be considered as "putting into circulation". This is irrespective of remuneration or profit; only the voluntary putting into circulation, and thus the risk created by the producer, is of significance. On the other hand the Directive concerning product liability does not regulate every risk which results from industrial production. It specifically provides provisions for product risks which arise through a consumer-specific determination of the purpose.

b) Manufacturer of a component part

6.16 Manufacturers of component parts are treated as producers (Article 3(1)). Thus they risk an extensive extension of liability if the component part supplied is defective and thus renders the entire product defective. The Directive assumes the producer and the manufacturer of a component part to be jointly and severally liable for the entire damage. However liability for manufacturers of a component part merely applies to the supply of parts or primary products and not to services.

Article 7(f) assumes an exemption of liability which is related to the person (6.27). However the defect must be attributable to the design of the product in which the component has been fitted, the causation of which needs to be established by the consumer by virtue of Article 4 of the Directive.

c) EU "importers"

6.17 The EC Directive makes liable any person who imports the product into the Union for the first time (EU importers). Thus the EC Directive goes further than the law of the Member States. This point of view focuses on the undertaking. Product liability which relates to the defect proceeds from the undertaking as an organisation rather than from individual misconduct. Thus an extension of the circle of persons who could possibly be liable ensues. Liability depends on the point at which the product is put into circulation within the territory of the EU. Furthermore the EU importer presents himself as the producer. This justifies his liability. The consumer shall thus be spared the costly and uncertain process of bringing an action against the producer beyond the Community's external borders.

Vice versa the EC Directive excludes product liability of the "importer" within the borders of the Union. This principle determines the interpretation of the provisions on the free movement of goods; in the internal market the role of the importer no longer applies in order to connect special legal consequences to his activities. He is merely subject to secondary liability as a supplier.

d) *Subsidiary liability of the supplier*

6.18 With regard to the supplier, the reasoning in favour of liability is less clear-cut as his responsibility is normally derived from unchanged national sales or tort law. He can only be included in the circle of persons who could possibly be held liable by virtue of a special provision. Liability has been designed as secondary liability as it concerns liability for the (unidentified) producer instead of liability for defects. It relates to a kind of liability for omitting to supply information. The supplier is required to meet this obligation within a particular period of time which is to be determined by the Member States; otherwise the supplier will become liable himself under Article 3(2). The Directive does not set out this period of time but refers instead to a reasonable time. In the Commission's report of 31 January 2001 a standardisation of a certain period of time has been rejected, even though numerous opinions have been in favour of it (see 6.3). However, it is not clear under the Directive whether the supplier will be liable if he provides false information; this case should be regarded as being similar to the situation in which he did not provide any information at all. On the other hand, he will not be liable if the producer cannot meet his obligations.[27]

Particular problems have arisen in the relationship of Article 3(3) of the Directive to more stringent national rules which put both the producer and the supplier under a joint regime of strict liability. In *Skov*, the referring Danish court asked whether the Directive is to be interpreted as precluding a national rule under which the supplier is answerable without restriction for the no-fault liability which the Directive establishes and imposes on the producer.[28] The ECJ held that the Directive must be interpreted as precluding a national rule under which the supplier is answerable, beyond the cases listed exhaustively in Article 3(3) of the Directive, for the no-fault liability which the Directive establishes and imposes on the producer. However, this does not preclude a national rule under which the supplier is answerable without restriction for the producer's fault-based liability. The AG and the ECJ deduce this consequence from a reverse conclusion of Article 3(3) under which the supplier is freed from his liability as a fictitious producer if he names the (for the moment unknown) producer or his retailer irrespective of whether the exemption of the liability via liability transfer concerns the correct and solvent party. The Danish law provides for the direct liability of the supplier; however, the supplier may be exempted from his liability by claiming recourse to the producer. The ECJ rejected the Danish ruling as running counter to the *effet utile* of the Directive which provides for complete harmonisation. This argument is, in our view, not convincing because the rule of the Directive extending the liability of the

---

27 See Reich, in: *Liber amicorum Alpa*, 853.

28 ECJ, 10 January 2006, C-402/03, *Skov* [2006] ECR I-199.

supplier in case of non-identification of the producer in order to give *additional protection* to the consumer is turned upside down by the ECJ in limiting his liability whenever he gives this information, whether effective or not for an enforcement of the claim of the consumer.[29] The original Danish solution, making the supplier liable but allowing him a recourse against the producer, is a much more adequate distribution of risks in line with the philosophy of Directive 85/374/EEC because it avoids the consumer being put in a *non liquet* situation by not being able to sue the supplier who has freed himself of this obligation by simply naming the producer, and not having an effective remedy against the supplier who can always argue that he is not the producer of the specific lot which caused the harm to the consumer. Such a result is against the consumer protection spirit of the Directive, which aims to avoid the consumer being caught in between the complexities of modern distribution which he cannot control and often does not even know about.

IV. EXEMPTIONS FROM LIABILITY

6.19 In the legal policy discussion about the Directive, exemption from strict liability for damages for product risks has almost played a more important role than the concept itself. The discussion has produced a number of such features – to be established as defences by the person being held liable – which do not produce a systematically uniform picture. They might arise from the product, the producer or the risk.

1. EXEMPTIONS RELATED TO THE PRODUCT

a) Agricultural products

6.20 The original version of the EC Directive contained a strongly disputed product-specific exemption which concerned natural agricultural and fishery products. Not only the interpretation of the wording, but also the existence of this exemption from liability has been problematic. With hindsight it can be said that it concerned an exceptional element which could not be justified by the facts and which in effect presented a case of "special interest lobbying". When this provision was enacted, the phenomenon of industrial agriculture had not been acknowledged. It had exclusively referred to the impossibility of considering the impact of the environment, which the producer cannot influence. The extensive use of pesticides and insecticides, the medicinal or hormonal treatment of animals, and the use of genetic technology was neglected entirely. Modification

29 Critique Reich, in: *Liber amicorum Alpa*, 854; Whittacker, 865.

of the original exception by the adoption of Directive 99/34/EC[30] was only done when consumers had been alerted by the outbreak of mad cow disease.

b) Dynamic concept of "product"

6.21 As a general principle under Community/Union law,[31] the exemptions provided by the Directive need to be interpreted strictly. In general the Directive assumes a wide interpretation of the term "product". Electricity is included without there being a need to expressly include gas, distant heating or water. For the application of the Directive it is irrelevant whether energy is "distributed" under public or private law. However, according to the Council of Ministers' explanation of Article 2, the defect should arise during the production process not during subsequent intervention, for example during the distribution (short circuit of the network). This interpretation is not legally binding. The time of "putting the electricity into circulation" is decisive; is it the time of generation or of distribution? As the mere generation is of no use for the consumer, disturbances occurring during distribution are included.

6.22 The producer cannot defend himself by arguing that the consumer merely had contact with the defective product in the scope of rendering the service. In that case the defectiveness of the product which had been used in the scope of rendering a service is concerned, not the defectiveness of the service itself.[32] On the other hand, liability is however limited to the supply of a defective product by the seller, not to its use by a hospital in the context of medical treatment which has not produced the product.[33]

The notion of "product" as contained in the Directive is a dynamic one, i.e. it relates to the progress of research and economy. Thus products of modern biotechnology, e.g. microorganisms, shall be regarded as products in terms of the Directive provided they have been produced or cultivated artificially, for example by genetic engineering. Software is also considered a product. This is consistent with the legal opinion of the Commission[34] which does not provide any reasoning. The issue had been intensively discussed in connection with the so-called "millennium bug". Component products, installed products, primary products and the like lead to specific liability, whereas immovable things (buildings, factories, bridges, etc., but also vessels, airplanes and satellites[35] as "movable things") will not entail liability. An extension of liability, according to

---

30 OJ L 414, 4 June 1999, 20.

31 Reich, *General Principles of EU Civil Law*, para 2.12.

32 ECJ, 10 June 2001, C-203/99, *Veedfald* [2001] ECR I-03569 at para 12.

33 ECJ, 21 December 2011, C-495/10, *Centre Hospitalier universitaire de Besancon (CHUB) v Thomas Dutrueux et al.* [2011] ECR I-14155.

34 OJ C 114, 8 June 1989, 42.

35 Cf. v. Westphalen, 63 ff.

the Directive concerning product liability in relation to immovable property, is considered inadequate in the report of the Commission of 2001 since there are existing special mandatory and regulatory provisions in the Member States or national contract law which are far-reaching. Moreover it is the purpose of the Directive to guarantee liability of the producers of mass-produced products, whereas real property concerns individual products which require different provisions.

6.23 With regard to movable things which are part of a building, the defect and the causation of the subsequent harm are to be specifically determined. If for example a defective steel cable causes the collapse of a building, then the producer of this part will be liable for personal injury caused to any injured party and for property damage caused to any consumer (the owner of the building is excluded unless it is used for private purposes in terms of Article 9(b)). According to the wording of the Directive, it is irrelevant that according to the law of the Member States, special ownership rights of the installed part of the building have ceased to exist. Product liability will generally remain independent of the legal destiny of the defective part.

2. EXEMPTIONS RELATED TO THE PERSON

a) The general problem

6.24 Exemptions related to the person refer to activities which should be excluded from a safety-based concept of liability for product risks. The discussion within the EC/EU differs noticeably from the law of the Member States, the latter of which is linked to duties of care rather than to the phenomenon of the risk potential as caused by industrial production. However, during the legal policy discussions on the EC proposals, the wording has changed, which illustrates the difficulties in demarcating the potential of the party causing the harm and thus the risk potential. The first proposal did not contain an exemption provision whereas the second proposal of 1979 expressly referred in Article 5(c) to the economic purpose of the production and the distribution in the scope of business activities. According to Article 7(c) of the 1985 Directive, the producer shall not be liable if he proves:

> "that the product was neither manufactured by him for sale or any form of distribution for economic purpose nor manufactured or distributed by him in the course of his business."

Thus it becomes evident that no-fault liability shall apply only if the defective product has been put into circulation for an economic purpose. The exemption of liability will not apply if the product is made available to the consumer free of charge provided that the economic and professional nature of production remains unaltered. Thus defective products which are distributed to the consumer in the scope of social security benefits by public authorities are subject to liability as provided by the EC Directive, as the ECJ confirmed in *Veedfald*.[36]

b) The decisive element: putting a product into circulation

6.25 Article 7(a) of the Directive offers an exemption from liability for damages which were caused by a product which the producer had not put into circulation yet. The ECJ had two occasions to give shape to the reach of the exemption. In *Veedfald* it held that Article 7(a) should mean that the producer is not liable if the use of the product is contrary to the will of the producer or a third party takes the product out of the manufacturing process. The provision, however, is not applicable if the consumer comes into contact with the product by entering the area which is controlled by the producer and if the particular product is used in the scope of a service provided by the producer. Based on a direct reference to *Veedfald*, the ECJ decided in *O'Byrne* that Article 11 of the Directive, dealing with the prescription period, is to be interpreted as meaning that a product is put into circulation when it is taken out of the manufacturing process operated by the producer and enters a marketing process in the form in which it is offered to the public to be used or consumed.[37] Both Article 7(a) and Article 11 refer to the moment at which the product has been put into circulation. Both require an identical interpretation. From the facts of *O'Byrne* it becomes clear that the product has not been put into circulation if the producer has sold it to its wholly-owned subsidiary.

c) "Non"-economic activity of the producer

6.26 Another exemption (6.24) concerns both "private" production and the non-commercial distribution of products. With regard to interpretation, it should be noted that the exemption of liability for the producer of arts and crafts articles, etc., as provided in the first proposals, does not apply to the Directive. Thus if the producer produces those articles in the scope of commercial or professional activities, the no-fault liability regime of Directive 85/374/EEC applies. The artisan potter who uses poisonous lead paint for the glaze is to be treated equivalently to an industrial producer. There is a presumption of commercial or professional activities; mere private activities exist only with regard to amateur painters, hobby artists, etc. Activities of artisans and self-employed persons in the scope of production and distribution are subject to no-fault liability.

---

36 ECJ, 10 June 2001, C-203/99, *Veedfald* [2001]ECR, I-3569 at para 21.

37 ECJ, 9 February 2006, C-127/04, *O'Byrne* [2006] ECR I-1313 at paras 24 and 32.

d) *Producer of component parts*

6.27 Article 7(f) has introduced a further exemption in favour of a manufacturer of a component. He shall not be liable if the defect is attributable to the actual manufacturer of the product.

The manufacturer of the component part has to meet strict requirements regarding the evidence in exoneration as per Article 7(f). In particular he has to prove that the defect is attributable to the design of the (final) product in which the component has been fitted or to the instructions given by the manufacturer of the product. If the component part as such is defective, then this defence will not apply. The component part supplier is the producer and will be liable for damages caused by the defect of the product. The so-called assembler who exclusively assembles primary products to create the final product, which is then marketed by him, is a producer under the terms of Article 3.

V. EXEMPTIONS RELATED TO RISKS: THE DEVELOPMENT RISK DEFENCE

1. THE ORIGINS OF THE DEBATE

6.28 In the debate, exemptions related to hitherto unknown risks have proved most controversial. The so-called development risk defence has been the focus of the interest. It concerns defects of a product – such as side-effects of pharmaceutical products – which according to the state of science and technical knowledge were not known or reported at the time of putting the product into circulation but which came to light subsequently. In US product liability cases, enormous awards have been granted by extending the traditional liability law, for example for long-term side-effects as a result of the administration of artificial hormones as medication or of workplaces contaminated with asbestos. The alleged "product liability crisis" in the United States has strained the European discussion considerably.

The viewpoint of the EC Commission as illustrated in the works on the Directive has been clear as development risks should also be subject to liability. This not only arose from the system of defect-related and no-fault liability but also from the consumer policy purpose of the proposals. The proposal of 1976 is unequivocal as:

> "The producer shall also be liable even if the state of scientific and technical knowledge at the time when he put the product into circulation was not such as to enable the existence of the defect to be discovered."

According to consumer associations, this constituted the core of the Directive and thus has been supported. A proposal of the Consumer Advice Council of the EEC of 1976 even demanded damage-related liability of the producer on whom the burden of the counter-proof has been placed to show that neither a defect nor causation of the defect played a role.[38]

On the other hand, industry has objected to the idea of strict liability for development risks by referring to the cost and risk burden, in particular with regard to newly developed products. In the European Parliament, industry was able make its point. Parliament rejected any liability for development risks. Instead Article 1(a) of the proposal of Parliament wanted to introduce a duty for the producer to observe the product and to react if necessary – similarly to tort law – which has, however, not been included in the Directive (see 6.8).[39]

Irrespective of this discussion, the proposal from the Commission of 1979 maintained strict liability for development risks. It provided upper limits for liability which constituted a certain limitation of the risk.

The debate about the Directive in the Council of Ministers is characterised by attempts to find a compromise which is acceptable for all Member States under the then existing unanimity requirement. However, the idea of approximation and consumer protection has been reduced. The producer will be liable for product defects; however, he can produce evidence that, "the state of scientific and technical knowledge at the time when he put the product into circulation was not such as to enable the existence of the defect to be discovered" (Article 7(e)).

Member States, however, maintained an option to waive the development risk defence. In order to avoid a possible falling apart of the national legal systems, Community law established particular proceedings under Article 15 (6.33). The discussion about the exclusion of liability for development risks has not yet been settled, as in the Green Paper from the Commission the question of whether to abolish this exemption had again been raised.[40] While undertakings and their associations were in favour of maintaining the exemption, consumer associations, in particular, demanded the abolishment of an exemption which is contrary to the system of no-fault liability. In its report the Commission was satisfied with the simple finding that there is only little knowledge of the practical effects and that the few decisions dealing with that area illustrated the difficulties of the burden of proof of the foreseeability of the defect being imposed on the manufacturer.

---

38 Doc. CCC/27/76 of 6 January 1976.

39 OJ C 127, 26 June 1979, 61.

40 COM (1999) 396 final, 24.

2. THE PRESENT SITUATION OF THE "DEVELOPMENT RISK" DEFENCE

6.29 According to the Directive, producers, quasi-manufacturers and suppliers under secondary liability will as such be liable for so-called development risks. They may invoke a defence according to Article 7(e), which refers to defects which "according to the state of scientific and technical knowledge at the time when the product was put into circulation were not such as to enable the existence of the defect to be discovered". The standard is set by a relative approach to the notion of "defect" (see 6.5–6.9). This general attribution of risk is not altered by the Directive because of its defect- and risk-related approach. The Directive enables the person who is liable to produce evidence of exoneration. This exception, which is legally very debatable, has to be interpreted strictly according to the general principles of Union law, which has a number of important consequences. In any case, the Directive imposes a safety obligation on the producer that has a corresponding right to compensation of the consumer in case of injury as covered by the Directive. This safety obligation, based on broad comparative research, was well described by Burton J in the *Hepatitis C* case:[41]

> "The blood products [contaminated by Hepatitis C infection] were non-standard products, and were unsafe by virtue of the harmful characteristics which they had and which the standard products did not have. They were not ipso facto defective ... but were defective because I am satisfied that the public at large was entitled to expect that the blood transfused to them would be free from infection. There were no warnings and no material publicity ... It is not material to consider whether any steps or any further steps could have been taken to avoid or palliate the risk that the blood would be infected." (paras 79–80)

In a similar reasoning, the German Federal Court in its well-known *Bottle* case[42] argued that the:

> "consumer expects a mineral water bottle to have no obvious or even microscopic damage which might lead it to explode. The fact that it is not technically possible to detect and repair such defects in the bottle does not alter the consumer's expectations."

The Directive will only allow an exemption from liability if the producer proves that according to the state of scientific and technical knowledge, the defect could

---

41 *A v The National Blood Authority* [2001] 3 All ER 289 at 342 per Burton J, comments by Mildred, 181–183; Brooke/Forrester, with Postscript by Underhill and Afterword by Burton, The use of comparative law, in: Fairgrieve at 13; Howells, Defect in English Law, in: Fairgrieve, 138 at 150–151.

42 BGH NJW 1995, 2161 – *Mineralwasser*, cited by Burton J in the *Hepatitis C* case at 321; critical comment by Brüggemeier at 439, arguing that the filler of the bottle is not the producer.

not have been discovered. It therefore depends on the foresight of experts, not on the actual or possible knowledge of the producer. Thus the expression "state of the art defence" is misleading as it is not the balancing of risk/benefit which is of concern. The determination of development risks not only depends on the possibility of knowledge according to the state of technical knowledge – which is often unilaterally influenced – but also and particularly according to the state of the *scientific knowledge*. This means that risk potentials as described by scientific minority opinions or as established by scientific criteria (for example with regard to medications and chemicals which are suspected to cause cancer) are apt to destroy the evidence in exoneration. The knowledge does not need to be common property.[43]

The "state of scientific knowledge" describes an open process in which risks are discussed, established and rejected. The producer bears the risk of indeterminacies of this process. If he fails to take minority opinions into consideration, then he acts on his own responsibility. This applies even if the source is remote as the requirement of "foreseeability" is connected to the respective state of scientific and technical knowledge without requiring the actual possibility of knowledge.[44] The required safety precautions are not restricted to what is technically possible or economically reasonable. According to our point of view, the defence does not contain an element of fault liability as it is connected to the general foreseeability in the market instead of specific foreseeability of the individual producer.

Moreover, it should be taken into consideration that the producer is also required to prove that at the time the product was put into circulation the defect could not have been discovered. Thus the question arises as to when the product had been put into circulation (cf. 6.13). Doubts on its timing are to be borne by the producer. Therefore the question remains whether according to the (strict) criteria of the state of scientific and technical knowledge whether the defect could have been discovered prior or subsequent to putting the product into circulation; if so the defence will fail.

If, however, the producer can produce the twofold evidence in exoneration to the full extent, then he will merely be liable for subsequent product risks under the principles of contract or tort law of the Member States. The limited solution of the Directive forces the consumer to eventually base his claim on two causes of action; the harmonisation effect of the Directive has been considerably reduced.

---

43 Cf. v. Westphalen, 54.

44 ECJ, 29 June 1997, C-300/95, *Commission v United Kingdom* [1997] ECR I-2649; the background of the proceedings is explained by Howells/Weatherill, 246–248.

VI. THE EFFECTS OF THE DIRECTIVE ON THE PRODUCT LIABILITY LAW OF THE MEMBER STATES

1. THE RELATION TO OTHER CLAIMS UNDER NATIONAL LAW

6.30 The relation of the Directive to other claims is governed by Article 13 according to which the Directive shall not affect any rights which an injured person may have according to the rules of the law of contractual or non-contractual liability or a special liability system existing at the moment when this Directive is notified. Article 13 names three legal areas where liability beyond the scope of the Directive can be invoked – namely claims arising from the law of contractual liability or non-contractual liability or a special liability system for product liability. According to the dominant opinion of legal scholars at the time of its enactment, the Directive does not claim to establish a uniform regime applicable in all Member States which replaces claims arising from other possible legal regimes. This reasoning was later reversed by arguing that within the area governed by the Directive, harmonisation is complete and final. In striking contrast to the Directives on consumer contracts, the Directive concerning product liability does not merely establish minimum standards. This has been the point of view of the case law of the ECJ, supported by the Commission.

The Commission has therefore sued Greece and France, charging their implementation provisions with providing excessive protection to the injured party.[45] A similar question resulted from a preliminary ruling before Spanish courts. It concerned the question of whether Spain could maintain stricter protective provisions within the scope of application of the Directive.[46] In the light of the three proceedings, the ECJ, in three identical judgments of 26 April 2002, had been given the opportunity to decide on two interlinked questions:

(1) Does the Directive purport complete harmonisation within its scope of application or can Member States invoke Article 153 EC (now Article 12/169 TFEU), in order to claim minimum harmonisation as a general principle of consumer protection?
(2) Which claims are covered by the exemption or in which circumstances can claims be said to have the *same* or a *different* basis?

The relevant decisive grounds are identical in each of the three decisions. From the recitals and the lack of a minimum protection clause, the ECJ argues that the

---

45 ECJ, 26 April 2002, C-52/00, *Commission v France* [2002] ECR I-3827; ECJ, C-154/00, *Commission v Greece* [2002] ECR I-3879.

46 ECJ, 26 April 2002, C-183/00, *González Sánchez v Medicina Asturia* [2002] ECR I-3901.

Directive purports complete harmonisation. This provision is not contrary to Article 153 EC, as its para (3)(a) refers to the internal market legislation of Article 95 EC. Furthermore it formulates an instruction for *future* shaping the policy of the Community/Union. The ECJ rejects the attempts of the Member States sued or of the Spanish claimant both of which insist that the principle of complete harmonisation must be supplemented in favour of the protection of the injured party. The verdict of the ECJ rejects the Greek preservation of unlimited liability without a minimum threshold of €500 for property damage, as well as the inclusion in French implementation act of the duty to observe the product and its equalisation of liability of sellers or suppliers and producers.

The ECJ did not really resolve the question of in which circumstances it is to be proceeded from an identical legal ground as it seems that Article 13 of Directive 85/374/EEC applies only if a special provision is of concern which is limited to a particular area of production. The Spanish preliminary decision would have been a good opportunity to further explore this issue. In its judgment, however, the ECJ proceeded from the fact that the assessment of the national courts on the different scope of the national liability provisions should apply. It is this assessment which would have had to be examined in order to find out what constitutes the same or different legal ground. Indirectly the ECJ is steadily narrowing down the scope of application of national tort law rules reaching beyond the Directive. This becomes clear in its narrow reading of Article 3(3) which concerns national rules on the strict liability of suppliers.

A similar approach was taken in the later decision in *Skov* (*supra* 6.18). However, the preclusionary effect does not extend to the use of a defective product by a hospital which is not the producer (*CHUB* case, *supra* 6.22).

The decisions of the ECJ are consistent with the opinion held by the Commission, which in the medium term wishes to abolish Article 13 in order to be able to use the provisions of the Directive as a basis for a European liability law. The ECJ has increased the pressure on the Member States to ensure that in a possible reform of the Directive, the liability provisions will cover all the relevant questions of substance. Product liability which excludes the observance of the product and excessively privileges the seller hardly seems in keeping with the times.

2. PRESCRIPTION PERIODS

6.31 The Directive contains a double mechanism regulating firstly the prescription period and secondly the extinction period. Article 10 obliges Member States to provide in their legislation that a limitation period of three years shall apply to proceedings for the recovery of damages. The limitation period begins to run from the day on which the plaintiff becomes aware or should reasonably have become aware of the damage, the defect and the identity of the producer. Member States, however, remain free to lay down suspension and interruption rules. Article 11 provides that the rights granted under the Directive will be extinguished upon expiry of a period of ten years from the date that the producer put the product into circulation which caused the damage, unless the injured person has in the meantime instituted proceedings against the producer. According to the ECJ, the product is put into circulation when it is taken out of the manufacturing process operated by the producer and enters a marketing process in the form in which it is offered to the public in order to be used or consumed.[47]

3. IMPLEMENTATION PROCEEDINGS

6.32 The Directive had to be implemented into national law by the Member States within a period of three years, i.e. by 1 August 1988, or for new Member States according to the dates set in the Accession Treaties. Some Member States implemented the Directive only with considerable delays and sometimes even incorrectly. France was the last of the old Member States to implement the Directive, with a delay of ten years. Prior to the implementation, the ECJ had condemned France three times: first for failure to fulfil its obligations in 1993,[48] second for extending product liability to product monitoring and supplier liability[49] (6.30), and third for not respecting the ECJ's reading of Article 13 in 2006.[50] The law of the Member States acceding after 2004 has been carefully analysed in a monograph by Tulibacka.[51]

The Directive was used as a model for non-Member States to modernise their product liability law. In 1994 Switzerland autonomously enacted the Product Liability Act after the failure of a referendum concerning membership of the European Economic Area which would have obliged Switzerland to assume the *acquis*. Australia[52] and several Asian countries have amended their product liability laws under the influence of the EC Directive.[53]

47 ECJ, 9 February 2006, C-127/04, *O'Byrne* [2006] ECR I-1313 at paras 24 and 32. According to ECJ, 2 December 2009, C-358/08, *Aventis Pasteur* [2009] ECR I-11395, Article 11 of the Directive "precludes national legislation, which allows the substitution of one defendant for another during proceedings, from being applied in a way which permits a 'producer', within the meaning of Article 3 of that directive, to be sued, after the expiry of the period prescribed by that article, as defendant in proceedings brought within that period against another person".

48 ECJ, 13 January 1993, C-293/91, *Commission v France* [1993] ECR I-1.

49 ECJ, 26 April 2002, C-52/00, *Commission v France* [2002] ECR I-3827.

50 ECJ, 14 March 2006, C-177/04, *Commission v France* [2006] ECR I-2461.

51 Tulibacka.

52 Harland, *JCP* 1992, 191; Howells, *supra* note 1, 276 ff.

53 For a critical account of the practical effects of the worldwide "success story", Reimann, *ERPL* 2003, 128; Kellam/Nottage, 217.

6.33 The Directive provides for special proceedings concerning the implementation of product and risk-related exemptions from liability, namely for agricultural products and development risks (Article 15). It expressly authorises Member States to "improve the law" irrespective of the binding effect of the Directive and the possible negative effects of such an extension of liability for the free movement of goods. In the course of the scandal concerning mad cow disease, the EC legislator decided to include primary agricultural products in the no-fault liability regime of Directive 85/374/EEC and to abolish the option allowing an exemption from liability. This purported to re-establish the trust of consumers in agricultural products. Simultaneously legal uncertainty considering the term "first processing" was to be abolished. Therefore, Directive 99/34/EC of 4 June 1999 was adopted and Member States were required to implement it by 4 December 2000.[54]

The inclusion of liability for development risks (6.28) by Member States required a particular "standstill" and coordination process similar to the one introduced by the EC in other regulative areas requiring safety measures such as in the area of technical standardisation.[55] The initiative of a Member State shall serve as an impulse to establish a higher level of protection within the entire area of the Community in order not to lose sight of the purpose of the approximation of the laws, namely to improve both free movement of goods and consumer protection. It remains to be seen whether this procedure, which is connected to the Commission's duty to inform and the Council's duty to make a decision, will be successful, which does not seem to be the case at the time of writing. So far only Luxembourg and Finland have availed themselves of this option, whereas Spain has limited itself to food and pharmaceutical products. In France, dealing with the question of development risks has led to delays in implementation.

So far the exemptions have only been of little practical significance.[56] According to the doctrine of "direct effect", courts are able to reduce exemptions from liability considerably by means of "directive conforming interpretation". Thus a similar result to the "standstill" clause in Article 15 is achieved. Unlike the national legislator, the courts are not bound by the procedural restrictions on the introduction of an "improvement of the law". A disintegration of substantive safety law by divergent case law cannot be prevented by the Community legislator unless the courts use the preliminary proceedings procedure as per Article 234 EC (now Article 267 TFEU) if the interpretation of the Directive is of concern. In conclusion this leads to "judicialising" safety law, a development which could already be seen in the area of traditional product liability law.

---

54 OJ L 141, 4 June 1999, 20.

55 Tulibacka, 265–266.

56 Cf. also the second report from the Commission of 31 January 2001, COM (2000), 893 final.

4. THE IMPACT OF THE DIRECTIVE ON THE SUBSTANTIVE LAW OF THE MEMBER STATES

6.34 So far only a few court decisions on the new product liability law have become public in the Member States; these decisions do not allow for a conclusion about the actual impact of the Directive on product risks in the Union. The impact on new Member States seems to be more important, according to the monograph by Tulibacka.[57] The fact that there is possibly a high number of out-of-court settlements between the injured consumer and the liable party may be an aggravating factor.

An indirect result of the Directive may be seen in developments of tort law in many Member States: it is in the process of changing from a subjective concept based on fault to a more objective concept of certain duties of undertakings in designing, producing and marketing their products. A similar concept of defect is emerging that is connected to the expectations of the typical consumer from a factual, territorial and timely point of view. The division of defects into construction defects, production defects and instruction defects becomes similar in modern tort law and in the Directive. A major difference remains, however: the Directive does not provide liability for the violation of the duty to observe and monitor the product (cf. 6.8). Thus it is not only conceivable but likely that in the individual case the recourse to liability based on the conduct of the producer may be advantageous for the injured consumer compared to the no-fault liability of the Directive. As a result of this discussion, Whittacker has rightly pointed out the paradox that the "harmonising effect of the Product Liability Directive is more formal than substantive … The difference between this liability [e.g. based on traditional concepts of fault] and liability under the Directive is indeed slight".[58]

The exclusion of a particular claim for damages for pain and suffering by virtue of Article 9 of the Directive[59] is especially detrimental to victims unless the national legislator "subsequently improves". This lack of protection is particularly critical since the injured consumer will mostly be interested in damages for pain and suffering from bodily injuries.[60]

With regard to material damage, traditional tort liability is applied to fill those gaps which have been left by the Directive. Thus the Directive provides a minimum threshold of €500 which was subject to procedures launched by the European Commission against France and Greece for failure to fulfil its obligation (6.10) – and only grants compensation in the event of damage to or

---

57 Tulibacka, 187, linking it to general tort law systems.

58 Whittacker, 868.

59 Different Article 6 of the second proposal of 1979.

60 The second report from the Commission contains an extensive assessment of the impact of the national provision and the likely inclusion of non-pecuniary damages is recommended but has not been taken up by the EU legislator.

destruction of any item of property which was "used mainly for private use or consumption" (Article 9(b)). The large field of industrial, professional and economic damages is exempted from liability by virtue of the Directive.

The Directive does not provide a definition of the term "damage" either. Thus Member States are authorised to have recourse to the national provisions regulating damages. The assessment of such harm is thus based on national law. The ECJ requires the Member States to guarantee appropriate and complete compensation – for personal injury as well as property damage provided they are covered by the Directive – for those injured by the product. Thus Member States are not authorised to restrict the types of harm to be compensated. In *Veedfald*[61] the Court wrote:

> "Article 9 of the Directive indicates that 'damage must cover both damage resulting from death or from personal injuries and damage to, or destruction of, an item of property. In the latter case, the damage must be of an amount exceeding EUR 500 whilst the item damaged must be of a type ordinarily intended for private use or consumption and must have been used as such by the injured person. Although it is left to national legislatures to determine the precise content of those two heads of damage, nevertheless, save for non-material damage whose reparation is governed solely by national law, full and proper compensation for persons injured by a defective product must be available in the case of those two heads of damage. Application of national rules may not impair the effectiveness of the Directive ... and the national court must interpret its national law in the light of the wording and the purpose of the Directive ... A Member State cannot therefore restrict the types of material damage, resulting from death or personal injury, or from damage to or destruction of an item of property, which are to be made good". (paras 26–28)

6.34a Compensation is only given for damage to property if the property is used by the injured person "mainly for his private use or consumption". However, Member States may extend this exclusion, since Directive 85/374/EC does "not preclude the interpretation of domestic law or the application of settled domestic case-law according to which an injured person can seek compensation for damage to an item of property intended for professional use and employed for that purpose, where that injured person simply proves the damage, the defect in the product and the causal link between that defect and the damage".[62]

Similarly the Directive does not alter the general provisions on the burden of proof of the defectiveness and causation (Article 4). The law of the Member State may be advantageous to the injured party by establishing certain facilitations of the burden of proof as regards defectiveness and causation, e.g. by a rule on *res ipsa loquitur*. Thus defectiveness and causation may be inferred from the

61 ECJ, 10 May 2001, C-203/99, *Henning Veedfald v Arhus Amtscommune* [2001] ECR I-3569 at para 28.

62 ECJ, 4 June 2009, C-285/08, *Société Moteurs Leroy Somer v Société Dalkia* France [2009] ECR I-4735 at para 32; critique Borghetti, *ZEuP* 2011, 928.

occurrence of damage. According to Article 21, every five years the Commission is to present a report to the Council on the application of this Directive.[63] Both reports so far have submitted appropriate proposals. The Commission, however, proceeds from the point of view that the Directive has resulted in a balanced system. Alterations should only be considered if objective reasons for reform emerge, and these are currently deemed not to exist.

6.35 Changes, however, can be seen in the concept of producer. In traditional tort law, liability of the producer focuses on the person. Liability of sellers and importers (quasi-manufacturers) is less restrictive than the liability of the actual producer. The responsibility of the supplier is determined according to the law on the sale of goods; secondary liability had not been known to any national law. The concept of the Directive is different: liability refers to the undertaking as an organisation which is involved in the marketing of a (defective) product. This is where the law of the Member States is to be amended. The additional conflict arising therefrom of contract law, tort law and product liability law for defects requires a thorough individual analysis which needs to be related to the respective national law. The liability of the producer arising from this Directive "may not be limited or excluded by a provision limiting his liability or exempting him from liability" (Article 12). As regards the terms of the provision, it is already in line with the substantive law of the Member States which normally prohibits exemption clauses in tort law and which are at least restricted in contract law in connection to standard business conditions.

5. LEGAL PROTECTION PROVIDED BY THE DIRECTIVE

6.36 The Directive only determines the area of applicability indirectly as it is addressed to the Member States (Article 22). This is not to say that the damage needs to occur within the territory of the EC or that the injured consumer is required to live in the EC or that the producer needs to have his seat in the EC. Instead the general provisions of private international law need to be applied as the Directive does not contain any conflict rule. This has recently been enacted by the Rome II Regulation 864/2007 which establishes special rules for product liability described in Chapter 7 of this book (7.27).

Jurisdiction in cross-border cases is determined by Regulation 44/2001 (7.42). Following this instrument, namely Article 5(3), claims in tort, including strict product liability law, are to be handled in the courts of the tortfeasor or of the habitual residence of the victim. This allows "forum shopping" in the case of cross-border product-related injuries.[64]

63 COM (1995) 617 final, 13 December 1995 as well as COM (2001) 893 final, 31 January 2001.

64 ECJ, 30 July 1976, C-21/76, *Mines de Potasse d'Alsace* [1976] ECR I-1736.

VII. LIABILITY FOR SERVICES

6.37 Subsequent to the enactment of the Directive concerning product liability, in 1985 the Community – in particular the Commission which is authorised to exercise the right to initiate legislation – addressed the issue of liability for "defective" services. An important step in this direction is Article 5 of Directive 90/314/EEC on package holidays which contains liability of presumed fault of the organiser, prohibits exclusion of liability and limits the restriction of liability.[65] Moreover there is the consideration that the purpose of establishing a single internal market for services by virtue of Article 14 EC (now Article 26(2) TFEU), similar to the single internal market for goods, requires harmonisation of liability rules in order to prevent a distortion of competition and to guarantee a minimum standard of consumer protection.

The proposal for a Council Directive on the liability of suppliers of services constituted the height of these efforts.[66] In its proposal the Commission pursued an objective fault liability scheme following French liability law. The proof requirements contained in the proposed Directive concerning services were less strict than those in the Directive concerning product liability. In the former the service provider was required to furnish evidence for his non-fault whereas in the latter the consumer is required to prove the defect. Regardless of the strong criticism of legal doctrine, doubts about the legitimacy of Community legislation in the area of liability law led to the withdrawal of the proposal.[67] These doubts followed the discussion on the principle of subsidiarity (cf. 1.9) which emerged subsequent to the ratification of the Maastricht Treaty. Instead of a comprehensive regulation, a sectoral approach was preferred, but no proposals have been presented. By means of the Treaty of Amsterdam the consumer political basis for negotiation has been strengthened by virtue of Article 153 EC (1.17, 1.19) on the basis of which the Commission established a consumer policy action plan for 2002–2006.[68] Definite proposals have not yet been made. At least DG SANCO has made this issue the subject of an extensive research programme. Thus in the medium term a new attempt from the Commission may be expected.[69]

6.38 The Service Directive 2006/123/EC[70] (SD) is meant to establish a common framework for the harmonisation of all those services which are not subject to sectoral regulation *d'un seul coup*. The Directive should be understood

---

65 Council Directive 90/314/EEC of 13 June 1990 on package travel, package holidays and package tours (1990), OJ L 158, 23 June 1990, 59.

66 COM (1990) 482 final, OJ C 12, 18 January 1991, 8.

67 COM (1994) 260 final.

68 COM (2002) 209 final.

69 See for possible perspectives Magnus/Micklitz.

70 OJ L 376, 27 December 2006, 36.

as a combination of the softened country of origin principle designed to establish freedom of services and freedom of establishment combined with a quasi-New Approach type of regulation, meant to shape the quality of services, including contractual rules.[71] The Directive has a limited scope of application by exempting, for example, labour law, services of general economic interest and health care services. However, the European Commission sticks to the idea of liberalising health care services as was originally foreseen in the Draft Service Directive.[72]

Although the approach chosen by the European Commission would have provided the opportunity to discuss whether and to what extent freedom of services and freedom of establishment might and should be backed by common rules on the liability for the quality and the safety of services, no such rules can be found in the SD. Instead the Directive refers to international private law rules, which are now enshrined in the Rome I and Rome II Regulations discussed in Chapter 7.

Rules on the liability of service providers are frequently accompanied by provisions on professional mandatory insurance. The SD, in Article 23, takes as a starting point the existing Member States' rules which may be different and thereby pose obstacles to cross-border provisions of services. Member States are free to require that providers whose services present a direct and particular risk to the health and safety of the recipient or a third person, or to the financial security of the recipient, subscribe to a professional insurance appropriate to the nature and extent of the risk, or provide a guarantee or similar which is equivalent or essentially comparable as regards its purpose (Article 23(1)). This provision also contains a "negative obligation": where these criteria cannot be fulfilled, Member States may not impose mandatory professional insurance, at least not against providers from other EU countries. This again implies a monitoring obligation on Member States. At the same time, Member States are obliged to recognise equivalent guarantees given by another Member State in which the provider is already established (Article 23(2)).[73] The Commission may establish common criteria for defining when equivalence is supposed to exist, subsequent to the "comitology procedure" (Article 23(4)). This may prove difficult if the risks covered are not identical.

It is here that the Commission's overall policy from pre-market control through public law to post-market control through private law becomes evident. The non-mandatory professional liability standards will compensate the consumer for the increasing risks which result from the open markets for services. However, not even professional liability insurance or guarantee is obligatory. That means Member States may equally decide not to put pressure on

---

71 Micklitz.

72 See in particular COM (2004), 2 final, 26 February 2004.

73 Roth, 169; Micklitz, 63–65.

service providers, in order not to cause their own national service providers to discriminate against the foreign service providers which might benefit from a laxer policy.

VIII. ANNEX: PROPOSED DRAFT FOR AN EC REGULATION/DIRECTIVE ON THE LIABILITY FOR THE SAFETY OF SERVICES[74]

1. GENERAL CONCEPT

a) Common system of combined contract and tort law

6.39 Services here under review comprise only services with a certain element of public offer, namely medical services, leisure and tourism services, and services of public utilities (meaning services of general economic interest). They have gained an ever-growing importance in the Member States and they pertain more than most other services to the essential interests of the recipient of the service. Therefore it is not at all surprising that the sheer number of conflicts has increased, too. The providers of these services may be private companies and/or public institutions like municipalities.

The comparison of the seven countries in Magnus and Micklitz's study demonstrates that accidents resulting in personal injuries through unsafe services come under the regime of civil law. Whilst the basic distinction between contract and tort law still exists, it is striking to recognise that the courts in present practice generally stay away from the differences and apply the same standards of care. Sometimes it is almost impossible to discover the legal basis on which the decision is based. Therefore it can safely be concluded that the distinction between tort and contract law has lost importance for most of the categories here under review.

---

[74] Magnus and Micklitz in their study *Liability for the Safety of Services,* 2006, 573–580, have concluded their comparative analysis of four major areas of services – medical services, leisure and tourism services, services of public utilities – with a draft EC regulation resp. directive on the liability for the safety of services which is reprinted here in full. The study concerned six EU countries: the UK, France, Germany, Spain, Italy and Sweden, as well as the US. The references to US law have mostly been eliminated. It takes a practical approach. From the beginning it was thought appropriate not to focus on a mere legal approach, but to look at actual disputes, be they in or out of the courts, in order to identify the true problems that a consumer might have to face in relation to unsafe services. The country reports are written around the available case law and based less on academic writing. The case law, representing actual disputes over the liability of the service provider, has been taken as the starting point for the country reports. They are not meant fully to present legal scholarship. They are, however, meant fully to document the relevant law in action.

(1) A liability system for bodily injuries resulting from unsafe services (medical malpractice, leisure, tourism and public utilities) is widely recognised and should be built on a combination of contract and tort law rules.

b) *Justification: social contact*

6.40 The relationship between the service provider and the recipient is based on *social contact.* Though a private contract is quite frequently concluded between the parties at the beginning of the relationship, it is not a necessary basis for a service provider–recipient relationship and the specific obligations under this relationship also arise irrespectively of the existence of a valid contract. The relationship is established by the mere fact that the recipient requests the service and that the provider accepts that request. The idea on which this concept is based has its roots mainly in the common law and the US legal system in so-called common callings. In the Middle Ages, certain professions, among them innkeepers, carriers and others who had easy access to the goods of their customers were for these reasons bound by law to observe rather far-reaching duties of care for their customers and even partly faced strict liability. The conclusion of the contract is no more than a starting point for social involvement; the duties of care are largely defined independently from the contractual rights and duties under the aspect that the service providers offer services to the public at large. The recipients of the services nearly entirely depend on the service providers' skills. It is the recipients' most valuable and vulnerable interests (life and health) which are at stake. If the service provider holds him or herself out to possess the necessary skills, often a risk of injury is involved.

(2) A mere factual service provider–recipient relationship suffices and the obligations of the provider with respect to the recipient's health and safety are mandatory and outside the parties disposal. Specific contractual obligations are imported into tort law where their violation results in tortuous liability.

2. ELEMENTS OF LIABILITY

a) *Type of liability*

6.41 The service provider's liability in the Member States depends mainly on negligence. With the exception of Spain and to some extent France, none of the countries rely on strict liability. However, even in France and Spain, strict liability is the exception to the rule. In France the "*obligation de résultat*" or the liability of the "*gardien*" shows up in exceptional cases. Spanish courts apply strict liability if, in the particular circumstances of the case, a blatant violation of the duty of care is at issue. The legal basis of the decisions is often not fully developed.

However, the French and Spanish approach is characteristic of the general attitude of courts in all the countries under review to raise the standard of liability beyond that of pure negligence. This tendency is triggered if one of three factual situations is present: (1) clear evidence of negligent behaviour, (2) clear evidence of a bodily injury typical for negligence or (3) clear evidence of causation between bodily injury and negligence. The facts of the case must be such that one of the three elements is clearly present. The courts then apply certain tools to find the missing link required to establish liability.

6.42 These tools are the following ones: often the legal systems and the courts tend to ease or to reverse the burden of proof for either causation or negligence if the other element exists. But none of the countries have gone so far as to reverse the burden of proof in its entirety. There is a certain preparedness in the courts to ease the burden of proof with regard to the missing link, be it through *presumed liability, prima facie evidence* or *res ipsa loquitur.* Beyond this tendency it is difficult to identify in the legal orders under review a further common core of legal principles.

(3) The liability for unsafe services is based on negligence. However, there is ample evidence to introduce a flexible system to alleviate the burden of proof with respect to causation and negligence according to the existence of either factual evidence of negligent behaviour, of a bodily injury typical of negligence or of causation between bodily injury and negligence.

b) Standard of care

6.43 The law in the seven countries imposes a general duty of care on the service provider to protect the health and safety of the recipient of the service. Whether the duty is to be found in contract law or in tort law is not important. The recipient's justified expectations set the standard of care irrespective of contract or tort. The standard of care corresponds to the type of service and its inherent risks.

All the countries under review start from an average standard of care. This standard requires that reasonable care and skill is exercised. It complies with whatever the standard formula might be, the behaviour of the *bon père de famille,* sensibly prudent and reasonable person, *buen padre de famille,* reasonable care or ordinary reasonable care. Generally this means a high level of care, which reflects the dangerousness of the respective service. In Sweden this yardstick seems to be even higher in certain medical malpractice cases.

The courts in all compared countries have developed a set of risk-related duties, which are imposed on the service provider and which flow from the service provider–recipient relationship. Three types of duties are at the forefront: the duty to organise the service so as to avoid unreasonable risks to the recipient, the duty to supervise and control any equipment, and last but not least the duty to provide assistance to the recipient, whether in the form of information, warnings or advice.

As far as the services are regulated by binding rules or even non-binding recommendations, the courts tend to refer to these rules though without feeling formally bound by the enshrined standards. They accept rules and regulations, national technical standards or even international standards on the organisation of services as a yardstick against which the behaviour of the service provider can be measured. Compliance with these rules and standards, however, does not automatically exempt service providers from liability.

The wide variety of cases makes it difficult to define a common denominator beyond the standard formula of the average standard of care, beyond classifying the mentioned duties and beyond reference to existing rules and recommendations. The courts link the standard of care to the type of service. Therefore different duties apply to passive recipients (visitors, patients) in comparison to active recipients (competitors, teammates, etc).

(4) *The general standard of care requires that reasonable care and skill is exercised. The standard must correspond to the respective service and its inherent risks. Therefore a high standard of care must be guaranteed. Non-binding rules or recommendations may provide guidance for fixing the standard of care. Compliance with such rules does not automatically exempt service providers from liability.*

c) *Scope of protection*

6.44 The distinction between contracting parties and mere bystanders is well-known to all legal systems discussed here. However, the circle of all those who are protected by the service provider–recipient relationship is broader. Such an approach is neither new nor unknown to the Member States. Their legal systems have already overcome the harsh doctrine of strict privity of contract. This is particularly true with regard to those third parties who are integrated into a services contract although they are not a party to the contract. The UK has quite recently changed the privity doctrine. France overrules the *non cumul* rule by the doctrine of implied consent. German law has traditionally developed a concept of contracts with protective effects for third parties. For mere bystanders who remain outside the contract and are violated more or less randomly, tortuous liability applies.

Within the concept of the service provider–recipient relationship, the classification of the customer according to his or her degree of involvement seems more appealing. The distinction is inspired by US law, which distinguishes for these purposes between invitees, licensees and trespassers. Only invitees (direct recipient of the service, family members and other intended beneficiaries) come under the full protection of the service provider–recipient relationship. They are engaged in a mutual consensual relationship. Mere licensees are allowed to use the service of the provider's premises or facilities but do so solely for their purposes and not to the advantage of the provider. They must only be warned of possible dangers. Trespassers, however, are those who enter the provider's premises or use his/her facilities without permission or justified reason. Here the service provider–recipient relationship is protected under general tort law.

(5) The scope of protection of the service provider–recipient relationship does not only include the direct recipient of the service but also those who are direct beneficiaries of the service. Those who come into contact with the service as mere licensees enjoy less protection and must only be warned of known dangers. Mere trespassers can only rely on general tort law.

d) Vicarious liability

6.45 Service providers are vicariously liable for acts by which their employees negligently injure third persons as long as these employees are acting within the scope of their employment. Member States' legal orders hold the service provider liable irrespective of whether the liability results from contract or tort law – with one notable exception: Germany. Under German law, the tortfeasor is still allowed to escape liability under §831 German Civil Code. Vicarious liability is extended even to cases where the service provider acts as a principal who employs independent contractors as his or her agents, such as in tourist services. Vicarious liability in this sense is well settled.

(6) Service providers are liable for wrongful conduct of their employees. This rule applies to principal–agent relations as well, even if the agent is an independent contractor.

e) Bodily injury

6.46 Three types of injuries have to be distinguished: mere bodily injury however severe, death and immaterial harm. The latter category concerns also situations in which a recipient of a service is not physically injured but where the injury results in non-physical, immaterial or psychological harm. It covers compensation for lost and spoilt holidays as well. With some differentiation in detail, all legal orders provide for compensation whatever the type of injury might be.

(7) *The recipient must be protected against personal injury, death and immaterial harm. Immaterial harm includes lost and spoilt holidays.*

f) Causation

6.47 All the compared countries agree that liability for services here under review requires causation between the recipient's injury and the service provider's negligence. But the general concept, which the compared countries apply with respect to causation, varies to some degree, though less so the final results when the question of causal nexus between these elements has to be answered. Remoteness (United Kingdom), adequacy (Germany), directness (France) or similar concepts are often not finally conclusive, but are supplemented by additional considerations. Despite the different dogmatic starting points, it is quite generally accepted that, first, the injury of the recipient must not have occurred without the act or omission of the service provider, and that further, mainly policy considerations might restrict causation to sufficiently close consequences.

(8) *Liability for services requires causation between the recipient's injury and the service provider's negligence. Despite varying concepts in legal doctrine, the final results are often similar. The main thrust lies in the proof of causation.*

g) Proof

6.48 In order to adapt liability to the reasonably required standard of care, the element of proof plays a particularly important role. The analysis of the law of the seven countries discussed has demonstrated that the courts use the rules on the burden of proof in a very flexible manner. This is true with regard to negligence – presumed liability, *prima facie* liability or the maxim of *res ipsa loquitur* and equally with regard to causation – *prima facie* liability and *res ipsa loquitur.* However, what is even more important is the courts' general policy of relating the type of liability to the type of standards of care, to the requirements of causation, and finally to the burden of proof.

This means in essence that in hard cases, the courts in fact come very close to strict liability or at least presumed liability. The higher the standards of care, the harder the case, i.e. the more blatant the violation of the duty of care. The same logic applies to causation. In the few cases where strict liability is at stake, the onus is on the customer to provide full evidence of causation. The concept can easily be turned upside down. The weaker the case, the stronger the plea of liability for negligence. The customer then has to prove not only the violation of the duty of care but also causation. In this respect, the courts have established a relatively well balanced system of liability.

(9) *The courts adapt, mainly by a flexible use of the instruments of proof, the required level of care to the desirable protection of persons injured during the provision of services. Whilst the type of liability varies in the countries between strict liability, negligence and presumed liability, due to the courts' flexible application of instruments to ease the burden of proof at the level of negligence and/or causation, the final outcome is often similar. A common European concept will have to combine liability for negligence with a flexible system to alleviate the burden of proof. Therefore a general reversal of the burden of proof or a general rule on presumed liability would go too far.*

(10) *Three variants have to be distinguished: (1) negligent behaviour will have to be presumed if there is clear factual evidence for wrongful conduct, (2) negligence will have to be presumed if there is factual evidence for a bodily injury typical for negligence, and (3) causation will have to be presumed if there is factual evidence for causal link between bodily injury and negligence.*

h) Compensation and damage

6.49 The recipient of a service is entitled to claim full compensation under the legal systems investigated for the restoration of his or her health, be it under contract law or under tort law. With the exception of Italy, all countries here under review also grant the recipient compensation for pain and suffering irrespective of the legal basis. Italy starts from a rather narrow understanding, where compensation for pain and suffering, if any, can be claimed only under tort law. The scope is further narrowed down as the Italian law usually binds compensation to the existence of a crime.

Caps or ceilings for compensation are mostly unknown in the Member States of the European Community. However, in Italy and in Germany there are limits to what the recipient might legitimately claim.

(11) *The recipient of service is entitled to full compensation of damage to his or her health and safety, including compensation for pain and suffering.*

(12) *In case of death the heirs of the deceased recipient are entitled to lost maintenance. Near relatives are entitled to compensation for the emotional distress.*

i) Contributory negligence

6.50 All the legal systems compared recognise contributory negligence as a defence. It is a common principle well-known all over the European Community and the United States. Courts refer to contributory negligence to varying degrees. Contributory negligence serves as a means to fine-tune the degree of the service providers' liability. Although somewhat overstated, one might distinguish between the tough Anglo-American recipient (in particular in sports) and the softer continental European counterpart. In this respect, contributory negligence helps to balance out cultural differences in civilised nations.

Whenever children are involved, the question arises as to what extent the claim for damage has to take into account a possible violation of the parents' supervisory duty. German law excludes the imputation of parents' negligence. In principle, courts are quite reluctant to assume contributory negligence of children and tend to fully protect the latter, even if they may be blamed for their negligent behaviour.

The doctrine of assumption of risk is well established. The prominent fields of application are sports and leisure services.

(13) *All the legal systems compared recognise contributory negligence as a defence. Contributory negligence with respect to personal injuries should be viewed with caution. If it has to be taken into account it should result in a proportionate reduction of damages.*

3. EXCLUSION OF LIABILITY

6.51 So far in the Member States, the rules on whether or not exclusion of liability is admissible or not very much depend on the traditional distinction between contractual and tort law relations. The European Community has intervened twice, with regard to unfair terms in consumer contracts in Directive 93/13/EEC (3.5) and with regard to package tours in Directive 90/314/EEC (1.27). Both directives are formally bound to contractual relations; however, the concrete provisions which turn down exclusion clauses reach beyond bilateral consensus, and have an impact on the recipient–service provider relationship.

Directive 93/13/EEC has defined a common standard for exclusion clauses in consumer contracts, whatever the type of services might be. They are forbidden as long as they are contained in pre-formulated terms, even though no case law of the ECJ exists yet. In theory they remain admissible if they are individually negotiated. Courts demonstrate a certain, though reluctant, preparedness to accept such exclusions in service provider–recipient relations, as long as they are clearly formulated, readable and related to the inherent risk of the service. Therefore exclusion clauses are hard to justify even if they form part of direct bilateral consensus. Directive 90/314/EEC prohibits exclusion clauses in tourist services. Within the scope of the Directive, i.e. within the recipient–service provider relationship, exclusion clauses are eliminated irrespective of their outer appearance, as standard business conditions or as individually negotiated terms.

In trespasser–service provider relations – the traditional tort law cases – the starting point seems different. The recipient may base his or her claim either on contract law or on tort law, except in France, where the recipient has to make a "wise" choice. Therefore in most countries it it is necessary to distinguish between cases where there is a contract which might exclude tortious liability and cases where there is no such contract. The former variant is dealt with under Directives 93/13/EEC or 90/314/EEC, the latter being mainly subject to the doctrine of assumption of risk. As the liability cannot be excluded, courts balance out the responsibility of the service provider and the trespasser-recipient under the aspect of contributory negligence. Therefore it might safely be concluded that there is a tendency to eliminate exclusion clauses for the liability of health and safety irrespective of the type of recipient–service provider relationship, be it the recipient-invitee, the recipient-licensee or the recipient-trespasser. The doctrine of contributory negligence helps to take the recipient's self-responsibility into consideration.

(14) *Exclusion clauses for the liability of health and safety are prohibited in recipient–service provider relationships.*

4. SPECIFIC ADR MECHANISMS

6.52 The seven countries under review demonstrate some preparedness to provide for out-of-court dispute settlement procedures. A relatively consistent policy can only be found in the field of sports, where mechanisms are available in particular if conflicts between teammates or between competitors are to be solved. The European Commission has established a relatively well-developed policy to create incentives for fostering the establishment of out-of-court dispute settlement procedures. The two Recommendations 98/257/EC and 2001/310/EC provide ample evidence of the Commission's intention to give form to a European dispute settlement procedure (8.19, 8.22). They will be supplemented by the Directive 2013/11/EU on Consumer ADR and Regulation (EU) 524/2013 on Consumer ODR (8.18, 8.23a–g).

(15) *Out-of-court dispute settlement procedures should be made available in recipient–service provider relationships. They should be shaped along the lines of Recommendations 98/257/EC and 2001/310/EEC (now Directive 2013/11/EU and Regulation 524/2013).*

CHAPTER 7

CROSS-BORDER CONSUMER PROTECTION

Norbert Reich

CONTENTS

Bibliography:

J. Basedow, Materielle Rechtsangleichung und Kollisionsrecht, in: Schnyder/Heiss/Rudisch (eds.), *Internationales Verbraucherschutzrecht*, 1995, 11; J. Basedow, *The Law of Open Societies - Private Ordering and Public Regulation of International Relations*, (General Course on Private International Law - The Hague Academy), 2013; P. Berger, *The Creeping Codification of the Lex Mercatoria*, 1999; M. Bogdan, *Concise Introduction to EU Private International Law*, 2nd ed. 2011; M. Bonell/R. Peleggi, Unidroit Principles of International Commercial Contracts and Principles of European Contract Law, *Uniform LRev* 2004, 315; G.-P. Calliess, *Grenzüberschreitende Verbraucherverträge*, 2006; G.-P. Calliess, Kollisionsrecht, Richtlinienrecht, oder Einheitsrecht, *ZEuP* 2006, 742; G.-P. Calliess (ed.), *Rome Regulations*, 2011; G.-P. Calliess/P. Zumbansen, *Rough Consensus and Running Code*, 2010; A. Dickinson, *The Rome II Regulation: The Law Applicable to Non-contractual Obligations*, 2008; U. Draetta, *Internet et commerce électronique*, 2004; F.J. Garcimartín Alférez, The Rome I Regulation: Much ado about nothing?, *The European Legal Forum* 2008, I-61; V. Gessner, Europas holperige Rechtswege - Die rechtskulturellen Schranken der Rechtsverfolgung im Binnenmarkt, in: *Liber amicorum N. Reich*, 1997, 163; M. Giuliano/P. Lagarde, Report on the Convention on the law applicable to contractual obligations, OJ C 282 of 31 October 1980 ("the Giuliano-Lagarde Report"); C. Joerges et al. (eds.), *Transnational Governance and Constitutionalism*, 2004; S. Klauer, *Das europäische Kollisionsrecht der Verbraucherverträge zwischen Römer EVÜ und EG-Richtlinien*, 2002; J. Kropholler/J.V. Hein, *Europäisches Zivilverfahrensrecht*, 9th ed. 2011; O. Lando/A. Nielsen, The Rome I Regulation, *CMLRev* 2008, 1687; X. Kramer, European Small Claims Procedure, *ZEuP* 2008, 355; S. Leible, Die neue EG-Verordnung über das auf außervertragliche Schuldverhältnisse anzuwendende Recht (Rom II), *RIW* 2007, 721; A. Maack, *Die Durchsetzung des AGB-rechtlichen Transparenzgebotes in internationalen Verbraucherverträgen*, Schriftenreihe des Zentrums für Europäische Rechtspolitik an der Universität Bremen, Vol. 38, 2001; U. Magnus, Rom I-VO, Einleitung und Art. 1–10, in: Staudinger, *Kommentar zum BGB*, revised ed. 2011; U. Magnus/P. Mankowski (eds.), *Brussels I Regulation*, 2nd ed. 2012; P. Mankowski, Entwicklung und Stand des europäischen Internationalen Verbraucherschutzrechts, in: Wagner/Wedl (eds.), *Bilanz und Perspektiven zum Europäischen Recht*, 2007, 325; D. Martiny, Europäisches Internationales Vertragsrecht in Erwartung der Rom I-Verordnung, *ZEuP* 2008, 79; M. Micheletti/A. Follesdal, Shopping for Human Rights, 2007, 167–175; H.-W. Micklitz, Der Vertragsbegriff in den Übereinkommen von Brüssel und Rom, in: Schulze/Schulte-Nölke (eds.), *Europäisches Vertragsrecht in den EG-Richtlinien*, Schriftenreihe der ERA, 2002, 65; MPI comments on the proposal of the European Commission for a Rome I Regulation, *RabelsZ* 2007, 225; H. Muir Watt, Integration and Diversity: The Conflict of

Laws as a Regulatory Tool, in: Cafaggi (ed.), *The Institutional Framework of European Private Law*, 2006, 107; T. Pfeiffer, Neues Internationales Vertragsrecht, *EuZW* 2008, 622. N. Reich, *General Principles of EU Civil Law*, 2013; N. Reich, EU Strategies in Finding the Optimal Consumer Law Instrument, *ERCL* 2012, 1; N. Reich, Transformation of Contract Law and Civil Justice in the New EU Member Countries: The Example of the Baltic States, Hungary and Poland, in: Cafaggi (ed.), *The Institutional Framework of European Private Law*, 2006, 271; N. Reich, Horizontal Liability in EC Law – "Hybridisation" of remedies for compensation in case of breaches of EC rights, *CMLRev* 2007, 705–742; N. Reich, More clarity after "Claro"?, *ERCL* 2007, 41; N. Reich, Competition between Legal Orders – A New Paradigm in EC Law?, *CMLRev* 1992, 882; N. Reich/A.P. Gambogi, Gerichtsstand bei internationalen Verbrauchervertragsstreitigkeiten im e-commerce, *VuR* 2001, 269–280; N. Reich/A. Halfmeier, Consumer Protection in the Global Village: Recent Developments in the German and European Law, *Dickinson LRev* 106 (2001), 111; W.-H. Roth, Case note to C-381/98, *Ingmar GB Ltd./Eaton Leonard Technologies Inc.*, *CMLRev* 2002, 369; D. Schiek, Private Rulemaking and European Governance – Issues of legitimacy, *ELRev* 2007, 443; M. Tenreiro, *La compétence internationale des tribunaux en matière de consommation. Les consommateurs protégés dans la société d'information,* 2004, 1093; K. Vassileva, 1968 Brussels Convention and EU Council Regulation 44/2001: Jurisdiction in Consumer Contracts Concluded Online, *ELJ* 2004, 129; H.L.E. Verhagen, The Tension between the party autonomy and European Union law: some observations on *Ingmar Ltd v Eaton Leonard Technologies Inc*, *ICLQ* 2002, 135.

I. GENERAL REMARKS

7.1 While in the past cross-border business was almost exclusively conducted by undertakings and traders, the internationalisation of consumption has led to an "internationalisation" of consumer transactions. The consumer as a tourist, shopper, bank client and investor, but also as a victim of cross-border product risks, will be involved in international settings in several ways. Cross-border conflicts will increase within the internal market, the paramount objective of which is to guarantee the mobility of persons, goods, capital and services.

For supporters of the single internal market, a uniform consumer law which governs these conflicts would be desirable; as a result Union-wide standards of consumer protection could be enforced. The Community and now Union has introduced a number of such standards in the form of directives which generally guarantee certain consumer rights. According to the prevailing view, this does not constitute a uniform Union consumer law as the directives do not establish obligations and rights which apply directly between consumers and traders (1.31). The provisions of the directives must be implemented into national law and must be harmonised with the existing norms, in accordance with Article 288 TFEU (ex-Article 249(3) EC). Rights and obligations arising indirectly out of directives will then be enforced under national – not Union – law.

The decision as to whether to apply these rights and obligations to situations which have a cross-border element will be made under the rules of private international law (PIL). This area of law, which originally formed part of national law, has recently become "Europeanised". It will only possess a specific consumer policy element where the consumer engages in cross-border transactions or becomes a victim of a cross-border tort. The need to protect the consumer arises out of the fact that he is not familiar with the foreign law – including its jurisdiction. Enforcement of the consumer's rights against the obligations of the trader therefore causes additional costs and risks. The best possible consumer protection in international settings could be brought about by a rule which exclusively refers to the domicile or residence of the consumer (*lex consumatoris* principle). On the other hand, this may impair the trader's access to the internal market by subjecting him to many different national regimes of consumer protection. Such a far-reaching provision, however, cannot be found in any system of PIL. Rather, it is characterised by different criteria which are distinguished according to the type of transaction or action, as well as legal traditions.[1] Only aspects of international – European – contract and tort law are of relevance in this context.

Traditionally in contract law the parties' autonomy to determine the proper law of their contract constitutes the most important connecting factor. Among traders this might be acceptable.[2] However, if consumers are involved it lacks legitimacy because of their structural weakness with regard to cross-border transactions, in particular when choice of law clauses are imposed by standard contract terms. Therefore the parties' autonomy needs to be restricted. With an increasing number of national laws governing consumer protection, the main objective of the specific provisions is to deter the seller or supplier, who is in a stronger bargaining position, from using the parties' freedom to unilaterally determine the law governing the contract, thereby waiving protective standards. Such minimum standards will establish a more consumer-friendly contract law. According to the counter argument, however, this protection should not be taken to the extreme, in particular not in favour of the active consumer who had deliberately opted for a foreign law under Article 26 TFEU (ex-Article 14 EC), e.g. by going abroad and making his transactions in a foreign jurisdiction.

These principles could originally be found in the Convention on the law applicable to contractual obligations opened for signature in Rome on 19 June 1980 (Rome Convention),[3] now supplemented by Regulation (EC) No 593/2008 of the EP and the Council of 17 June 2008 on the law applicable to contractual

1 For an overview of the different approaches in private international law see now Basedow, *The Law of Open Societies*, 351.

2 Giuliano/Lagarde, 15 ff with regard to Article 3 of the Rome Convention which enshrines freedom of choice of law recognised by all EU Member States for commercial transactions.

3 OJ L 266, 9 October 1980, 1.

obligations (Rome I)[4] for most of the contracts governed by the law of obligations. It applies to contracts concluded after 17 December 2009, with an opt-out for Denmark. The Rome Convention will therefore keep its importance for a number of years and needs to be discussed in this context.

Special provisions can be found in some consumer protection directives, for example Directive 93/13/EEC on unfair terms in consumer contracts (3.30), Directive 99/44/EC on the sale of consumer goods (4.33), and distance marketing of financial services 2002/65/EC.[5] A similar provision is contained in Article 22(4) of the Consumer Credit Directive 2008/48/EC of 23 April 2008 (CCD: Chapter 5)[6] and more recently in the new Consumer Rights Directive 2011/83/EU of 25 October 2011 (see Chapter 9).[7] These contract law directives take a different approach; they establish a special connecting factor, the compatibility of which with general PIL is rather questionable, especially after the adoption of Regulation 593/2008. Their main focus is the protection of the EU consumer against choice of a third country law if the contract has a close connection with the EU (7.20–7.25).

Tort law is concerned with the protection of the victim. It also purports to develop adequate rules applicable to cross-border settings, for example in relation to product liability under Directive 85/374/EEC[8] (6.36). Consumer protection is sought by the Union through approximation of substantive law. For conflict situations, the EC legislator has adopted Regulation (EC) No 864/2007 of the European Parliament and the Council of 11 July 2007 on the law applicable to non-contractual obligations (Rome II, *infra* 7.26), which came in effect on 11 January 2009.[9]

II. THE ROME CONVENTION

7.2 Through the Rome Convention a Community-wide PIL on contractual obligations had been established; although based on international law it was intended to be applicable to all Member States. It came into force on 1 April 1991 and was applicable to all former EU Member States, and since 29 November 1996 it also applied to the then acceding states Finland, Austria and Sweden. An accession agreement was concluded with the new Member States on 14 May

---

4 OJ L 177, 4 July 2008, 6.

5 Directive 2002/65/EC of the European Parliament and of the Council of 23 September 2002 concerning the distance marketing of consumer financial services and amending Council Directive 90/619/EEC and Directives 97/7/EC and 98/27/EC, OJ L 271, 9 October 2002, 17.

6 OJ L 133, 22 May 2008, 66.

7 OJ L 304, 22 November 2011, 64.

8 Council Directive 85/374/EEC of 25 July 1985 on the approximation of the laws, regulations and administrative provisions of the Member States concerning liability for defective products OJ L 210, 7 August 1985, 29.

9 OJ L 199, 31 July 2007.

2005, which entered into force on 1 May 2006, but had not yet been ratified by all Member States.[10] It applied to all contractual and quasi-contractual obligations including subsequent claims (Article 10) but not to statutory obligations, in particular tort. Under Article 1(3) contracts of insurance which cover risks arising on the territories of the Member States are excluded. Under Article 20 the Convention shall not affect the application of provisions which lay down choice of law rules relating to contractual obligations under either primary or secondary law, in particular the consumer contract law directives.

The interpretation of the Rome Convention has been left to Member State courts because the interpretation protocols conferring such powers to the ECJ have entered into force only on 1 August 2004. Guidelines may be found in the practice of the ECJ under the Brussels Convention (7.31), especially as such civil law concepts like "contract", "consumer" and "choice of laws" respectively jurisdiction clauses are concerned.

Its relation to the Rome I Regulation 593/2008 is determined by Article 24. It remains in force in Denmark (7.16).

1. FREEDOM OF CHOICE: ARTICLE 3 TAKEN WITH ARTICLES 8 AND 4 OF THE ROME CONVENTION

7.3 The Convention is based on the overriding objective to put both contractual parties in a position to make autonomous and responsible decisions. This explains the central position of Article 3 of the Convention and its requirements ensuring an effective choice of the applicable law. Choice of the applicable law and the main contract are considered as two separate contractual provisions. This approach causes difficulties in particular in consumer contracts where the choice of the applicable law is governed by standard terms, or where the contract is silent on the choice of law and an inference can be drawn from attached jurisdiction clauses. Therefore the interrelation of Articles 3 and 8 of the Rome Convention is of paramount importance.

If, however, there is no agreement on the applicable law, the law which will apply will be determined according to the objective criterion of the closest connection (Article 4 of the Convention (7.7)).

a) Requirements for the choice of law in Article 3 of the Rome Convention

7.4 The choice of law is the central focus of the Convention. It attaches quasi-statutory weight to the parties' autonomy to determine the proper law, which is subject to only one exception under Article 3(3): if the contract is merely

10 Martiny, *ZEuP* 2008, 79; Bulgaria and Romania acceded with their membership treaties coming into effect on 1 January 2007. Croatia became an EU member on 1 July 2013.

connected with one legal system, then its mandatory provisions cannot be circumvented by choosing a foreign law.[11] Within these restrictions the choice of law may be made expressly (Article 3(1) s. 2 first alternative) or by way of an agreement which is derived "with reasonable certainty from the terms of the contract or the circumstances of the case" (Article 3(1) s. 2 second alternative). In Article 3(1) s. 1 the Convention presumes a certain basic knowledge of the term "choice of law". The wording only implicitly states that the parties can enter into an agreement either expressly or implicitly. Article 3(2) only contains the formulation "agree" – without giving a further definition. If one refers to the Giuliano-Lagarde Report, then the concept of the choice of law can be explained with the help of the parties' autonomy to determine the proper law as rooted in the signatory states. To that extent the attempts to find an explanation go around in circles. The situation is different for the second alternative. Here the Report purports to clarify matters because it is crucial to allow for the intentions of the parties. Guiliano/Lagarde[12] unequivocally state that Article 3(1) s. 2 second alternative does not give the judge the discretion to imply a choice of law by the parties if they had no intention to make such a choice. The choice may be express or inferred. Moreover, it need not to be in writing. The Giuliano-Lagarde Report provides a number of examples of situations where a court may draw an inference as to the parties' intentions:

- a jurisdiction or arbitration clause;
- the place of conclusion or performance of the contract;
- previous contracting;
- parties' domicile or business seat.

Issues in relation to the validity and existence of consent are, however, determined in accordance with special rules relating to formal validity and incapacity.[13]

Furthermore, where no choice can be inferred, the provisions of Article 4 of the Convention will apply to the contract (objective connection: 7.7).

b) Separation of choice of law and main contract

7.5 From today's perspective the choice of law is generally regarded as an individual contract existing alongside the main contract.[14] As regards the matter of transparency, the fact that there are two separate contracts and the law which applies respectively would need explaining to the parties. In practice it is

---

11 Lando, *CMLRev* 1987, 159.
12 Giuliano/Lagarde, 17.
13 Per Article 3(4) of the Rome Convention.
14 Martiny, *ZEuP* 1997, 107 ff, 114.

likely that the non-professional – typically the consumer – who enters into a cross-border contract will not be aware that he or she has entered into two contracts. Therefore the question of the intended choice of law is to be determined on the merits of the case, in particular the circumstances when entering into the contract – and not the formal separation of the two contracts. The model of separation as supported by the prevailing legal doctrine is also problematic, since under Article 8(1) the contract governing the choice of law would be subject to the law to be applied – an obviously circular argument. Therefore, in essence, the individual contract governing the choice of law would be ineffective.[15] The model of separation and the principle of transparency would be rendered redundant.

If case law and the prevailing legal doctrine were to give up the model of separation, then this would have a significant impact. The choice of law in contracts creating mutual obligations would no longer be bound to an agreement which needs to be effective under the law of at least one legal system. Rather, the substantive requirements should and could be determined autonomously, i.e. related to a context under Community law. To this extent case law, turned upside down, accidentally opens perspectives that have parallels to the assessment of jurisdiction clauses under the Brussels Convention. In that area Advocate General Alber in *Mainschifffahrts-Genossenschaft eG (MSG)*[16] paved the way for the ECJ in *Trasporti Castelletti*,[17] when deciding on the validity of a jurisdiction clause to take into account substantive requirements. These considerations are based on the aim of finding objective solutions for the Brussels Convention which are tailored to its objectives. Article 8(2) of the Rome Convention normally allows for a modification of the agreement on the choice of law. If it appears unjustifiable to determine the conduct of one party according to that law, then this party can rely on the law of its habitual residence when claiming that it had not agreed to the choice of law. Article 8(2) functions as a substantive correction. It would, however, not be sought in the forum state but be derived autonomously from the law of conflicts. A parallel approach with the Brussels Convention would be possible. In that area case law has already paved the way for the formulation of a control mechanism against abuse under Article 17 of the Brussels Convention if it can be shown that there is no agreement.[18]

---

15 Stoll, in: *Liber amicorum Heini*, 1995, 434; also Martiny, *ZEuP* 1997, 112 ff raises the question of the extent to which the choice of the law shall be without restrictions. In particular the question is posed as to whether the boundaries arising from the contractual obligations under contract law also apply to the choice of law.

16 ECJ, 20 February 97, C-106/95, [1997] ECR I-911.

17 ECJ, 16 March 1999, C-159/97, [1999] ECR I-1597.

18 Micklitz, 54.

c) *Choice of law in standard terms and conditions: Article 8(1) and (2)*

7.6 There is a great degree of uncertainty concerning the rules applicable to choice-of-law clauses in standard terms, which results from the fact that the Rome Convention allows such choice in consumer contracts in principle and fails to provide for a review mechanism. The German author Maack[19] has convincingly established that a justified need for consumer protection can only be derived from Article 8(2) if the consequences of the foreign statutory provision are not recognisable to him. This would mainly concern cases where the consumer remains silent as to the choice of law clause in the standard terms, but where silence cannot be implied as consent, as well as cases where the standard terms have not been provided in the correct language. This is supported by the requirement of transparency which is derived from Article 8 of the Convention. With the help of this approach it is possible to assess choice of law clauses against standard terms, which need to be avoided under the Rome Convention.

So far this solution is predominantly applied by practice and doctrine in the field of national consumer laws. To resolve a dispute, it is necessary to answer the question of whether and to what extent the provisions on standard terms apply to choice of law clauses with or without coordination with the Rome Convention.

The main argument of the approach taken here lies in the interrelation of the principle of transparency as derived from Article 8 of the Rome Convention with the similar principle as contained in Directive 93/13/EEC (3.16). Article 7 of the Rome Convention allows making the protective provisions which are derived from EC law internationally mandatory and therefore would need to be applied by the courts irrespective of the *lex causae*.[20]

The extent of the requirement of transparency is textually restricted as it only applies to situations which are unclear. If the consumer is, however, clearly informed about the loss of his protection under national law by entering into a choice of law agreement, his protection is limited by substantive law. These will only reveal their full potential if the choice of law agreement and the main contract are not regarded as two separate agreements and an autonomous interpretation of the choice of law agreement is sought. If it were regarded as sufficient to have an autonomous statement that the parties actually intend to apply a particular legal system and document this intent when concluding the contract, then the question would arise as to whether it would be sufficient to hide this agreement within the standard terms. It could be argued that in that case it is not a real agreement. Therefore a review of unfairness would be available under Community/Union law similar to choice of law agreements under the Rome Convention.

---

19 Maack, 239–240.

20 Maack, 207.

d) *Objective applicable law in the absence of a choice: Article 4 of the Rome Convention*

7.7 To the extent that the law applicable to the contract has not been chosen, the contract shall be governed by the law of the country with which it is most closely connected under Article 4.[21] For consumer contracts this will normally be the place of business, or the branch of the seller or party providing the service, and not the domicile or habitual residence of the consumer. The Rome Convention thereby established a country-of-origin principle which can however be waived by agreement of the parties. In cross-border transactions the consumer needs to be aware of the applicability of foreign law, unless Article 5 applies or the circumstances show that the contract has a closer connection with another state.[22] Special provisions apply to contracts on rights to or the use of immovable property; here the law of the *situs* of the property applies (principle of *lex rei sitae*).

2. SCOPE OF APPLICATION AS REGARDS THE PERSON AFFECTED: CONSUMER CONTRACTS (1)

7.8 Article 5 of the Rome Convention regulates consumer contracts without properly defining key terms, for example, "contract". The German Federal Court has taken a narrow approach, thereby excluding unilateral promises of prizes (*Gewinnzusagen*) from its scope of application.[23]

The question of whether a person qualifies as a "consumer" is determined according to the purpose of the transaction. Subjectively there will only be a consumer contract if it has been entered into by a person for a purpose which can be regarded as being outside his trade or profession. The contract must enter the private, non-professional sphere of the consumer. The Convention intentionally refers to the definition of a consumer as contained in the Brussels Convention.[24]

This broad definition has caused a number of disputes which *inter alia* concerned the question of who should be considered a consumer – natural or legal persons, natural persons as non-professionals, non-contractual third

---

21 Martiny, The Applicable Law to Contracts in the Absence of Choice, in: *Estudios sobre Contraction Internacional*, 2006, 11.

22 LG Köln, *VuR* 1992, 156: German law is applicable if the service of a foreign agent of holiday homes has been provided in Germany.

23 BGH NJW 2006, 230, applying instead the law of the place where the obligation has to be performed in analogy to Article 5(1) Brussels Regulation 44/2001, namely the place of residence of the addressee (consumer); the ECJ has taken a similar view with regard to the Brussels Convention in Engler, ECJ, 20 January 2005, C-27/02 [2005] ECR I-481 (*infra* 7.37); for a discussion see Martiny, *ZEuP* 2008, 85.

24 See the official Guiliano/Lagarde Report, 23–25.

parties, related contracts, agents appointed by the consumer and contracts in favour of (private) third parties. Moreover the definition does not specify what is meant by "for a purpose which can be regarded as being outside his trade or profession", including the time and the criteria for determining the purpose. It is not clear how one would categorise so-called *mixed or double purpose contracts* (purchase of a car by a lawyer, the trader's sale of his business). Under the Rome Convention, Article 3 of which concerns the freedom of choice of law and Article 4 of which considers the application of the law of the characteristic obligation as the norm (and consumer protection as the exception), the consumer bears the burden of proving that the contract falls within his private sphere. This might be inferred from the circumstances in which the contract was concluded or from the subject matter of the contract. Some answer could be found in the interpretation of the similar provision in Article 13 of the Brussels Convention of 1968 (now Article 15 of the Brussels Regulation 41/2001, *infra* 7.36). In the case of so-called "mixed contracts", the Court in *Gruber*[25] stated that Article 13 should only be applied in cases where the professional activity to which the contract is related is only marginal and ancillary (for criticism see 1.36). AG Jacobs, in his opinion of 8 July 2004, expressly referred to the Giuliano-Lagarde Report[26] where it is stated that:

> "If such a (private) person acts partly within, partly outside his trade or profession the situation only falls within the scope of Article 5 if he acts primarily outside his trade or profession. Where the receiver of goods or services in fact acted primarily outside his trade or profession but the other party did not know this and, taking all circumstances into account should not reasonably have known it, the situation falls outside the scope of Article 5. Thus if the receiver of goods or services holds himself out as a professional, e.g. by ordering goods which might well be used in his trade or profession on his professional paper the good faith of the other party is protected and the case will not be governed by Article 5."

Should the consumer deceive the counterparty as to the true character of the contract – for example he pretends the contract to be part of a professional activity even when this part is only minor – he has waived his protection and the good faith contract partner does not enjoy the protective provision in Article 5. This approach is, however, somewhat too narrow and does not respect the protective ambit of Article 5 of the Rome Convention, which is mandatory and does not allow the consumer to opt out, unless his behaviour obviously contradicts prior action (*venire contra factum proprium*).[27]

---

25 ECJ, 20 January 2005, C-464/01, *Johann Gruber v BayWa AG* [2005] ECR I-439.

26 Giuliano/Lagarde, 23.

27 Reich, *EuZW* 2005, 244; for a different supporting view, see Garcímartin, I-61 at 71.

3. SCOPE OF APPLICATION AS REGARDS THE SUBJECT MATTER: CONSUMER CONTRACTS (2)

7.9 Objectively there would only be a consumer contract under the Rome Convention if movable goods are delivered (i.e. transactions concerning immovable property, securities, assignment of claims and other rights are excluded) or services and financing of those services are provided. The German Federal Court has held that the management of a business by a trustee who manages the shares of the persons in the course of a sale of timeshare rights amounted to a service.[28] That means that even if the sale of a property or the purchase of a share in a business will not be subject to Article 5 of the Rome Convention, the financing of the service, however, which is a prerequisite for the purchase, constitutes a consumer contract in terms of the Convention.

According to the wording of Article 5 of the Rome Convention, simple consumer credit contracts not attached to the financing of goods or services will not come under the definition of a consumer contract – an exemption which was clearly inappropriate and could only be explained by referring to the origin of the Convention. Simple consumer credit contracts were then practically unknown. At the very least they were typically combined with another transaction (financed purchase or service). This ambiguity could be remedied in two different ways. Either credit contracts are generally qualified as services, or consumer protection would be ensured by inserting a reference to the mandatory provisions in terms of Article 7(2). The CCD (*supra* 7.1) tries to solve this problem by complete harmonisation and by a separate clause forbidding choice of law of a third country if the contract has a close connection to the EU (7.17).

It follows from these considerations that the term "service" is to be interpreted widely and needs to be determined as per general Community/ Union law, provided there are no special exceptions in existence, as for insurance (Article 1(3) of the Rome Convention).[29]

4. SPECIAL CONNECTING FACTORS IN CONSUMER CONTRACTS (3)

7.10 Article 5 of the Rome Convention contains the central protection provision in practice for cross-border consumer transactions. It purports to guarantee a minimum level of protection of the consumer (*supra* 7.8) under PIL even where another law as of choice of law or closest connection would otherwise be applicable.

---

28 BGH, NJW 1994, 262.

29 For details of the earlier law in the insurance directives see SMULDERS/GLAZENER, 775.

a) *Protection of the "passive consumer"*

7.11 As Article 5(2) shows, the Convention protects the passive consumer only. Three different cases are distinguished:

- in "that country" (i.e. the country of the habitual residence of the consumer) the conclusion of the contract was preceded by a specific invitation addressed to the consumer or by advertising, and the consumer had taken in "that country" all the steps necessary on his part for the conclusion of the contract; or
- the other party or his agent received the consumer's order in "that country"; or
- the contract was for the sale of goods and the consumer travelled from "that country" to another country and there made his order, provided that the consumer's excursion was arranged by the seller for the purpose of inducing the consumer to buy.

The wording referred to particular facts, the domestic connection of which is so substantial that it pushes aside the provision on "choice of law" or "closest connection". According to its wording, Article 5(2) does not apply where the consumer, having regard to the criteria allowing for a restriction of the choice of law, was not in his country of residence but in another country even if there are close ties with the country of residence. Such close ties may be present where:

(1) the order was made by mail order, by phone or over the internet while the consumer was abroad, even if the stay abroad was merely temporary (first alternative);
(2) the contract was initiated and concluded at the consumer's holiday residence by way of "door-to-door selling" but is to be performed at the consumer's domicile (first alternative);
(3) the consumer orders the goods or requests services during a sales event (for example a trade fair) abroad (second alternative);
(4) the final destination of the excursion is a third country, but the contract is concluded in another country (third alternative); or
(5) the excursion does not start in the country of residence but in another country (third alternative).

In other circumstances Article 5(1) will not apply, having regard to its wording, e.g.:

(6) the contract is concluded "on the occasion" of an excursion without providing that it was conducted for the purpose of concluding a contract (third alternative);
(7) the excursion only results in the conclusion of a contract for services or on real property such as trust units or part-time property (third alternative).

b) *Application of Article 5 beyond its strict wording*

7.12 Because of the strict wording of Article 5(1) and (2) of the Rome Convention, it could be argued that the protection provided by Article 5(1) will only apply if all facts are established completely. In the cases outlined above, the consumer would be deprived of the protection of the law of his country of residence if he was abroad on a temporary basis; this would even be the case where an entrepreneur initiated the conclusion of the contract whilst aware that the consumer is tied to another legal system or where the contract is concluded on the occasion of an excursion abroad or relates to the provision of services.

Therefore, legal doctrine controversially discussed the possibility of applying Article 5 *per analogiam* to situations which require protection of consumers exposed to aggressive selling even if there is no close connection to the country of residence according to the strict wording of the Convention. Some courts and authors avoided dealing with the issue by applying the consumer's home country protection provisions as mandatory law in the sense of Article 7(2) of the Rome Convention.[30] This approach was clearly rejected by the German Federal Court preferring a narrow reading of Article 7(2), the so-called *lois de police*; at the same time, it also rejected an extensive interpretation of Article 5(2) to contracts or situations not expressly covered in paras 1–3.[31]

In *Arblade*,[32] the European Court found that these *lois de police*, namely the

> "term (i.e. public-order legislation) must be understood as applying to national provisions compliance with which has been deemed to be so crucial for the protection of the political, social or economic order in the Member State concerned as to require compliance therewith by all persons present on the national territory of that Member State and all legal relationships within that State". (para. 30)

In *Ingmar* the ECJ[33] made a first step in this direction. The case concerned a choice of law clause in a contract with a commercial agent doing business in the UK and a US principal, according to which Californian law was to apply. The litigation before the UK courts was concerned with the question whether the mandatory rules on compensation after termination of the contract could be waived by a choice of law clause, a consequence which the ECJ rejected, relying both on the harmonisation aspect and on protection of the commercial agent by

---

30 OLG Celle, decision 28 August 1990, *EuZW* 1990, 550.

31 BGH NJW 1997, 1697; NJW 2006, 762; French law takes a different view and regards consumer protection provisions as *lois de police*, see Martiny, *ZEuP* 2008, 95 with reference to Cass. civ., 23 May 2006, *Rev. crit. dr. int. pr.* 2007, 85.

32 ECJ, 23 November 1999, C-369+376/96, *Arblade and Leloup* [1999] ECR I-8453.

33 ECJ, 9 November 2000, C-381/98, *Ingmar GB Ltd. V Eaton Leonard Technologies Inc.* [2000] ECR I-9305.

mandatory rules of Directive 86/653/EEC.[34] Under conflict rules, this could be read so as to imply that Article 7 of the Rome Convention could be a provision having both theoretical and also practical impact for consumer protection.[35] By applying Article 7, mandatory provisions of harmonised contract law could be made unavailable for opting-out by choice of law clauses referring to third countries, if a close connection existed with the EU.[36] This understanding would impose a unilateral conflict rule on consumer contracts which is, however, not in accordance with the Rome Convention and the later Rome I Regulation, but can be found in specific consumer contract directives (*infra* 7.22).[37]

c) *Consequences of Article 5*

7.13 In the event that the application of Article 5 of the Convention is possible in favour of the (passive) consumer, then the extent of the reference to the law of habitual residence of the consumer depends on whether or not there is a choice of law clause. If there is no such choice, then the law of the consumer applies to its full extent (Article 5(3)). If, however, a valid choice of law has been made, then Article 5(2) merely provides a balancing test: the consumer must not be deprived of the protection provided by the mandatory provisions of his country of habitual residence. In the case of equal protection, the provisions chosen will prevail.[38] The remaining (non-mandatory) contractual terms will also be governed by the law chosen. Mandatory provisions are those which are established by Community/Union law; additionally they extend to the (different) legal framework of the consumer protection laws of the Member States within the general boundaries of Community/Union law. Article 5(4) of the Rome Convention contains an exception for transport contracts as well as contracts for services which need to be executed in the other country (e.g. hotel accommodation and language courses) which will always be governed by Article 3 or 4. An "exception to the exception" (i.e. application of the general rule of Article 5(1) to (3) is made for package holidays which are regarded as consumer contracts for the purposes of the Convention (para 5).

---

34 OJ L 382, 31 December 1986, 17.

35 Cf. more detailed view on the topic: Micklitz, 71.

36 Cf. positively supportive Reich, commentary to ECJ, 9 November 2000, C-381/98, *Ingmar*, *EuZW* 2001, 51; critique by Roth, 369 (382); Verhagen, *ICLQ* 2002, 135, 151: "Unfortunately, it must now be concluded that this decision does not correctly reflect current EU law".

37 For a general critique of the unilateral approach see Basedow, *supra* note 1, 366.

38 Reich/Halfmeier, 118; Basedow, *supra* note 1, 364 mentions that usually the judge will apply "his" law, not a foreign law even if this might be more protective; comparison of different laws is simply too time consuming.

III. ROME I REGULATION (EC) 593/2008

1. ISSUES FOR REFORM OF PIL

7.14 The PIL of consumer contract law had been in urgent need of reform. Concerning the proposed reform, the following issues had arisen:

- whether, unlike in Article 5 of the Rome Convention, the protective provisions should differentiate between contracts concluded within the EU and those concluded outside it;[39]
- whether goods and services are covered uniformly;[40]
- how to deal with the individual situations in which Article 5 of the Convention imposes a special connection, and with contracts concluded on the internet;
- how to ensure the harmonisation of the reform with the provision of Article 15 of Regulation (EC) No 41/2001 which contains a paradigm change from the "passive consumer" to the "active trader" (*infra* 7.39).

2. TRANSFORMING THE CONVENTION INTO A REGULATION: COMMISSION PROPOSAL OF 15 DECEMBER 2005 AND AMENDED EP PROPOSAL OF 29 NOVEMBER 2007

7.15 In the course of the reform, the Rome Convention should, according to the model of the Brussels Convention of 1968 becoming Regulation (EC) No 44/2001, be transformed into a Regulation. A step in this direction would undoubtedly allow further integration of Europe even if the different laws were already very much alike; it would automatically include the new Member countries which had acceded to the EU since 2004. By way of a Regulation a majority of the problems arising from the application of the law would be resolved and more legal certainty created, in particular in regard to consumers. Nonetheless, the difficulty would remain as to how to deal with the special provision of Denmark and the possible opt-out of the UK and Ireland. The principle of universal application should be retained. The Commission had published a Green Paper preparing such a proposal in 2002.[41]

On 15 December 2005, the Commission made known its proposal for a "Regulation … on the law applicable to contractual obligations (Rome I)", having

---

39 In support Basedow, in: Schnyder/Heiss/Rudisch (eds.), 11; contrary view, Leible, in: Schulte-Nölke/Schulze (eds.), *Europäische Rechtsangleichung*, 353, 383 ff; Klauer.

40 Europäische Gruppe für IPR, *IPRax* 2001, 64 ff.

41 COM (2002) 654.

held extensive hearings with stakeholders and experts.[42] It was based on the Rome Convention, but included some important innovations which are of importance for consumer contracts. Its legal basis was Article 65/61 EC (now Article 81 TFEU) which meant that Denmark would not participate, while the UK and Ireland could opt in. It would be directly binding upon Member States without the need for specific ratification, as was the case under the Rome Convention.

Article 3(1) of the proposal contained the basic principle of freedom of choice of law. This could be extended to "principles and rules of substantive law of contract recognised internationally or in the Community", such as UNIDROIT or the European principles of contract law:[43] Article 3(2). Article 3(4) continued the well-known rule that mandatory rules cannot be contracted out if all elements of the contract relate to one jurisdiction. Article 3(5) consolidated secondary law concerning choice of the law of a non-Member country: such choice was permitted, but "shall be without prejudice to the application of such mandatory rules of Community law as are applicable to the case". This confirms the *Ingmar* case law cited above (7.12).

Article 5 of the proposal would substantially modify the rules on consumer protection by taking up some of the criticism voiced against the Rome Convention but perhaps going beyond the internal market requirements, as some authors complained.[44] The basic rule would be that within the EU, the consumer contract will be governed by "the law of the Member State in which the consumer has his habitual residence". There would be no more distinction over whether the applicable law is determined by a valid choice of law clause or by objective circumstances under Article 4 (7.13). Such a rule should be welcomed as a clarification and simplification of the existing law, even if it may make it difficult for traders to develop uniform marketing standards in the internal market. Article 5(2) then defined the concept of "consumer contract" which is identical to the one already used by secondary law; it was however not limited to the supply of goods and services, but also included credit contracts, without special reference to instalment transactions. The basic criteria for applying the law of residence of the consumer was the fact that the "contract has been concluded with a person who pursues a trade or profession in the Member State in which the consumer has his habitual residence or, by any means, directs such activities to that Member State or to several Member States including that Member State, and the contract falls within the scope of such activities, unless the professional did not know where the consumer had his habitual residence and this ignorance was not attributable to his negligence". This abandoned the former approach of merely protecting the "passive consumer" (7.11).

---

42 COM (2005) 650 final; MPI comments, *RabelZ* 2007, 225.

43 For a comparison, see Bonell/Peleggi, *Uniform LRev* 2004, 315.

44 Calliess, *ZEuP* 2006, 742, contra Reich, *ZEuP* 2007, 180.

This formula followed Article 15 of the Brussels Regulation 44/2001 (7.39) closely, with one important exception: the professional who did not know or could not have known that the residence of the consumer would not be subject to Article 5; the applicable law would then be determined either by a choice of law clause or by the principle of closest connection, which will usually be the law of the home country of the professional. This new rule was meant to "protect" the seller in distance contracts or e-commerce who has been misled about the consumer's residence. It contradicted to some extent the mandatory character of these rules, but seemed to take up the case law of the Court in *Gruber.*[45]

Article 5(3)contained the well-known exceptions for:

- contracts for the supply of services where the services are to be supplied to the consumer exclusively in a country other than that in which he has his habitual residence, e.g. hotel and accommodation services, study courses, etc.;
- contracts of carriage with the exception of package travel; and
- contracts on immovable property with the exception of time-share.

3. ROME I REGULATION: RELATION TO THE CONVENTION

7.16 After long and controversial debates, the European Parliament adopted a modified proposal for a Rome I Regulation on 29 November 2007.[46] Articles 3 and 5 in the Commission proposal, which met strong opposition from both stakeholders and governments, had been redrafted. The criticism was concerned with a reference to the choice of "soft law" in Article 3 and to the "consumer country principle" in Article 5. The European Parliament went back to a great extent to the formulations in the original Rome Convention, in particular Article 3. Choice of non-state law was excluded, but Recital (13) of the Regulation clarified that the parties are always allowed by a reference in their contract to incorporate a non-state body of laws or an international agreement, but within the limits of the mandatory state law applicable to the contract. The aspects of the choice of law clauses relating to the existence and validity of the parties' consent shall be determined by national law designated by Articles 10, 11 and 13 of the Regulation (Article 3(5)).

The default rules of Article 4 had been extended to cover a catalogue of types of contract; usually the law of the seller or provider of services will apply. A contract to a right *in rem* in immovable property or to a tenancy of immovable property shall be governed by the law of the country where the property is located, with an exception of tenancy of less than six months.

---

45 ECJ, 20 January 2005, C-464/01, *Johann Gruber v BayWa AG* [2005] ECR I-439.

46 A6–0450/2007.

Special rules had been inserted for contracts of carriage (Article 5) and insurance contracts (Article 7). The general norm for consumer contracts will be a new Article 6 which read as follows and became law subsequently:

> "(1) … a contract concluded by a natural person for a purpose which can be regarded as being outside his trade or profession (the consumer), with another person acting in the exercise of his trade of profession (the professional) shall be governed by the law of the country where the consumer has his or her habitual residence provided that the professional:
> (a) pursues his commercial or professional activities in the country where the consumer has his habitual residence, or
> (b) by any means, directs such activities to that country or to several countries including that country,
> and the contract falls within the scope of such activities.
> (2) Notwithstanding this, the parties may choose the law applicable to a contract to which this Article applies, in accordance with Article 3. Such a choice may not, however, have the result of depriving the consumer of the protection afforded to him by provisions that cannot be derogated from by contract by virtue of the law which, in the absence of choice, would have been applicable on the basis of para. 1."

4. REFORMULATION OF CONSUMER CONTRACTS

7.17 After the European Parliament's proposal had been accepted as a compromise by the Council, Rome I was adopted as Regulation (EC) 593/2008 of 17 June 2008.[47] The UK had originally decided not to opt in but did so later. Denmark will continue to be subject to the Rome Convention.

Article 6 on consumer contracts as defined by the European Parliament has universal application, that is it applies whether or not consumers reside in the EU.[48] It had been modified in two important ways that closely follow Article 15 of the Brussels Regulation 44/2001 (7.35–7.39); Recital (7) of the Rome I Regulation requires consistent interpretation:

- it applies now to *any* consumer contract, thus replacing the narrow formulation in Article 5 of the Rome Convention which was limited to the sale of goods and the provision of services and their financing, but not to simple consumer credit; there are exceptions for certain types of financial instruments which need to be governed by "a single law" according to Recital (29) (Article 6(4)(d) and (e)); contracts relating to *rights in rem* including lease and tenancy (Article 6(4)(c)) are also excluded;[49]
- it is sufficient that the "professional" *directs* its marketing activities to the country of the consumer's habitual residence.

---

47 OJ L 177, 4 July 2008, 6.

48 Garcímartin Alférez, I-61 at 71.

49 For details Garcímartin, 72–73.

On the other hand, the balancing test of the Rome Convention in the case of choice of law has been maintained (7.13). The main reason is not to impede the trader from doing cross-border business on the internet and submit him to all the provisions of the consumer's country of residence; this was regarded as an unnecessary impediment to cross-border marketing. This rule applies notwithstanding whether the professional is doing business from "inside" or "outside" the EU since the Regulation enjoys universal application according to Article 2.

The concept of "directing" activities which was left unclear in the Brussels Regulation particularly with regard to e-commerce (*infra* 7.24) was defined in Recital (24) by reference to a joint declaration of the Council and the Commission to the prior Article 15:

> "for Art. 15 (1) to be applicable it is not sufficient for an undertaking to target its activities at the Member State of the consumer's residence, or a number of Member States including that Member State; a contract must also be concluded within the framework of its activities...the mere fact that an Internet site is accessible is not sufficient for Art. 15 to be applicable, although a factor will be that this Internet site solicits the conclusion of a distance contracts and that a contract has actually been concluded at a distance, by whatever means. In this respect, the language or currency which a website uses does not constitute a relevant factor."

Article 9(2) contains the provision on the application of the mandatory provisions of the law of the forum which are now reformulated to "overriding mandatory provisions", thus taking up the case law of the ECJ in *Arblade* (7.12), referring to such provisions which are regarded "as crucial by a country for safeguarding its political, social or economic organisation, to such an extent that they are applicable to any situation falling within their scope, irrespective of the law otherwise applicable to the contract under his Regulation". This is quite a narrow definition which must be interpreted strictly according to Recital (37), thus excluding most consumer protection norms of Member States beyond EU law. Article 9(3) allows the application of "overriding mandatory provisions of the law of the country where the obligations arising out of the contract have to be or have been performed". The application is however not imposed on Member countries, but is only optional.

7.17a The new concept of "directing activities" has been interpreted by the ECJ in its *Pammer* judgment of 7 December 2010:[50]

> "The following matters, the list of which is not exhaustive, are capable of constituting evidence from which it may be concluded that the trader's activity is directed to the

[50] ECJ, 7 December 2010, Joined Cases C-585/08 + C-144/09, *Peter Pammer et al v Reederei Karl Schlüter et al.* [2010] ECR I-12527.

> Member State of the consumer's domicile: the international nature of the activity, mention of itineraries from other Member States for going to the place where the trader is established, use of a language or a currency other than the language or currency generally used in the Member State in which the trader is established with the possibility of making and confirming the reservation in that other language, mention of telephone numbers with an international code, outlay of expenditure on an internet referencing service in order to facilitate access to the trader's site or that of its intermediary by consumers domiciled in other Member States, use of a top-level domain name other than that of the Member State in which the trader is established, and mention of an international clientele composed of customers domiciled in various Member States. It is for the national courts to ascertain whether such evidence exists".

It should be kept in mind that the ECJ only gives examples for defining the *direction* of the marketing activity of the trader; it remains a question of fact how it can be established in a concrete case. This will depend on his business strategy. The most frequent case seems to concern mail-order sales by catalogue. In the past, this was done by distributing a printed catalogue to existing and potential customers on an annual or semi-annual basis, usually including the general contract terms of the trader, containing an order card to be filled out by the consumer and to be sent to the trader who would be free to accept or not accept the order on his terms of contracting. Today's business practice tends to substitute the paper format for an e-catalogue which can be downloaded on the internet and complemented by an electronic order scheme which will usually be communicated to the trader by e-mail. The consumer will have to accept the terms of the trader by clicking on an icon; if he refuses to do so the trader will usually refuse to contract with him. Payment can be made either by credit card, by Paypal or by sending out bills, depending on the marketing strategy of the trader and on the type of customer. Does this practice suffice to make Article 6(1) of Rome I applicable in the interpretation given in *Pammer*?

The mere accessibility of the website of the trader does not suffice; the trader must "have manifested its intention to establish commercial relations with consumers from one or more other Member States, including that of the consumer's domicile, mind(ing) to conclude a contract with those consumers", according to the ECJ (paras 75–76). This must be read as a differentiation of commercial activities according to their territorial scope from the perspective of a potential customer: if they are clearly limited to one Member state, namely the trader's place of residence, then Article 6(1) Rome I – which is worded in a similar way as Article 13 of the Brussels Regulation 44/2001, which was part of the *Pammer* litigation – is not applicable. If the internet presentation by the trader, by an intermediary or by a reference system on a search engine gives the potential consumer the *impression of an international activity* (for example by the use of a language, a choice of languages, or a currency different than that of the trader, the use of international telephone numbers or top-level domains) then the trader must be regarded as *"directing" his activity at the consumer's country* of habitual residence. In the case of sales by an e-catalogue, this depends on the nature of the catalogue itself: is it targeted at a purely national or also at an international (European) consuming public? To put it the other way around: if the trader wants to expand its distance marketing to other EU countries beyond its place of business, he will be regarded as "directing" its activities to potential customers in these countries and will be subject to the provisions of Article 6 Rome I.

The scope of the *Pammer* judgment was clarified in *Mühlleitner*[51] where the Court insisted that Article 15(1)(c) does not require that the contract be concluded at a distance.

Once the trader has "directed" his marketing activity to the consumer's country of habitual residence, the first and all following transactions will come under the scope of Article 6 Rome I. Subsequent sales will therefore not change the regime of applicable law even if done by the initiative of the consumer; they are all based on the original "direction" of the activity of the trader. This will ensure the continuity of the contract regime in the interests of both the trader and the consumer.

7.17b The consequences of the application of the consumer's law of habitual residence under the above mentioned criteria differ according to whether there has been a (valid) choice of law clause or not; Article 6(1) and (2) Rome I basically follow the principles contained in Article 5 of the Rome Convention (7.17). If there has been *no choice of law*, the consumer's home law applies in full. If there has been *a choice of the law* – normally the law of the trader – then the consumer cannot be deprived of the protection of the (mandatory consumer) law provisions (of his home country) according to Article 6(2) Rome I. This requires a comparison between the different levels of protection of the chosen law and the law of the consumer – to some extent a difficult task for the *judex a quo*. In the opinion of this author, an *equivalence test* in an EU-conforming interpretation should be applied, at least in areas which have been harmonised by EU law.[52] There is a presumption that both laws allow an equivalent degree of protection. Such an interpretation would both guarantee a sufficient level of consumer protection, and avoid at the same time unnecessary search costs of the trader to find out exactly what the law of the consumer's home country is.

---

51 ECJ, 6 September 2012, C-190/11, *D. Mühlleitner v A. u. W. Yusufi* [2012] ECR I-nyr; see now ECJ, 17 October 2013, C-218/12, *L. Emrek v V. Sabranovic* [2013] ECR I-nyr rejecting the requirement of a causal relationship between the "directing activity" of the trader and the contract conclusion by the consumer. For a differing view see Magnus, in: Staudinger, Art. 6 Rom I-VO para 120.

52 Reich, *ERCL* 2012, 24 with further references.

5. SPECIAL RULES FOR PERSONAL PASSENGER CONTRACTS

7.18 Carriage of passengers is regulated in a new way by Article 5(2). The passenger need not fulfil the narrow criteria of "consumer" in the sense that the purpose of the contract for carriage is not relevant; this conforms to the proposals to use a broad concept of "user" beyond the concept of "consumer" (1.39). The Regulation allows a limited choice of law of the country where:

- the passenger has his habitual residence;
- the carrier has his habitual residence;
- the carrier has his place of central administration;
- the place of departure is situated;
- the place of destination is situated.

If there is no choice, the law of the passenger's residence will apply where either the place of departure or of destination is situated in this country. If these requirements are not met, the law of the country where the carrier has his habitual residence shall apply. It can be supposed that the carrier, in order to have a uniform regime for its passengers, will always choose the law of their habitual residence or central administration (which can be the law of a country outside the EU). The consumer/passenger may therefore be confronted with a law containing a lower protection than the law of his country of residence.

6. RELATION TO SPECIAL EC/EU INSTRUMENTS

7.19 Article 23 provides for the priority of specific EU instruments if they "lay down conflict-of-law rules relating to contractual obligations". This is particularly important with regard to the existing and continuing special conflict rules in certain directives (7.20), including those said to contain a "country of origin" principle like in e-commerce (7.24). Recital (40) insists that the "application of provisions of the applicable law designated by the rules of this Regulation should not restrict the free movement of goods and services as regulated by Community instruments such as Dir. 2000/31".

IV. PIL IN SECONDARY COMMUNITY/UNION LAW

7.20 In the course of time directives governing contractual relationships have developed alongside the Rome Convention, the former of which claims to take precedence over the Convention. In particular, consumer law-related directives had substantially supplemented the provisions of the Convention.[53] This has continued after the adoption of Regulation 593/2008, as rightly criticised by Garcímartin.[54]

1. SPECIAL PROVISIONS IN THE CONSUMER LAW REGULATIONS

7.21 Contractual provisions in the form of regulations which would take precedence under Article 20 only exist to a minimal extent with the exception of the law governing transport: if there are claims based on transport law for damages suffered because of overbooking, cancellation or long delays, the status of the contract need not be determined; flights departing from or going into a EU Member State are subject to the Council Regulation 261/2004,[55] based on Article 80(2) EC (now Article 91 TFEU). Delays, missed connections and cancellations of railway passengers are covered by Articles 15–18 Regulation 1371/2007.[56]

2. DIRECTIVES

a) *The approach taken in directives*

7.22 Due to the different provisions in the directives and the respective national implementations, the legal situation is comparatively opaque. To date the Community has failed to establish a consistent approach within Directive law.

This lack of transparency mostly results from the fact that not all directives contain conflict of laws provisions. The first consumer directives – Directive 85/577/EEC on door-to-door selling,[57] Directive 87/102/EEC on consumer credit[58] and Directive 90/314/EEC on package holidays[59] – did not contain any

---

53 Martiny, *ZEuP* 2001, 312 with further references.

54 Garcímartin, I-66. Similar Pfeiffer, *EuZW* 2008, 626.

55 Regulation (EC) No 261/2004 of the European Parliament and of the Council of 11 February 2004 establishing common rules on compensation and assistance to passengers in the event of denied boarding and of cancellation or long delay of flights, and repealing Regulation (EEC) No 295/91 [2004] OJ L 4; for its legality, see ECJ, 10 January 2006, C-344/04, *IATA and ELFAA v Department for Transport* [2006] ECR I-403.

56 Regulation (EC) No 1371/2007 of the EP and the Council of 23 October 2007 on rail passengers' rights and obligations, OJ L 315, 3 December 2007, 14.

57 Council Directive 85/577/EEC of 20 December 1985 to protect the consumer in respect of contracts negotiated away from business premises, OJ L 372, 31 December 1985, 31.

58 Council Directive 87/102/EEC of 22 December 1986 on the approximation … concerning consumer credit, OJ L 42, 12 February 1987,48; BGH NJW 2006, 762 rejects an extension of the PIL contained in later directives to consumer credit not covered by Directive 87/102/EEC.

59 Directive 90/314/EEC on package holidays, OJ L 158, 23 June 1990, 59.

such special provisions. It appears that at the time these directives were enacted, the need for regulation of conflicts of laws had not yet been recognised. As regards these directives, the provisions of the Rome Convention would prevail.

Subsequent directives in the field of consumer protection contained conflict of law provisions, namely Directive 93/13/EEC on unfair terms in consumer contracts (3.30), Directive 94/47/EEC on time sharing (in the meantime replaced by Article 16 of Directive 2008/122/EC),[60] Directives 97/7/EC and 2002/65/EC on distance selling (7.1), Directive 99/44/EC on the sale of consumer goods (4.33), and the Consumer Credit Directive (CCD) 2008/48 (5.4). The more recent Consumer Rights Directive (CRD) 2011/83/EU has repealed Directives 85/577/EEC and 97/7/EC and now contains a conflict-of-law provision in Article 25. These directives deal with consumer law. By inserting special conflict of law provisions they aim to protect the consumer against opt-out clauses with regard to third countries.

The wording of the relevant provision, namely Article 6(2) of the Directive on unfair terms in consumer contracts, reads as follows:

> "Member States shall take the measures needed to ensure that the consumer does not lose the protection granted by this directive by virtue of the choice of the law of a non-member country as the law applicable to the contract, if the latter has a close link with the territory of the Member States."

The wording of the conflict of laws provision contained in Article 7(2) of Directive 99/44/EC on the sale of consumer goods diverges slightly from the above wording, but also requires a close link with the territory of one or more Member States. The same is true with regard to Article 22(4) of Directive 2008/48. Article 25 of the CRD has a somewhat different wording:

> "If the law applicable to the contract is the law of a Member State, consumers may not waive the rights conferred on them by the national measures transposing this Directive. Any contractual terms which directly or indirectly waive or restrict the rights resulting from this Directive shall not be binding on the Consumer."

b) *Similarities of the conflict of law provisions as contained in the different directives*

7.23 The directives were similar in that they do not contain their own concrete conflict of laws provision but instead leave it to the Member States to take the "appropriate measures". Article 25 of the recent CRD is somewhat more concrete by applying only when the law of a Member State is applicable under Rome I, not

---

[60] Directive 2008/122/EC of 14 January on the protection of consumers in respect of certain aspects of timeshare, long-term holiday product, resale and exchange, OJ L 35, 3 February 2009, 10.

if the law of a non-EU country applies. The consequences of Article 25(2) and of Article 6(2) of Rome I are to some extent similar.

Unfortunately for the consistency of Union PIL, the special unilateral provisions of directives create a certain tension with the general bilateral conflict rules as contained in the Rome I Regulation; they had been implemented in widely divergent ways in the several Member countries. The legislator of the Rome I Regulation, however, did not seize the opportunity to clarify the confusing state of law by eliminating the special provisions in the directives, but maintained their priority in Article 23 of Regulation 593/2008 according to which:

> "this Regulation shall not prejudice the application of provisions of Community law which, in relation to particular matter, lay down conflict-of-law rules relating to contractual obligations."

Basedow[61] wants to restrict the unilateral approach to "a contract such as a contract for services to be supplied abroad (which) falls outside the substantive scope of Art. 6. Here, the unilateral conflict rule of a directive may indeed provide protection to the consumer".

c) *The special case of e-commerce: a "country-of-origin" principle?*

7.24 Not all directives which are of relevance to the consumer contain special conflict of laws provisions. Directive 2000/31/EC on electronic commerce[62] returns to the initial draft of the Directive without a special conflict of laws provision. It deals with the conclusion of contracts by "information society services" which follow the so-called "country-of-origin principle" in Article 3(1) and (2). Reality though is different. This is due to an inherent contradiction of the Directive: on the one hand, according to its Article 1(4) it does not purport to set new rules on PIL or jurisdiction, and expressly excludes consumer contracts from the "country-of-origin" principle of Article 3. On the other hand, different consumer law standards in the Member countries, e.g. on consumer information, may very well create obstacles to the free circulation of information society services, especially if they go beyond the minimum protection offered by Community directives. This must however be determined on a case-by-case basis. The "country-of-origin" principle is not appropriate for consumer contract matters and should therefore be restricted to rules on marketing and advertising.[63] It remained however an open question whether Recital (40) of

61 Basedow, supra note 1, 370.

62 Directive 2000/31/EC of the European Parliament and of the Council of 8 June 2000 on certain legal aspects of information society services, in particular electronic commerce, in the Internal Market, OJ L 178, 17 July 2000, 1.

63 Reich/Halfmeier, 133; a different view has been taken by Leible, 729.

Regulation 593/2008 in connection with Article 23 would require a different interpretation (*supra* 7.19). In the meantime, the *eDate* judgment of the ECJ[64] rejected its characterisation as a "specific conflict of law rule" (para 63), insisting that it only "precludes… an electronic commerce service provider from being made subject to stricter requirements than those provided for by the substantive law in force in the Member state in which that service provider is established" (para 68).

V. ROME II REGULATION (EC) 864/2007 ON PIL ARISING OUT OF NON-CONTRACTUAL OBLIGATIONS

7.25 International tort law and other obligations arising out of non-contractual relations had not been codified before in any shape or form within the European Union. A political agreement on the need for an EU instrument was reached during the meeting of the European Council in Tampere on 15/16 October 1999. On 22 July 2003, the Commission published a proposal for a Council Regulation on the Law applicable to non-contractual obligations (Rome II).[65] The proposal was based on the provisions of the Amsterdam Treaty concerning judicial cooperation in civil matters, Article 65 EC (now Article 81 TFEU), similar to the Brussels Regulation (EC) No 44/2001. After the debate in the European Parliament which suggested a number of modifications, an amended proposal was published on 21 February 2006.[66] Regulation (EC) No 864/2007 of the EP and the Council on the law applicable to non-contractual obligations (Rome II) was adopted on 11 July 2007 and applied from 11 January 2009.[67]

According to Article 1, the Regulation shall be applicable to non-contractual obligations (e.g. tort, unjust enrichment, *negotiorum gestio*, *culpa in contrahendo*) in civil and commercial matters in situations involving a conflict of laws. The Regulation will be universally applicable and not be limited to situations occurring within the EU. According to Article 3 any law specified by the Regulation shall be applied whether or not it is the law of a Member State. It will also apply to non-contractual obligations that are likely to arise and may give rise to an injunction or a restraining order. Certain areas are excluded, e.g. the most controversial one relating to non-contractual obligations arising out of violations of privacy and rights relating to personality, including defamation (Article 1(2)(g)).

---

64 ECJ, 25 October 2011, Joined Cases C-509/09 + 161/10, *eDate Advertising et al.* [2011] ECR I-10269.

65 COM (2003) 427 final.

66 COM (2006) 83.

67 OJ L 199, 31 July 2007, 40. COM (2006) 83.

1. GENERAL APPLICATION OF THE *LEX LOCI DELICTI*

7.26 The Regulation clearly acknowledges, just like earlier drafts, the *lex loci delicti commissi*. Article 4(1), with some exceptions resulting from the "closer connection principle", rules that, irrespective of where the action giving rise to damages occurred and irrespective of the country in which the indirect consequences of that event arise, the law of the country applies in which the damage arises or is likely to arise (usually the place of residence of the victim). This rather traditional rule might seem relatively surprising having regard to the long debate on alternatives, e.g. the country-of-origin principle. However, as tort law is mostly about compensation, the rule seems to be reasonable since the loss can best be assessed and compensated according to the law of the country where the damage has occurred.

2. THE SPECIAL CASE OF PRODUCT LIABILITY

7.27 Article 5 introduces a provision dealing with product liability, whether emanating under Directive 85/374/EEC or under general principles of tort law. The rules which emanated from a compromise formula are quite difficult to understand and rather contradictory:

- under Article 5(1)(a) the general law is the law of the country in which "the person sustaining the damage had his or her habitual residence when the damage occurred, if the product was marketed in that country";
- if the product was acquired in another country and marketed there, then this will determine the applicable law, Article 5(1)(b);
- finally, the law of the country will be applicable in which the damage occurred if the product was marketed in that country, Article 5(1)(c);
- if the person claimed to be liable could not reasonably foresee the marketing of the product in one of those countries, then "the applicable law shall be that of the country in which the person claimed to be liable is habitually resident";
- Article 5(2) contains a "closer connection rule", e.g. by a prior contract between the parties. This provision which became more complex during the legislative process aims to exclude "forum shopping",[68] unlike environmental liability according to Article 7;
- as a safeguard clause, Article 17 provides that "in assessing the conduct of the person claimed to be liable, account shall be taken, as a matter of fact and insofar as it is appropriate, of the rules on safety and conduct which were in force at the place and time of the event giving rise to the damage". This is a limited reference to the country-of-origin principle, but not as a matter of law but of fact.

---

68 Leible, 727.

As a result of this somewhat complex regulatory scheme, one will have to acknowledge a combination of the *lex loci delicti* rule with the market principle. The victim of an injury caused by a defective product outside a contractual relationship can rely on his "home law" only when the product was marketed there. If the marketing was not foreseeable by the producer or was even prohibited by him in the consumer's country, e.g. use of medicines for testing, not sales purposes, then the law of the producer will apply. Within the EU it must however be respected that the producer may not artificially prevent its product from being sold in another EU country – this would contradict the very heart of free movement of goods. However, if the consumer acquired the defective product in another country where it was marketed, e.g. at an airport, then the law of his country will apply. Finally, if the damage occurred in another country where the product was marketed then this law will be applicable. This relates to cases where the consumer was injured as a mere bystander" without having purchased the product himself.[69]

This scheme does not seem very convincing *vis-à-vis* EU attempts at harmonising product liability law, including the recent ECJ case law on "complete harmonisation" in areas covered by Directive 85/374/EEC (6.30). In these cases it should not make any difference where the product was marketed. The general principle of *lex loci delicti* should be applicable here as foreseen in the original Commission proposal of Regulation 864/2007, e.g. the law of the country where the damage occurred, whether or not this is the place of residence of the consumer (which may be irrelevant to the producer). The place of marketing should not be determined either because of the free flow of goods within the EU – a product once put on the market of the EU can circulate freely in the entire Union; therefore the producer will have to respect the liability regimes in all EC countries as a corollary, and the victim should have a certain choice of jurisdiction and applicable law if there is a close link like domicile or place of injury. This is particularly true for multi-state injuries where some forum shopping should be allowed to the injured person as compensation for the free movement of goods which the producer enjoys under EC law.

3. UNFAIRNESS: THE "MARKET PRINCIPLE" VS. COUNTRY OF ORIGIN

7.28 Claims arising from unfair competition (or other marketing practices harmful to consumers) are assessed under the law of the country where the competitive relations or the collective interests of consumers (Article 6(1)) are, or are likely, to be affected. Rome II codifies the well-established "market rule", e.g. applicability of the law of the market where the competitive relations or collective

69 Leible, 728 prefers the application of the country where the person was injured.

consumer interests are affected. This provision again refers to the place of commission and thus follows Article 4(1). However, it is not always a given that there is congruency. It seems possible that the damage occurs in a country other than the country where the competition has been distorted.

A special rule concerning the country-of-origin principle, e.g. for acts of unfair competition arising out of electronic commerce was originally reserved in Article 3(d) of the first Commission proposal, namely for Community acts to "promote the smooth operation of the internal market, where such rules cannot apply at the same time as the law designated by the rules of private international law". This reference has been omitted in the final text which in Article 27 only provides that "[t]his regulation shall not prejudice the application of provisions of Community law which, in relation to particular matters, lay down conflict-of-law rules relating to non-contractual obligations". It was a debated question how far this relates to E-Commerce Directive 2000/31 (*supra* 7.24), or whether the rules of Regulation 864/2007 will apply in this context; some authors prefer the application of the "country-of-origin" principle,[70] while this author has suggested a more differentiated approach as can be seen with TV advertising.

However, it should always be kept in mind that the law applied under the "market rule" must comply with other substantive EU law provisions, e.g. on the free movement of goods and services, or relating to special rules for certain goods or services. This can be shown with regard to the advertising rules contained in TV Directive 89/552/EEC as amended.[71] The *de Agostini* litigation[72] concerned, amongst other issues, whether the country-of-origin principle applied to the Swedish ban on TV advertising to children against a broadcaster or advertiser established in the UK. The advertising had been presented in the Swedish language to attract Swedish children. The Consumer Ombudsman based the prohibition on the special rules of Swedish TV advertising legislation and on the general clause of the Act against unfair practices. AG Jacobs applied the country-of-origin principle both to the special rules on TV advertising and to the prohibition contained in the general clause. This would have meant that only British authorities are competent to control whether the broadcast violated British rules on children's advertising, and on deceptive advertising, not having regard to the fact that the British authority did not understand Swedish. The Court preferred a more differentiated approach:

---

70 Leible, 729.

71 OJ L 298 of 1989, 23, as amended by Directive 97/36/EC, OJ L 202, 30 July 1997, 60 and Directive 2007/65/EC of 11 December 2007 on audio-visual media services, OJ L 332, 18 December 2007, 27. Now Directive 2010/13/EU of 10 March 2010 on Audiovisual Media Services, OJ L 95, 15 April 2010, 1.

72 ECJ, 9 July 1997, C-34–36/95, *Konsumentombudsmannen v De Agostini Forlag AB and TV Shop i Sverige AB* [1997] ECR I-3843.

- Since the Directive only attempts a partial harmonisation, the country-of-origin principle is limited to the harmonised field. Here, this was TV advertising to children. Swedish authorities are prohibited from applying their (stricter) rules.
- The Directive does not in principle preclude application of national rules with the general aim of consumer protection. However, this is on condition that they do not involve a second control of TV broadcasts in fields already controlled by the country of origin. Therefore, the general ban on misleading and unfair advertising is not caught by the country-of-origin principle, and may be enforced by the Ombudsman according to Swedish legislation and in private litigation by consumer associations under Article 6 of Regulation 864/2007.

A different scenario arose in the *Bacardi* case,[73] which concerned the interdiction of indirect alcohol advertising by the French *loi Envin* arising from the appearance on screen of hoardings during the transmission of bi-national sporting events and its effects on cross-border TV broadcasts. The Court found that indirect advertising is not caught by the country-of-origin principle of Directive 89/522. A possible restriction of cross-border marketing of services is justified by health concerns: "it is for the Member States to decide on the degree of protection which they wish to afford to public health and on the way in which that protection is to be achieved" (para. 33). They must of course observe the principle of proportionality. The applicable market rule would allow the application of stricter French rules to the advertising because it affects the French consumer market.

4. RESTRAINTS OF COMPETITION

7.29 Acts restraining competition in the sense of Recital (23) are judged according to the market affected, or, if more than one market is affected, by the law of the forum if the injured party so chooses, provided that this market is amongst those directly and substantially affected. In the case of multiple claims, the injured party "can only choose to base the claim on the law of the court (seised) if the restriction of competition on which the claim against each of these defendant relies directly and substantially affects also the market in the Member State of that court" (Article 6(3)(b)). This "last minute" amendment aimed to avoid multiple jurisdictions in case of restraints of competition affecting several jurisdictions in the EU. It may also be important for consumer claims arising out of acts restraining competition (8.13).[74]

---

73 ECJ, 13 July 2004, C-429/02, *Bacardi-France v TF1 et al.* [2004] ECR I-6613.

74 Basedow, *supra* note 1, 467 referring to the effects doctrine as a bilateral conflict rule; substantive law issue are discussed by Reich, *CMLRev* 2007, 740. See also Commission

5. OTHER NON-CONTRACTUAL OBLIGATIONS: LIMITED FREEDOM OF CHOICE

7.30 Chapter III of the Regulation deals with "non-contractual obligations arising out of unjust enrichment, *negotiorum gestio*" and also *culpa in contrahendo*. This seems justified within a European framework because of the different definition of this term. The inclusion of *culpa in contrahendo* seems to refer to the case law of the ECJ under the Brussels Convention that puts it under the tort jurisdiction of Article 5(3),[75] but at the same time refers to the law that applies to the contract "or that would have been applicable to it had it been entered into" (Article 12(1)). There are some exceptions where the *lex contractus* cannot be established (Article 12(2)).

Pursuant to Article 14 of the Regulation the parties may agree to submit non-contractual obligations to the law of their choice, either by an agreement entered into after the event giving rise to the damage occurred, or, where all the parties are pursuing a commercial activity, also by an agreement freely negotiated before the event giving rise to the damage occurred. If they are not, such an agreement is only valid if it is entered into after the event giving rise to the damage occurred. This protects consumers against agreements taking away the protection of their *lex loci delicti* before the event has happened.

VI. JURISDICTION IN CROSS-BORDER LITIGATION

1. THE IMPORTANCE OF THE BRUSSELS CONVENTION AND REGULATION

a) *The Brussels Convention of 1968 as amended*

7.31 Judicial protection presumes that a party subject to a dispute should be able to bring legal proceedings in a court of law (or other body responsible for resolving legal disputes), knowing that the decision taken by such a body will be recognised and enforced across the entire European Union. Sometimes this should be done in a State other than that where the claimant is established or domiciled. Therefore questions of jurisdiction, recognition and enforcement of judgments throughout the Community are crucial to ensure effective protection of rights derived from Community law. These also form part of an effective

Proposal of 11 June 2013 for a Directive on certain rules governing actions for damages under national law for infringements of the competition law provisions of the Member States and the EU, COM (2013) 404 final.

75 ECJ, 17 September 2002, C-334/00, *Fonderie Officine Meccaniche Tacconi SpA v Heinrich Wagner Sinto Maschinenfabrik (HWS)* [2002] ECR I-7357.

internal market presupposing a "free flow of judgments", at least in civil and commercial matters.

Within the EU, the above-mentioned questions had been regulated first by the 1968 Brussels Convention on Jurisdiction and the Enforcement of Judgments in Civil and Commercial Matters.[76] The original EEC Treaty was mostly concerned with the establishment of the Common Market and contained virtually nothing about private international law and jurisdiction, except for Article 220 EEC (now repealed by the Lisbon Treaty), which stated that:

> "Member States shall, so far as is necessary, enter into negotiations with each other with a view to securing for the benefit of their nationals ... the simplification of formalities governing the reciprocal recognition and enforcement of judgments of courts or tribunals and of arbitration awards."

The only instrument that could be adopted under these provisions was an international treaty. Therefore, the Brussels Convention was adopted as an international law instrument and ratified by all Member States. As stated previously, the Convention provided a set of uniform and directly applicable rules. These form part of the law of every Member State party to the Convention. The courts of those Member States are under an obligation to apply these rules while considering issues on jurisdiction. Moreover, they should give virtually automatic recognition and enforcement of judgments in civil and commercial matters issued in other States party to the Convention.

7.32 Not only is it the national courts of Member States of the European Union that have applied the Convention on a consistent basis; indeed, the European Court of Justice has also delivered preliminary rulings interpreting the Convention which are still important today. This right was conferred upon the Court by the 1971 Protocol, thus promoting a more uniform application and autonomous interpretation of the Convention throughout Member States. A substantial body of case law exists on the Brussels Convention, from references by the original six Contracting States to the ECJ, and more recently from references from other Contracting States.[77] The Court stressed its interpretative role of the Convention in the *HWS* case:[78]

> "Only such [autonomous] interpretation [of the concepts of contract and tort in Article 5(1) and (3) of the Brussels Convention] is capable of ensuring the uniform

---

[76] 1968 Brussels Convention on jurisdiction and the enforcement of judgments in civil and commercial matters OJ C 27, 27 January 1998, 1 (consolidated version); Protocol on the interpretation of the 1968 Convention by the Court of Justice, OJ C 27, 27 January 1998, 28.

[77] Fawcett/North, *Cheshire and North's Private International Law*, 1999, 184.

[78] ECJ, 17 September 2002, C-334/00, *Fonderie Officine Meccaniche Tacconi SpA/Heinrich Wagner Sinto Maschinenfabrik (HWS)* [2002] ECR I-7357.

application of the Brussels Convention, which is intended in particular to lay down common rules on jurisdiction for the courts of the Contracting States and to strengthen the legal protection of persons established in the Community by enabling the claimant to identify easily the court in which he may sue and the defendant reasonably to foresee in which court he may be sued". (para. 20)

The principal objectives of the Convention may be traced through the substantial ECJ case law interpreting the Convention. These include:

- determination of international jurisdiction of (national) courts in the European Community;[79]
- simplification of formalities governing reciprocal enforcement of judgments;[80]
- procedural provisions for these purposes;[81]
- avoidance of multiplicity of jurisdictions;[82]
- prohibition of the English doctrine of *forum non conveniens* where the case has a closer connection with the courts of a non-Member State, or the practice of issuing anti-suit injunctions" against alleged frivolous litigation in other Member countries;[83]
- the need to strengthen the legal protection of the rights of defendants;[84]
- protection of socially or economically weaker parties.[85]

Finally, the provisions of the Brussels Convention were repeated in the Lugano Convention concluded between the EEC countries and members of the European Free Trade Association. In opinion 1/03[86] the Court was asked by the Council whether the EU had concurrent or exclusive competence to conclude the new Lugano Convention on jurisdiction and recognition and enforcement of judgments. Since the Community had already enacted Regulation 44/2001 (7.34), competence to conclude an international agreement extending its mechanisms to third countries, namely those of the EFTA (Switzerland, Norway and Iceland) had been transferred to the EU alone. This was justified by ensuring the "uniform and consistent application of the Community rules and the proper

79 ECJ, 7 October 1976, C-14/76, *A. De Bloos, SPRL v Société en comandite par actions Boyer* [1976] ECR I-1497.

80 ECJ, 22 February 1979, C-133/78, *Gourdain v Nadler* [1979] ECR I-733 at para 3.

81 ECJ, 7 March 1985, C-48/84, *Spitzley v Sommer Exploitation SA* [1985] ECR I-787 at para 21.

82 C-14/76, *A. De Bloos, supra* note 79.

83 ECJ, 1 March 2005, C-281/02, *Andrew Owusu v N.B.Jackson et al.* [2005] ECR I-1383; ECJ, 27 April 2005, C-159/02, *Gregory Paul Turner v Felix Fareed IsmailGrovit et al.* [2005] ECR I-3565.

84 ECJ, 15 May 1980, C-125/79, *Denilauer v SNC Couchet Frères* [1980] ECR 1553 at para 13.

85 ECJ, 21 June 1978, C-150/77, *Bertrand v Paul Ott KG* [1978] ECR 1431 at para 21; ECJ, 14 July 1983, C-201/82, *Gerling Konzern Speziale Kreditversicherungs-AG v Amministrazione del Tesoro dello Stato* [1983] ECR I-2503 at para 17.

86 ECJ, 7 February 2006, opinion 1/03 [2006] ECR I-1145.

functioning of the system which they establish in order to preserve the full effectiveness of Community law" (paras 128, 133 and 161).

7.33 The well-known international law rule *actor sequitur forum rei* is the general principle of jurisdiction of the Brussels Convention, per Article 2. This means that a person should be sued in the court of the place where he is domiciled. This rule may be derogated from and a person may be sued in the courts of other States that are party to the Convention only by virtue of the rules on "special jurisdiction" stated in the Convention. These rules state that person may also be sued:

- in the courts of the state where the contract obligation was performed (Article 5(1);
- where a harmful event has occurred (in matters related to delict) (Article 5(3)) (*infra* 7.34);
- where a branch or agency is situated (in matters related to operations of a branch, Article 5(5)).

Persons who are not nationals of the state in which they are domiciled shall be governed by the rules of jurisdiction applicable to nationals of that state. In addition, parties to the contract may enter into an agreement on jurisdiction, subject to provisions of Section 6 of the Convention.

The Convention also determined the rules on "exclusive jurisdiction" (Article 16). This, unlike general and special jurisdiction, is linked not to the courts of the state where the party is domiciled but where immovable property is situated, where the company has its seat or where the public register is kept. The courts, which have exclusive jurisdiction under the Convention, cannot be excluded from the proceedings by an agreement on jurisdiction. Article 16(1)(a) does not apply to a club membership contract which, in return for a membership fee which represents the greater part of the total price, allows members to acquire a right to use, on a timeshare basis, immoveable property of a specified type in a specified location and provides for the affiliation of members to a service which enables them to exchange their right of use.[87]

b) Brussels Regulations 44/2001 and 1215/2012

7.34 However, such legislation through an international convention remained the only possible approach to jurisdiction rules in the EU until the Amsterdam Treaty introduced Article 65(b) EC (now Article 81(1) and (2) TFEU with more details), which contained a provision on:

[87] ECJ, 13 October 2005, *B. and M. Klein v Rhodos Management* [2005] ECR I-8667.

> "measures in the field of judicial cooperation in civil matters having cross-border implications, to be taken ... promoting the compatibility of the rules applicable in the Member States concerning the conflict of laws and of jurisdiction."

Hence, the private international law and jurisdiction rules in the European Union were brought within the remit of the First Pillar. This article was used as a basis for adoption of Council Regulation (EC) No 44/2001.[88] The Regulation replaced the Convention as of 1 March 2002 for 14 Member States of the EU. Article 68 of Regulation 44/2001 provides:

> "[The] Regulation shall, as between the Member States, supersede the Brussels Convention. ... In so far as this Regulation replaces the provisions of the Brussels Convention between Member States, any reference to the Convention shall be understood as a reference to this Regulation."

However, the Brussels Convention continued to apply in relations between Denmark and the other Member States that are bound by the Regulation, and to the territories of the Member States that fall within the territorial scope of the Convention and which are excluded from this Regulation pursuant to Article 299 EC.[89] On 10 October 2005, the Community and Denmark signed an agreement concerning the extension of the Brussels Regulation 44/2001 to Denmark. This agreement entered into force on 1 July 2007.[90]

In the meantime, a new Regulation 1215/2012[91] was adopted, applicable to proceedings initiated on or after 10 January 2015 without changing the consumer protection provisions which are of concern in this chapter.

Despite the fact that the Convention ceased to govern relations between most Member States, it will remain important for the purpose of uniform interpretation and application of the Regulation, since "[c]ontinuity between the Brussels Convention and this Regulation should be ensured".[92] The case law of the ECJ interpreting provisions of the Brussels Convention that were transferred unchanged into the Regulation should remain a valid source for interpreting the provisions of the Regulation. For this reason, the existing case law of the ECJ,[93]

---

88 Council Regulation (EC) No 44/2001 of 22 December 2000 on jurisdiction and the recognition and enforcement of judgments in civil and commercial matters OJ L 12, 17 January 2001, 1.

89 Recitals (21) and (22) of the Regulation.

90 Council Decision 2006/325/EC, OJ L 120, 2006, 22.

91 Regulation (EU) No 1215/2012 of the EP and of the Council of 12 December 2012 on jurisdiction and recognition and enforcement of judgments in civil and commercial matters (recast), [2012] OJ L 351/1.

92 Recital (19) of Regulation 44/2001.

93 For an example cf. ECJ, 1 October 2002, C-167/00, *Verein für Konsumenteninformation v Karl Heinz Henkel* [2002] ECR I-8111 concerning the question on whether Article 5(3) is also applicable to injunctions to prevent an illegal act, which the ECJ answered in the affirmative by referring to the amended text in Article 5(3) of Regulation 44/2001.

as well as the Official Reports on the Convention,[94] have retained their importance and will be cited here.

2. JURISDICTION OVER CONSUMER CONTRACTS UNDER THE CONVENTION/REGULATION

7.35 The Brussels Convention had a special section entitled "Jurisdiction over consumer contracts" in Articles 13–14. Similar articles can be found in the Lugano Convention. This has been superseded by Articles 15–16 of Regulation 44/2001, now Articles 17–18 Regulation 1215/2012. Jurisdiction clauses in cross-border litigation within the EC in consumer contracts were regulated in Article 15 of the Convention, superseded by an identical Article 17 of the Regulation 44/2001 and Article 19 of Regulation 1215/2012 (7.40) which should be extended to arbitration clauses (7.41).

Article 13 provided:

> "In proceedings concerning a contract concluded by a person for a purpose which can be regarded as being outside his trade or profession, hereinafter called "the consumer", jurisdiction shall be determined by this Section, without prejudice to the provisions of point 5 of Articles 4 and 5, if it is:
> (1) a contract for the sale of goods on instalment credit terms; or
> (2) a contract for a loan repayable by instalments, or for any other form of credit, made to finance the sale of goods; or
> (3) any other contract for the supply of goods or a contract for the supply of services, and
>   (a) in the State of the consumer's domicile the conclusion of the contract was preceded by a specific invitation addressed to him or by advertising and
>   (b) the consumer took in that State the steps necessary for the conclusion of the contract.
>
> Where a consumer enters into a contract with a party who is not domiciled in a Contracting State but has a branch, agency or other establishment in one of the Contracting States, that party shall, in disputes arising out of the operations of the branch, agency or establishment, be deemed to be domiciled in that State.
> This section shall not apply to contracts of transport."

The first paragraph of Article 14 of the Brussels Convention provided:

> "A consumer may bring proceedings against the other party to a contract either in the courts of the Contracting State in which that party is domiciled or in the courts of the Contracting State in which he is himself domiciled.

94 SCHLOSSER Report, OJ C 59, 1979; JENARD Report OJ C 59, 1979; EVRIGENIS AND KERAMEUS Report, OJ C 298, 1986; ALMEIDA CRUZ, DESANES REAL, JENARD Report, OJ C 189, 1990.

> That rule of jurisdiction may be departed from only if there is compliance with the conditions laid down in Article 15 of the Brussels Convention."

The Court has on several occasions had opportunity to interpret the relevant provisions of Articles 13–15. As a starting point, it insisted on an independent yet strict interpretation because of its exceptional character to the normal rules on jurisdiction, especially the *actor sequitur forum rei* principle enshrined in Article 2.[95] This has a number of consequences.

a) *The concept of "consumer" in the Convention and the Regulation*

7.36 The Court[96] has repeatedly held that the special rules introduced by the provisions of Title II, Section 4, of the Brussels Convention – and in a similar sense in Articles 15–17 of the Brussels Regulation 44/2001 – which derogate from the general rule laid down in the first paragraph of Article 2, and from the rules of special jurisdiction for contracts in general enshrined in Article 5(1) of the Convention:

> "serve to ensure adequate protection for the consumer as the party deemed to be economically weaker and less experienced in legal matters than the other, commercial, party to the contract, who must not therefore be discouraged from suing by being compelled to bring his action before the courts in the Contracting State in which the other party to the contract is."

The Court has concluded

> "that those provisions only cover private final consumers, not engaged in trade or professional activities, as the benefit of those provisions must not be extended to persons for whom special protection is not justified … [R]eference must be made to the position of the person concerned in a particular contract, having regard to the nature and aim of that contract and not to the subjective situation of the person concerned, since the same person may be regarded as a consumer in relation to certain supplies and as an economic operator in relation to others. The Court held that only contracts concluded outside and independently of any trade or professional activity or purpose, solely for the purpose of satisfying an individual's own needs in terms of private consumption, are covered by the special rules laid down by the Convention to protect the consumer as the party deemed to be the weaker party. Such protection is unwarranted in the case of contracts for the purpose of a trade or professional activity."

In its *Vapenik* judgment,[97] the ECJ insisted that the provisions of the Brussels Regulation and related instruments like the Regulation (EC) No 805/2004 on

---

95 Since ECJ, 21 June 1978, C-150/77, *Bertrand v Ott* [1978] ECR I-1431.

96 ECJ, 20 January 2005, C-464/01, *Johannes Gruber v BayWa* [2005] ECR I-439 at paras 34–37.

97 ECJ, 5 December 2013, C-508/12, *Vapenik v Thurner* [2013] ECR I-nyr.

uncontested claims[98] apply only where the counterpart of the consumer is a trader, not a consumer in a similar position as the plaintiff. The Court went on to say:

> "That interpretation is supported by the structure and broad logic of the rules of special jurisdiction over consumer contracts laid down in Article 16(1) and (2) of Regulation No 44/2001, which provides that the courts for the place where the consumer is domiciled are to have jurisdiction with respect to actions brought by and against him. It follows that that provision is applicable only to contracts in which there is an imbalance between the contracting parties". (para 34)

This has a number of practical consequences for cross-border litigation:

- only the consumer himself – not his assignee – comes under the protection of Article 13,[99] even if this is a private person or association;
- if the consumer is in the process of starting a business (so called start-up contracts), he will not be protected by Article 13 even if he lacks business experience;[100]
- in cases of a so-called "mixed or double purpose contract" (7.8), the Court held in *Gruber*[101] that "a person who concludes a contract for goods intended for purposes which are in part within and in part outside his trade or profession may not rely on the special rules of jurisdiction laid down in Articles 13 to 15 of the Convention, unless the trade or professional purpose is so limited as to be negligible in the overall context of the supply, the fact that the private element is predominant being irrelevant in that respect";
- if the person who claims to be a consumer behaved in such a way as to give the other party to the contract the legitimate impression that he was acting in a business capacity he will not be protected by Article 13, and is thus able to waive the protection;
- it is not yet clear whether a legal person can also come under the privileged jurisdiction rules of Article 13, but case law from other Community instruments, in particular Directive 93/13/EEC on unfair contract terms (3.14), seems to rule out this possibility.

In the opinion of this author, the approach of the ECJ is rather too narrow. This is particularly so in the case of so-called "mixed contracts" where the Court puts the burden of proof entirely on the (usually weaker) private party alleging to be a consumer and even allows a contracting out of the protection (1.25).[102]

---

98 [2004] OJ L 143/15.
99 ECJ, 19 January 1993, C-89/91, *Shearson Lehmann Hutton* [1993] ECR I-139.
100 ECJ, 3 July 1997, C-269/95, *Benincasa* [1997] ECR I-3767.
101 ECJ, 20 January 2005, C-464/01, *Johann Gruber v BayWa AG* [2005] ECR I-439 at para 54.
102 Reich, *EuZW* 2005 at 244 – critical remarks on the *Gruber* case.

b) *Concept of consumer contract under the Convention*

7.37 Article 13 related to three types of contracts:

- contracts for the sale of goods whereby payment is made in instalments;
- credit contracts made to finance the sale of goods (not services);
- any other contract for the supply of goods or services with a consumer.

The two first points have lost importance in today's marketing practices because they only cover specific forms of credit related to the sale of goods and not a sales contract to be performed after the price is discharged by way of several payments.[103] It was also not applicable to independent credit contracts. A credit contract without a specific purpose can be subsumed under Article 13(3), namely a contract for the supply of a (financial) service (7.9 with regard to the Rome Convention).

The third has gained practical relevance in (unilateral) cross-border prize promises by professional traders. The Court has dealt with such cases in two apparently different situations.

In *Gabriel*,[104] the trader notified the consumer that they would win a prize on the condition that they had ordered goods. Since the consumer would get the prize only when placing an order, the Court was satisfied that a "contract was concluded" in the sense of Article 13(1)(c). In *Engler*,[105] the trader only promised a prize without the requirement of the consumer placing an order. The Court refused to interpret this as the conclusion of a contract, even though it applied Article 5(1) of the Brussels Convention to the case at hand where a broader concept of "contract" is used. The two cases seem to make a distinction which does not conform to marketing practices. The consumer has to react positively in both cases to "win" the prize promised to him (which is usually a gimmick to attract attraction and personal data from the consumer). Whether this depends on the prior sales of goods or not seems to be irrelevant.

c) *Protection of the "passive consumer" only in the Convention*

7.38 Article 13(1)(c) did not cover all consumer contracts, but only those where the conclusion of the contract was "preceded by a specific invitation addressed to him or by advertising". The wording is with some nuances similar to Article 5(2) of the Rome Convention (7.12). The Court did not have a chance to interpret

---

103 See ECJ, 27 April 1999, C-99/96, *Mietz* [1999] ECR I-2277.

104 ECJ, 11 June 2002, C-96/00, *Gabriel* [2002] ECR I-6367.

105 ECJ, 20 January 2005, C-27/02 *Engler* [2005] ECR I-481; a broader view has been taken by AG Trstenjak in her opinion of 11 September 2008 in C-180/06, *Renate Ilsinger v Martin Dreschers*, based on the new formulation in Article 15(1)(c) of Regulation 44/2001, *infra* 7.39.

these characteristics. In *Gruber*, AG Jacobs[106] gave some hints on how to interpret these notions saying that:

> "where in the State of his domicile a consumer receives a specific offer by telephone from a supplier in another State, and subsequently acquires from that supplier the goods or services thus offered, the conclusion of the contract must be regarded as preceded by a specific invitation within the meaning of Article 13 (3) (a) of the Brussels Convention even if the actual terms of the contract are based on a subsequent offer not received in the State of the consumer's."

The difference between advertising and "specific invitation" does not seem to be relevant because both are treated in the same way.

d) *Modifications by Article 15 of the Brussels Regulation 44/2001: the concept of "active trader"*

7.39 Article 15(1)(c) of Regulation (EC) No 44/2001 (Article 17(1)(c) Regulation 1215/2012) replaced the former conditions with the following: the consumer may sue the trader either at his place of domicile or at the business seat if:

> "the contract has been concluded with a person who pursues commercial or professional activities in the Member State of the consumer's domicile or, by any means, directs such activities to that Member State or several States including that Member State."

The new provision is no longer concerned with whether the consumer is active or passive, but with the activity of the trader.[107] This provision has aroused intense debate with regard to e-commerce, since it may be interpreted in such a way that the mere accessibility of the website of a company situated in one Member State by a consumer domiciled in another Member State may give such consumer the right to sue the company in the consumer's domicile – a result which makes marketing in e-commerce subject to different and divergent jurisdictions. Therefore, the ECJ in its *Pammer* judgment (7.17a) distinguishes between the mere accessibility of a website which does not suffice to qualify as "directing activities", and a number of non-exclusive criteria where such a qualification is possible and must be established by the competent national court.[108] The trader may avoid this multiplicity of jurisdictions by making clear his intention to market his product or service only in certain countries to the exclusion of others, or by not making his website available in such a country.

---

106 *Gruber, supra* note 101, opinion of 8 July 2004, para 67.

107 Tenreiro, 1093.

108 For an overview of the earlier debate see Mankowski, in: Wagner/Wedl (eds.), 325; critique Nielsen in: Magnus/Mankowski (eds.), *Brussels Regulation I*, 2007, Article 15 para. 36.

Such a rule on multiplicity of jurisdictions may, on the other hand, encourage the establishment of alternative dispute settlement (ADR) mechanisms which is one of the aims of Directive 2013/11/EU on consumer ADR and Regulation 524/2013 on consumer ODR (8.23a–g).[109]

e) *Jurisdiction clauses*

7.40 Jurisdiction clauses are now regulated in Article 17 of Regulation 44/2001/ Article 19 Regulation 1215/2012. The main objective of this provision is that such clauses in consumer contracts cannot be enforced before the litigation has started. A consumer does not lose his privileged access to courts under Articles 15/16 because of the jurisdiction clause. This is in contrast to the general rule in Article 23 (Article 25 of Regulation 1215/2012) which allows jurisdiction clauses to be enforced if entered into in writing or by electronic means.

f) *Arbitration clauses*

7.41 As a general rule, arbitration is exempt from the applicability of the Brussels Convention respectively Regulation 44/2001: Article 1(2)(d). On the other hand, the effect of jurisdiction clauses in consumer contracts has been severely limited in the Convention respectively Regulation (*supra* 7.40). These principles should be applied *per analogiam* to arbitration clauses which may have a similar effect on the consumer's right to have his case heard in his home jurisdiction if the conditions of Article 15 of the Convention or Article 17 of Regulation 44/2001 are met. There is indeed no reason to argue against such analogy because for the consumer it does not make any difference whether the denial of his home jurisdiction before litigation is effected through a jurisdiction or an arbitration clause.[110] The exemption of arbitration from the scope of application of the Brussels instruments aims to privilege commercial arbitration, but not deprive the consumer of his right to a defence and a fair hearing. This has three legal consequences:

- Cross-border arbitration clauses within the sphere of application of Regulation 44/2001 should be treated in analogy to jurisdiction clauses according to Articles 17/23, but the case law of the ECJ is still lacking. This means that an arbitration clause cannot force the consumer, who has been subjected to business activity by the trader pursuant to Article 15(1)(c), to go to arbitration outside his country of domicile unless the clause has been concluded after the litigation arose.
- Cross-border arbitration clauses outside the scope of application of Regulation 44/2001 follow general conflict rules. Under the Rome I

---

109 For the earlier debate see VASSILEVA, 129.

110 REICH, *ERCL* 2007, 45.

Regulation 593/2008 this will be Article 11 concerning form[111] and Articles 3 and 6 regarding substance. Choice of arbitration clauses are therefore possible, but must respect the (more favourable) protection provisions of the country of habitual residence of the consumer in the sense of Article 6(2). Their validity will depend on the law applicable to an arbitration clause, which differs between Member States.[112]

- Arbitration clauses in a national context, even if not coming under the Convention respectively Regulation, should be treated as unfair under Annex 1(q) of Directive 93/13/EEC; the enforcement of arbitration awards against consumers should be subject to the *ordre public* proviso, as defined by the ECJ in its seminal *Claro* case[113] (8.25).

The Directive on Consumer ADR 2013/11/EU (8.18) has modified the law of consumer arbitration and will be discussed in this context (8.23c–e). It is not limited to cross-border claims.

3. ACTIONS IN TORT/QUASI-DELICT

7.42 Article 5(3) contains a specific provision "in matters relating to tort, delict or quasi-delict", where "the courts for the place where the harmful event occurred" have jurisdiction, parallel to the courts at the domicile or business seat of the defendant under Article 2. The concepts of "tort, delict or quasi-delict" have to be interpreted autonomously by Union law. They include all actions which seek to establish the liability of a defendant and which are not related to a contract in the sense of Article 5(1) like *culpa in contrahendo*.[114] This is the case for instance with:

- the French *action directe* which extends contractual liability for defective products to third parties in the line of distribution;[115]
- however, mere consequential damages arising out of a tort towards another person are not covered by Article 5(3).[116] In the *Kronhofer* case[117] the Court insisted on a narrow interpretation of Article 5(3) as an exception to the general rule of Article 2 Brussels Convention. In tort actions regarding the

111 For German law, see BGH NJW 2005, 3499.
112 Reich, *ERCL* 2007, 44–48.
113 ECJ, 26 October 2006, C-168/05, *Claro* [2006] ECR I-10421; see also ECJ, 6 October 2009, C-40/08, *Asturcom v Christina Rodrigues Nogueria* [2009] ECR I-9579.
114 ECJ, 27 September 1988, 189/87, *Kalfelis* [1988] ECR 5565 at para 16; ECJ, 17 September 2002, C-334/00, *Fonderie Officine Meccaniche Tacconi SpA/Heinrich Wagner Sinto Maschinenfabrik (HWS)* [2002] ECR I-7357.
115 ECJ, 17 June 1992, C-26/91, *Handte* [1992] ECR I-3967.
116 ECJ, 11 January 1990, C-220/88, *Dumez-France v Helaba* [1990] ECR I-49.
117 ECJ, 10 June 2004, C-168/02, *Rudolf Kronhofer v Marianne Maier et al.* [2004] ECR I-6009.

marketing of financial services, the mere fact that the claimant had its business seat or assets in one Member State is not sufficient to constitute the "place where the harmful event occurred".

In a product liability case, the words "place where the harmful event occurred" designate the place where the initial damage occurred as a result of the normal use of the product for the purpose for which it was intended.[118]

Under Article 5(3), the plaintiff is allowed to profit from *forum shopping*, namely to commence the action:

- in the country of the domicile of the defendant; or
- in the country where the harmful event occurred, that is where the legally protected interests (life, limb and property) have been injured, usually the domicile of the plaintiff.

Forum shopping, which the ECJ allowed for cross-border environmental and product liability in the *Mines de Potasse* case,[119] is particularly important where access to justice and applicable law differ between Member countries. It puts the producer at particular risk in the case of multi-state product-related risks. However, Article 5(3) of Regulation 44/2001 has maintained the existing state of the law and extended it to preventive injunctions (8.40).

VII. SPECIFIC UNION PROCEDURES ALSO INVOLVING CONSUMERS

1. ORDER FOR PAYMENT PROCEDURE

7.43 The European Parliament and Council have, after a modified proposal of the Commission, adopted Regulation (EC) No 1896/2006 of 12 December 2006 creating a European order for payment procedure.[120] The purpose of this instrument is to simplify and speed up litigation concerning uncontested claims in cross-border cases and to reduce costs by establishing a European order for payment, not necessarily a small claims procedure (7.44). According to Recital (12), Member States should "take due account of need to ensure access to justice". Recital (6) describes the objective of the Regulation with the following words, thus excluding consumer policy aspects:

---

118 ECJ, 16 July 2009, C-189/08, *Zuid Chemie v Phillippos Mineralenfabriek* [2009] ECR I- 6917 at para 32.

119 ECJ, 30 November 1976, 21/76, *Mines de Potasse* [1976] ECR I-1735.

120 OJ L 399, 30 December 2006, 1; for the Common Position of the Council of 30 June, see Doc. No 7535/06, adopted by the Commission, COM (2006) 374.

> "The swift and efficient recovery of outstanding debts over which no legal controversy exists is of paramount importance for economic operators in the EU, as late payments constitute a major reason for insolvency threatening the survival of businesses, particularly small and medium sized enterprises, and resulting in numerous job losses."

This Regulation, which entered into force on 12 December 2008 for all EU Member countries with the exception of Denmark, applies to civil and commercial matters in cross-border cases, whatever the nature of the court or tribunal. Litigation on revenue, customs or administrative matters or the liability of the State for acts and omissions in the exercise of state authority (*acta iure imperii*) is excluded from the scope of application. A claimant will commence the European payment order procedure by completing a claim form set out in the Annex to the text and lodging it at the competent court or tribunal directly, by post or by any other means of communication such as fax or e-mail acceptable to the Member State in which the procedure is commenced. The claim form will include a description of evidence supporting the claim and be accompanied, where appropriate, by any relevant supporting documents.

The competence for the procedure is determined by reference to the rules of Regulation 44/2001. This means that the court of domicile of the defendant is usually competent, unless the specific provisions of Article 5 are applicable. According to Article 6(2) an order against the consumer can only be sought in the court where the consumer is domiciled. However, once a national authority has issued a payment order in a simplified procedure, any opposition concerning competence must be lodged in the country where the procedure was commenced. Once the order has become enforceable in the Member State of origin, according to Article 19 it also becomes enforceable in the other Member States without the need for a declaration of enforceability and without "any possibility of opposing its recognition". In "normal cases" the consumer should be sufficiently protected by the obligation of the court to examine *ex officio* its jurisdiction under Article 6(2) and thereby exclude inadmissible claims. According to Article 8, this examination can, however, be done via an automated procedure which *de facto* limits the power of the court to exclude inadmissible claims. One may be satisfied with the argument that consumer protection is secured by the possibility of the consumer to oppose the claim in his country of domicile within 30 days after service of the order. Problems may exist with "mobile" consumers domiciled in several countries or in cases of a wrong declaration of domicile by the applicant. The exclusive jurisdiction of the court of the country of origin may substantially diminish the rights of defence of the consumer. This may also be the case if the capacity of the consumer cannot be clearly discovered during the automated procedure, especially where traders do not provide adequate information in this respect; it will greatly vary from Member State to Member State.

It is clear that the European payment order procedure is not intended to particularly protect consumers because it can (and probably will) mostly be used against them. On the other hand, the consumer may have an instrument which enables him to enforce cross-border claims without involving substantial litigation costs,[121] a problem which exists under the existing Brussels regime.[122]

2. SMALL CLAIMS PROCEDURE

7.44 Another project in the legislative process more or less followed the logic of Directive 2002/8/EC on legal aid (8.16)[123] – that is, it is based on Article 65 EC, applied to civil and commercial matters in cross-border cases, and is concerned with a small claims procedure.[124] In the meantime, a specific cross-border small claims procedure has been established via the new Regulation 861/2007 and was applicable from 1 January 2009.[125] According to Recital (7), the Regulation aims "to facilitate access to justice". The procedure is determined by the principles of "simplicity, speed and proportionality" – principles put forward in the detailed rules of the Regulation. It is meant to be a written procedure to be completed in a short time (Recital (14)). The procedure is not particularly targeted at consumer claims, but will certainly be used either by consumers as creditors or against consumers as defendants; the later case should be relatively rare because of today's business practice of requiring the consumer to pay in advance by credit card or some other payment instrument. It is available for cross-border cases where the value of a claim does not exceed €2,000. It is available only in civil and commercial matters with some exceptions listed in Article 2(2), e.g. arbitration, employment law, violations of privacy and personality rights. This implies that most consumer claims – whether active or passive – will be covered by the procedure. However, the exclusion of "arbitration" is not clear: does it mean that an arbitration clause pre-empts access to the small claims procedure and that its validity must be determined by arbitration or must the principles of the *Claro* judgment[126] be applied, requiring the *judex a quo* to examine *ex officio* the validity of the arbitration clause (7.41)? The procedure is started by filling out a form, which is appended to the Regulation, with the court or tribunal with jurisdiction (Article 4(1)). This jurisdiction is determined by the general rules of Regulation 44/2001 (7.31). If a consumer claims in the sense of Article 15, the consumer may bring the claim either in his home jurisdiction or in the jurisdiction of the

121 Hondius, 137.

122 Gessner, in: *Liber amicorum N. Reich*, 163.

123 OJ L 26, 31 January 2003, 41.

124 COM (2005), 87 final, 15 March 2005; see Mankowski, *supra* note 108, 353.

125 Regulation (EC) No 861/2007 of the EP and the Council of 11 July 2007 establishing a European Small Claims Procedure, OJ L 199/1, 31 July 2007; comments by Kramer, 355.

126 ECJ 27 October 2006, case C-168/05, *Claro* [2006] ECR I-10421; Reich, *ERCL* 2007. 41.

defendant. This rule will certainly make it easier for consumers to enforce eventual claims of restitution or compensation against traders who have violated his rights. The Regulation contains detailed rules on procedure, evidence, appeals, costs and enforcement. Future practice will determine the effectiveness of these rules.

VIII. OUTLOOK: "TRANSNATIONAL CONSUMER LAW" AS AN ALTERNATIVE TO CONFLICT RULES?

1. *LEX MERCATORIA ELECTRONICA* AS EMERGING "TRANSNATIONAL LAW"?

7.45 International commercial law has already had to face the challenges of globalisation for many years because trade is by its very nature directed across borders; the emerging *lex mercatoria* has seemingly been an answer to these challenges. The concept of *lex mercatoria* is quite controversial and cannot be discussed here in detail.[127] It relates to a set of norms, practices, and standards in international trade and conflict resolution mechanisms (mostly through arbitration) which have evolved through commercial usage and customs, and have to some extent been "codified" by private international organisations like the International Chamber of Commerce (ICC), international standardising organisations like ISO, international law harmonising institutions like UNIDROIT, and specialised organisations for certain trades or communication systems, in particular the internet, like ICANN.[128] The basis of applicability in commercial contracts is not state law or an international treaty, but usually agreement of the parties which need not be express and formalised, but can be implied. This practice may result in *general principles* which are accepted by the relevant business community as guidelines for their commercial transactions. They will usually be enforced in arbitration; arbitrators will use them in contract interpretation and decision-making unless the arbitration agreement provides for the contrary. Therefore, some authors talk of a "private ordering" in the sense of a law created by the economic agents themselves which results in a "global governance" of self-regulation.[129] Other authors refer to a "global civil society"

---

127 See Berger, *The Creeping Codification of the Lex Mercatoria*, 1999; contributions in: Berger (ed.), *The Practice of Transnational Law*, 2001; Basedow, *supra* note 1, 137, 140.

128 See Teubner, Societal Constitutionalism: Alternatives to State Centred Constitutional Theory?, in: Joerges et al. (eds.), *Transnational Governance and Constitutionalism*, 2004, 18; somewhat more critical v. Bernstorff, The Structural Limitations of Network Governance: ICANN as a Case in Point, ibid at 257. This is not the place to discuss these concepts.

129 See Calliess, *Grenzüberscheitende Verbraucherverträge*, 196.

which emerges as a "law creating instance" via a "creeping codification of transnational law".[130]

These concepts seem, however, to be somewhat exaggerated and misleading because, in the end, the basis of their applicability to international commercial transactions is the free will of the parties. The parties can always opt out of these "standards", "principles", etc., although there may be no incentives to do so or transaction cost economics will force the parties to subscribe to these standards. It may also be imputed that, if the parties do not come to an agreement on applicable law or if there are doubts as to interpretation, the *lex mercatoria*, like the UNIDROIT principles, will be applicable as "general principles", commercial practice or custom, in particular in commercial arbitration.[131]

7.46 Can these concepts of *lex mercatoria*, of "private ordering of markets", and of "global governance via self-regulation" be transferred to consumer law? This is indeed the thesis of the German author Calliess, who proposes them as an alternative to the erosion of national (and EU) consumer law in a globalised context. He mentions a number of initiatives and mechanisms which seem to confirm his theory:

> "By establishing a global civil constitution for a transnational consumer contract law, reflexive institutions must be created which organise the phenomena of self-regulation and of private ordering in such a way, that on the one hand they promote effective legal protection via alternative consumer protection mechanisms, and on the other guarantee fairness and justice of such procedures via-à-vis the consumer."[132]

This radical separation of (transnational) consumer law from the state (or the EU) – and as a consequence from the existing state-controlled mechanisms of consumer protection – provokes criticism because of the central weakness of such a concept, namely that no representative consumer association exists worldwide which could promote, or at least monitor and support, these standards in some sort of collective consumer interest. Neither state power nor collective action by social partners can guarantee the promises which Calliess sets out.[133] There is no consumer consensus to accept standards unilaterally imposed by the international "business" or "e-commerce" community. Although a "global civil society" may exist on the business side of things via the internet (even though this seems quite doubtful due to conflicting interests as

130 Berger, in: Berger (ed.), *The Practice of Transnational Law*, 2001, 12–19.

131 For the UNIDROIT principles see Bonell, in: Berger (ed.), *The Practice of Transnational Law*, 2001, 28–36.

132 Calliess, 340; author's own translation.

133 See Schiek, *ELRev* 2007, 443 concerning the need for (collective) autonomy to justify private rulemaking in the EU context; this also applies to international law.

v. Bernstorff has shown with regard to ICANN),[134] it certainly is not true with regard to highly fragmented consumer markets.

In his search for an alternative of the traditional state-oriented consumer law, Calliess would be satisfied if the soft-law mechanisms of "transnational consumer law" at least manage to provide what he calls "rough justice"[135] – probably meaning lower standards of protection than already guaranteed within existing consumer law. This must be achieved through different ADR mechanisms (see 8.17–8.23e), including possibly consumer arbitration (7.41). What are the standards by which these mechanisms are supposed to function? What about the third-party effects of these "private orderings" *vis-à-vis* consumers (as individuals or as a group) which must be legitimised either by democratic processes or by agreement of those concerned? Is there an international consensus on certain minimal standards for consumer protection? How far is the principle of freedom of contract, which is indeed a basic rule of international commercial transactions, extended to consumer transactions, which are, as we have seen, excluded both from the "hard law" of the CISG and the "soft law" of the UNIDROIT principles? What about the effects on competition, which according to the ECJ belongs to the *ordre public* rejecting recognition of foreign judgments or arbitration awards in violation of EC competition law?[136]

"Rough justice" in the sense intended by Calliess certainly means "rough justice" – only a vague guarantee of certain consumer expectations which can hardly be called "rights" and which can usually be "enforced" only via private arbitration that is not subject to any public control or transparency, and without clear rules on the applicable law. The concept of "transnational law" remains unclear. It is already doubtful whether it can really be called "law" at all, since law requires either some state monitoring or a minimum consensus between the parties – two elements clearly set out in Article 1134 of the French Code Civil, whereby "*les conventions légalement formées tiennent lieu de loi à ceux qui les ont faites*".

Calliess defends his concept with the following words:

> "Transnational law describes a third category of autonomous legal systems beyond the traditional categories of national or international law. Transnational law is created and developed by the legal creative acts (*Rechtsschöpfungskräfte*) of a global civil society. (1) It is based (a) on general principles of law and (b) on their condensation and confirmation in civil society practice and custom. (2) Its application, interpretation and development are regularly *conferred* [emphasis added] to private providers of dispute resolution mechanisms. (3) Its mandatory character is based on legally

134 *Supra* note 128, 274–281.

135 Calliess, 351.

136 ECJ, 1 June 1999, C-126/97, *Eco Swiss China Time Ltd v Benetton International NV* [1999] ECR I-3055.

> (*rechtsförmig*) organised orders and enactment of social-economic sanctions. (4) A codification of transnational law – if at all – occurs in the form of general catalogues of principles and rules, standardised contract forms and codes of conduct which are established by private standard setting institutions (*Normierungsinstitutionen*)."[137]

This definition may be true for classical *lex mercatoria* but always requires some express or tacit act of agreement between the parties for *lex mercatoria* to be applicable in their relations if there has been no constitutionally delegated power behind its enactment. It cannot be used against third parties like consumers who have not participated in the elaboration of this "transnational law", either personally or via their representatives. We are not arguing that law always requires state enactment, but if this is not the case, there must at least be some other mechanisms substituting the decision of the legislator – this can only be party autonomy of those concerned, whether individual or collective. Even the argument of Calliess set out above requires some sort of "conferral" of power to (binding) dispute resolution mechanisms, but it does not tell us who can validly effect this transferral to the detriment of state or other legitimate mechanisms. The idea of an "international civil society" is too vague and to abstract to have this power of conferral. Therefore, the concept of "transnational law" cannot easily be transferred to consumer transactions even in a globalised setting without the involvement state, because of the lack of equality of the parties and the limited freedom of choice of consumers themselves.

In a more recent paper,[138] Calliess seems to limit his approach to e-commerce in B2C transactions that are done mostly cross-border and are not limited to the EU. "Private ordering" is not so much done via law – whether substantive or international private law, as described in this book – but by other mechanisms like "online reputation", "trustmarks and codes of conduct", online ADR, and credit security via charge back systems. Calliess believes in the rational self-interest of business to accept and impose such "soft law" standards in consumer transactions done via e-commerce B2C. He writes:

> "Thus, private ordering has proven to be a valuable alternative to state law not only in the apolitical domain of merchant law, but might as well contribute to the solution of regulatory problems in the area of consumer law, where the protection of weaker parties is at stake."[139]

At the same time he points to the "need for transparency with regard to the offered level of protection as well as the effectiveness and fairness of such regimes. In other words, there is a need for substantive as well as procedural

137 Calliess, 371; author's own translation.
138 Calliess/Zumbansen, 153.
139 Ibid, 179.

minimum standards regarding the private provision of consumer-protecting services, ie 'law-consumer protection'". Who could not agree more with him?

It is interesting to see that the so-called institutions of an international "civil society" upon which Calliess relies for his concept of "transnational law" refer themselves to mandatory standards which are set by state (or international,[140] namely supranational) law. It seems that the international "civil society" (which is, in my opinion, a fiction anyhow) cannot exist without the state, as will be shown in the following section.

2. THE EVOLUTION OF "SOFT LAW" STANDARDS: AN ALTERNATIVE TO "HARD" LAW CONCERNING CROSS-BORDER TRANSACTIONS?

7.47 It is perhaps useful to take a look at some of these "soft law" standards which have been developed by (mostly American) providers of internet services, since they are the main players on the global market for e-commerce. The surprising point of all these systems seems to be that they offer the consumer certain mechanisms to guarantee satisfaction and to resolve disputes, but that they do not completely do away with traditional, state bound consumer law and protection. Take the following examples documented by Calliess in his 2006 study and somewhat critically evaluated in the later 2010 publication[141]:

- Better Business Bureau*OnLine* "Code of Online Business Practice":[142] this contains five principles, including consumer satisfaction. It recommends informal dispute settlement mechanisms, including non-binding or conditionally binding arbitration (under which the decision is binding on the company if the consumer elects to accept the decision, thereby making it binding on the consumer as well), without pre-empting further governmental actions in this field; the critical point for arbitration is obviously the "election by the consumer" – can it be done in general contract terms communicated electronically to the consumer? This question is not answered by Calliess.
- Agreement between Consumers International and the Global Business Dialogue on Electronic Commerce – Alternative Dispute Resolution Guidelines:[143] ADR mechanisms are greatly encouraged; dispute resolution may be based on equity or codes of conduct. Binding arbitration before the dispute is to be avoided "where such commitment would have the effect of

140 The need for mandatory international standards has been emphasised by the International Council of Human Rights, *Beyond Voluntarism*, 2002; see also Micheletti/Follesdal, *JCP* 2007, 167.

141 Calliess, *supra* at note 129 pp. 169.

142 Ibid, at 422.

143 Ibid, at 439.

depriving the consumer of the right to bring an action before the courts." Development of ADR is left to governments. The guidelines contain a plea for deregulation of formal requirements for ADR and for a clarification of rules on jurisdiction and applicable law to be dealt with in "a manner that encourages both business investment and consumer trust in electronic commerce".

- American Bar Association (Task Force) Recommendation on Best Practices for Online Dispute Resolution Service (ODR) Providers:[144] this clearly states that ODR providers "should disclose the jurisdiction where complaints against the ODR provider can be brought, and any relevant jurisdictional limitations."
- ICC "Resolving disputes online" – Best practices for ODR in B2C and C2C transactions:[145] they insist that "companies should not obligate consumers to agree to use binding dispute resolution processes prior to the materialisation of a dispute".

The examples show that a concept of "transnational consumer law" based on self- or co-regulation by "civil society" does not conform to reality. Therefore, the main argument against such *lex mercatoria electronica* is still the binding force of state consumer law and consumer protection mechanisms which are part of the constitutional heritage of Member states and the Union under Article 6(3) TEU, Article 6 ECHR, Article 47 of the EU Charter of Fundamental Rights, and Article 19(1)(2) TEU, as recognised by Calliess himself.[146] Traders may of course make consumer satisfaction and dispute resolution easier by encouraging ADR mechanisms, a policy explicitly supported by EU initiatives. Consumers should be allowed easy access to ADR mechanisms provided they are fair and transparent as proposed in EU Recommendations 98/257/EC and 2001/310/EC (8.22) and now by Directive 2013/11/EU and Regulation (EU) 524/2012 (8.23a–g). But the final arbiter in a consumer dispute – even under transnational conditions – that cannot be resolved by ADR should always be a court of law. The consumer should not be barred from eventual access to courts of law even if this happens rarely. This insistence on legal proceedings as a final "protective net" for consumers may create obstacles and difficulties to e-commerce in a globalised "virtual" marketplace; it may also be difficult and ultimately impossible to enforce. But this is not an argument against national or EU consumer law, and it is anyhow the price to be paid for such globalisation allowing greater access for traders to world markets that does not automatically tear down legal barriers.

---

144 Ibid, at 448.

145 Ibid, at 458.

146 See now CALLIESS, *supra* note 129, 174; now REICH, *General Principles of EU Civil Law*, paras 4.3–4.10.

CHAPTER 8

LEGAL PROTECTION OF INDIVIDUAL AND COLLECTIVE CONSUMER INTERESTS

Norbert Reich

CONTENTS

Bibliography:

A. Albors-Llorens, Consumer Law, Competition Law, and the Europeanisation of Private Law, in: Cafaggi (ed.), *The Institutional Framework of European Private Law*, 2006, 245; R. Alderman, Consumer Arbitration: The Destruction of the Common Law, *Journal of American Arbitration* 2002, 1; R. Alderman, The Future of Consumer Law, in: the US. Univ. of Houston Public Law and Legal Theory Series 2008-A-09; C. Barnard, The Service Directive 2006/123/EC, *CMLRev* 2008, 323; J. Basedow et al., *Die Bündelung gleichgerichteter Interessen im Prozess – Verbandsklage und Gruppenklage*, 1999; J. Basedow (ed.), *Private Enforcement of EC Competition Law*, 2007, 2011; H. Beuchler, *Class Actions and Securities Class Actions in the USA*, 2008; G.-P. Calliess, *Grenzüberschreitende Verbraucherverträge*, 2006; F. Cafaggi/H.-W. Micklitz (eds.), *New Frontiers of Consumer Protections*, 2009; R. Caranta, Judicial Protection against Member States: A New Ius Commune takes Shape, *CMLRev* 1995, 703; V. Christianos, La recevabilité des actions de groupe devant la Cour de Justice des CE, in: Bourgoignie (ed.), *Group actions and consumer protection*, 1992, 217; P. Craig/G. de Burca, *EU Law*, 5th ed. 2012;

T. Eilmannsberger, The Green Paper on Damages Actions for Breach of the EC Antitrust Rules and Beyond: Reflections on the Utility and Feasibility of Stimulating Private Enforcement Through Legislative Action, *CMLRev* 2007, 431; W. van Gerven, Of Rights, Remedies and Procedures, *CMLRev* 2000, 501; W. van Gerven, Bridging the Gap between Community and National Laws: Towards a Principle of Homogeneity in the Field of Legal Remedies?, *CMLRev* 1995, 679; A. Hartkamp, *European Law and National Private Law*, 2012; C. Hodges et al., *Consumer ADR in Europe*, 2012 (review Reich, *CMLRev* 2013, 913); G. Howells/H.-W. Micklitz/T. Wilhelmsson, *European Fair Trading Law*, 2006; G. Howells/T. Wilhelmsson, *EC Consumer Law*, 1997; F.G. Jacobs, Remedies in National Courts for the Enforcement of Community Rights, in: *Liber Amicorum for Don Manuel Diez de Velasco*, 1993, 969; S.E. Keske, *Group Litigation in European Competition Law – A Law and Economics Perspective*, 2010; H. Koch, Die Verbandsklage in Europa, *ZZP* 2000, 413; H. Koch, *Verbraucherprozessrecht*, 1990; P. Komninos, New prospects for private enforcement of EC competition law: Courage v Crehan and the Community right to damages, *CMLRev* 2002, 447; L. Krämer/H.-W. Micklitz/K. Tonner (eds.), Law and Diffuse Interests in the European Legal Order – Recht und diffuse Interessen in der Europäischen Rechtsordnung, in: *Liber amicorum Norbert Reich*, 1997; C. Liebscher, Comment to Claro, *CMLRev* 2008, 545; J. Lindholm, *State Procedure and Unions Rights*, 2007; H.-W. Micklitz, *Internationales Produktsicherheitsrecht*, 1995; C. Meller-Hannich/A. Höland/E. Krausbeck, "ADR" und "ODR": Kreationen der europaïschen Rechtspolitik. Eine kritische Würdigung, *ZEuP* 2014, 8; H.-W. Micklitz, The Maastricht Treaty, the Principle of Subsidiarity and the Theory of Integration, *Lakimies* 1994, 508; H.-W. Micklitz/N. Reich (eds.), *Public Interest Litigation before European Courts*, 1996; H.-W. Micklitz/N. Reich/S. Weatherill, EU Treaty Revision and Consumer Protection, *JCP* 2004, 367; H.-W. Micklitz/A. Stadler, *Das Verbandsklagerecht in der Informations- und Dienstleistungsgesellschaft*, 2005; H.-W. Micklitz/A. Stadler, The Development of Collective Legal Actions in Europe, Especially in German Civil Procedure, *EBLRev* 2006, 1473; N. Reich, The Courage-doctrine: encouraging or discouraging compensation for antitrust injuries?, *CMLRev* 2005, 35; N. Reich, Horizontal liability in EC law: "Hybridisation" of remedies for compensation in case of breaches of EC rights, *CMLRev* 2007, 705; N. Reich, Individueller und kollektiver Rechtsschutz im EU-Verbraucherrecht – Von der "Nationalisierung" zur "Konstitutionalisierung" von Rechtsbehelfen, in: *Schriftenreihe der Juristischen Studiengesellschaft Hannover* Vol. 51, 2012; N. Reich, The interrelation between rights and duties in EU Law: Reflections on the state of liability law in the multilevel governance system of the Union – Is there a need for a more coherent approach in European private law?, in: *Oxford Yearbook of European Law (YEL)*, 2010, 112; N. Reich, *General Principles of EU Civil Law*, 2013; N. Reich, *Bürgerrechte in der Europäischen Union*, 1999; N. Reich, "Federalism" and effective legal protection, in: Liber amicorum Brüggemeier, 2009; N. Reich, AGM-COS.MET or: who is protected by EC safety regulation?, *ELRev* 2008, 85; H. Rösler, Auslegungsrobleme des Europäischen Verbraucherprivatrechts in Theorie und Praxis, *RabelsZ* 2007, 495; H. Rösler, *Europäische Gerichtsbarkeit auf dem Gebiet des Zivilrechts*, 2012; P. Rott, Injunctions for the protection of consumers' interests after the implementation of Directive 98/27/EC into German and English law, *JCP* 2001, 401; P. Rott, Consumers and Services of General Interest: Is EC Consumer Law the Future?, *JCP* 2007, 49–60; P. Rott, Effective

Enforcement and Different Enforcement Cultures in Europe, in: WILHELMSSON/PUNIO/POJOLAINEN, *Private Law and the Many Cultures of Europe*, 2007, 305; P. ROTT, The ECJ's Principle of Effectivness and its Unforseeable Impact on Private Relationships, in: D. LECZYKIEWICZ/S. WEATHERILL (eds.), *The Involvement of EU Law in Private Law Relationships*, 2013, 181; R. SCHULZE (ed.), *Compensation of Private Losses*, 2011; R. SCHULZE, *European Private Law – Current Status and Perspectives*, 2011; V. TRSTENJAK/E. BEYSEN, European Consumer Protection Law: Curia semper dabit remedium?, *CMLRev* 2011, 95; F. SNYDER, The Effectiveness of European Community Laws: Institutions, Processes, Tools and Techniques, *MLR* 1993, 19; J. STUYCK, Comment Courage v Crehan, *ERCL* 2005, 228; J. STUYCK et al., *An analysis and evaluation of alternative means of consumer redress other than redress through ordinary judicial proceedings*, 2007; K. TONNER, ADR in the EU, *New Zealand Business Law Quarterly* 2002, 414; T. TRIDIMAS, Liability for breach of community law: Growing up and mellowing down?, *CMLRev* 2001, 301; T. TRIDIMAS, *The General Principles of EC Law*, 2nd ed. 2006; S. WEATHERILL, *EU Consumer Law and Policy*, 2005, 2nd ed. 2013; T. WILHELMSSON/A. HURRI, *From Dissonance to Sense: Welfare State Expectations, Privatisation and Private Law*, 1999; T. WILHELMSSON/E. PUNIO/A. POHJOLAINEN (eds.), *Private Law and the Many Cultures of Europe*, 2007.

I. EFFECTIVE AND APPROPRIATE LEGAL PROTECTION AS A GENERAL EU LAW PRINCIPLE

8.1 The legal position of the consumer within the Community/Union can be improved if the substantive consumer rights which are embedded in Article 12/169 TFEU, Article 38 EU Charter of Fundamental Rights (*supra* 1.11–1.19) can be effectively enforced. The legal protection of the individual is the responsibility of Member States in order to make rights under Union law directly applicable against the supplier or other undertakings acting in consumer markets. Liability of the Union as per Article 340(2) TFEU has not proved relevant to consumer protection thus far, but may gain in importance with regard to Articles 12 and 169 TFEU (cf. 8.15). Effective individual legal protection, which might enhance the legal position of the individual consumer before national courts and the enforcement of Union consumer rights, constitutes the main focus of this chapter. It will be supplemented by remarks on collective consumer protection by consumer associations (8.26–8.43).

The Community/Union legislator has remained in the background where effective legal protection is concerned. The ECJ represents the key force in developing the principle of effective and equivalent legal protection as a general obligation of Member States under Article 4(3) TFEU (ex-Article 10 EC) not limited to consumer protection, but certainly taking on a special significance here (1.18).

1. OVERVIEW OF THE DEVELOPMENT OF THE CASE LAW

8.2 Even at an early stage the ECJ realised that the institutional and procedural autonomy of Member States is potentially in conflict with the practical effect (*effet utile*) and the effective application of (then) Community law. In order to resolve this "indirect collision" the ECJ developed the principle of *effective legal protection* which is intended to ensure the protection of those individual rights based on directly applicable Community law.[1] From a theoretical point of view this approach is established as per Article 4(3) TEU whereas the ECJ can see its basis in the constitutional traditions of Member States and in Articles 6 and 13 ECHR, and thus proceeds from a general principle of Union law.[2] Uniform enforcement of Union law and effective legal protection of the individual are the crucial principles which Member States are required to ensure within directly effective Union law. Both principles are interrelated but have a separate meaning.

The first cases (in particular *REWE*,[3] and *Simmenthal*)[4] concerned the interpretation of national legal provisions in relation to Community law. Since then the principles of equivalence and effectiveness have become particularly important for almost all national legal provisions in the enforcement of Community/Union law rights, including those relating to consumer protection. These principles are illustrated by the ECJ in *Comet*[5] and *Palmisani*.[6] Later cases like *Factortame*,[7] *Francovich*[8] and *Zuckerfabrik Süderdithmarschen*[9] represent a major turning point in the case law. Not least because, as a result of the obvious *lacunae* in the enforcement of Union law, the ECJ has gradually developed a Union-wide system of legal protection, the potential of which has yet to be exploited by the individual consumer or consumer associations.

---

1 Reich, *General Principles of EU Civil Law*, Chapter 4; Rott, in: Wilhelmsson/Punio/Pojolainen, 305; Lindholm; Craig/de Burca, 305–328; Tridimas, *The General Principles of EC Law*, 418.

2 ECJ, 15 May 1986, 222/84, *Johnston* [1986] ECR 1651, 1682 at para 18; ECJ, 13 March 2007, C-432/05, *Unibet v Justitiekanslern* [2007] ECR I-2271 at para 37.

3 ECJ, 16 December 1976, 33/76, *REWE v Landwirtschaftskammer Saarland* [1976] ECR 1989.

4 ECJ, 9 March 1978, 106/77, *Simmenthal* [1978] ECR 68.

5 ECJ, 16 December 1976, 45/76, *Comet*, [1976] ECR 2043.

6 ECJ, 10 July 1997, C-261/95, *Palminisani* [1997] ECR I-4025.

7 ECJ, 19 June 1990, C-213/89, *Factortame I* [1990] ECR I-2433.

8 ECJ, 19 November 1991, Joined Cases C-6/90 + C-9/90, *Francovich* [1991] ECR I-5358.

9 ECJ, 21 December 1991, Joined Cases C-143/88 + C-92/89, *Zuckerfabrik Süderdithmarschen* [1991] ECR I-415.

2. THE PRINCIPLES OF EQUIVALENCE AND EFFECTIVENESS

8.3 The first judgments on individual legal protection have been characterised by a certain amount of restraint on the part of the ECJ. The main focus was on the effectiveness of Community law and the obligation, as expressed in Article 4(3) TFEU (ex-Article 10 EC), of Member States' loyalty to the Union.

In *REWE*[10] and *Comet*[11] the ECJ recognised the principle of procedural autonomy of Member States, according to which:

> "in application of the principle of cooperation laid down in article 5 of the Treaty (now Article 4 (3) TEU NR), national courts are entrusted with ensuring the legal protection conferred on individuals by the direct effect of the provisions of community law."[12]

The scope of autonomy is nonetheless restricted. The ECJ held that:

> "in the absence of any relevant community rules, it is for the national legal order of each member state to designate the competent courts and to lay down the procedural rules for proceedings designed to ensure the protection of the rights which individuals acquire through the direct effect of community law."

However these provisions must not be:

> "less favourable than those governing the same right of action on an internal matter. The position would be different only if those rules and time limits made it impossible in practice to exercise rights which the national courts have a duty to protect."[13]

While in *Comet* the principle of effectiveness was the major focus, in *Palmisani*[14] the ECJ dealt extensively with the principle of *equivalence*. In *Comet* the ECJ held that preclusive periods must not render the bringing of an action under Community law "practically impossible".[15] In *Palmisani* the ECJ stated that the substantive and formal requirements must not be less advantageous than for similar claims which only concern national law. The ECJ left the concrete assessment as to whether the principle of equivalence had been

---

10 ECJ, 16 December 1976, 33/76, *REWE v Landwirtschaftskammer Saarland* [1976] ECR 1989 at para 5.

11 ECJ, 16 December 1976, 45/76, *Comet* [1976] ECR 2043 at paras 11, 18.

12 ECJ, 9 March 1978, 106/77, *Simmenthal* [1978] ECR 67 at para 5; ECJ, 16 December 1976, 45/76, *Comet* [1976] ECR 2043 at para 12.

13 ECJ, 9 March 1978, 106/77, [1978] *Simmenthal*, ECR 67, para 5; 16 December 1976, 45/76, *Comet*, [1976] ECR 2043, para 13, 16.

14 ECJ, 10 July 1997, C-261/95, *Palmisani*, [1997] I ECR -4028.

15 ECJ, 16 December 1976, 45/76, *Comet* [1976] ECR 2043 at paras 11, 18.

guaranteed to the discretion of the submitting court. *Francovich*[16] tightens the requirements to the extent that national provisions:

> "must not be so framed as to make it virtually impossible or excessively difficult to obtain reparation."

In this first phase of development the ECJ did not go so far as to dictate to national courts the sanctions and remedies which would be required to provide effective legal protection.[17] The EC Treaty did not purport to "to create new remedies in the national courts to ensure the observance of community law other than those already laid down by national law".[18] However, this conclusion is not compatible with *Simmenthal*,[19] according to which the national judge is obliged to:

> "apply community law in its entirety and protect rights which the latter confers on individuals and must accordingly set aside any provision of national law which may conflict with it."[20]

In this case the effectiveness of Community law might have been the focus of interest. In the same judgment, however, the ECJ held that the directly applicable provisions obliged the authorities and in particular the competent Member State judges to safeguard the interests of an individual who might be affected by a possible violation of the relevant provisions by providing direct and immediate protection.[21]

The principle of equivalence has been affirmed in Article 340 TFEU (formerly Article 288(2) EC) as well as in the "Explanation of the application of Community law" as attached to the Maastricht Treaty.[22] In numerous judgments the ECJ has had the opportunity to outline the principle of equivalence and effectiveness. According to *Peterbroeck*[23] and *van Schijndel*[24] the assessment of the "unreasonable impediment" depends on the position of the national provision within the proceedings, the course of proceedings and the particularities of the proceedings before the different national authorities. The principles – for example, the protection of the right to defence, legal certainty and due process of law – which the national legal protection system is based upon, need to be taken into consideration. Further judgments deal with national time limits; in addition,

---

16 ECJ, 19 November 1991, Joined Cases C-6/90 + C-9/90, *Francovich* [1991] ECR I-5357 at para 43.
17 Caranta, *CMLRev* 1995, 705.
18 ECJ, 18 August 1981, 158/80, *REWE v Hauptzollamt Kiel* [1981] ECR 1805 at para 44.
19 ECJ, 9 March 1978, 106/77, *Simmenthal* [1978] ECR 68.
20 Ibid, at paras 21, 23.
21 Ibid.
22 Cf. Reich *supra* note 1, para 4.3.
23 ECJ, 14 December 1995, C-312/93, *Peterbroeck* [1995] ECR I-4599 at para 14.
24 ECJ, 14 December 1995, Joined Cases C-430/93 + C 431/93, *van Schijndel* [1995] ECR I-4705 at para 19.

conditions for admission, provisions governing the process of setting-off, statutes of limitations and provisions on the burden of proof are also of concern. The latter types of provisions need to remain inapplicable if they render the reimbursement of financial penalties which have been imposed in violation of Community law practically impossible or excessively difficult.[25] National time limits need to be ignored if they prevent the restitution of an unlawful state aid.[26] A provision contained in national procedural law which prevents the court from reviewing *ex officio* the compatibility of a national legal instrument with a European provision may also be inapplicable if no person interested in the proceedings has invoked Union law within a certain period.[27]

Case law prohibits the application of any national law which contravenes Union law; however, it does not establish new remedies *per se*. This is a matter for Member State law under its obligation according to Article 4(3) TEU. Caranta[28] compares this situation with the English "doctrine of equity" as the principle of effective legal protection has the effect of a shield and not a sword.

The Charter of Fundamental Rights of the European Union, now integrated into the Lisbon Reform Treaty per Article 6(1) TEU, states in Article 47:

> "Everyone whose rights and freedoms guaranteed by the law of the Union are violated has the right to an effective remedy before a tribunal ... Legal aid shall be made available to those who lack sufficient resources insofar as such aid is necessary to ensure effective access to justice."

Article 19(1) s. 2 TEU puts the responsibility for "providing remedies sufficient to ensure effective legal protection in the fields covered by Union law" on Member States from the perspective of their courts of law being "Union courts". A similar provision was contained in Article I-29(1) of the Draft EU Constitution which was rejected in the Dutch and French referenda, but which later formed the basis of the TEU.[29]

A good example of the importance of Article 47 of the Charter in the ECJ case has been the *Alassini* case:[30] it concerned an Italian requirement for consumer complaints against telecommunication operators to first undertake an ADR/ODR proceeding as foreseen in Directive 2002/22[31] before going to

---

25 ECJ, 25 February 1988, Joined Cases 331, 376 + 378/85 *Bianco and Girard* [1988] ECR 1099 at para 12.

26 ECJ, 20 March 1997, C-24/95, *Alcan* [1997] ECR I-1591 at para 38.

27 ECJ, 14 December 1995, C-312/93, *Peterbroeck* [1995] ECR I-4599 at para 20.

28 Caranta, *CMLRev* 1995, 706.

29 Tridimas, *supra* note 1, 419; the more recent study by Poelzig, *Normsetzung durch Privatrecht*, 2013, 270 analyses the principle of effectiveness as starting point for individual enforcement of Union law, but does not even mention Article 47 of the Charter.

30 ECJ, 18 March 2010, C-317/07, *Alassini v Telecom Italia* [2010] ECR I-2214; Reich, *supra* note 1, para 4.5.

31 Directive 2002/22/EC of 7 March 2002 of the EP and of the Council on Universal Services in Electronic Communications [2002] OJ L 108/51.

court. The Court discusses this requirement in relation to both the equivalence and effectiveness principles and also in relation to Article 47, but did not find a violation. It wrote:

> "In those circumstances, it must be held that the national legislation at issue in the present case complies with the principle of effectiveness in so far as electronic means is not the only means by which the settlement procedure may be accessed and in so far as interim measures are possible in exceptional cases where the urgency of the situation so requires". (para 60)

3. IMPROVEMENT OF EFFECTIVE LEGAL PROTECTION OF THE INDIVIDUAL

8.4 The case law as established by the ECJ has developed over the years; Member States are required to grant both interim legal protection and compensation of damage provided certain requirements have been met. Lindholm[32] has been critical to the approach of the ECJ as encroaching too much on Member State competence in comparison to the federal situation in the USA.

a) Interim legal protection

8.5 In *Factortame*[33] the ECJ obviously intervened with national law. The case concerned the question of whether Community law would require the temporary suspension of measures imposed by the British Parliament under its sovereign powers by the means of an interim injunction issued by the (British) courts. Advocate General Tesauro[34] extensively deals with the significance of interim legal protection and stresses the fact that the emphasis is not on the relationship between national law and Community provisions but rather:

> "it relates to the requirement for, and the very existence of, the interim protection of a right which is not certain but whose existence is in the course of being determined in a situation where there is a conflict between legal rules of differing rank."

In *Zuckerfabrik Süderdithmarschen*[35] the ECJ produced the elements of the new legal instrument by virtue of Articles 242 and 243 EC (now Articles 278 and 279 TFEU) concerning the suspensive effect of actions before, and interim measures taken by, European courts which may, under certain conditions, also

---

32 Lindholm, 327–332; an overall discussion by Reich, in: *Liber amicorum Brüggemeier*, 381.
33 ECJ, 19 June 1990, C-213/89, *Factortame I* [1990] ECR I-2433.
34 Opinion of AG Tesauro, in C-213/89, *Factortame I*, at para 15.
35 ECJ, 21 February 1991, Joined Cases C-143/88 + C-92/89, *Zuckerfabrik Süderdithmarschen* [1991] ECR I-415 at paras 16–20.

be applied by national courts, despite the monopoly of the ECJ on voiding EC acts as, developed in *Foto Frost*:[36]

> "The interim legal protection which Community law ensures for individuals before national courts must remain the same, irrespective of whether they contest the compatibility of national legal provisions with Community law or the validity of secondary Community law, in view of the fact that the dispute in both cases is based on Community law itself."

The ECJ stresses the necessity of effective legal protection as:

> "the legal protection guaranteed by Community law includes the right of individuals to challenge, as a preliminary issue, the legality of such regulations before national courts and to induce those courts to refer questions to the Court of Justice for a preliminary ruling."

That right would be compromised if:

> "individuals were not in a position, where certain conditions are satisfied, to obtain a decision granting suspension of enforcement which would make it possible for the effects of the disputed regulation to be rendered for the time being inoperative as regards them."

According to *Atlanta Fruchthandelsgesellschaft*[37] interim legal protection can be granted by a national court against a Community legal act only if:

(1) that court entertains serious doubts as to the validity of the Community act and, if the validity of the contested act is not already an issue before the Court of Justice, itself refers the question to the ECJ;
(2) there is urgency, in that the interim relief is necessary to avoid serious and irreparable damage being caused to the party seeking the relief;
(3) the court takes due account of the Community interest; and
(4) in its assessment of all those conditions, it respects prior decisions of the Court of Justice or the Court of First Instance ruling on the lawfulness of the regulation or on an application for interim measures seeking similar interim relief at Community level.

By applying this case law the ECJ requires Member States, if necessary, to grant interim legal protection even if it has not been provided for in national law. The

---

36 ECJ, 22 October 1987, 314/85, *Foto Frost* [1987] ECR 4199; see also ECJ, 10 January 2006, C-344/04, *IATA and ELFAA v Department for Transport* [2006] ECJ I-403 at para 27.

37 ECJ, 9 November 1995, C-465/93, *Atlanta Fruchthandelsgesellschaft* [1995] ECR I-3761 at para 51; confirmed by ECJ, 6 December 2005, C-453/03, *ABNA et al. v Secretary of State for Health et al.* [2005] ECR I-10423.

rules stated in *Zuckerfabrik Süderdithmarschen* and *Atlanta Fruchthandelsgesellschaft* are based upon Community law and are binding upon all Member States. With these cases the ECJ has established the foundation for a new *ius commune* in the field of legal protection against the state,[38] the effects of which can be seen in consumer law.

8.5a In a more recent consumer case – *Aziz*[39] – the Court was confronted with the protection of debtors defaulting on an outstanding mortgage loan who under existing Spanish law could not oppose the claim of the creditor for execution even if clauses in the contract on acceleration, default interests and unilateral determination of the amount of unpaid debt were found to be unfair under Article 3 of Directive 93/14/EEC (*supra* 3.16). In her opinion of 8 November 2012, AG Kokott referred to the principle of effective legal protection of the debtor which must give the judge the possibility to stay execution proceeding in order to find out whether the incriminated clause is abusive or not (para 57). The Court in its judgment of 14 March 2013 followed suit, stating that the principle of effectiveness must be assessed "by reference to the role of that provision in the procedure, its progress and its features, viewed as a whole, before the various national bodies" (para 53).

b) Damages for breach of directly effective EU law: state liability

8.6 In *Francovich*[40] the ECJ established a new legal instrument on state liability for breaches of Community law which did not exist uniformly in national legal systems. *Francovich* needs to be seen against the background that the direct applicability of Community law constitutes the regular legal instrument of consumer protection as developed by the ECJ. An individual can invoke Community law if it is clear, unambiguous and unconditional. This principle, however, clutches at thin air as regards directives, as the direct "horizontal" applicability of the latter is prohibited by virtue of Article 288 TFEU (1.31–1.32). According to case law, directives have only limited direct effect so that there is a gap as regards remedies. Article 340(2) TFEU, which regulates Union liability but not the liability of Member States, constitutes the only applicable provision under Union law which provides damages for a violation of EU law which should be applied in analogy to States. For this reason in *Francovich* the ECJ strengthened the position of the individual by vertically granting the individual rights against the state.[41] The basis and requirements for a claim arise from Community law.[42] Liability is not only

38 Caranta, *CMLRev* 1995, 715.

39 ECJ, 14 March 2013, C-415/11, *Aziz v Catalunyacaixa* [2013] ECR I-(14.03.2013).

40 ECJ, 19 November 1991, Joined Cases C-5/90 + C 9/90, *Francovich* [1991] ECR I-5358.

41 Reich, *Bürgerrechte*, 1999, 142–144; Hartkamp, para 10.

42 ECJ, 19 November 1991, Joined Cases C-5/90 + C 9/90, *Francovich* [1991] ECR I-5357 at paras 38 *et seq*.

based on the *effet utile* but also on the principles of effective legal protection of the individual.

> "National courts whose task it is to apply the provisions of Community law in areas within their jurisdiction must ensure that those rules take full effect and must protect the rights which they confer on individuals."[43]

The initial restrictive case law of the ECJ has become obsolete since *Francovich*, most recently. According to the initial case law the EC Treaty did not purport to establish new possible remedies – applying alongside existing remedies under national law – in order to ensure that Union law is applied by the national courts.[44]

8.7 Claims arising from state liability have been concretised and extended in a number of decisions. According to the seminal *Brasserie du Pêcheur* judgment[45] they depend on three conditions:[46]

- the EC/EU Act that was not or incorrectly implemented by the Member State intended to give rights to individuals;
- the breach must be "sufficiently serious"; and
- a direct causal link must exist between the breach and the damage.

Such claims may be justified if a national legislative organ violated directly applicable Treaty provisions (*Brasserie*), in the case of a violation of the obligation to implement directives (*Francovich* and *Dillenkofer*)[47] and in case of administrative bodies violating Community law (*Hedley Lomas*).[48] This is also true for an administrative failure to act which is in violation of Union law.[49] In *Köbler*,[50] the Court confirmed the principle of state liability in the case of a "manifest breach" of Community law by the highest court of a Member State. Such a breach had to be established by considering a number of factors like the "degree of clarity and precision of the rule infringed, whether the infringement was intentional, whether the error of law was excusable or inexcusable, the position taken, where applicable, by a Union institution and compliance by the court in question with its obligation to make a reference for a preliminary ruling

43 Ibid, at para 32.
44 *Supra* note 18.
45 ECJ, 5 March 1996, Joined Cases C-46/93 + C-48/93, *Brasserie du Pêcheur and Factortame* [1996] ECR I-1029.
46 For an overview of the intense discussion see HARTKAMP, *supra* note 41, para 73; TRIDIMAS, *supra* note 1, 516–521; VAN GERVEN, *CMLRev* 2000, 520.
47 ECJ, 8 October 1996, C-178/94 et al., *Dillenkofer* [1996] ECR I-4845.
48 ECJ, 23 May 1996, C-5/94, *Hedley Lomas* [1996] ECR I-2552.
49 ECJ, 9 December 1997, C-265/95, *Commission v France* [1997] ECR I-6959.
50 ECJ, 30 September 2003, C-224/01, *G. Köbler v Austria* [2003] ECR I-10239.

under Article 267(3) TFEU (ex Article 234 EC)" (para 55). The infringement will be sufficiently serious "where the decision concerned was made in manifest breach of the case law of the Court in the matter" (para 56). This was confirmed in *Traghetti*.[51] The Court defended in very strong words its *Köbler* judgment and severely criticised Italian legislation and case law of the Corte Suprema di Cassazione (the highest Italian court in civil and criminal matters) to exclude liability in cases where the infringement results from an interpretation of provisions of law or an assessment of facts or evidence, and to limit it to "intentional fault and serious misconduct". Such a general exclusion makes the defence of Community rights against the highest court of a country impossible and meaningless; it would deprive the principles set out in *Köbler* "of all practical effect with regard to manifest infringements of Community law for which courts adjudicating at last instance were responsible" (para 40). As a result, "[a]ccordingly, although it remains possible for national law to define the criteria relating to the nature or degree of the infringement which must be met before State liability can be incurred for an infringement of Community law attributable to a national court adjudicating at last instance, under no circumstances may such criteria impose requirements stricter than that of a manifest infringement".

On the other hand, it should not be overlooked that too a strict liability of Member States may in the end impair consumer rights, as can be shown in the *AGM COSMET* judgment.[52] It was concerned with state (Finland) and personal liability for an official's incorrect statements against the instructions of his ministry in a TV broadcast concerning risks of a product that did not comply with the safety clause of Article 7 of Machinery Directive 98/37/EC.[53] EC law is only concerned with state liability, not with the personal liability of the official. The statements must be made by the official "within the authority of his office" (para 57), which must be determined by a number of criteria, in particular whether the person to whom those statements are addressed can be "reasonably supposed" to have such authority. Since the Machinery Directive exhaustively harmonises the procedures to be taken in case of a safety risk of a product covered by the Directive (vehicle lift charged to be unstable when lifting vehicles), Member State officials cannot go to TV to warn about risks without meeting these requirements. Such action is neither justified by the freedom of expression of the official nor by safety concerns. Since Directive 98/37/EC confers rights on individuals (right to market access once the conditions are met and the *"CE"* label is correctly attached), the state must adequately compensate the company that has suffered damage from the critical remarks of the state's officials, setting

51 ECJ, 13 June 2006, C-173/03, *Traghetti del Mediterrano SpA v Italian Republic* [2006] ECR I-5177.

52 ECJ, 17 April 2007, C-470/03, *A.G.M. COSMET* [2007] ECR I-2749.

53 OJ L 207, 22 June 1998, 1.

aside any additional conditions which Member State law imposes on liability. The judgment does not even consider the position of persons who may be injured by a device which does not comply with the state of the art because the vehicle lift subject to (unauthorised) criticism from a state official did not guarantee stability if a car was driven on it in both directions, as required by the relevant technical standards, whereas the producer limited this to driving forwards.[54]

The basic requirement of state liability is always that a rule of directly applicable EU law is intended to confer *rights* upon an individual, whether business, worker or consumer. In the *Peter Paul* case the Court held that the EU banking directives do not preclude a Member State from ruling that the functions of the national authority responsible for supervising credit institutions are to be fulfilled only in the public interest, which excludes individual claims in compensation for damage resulting from defective supervision on the part of the authority. These directives do not confer rights on depositors or consumers in the event that their deposits are unavailable as a result of defective supervision – a supervision which is directed at safeguarding the stability of financial markets.[55]

The only field which the process of the approximation the laws of damages has not yet touched upon is the extent of damages.[56] Until recently the ECJ has been of the opinion that it is at the discretion of Member States to determine the extent of damages. In *Brasserie du Pêcheur* and *Factortame* the ECJ held that the exclusion of compensation for loss of profit was inadmissible.[57] The principle of equivalence requires that compensation for infringements of EC rights should be commensurate to infringements of national rights; the comparison will not always be easy to draw, as *Palmisani*[58] shows.

This new hybrid element of liability represents the third pillar alongside Article 340(2) TFEU and the national rules on state liability. Furthermore, it strengthens the subjective legal position of the Community citizen and forms part of the *acquis communautaire*, based also on the principle of primacy of EU law.[59]

4. THE MEANING OF EFFECTIVE LEGAL PROTECTION IN CONSUMER LAW

8.8 The principle of effective legal protection in the field of consumer protection may gain in importance in very different ways. The most important

54 See the critique by Reich, *ELRev* 2008, 85; for a more positive view see de Vries, *CMLRev* 2008, 569.

55 ECJ, 12 October 2004, C-222/02, *Peter Paul et al. v Federal Republic* [2004] ECR I-9425.

56 This argument has been put forward by van Gerven, in: Micklitz/Reich (eds.), *Public Interest Litigation*, 87.

57 ECJ, 5 March 1996, Joined Cases C-46/93 + C-48/93, *Brasserie du Pêcheur and Factortame* [1996] ECR I-1157 at para 87.

58 ECJ, 10 July 1997, C-261/95, *Palminisani* [1997] ECR I-4025.

59 Tridimas, *supra* note 1, 503.

question is whether the individual consumer can claim compensation where a Member State has failed to enact legislative measures necessary to develop a legal system in the first place. This requires that concrete minimum requirements can be derived from the principle of effective legal protection. In many cases this will only be possible with the help of secondary Union law. It concerns possible liability for legislative wrongs which is entirely in line with *Francovich*. Liability of Member States for compensation of the damage which results from its failure or partial failure to implement a directive, and which constitutes a subjective right in favour of the consumer is less problematic as it is legally secured and part of the *acquis communitaire* (1.33). This is the premise that most proceedings have been based upon, particularly in the *Dillenkofer* case[60] (*infra* 8.10). However Member States' liability for faulty application of a directive is less clear cut; it primarily concerns the neglect of supervisory powers. The development in this area is still in its infancy, as can be seen from the above-mentioned *Peter Paul* case (8.7).

a) *Legal consequences for breach by Member States of the obligation to provide effective legal protection*

8.9 By virtue of primary law, Member States are obliged to provide effective legal protection in consumer law. The rights which are granted to the consumer by virtue of Article 169(1) TFEU and the sectoral clause of Article 12 TFEU (ex-Article 153(2) EC) would be redundant were the individual consumer unable to enforce those rights. National courts are obliged to interpret national legal provisions in a way that the practical effect of consumer rights of Article 169 TFEU is guaranteed (1.32). According to *Factortame* and *Zuckerfabrik Süderdithmarschen*, courts are required to establish new legal instruments which had not been known before under the so-called "remedial function" of the effectiveness principle.[61]

The guarantee of legal protection of the individual by Member States results in an increased power of self-assertion of Union law. The interplay of the principles of practical effect of Union law and effective legal protection becomes particularly evident in consumer protection law. Article 169 TFEU sets out the Member States' obligation to act. According to Article 12 TFEU and Article 4(3) TEU, Member States are required to *provide not only a minimum but an "adequate" standard.* If Member States fail to provide the legislative measures necessary to ensure this minimum standard or go below it, then they violate their primary legal obligation. The same applies if Member States violate their obligation to protect consumers which arises from Article 36 and Article 114 TFEU concerning the safety of products.[62]

---

60 ECJ, 8 October 1996, C-178/94, *Dillenkofer* [1996] ECR I-4845.

61 Reich, *supra* note 1, paras 4.10–4.11.

62 Micklitz, *Internationales Produktsicherheitsrecht*, 220 ff.

The principle of effective legal protection is of assistance in concretising the remedies necessary, including an "upgrading" of national provisions which leads to a "hybridisation" of remedies.[63] While possible liability for harm is rather straightforward, the derivation of preventative actions incurs substantially more problems. A possible direct effect of Union law does not oppose the creation of a claim for damages as the latter constitutes a minimum guarantee. If Member States fail to fulfil this obligation they will be liable for a legislative wrong according to *Brasserie du Pêcheur.* Consumer harm may not always be compensated by pecuniary means. The obligation to enact necessary legislative measures would constitute an appropriate means as, for example, by way of *preventative legal action.* In *Unibet*,[64] the Court was, however, hesitant to require such a remedy: here, the Court was asked whether the principle of effectiveness required national law to introduce a "free-standing action" which seeks primarily to dispute the compatibility of national provisions with Community/Union law. The Court denied such an obligation if it did not exist in national law (para 52). On the other hand, such a claim may be brought incidentally in an action for damages or illegality. However,

> "if … it was forced to be subject to administrative or criminal proceedings and to any penalties that may result as the sole form of legal remedy for disputing the compatibility of the national provision at issue with Community law, that would not be sufficient to secure for it such effective judicial protection". (para 64)

National law must allow for "interim relief necessary to ensure those rights are respected" (para 72). The conditions must be laid down by national law.

b) *Damages for failure to implement directives*

8.10 If a Member State fails to fulfil its obligation to implement a directive as governed in Article 288(2) TFEU (ex-Article 249(3) EC), then an individual might have a claim for compensation by virtue of *Francovich*, provided that the directive establishes subjective rights which are specific and unconditional. The consumer rights which are embedded in primary Community law become subjective rights in the sense of Article 12 TFEU.[65] Failure to implement directives properly or in time may cause substantial harm to the individual consumer. The most important case so far which has been decided by the ECJ concerned the Package Travel Directive 90/314/EEC (1.27). In *Dillenkofer* the ECJ easily adjudicated that the individual had a subjective legal position, which entailed state liability of the Federal Republic of Germany which had failed to make arrangements for possible insolvency of the tour organiser as required by

---

63 Reich, *YEL* 2010, 112; Reich, *supra* note 1, para 4.33.

64 ECJ, 13 March 2007, C-432/05, *Unibet v Justitiekanslern* [2007] ECR I-2271.

65 Reich, *VuR* 1999, 3.

Article 7 of the Directive. A later decision concerned a similar failure by the Austrian government which tried to improperly limit compensation.[66] The cause also concerned the question of causation. Austria, which had not correctly implemented Article 7 of Directive 90/314, claimed *inter alia* unforeseeable circumstances and lack of causation to avoid state liability under the *Brasserie* doctrine. The ECJ has however argued differently:

> "In those circumstances, the Member State's liability for breach of Article 7 of the Directive (90/314) cannot be precluded by imprudent conduct on the part of the travel organiser or by the occurrence of exceptional and unforeseeable events. Such circumstances, in as much as they would not have presented an obstacle to the refund of money paid over or the repatriation of consumers if the guarantee system had been implemented in accordance with Article 7 of the Directive, are not such as to preclude the existence of a direct causal link". (paras 75–76)

In both cases it was beyond doubt, however, that the Directive grants the consumer subjective rights. This requirement is always problematic if the relevant directives set out primarily supervisory obligations for Member States, adherence to which serves the protection of consumers as a whole without clearly illustrating whether the individual consumer is granted a subjective legal position, as could be demonstrated by the *Peter Paul* decision (*supra* 8.7). Similar problems exist with regard to consumer safety law.[67]

The legal assimilation of the effects of a directive which had not been implemented properly or within an appropriate period of time, and which cannot be compensated for monetarily, remains similarly open. As the practical effect of consumer rights arising from Article 12 TFEU is in the foreground, other remedies need to be taken into consideration in order to ensure adequate legal protection of the consumer. Interim legal protection may be necessary if the Directive which is to be implemented purports to protect the consumer against hazardous products. A directive which has not been implemented in a timely manner may lead to substantial, irreparable harm. To reduce legal protection to subsequent pecuniary compensation would substantially interfere with the consumer rights of Article 12 TFEU. The principle of effective legal protection of the individual requires an intervention prior to harm to the consumer. To the extent that directives constitute subjective rights, interim legal protection must be ensured.

c) Legal protection in the case of faulty applications of the consumer protective directives

8.11 The discussion about which rights and obligations result directly from Article 12 TFEU is still in its infancy. This is the reason why this question is to be

---

66 ECJ, 15 June 1999, C-140/95, *Rechberger v Austria* [1999] ECR I-3499.

67 Reich, *ELRev* 2008, 98.

answered by considering both primary and secondary legal obligations. This issue becomes particularly evident with regard to faulty application of directives which have been properly implemented, but where official practice may possibly not fulfil the requirements of the directives. Administrative acts which do not sufficiently consider the conditions as set out in the directives may interfere with consumer interests. This raises the question of compensatory claims against Member States whose conduct violates Union law, provided the respective directive provides such a subjective right.

In the aftermath of *Francovich* and its consecutive judgments, a comprehensive legal protection system has been established, the requirements of which may be directly derived from Union law. Case law allows one to draw the conclusion that the duty to compensate is not limited to a violation of the duty to implement. A State will be liable for any violation of Union law; the violation of the duty to implement appears to be a sub-category. The fact that the duty to compensate has the character of a general liability principle has been emphasised by the ECJ in *Brasserie*; liability may occur in "any case in which a Member State breaches Community law, whatever be the organ of the State whose act or omission was responsible for the breach."[68] This breach must however be "sufficiently serious", which is usually a matter for the national court to decide and depends very much on the facts of the case.[69]

It is always crucial to decide whether the directive in question intends to establish individual rights. The case law of the ECJ will be of guidance here.

II. THE IMPROVEMENT OF THE LEGAL PROTECTION OF THE INDIVIDUAL IN HORIZONTAL RELATIONSHIPS AGAINST UNDERTAKINGS

1. CLAIMS FOR COMPENSATION UNDER UNION LAW

8.12 While the basis for a state liability claim is originally derived from Community law, it is questionable whether liability of the individual business undertaking for violations of Union law also constitutes a Union law principle, or if the basis for a claim is to be derived from national legal systems which is then to be concretised according to the principle of equivalence and effectiveness and whether, eventually, the consumer can profit from such an action.

---

68 ECJ, 5 March 1996, Joined Cases C-46/93 + C-48/93, *Brasserie du Pêcheur and Factortame* [1996] ECR I-1029 at para 32.

69 Tridimas, *supra* note 1, 491.

As far as apparently the question had been submitted to the ECJ for the first time in *Banks*,[70] a competition case under the old ECSC Treaty, AG van Gerven suggested that the claim for damages was based on Community law, not national law.[71] The principles developed in *Francovich* for a state liability claim accordingly would also apply:

> "where an individual infringes a provision of Community law to which he is subject, thereby causing loss and damage to another individual. The situation then falls within the terms stated by the Court in paragraph 31 of the Francovich judgment …, namely breach of a right which an individual derives from an obligation imposed by Community law on another individual. Once again, the full effect of Community law would be impaired if the former individual or undertaking did not have the possibility of obtaining reparation from the party who can be held responsible for the breach of Community law."[72]

In its final judgment the ECJ denied liability; it refrained, however, from taking a point of view with regard to the issue in question. According to the decision of the ECJ the relevant provisions of the ECSC Treaty were not directly effective, i.e. there were no rights to be derived therefrom which needed to be taken into consideration by national courts.

An indication of a different assessment could already be seen in *Brasserie du Pêcheur* in which the ECJ reasoned that an extension of state liability for a violation of directly applicable Community law granted the right to compensation. This represented the corollary to the direct effect of the provision the violation of which caused the damage. This principle could also apply to the right (to damages) of the individual as directly applicable provisions of Union law imposed on undertakings' obligations from a horizontal relationship under private law (with consumers, competitors or other private parties). The basis for a claim is identical for horizontal and vertical relationships. It concerns the legally binding effect of the EU provisions and the principle of practical effect (*effet utile*) of Union law. The principles as established in *Brasserie* are thus transferable to claims arising in the horizontal relationship (the basis for such a claim would be Articles 101/102 TFEU).[73] In *Bosman*[74] the ECJ held that Article 39 EC (now Article 45 TFEU) on free movement of workers is not only binding upon Member States and Community organs but also upon legal subjects of private law, in particular sporting associations. Therefore a claim for damages directly based on Article 45 TFEU could succeed against undertakings or associations before a national court. In *Raccanelli*[75] the Court said:

---

70 ECJ, 13 April 1994, C-128/92, *Banks* [1994] ECR I-1209.

71 Opinion of AG van Gerven, 28 October 1993, C-128/92, *Banks*, para 36.

72 Opinion of AG van Gerven, 28 October 1993, C-128/92, *Banks*, para 43.

73 Van Gerven, *CMLRev* 2000, 530 ff.

74 ECJ, 15 December 1995, C-415/93, *Bosman* [1995] ECR I-4921 at paras 83 *et seq.*

75 ECJ, 17 July 2008, C-94/07, *Raccanelli vs. MPG* [2008] ECR I-5939; see also Van Gerven, *CMLRev* 2000, 531.

> "The Court has thus held, with regard to Article 39 EC [now Article 45 TFEU], which lays down a fundamental freedom and which constitutes a specific application of the general prohibition of discrimination contained in Article 12 EC [now Article 18 TFEU], that the prohibition of discrimination applies equally to all agreements intended to regulate paid labour collectively, as well as to contracts between individuals ... It must be held, therefore, that the prohibition of discrimination based on nationality laid down by Article 39 EC applies equally to private-law associations such as MPG". (paras 45–46)

In the judgments in *Viking* and *Laval*[76] the Court reaffirmed the direct effect of the fundamental freedoms of establishment and service provision against social action by labour unions which may, however, be justified on fundamental rights principles under Article 28 of the EU Charter of Fundamental Rights: the Court insisted that the fundamental freedoms of Article 49 TFEU (ex-Article 43 EC) and Article 56 TFEU (ex-Article 49 EC) also apply in horizontal relations to "rules of any other nature aimed at regulating in a collective manner gainful employment, self-employment and the provision of services". In *Viking* this is justified by the fact that in some Member States, working conditions are governed by law, in others by collective agreements; an exemption of the latter from the applicability the fundamental freedoms would "risk inequality in its application" (para 34). In *Laval* a more functional argument is used, namely that the abolition of "obstacles to the freedom to provide services would be compromised if the abolition of State barriers could be neutralised by obstacles resulting from the exercise of their legal autonomy by associations and organisations not governed by public law" (para 99). Articles 43 and 49 EC have direct effect and confer rights on individuals whose freedoms are violated by social action of labour unions, like in *Viking* where the Finnish ship owner Viking Line was prevented from re-flagging the vessel Rosella, and in *Laval* where the construction company Laval suffered loss from a boycott when posting its workers in Sweden. The Swedish Arbetsdomstolen, in its judgment of 2 December 2009, therefore awarded damages to Laval against the Swedish trade unions.[77]

8.13 A specific remedy for breach of horizontally applicable EC law provisions has been reaffirmed in *Courage*.[78] The case concerned claims for damages arising from a tying agreement which in an alleged violation of Article 81 EC (now Article 101 TFEU) had been entered into between English licensed pubs

---

76 ECJ, 11 December 2007, C-438/05 *International Transport Workers Federation (ITF) and Finnish Seaman's Union (FSU) v Viking Line* [2007] ECR I-10779; and ECJ, 18 December 2007, C-341/05, *Laval v Svenska Bygnaddsarbetereförbundet et al.* [2007] ECR I-11767; for comment Reich, *German Law Journal* 2008, 123.

77 Details Bernitz/Reich, *CMLRev* 2011, 603.

78 ECJ, 20 September 2001, C-453/99, *Courage v Crehan* [2001] ECR I-6298; the consequences are discussed in Reich, *CMLRev* 2007, 705.

and a brewery. As English law did not provide damages in this case because of the *in pari delicto* defence of the brewery, the Court of Appeal submitted to the ECJ according to Article 234 EC (now Article 267 TFEU) the question of whether this national principle was compatible with Article 81 EC (now Article 101 TFEU). The ECJ confirmed the duty to compensation between the parties involved. Arguing beyond the case at hand, the Court insisted on effective remedies such as compensation for better enforcing competition rules, including in favour of consumers. The Court wrote:

> "It follows from the foregoing considerations that *any individual* [emphasis added] can rely on a breach of Article 85(1) [now Article 101] ... before a national court even where he is a party to a contract that is liable to restrict or distort competition within the meaning of that provision ... Indeed, the existence of such a right strengthens the working of the Community competition rules and discourages agreements or practices, that are frequently covert, that are liable to restrict or distort competition. From that point of view, actions for damages before the national courts can make a significant contribution to the maintenance of effective competition within the Community". (paras 25–27)

The Court makes it very clear that actions for damages are an important contribution to governance of undertakings in the field of competition. This action is based directly on Community/Union law, not on national law,[79] even though the procedural features, as well as the determination of the competent court, are subject to national law. It has to be seen how far individual consumers who are harmed by anti-competitive practices can make use of this remedy.

This reasoning was reaffirmed in *Manfredi*.[80] The Court reiterated the importance of private law remedies in enforcing the competition rules, including absolute nullity under Article 81(2) by claims for compensation by "any individual" (para 61) – in the case at hand, individual consumers who had to pay premium increases in their car insurance because of a price cartel. There must be a *causal relationship* between that harm and an agreement prohibited under Article 81 which is for the national courts to establish. The compensation must include *damnum emergens* and *lucrum cessans* (lost profit) as well as interest (para 95). Punitive damages are only owed if similar national law provides for them. Community law does not entail the unjust enrichment of those who enjoy a right of compensation (para 94). Limitation periods must not make the exercise of the right to seek compensation practically impossible, particularly when the limitation period begins to run from the day on which the agreement or concerted practice was adopted (para 78).

---

79 Komninos, *CMLRev* 2002, 473; Reich, *CMLRev* 2005, 54.

80 ECJ, 13 July 2006, C-295–298/04, *Vicenzo Manfredi et al v Lloyd Adriatico Asssicurazioni SpA et al.* [2006] ECR I-6619; similar now ECJ, 6 November 2012, C-169/11, *EU v Otis* [2012] ECR I-nyr concerns claims of the EU itself as client against a price fixing cartel.

2. EFFECTS ON CONSUMER PROTECTION: PROPOSED EU ACTION

8.14 The discussion about a basis for a claim originating from Union law and the ECJ rulings in *Courage* and *Manfredi* clearly show that enforcement under the law of compensation of Community rights of the individual is of increasing significance. This has to some extent been recognised by Council Regulation (EC) 1/2003 of 16 December 2002 on the implementation of the rules on competition.[81] According to Recital (7), national courts have an essential part to play in applying Community competition rules. When deciding disputes between private individuals, they protect subjective rights under Community law, for example by awarding damages to the victims of infringements. However, Regulation 1/2003 does not contain any rules on compensation. This must be determined by applicable Member State law.[82]

The extension of the scope of protection of EU competition law to private parties constitutes a substantial contribution to improved consumer protection. Consumer protection gains in importance in part by virtue of the sectoral clause in Article 12 TFEU (ex-Article 153(2) EC). Consumers can directly invoke Articles 101 and 102 TFEU (1.39) and assert that their (consumer) rights have been violated by anti-competitive action directed against them, for example price fixing and discrimination, artificial segregation of markets or limitations of supply and output (see the examples in Article 1011(1)(a) to (c) EC itself).[83] The sanction which increases the powers of self-assertion of Union law must be the one chosen. It needs to be tailored to the hypothetical conduct of the parties participating in the restriction of competition. The sanction chosen by the consumer against the undertaking thus has a deterrent effect.

In 2005, the Commission itself published a short Green Paper outlining future options for improving private enforcement of competition law, to which was appended a staff working paper including comparative and economic information on remedies against breaches of antitrust provisions.[84] A White Paper[85] on "Damages actions for breach of the EC antitrust rules" discussed several options on how to improve private enforcement, but did not make any legislative proposals (see also *infra* 8.43 for collective redress). The Commission insists that "any person" injured by breaches of antitrust provisions, including indirect purchasers, such as consumers, should be able to receive compensation. On 11 June 2013 the Commission proposed a directive on "certain rules

---

81 OJ L 1 April 2003, 1.

82 Reich, *CMLRev* 2005, 35.

83 Reich, *supra* note 1, 4.28.

84 COM (2005) 672 final, 19 December 2005; for a discussion see the contributions to Basedow (ed.), *Private Enforcement of EC Competition Law*, 2007; 2011.

85 COM (2008) 165 final of 2 April 2008; accompanied by a Staff Working Paper SEC (2008) 404 of 2 April 2008.

concerning actions for damages under national law for infringements of the competition provisions of the Member States and the EU",[86] expressly including claims of so-called "indirect purchasers" and consumers.

The recognition of consumer claims against discriminatory and overcharging undertakings is supported by a similar discussion in the field of the internal market for electricity. In that area consumers are entitled to assert claims for the supply of electricity. In the case of denial of the latter or requiring above-average fees, the consumer can claim for damages *inter alia* by virtue of the direct effect of Article 102 EC because of an abuse of a dominant position.[87]

III. EFFECTIVE LEGAL PROTECTION OF THE INDIVIDUAL AND LIABILITY OF THE UNION

8.15 The non-contractual liability of the Union as per Article 340(2) TFEU over which the General Court has jurisdiction has not yet played an important role in consumer law. On the one hand this might result from the restrictive handling of the requirements for bringing a claim; on the other hand the focus is on the legal protection of the individual by the courts of Member States, which need to ensure claims under civil law against Member States and private undertakings. This understanding is compatible with the principle of subsidiarity in Article 5(3) TEU (1.10).

Liability of the Union arises in accordance "with the general principles common to the laws of Member States". With regard to regulatory provisions, the enactment of which require economic policy decisions, liability of the Union can only arise – according to the case law of the ECJ – if there is a sufficiently serious violation of a regulatory provision purporting to protect the individual. In *Francesconi*,[88] the only case so far dealing with consumer protection, the ECJ rejected liability of the Community as the information system allowing the monitoring of the wine market as introduced by the Community leaves it to national authorities to inform the consumer about hazardous products. The case concerned liability under Article 288(2) EC (now Article 340 TFEU) for failure of the Community organs to take measures to recall hazardous products (alcohol adulterated with diethylene glycol, the consumption of which resulted in several deaths in Italy). The ECJ referred to the primary responsibility of Member States which excludes a sanctioned duty to protect of the Community as such:

> "Finally, the applicants submit that the Commission ought … to have taken steps to withdraw wines from the market, inform consumers of the scandal of adulterated

86 COM (2013) 404 final.

87 Micklitz/Rott, *VuR* 2000, 389.

88 ECJ, 7 April 1989, 326/86 + 66/88, *Francesconi* [1989] ECR 2088.

> wines and increase checking by the competent national authorities in their supervision of the Community system of distillation.
> It must first of all be observed that the Commission has no power to withdraw adulterated from the market, that being a matter for the national authorities. The Commission is under no obligation to publish the identity of traders who may be involved in scandals. The information system established to detect fraud and irregularities in the wine sector and to avert dangers which might arise from the use of consumable products leaves it to the national authorities to take steps to inform the consumer."

Since 1989 – the year in which *Francesconi* was decided – the balance of power has shifted. The Union may be authorised to order EU-wide measures and it may be required to comply with the duties to protect consumer's health and safety as set out in Articles 12, 36 and 114 TFEU. The Commission has become increasingly competent; however, it has exposed itself to the risk of becoming subject to liability claims. It seems that the narrow interpretation of Union law needs to also be modified in other areas of Union policy and law, given that the Union has been recognised as being responsible in areas such as the admission of pharmaceutical products and in monitoring product safety in the internal market. At the least, a joint and several liability of the Union and the Member State in question should be debated. Article 12 TFEU might play a key role. Article 12 is addressed to the Union, i.e. an unrestricted referral to the discretion of Member States by virtue of *Francesconi* is impossible. However, where the Union merely makes a "contribution", Member States are primarily responsible. If the latter fail to fulfil their obligation, then the practical effect of the consumer rights will be in conflict with the then increasingly important duty to promote the Union. This interplay of different levels of responsibility is supported by the provision, as contained in Article 169(2)(b) TFEU, according to which the Union shall contribute through measures which support, supplement and monitor the policy pursued by Member States (1.23). To that extent a duty to act for the Union could be established from Article 12 TFEU taken with provisions under secondary law which would result in liability as per Article 340(2) TFEU.

IV. IMPROVING CONSUMERS' ACCESS TO JUSTICE

1. LEGAL AID IN CROSS-BORDER CONFLICTS

8.16 Based upon the provisions on judicial cooperation in civil matters (1.18), the Community adopted Directive 2002/8/EC of 27 January 2003 concerning legal aid in cross-border disputes.[89] It is not, like all provisions under this

[89] OJ L 26, 31 January 2003, 41.

competence, targeted specifically at consumers, but it may be particularly important if consumers engage or are forced to engage in cross-border consumer litigation. The Directive contains minimum rules based on the principle of non-discrimination. It establishes a right to legal aid for natural persons who are wholly or partly unable to meet the costs of pre-litigation advice "with a view to reaching a settlement prior to bringing legal proceedings" (Article 3(2)(a)) and legal assistance and representation in court in cross-border disputes relating to civil and commercial matters. It does not define the ceiling itself but leaves it to Member States to decide appropriate thresholds with respect to the non-discrimination principle which applies both to Union citizens and to third-country nationals residing lawfully in a Member State (Article 4). Legal aid must be granted to persons who are partly or totally unable to meet the costs of proceedings "as a result of their economic situation, in order to ensure their effective access to justice" (Article 5(1)). The right to legal aid is applicable to extra-judicial procedures if the law requires the parties to use them or if the parties to the dispute are ordered by the court to have recourse to them (Article 10). The Directive, being a measure under the provisions of judicial cooperation, does not apply to Denmark. The UK and Ireland opted in here.

2. ALTERNATIVE DISPUTE RESOLUTION (ADR): DIRECTIVE 2013/11/EU AND REGULATION (EU) 524/2013

8.17 Most consumer disputes involve relatively small sums of money, and the traditional mechanisms of legal protection in Member States may either not be adequate or simply be unviable for consumers. For these reasons the consumer movement in the US[90] and later in Europe,[91] put great emphasis on developing ADR mechanisms which would allow the consumer to proceed with his claims in a speedy and effective way without incurring the costs and risks of "normal" litigation. Member States have developed several models, some like in the Scandinavian countries sponsored and supported by the State, some relying on self-regulation as in Germany and the UK, and others on cooperation between business and consumer associations as in the Netherlands. This is not the place to even try to give an overview of the many initiatives and experiences developed in this field.

---

90 Reich, *Staatliche Regulierung*, 1984, 115 ff.

91 Tonner, 414; overview in the study of Stuyck *et al.* done for the EC Commission: an analysis and evaluation of alternative means of consumer redress other than redress through ordinary judicial proceedings, 2007; Hodges et al., *Consumer ADR in Europe.*

8.18 The Union does not enjoy original competence in this area. However, as far back as 1975, the resolution of the Council regarding the preliminary Programme of the European Commission for consumer protection and information policy, affirms "the right to compensation for damages through fast, efficient and cost-effective proceedings" as being one of the five rights of the consumer (1.3). The Commission therefore first took recourse to soft-law instruments like recommendations, support of voluntary programmes, encouragement of Codes of conduct and practice by business associations, possibly in cooperation with consumer associations and the like.

Legally binding Union measures were adopted only recently, the most important being Directive 2013/11/EU of 21 May 2013 on consumer ADR[92] (details *infra* 8.23a, consumer arbitration at 8.23c–e) and Regulation (EU) No 524/2013 of 21 May 2013 on consumer ODR[93] (details 8.23g). They are still directly linked to the objective of achieving the internal market – at least formally, and therefore based on Article 114, not 81 TFEU. The following lines will give an overview of the importance of the new instruments on imposing solutions on consumers by ADR entities (8.23c–e) and conclude with an outlook for EU and US case law on ADR and consumer arbitration as a coming "privatisation of (consumer) justice" (8.24).

8.19 Recommendation 98/257/EC of the Commission of 30 March 1998 regarding principles applicable to bodies responsible for out-of-court consumer dispute settlements[94] aims at encouraging respect for certain essential principles by bodies responsible for alternative consumer dispute resolution systems that already exist or are to be created within the European Union. The adoption of these principles (the independence and transparency of ADR mechanisms, the adversarial system, efficiency principle, principle of legality, freedom of access, and the principle of representation) tends to ensure the protection of consumer rights and to increase confidence in ADR systems. *Alassini*[95] gave it a sort of quasi-legal importance, insisting that recommendations can produce legal effect in areas where Member States use recommendations for legally binding policy decisions.

8.20 The European complaint form attached to the Recommendation of 30 March 1998 has been designed as an instrument of dialogue between the consumer and the professional in the event of litigation. Should an out-of-court settlement be arrived at, this form constitutes a means of facilitating and rationalising the commencement of a procedure before extra-judicial authorities

---

92 OJ L 165, 18 June 2013, 63. Critical evaluation by Meller-Hannich et al., *ZEuP* 2014, 8 (30).

93 OJ L 165, 18 June 2013, 1.

94 OJ L 115, 18 April 1998, 31.

95 ECJ, 18 March 2010, C-317/07, *Alassini v Telecom Italia* [2010] ECR I-2214.

for the settlement of consumer disputes. This European complaint form is available on the internet in all the official languages of the EU.[96] It is not known whether and how it has been used.

8.21 The Resolution of 25 May 2000[97] established the European Extra-Judicial Network, the *EEJ-Net*. This initiative is strongly related to the adoption of the E-Commerce Directive 2000/31/EC (7.24)[98] and the euphoria at that time over the prospects of the internet and more particularly the new economy. Member States are invited to set up central contact points which are to function as a clearing house. In the national context this clearing house shall provide the consumer with assistance in finding a competent national ADR system for the particular conflict. In the international context the clearing house shall inform the consumer who is involved in a cross-border conflict on ADR systems in the respective Member States. The mechanism encourages Member States to gain a full picture of the diverse national ADR systems and exchange the information via the contact points. National clearing houses support the consumer in filing his complaints.

The EEJ-Net is supplemented by the FIN-NET. On 1 February 2001, the European Commission launched an out-of-court complaints network for financial services to help businesses and consumers resolve disputes in the internal market rapidly and efficiently by avoiding, where possible, lengthy and expensive legal action. This network, called FIN-NET, has been designed particularly to facilitate the out-of-court resolution of consumer disputes when the service provider is established in an EU Member State other than that of the consumer. The network brings together more than 35 different national schemes that either cover financial services in particular (e.g. banking and insurance ombudsmen schemes) or handle consumer disputes in general (e.g. consumer complaint boards). Both online and offline services are covered.

8.22 Recommendation 2001/310/EC of the Commission of 4 April 2001 regarding principles applicable to the out-of-court bodies involved in the consensual resolution of consumer disputes[99] states that principles are to be respected within any procedure initiated by a third party (irrespective of its denomination), facilitates the resolution of a consumer dispute by bringing the parties together in an attempt to persuade them to find a solution by common agreement, and does not interfere with the principles set up by Recommendation 98/257/EC, which have to be respected within the scope of out-of-court

---

96 www.europa.eu.int/comm/consumers/index_fr.html.

97 OJ C 155, 6 June 2000, 1.

98 Directive 2000/31/EC of the European Parliament and of the Council of 8 June 2000 on certain legal aspects of information society services, in particular electronic commerce, in the Internal Market ("Directive on electronic commerce") OJ L 178, 18 August 2000.

99 OJ L 109, 19 April 2001, 56.

procedures. These procedures, independent of their denomination, result in the resolution of disputes via active third-party intervention to propose or impose a solution which may or may not be binding on the parties concerned. The principles encouraged by this Recommendation are fairness, transparency, efficiency and equity.

8.23 The European Commission has a long-standing policy of inviting Member States to initiate action within professional bodies on the development of appropriate dispute settlement mechanisms. It is therefore a prominent field of self-regulation which has recently been taken up in Directive 2006/123/EC of 12 December 2006 on services in the internal market (SD, 1.27). However, the rules on dispute settlement in the SD remain rather scarce and "take a light touch approach".[100] There is no reference to dispute settlement in the recitals and only one modest one in Article 27 in the text, which runs as follows:

> "1. Member States shall take the general measures necessary to ensure that providers supply contact details, in particular a postal address, fax number or e-mail address and telephone number to which all recipients, including those residents in another Member State, can send a complaint or a request for information about the service provided. Providers shall supply their legal address if this is not their usual address for correspondence. Member States shall take general measures necessary to ensure that providers respond to the complaint referred to in the first subparagraph in the shortest possible time and make their best efforts to find a satisfactory solution.
> 2. Member States shall take the general measures necessary to ensure that providers are obliged to demonstrate compliance with the obligations laid down in this Directive as to the provision of information and to demonstrate that the information is accurate.
> 3. Where a financial guarantee is require for compliance with a judicial decision, Member States shall recognise equivalent guarantees lodged with a credit institutions or insurer established in another Member State. ...
> 4. Member States shall take the general measures necessary to ensure that providers who are the subject to a code of conduct, or are members of a trade association or professional body, which provides recourse to a non-judicial means of dispute settlement inform the recipient thereof and mention that fact in any document which presents their services in detail, specifying how to access detailed information on the characteristics of and conditions for, the use of such a mechanism."

Empirical evidence has shown that consumers all over the European Union are very much concerned about the enforceability of their rights outside their home country. The SD neither mentions these concerns, nor refers to already

---

100 See Barnard, *CMLRev* 2008, 374.

established Europe-wide dispute settlement mechanisms, such as the EEJ-Net, nor underlines the importance of the relevant Recommendations 98/257/EC and 2001/310/EC which lay down minimum requirements for out-of-court dispute settlement procedures.

The reason might be that the approach chosen in the SD is extremely narrow. Contrary to Article 26 SD, which concerns quality, Article 27 addresses Member States only; it does not define the role of the European Commission and it deals only with in-house dispute settlement through the service provider himself and not through dispute settlement bodies as established by professional bodies. These service providers will use their best efforts. Member States are not obliged to set up ADR mechanisms, but must "ensure that providers supply contact details ... to which a complaint can be sent or information about the service can be requested."

It is true that the European competence on enforcement matters is indeed shaky. However, the European Commission has quite successfully combined the regulation of the substance of the matter, such as services, with introducing appropriate enforcement mechanisms. It seems as if the intended "high level of protection of the general interest objectives, especially protection of consumers", as spelt out in Recital (7), does no more than pay lip service to the Treaty without taking measures to give shape to that policy.

Directive 2008/48/EC of 23 April 2008 on credit agreements for consumers[101] (5.4) states in Article 24 that:

> "1. Member States shall ensure that adequate and effective out-of-court dispute resolution procedures for the settlement of consumer disputes concerning credit agreements are put in place, using existing bodies where appropriate.
> 2. Member States shall encourage those bodies to cooperate in order to also resolve cross-border disputes concerning credit agreements."

8.23a Directive 2013/11/EU is a comprehensive document committed to creating uniform and transparent rules on consumer ADR in the internal market. Together with Regulation 524/2013 (*infra* 8.23g) it builds on the preceding unsatisfactory experiences with non-binding instruments and puts them into a legally binding form, with the result that the Directive is to be implemented by the Member States before 9 July 2015. The Directive somewhat surprisingly also covers ADR entities which may impose solutions (binding consumer arbitration, 8.23c–e). Recital (4) states the main objective of these EU initiatives:

> "Ensuring access to simple, efficient, fast and low-cost ways of resolving domestic and cross-border disputes which arise from sales or service contracts should benefit consumers and therefore boost their confidence in the market. That access should

101 OJ L 133, 22 May 2008, 66.

apply to online as well as offline transactions, and is particularly important when consumers shops across borders."

The Directive is directed at Member States who, under Article 5, have a twofold obligation:

- to facilitate access by consumers to ADR procedures; and
- to guarantee that disputes between consumers and traders can be submitted to an ADR entity that complies with the requirements of this Directive.

It is not clear from the wording whether Member States are required under EU law to set up such entities; this, however, seems contradictory to the voluntary nature of such institutions and the freedom of the parties to submit their disputes to them. The Directive is meant to be a *facilitative, not a mandatory instrument* with regard to the establishment of ADR entities, despite the somewhat ambiguous wording of Article 5(1). Once ADR entities exist – and many of them exist in a rather confusing manner and with widely different jurisdictions in the Member States, as recent studies have shown – they must fulfil the requirements set out in the Directive.

8.23b Article 2 of Directive 2013/11/EU defines the *scope* of the Directive. There are several elements defining and at the same time limiting the "jurisdiction" of ADR entities:

- they are open to C2B, not B2C disputes;
- these disputes must arise out of sales or services contracts; according to Recital (14), contracts on digital content as envisaged in Articles 5(1)(g) and (h) and 6(1)(r) and (s) of the Consumer Rights Directive 2011/83/EU are also included;
- certain contractual or quasi-contractual disputes are excluded, e.g. disputes over health services, public higher education or non-economic services of general interest; Member States may however extend their ADR mechanisms to handle these disputes, which will then follow their own rules;
- ADR mechanisms established and financed exclusively by traders or their associations, e.g. the many ombudsmen systems in the financial services industry in Germany and the UK, may come under the Directive if they fulfil the impartiality requirements specified in Article 6(3); and
- ADR entities will usually only *propose* solutions to the parties to a conflict; Member States may however allow them to *impose* a solution, thereby being regarded as binding consumer arbitration. A certain number of – still insufficient – safeguards are attached to this option (see 8.23d–f).

8.23c Articles 6–10 contain a sort of "Magna Charta" of ADR procedures, thus continuing the approach in Recommendations 98/257 and 2001/310, as well as following the directions under the *Alassini* case law referring to Article 47 of the EU Charter of Fundamental Rights. They are, in brief, the following:

- Article 6 is concerned with *expertise, independence* and, *impartiality.* Members of ADR entities do not need to be trained in law; a "general understanding of law" (not necessarily consumer law) is sufficient;
- Article 7 is concerned with *transparency,* requiring ADR entities to make publicly available "clear and easily understandable information" on 15 specific items;
- Article 8 tries to ensure *effectiveness* by requiring procedures free of charge or requiring only "nominal charges"; the outcome of an ADR procedure should be made available within 90 days; an exception may be possible for "highly complex disputes";
- Article 9 imposes rules on *fairness*, e.g. a "right to be heard" within the limits of the chosen procedure, the possibility (but not the need) for the consumer to be represented by a lawyer or other persons, and the right to be notified of the outcome;
- Article 10(1) contains a rule concerning the *liberty* of the parties to submit their conflict to an ADR entity by agreement. The agreement is not binding on the consumer if "it was concluded before the dispute has materialised and if it has the effect of depriving the consumer of his right to bring an action before the courts for settlement of the dispute". At the same time, the judicial proceedings will not be subject to limitation or prescription periods during the on-going ADR procedure, Article 12.

8.23d EU Directive 2013/11/EU is also important for the development of *binding consumer arbitration* in the EU. This is based on the establishment of a two-tier mechanism of out-of-court settlement of consumer disputes "*proposing and imposing solutions*", which are described in Article 2(1) as follows:

> "This Directive shall apply to procedures for the out-of-court resolution of domestic and cross-border disputes concerning contractual obligations stemming from sales contracts and service contracts between a trader established in the Union and a consumer resident in the Union through the intervention of an ADR entity which proposes or imposes a solution or brings the parties together with the aim of facilitating an amicable solution."

A seemingly contradictory statement relating to the "optional character of ADR entities imposing solutions" in Article 2(4) of Directive 2013/11/EU reads:

> "This Directive acknowledges the competence of Member States to determine whether ADR entities established on their territories are to have power to impose a solution."

Member States are therefore free to set up ADR entities with the power to impose solutions, to continue existing instruments, or to completely abstain from doing so. In the following, they will be called instruments of (*binding*) *consumer arbitration*. If Member States take an active approach to consumer arbitration, they are bound by the requirements of Directive 2013/11/EU. These provisions will only apply in cases where the consumer as "plaintiff" is party to a valid arbitration agreement, not if the trader himself initiates a claim in arbitration because in these cases Directive 2013/11 is not applicable: Article 2(2)(g). It is limited to actions in contract (with the exception of non-economic services of general interest), excluding actions in tort and restitution. Injunctions against illegal behaviour of traders sought by consumer associations are also excluded; they come under other EU law instruments, in particular Directive 2009/22/EU on injunctions (8.33).

The principles contained in Directive 2013/11/EU are *minimum requirements* under Article 2(3). Within these limits, Member States are free to regulate consumer arbitration, e.g. regarding competence, costs, choice of arbitrators etc. This is part of their so-called "procedural autonomy" which has been recognised by the ECJ as a general principle of EU law (8.3). On the other hand, Member States must respect the principles of effectiveness and equivalence which are now part of Article 47 of the EU Charter of Fundamental Rights.

A consumer wanting to put his claim against a trader located in another EU country under an arbitration agreement cannot rely on the jurisdiction of his home country, as would be the case under the Brussels regime (7.35). Directive 2013/11/EU does not contain any rules on jurisdiction in cross-border conflicts. Article 7(1)(a) only requires ADR entities to "make publicly available on their website, … clear and easily understandable information on their contact details, including postal address and e-mail address". The most important protective provision of Directive 2013/11/EU, namely Article 10(2), follows the classical paradigm of the "informed EU consumer".[102] It is quite explicit about this minimum requirement for an arbitration clause in a C2B dispute which may be extended by Member States both horizontally to a B2C conflict and vertically by imposing additional requirements on this *specific acceptance*. Article 10(2) reads:

> "Member States shall ensure that in ADR procedures which aim at resolving a dispute by imposing a solution the solution imposed may be binding on the parties only if they were informed of its binding nature in advance and specifically accepted this. Specific acceptance by the trader is not required if national rules provide that solution are binding on traders."

What does mean "specific acceptance" (in German: "*ausdrücklich akzeptiert*")? Recital (43) does not provide an answer. It may be concluded in electronic form,

[102] See Weatherill, *EU Consumer Law and Policy*, 92.

but the trader must provide the consumer with a confirmation of that agreement on a durable medium; a mere link on the website is not sufficient.[103] On the other hand, it cannot form part of the general contract terms, but must be clearly separated from them. "Click-wrap clauses", popular in US e-contracting and licensing agreements (which come under Directive 2013/11/EU according to Recital (16)) whereby the simple click on an icon indicating the acceptance of general contract terms, including an arbitration agreement, are not sufficient for EU law.

It is not clear whether the term "specific acceptance" excludes *pre-dispute arbitration clauses*. The wording of Article 10(2) refers to a "dispute" to be resolved. Before conclusion of the contract there is, under a strict literal construction, no "dispute" that can be resolved. This is only the case once the contract is operating and the consumer is complaining about a defect, a misrepresentation and the like. Arbitration clauses therefore take their importance only once a specific dispute has arisen between the trader and the consumer. Both parties may have good reasons to take their conflict to arbitration, e.g. because of the speed or lower costs of getting a (binding) decision, but the consumer should not be forced to do so before a concrete dispute has arisen.

"Specific acceptance" has imposed an EU standard subject to interpretation by the CJEU. This warrants a critical appraisal of the traditional rule of (commercial) arbitration that the arbitrator, not the court, has *competence-competence* concerning the validity of the arbitration agreement. The EU unfair terms legislation (3.29) should be applied beyond the mere information model of Directive 2013/11/EU. A national court would be required to control *ex officio* under the unfairness test arbitration clauses imposing substantial inconveniences on the consumer by charging him excessive costs for arbitration or forcing him to take the case to an ADR entity far away from his residence. As is well known, EU law has been quite strict in banning jurisdiction clauses which force the consumer to take his case to a court away from his habitual residence and result in a *de facto* denial of access to justice. The same rules should apply to pre-contractual arbitration clauses (3.21).

8.23e Under traditional arbitration law, in particular in commercial matters, the parties are free to determine the applicable law, including commercial usages or simply principles of equity. Article 7(1)(i) has put this problem under the heading of "transparency" for all ADR entities, including consumer arbitration as defined above which reads:

> "Member States shall ensure that ADR entities make publicly available on their websites, on a durable medium, or by any other means they consider appropriate, clear and easily understandable information on … the types of rules the ADR entity

103 ECJ, 5 July 2012, C-49/11, *Content Service* [2012] ECR I-nyr.

may use as a basis for the dispute resolution (for example legal provisions, considerations of equity, codes of conduct)."

This freedom on the applicable rules is however limited concerning the *application of mandatory provisions of consumer law*, in particular EU law. This is regulated in the provisions on "legality" of Article 11. It concerns two situations: (a) purely internal ones where the mandatory consumer law provisions must be applied even if contracted out, and (b) cross-border disputes where the rules on applicable law in Regulation 593/2008 are normally excluded for arbitration agreements (7.15). Article 11(1)(a) to (b) provide as follows:

> "Member States shall ensure that in ADR procedures which aim at resolving the dispute by imposing a solution on the consumer: (a) in a situation where there is no conflict of laws, the solution imposed shall not result in the consumer being deprived of the protection afforded to him by the provisions that cannot be derogated from by agreement by virtue of the law of the Member State where the consumer and the trader are habitually resident; (b) in a situation involving conflict of laws, where the law applicable to the sales or service contract is determined in accordance with Article 6(1) and 6(2) of Regulation 593/2008, the solution imposed by the ADR entity shall not result in the consumer being deprived of the protection afforded to him by the provisions that cannot be derogated from by agreement by virtue of the law of the Member State in which he is habitually resident".

The legality requirement of consumer arbitration can only be fulfilled if Member States grant a remedy to the consumer to challenge an incorrect application of mandatory provisions by the arbitrator. The following situations may arise:

- The consumer (or a group of consumers) brings a claim against the trader before a court of law, but the trader falsely invokes the arbitration agreement.
- The claim of the consumer is rejected (or reduced) by the arbitrator based on a false application of mandatory consumer law against Article 11 of Directive 2013/11/EU; the consumer wants to challenge this rejection before courts of law which may be impossible or difficult under existing arbitration legislation relying on the *competence-competence principle* of the arbitrator.
- In practice the most frequent situation is concerned with the trader – in particular in a long-term contract – using the arbitration mechanism to enforce his claims, as could be seen from the *Claro* and *Asturcom* cases. These situations are however not caught directly by Directive 2013/11/EU which may however be *applied by analogy*.

8.23f Directive 2013/11/EU also contains some protective provisions in Article 8 which, however, do not have force of law but rather form standards of good ADR practice subject to monitoring and reporting under Article 20. They include:

- the ADR procedure is free of charge or available at a nominal fee for consumers: Article 20(c);
- the outcome of the ADR procedure is made available within a period of 90 calendar days from the date on which the ADR entity has received the complete complaint file. In the case of highly complex disputes, the ADR entity in charge may, at its own discretion, extend the period of 90 calendar days. The parties shall be informed of any extension of that period and of the expected length of time that will be needed for the conclusion of the dispute.

These are very flexible formulations which are also applicable to consumer arbitration. It is up to Member States whether and how they implement them. It can be presumed that they contain basic rules to enable a good functioning of ADR systems as an alternative to going to court, namely to provide for inexpensive and quick justice. Where practice shows that this objective cannot be obtained by the existing consumer arbitration mechanism in one country and market, it would be unfair to force the consumer to refer his claims to such arbitration even if the standards of "specific acceptance" under Article 10(2) of Directive 2013/11/EU are met. As recommendations they can be used to interpret Member State law "implementing" EU provisions under the *Grimaldi* doctrine.[104]

8.23g Directive 2013/11/EU is not concerned with *collective redress mechanisms* which exist in some Member States like the Netherlands.[105] Recital (27) makes clear that this option is not precluded by the Directive. It merely says that "the existence of an effective system for collective claims and easy recourse to ADR should be complementary and they should not be mutually exclusive procedures."

8.23h Regulation 524/2013 is of a more technical nature because it aims to give businesses and consumers trading electronically an online platform to solve their disputes by referring them to existing ADR entities. According to Article 2(1) it applies to "the out-of-court resolution of disputes concerning contractual obligations stemming from online sales or service contracts" from EU-resident consumers and traders. The Member State of the consumer may extend it to B2C disputes, i.e. disputes brought by the trader against the consumer. The ODR platform is supposed to be a "single point of entry" (Article 5(2)) for consumers and traders. The complainant party shall fill in "the electronic complaint form": Article 8(1). Most of the other parts of the Regulation concern a reference to the requirements of Directive 2013/11/EU on ADR

104 ECJ, 13 December 1989, 322/88, *Grimaldi v Fonds de Maladies Professionnelles* [1989] ECR 4497.

105 Hodges et al., 148.

entities. Article 9 regulates in great detail the processing and transmission of a complaint, and Article 10 provides for a resolution of the dispute by the chosen ADR entity without the parties' "physical presence".

3. CASE LAW ON ADR AND CONSUMER ARBITRATION

8.24 In the *Nordsee* case,[106] the Court refused to answer a preliminary question raised by an arbitrator because the Court deemed that an arbitrator cannot be considered a national jurisdiction in the sense of Article 234 EC.

This reading has been confirmed in *Denuit/Cordenier v Transorient.*[107] The submission of the matter to the arbitration panel of the travel dispute committee stemmed from an arbitration agreement entered into between the parties. The ECJ held that since the parties are under no obligation, in law or in fact, to refer their disputes to arbitration and the Belgian public authorities are not involved in the decision to opt for arbitration, the *Collège d'arbitrage de la Commission de Litiges Voyages* cannot be regarded as a court or tribunal of a Member State for the purposes of Article 267 TFEU.

8.25 In the *Claro* case[108] the Court had to decide whether the national court, in an action for annulment of an arbitration award against a consumer, can on its own motion determine the unfairness of the arbitration clause. The Court answered positively, thereby expressly excluding the question of whether the clause as such was violating Directive 93/13/EEC which it left to the national court (3.21). Once this court is convinced of the unfairness of the clause, overriding concerns of consumer protection according to Article 3(1)(t) EC (1.10) as implemented by Directive 93/13/EEC, "a measure which is essential to the accomplishment of the tasks entrusted to the Community and, in particular, to raising the standard of living and the quality of life in its territory", require the court "to assess of its own motion whether a contractual term is unfair, compensating in this way for the imbalance which exists between the consumer and the seller or supplier" (para 37). *Claro* has not ruled out the use of arbitration clauses in consumer contracts, this being a matter of Member State law, but it has obliged the judge in enforcement proceedings to raise on its on own motion the defence of *ordre public* if the arbitration award does not meet certain standards and has effectively curtailed consumer remedies under national law.

---

[106] ECJ, 23 March 1982, C-102/81, *Nordsee v Reederei Mond* [1982] ECR I-1095.

[107] ECJ, 28 January 2005, C-125/04, *Denuit/Cordenier v Transorient* [2005] ECR I-923.

[108] ECJ, 26 October 2006, C-168/05, *Elisa Maria Mostaza Claro v Centro Movil Milenium* [2006] ECR I-10421; the importance has been stressed by Reich, *ERCL* 2007, 41; criticism has been voiced by Liebscher, *CMLRev* 2008, 545.

The importance of *Claro* for effective consumer protection should not be underestimated. It is also important to allow the judge in consumer cases to reject *ex officio* the trader's defence that according to a clause in a standard form contract the case should be taken to arbitration (7.41). This case law was continued in *Asturcom,* concerning the complete inertia of a consumer drawn into arbitration whereby the award had become final.[109] Under the principle of "equivalence" (8.3) the Court insisted that the award should be set aside for EU policy reasons if this is possible under national law.

8.25a The restrictive ECJ case law on arbitration clauses in consumer contracts – which may be modified after implementation of Directive 2013/11 (8.23a) – must also be seen against US tendencies that allow consumer disputes to be referred by standard form clauses to binding arbitration and to thus effectively undermine state consumer protection legislation. In the words of the Supreme Court in *Southland Corp. v Keating,*[110] the Federal Arbitration Act (FAA – 9 U.S.C. Sections 1–16) "declared a national policy favoring arbitration and withdrew the power of the states to require a judicial forum for the resolution of claims which the contracting parties agreed to resolve by arbitration". Therefore, US law usually takes a very liberal view towards arbitration clauses agreed "in commerce" without making a distinction between commercial and consumer arbitration. This was confirmed by a controversial decision of the Supreme Court in *Green Tree Fin. Corp.-Ala. v Randolph*[111] in a consumer case, including the defence of statutory rights under state law. Consumers bear the burden of proving that the arbitral forum is financially inaccessible to them.

The recent Supreme Court decision of 21 February 2006, *Buckleye Check Cashing Corp. v John Cardegna*[112] seemed unconcerned by attempts to limit the effects of arbitration clauses in consumer contracts. The litigation concerned a class action suit brought against usurious terms in a consumer credit agreement which contained a broad arbitration clause. The Florida Supreme Court[113] set aside the arbitration clause reasoning that to enforce an agreement to arbitrate in a contract challenged as unlawful "could breathe life into a contract that not only violates state law, but is criminal in nature".

The Supreme Court, per Justice Scalia, quashed the judgment, distinguishing two cases where arbitration clauses could be challenged before courts of law, namely where:

---

109 ECJ, 6 October 2019, C-40/08, *Asturcom v Christina Rodrigues Nogueria* [2009] ECR I-9579; comment Schebasta, *ERPrL* 2010, 847,.

110 465 U.S. 1, 10 = 104 S. Ct. 852, 858 (1984).

111 531 U.S. 79 = 121 S. Ct. 513, 521 (2000).

112 546 U.S. 440 = 126 S. Ct. 1204 (2006).

113 894 So.2nd 860, 862 (2005).

- the arbitration clause is unlawful as such; and
- the entire contract is invalid from which the arbitration clause cannot be severed which was not the case in a usurious credit agreement.

As a consequence, Justice Scalia held:

> "We reaffirm today that, regardless of whether the challenge is brought in a federal or state court, a challenge to the validity of the contract as a whole, and not specifically to the arbitration clause, must go to the arbitrator."

Consumer protection therefore depends on the willingness of arbitrators to apply and enforce consumer protection provisions in particular of state law; their awards are not subject to critical public and academic debate. It seems that there is no remedy under US law against an arbitration award disregarding mandatory consumer protection provisions, similar to the approach of the ECJ in *Claro*. Arbitration clauses thereby have become a prominent and "popular" instrument to avoid the application of consumer protection provisions, at least in contract litigation between business and consumers, in particular against class action suits – a situation which does not exist as such in the EU. Exceptionally, an arbitration clause may be considered as "substantially unconscionable" as in the Pennsylvanian *Bragg* case[114] because of the one-sidedness and non-transparency of the clause, additional costs to the consumer to go to arbitration, etc.

8.25b The relationship between arbitration clauses in consumer contracts and the prohibition of class actions was more recently again before the Supreme Court in its *AT&T* judgment of 17 April 2011.[115] The Supreme Court held that the dispute must go to arbitration, and should not proceed as a class action. Prior to that holding, the state courts in California had maintained the opposite rule:[116] they had ruled that consumers must have the right to proceed with a class action, and shall not be forced into arbitration. Justice Antonin Scalia framed the *AT&T* case as a clash of two policies. On the one hand, the policy of the Californian courts favoured class actions. On the other hand, the policy of the Federal Arbitration Act favoured arbitration. By a vote of 5–4, the US Supreme Court held that the federal arbitration statute preempts the state court class action rule. The dissenting opinion written by Justice Breyer insisted that due to the small amount of the claim of the consumers before the court ($30.22), a denial of class actions practically meant a denial of justice – an argument

114 *Bragg v Linden Research*, 487 F.Supp. ed 593 (E.D. Pa. 2007); for a discussion of US practice see Lastowka, *Virtual Justice*, 2010, 17, 94.

115 *AT&T Mobility LLC v Concepion et al.*, 563 US, 131 S. Ct. 1740 (2011).

116 The so-called "Discover rule" of the California Supreme Court, *Discover Bank v Superior Court*, 113 P.3d 110 (2005).

which did not convince the majority opinion which found that class actions in arbitration proceedings as well are not a useful and manageable remedy.

The most recent *American Express* case before the Supreme Court decided by a judgment of 20 June 2013[117] concerned a commercial case with an arbitration clause also excluding anti-trust claims from being brought by class actions. Again Justice Scalia reiterated the liberal opinion of the Court majority favoring arbitration as "matter of contract" even against mandatory provisions of federal anti-trust laws. The dissenting opinion written by Justice Kagan in my opinion quite correctly insisted on the "effective vindication" rule established in prior case law limiting arbitration clauses where they effectively prevent enforcement of "congressionally created rights." This is done by the arbitration clause which *de facto* prevents compensation of anti-trust claims and undermines the deterrent effect of compensation for anti-trust infringements.

The case law of the US Supreme Court limits effective consumer protection as provided by federal (anti-trust) or state (the California *Discover* rule) law. It also seems to contradict the very wording of §2 of the Federal Arbitration Act which reads:

> "A written provision in any … contract evidencing a transaction involving commerce to settle by arbitration a controversy thereafter arising out of such contract or transaction … shall be valid, irrevocable and enforceable, save upon such grounds as exist at law or equity for the revocation of any contract."

US law itself therefore allows limits on arbitration in consumer (and commercial) matters based on such defences as fraud, duress, unconscionability and mandatory (federal and/or state) law which had in part been developed by state courts but had been regarded with hostility by the Supreme Court majority. This practice creates, as the minority in *American Express* pointed out, areas of *de facto immunity from law.* Justice Breyer wrote:

> "That statute [the FAA] reflects a federal policy favoring actual arbitration – that is, arbitration as a streamlined 'method of revolving disputes', not as a foolproof way of killing off valid claims."

In public opinion, criticism has been voiced against the "excessive use" of arbitration clauses in consumer contracts as supported by the majority opinion of the US Supreme Court.[118] Their disadvantages seem to be greater than the frequently invoked advantages of arbitration, namely:

---

117 *American Express Co. et al. v Italian Color Rest. et al.* 570 US (2013).

118 For details see ALDERMAN, Consumer Arbitration: The Destruction of the Common Law, *Journal of American Arbitration* 2002, 1; ALDERMAN, *The Future of Consumer Law in the US – Arbitration and the Destruction of Common Law*, University of Houston Public Law and Legal Theory Series 2008-A-09; with regard to then existing small claims procedures, see

- no possibility of a rational decision for or against arbitration before the dispute arises;
- the trader can always amend the arbitration clause unilaterally;
- no legal representation, no class actions, limited possibilities for bringing evidence, no legal dispute insurance;
- arbitrators cannot be formally obliged to apply state consumer protection legislation;[119]
- only limited access to documents which are usually in the hands of the trader, no pre-trial discovery procedure;
- no jury; only limited appeal possibilities;
- frequently excessive costs, compared with existing small claims procedures; and
- the place of arbitration may be far away from the residence of the consumer.

V. ENFORCEMENT OF COLLECTIVE CONSUMER INTERESTS

1. GENERAL PRINCIPLES UNDER UNION LAW

8.26 The communications published and actions taken by the Community/Union organs with regard to consumer legal protection show that collective legal protection plays a significant role alongside individual legal protection. Protective positions as guaranteed by substantive law can only be enforced if effective legal protection is possible. Given the lack of active engagement of individual consumers in building up the market, new innovative remedies allowing for enhanced access to the law appear particularly appropriate. The question of the accessibility of the law revolves around the enforcement of existing rights.

Practice shows that the individual judicial process is not always suited to sufficiently supervising obedience of the laws. In general, the consumer as an individual will avoid legal proceedings for a number of reasons. Often legal proceedings are not commenced as the damage is only minor, and assertion of a claim by an individual would not be worth it. There is also a certain wariness of legal institutions as well as the fear of bringing a claim against a well-known undertaking. This is to the detriment of the collective interest of consumers, as the passivity of consumers allows undertakings to continue their illegal practices

Reich, *Staatliche Regulierung zwischen Marktversagen und Politikversagen*, 1988, 129. A critical view (without citing the harsh case law of the US Supreme Court) has also been voiced by Calliess, 308–314.

119 The AAA Consumer Due Process Protocol contains such an obligation, while the rules of the ABA and the ICC are silent on that point, Calliess, 359.

and in so doing harm an unidentifiable number of consumers. So far, collective legal protection has failed as a result of consumers' lack of power as a genuine counterpart to business, itself a result of the lack of organisation of the consumers as a group. The falling apart of objective law and subjective legal protection of the individual justifies the introduction of collective legal protection.

Collective legal protection relates to the "abstract" competence of consumer associations to assert a claim and bring an action; these associations need not be in a legal relationship with the defendants. Consumer associations can take action without having to satisfy the requirement that the review of the conduct in question is in their own legal interest. In fact, the protection of individual interests is of little concern; this, however, does not prevent the establishment of a competence based on a public interest test. Asserting a claim for "de-individualised" consumer rights by bringing a legal action results in an institutional "system of guarantees" for the protection of the consumer. Collective protection leads to a transition from an individual's subjective rights being affected to a wider group of consumers being affected collectively, for example by unfair terms or misleading advertising, thus synchronising public and private law. As the ECJ wrote in its *Henkel* case[120] concerning jurisdiction for actions of consumer associations under the Brussels Convention (7.34):

> "The legal basis for its action [of the consumer association] is a right conferred by statute for the purpose of preventing the use of terms which the legislature considers to be unlawful in dealings between a professional and a private final consumer".

However, in its recent *ACI* judgment of 5 December 2013[121] the ECJ did not object to national (Spanish) procedural rules to limit the competence of the court for actions of consumer associations to the place of the establishment of the defendant (critique 3.27).

8.27 By facilitating the access to justice for groups of persons, the legal position of the consumer can be strengthened; this ultimately has the result of establishing a counterbalance to business. Substantive legal provisions regulating consumer protection are insufficient. Only by building up the access to justice can the effectiveness of substantive law be strengthened.[122] Collective protection can be used to overcome individual lack of interest, to minimise legal costs and to contribute to the furtherance of legal awareness.

---

120 ECJ, 1 October 2002, C-167/00, *Verein für Konsumenteninformation (VKI) v Karl Heinz Henkel* [2002] ECR I-8111 at para 39.

121 ECJ, 5 December 2013, C-413/13, *Ass. de Consumidores Independientes (ACI) de Castilla y Leon v Anuntis Segundanamo Esp.* [2013] ECR I-nyr.

122 Koch, *ZZP* 2000, 416 ff.

Effective legal protection is a fundamental requirement in a legal system which not only proclaims but also guarantees the law; it is therefore sometimes referred to as being an economic and social fundamental right, but is not protected by Article 47 of the Charter with this individual conception of a "right under Union law".[123] However, from a consumer policy point of view, consumer protection as a whole can be increased by providing an effective guarantee of substantive and procedural consumer protection provisions. It should be emphasised – irrespective of whether legal actions taken by consumer associations are to be characterised as procedural or substantive – that both areas are interrelated and that substantive provisions in particular can – by granting effective access to justice – serve the general cause of consumer protection.

With regard to compensation of costs for an NGO's support of proceedings before EU institutions, in particular the European Ombudsman, the ECJ[124] declined any liability of the EC under Article 288(2) EC:

> "the causal link required under the second paragraph of Article 288 EC is established where the damage is the direct consequence of the wrongful act in question ... With regard a claim for compensation for material damage which an applicant alleges to have suffered on account of the costs incurred in seeking legal advice at the pre-litigation stage of the procedure governed by Article 90 of the Staff Regulations, the Court of Justice held that, since in particular the contents of administrative complaints lodged under that provision must be interpreted and understood by the administration with all the care that a large and well-equipped institution owes to those having dealings with it, including members of its staff, although it is not possible to prohibit those concerned from seeking legal advice even at that stage, it is their own decision and the institution concerned cannot be held liable for the consequences. Thus, there is no causal link between the damage alleged, namely the lawyers' fees, and the act of the institution concerned". (paras 23–24)

2. ABSENCE OF COLLECTIVE REDRESS MECHANISMS IN PRIMARY EU LAW

8.28 Article 169(1) TFEU guarantees consumers the freedom of association (1.16). They are also protected by the non-discrimination principle of Article 18 TFEU. It does not, however, say anything about their competences under consumer law. This is usually left to Member States, which have developed rather different traditions and mechanisms.[125]

---

123 Reich, *supra* note 1, para 4.37.

124 ECJ, 28 June 2007, C-331/05P, *Internationaler Hilfsfonds v Commission* [2007] ECR I-5475.

125 See for recent trends in Member States, Micklitz/Stadler, *EBLR* 2006, 1473; Micklitz/Stadler, *Das Verbandsklagerecht in der Informations- und Dienstleistungsgesellschaft*, 2005.

One could argue that reading the sectoral clause in Article 12 TFEU, which insists on the importance of consumer protection in defining and implementing Union policies, together with the principle of effective legal protection as developed by the ECJ as a general principle of the Union could be interpreted as guaranteeing consumer associations an action for injunction as a minimum right to enforce consumer law. On the other hand, the ECJ has ruled on several occasions that Article 153 EC (now Article 169 TFEU) does not enjoy direct applicability as a result of its rather imprecise character;[126] it needs to be implemented and concretised in secondary law in order to create individual or collective rights of action. But Article 169 read in conjunction with Article 12 TFEU may be used for interpretative purposes in the context of a "dynamic interpretation" in order to optimise existing consumer protection law.[127] Last but not least, Article 38 of the EU Charter of Fundamental Rights insists that "Union policies shall ensure a high level of consumer protection"

The competence of the Union to enact measures to improve collective consumer protection is based either on the internal market competence as being ancillary to substantive protection rules, on Article 169(2)(b) TFEU in supporting Member States' measures, or, particularly in a cross-border context, on the provisions of the Amsterdam Treaty and now Lisbon Treaty on judicial cooperation in civil matters (1.18). In the following we refer to important measures taken under secondary law.

3. SECONDARY LAW

a) *Directives 84/450/EEC and 2006/114/EC on misleading advertising*

8.29 Directive 84/450/EEC on misleading advertising[128] was of a pioneering character in the building up of collective legal protection by way of an action for injunction. The Directive prohibits misleading advertising in the interest of the public, competitors and – until Directive 2005/29/EC was adopted (2.5; *infra* 8.32) – consumers. Directive 84/450/EEC has been amended by Directive 97/55/EC[129] and codified by Directive 2006/114/EC.[130] Comparative advertising has been included. Article 4(1) of Directive 84/450/EEC, now Article 5 of Directive 2006/114/EC, requires Member States to take adequate and effective means for

126 ECJ, 7 March 1996, C-192/94, *El Corte Ingles v Rivero* [1996] ECR I-1281.

127 Rösler, *RabelsZ* 2007, 508; ECJ, 26 October 2006, C-168/05, *Elisa Maria Mostaza Claro v Centro Movil Milenium* [2006] ECR I-10421; Reich, *EJCL* 2007, 42.

128 Council Directive 84/450/EEC of 10 September 1984 relating to the approximation of the laws, regulations and administrative provisions of Member States concerning misleading advertising OJ L 250, 19 September 1984, 18.

129 OJ L 290, 23 October 1997, 18.

130 OJ L 376, 27 December 2006, 21.

the control of misleading advertising. Such means shall include legal provisions under which persons or organisations regarded under national law as having a legitimate interest in prohibiting misleading advertising may take legal action against such advertising (Article 4(1)(a)) and/or bring such advertising before an administrative authority (Article 4(1)(b)). Article 4(1)(2) expressly states which of these options (judicial legal protection or administrative authority) shall be granted.[131] The Proposal from 1979 contained a right for consumer associations to sue, which was watered down in particular by virtue of opposition from the UK. At the same time there were opinions which denied the Member State any discretion in the transposition process.[132] Nonetheless, due to its history, Articles 4 and 5 are to be interpreted in terms of minimum procedural protection in that the principle of effective, preventive and speedy legal protection, and the principle of participation of consumer associations are recognised. The latter principle, however, is not constituted under Community law but remains at the discretion of Member States.[133]

b) Directive 93/13/EEC on unfair terms in consumer contracts

8.30 Article 7 of Council Directive 93/13/EEC on unfair terms in consumer contracts (3.27)[134] purports to create effective and *supra*-individual instruments to eliminate consumer transactions from unfair clauses.[135] Article 7(2) provides that these means shall include provisions "whereby persons or organisations, having a legitimate interest under national law in protecting consumers, may take action according to the national law concerned before the courts or before competent administrative bodies for a decision as to whether contractual terms drawn up for general use are unfair, so that they can apply appropriate and effective means to prevent the continued use of such terms". The question arose as to whether legal actions taken pursuant to Article 7(2) are discretionary or mandatory. This question was presented to the ECJ by the UK High Court at an early stage.[136] After the political change, the UK incorporated a right for consumer associations to take legal action into the Consumer Contracts

131 Grabitz/Hilf-Micklitz, Vol. 3, A 3, para 150; for a different view, Hoffmann, *Consommation – Publicité et protection des consommateurs en droit européen*, 1987, Fasc. 905, No. 46.

132 Hoffmann, *supra* note 131, 115.

133 Reich, *RabelsZ* 1992, 450 ff.

134 OJ L 25, 21 April 1993, 29; the history of origin cf. Howells/Wilhelmsson, *EC Consumer Law*, 121 ff.

135 Grabitz/Hilf-Pfeiffer, Vol. 3, A 5, Article 7, para 1.

136 The question was: "Does Article 7 Abs. 2 of the Directive 13/93 impose obligations on Member States to ensure that national law, (1) states criteria to identify private persons or organisations having a legitimate interest in protecting consumers, and (2) allows such private persons or organisations to take action before the courts or before competent administrative bodies for a decision as whether contractual terms drawn up for use are unfair?"

Regulations 1999 so that the claim brought by *Which Ltd* was rendered obsolete.[137]

8.31 However, this has not rendered the entire issue obsolete, as not all Member States provide a right for consumer associations to take legal action. In legal literature the prevailing opinion assumes such an obligation. It should be interpreted together with Article 12 TFEU (ex-Article 153(2) EC) and the *effet utile* principle, which leads to the conclusion that such an obligation could be assumed to exist. The wording in Article 7 itself provides such hints. Taken with Recital (23), Article 7 can be interpreted to mean that consumer associations have a right to take legal action.[138] For the first time Directive 93/13/EEC indicates an extension of possible legal remedies. The request for "appropriate means" in Article 7(1) is not bound to be limited to an application for an injunction.

c) *Directive 2005/29/EC on unfair commercial practices and Directive 2011/83 on consumer rights*

8.32 The contents of Articles 11 and 12 of Directive 2005/29/EC[139] correspond in reverse order to Articles 4 and 6 of Directive 84/450/EEC. The Community legislator avoided tackling the question of whether Member States are obliged to introduce, as a minimum, an action for injunction granted to consumer associations and trade associations. Article 11(1) restricts the obligation on Member States to ensure that adequate and effective means exist to combat unfair commercial practices in order to enforce compliance with the provisions of the Directive in the interest of consumers. The reference contained in Article 4(1) of Directive 84/450/EEC to the interests of competitors and the public interest has been abandoned. Recital (21) only refers to collective monitoring mechanisms in general terms. Persons and organisations must have legal remedies for initiating proceedings against unfair commercial practices, without saying who is actually being referred to. It is possible to argue that trade associations shall be denied the right to take actions in consumer disputes. Such a distinction would be in line with the limited scope of application of the unfair commercial practices Directive. Consumer associations shall be competent for violations of the law in business-to-consumer (B2C) relationships and trade associations in business-to-business (B2B) relationships. This distinction appears

137 In detail: Grabitz/Hilf-Micklitz, *supra* note 135 with further references.

138 Wilhelmsson, in: Micklitz/Reich (eds.), *Public Interest Litigation before European Courts*, 385 ff, 387; as well as Willett, in: Micklitz/Reich (eds.), *Public Interest Litigation before European Courts*, 403; Dickie, 112.

139 Directive 2005/29/EC of the EP and the Council of 11 May 2005 on unfair commercial practices, OJ L 149, 11 June 2005, 22; Micklitz, in: Howells/Micklitz/Wilhelmsson, *European Fair Trading Law*, 322–328.

to be dramatic in the light of full harmonisation as purported by Directive 2005/29/EC. Trade associations would be excluded from taking actions in B2C relationships.

There are two systematic considerations which contradict such an understanding. First, Article 11(1) explicitly names competitors as having a legitimate interest. If this were true, then it seems irrational to exclude trade associations from taking action in the interest of consumers. At the same time, persons and organisations regarded under national law as having a legitimate interest shall be entitled to take legal action. The reference to national law only concerns the "how" of the right to take action but not the "whether". It seems that, pursuant to the ambiguous wording of Article 11(1), which does not explicitly refer to trade associations but which does not exclude them either, those organisations shall be entitled to take legal action in the interests of the consumer to apply for an injunction of unfair commercial practices.

8.32a The recently adopted Consumer Rights Directive 2011/83/EU of 25 October 2011[140] has included a general clause on enforcement in Article 23 (2) similar to the ones discussed above. It thereby greatly extends the scope of collective actions by consumer or professional organisations "having a legitimate interest in acting", in particular in the field of off-premises and distance contracts, and of other obligations contained in the Directive analysed in Chapter 9, in particular information requirements under Article 5 that are valid for all consumer contracts.

d) Directive 2009/22/EC (ex-Directive 98/27/EC) on injunctions for the protection of consumers' interests

8.33 Directive 2009/22/EC of 23 April 2009,[141] codifying the former Directive 98/27/EC of 19 May 1998 on injunctions for the protection of consumers' interests,[142] pursues as an objective the access of consumers and consumer associations to justice; it could have been based on Article 169 TFEU (ex-Article 153 EC). As has been argued (1.23), this Article authorises the Community to promote consumer interests and the right of consumers to form organisations in order to safeguard their interests. The Economic and Social Committee wanted to base the Directive on this provision;[143] the Preamble of the Directive, however, refers to Article 114 TFEU (ex-Article 95 EC) as its legal basis. This illustrates the objective of approximating the laws in the interest of the internal market to facilitate the cross-border enforcement of consumer

140 OJ L 304, 22 November 2011, 64.
141 OJ L 110, 1 May 2009, 30.
142 OJ L 166, 11 June 1998, 51.
143 Opinion on the Proposal for a Directive, OJ C 30, 30 January 1997, 112 (sub 3.1).

rights.[144] By regulating the right of consumer associations to take legal action, the Directive also applies to purely national circumstances. This represents a further step in approximating the procedural provisions. In this context Article 81 TFEU (ex-Article 65 EC) is of significance: Article 81(2)(c) requires the Union to "promote the compatibility of the rules on civil procedure applicable in Member States". The national civil procedure rules are therefore considered the framework conditions for the development of the substantive law.

8.34 Directive 2009/22/EC, just like its predecessor Directive 98/27/EC, contains minimum standards concerning the right of qualified EU-based entities to take legal action in all Member States, and it governs certain procedural aspects.[145] Article 1 clarifies that it is the purpose of the Directive to approximate the laws, regulations and administrative provisions of Member States relating to actions for an injunction aimed at the protection of the collective interests of consumers provided by the (consumer) directives listed in the Annex, with a view to ensuring the smooth functioning of the internal market. Pursuant to Article 2, Member States are obliged to designate the courts or administrative authorities competent to rule on proceedings commenced by qualified entities – and these are defined in Article 3 as any body or organisation which, being properly constituted according to the law of a Member State, has a legitimate interest in ensuring the protection of the collective interests of the consumers. This follows from the objective of the Directive (consumer protection), meaning that business organisations are excluded. Article 4 governs the right of consumer associations to take legal action in the event of intra-Community infringements; the proof of this right is to be found in a list published in the Official Journal of the European Union. The right to take legal action will only be available if the alleged infringement concerns directives listed in the Annex which is updated regularly with new directives. Pursuant to Article 7, Member States are allowed to adopt or maintain provisions designed to grant more extensive rights to bring an action at a national level.

e) Relationship of Directive 2009/22/EC to individual provisions contained in other directives

8.35 At the time of writing, the updated Annex to Directive 2009/22 lists 16 directives which in part contain provisions on applications for injunctions, but which do not always comply with the current solution of the right of consumer associations or administrative authorities to take legal action.[146] Included in the Annex are Directive 99/44/EC on the sale of consumer goods (4.1), Directive

144 Koch, *ZZP* 2000, 433; Green Paper, Access to justice, COM (1993) 576 final, 88.
145 In detail: Rott, *JCP* 2001, 401; Weatherill, 300.
146 Koch, *ZZP* 2000, 436 ff.

2005/29/EC on unfair commercial practices (2.5), Directive 2006/123/EC on services in the internal market (1.27) and Directive 2011/83/EU on consumer rights (Chapter 9), but not Directive 2008/48/EC on consumer credit (5.4). Directive 2009/22/EC purports to regulate the collective right to take legal action, meaning that it prevails over individual directives containing provisions on the right of consumer associations to take legal action. National provisions concerning this right which are not required under Union law remain unaffected due to the principle of minimum harmonisation.

4. RIGHT OF ACTION AND STANDING TO SUE (LEGITIMATE INTEREST TO TAKE LEGAL ACTION)

8.36 Directive 2009/22/EC allows, in conformity with French law, for the distinction of three levels. (1) The question of the right of action (*qualité d'agir*), which is determined by the *lex fori*. Here, Directive 2009/22/EC concerning actions for cross-border injunctions brings clarity by providing mutual recognition of national consumer organisations which have a right of action. (2) Standing to sue (*intérêt pour agir* – under Union law it appears to make more sense to speak of a legitimate interest to take legal action instead of claim), which is determined by the *lex fori delicti*, given the nature – as regards the law of tort/delict or the law of quasi-delict – of actions by consumer associations concerning general terms and conditions. Here, the discussion about the rule as to market effect has its place (7.28), but it is also limited under Union law. And (3) the determination of the substantive law to be used under EU private international law, for which Directive 2009/22/EC provides a regulation of little satisfaction (on the potential implications of Rome II Regulation 864/2007, see 7.21).

a) Right of action

8.37 The aim of Directive 2009/22/EC is to fix, in respect of cross-border infringements within the Community, the principle of mutual recognition for entities qualified to bring an action. Member States are required, on application by their national entities, to inform the Commission of the name and purpose of national entities which, in that country, have a right to bring an action. This list is published in the Official Journal Part C. Article 2(1) leaves it to Member States to designate the entities qualified to bring an action. New legal remedies are not created through the Directive. Article 4 obliges Member States to take all measures necessary to ensure that, in the event of an infringement originating in that Member State, any qualified entity from another Member State, where the interests protected by that qualified entity are affected by the infringement, may seize the court or administrative authority referred to in Article 2, on presentation of the list provided for in paragraph 3.

b) *Standing to sue (legitimate interest to take legal action)*

8.38 Directive 2009/22/EC does not (i) make a statement in respect of standing to sue, nor (ii) define concrete requirements for standing to sue (the legitimate interest to take legal action), nor (iii) make arrangements concerning the applicable law. Hence, the solution is to be found under national law. The starting point is the legal nature of the claim to compel someone to refrain from doing something, which, based on Union law, is to be classified as falling under tort/delict or quasi-delict respectively.[147] If one puts both types of action on the same level, the means of determining the applicable law already appears to be designated. According to Article 6(1) of the Rome II Regulation 864/2007 (7.28) the applicable law is to be inferred from the *lex loci delicti*, which, in the law concerning general terms and conditions, is typically the place where the user has employed the general terms and conditions. In the field of advertising it is the marketplace where the advertising measure has its effects on consumers as a whole. In case of multi-state marketing, every country where the measure injures consumer interests must be regarded as determining the *lex loci delicti*.

8.39 The rule as to market effect, however, must be modified under Community law, as seems to be suggested under Article 27 of the Rome II Regulation 864/2007 (7.28). The – limited – principle of the country of origin guarantees free access to the European internal market for all products and services that have lawfully been placed onto the market in the country of origin.[148] The privilege of access is made impossible where the product or service has been placed upon the market unlawfully. A Member State – and this is the crucial conclusion of the interplay between lawful and unlawful – has a responsibility at source.[149] As a result of the principle of the country of origin, a Member State must ensure that there are no risks originating in its territory which endanger the citizens in the other Member States. The principle of the country of origin ensures the application of national law that conforms to EC law in order to eliminate the cause at its root, i.e. in the country of origin, where the full damaging effect is only felt in the country of designation. Improper marketing practices also have to be dealt with where the commercial activity has its starting point. This does not mean, however, that the courts of the country of activity cannot take appropriate measures under the applicable jurisdiction rules

---

147 ECJ, 1 October 2002, C-167/00, *Verein für Konsumenteninformation (VKI) v Karl Heinz Henkel* [2002] ECR I-8111.

148 Cf. particularly clearly in ECJ, 20 February 1979, 120/78, *REWE v Bundesmonopolverwaltung für Branntwein (Cassis de Dijon)* [1979] ECR 649 at para 14; and ECJ, 12 March 1987, 178/84, *Commission v Germany, (purity of beer case)* [1987] ECR 1227 at para 52; and Reich, *supra* note 118, 492.

149 Cf. Reich, *RabelsZ* 1992, 509; more reserved about the extra-territorial extension of competence Roth, *RabelsZ* 1991, 668.

of the Brussels Regulation 44/2001 (7.42/8.40) and the applicable substantive law, provided those measures comply with free movement requirements of EC law.

5. INTERNATIONAL JURISDICTION AND ENFORCEMENT IN ACTIONS FOR CROSS-BORDER INJUNCTIONS

8.40 The determination of international jurisdiction should be comparatively simple, even though Articles 15 *et seq.* of Regulation 44/2001 are not applicable to legal actions taken by a consumer protection association because the association is not the ultimate consumer and hence does not need the special protection provided by the regulation on jurisdiction in matters concerning consumers.[150]

International jurisdiction in respect of unlawful advertising measures across national borders, such as unwanted telephone calls from one EU state to another or of television broadcasts with unlawful portions of advertising, is determined by Regulation 44/2001 if a "civil and commercial matter" for the purposes of Article 1(1) is shown. In cases of wide-ranging violations against consumer protection provisions, a tort, delict or quasi-delict in accordance with Article 5(3) of Regulation 44/2001 may exist, which is covered by a special jurisdiction in the place where the harmful event occurred, similar to the market effect rule in private international law.[151] In this respect, there has been no change from the Brussels Convention (7.34). In *Henkel* the Court wrote:

> "The concept of harmful event within the meaning of Art 5 (3) of the Brussels Convention is broad in scope... so that, with regard to consumer protection, it covers not only situations where an individual has personally sustained damage but also, in particular, the undermining of legal stability by the use of unfair terms which it is the task of associations such as the VKI to prevent". (para 42)

The same applies to adhesional actions.[152] Thus the courts in the place of the business seat of the tortfeasor and in the place where the harmful event occurred to the collective detriment of consumer interests both have jurisdiction. This, in principle, allows for *forum shopping*. This can however be limited by national procedural rules putting jurisdiction for actions by consumer associations exclusively to courts of the establishment of the defendant (8.26).

A similar interpretation will prevail in cases where consumer associations take action against misleading advertising, deceptive omissions of information

150 ECJ, 1 October 2002, C-167/00, *Verein für Konsumenteninformation (VKI) v Karl Heinz Henkel* [2002] ECR I-8111 at para 33.

151 Reich, *supra* note 118, 148.

152 ECJ, 21 April 1993, C-172/91, *Sonntag* [1993] ECR I-1963.

requirements in secondary Union law (for example on a right to withdrawal), and unfair commercial practices under Directive 2005/29/EC.

8.41 In the case of an action for an injunction being brought in the country where harm is caused, i.e. in the country where advertising misleadingly affects consumers or unfair terms are used in consumer transactions, court decisions – so far as the opposing party can be heard – are capable of being recognised in principle according to Regulation 44/2001 as well as (formerly) the Brussels Convention.[153] Payments by way of a penalty are enforced in accordance with Article 49 of Regulation 44/2001. That provision reads:

> "A foreign judgment which orders a periodic payment by way of penalty shall be enforceable in the Member States in which the enforcement is sought only if the amount of the payment has been finally determined by the courts of the Member State of origin."

These principles, in theory, allow for the prosecution of misleading advertising, unfair contractual provisions or unfair practices across national borders through national consumer organisations, which, because of this, become "officials of Union law".[154] If one follows the opinion outlined here, actions could be brought both in the state of origin (country of origin principle) and in the state where the infringement takes effect (marketplace rule). The basis for this is the mutual recognition of the rights of action of the respective national consumer associations in the forums of Member States. Practical experiences with this *Cassis* principle in the field of the bringing of legal action, however, must first be developed through test cases,[155] which will help enforce the "diffuse interests of consumers" in collective legal enforcement.

6. COOPERATION ON CONSUMER PROTECTION

8.42 In order to fight cross-border violations of consumer interests more effectively, the Commission, in July 2003, adopted a proposal for a regulation on consumer protection cooperation.[156] In October 2004, it was finally adopted as Regulation (EC) No 2006/2004 on cooperation between national authorities responsible for the enforcement of consumer protection laws.[157] Its legal basis is Article 95 EC (now Article 114 TFEU). It has applied from 29 December 2005

---

153 ECJ, 21 May 1980, C-125/79, *Denilauler* [1980] ECR I-1553.
154 Reich, *supra* note 118, 503.
155 On their relevance, cf. Koch, *Verbraucherprozessrecht*, 29 ff; on this Reich, *JCP* 1990, 484.
156 COM (2003) 443.
157 OJ L 364, 9 December 2004, 1.

onwards, but the provision on mutual assistance has only applied from 29 December 2006.

Article 4 obliges Member States to designate certain authorities competent for consumer protection matters listed in the annex. They must have the following powers (Article 4(6)):

> "The powers referred to in paragraph 3 shall only be exercised where there is a reasonable suspicion of an intra-Community infringement and shall include, at least, the right:
> (a) to have access to any relevant document, in any form, related to the intra-Community infringement;
> (b) to require the supply by any person of relevant information related to the intra-Community infringement;
> (c) to carry out necessary on-site inspections;
> (d) to request in writing that the seller or supplier concerned cease the intra-Community infringement;
> (e) to obtain from the seller or supplier responsible for intra-Community infringements an undertaking to cease the intra-Community infringement; and, where appropriate, to publish the resulting undertaking;
> (f) to require the cessation or prohibition of any intra-Community infringement and, where appropriate, to publish resulting decisions;
> (g) to require the losing defendant to make payments into the public purse or to any beneficiary designated in or under national legislation, in the event of failure to comply with the decision."

It also puts in place a system that is designed to ensure the sharing of information and pattern of mutual assistance between enforcement authorities in different Member States. The designated bodies are to be linked according to a model that empowers authorities in one Member State to obtain action from their counterparts in another. Consumer organisations only indirectly participate in that network, but are encouraged to cooperate with competent authorities. They do not enjoy rights of their own.

7. COLLECTIVE REDRESS IN EU LAW: A NEW TENDENCY TOWARDS LAW ENFORCEMENT?

8.43 In its Consumer Policy Strategy 2007–2013[158] the Commission wrote that it will consider taking action on collective redress mechanisms for consumers both for infringements of consumer protection rules and for breaches of EU antitrust rules in line with the 2005 Green Paper on private damages actions (8.13). To date no concrete proposal has been put forward.

158 COM (2007) 99 final of 13 March 2007, 11.

In the meantime, the European Economic and Social Committee has delivered its own-initiative opinion on "Defining the collective actions system and its role in the context of Community consumer law".[159] The opinion discusses a number of issues without making concrete proposals. It clearly rejects the US system of class actions,[160] which better serves the interests of lawyers in legal fees than that of consumers in effective legal protection. The procedural "environment" towards class actions is much more restrictive in EU Member countries than in the US. On the other hand, class or rather collective actions (*Sammelklagen*) must be regarded as an effective means of consumer redress and access to justice. Whether an *opt-in* (all plaintiffs must agree to join the action beforehand) or *opt-out* scheme (one plaintiff or his lawyer takes the action on behalf of himself and the other injured consumers who may later decide not to join in if they do not want to share the risks and costs of the proceedings) is chosen to determine the group of plaintiffs depends on the nature of the claim: small claims can only be effectively enforced under an opt-out system; larger claims (e.g. those arising out of product liability) will require an opt-in scheme. The EU law instrument can either be a regulation under its competence for judicial proceedings in civil matters, or a directive under Article 169 TFEU specifically serving the consumer interest (*supra* 1.24). So far the Commission has not yet taken up this initiative.

As a second step in a similar direction, the Commission White Paper on "Damages actions for breach of the EC antitrust rules" of 2 April 2008,[161] accompanied by a more detailed Staff Working Paper,[162] puts forward suggestions for, either:

- representative actions brought by qualified entities, e.g. consumer associations, state bodies or trade associations, on behalf of identified or, in restricted cases, identifiable victims; or
- opt-in collective actions in which victims expressly decide to combine their individual claims into one single action.

However, the White Paper is not accompanied by a legislative proposal. It does not discuss the legislative basis of EC action in this field.[163] The recently adopted proposal for a Directive on damages actions for infringements of EU competition

---

159 CESE 258/2008 of 13/14.42.2008.

160 For an overview see the excellent study by BEUCHLER.

161 COM (2008) 165 final of 2 April 2008.

162 SEC (2008) 404 of 2 April 2008.

163 See the different evaluation by EILMANNSBERGER, The Green Paper on Damages Actions for Breach of the EC Antitrust Rules and Beyond: Reflections on the Utility and Feasibility of Stimulating Private Enforcement Through Legislative Action, *CMLRev* 2007, 431 at 2.4; REICH, *CMLRev* 2007, 742.

law on 11 June 2013[164] (*supra* 8.14) does not contain any provisions on collective redress, not even in an opt-in version.

8.44 Some Member States have introduced different schemes for collective redress of consumer injuries, but an overview of the existing law and practice in Member States in the study by Stuyck[165] done before 2007 summarises the findings as follows:

> "Contrary to class actions, as they exist in the US, Canada and Australia, there is no common form of collective action for damages in Europe."[166]

This state of law has not changed very much since then.[167] The general discussion in the European Parliament on collective redress has been rather hostile, as a report of the legal committee of 12 January 2012 shows:

> "a collective redress system where the victims are not identified before the judgment is delivered must be rejected on the grounds that it is contrary to many Member States' legal orders and violates the rights of any victims who might participate in the procedure unknowingly and yet be bound by the court's decision". (para 20)

The Commission has therefore not made any legislative proposals on that subject, and instead only released a Recommendation on 11 June 2013[168] rejecting any type of opt-out solution and leaving it to Member States to define standing, admissibility and funding, and containing, surprisingly, a prohibition on punitive damages and contingency fees. Unfortunately, the Recommendation does not show any sincere concern for collective redress of violations of consumer law and may even discourage Member States from advancing legal reform; instead it seems to aim only at rejecting any US class-action initiative.

---

164 COM (2013) 404 final.

165 Stuyck et al., *An analysis and evaluation of alternative means of consumer redress*, 260–320.

166 Ibid, at 321.

167 For a discussion see Reich, *Individueller und kollektiver Rechtsschutz im EU-Verbraucherrecht*, 54.

168 COM (2013) 3539/3 [2013] OJ L 260/60.

CHAPTER 9

THE CONSUMER RIGHTS DIRECTIVE AND ITS IMPACT ON INTERNET AND OTHER DISTANCE CONSUMER CONTRACTS

Klaus TONNER

CONTENTS

Bibliography:
J.M. Bech Serrat, *Selling tourism services at a distance*, 2012; T. Brönneke/K. Tonner, *Das neue Schuldrecht: Verbraucherrechtsreform 2014*, 2014; O. Calliano, A Critical First Glance at the CESL Project by the Digital Consumer Law Approach, in: Moccia, *The Making of European Private Law: Why, How, What, Who*, 2013, 217; J. Dickie, *Producers and Consumers in EU E-Commerce Law*, 2005; E. Hall/G. Howells/J. Watson, The Consumer Rights Directive – an assessment of its contribution to the development of European consumer contract law, *ERCL* 2012, 139; N. Helberger et al., *Digital consumers and the law – towards a cohesive European framework*, 2013; N. Helberger et al., Digital content contracts for consumers, *JCP* 2013, 37–57; G. Howells/R. Schulze, Overview of the proposed Consumer Rights Directive, in: G. Howells/R. Schulze, *Modernising and harmonising consumer contract law*, 2009, 3; J. Karsten, Travel law, in: Twigg-Flesner, *The Cambridge Companion to European Private Law*, 2010, 201; H.-W. Micklitz/N. Reich, Cronica de una muerte anunciada: The Commission proposal for a "Directive on Consumer Rights", *CMLRev* 2009, 471; H.-W. Micklitz/N. Reich, The Commission proposal for a "Regulation on a Common European Sales Law (CESL)" – Too broad or not broad enough?, in: Moccia (ed.), *European Private Law: Why, How, What, Who*, 2013, 21; J. Pisulinski, The application of the CESL to a contract for the supply of digital content (e.g. software), in: Moccia (ed.), *The Making of European Private law: Why, How, What, Who*, 2013, 205; N. Reich, *General Principles of EU Civil Law*, 2013; N. Reich, From minimal to full to "half" harmonization, in: Devenney/Kenny (eds.), *European Consumer Protection*, 2012, 3; longer version in German: Von der Minimal- zur Voll- zur Halbmodernisierung, *ZEuP* 2010, 7; G. Rossoni, The impact of the Consumer Rights Directive on tourism, *IFFTA Law Rev* 2013, 10 (supplement to *Reiserecht aktuell* 2013(4)); P. Rott, Consumers and services of general interest, *JCP* 2007, 53; P. Rott, The balance of interests in distant selling law, *ERPL* 2010, 185–194; P. Rott/E. Terryn, The proposal for a Directive on Consumer Rights: no single set of rules?, *ZEuP* 2009, 456; K. Tonner/K. Fangerow, Directive 2011/83/EU on consumer rights: a new approach to European consumer law?, *EUVR* 2012, 67; K. Tonner/M. Tamm, Der Vorschlag einer Richtlinie über Rechte der Verbraucher und seine Auswirkungen auf das nationale Verbraucherrecht, *JZ* 2009, 277; O. Unger, Die Richtlinie über die Rechte der Verbraucher: eine systematische Einführung, *ZEuP* 2012, 270; S. Weatherill, The Consumer Rights Directive: how and why a quest for "coherence" has (largely) failed, *CMLRev* 2012 1279; T. Wilhelmsson, The abuse of the "confident consumer" as justification for EC consumer law, *JCP* 2004, 317.

I. INTRODUCTION

9.1 This chapter deals in particular with the special requirements for the conclusion of consumer contracts by electronic means, especially via the internet. There are three Directives which are of relevance: the E-Commerce Directive 2000/31/EC and the Consumer Rights Directive 2011/83/EU (CRD), and, to a limited extent, the Services Directive 2006/123/EC. The Consumer Rights Directive is the successor of two Directives from 1985 and 1997, the

Doorstep Sales Directive 85/377/EEC and the Distance Selling Directive 97/7/EC. The transposition period of the CRD has only just expired at the time of writing, so there is not yet any experience with its implementation.

The scopes of the E-Commerce Directive and of the CRD are anything but coherent. This is because the E-Commerce Directive is based on the provisions of freedom to provide services, whereas the CRD is part of consumer policy. But in a core matter both Directives overlap: they have to be applied in consumer contracts, which are or are to be concluded through electronic means. Electronic means are not defined; the E-Commerce Directive includes only the term "service of the information society" (9.18). A trader, who wants to sell a good or a service to a consumer via the internet, has to fulfil the requirements of both Directives. This is why both have to be dealt with here.

Moreover, the scopes of the two Directives are different. The E-Commerce Directive is applicable to all contracts, whereas the CRD is only applicable to B2C contracts. On the other hand, the E-Commerce Directive is limited to contracts concluded through electronic means, whereas the CRD is open to all distance contracts, even those which are concluded through traditional means like a posted letter. This is because the CRD follows the approach of the Distance Selling Directive of 1997.

II. CONSUMER RIGHTS DIRECTIVE

1. SHORT LEGISLATIVE HISTORY OF THE CRD

9.2 On 25 October 2011 the CRD was adopted.[1] Member States have to transpose the Directive to their national law until 13 December 2013, whereas the transposition rules have to be applied from 13 June 2014 for contracts concluded after that date (Article 28).

According to the original intention of the Commission the CRD should have become the cornerstone of a second generation of consumer contract law directives as envisaged in the Commission's Consumer Policy Strategy 2007–2013.[2] The Commission distinguished so-called vertical and sectoral Directives. The Doorstep Selling Directive,[3] the Distance Selling Directive,[4] the Unfair

1 Directive 2011/83/EU of the European Parliament and of the Council of 25 October 2011 on consumer rights, amending Council Directive 9313/EEC and Directive 1999/44/EC of the European Parliament an of the Council and repealing Council Directive 85/577/EEC and Directive 97/7/EC of the European Parliament and of the Council, OJ L 304 of 22 November 2011, 64.

2 COM (2007) 99.

3 Directive 85/577/EEC of 20 December 1985, OJ L 372 of 31 December 1985, 31.

4 Directive 97/7/EC of 20 May 1997, OJ L 144 of 4 June 1997, 19.

Contract Terms Directive[5] and the Consumer Sale of Goods Directive[6] were regarded as "vertical" directives, which should be combined into one Directive, whereas the other directives with contractual contents (consumer credit, timeshare and package tours) should remain separate directives, but undergo a review. Following this structure the CRD should have deserved its ambitious title, because it would have been the centre of the new consumer contract law. The main characteristic of this second generation should be the step from minimum standard harmonisation of the first generation directives of the 1980s and 1990s to full harmonisation.

In 2008 the Commission adopted its proposal for a CRD, which should replace the four "vertical" directives mentioned.[7] The proposal attracted a lot of criticism from Member States and legal writers,[8] which was not directed against the systematic approach – quite the contrary, a bit more coherence of consumer law was welcomed – but against the full harmonisation principle. Member States were not only afraid of losing their influence over consumer law, but the more advanced Member States also feared being forced to reduce some of their existing law beyond the level of the existing directives. Parliament welcomed the idea of full harmonisation on the one hand, but stressed on the other hand the principle of a high level of consumer protection as laid down in Article 114 TFEU,[9] which should not force any Member State to reduce its existing level of consumer protection.[10]

The outcome of long discussions between Council and Parliament within the conciliation procedure according to Article 294 TFEU was a serious reductionism of the proposal, if not a failure of the Commission's original approach.[11] The CRD as it was finally adopted replaces only the Doorstep Selling Directive and the Distance Selling Directive, whereas the Unfair Contract Terms Directive and the Sale of Consumer Goods Directive were – with slight adaptations to the CRD – left as they are, including the minimum standard principle. This is not the end of the story of the review of consumer sales law, as the proposal for a CESL shows, which is briefly discussed elsewhere in this book (1.43b).[12] But for the moment existing law is only the CRD with its limited scope and the two "old" Directives from 1993 and 1999.[13]

---

5 Directive 93/13/EC of 5 April 1993, OJ L 95 of 21 April 1993, 12.

6 Directive 1999/44/EC of 25 May 1999, OJ L 171 of 7 July 1999, 12.

7 COM (2008) 614.

8 Micklitz/Reich, *CMLRev* 2009, 471; Howells/Schulze, 3, 25; Rott/Terryn, *ZEuP* 2009, 456.

9 Article 114 is the legal basis not only of the CRD, but of all consumer protection directives, cf. 1.9.

10 Report of the Committee on Legal Affairs, PE 445.885, 24 January 2011.

11 This is the general opinion in literature, cf. Weatherill, *CMLRev* 2012, 1279.

12 Cf. also Micklitz/Reich, in: Moccia, 21.

13 For the relevance of the CRD for consumer contract law cf. Hall/Howells/Watson, *ERCL* 2012, 139.

Nevertheless, the CRD is not only of relevance within the scope of the former Doorstep Selling and Distance Selling Directives. The CRD also includes some provisions with relevance for sales law (9.16), and in particular it provides for information duties not only in an off-premises or distance selling context, but also for traditional shopping.

2. SCOPE OF APPLICATION

9.3 The scope of the Directive is limited to (contractual) relations between consumers and traders. The definition of "consumer" is the traditional one: a natural person, acting outside his trade, business, craft or profession (Article 2 (1); for the term "consumer" cf. 1.37). The wording of this provision does not address the dual use problem, but Recital (17) does. According to this Recital, a person should be considered a consumer even if a trade purpose is so limited as not to be predominant in the overall context of the contract. This is broader than the approach of CJEU in *Gruber*, dealing with the term of consumer of the Brussels Convention/Brussels I Regulation,[14] according to which a consumer protection rule is only applicable if "the trade or professional purpose is so limited as to be negligent in the overall context of the supply."[15] It remains to be seen whether the CJEU will adapt its jurisdiction to Recital (17) of the CRD or whether it will insist on its definition within the scope of the Brussels I Regulation.[16]

The CRD follows, as expressed by the Consumer Strategy 2007–2013, a "vertical" approach. This is to say that it is applicable "to any contract concluded between a trader and a consumer" (Article 3(1)). From the point of view of legal orders such as the German BGB it may be surprising that sales law is part of a vertical and not of a sectoral directive, as such legal orders distinguish general rules on contract law from rules on specific types of contract, of which a sales contract is only one of a fairly large number of types of contract. It must be stressed that the distinction between "vertical" and "sectoral" in EU consumer contract law is not the same as between general and specific parts in codifications like the BGB. For a national legislator who wants to maintain the traditional approach of general parts it is difficult to comply at the same time with the approach of the new consumer contract Directives and their distinction between "vertical" and "sectoral", as the present implementation of the CRD in Germany clearly shows.[17]

---

14 Regulation (EC) No 44/2001 of 22 December 2000, OJ L 12 of 16 January 2001, 1.

15 ECJ 20 January 2005, C-464/01, *Johann Gruber v BayWa AG* [2005] ECR I-439; see also 1.36, 7.8.

16 A broader discussion of this issue can be found in TONNER/FANGEROW, *EUVR* 2012, 67, 72. Cf. also 1.38.

17 Cf. Gesetz zur Umsetzung der Verbraucherrechterichtlinie, Bundesgesetzblatt 2013 I 3642 (Act transposing the Consumer Rights Directive, [German] Federal Official Journal 2013 I, p. 3642; discussed in BRONNEKE/TONNER.

9.4 The statement that the Directive is applicable to "any" contract is very much mitigated, if not contradicted, in the following sections of the CRD. The list of exemptions is long and contradicts the pretention of the proposal to provide for more coherence within consumer contract law.[18] The basic rule is that rules for specific sectors prevail (Article 3(2)). This means that the CRD does not create general principles of consumer contract law which are applicable for all consumer contracts, but rather that such principles are applicable only within the scope of the CRD. Legal instruments governing specific sectors in the sense of Article 3(2) create their own system and must not be amended by principles derived from the CRD. This means that the CRD is not at a somewhat "higher" level than the other consumer contract directives, but that it is just one among a set of "equal" Directives – and so does not deserve its title.[19]

This makes it even more important to have a close look at the exemptions. Among the list in Article 3(3) are all the "sectoral" Directives, which are part of the review according to the 2007–2013 Strategy. Two of them were revised – the law of timesharing by Directive 2008/122/EC[20] and provisions on consumer credit by Directive 2008/48/EC[21] (5.3) – whereas the review of the Package Travel Directive[22] has been delayed (a proposal was published only in July 2013).[23] It should be noted that the CRD is applicable within the scopes of the Unfair Contract Terms Directive and the Sale of Consumer Goods Directive. The precedence of the Consumer Credit Directive means, that the *Heininger* case law of the CJEU, dealing with the applicability of the Doorstep Sales Directive in credit contracts, is no longer applicable.[24]

It is doubtful whether the Consumer Credit Directive or the CRD is applicable for consumer guarantees to credit contracts. According to *Dietzinger*, such a consumer guarantee is under the scope of the (former) Doorstep Sales Directive only, if the "main contract", this is to say the credit contract, is a consumer credit contract.[25] The *Dietzinger* doctrine is still applicable. A guarantee is no credit contract and so not under the scope of the Consumer Credit Directive, meaning that the rule of the CRD, which provides for the precedence of the Consumer Credit Directive, does not apply and the consumer has a right to withdraw if the prerequisites of an off-premises contract or a distance contract are fulfilled.

---

18 Weatherill, *CMLRev* 2012, 1279.

19 According to Weatherill, *CMLRev* 2012, 1279 the title is even misleading.

20 Directive 2008/122/EC of 14 January 2009, OJ L 33 of 3 February 2009, 10.

21 Directive 2008/48/EC of 23 April 2008, OJ L 133 of 22 May 2008, 66.

22 Directive 90/314/EEC of 13 June 1990, OJ L 158 of 23 June 1990, 59.

23 COM (2013) 512.

24 ECJ 22 April 1999, C-423/97, *Travel Vac* [1999] ECR I-2196; ECJ, 13 December 2001, C-481/99, *Heininger* [2001] ECR I-9945; in more detail 9.13; Reich, *General Principles of EU Civil Law*, 4.21.

25 ECJ 17 March 1998, C-45/96, *Dietzinger* [1998] ECR I-1199.

Further sectors that are excluded are social services, healthcare, gambling, financial services, immovable property, contracts established by a public office holder, supply of foodstuff for current consumption supplied by a mobile trader, passenger transport services,[26] contracts concluded by automatic vending machines and contracts concluded with telecommunications operators through public payphones. Included are contracts for the supply of water, gas, electricity or district heating. This is a step in building a bridge between the many EU legal instruments in the field of services of general interest and the body of consumer law, which is also underpinned by the new European Consumer Agenda.[27]

9.5 The different approach of the CRD concerning its relation to other consumer contract Directives results in some changes especially with regard to information in e-commerce. Under the "old" regime, this is to say the Distance Selling Directive, a trader who wants to sell goods or services through the internet has to fulfil information duties according to the Distance Selling Directive and the E-Commerce Directive (9.18), whatever the goods or services were. In particular, travel and tourism services were not excluded from the information obligations of the Distance Selling Directive. After the Distance Selling Directive had expired, there was a general obligation for a trader only to act in conformity with the E-Commerce Directive. Secondly, the internet trader has to ascertain which Directive applies for his business. This is not necessarily the CRD. In the tourism sector, for example, the trader has to find out whether he is a tour operator. If so, only information duties according to the Package Travel Directive apply; but if not, because, for example, he sells only a single service, the CRD applies.[28] Most probably, the trader will sell package tours and single services as well. Does his website in this case have to be in line with the information requirements of the "vertical" and the "sectoral" Directive? The same is true for a bank selling consumer credit. Undoubtedly, the idea of providing different sets of information duties will lead to much confusion in practice.

Even more confusion may arise, as according to the E-Commerce Directive the trader (in the words of the E-Commerce Directive: the service provider, 9.18) has to fulfil the information duties *vis-à-vis* every client, whereas according to the CRD only *vis-à-vis* a consumer. What about the trader whose website is addressed to the general public? Must he provide two websites, one for consumers and one for other clients? Obviously this cannot be the answer. But it indicates that the Commission's promise of more coherence fails.

---

26 Meanwhile, the EU has adopted a full set of passengers' rights regulations under the auspices of transport policy, not consumer policy; for an overview cf. KARSTEN, in: TWIGG-FLESNER (ed.).

27 In COM (2012) 225 nos. 4.3 and 4.4., among others, the energy market is stressed. Cf. already ROTT, *JCP* 2007, 53.

28 For the relation between CRD and travel law cf. BECH SERRAT, 29; ROSSONI, *IFTTA Law Rev* 2013, 10.

3. FULL HARMONISATION

9.6 The CRD is not the first consumer contract law directive, which follows the model of full harmonisation as developed in the Consumer Policy Strategy 2007–2013. The Directive concerning the distant marketing of financial services was the first (2002), followed by the Consumer Credit Directive and the Timeshare Directive (both 2008). But it was the CRD that caused a comprehensive discussion about the shift from minimum to full harmonisation. The author of this chapter, for example, argued that the TFEU provides for a shared responsibility between the EU and Member States in the field of consumer policy. This is to say that there has to be left some autonomy to Member States.[29] But the time of minimum harmonisation in the traditional way, that is to say as a minimum standard clause for a whole directive, is over; it is an unhistorical idea to try to revitalise it, so we do not want to repeat here our former arguments for a minimum standard approach (cf. 1.44 for the debate on minimum and full harmonisation). This does not exclude other technical means to leave some space to the transposing national legislators from being made available and in fact being available.

The Commission's answer to Member States that were reluctant to follow the full harmonisation process was a so-called *targeted full harmonisation*. The term as such is never explained by the Commission. In practice it means that Member States are allowed to extend the scope of a legal instrument, e.g. from a mere B2C instrument to other transactions, or that certain obligations on a trader that have been foreseen in a Directive may also be provided for by the national legislator in cases that have not been foreseen in the Directive. But the obligation as such must not be extended in favour of the consumer. The most important examples are time limits: the 14-day period to withdraw from a contract must not be extended by a Member State. Targeted full harmonisation is one step back after two steps towards full harmonisation.[30]

The CRD is an excellent example to explain what targeted full harmonisation means in practice. It cannot be derived from the wording of the Directive, but from the recitals. Recital (13) is clear enough to be quoted word-for-word:

> "Member States should remain competent, in accordance with Union law, to apply the provisions of this Directive to areas not falling within its scope. Member States may therefore maintain or introduce national legislation corresponding to the provisions of this Directive, or certain of its provisions, in relation to contracts that fall outside the scope of this Directive. For instance, Member States may decide to extend the application of the rules to legal persons who are not consumers within the meaning of this Directive, such as non-governmental organisations, start-ups or

[29] Tonner/Fangerow, *EUVR* 2012, 67, 76.

[30] Reich, in: Devenney/Kenny, 3, who calls it half harmonisation.

> small and medium-sized enterprises. Similarly, Member States may apply the provisions of this Directive in contracts that are not distance contracts within the meaning of this Directive, for example because they are not concluded under an organised distance sales or service-provision scheme. Moreover, Member States may also maintain national provisions on issues not specifically addressed in this Directive, such as additional rules concerning sales contracts, including in relation to the delivery of goods, or requirements for the provision of information during the existence of a contract."

This Recital sounds almost like a guideline for the implementing national legislator.

In addition, Recital (14) limits the concept of strict full harmonisation. According to this Recital the Directive should be without prejudice to national law regulating for instance the conclusion or the validity of a contract. This means that, for example, national provisions about invalidity because of immorality may apply. The German Bundesgerichtshof (BGH) paid more heed to the *acquis*: though the sale of a radar trap warning device is regarded as immoral and hence null and void, the Bundesgerichtshof allowed the buyer to withdraw from the (strictly speaking non-existent) contract according to the rules of the Distance Selling Directive. The judges did not expressly address the prejudice of Union law, but obviously wanted to avoid a conflict with the scope of the Distance Selling Directive.[31] Under the CRD, it is not mandatory to decide in this way. The CRD allows the national court to apply the national rule on invalidity of a contract and so to declare the contract void, without granting the right to withdraw, as there is no contract from which the consumer could withdraw.

4. INFORMATION DUTIES

a) *General rules and rules for other than off-premises and distance selling*

9.7 The CRD does not only combine the information duties of the former Doorstep Selling and Distance Selling Directives, but introduces additional duties for "other than distance and off-premises contracts". This is one of the few "leftovers" of the original proposal regulating consumer sales law.

These information duties are provided for by Article 5 of the CRD. Speaking exactly, they are pre-contractual information duties, as the trader has to give the information "before the consumer is bound by a contract". The trader has to inform the consumer of: the main characteristics of the goods or services; his identity; the total price of the goods or services; the arrangements for payment,

[31] BGH 25 November 2009, VIII ZR 318/08. The BGH did not seek for a preliminary ruling of the CJEU.

delivery and performance; a legal guarantee for the conformity of the goods; after-sales services and commercial guarantees; the duration of the contract; and the functionality of digital content and the interoperationality of digital content with hardware or software.

Specific pre-contractual information duties for "digital content" are new.[32] There is no definition of "digital content" in the Directive itself, but according to Recital (19) it means "data which were produced and supplied in digital form, such as computer programs, applications, games, music, videos or texts, irrespective of whether they are accessed through downloading or streaming, from a tangible medium or through any other means." The same Recital declares a tangible medium to be a good, but did not answer the question of what an intangible medium is. Nevertheless the Recital clearly states that contracts for the supply of digital content should fall within the scope of the Directive. The question of whether such contracts are sales or services contracts is left open. As long as all such contracts are under the scope of the CRD and no specific legislation on digital content prevails, this does not play a practical role.[33]

In the past the European legislator was often criticised because of the information overload of consumer protection directives.[34] It was not only argued that the consumer is not able to read them, but – more generally – that the "information model" of European consumer law is a model, but not a reality.[35] Until now, the legislator was not really affected by such criticism,[36] and so the CRD does not reduce the quantity of information duties in the two preceding Directives. Following research on social behaviourism, it was recently suggested that information should be "framed",[37] which is to say that there must be correct timing and contextualisation of information, so that the consumer has the information at hand he needs for the decision he is actually making.

Article 5(4) expressly determines that Article 5 is a minimum standard provision. Recital (34) not only explains the meaning of the provision but, in addition to the wording of Article 5, obliges the trader to take into account the specific needs of vulnerable consumers because of their mental, physical or psychological infirmity, age or credulity. So the concept of the vulnerable consumer (1.36a, 2.27) is already part of the Directive, but not with regard to

---

32 For a discussion of digital content and CRD cf. Helberger et al., *JCP* 2013, 47.

33 This may change if the CESL comes into force, as the proposal of the CESL includes rules on digital content, which are far more debated in legal literature than the rule of the CRD, though the CRD is law in force, whereas the CESL is only a proposal, cf. e.g., Pisulinski, in: Moccia, 205.

34 For a recent discussion of these insights of social behaviourism cf. Helberger et al., *Digital Consumers and the Law*, Chapter 4.

35 Wilhelmsson, *JCP* 2004, 317.

36 This may change, as the new European consumer agenda shows some insight to adapt information more to the needs of consumers, COM (2012) 225.

37 Helberger et al., *JCP* 2013 49; Helberger et al., *Digital Consumers and the Law*, Chapter 4.

being economically vulnerable. It should be emphasised that recitals are guidelines for the interpretation of a directive.

The Directive also stipulates that the pre-contractual information given according to the Directive is binding for the contract (Recital (35)). Nevertheless, the parties may expressly alter them after the conclusion of the contract. It is astonishing that such an important provision is part of the recitals only and not of the wording of the Directive itself; the wording of Article 5(1) is not clear in this respect. The concept as such is not new. The old Package Travel Directive of 1990 already provided for pre-contractual information which is binding for the contract. The same is true for the original Timesharing Directive of 1994.

9.8 The Unfair Commercial Practices Directive (UCPD) prohibits misleading commercial practices. This also includes, according to Article 7, misleading omissions (for more details, see 2.34). Article 7(4) includes a list of information which must be given in the event of an invitation to purchase. The first four letters are identical with Article 5(1) of the CRD. This is to say that one has to distinguish whether information is given in the stage of invitation to purchase – in which case the UCPD applies – or in a pre-contractual stage – then the CRD applies. The distinction will not be easy. In both cases consumer associations have a right to take action, but only in the event of a violation of the CRD does the consumer have an individual right – which is to say to be provided with that information or to seek damages if it is not provided.

b) Off-premises and distance selling information duties

9.9 Article 6 also provides for information for distance and off-premises contracts. In the past, only the Distance Selling Directive provided for a significant number of information duties, whereas the Doorstep Sales Directive was adopted at a time (1985), when information did not play such an important role in European law as it has done more recently. So for doorstep sales – or off-premises sales as they are called by the CRD[38] – the amount of information to be provided is new. Article 6 is not a special or additional provision to Article 5, but is exclusive, so that one cannot fall back on Article 5. But in fact, most if not all of the information provided for in Article 5 is echoed in Article 6. In fact, Article 5 is a sample of Article 6. This is to say that the EU legislator provides for some basic information for traditional selling in face-to-face situations, whereas distance and off-premises selling is considered to need more information. Article 6(7) of the Directive expressly allows Member States to maintain or introduce language requirements.

The CRD integrates the former Doorstep and Distance Selling Directives as equal "sisters", but in fact distance selling is of far more relevance today than off-

[38] The new term does not alter the goal of the original Doorstep Sales Directive, cf. Recital (21).

premises selling. The Doorstep Sales Directive was adopted in the days when cold calling at the door of vulnerable consumers like elderly people was a widespread commercial practice. Such practices do not play a significant role any longer, as hard selling methods changed to cold calling via telephone and so are covered by distance selling regulations. Nevertheless off-premises rules cannot be repealed without substitution, as doorstep selling did not disappear completely.

c) *Formal requirements for off premises transactions*

9.10 Whereas there is no difference in the kind of information which must be stipulated by the trader, the Directive distinguishes between off-premises and distance selling with regard to "formal requirements". They are regulated in Articles 7 and 8.

Most of the information that is identical with the information requirements of Article 5 deals with the right of withdrawal. We will have a closer look at that in the next section of this chapter. The remaining requirements are only a few. The trader has to provide the consumer with his telephone and fax number and with his e-mail address, about the conditions for a deposit, and about a possible recourse to an out-of-court complaint and redress mechanism.

According to Article 7 the trader has to give the information on paper or another durable medium. He has to provide the consumer with a copy of the signed contract. The provision allows for some deviations from the information duties in repair and maintenance contracts and determines that it is a full harmonisation provision (Article 7(5)).

d) *Distance selling requirements*

9.11 In distance selling contracts the same information duties apply as in off-premises contracts (Article 6). But Article 8 provides for different "formal requirements". Article 8 is an important provision because it tries to protect the consumer who is concluding a contract via the internet or telephone. Compared with the former Distance Selling Directive, the requirements are new and try to adapt the Directive to the challenges of the e-commerce world. Article 8(1) includes a general rule, which is followed by special provisions on internet selling (Article 8(2) to (4)) and telephone selling (Article 8(5) and (6)). Article 8(7) provides for the confirmation of the contract, and Article 8(10) declares the provision to be a full harmonisation rule, this is to say that Member States must not impose more obligations on traders.

According to the general rule (Article 8(1)) the information must be made available to the consumer in plain and intelligible language in a way that is appropriate to the means of distance communication used. This principle was already stipulated in other Directives.

But the requirements for internet selling are new. The information on the main characteristics of the goods, the total price and the duration of the contract must be given "directly before the consumer places his order". This does not mean that the trader must not use a hyperlink to the information, but the hyperlink must be placed directly before the order and not anywhere on the website. Even more important is that a button by which a consumer places an order "shall be labelled only with the words 'order with obligation to pay'." There is a strict sanction for this requirement: if it is not met, the consumer is not bound to the contract or his order (Article 8(2)). It should not be underestimated that in this respect the CRD makes significant progress in consumer protection.

Interestingly enough, the Directive includes a special rule for smartphones. Article 8(4) allows restriction of the mandatory information on the main characteristics of the goods, the identity of the trader, the total price, the right of withdrawal and the duration of the contract, when "a means of distance communication which allows limited space" is used. The other information can be given through a toll-free telephone line or a hyperlink (Recital (36)).

With regard to contracts which shall be concluded by telephone, Article 8(5) obliges the trader to disclose his identity at the beginning of the conversation. Not disclosing the identity is also an unfair commercial practice according to Article 7(4)(b) of the UCPD. Neither the CRD nor the UCPD forbid "cold calling", but the UCPD is expressly without prejudice to the Directive on Privacy and Electronic Communication,[39] and this Directive leaves Member States the choice between opt-out and opt-in, so that national opt-in legislation does not contradict Union law.

Article 8(6) allows Member States to determine that the consumer is only bound if he has signed the offer or has sent his written consent. This means that the CRD provides for only a minimum standard for concluding a contract by telephone.

The trader shall provide the consumer with the confirmation of the contract on a durable medium (Article 8(7)). The confirmation shall include all information referred to in Article 6(1). This is not necessary if the information is already provided on a durable medium before the conclusion of the contract, for example if the trader has fulfilled his pre-contractual information duties by sending an e-mail attachment to the consumer or when the consumer concludes the contract by phone on the basis of a printed brochure. Article 2(10) of the Directive gives a definition of "durable medium". In this case the trader is not obliged to repeat the information in the confirmation. But usually the pre-contractual information in e-commerce is available on a website only, which is not a durable medium, so that the trader may change its contents after conclusion of the contract. In cases of conclusion of the contract via the internet the

39 Directive 2002/58/EC of 12 July 2002, OJ L 201 of 31 July 2002, 37 as amended by Directive 2009/136/EC of 25 November 2009, OJ L 337 of 18 December 2009, 11.

exemption will usually not take place, meaning that the trader has to give the full information in the confirmation.

The approach is not new that pre-contractual information has to be repeated in a confirmation if it has not been already provided on a durable medium before conclusion of the contract. Similar systems had already been included in the Package Travel Directive and the Timesharing Directive in 1990 and 1994.

5. RIGHT OF WITHDRAWAL

a) *Information about the right to withdraw*

9.12 The obligation to inform about the right to withdraw is part of the pre-contractual information duties according to Article 6 of the CRD. The trader has to inform the consumer about the conditions, time limit and procedures for exercising that right (Article 6(1)(h)). Further, he has to inform him about the model withdrawal form of Annex I(B) of the Directive and the costs of returning the goods. According to Article 6(4) the trader may use the model instructions set out in Annex I(A). He is not obliged to make use of this form, but there is a high incentive: if he correctly fills in the form, he shall have fulfilled the information requirements with regard to the consumer's right of withdrawal.

b) *Withdrawal period*

9.13 The consumer has a period of 14 days from the conclusion of the contract (Article 9(1)). The harmonisation of the withdrawal period is one of the most important advantages of the Directive. The length of the period must not be subject to any alteration by the implementing legislation of the Member States. According to the former Directives the period was seven days (Doorstep Sales Directive) and seven *working* days (Distance Selling Directive). As Member States have different public holidays, the working days rule of the Distance Selling Directive could lead to a different calculation of the period in different Member States. This problem is now solved. The first Directive providing for a 14-day period was the Directive concerning the distant marketing for consumer financial services,[40] followed by the reviewed Timesharing and Consumer Credit Directives in 2008.

The provision about the beginning of the period (Article 9(2)) is more or less the same as in the former Distance Selling Directive. In the case of sales contracts it is the day on which the consumer acquires physical possession of the goods. Recital (37) gives the reason for the right to withdraw: the consumer is not able to see the goods before concluding the contract and shall have the

---

[40] Directive 2002/65/EC of 23 September 2002 OJ L 271 of 9 October 2002, 16.

possibility to inspect them. In cases of off-premises contracts it is the potential surprise element and/or psychological pressure.

There is a strict sanction for the trader if he does not inform the consumer of his right to withdraw (Article 10). In this case an additional period of 12 months begins at the end of the initial withdrawal period. If the consumer receives the information late, but within this period, the period ends 14 days after the consumer receives that information.

Contrary to the former Distance Selling Directive, the CRD includes no additional period in the case of breach of other information duties than the one about the right to withdraw. This is a serious deviation from the original *acquis*, to the detriment of the consumer. The former Doorstep Sales Directive did not limit the withdrawal period if the consumer was not informed about his right to withdraw. It simply determined that the period began at the time of information about the right to withdraw. The CJEU decided that Member States were not entitled to limit the period, but that an unlimited period follows from the Doorstep Directive.[41] As a consequence, Member States that provided for any limitation had to delete such provisions from their national law. Now in implementing the CRD they have to introduce or, as the case may be, to re-introduce the limitation period.[42] The new approach may be more coherent and systematic, but in fact the disappearance of an unlimited period to withdraw is to the detriment of the consumer. But the *Heininger* rule is still applicable in the field of financial services and consumer credit (cf. 5.22).

c) *Exercise of the right of withdrawal*

9.14 There are no formal requirements for the exercise of the right of withdrawal. The consumer may use the form which is attached to the Directive as Annex I(B). The trader has to inform him about that form (Article 6(1)(h)). But the consumer is free to decide whether or not to use the form; he can "make any other unequivocal statement" (Article 11(1)(b)). This includes oral statements or statements by telephone, but the consumer should not be advised to do so, as according to Article 11(4) he bears the burden of proof that he exercised his right. So he is on the safe side only if he uses the form. The trader may provide the form on his website, so that the consumer may fill it in electronically (Article 11(3)).

As the exercise of the right of withdrawal terminates the contract (Article 12), the trader has to reimburse all payments to the consumer within 14 days (Article 13(1)). The provision includes special rules on delivery costs.

The consumer has to send back the goods (Article 14(1)). The principle rule is that the consumer has to bear the direct cost of returning (Article 14(2)). The

41 ECJ, 22 April 1999, C-423/97, *Travel Vac* [1999] ECR I-2196; ECJ, 13 December 2001, C-481/99, *Heininger* [2001] ECR I-9945.

42 The example is Germany, cf. Tonner/Fangerow, *EUVR* 2012, 76.

trader may claim compensation for the diminished value of the goods only in a very limited way: the consumer is allowed to "establish the nature, characteristics and functioning of the goods" and is liable for a diminished value only if his use of the goods exceeds this right. (Article 14(3)). Probably it will be difficult in practice to draw the line between inspecting the goods and using them. The trader has no claim for diminished value at all, if he did not inform the consumer about his right to withdraw. The Directive includes special rules for services and digital content (Article 14(4)).

Article 14 was not part of the former Directives. It seems to have been inserted into the CRD as a consequence of the *Messner* case of the CJEU.[43] This case dealt with Article 6 of the former Distance Selling Directive. The CJEU was asked by a German local court whether a trader may require compensation for the use of a good when the consumer returns it to the seller exercising his right of withdrawal. The Court stated that the consumer has a right to examine and to test the good and must not be obliged to pay compensation in that respect. But on the other hand, according to the Court the Directive "is not intended to grant [the consumer] rights going beyond what is necessary to allow him effectively to exercise his right of withdrawal." To draw a line the CJEU declares that Member States' law may require the consumer to pay fair compensation if he had used the goods "in an manner incompatible with the principles of civil law, such as those of good faith or unjust enrichment." It is left to the national court to establish what this means in detail. But the obligation to pay under these conditions "may not adversely affect the efficiency and effectiveness of the right of withdrawal." For that reason the trader may not "place on the consumer the onus of proofing that he did not use those goods" in such a way.

According to Article 15 any ancillary contracts shall be automatically terminated. This provision plays a role when a credit contract is combined with a sales contract. The Consumer Credit Directive includes a corresponding rule, Article 15. Details are left to Member States (Article 15(2)).

9.15 Article 16 of the CRD includes a long list of exemptions from the right of withdrawal. This is more or less an updated version of the list of the former Distance Selling Directive. There is no right of withdrawal, for example, for service contracts after the service has been fully performed with the consumer's prior consent, the supply of goods made to the consumer's specifications, the supply of sealed audio or video recording or sealed computer software, contracts concluded at a public auction, the provision of accommodation, transport of goods, car rental services,[44] catering or services related to leisure activities, or the supply of digital content that is not supplied on a tangible medium, if the performance has begun with the consumer's prior consent.

43 CJEU, 3 September 2009, C-489/07, *Messner* [2009] ECR I-7315; cf. also Rott, *ERPrL* 2010, 185.

44 The exclusion of car rental services goes back to ECJ 10 March 2005, C-336/03, *easy car* [2005] ECR I-1947.

Article 16 means that the Directive includes two lists of exceptions, one list (Article 3(3)), where the Directive is not applicable at all, and a second list (Article 16), where the core remedy of the CRD, the right of withdrawal, is not applicable, but the provision of other duties, in particular information duties, are applicable. This does not make it easy to apply the Directive correctly. To give an example from the tourism industry: if a supplier offers two combined services, he is under the obligations of the Package Travel Directive only, as he sells a "package" in the sense of the Directive. He has to observe the information duties of the Package Travel Directive only, not those of the CRD, and he has no obligation to grant a right of withdrawal to the consumer. This follows from Article 3(3). But when the same supplier offers a single service, for example, hotel accommodation, he does not act under the Package Travel Directive, but under the CRD. He has to observe the information duties of the CRD, but he has no obligation to grant a right of withdrawal, which follows in this case from Article 16(m) of the CRD.[45]

6. PROVISIONS WITH RELEVANCE FOR SALES CONTRACTS

9.16 Whereas the earlier sections of this chapter deal with those parts of the CRD which are, so to speak, the successors of the former Doorstep Selling and Distance Selling Directives, Articles 17 *et seq.* are "leftovers" of the original proposal, which also intended to replace the Sale of Consumer Goods Directive and the Unfair Contract Terms Directive. Articles 18–20 are provisions dealing with sales contracts, and Articles 19–21 with sales and services contracts. This is not uncomplicated. The Sale of Consumer Goods Directive is still in force, but additionally three provisions of the CRD specific to consumer sales law apply. Whereas the Sale of Consumer Goods Directive follows the minimum standard principle, Articles 18–20 of the CRD leave no discretion for the implementing national legislator.

Article 18(1) determines the time of delivery and stipulates legal remedies for the consumer in case of late delivery. If the parties did not agree on the time of delivery the goods have to be delivered "without undue delay, but not later than 30 days from the conclusion of the contract." It is more than questionable whether the 30-day period really constitutes progress for consumers in all Member States.

If delivery is late, the consumer is entitled to terminate the contract after he has given additional time to the trader. Additional time is not necessary if the

45 For the complex relation between the Package Travel Directive and the CRD, cf. Bech Serrat, 29; Rossoni, *IFTTA Law Rev* 2013, 10.

agreed delivery period is essential (Article 18(2)). Member States may additionally provide for other remedies (Article 18(4)). Place and modalities of delivery and rules concerning the transfer of the ownership remain subject to national law (Recital (51)).

Article 20 provides for passing of risk. Risk passes when the consumer has acquired the physical possession of the goods. There is one exemption: if the carrier was commissioned by the consumer, risk already passes upon delivery to the carrier.

In cases of unsolicited supply of goods or services (inertia selling) the consumer is exempted from an obligation to provide any consideration. This provision was already part of the former Distance Selling Directive (Article 9). It corresponds with the UCPD, according to which such inertia selling is an unfair practice, but adds a contractual remedy to the unfair commercial practices rule (cf. Recital (60) of the CRD).

7. ENFORCEMENT

9.17 The most important means for enforcement of the Directive is the right for associations to take action. The CRD does not amend the list in the Injunctions Directive,[46] as former consumer protection directives did, but includes its own provision: according to Article 23, public bodies, consumer associations with a legitimate interest in protecting consumers and professional organisations with a legitimate interest in acting may take action before the courts or competent administrative bodies to ensure that the national provisions transposing this Directive are applied. Contrary to the Injunctions Directive, Article 23 of the CRD is not limited to protecting the collective consumer interest, as the Injunctions Directive is, but also takes into account the legitimate interest of the professional organisations – surprising in a consumer protection directive. The term "legitimate interest" as such is inherited from the Injunctions Directive (cf. 8.33).

The Directive does not expressly provide for individual rights beyond the right of withdrawal. In particular there are no specific rights in the event of a violation of the many pre-contractual information duties. From the principle of an effective transposition of the Directive (Articles 23(1) and 24) it follows that national law must provide for sanctions for infringements in this regard. There is some discretion for the national legislator, which is compatible with the full harmonisation principle of the CRD. For example, damages for violation of a pre-contractual obligation (*culpa in contrahendo*) may apply.

---

[46] Directive 2009/22/EC of 23 April 2009, OJ L 110 of 1 May 2009, 30, consolidating Directive 98/27/EC of 19 May 1998, OJ L 166 of 11 June 1998, 51.

Contrary to other Directives, the CRD does not provide for out-of-court settlements in favour of consumers, but the ADR Directive 2013/11/EU (8.23a) will be applicable from 9 July 2015 onwards. A special conflict-of-law provision is contained in Article 25 of the CRD (7.22).

III. INFORMATION DUTIES OF THE SERVICES DIRECTIVE AND THE E-COMMERCE DIRECTIVE

9.18 Article 6(8) of the CRD stipulates that the information requirements of the CRD have to be applied additionally to the information duties of the Services Directive[47] and the E-Commerce Directive.[48] In the event of a contradiction, the CRD applies (Article 6(8) para 2). This is in line with Article 1(3) of the E-Commerce Directive, according to which this Directive is without prejudice to consumer protection provisions.[49] This is to say that a service supplier who sells his services via the internet has to observe all three Directives if his website is addressed – at least partly – to consumers.

According to Article 22 of the Services Directive the service provider has to inform the recipient of his name and geographical address, his inclusion in a public register (if he is registered), the name of the competent authority (if his activity is subject to an authorisation scheme), his VAT identification number, and any professional body with which he is registered. Further, he has to inform the recipient about his contractual clauses, after-sales guarantees, the price of the service and its main features and insurance or guarantee if applicable.

The CRD is limited to B2C relations, whereas there is no such limitation of the personal scope in the E-Commerce Directive. The E-Commerce Directive is applicable if a service provider acts. The Directive refers to the Directive for the provision of information in the field of technical standards,[50] according to which such a service is "any service normally provided for remuneration at a distance, by electronic means and at the individual request of a recipient of services" (Article 1(2)). He has to observe the E-Commerce Directive only if he wishes to sell goods solely to professionals, as well as the Services Directive if he intends to also sell services to professionals. If he wants to go into the consumer business, he has to observe the E-Commerce Directive and the CRD if he wants to sell goods only, and the E-Commerce Directive, the Services Directive and the CRD if he wants to sell services to consumers as well. More precisely, he does not have to observe all these directives but rather the national law transposing the

47 Directive 2006/123/EC of 12 December 2006, OJ L 376 of 27 December 2006, 36.

48 Directive 2000/31/EC of 8 June 2000, OJ L 178 of 17 July 2000, 1.

49 For the relation between the E-Commerce Directive and consumer policy cf. Dickie.

50 Directive 98/34/EC of 22 June 1998, OJ L 204 of 21 July 1998, 37.

directives, and he has to ascertain which national law is applicable. This question is regulated by private international law, which is also not easy to understand (7.14). This is, in short, the legal programme a trader has to complete before he can go to business on the internet.

The E-Commerce Directive provides for two types of information requirements. The first is pre-contractual information, which is known from the UCPD and the CRD, whereas the second type is specific: this is information which must be provided during the process of concluding the contract.

According to Article 5, the service provider has not only to provide information about his name and geographical address, but also has to provide further details such as whether he is registered in a public register or with a professional body and his VAT registration number. Prices have to be indicated, in particular whether they include tax and delivery costs. Commercial communication has to be identifiable as such, especially promotional offers and promotional competitions and games (Article 6).

For the conclusion of a contract by electronic means, Articles 10 and 11 are of utmost importance. Article 10 obliges the service provider to provide information about the technical steps to follow to conclude the contract, whether the contract will be filed by the service provider, technical means to correct input errors, and the languages in which the contract is offered. Contract terms and general conditions must be made available in a way that allows the recipient to store them. According to Article 11, the service provider has to acknowledge receipt of the recipient's order without undue delay and by electronic means. The order and the acknowledgement of receipt are deemed to be received when the parties to whom they are addressed are able to access them. Article 11 carefully avoids using the terms "offer" and "acceptance". An order is not necessarily an offer, and an acknowledgement is not necessarily an acceptance. It is left to national law to decide whether or not order and offer, and acknowledgement and acceptance, are identical. At the time of the adoption of the E-Commerce Directive the legislator did not want to regulate the conclusion of the contract. Now such provisions can be found in the proposal for a CESL.

IV. CONCLUSION

9.19 The CRD deserves some criticism as it is not *the* Consumer Rights Directive, as the title might suggest, but only one of a set of directives dealing with consumer law. This is due to the reductionism that affected it on its way from the Commission's proposal to the finally adopted Directive. But after the CRD came into force, the final Directive, and not the proposal and its original approach, should be the focus.[51] The final outcome as such must be judged, that

[51] Contrary, Weatherill, *CMLRev* 2012, 1279 assesses the original approach.

is to say whether the CRD is an appropriate successor to the Doorstep Sales and the Distance Selling Directives, and one which meets the challenges posed by the internet.

In this respect, the CRD is not a failure.[52] It is more than a "codification" of the two predecessors with a more "coherent" approach than the Directives from 1985 and 1997. It takes into account "digital content" with specific information duties, it provides for general information duties even for contracts in a high street shop and so creates coherence with the UCPD, it provides for a duty to inform that there is an obligation to pay when the consumer places his order (Article 8(2)),[53] and it integrates the *Messner* case for the compensation – and its limits – the consumer has to pay in case of withdrawal. There is at least a modest improvement of the level of consumer protection, and it would be unfair to say that the commitments of the Commission to a high level of consumer protection according to Article 114 TFEU is only lip service. But more could have been done – and should be done in the near future.

But though there is now coherence within the fields of off-premises and distance selling contracts, even the right to withdraw is different in each Directive, which provides for such a right. The 14-day period is the same in all the three relevant Directives (CRD, consumer credit, timesharing), but details differ. The list of exemptions in the CRD is so long that there is no real coherence. With regard to internet shopping, the parties do not have to take into account only the CRD, but also the E-Commerce Directive and – to a limited extent – the Service Directive. The personal scope of these two Directives is not the same. The E-Commence Directive is addressed to every "recipient of the service", whereas the CRD is limited to consumers.

The idea of leaving a review of the "leftovers" of the Consumer Rights Directive, that is to say the Sales of Consumer Goods Directive and the Unfair Contract Terms Directive, on the agenda is without real hope, as the Commission expressly relies on the optional CESL and not on further reviews of existing consumer law. The question is what realistic alternatives exist, but this has been discussed in the general parts of this book (1.43b).

The CRD is an update to the Distance Selling Directive for the needs of concluding contracts by electronic means with some slight improvements in favour of consumers, but it does not provide for coherence in consumer law. The list of exemptions is too long, and the lack of harmonisation with the E-Commerce Directive makes its application difficult.

The EU *acquis* does not meet the challenges of consumer contracts concluded via the internet with one legal instrument. The E-Commerce Directive also has to be applied. As the E-Commerce Directive is not a consumer protection

---

52 Cf. also Hall/Howells/Watson, *ERCL* 2012, 139.

53 This is an example of "framing" information in the sense of the demands of Helberger et al., *Digital Consumers and the Law*, Chapter 4.

instrument, but rather is applicable to all "recipients", the question has to be raised as to whether the goal of consumer protection of the CRD at least radiates to the E-Commerce Directive, in particular in favour of the vulnerable consumer, so as to create at least some coherence for the consumer in the virtual world.

INDEX*

* The numbers refer to paragraph numbers.

IUS COMMUNITATIS SERIES

Published titles within the series:

1. Stefan Grundmann, *European Company Law. Organization, Finance and Capital Markets*, 2nd edn., Cambridge-Antwerp-Portland, Intersentia, 2012
ISBN 978-1-78068-019-4
2. André Klip, *European Criminal Law. An Integrative Approach*, 2nd edn., Cambridge-Antwerp-Portland, Intersentia, 2012
ISBN 978-1-78068-001-9
3. Pieter Boeles, Maarten den Heijer, Gerrie Lodder and Kees Wouters, *European Migration Law*, Antwerp-Oxford, Intersentia, 2009
ISBN 978–90–5095–953–7
4. Karl Riesenhuber, *European Employment Law. A Systematic Exposition*, Cambridge-Antwerp-Portland, Intersentia, 2012
ISBN 978-1-78068-080-4